THE OXFORD H.

JEWISH ETHICS AND MORALITY

THE OXFORD HANDBOOK OF
JEWISH ETHICS AND MORALITY

Edited by
ELLIOT N. DORFF
and
JONATHAN K. CRANE

OXFORD
UNIVERSITY PRESS

Oxford University Press is a department of the University of Oxford.
It furthers the University's objective of excellence in research, scholarship,
and education by publishing worldwide.

Oxford   New York
Auckland   Cape Town   Dar es Salaam   Hong Kong   Karachi
Kuala Lumpur   Madrid   Melbourne   Mexico City   Nairobi
New Delhi   Shanghai   Taipei   Toronto

With offices in
Argentina   Austria   Brazil   Chile   Czech Republic   France   Greece
Guatemala   Hungary   Italy   Japan   Poland   Portugal   Singapore
South Korea   Switzerland   Thailand   Turkey   Ukraine   Vietnam

Oxford is a registered trademark of Oxford University Press
in the UK and certain other countries.

Published in the United States of America by
Oxford University Press
198 Madison Avenue, New York, NY 10016

© Oxford University Press 2013

First issued as an Oxford University Press paperback, 2016

All rights reserved. No part of this publication may be reproduced, stored in a
retrieval system, or transmitted, in any form or by any means, without the prior
permission in writing of Oxford University Press, or as expressly permitted by law,
by license, or under terms agreed with the appropriate reproduction rights organization.
Inquiries concerning reproduction outside the scope of the above should be sent to the
Rights Department, Oxford University Press, at the address above.

You must not circulate this work in any other form
and you must impose this same condition on any acquirer.

Library of Congress Cataloging-in-Publication Data
The Oxford handbook of Jewish ethics and morality / edited by Elliot
N. Dorff, Jonathan K. Crane.
p. cm.
Includes index.
ISBN 978-0-19-973606-5 (hardcover : alk. paper); 978-0-19-060838-5 (paperback : alk. paper)
1. Jewish ethics.
I. Dorff, Elliot N.   II. Crane, Jonathan K. (Jonathan Kadane)
BJ1285.2.O935 2013
296.3'6—dc23
2012011555

For our wives
Marlynn
And
Lindy
Whose love enriches our lives in untold ways

Contents

Contributors	xi
Abbreviations	xxi
Acknowledgments	xxiii

Introduction: Why Study Jewish Ethics?	1
ELLIOT N. DORFF AND JONATHAN K. CRANE	

PART I JEWISH ETHICAL THEORIES

Introduction to Part I	27
1. Ethical Theory and Practice in the Hebrew Bible ELAINE ADLER GOODFRIEND	35
2. Ethical Theories in Rabbinic Literature CHARLOTTE ELISHEVA FONROBERT	51
3. Ethical Theories in Jewish Mystical Writings JOSEPH DAN	71
4. Ethical Theories among Medieval Jewish Philosophers WARREN ZEV HARVEY	84
5. Spinoza and Jewish Ethics DAVID NOVAK	102
6. Mussar Ethics and Other Nineteenth-Century Jewish Ethical Theories IRA F. STONE	118
7. Ethical Theories of Hermann Cohen, Franz Rosenzweig, and Martin Buber JONATHAN K. CRANE	134
8. Ethical Theories of Mordecai Kaplan and Abraham Joshua Heschel MATTHEW LaGRONE	151

9. Ethical Theories of Abraham Isaac Kook and
   Joseph B. Soloveitchik   166
   LAWRENCE KAPLAN

10. Ethical Implications of the Holocaust   186
    MICHAEL BERENBAUM

11. Ethical Theories in the Reform Movement   206
    MICHAEL MARMUR

12. Ethical Theories in the Conservative Movement   225
    SHAI CHERRY

13. Ethical Theories in the Orthodox Movement   241
    DAVID SHATZ

14. Ethical Theories in the Reconstructionist Movement   259
    DAVID A. TEUTSCH

15. Feminist Jewish Ethical Theories   272
    JUDITH PLASKOW

16. Postmodern Jewish Ethical Theories   287
    MARTIN KAVKA

PART II   TOPICS IN JEWISH MORALS

Introduction to Part II   305

17. Jewish Bioethics: The Beginning of Life   313
    ELLIOT N. DORFF

18. Jewish Bioethics: The End of Life   330
    DANIEL B. SINCLAIR

19. Jewish Bioethics: The Distribution of Health Care   345
    AARON L. MACKLER

20. Jewish Bioethics: Current and Future Issues in Genetics   351
    LAURIE ZOLOTH

21. Jewish Business Ethics   367
    BARRY J. LEFF

22. Jewish Sexual Ethics   383
    DANYA RUTTENBERG

23. Jewish Environmental Ethics: Intertwining *Adam* with *Adamah* ARTHUR WASKOW	401
24. Jewish Animal Ethics AARON S. GROSS	419
25. Jewish Ethics of Speech ALYSSA M. GRAY	433
26. Jewish Political Ethics in America JILL JACOBS	445
27. Jewish Political Ethics in Israel REUVEN HAMMER	459
28. Judaism and Criminal Justice LAURIE L. LEVENSON	472
29. Jewish Ethics and War ASA KASHER	487
Biblical Sources: Rabbinic and Selected Medieval Citations	501
Subject Index	509

Contributors

Michael Berenbaum is the director of the Sigi Ziering Institute: Exploring the Ethical and Religious Implications of the Holocaust, and Professor of Jewish Studies at the American Jewish University in Los Angeles. He was Executive Editor of the Second Edition of the *Encyclopaedia Judaica*, which was awarded the Dartmouth Medal of the American Library Association for the outstanding reference publication of 2006. He has been a visiting professor of Holocaust studies at Chapman University, Richard Stockton College, Clark University, and Claremont-Mckenna College. From 1988 to 1993 he served as Project Director of the United States Holocaust Memorial Museum, overseeing its creation, and later worked as Director of its Research Institute. He has helped conceive and develop holocaust museums around the world, including in Illinois, Poland, and Macedonia. Author or editor of twenty books, he has also co-produced the award-winning *One Survivor Remembers: Gerda Weissman Klein Story*. Berenbaum is a graduate of Queens College (B.A., 1967) and Florida State University (Ph.D., 1975) and also attended The Hebrew University, the Jewish Theological Seminary, and Boston University.

Shai Cherry (Ph.D., Brandeis University; Rabbi, Ziegler School of Rabbinic Studies, American Jewish University) directs *Shaar Hamayim*, a Jewish Learning Center based in San Diego. Previously he taught for four years at Vanderbilt University and four years at the University of California, Los Angeles. He is the author of *Torah through Time: Understanding Bible Commentary from the Rabbinic Period to Modern Times* and numerous articles on Judaism, creation, and evolution. He is the featured lecturer for The Teaching Company's Introduction to Judaism course and is currently at work on a Jewish theology of nature.

Jonathan K. Crane is the Raymond F. Schinazi Junior Scholar in Bioethics and Jewish Thought at the Center for Ethics at Emory University. He holds an A.B. degree in International Relations from Wheaton College (Norton, MA); an M.A. in International Peace Studies from the University of Notre Dame (Indiana); an M.Phil. in Gandhian Thought from Gujarat Vidyapith (Ahmedabad, India); an M.A. in Hebrew Literature and Rabbinic Ordination from Hebrew Union College–Jewish Institute of Religion (New York); and a Ph.D. in Religion from the University of Toronto (Ontario, Canada). He has presented at conferences and taught around the world on themes relating to Judaism and ethics, bioethics, theology, social and political ethics, warfare ethics, interfaith relations, and Gandhian philosophy.

Recent publications can be found in *The Journal of Law and Religion, AJS Review, The Journal of Religious Ethics, Theology & Sexuality, CCAR Journal, The Review of Rabbinic Judaism, Anasakti Darshan,* and *The Journal of the Society of Christian Ethics.* He serves on the Executive Board of the Society of Jewish Ethics and the Editorial Board of the *The Journal of the Society of Christian Ethics.*

Joseph Dan (Ph.D. Hebrew University, 1964) is the Gershom Scholem Professor of Kabbalah, emeritus, in the Department of Jewish Thought at the Hebrew University of Jerusalem. Winner of the Israel Prize in Jewish Thought (1997), his many books include *The Heart and the Fountain: Jewish Mystical Experiences, The Early Kabbalah,* and *The Teachings of Hasidism.*

Elliot N. Dorff (A.B. Columbia College, 1965; M.H.L. and Rabbi, Jewish Theological Seminary, 1970; Ph.D. in Philosophy, Columbia University, 1971) is Rector and Sol and Anne Dorff Distinguished Service Professor of Philosophy at American Jewish University and a Visiting Professor at UCLA School of Law. He has been awarded four honorary doctoral degrees and has chaired four scholarly organizations—the Jewish Philosophy Association, the Jewish Law Association, the Society of Jewish Ethics, and the Academy of Judaic, Christian, and Islamic Studies. He has served on federal advisory commissions on health care, sexual ethics, and the ethics of research on human subjects, and he currently serves on the California Advisory Commission on Stem Cell Research. Author of over 200 published articles and twelve books on Jewish thought, law, and ethics, he has edited or co-edited fourteen other books as well. Among the latter is the book he co-edited with Louis E. Newman for Oxford University Press, *Contemporary Jewish Ethics and Morality: A Reader* (1995) and six books in the *Jewish Choices, Jewish Voices* series, each on moral issues arising in a particular area of life: body, money, power, sex, war, and social justice. In addition to books on Jewish theology and law, Dorff has written a number of books on Jewish ethics: *Matters of Life and Death* (on medical ethics), *To Do the Right and the Good* (on social ethics), *Love Your Neighbor and Yourself* (on personal ethics), and *The Way into Tikkun Olam (Repairing the World).*

Charlotte Elisheva Fonrobert (Ph.D., Graduate Theological Union, 1995) is Associate Professor of Religious Studies and Jewish Studies, with a courtesy appointment in Classics, at Stanford University, and Visiting Professor of Talmud at the Graduate Theological Union in Berkeley. Having written numerous articles on rabbinic and talmudic literature and culture, she is the author of *Menstrual Purity: Rabbinic and Early Christian Reconstructions of Biblical Gender* (2000), which was awarded the Baron Prize for a first book in Jewish Studies, and was a finalist for the National Jewish Book Award for Jewish Studies. She is co-editor of *The Cambridge Companion to the Talmud and Rabbinic Literature* (2007), as well as of the English edition of Jacob Taubes's *From Cult to Culture* (2010). Her current book project, *Re-Placing the Nation: Judaism, Diaspora and Neighborhood,* is a study of the politics of the rabbinic *eruv.*

Elaine Adler Goodfriend is a lecturer in Hebrew Bible and Jewish History at California State University, Northridge, and Loyola Marymount College. She has an M.A. and Ph.D. in Near Eastern Studies from the University of California at Berkeley, and a B.A. in Semitic Languages and Literature from Cornell University. Her publications can be found in *Anchor Bible Dictionary, Women's Commentary on the Torah, Women in Scripture: A Dictionary of Named and Unnamed Women in the Hebrew Bible, Apocrypha, and New Testament,* and *Cambridge Dictionary of Judaism.*

Alyssa M. Gray is Associate Professor of Codes and Responsa Literature at Hebrew Union College–Jewish Institute of Religion in New York. She holds law degrees from Columbia and Hebrew Universities, and a Ph.D. from the Jewish Theological Seminary. She has written and lectured widely on many topics, notably including martyrdom, the formations of the Babylonian and Jerusalem Talmuds, the relationship of *halakhah* and law, liturgy, and charity. Her essays have or will appear in *Conservative Judaism, Journal of Jewish Studies, AJS Review, Jewish Studies Quarterly,* and *Diné Israel.* She is also the author of *A Talmud in Exile: The Influence of Yerushalmi Avodah Zarah on the Formation of Bavli Avodah Zarah.*

Aaron S. Gross is Assistant Professor of Theology and Religious Studies at the University of San Diego. He holds a Masters of Theological Studies from Harvard Divinity School and a Ph.D. in religious studies with a specialization in modern Judaism from the University of California, Santa Barbara. Gross has lectured at academic conferences and universities around the world on issues related to animals and religion, and food and religion. He co-chairs the American Academy of Religion Consultation on Animals and Religion, serves on the board of the Society of Jewish Ethics, and is the founder and CEO of the nonprofit Farm Forward. Gross collaborated with novelist Jonathan Safran Foer on Foer's international best seller, *Eating Animals* (2009). His publications have appeared in *The Central Conference of American Rabbis Journal, The Encyclopedia of Film and Religion, The Huffington Post, Shofar: An Interdisciplinary Journal of Jewish Studies,* and *Tikkun Magazine.* Gross's forthcoming co-edited volume, *Animal Others and the Human Imagination,* came out in Spring 2012.

Reuven Hammer received his rabbinic ordination and doctorate in theology from the Jewish Theological Seminary of America as well as a Ph.D. in the field of special education from Northwestern University. After moving to Israel in the summer of 1973 he taught and worked for many years in the field of special education at the Hebrew University, David Yellin College, and other institutions and served as an advisor to the Ministry of Education. For eighteen years he was the Dean of the Israel programs of the Jewish Theological Seminary in Jerusalem and Professor of Rabbinic Literature. He was the founding director of the Institute for Jewish Studies, today the Schechter Institute. He has been a professor of Rabbinic Literature at Schechter and has also taught Rabbinics at The Jewish Theological

Seminary of America, Oranim College, the Hebrew University Rothberg School, the Seminario Rabinico Latinoamericano, and the Moscow State University of the Humanities. Two of his books, *Sifre, A Taanaitic Commentary on Deuteronomy* and *Entering the High Holy Days*, were awarded the National Jewish Book Council prize as the best book of scholarship for the year. He has also written *The Jerusalem Anthology, Entering Jewish Prayer, The Classic Midrash* and *Or Hadash*, a two-volume commentary on the prayerbook. His latest books are *Entering Torah* and *The Torah Revolution: Fourteen Truths That Changed the World*. He has also published numerous scholarly articles in the fields of Midrash and Liturgy in professional journals and various Jubilee volumes.

Warren Zev Harvey (Ph.D., Philosophy, Columbia University, 1973) is Professor Emeritus of Jewish Thought at the Hebrew University of Jerusalem, where he has taught since 1977. He previously taught at McGill University (1972–1977) and has been a visiting professor at several institutions, including Columbia University, the University of Pennsylvania, Queens College (CUNY), Yeshiva University, Yale University, and the École des Hautes Études en Sciences Sociales. He is the author of more than 150 studies on medieval and modern Jewish philosophy. Among his books is *Physics and Metaphysics in Hasdai Crescas* (1998). He is an EMET Prize laureate in the Humanities (2009).

Jill Jacobs is the Executive Director of Rabbis for Human Rights–North America. She is the author of *Where Justice Dwells: A Hands-On Guide to Doing Social Justice in Your Jewish Community* (2011) and *There Shall Be No Needy: Pursuing Social Justice through Jewish Law and Tradition* (2009). She has taught about Judaism and social justice throughout North America and around the world. Her writings on issues of housing, labor, and health care from a Jewish perspective have appeared in more than two dozen magazines, journals, and anthologies. Rabbi Jacobs has been named to The *Jewish Daily Forward*'s list of fifty influential American Jews (2006, 2008), *Newsweek*'s list of the fifty most influential rabbis in America (2009, 2010, 2011), *The Jewish Week*'s first list of "36 under 36" (2008), and the *Forward*'s list of the fifty most influential women rabbis (2010). Rabbi Jacobs received rabbinic ordination and an M.A. in Talmud from the Jewish Theological Seminary, where she was a Wexner fellow. She also holds an M.S. in Urban Affairs from Hunter College and a B.A. in Comparative Literature from Columbia University.

Lawrence Kaplan is Professor of Rabbinics and Jewish Philosophy in the Department of Jewish Studies of McGill University, where he has taught since 1972. He received his B.A. from Yeshiva College, Rabbinical Ordination from the Rabbi Isaac Elchanan Theological School of Yeshiva University, and M.A. and Ph.D. from Harvard University. Kaplan specializes in both medieval and modern Jewish thought and has published widely in both scholarly and popular journals. He is widely acknowledged as the leading translator of the Hebrew writings of R. Joseph B. Soloveitchik and as one of the leading scholars of his thought. He is co-editor of *The Thought of Moses Maimonides and R. Abraham Isaac Kook* and *Jewish Spirituality* and is currently completing a monograph "Halakhah and Religious Experience in the Thought of R. Joseph Soloveitchik." In 2005 he was a Harry Starr Fellow in Judaica at the Center for Jewish Studies of Harvard University, and in 2011–2012 was a Fellow in the Tikvah Center of the New York University Law School.

Asa Kasher (Ph.D., Hebrew University of Jerusalem) is Laura Schwarz-Kipp Professor Emeritus of Professional Ethics and Philosophy of Practice and Professor Emeritus of Philosophy at Tel Aviv University. He won the highest Israeli national honor, the Prize of Israel (2000), for his contributions to philosophy and ethics, the Izhak Sade Military Literature Prize for his book *Military Ethics,* and an honorary degree. He has written about 250 papers in philosophy of language, professional ethics, and other areas and many ethical documents, as well as several books, including *Judaism and Idolatry* and *A Small Book on the Meaning of Life.* He co-authored the first code of ethics of the IDF, a code of military ethics of fighting terrorism, and many others, including those of the Government ministers and the Knesset members. He has served on many governmental committees, including the National Bio-ethics Council.

Martin Kavka (Ph.D. Rice University, 2000) is Associate Professor of Religion at Florida State University. His publications include *Jewish Messianism and the History of Philosophy,* which was awarded the Jordan Schnitzer Book Award in Philosophy and Jewish Thought by the Association for Jewish Studies in 2008, numerous essays and articles in Jewish philosophy, and three edited volumes: *Tradition in the Public Square: A David Novak Reader* (co-edited with Randi Rashkover), *Saintly Influence: Edith Wyschogrod and the Possibilities of Philosophy of Religion* (co-edited with Eric Boynton), and *The Cambridge History of Jewish Philosophy: The Modern Era* (co-edited with Zachary Braiterman and David Novak). He is currently co-editor of the *Journal of Religious Ethics* and is completing a manuscript on the structural problems of covenant theology.

Matthew LaGrone is the Yetta Chaiken Teaching Fellow and Visiting Assistant Professor at the University of Delaware's Jewish Studies Program. He received his B.A. from the University of Alabama, M.A. from the Florida State University, and Ph.D. from the University of Toronto. His scholarship focuses on "Atlantic" Judaism and Jewish–Christian relations, and he is presently writing the first biography of Chief Rabbi Joseph Hertz.

Barry J. Leff is a business executive and rabbi. He is the General Manager for Innodata Isogen Israel, Ltd., an outsourcing company. He also serves as the Chairman of the Board of Directors for Rabbis for Human Rights, and he serves on the Board of Trustees (and is chair of the audit committee) of the Schechter Rabbinical Seminary in Jerusalem. He holds a Doctorate of Business Administration and an M.B.A. from Golden Gate University in San Francisco, and he was ordained as a rabbi and awarded an M.A. in Rabbinic Studies from the Ziegler School of

Rabbinic Studies of the American Jewish University in Los Angeles. He has over twenty-five years' experience as an entrepreneur and executive and has served as a congregational rabbi in Tucson, Arizona, Vancouver, BC, and Toledo, Ohio. He is the author of a chapter on relations between co-workers in the *The Observant Life*. He has written three *teshuvot* (Jewish legal opinions) that have been approved by the Conservative Movement's Committee on Jewish Law and Standards, two of which deal with issues of business ethics. He is a regular op-ed contributor to the *Jerusalem Post*, and he blogs on Israel and Judaism at www.neshamah.net.

Laurie L. Levenson is the David W. Burcham Chair in Ethical Advocacy at Loyola Law School, where she teaches evidence, criminal law, criminal procedure, and ethics. She also serves as the Director of Loyola's Center for Ethical Advocacy. She served for eight years as an Assistant United States Attorney in Los Angeles. She received her J.D. in 1980 from UCLA School of Law and her undergraduate degree from Stanford University in 1977. She was Chief Article Editor of the UCLA Law Review and a clerk for the Honorable Judge James Hunter, III, of the U.S. Court of Appeals for the Third Circuit. She has authored over a hundred articles and nine books. She recently contributed an article on capital punishment to *Jewish Choices, Jewish Voices: Social Justice* (edited by Elliot N. Dorff and Danya Ruttenberg). Finally, she is an international commentator on high-profile cases and criminal justice.

Aaron L. Mackler is Associate Professor of Theology at Duquesne University in Pittsburgh, where he teaches in the Center for Healthcare Ethics. He currently serves as President of the Society of Jewish Ethics and as a member of hospital ethics committees in the Pittsburgh area. He received a B.A. from Yale University, an M.A. and rabbinic ordination from the Jewish Theological Seminary of America, and a Ph.D. from Georgetown University. He served as Staff Ethicist for the New York State Task Force on Life and the Law and taught as Visiting Assistant Professor at the Jewish Theological Seminary of America. He was a member of the Rabbinical Assembly's Committee on Jewish Law and Standards (1991–2011), for which he served as Chair of the Subcommittee on Bioethics. He has spoken on health care ethics and theology for numerous professional societies and other audiences. Dr. Mackler's publications include *Introduction to Jewish and Catholic Bioethics: A Comparative Analysis* (2003), and an edited volume, *Life and Death Responsibilities in Jewish Biomedical Ethics* (2000). He also has written numerous articles in the fields of Jewish theology, ethics, and bioethics.

Michael Marmur is the Vice-President for Academic Affairs of the Hebrew Union College–Jewish Institute of Religion, where he also teaches Jewish Theology. He holds a B.A. degree from Oxford University, M.A. and Ph.D. degrees from the Hebrew University of Jerusalem, and Rabbinic Ordination from the Jerusalem School of the Hebrew Union College–Jewish Institute of Religion. Specializing in the thought of Abraham Joshua Heschel, he has lectured widely on modern Jewish thought, homiletics, Reform Zionism, and pluralistic Jewish education. His articles can be found in *The Jewish Quarterly Review, Shofar, The CCAR Journal, Manna*, and publications such as *Jewish Theology in Our Time* and *New Essays In American Jewish History*.

David Novak holds the J. Richard and Dorothy Shiff Chair of Jewish Studies as Professor of Religion and Philosophy at the University of Toronto. He was previously the Edgar M. Bronfman Professor of Modern Judaic Studies at the University of Virginia. He is a Fellow of the Royal Society of Canada, a Fellow of the American Academy for Jewish Research, and a Founder and Vice-President of the Union for Traditional Judaism. He received his A.B. from the University of Chicago, his M.H.L. and rabbinical diploma from the Jewish Theological Seminary of America, and his Ph.D. (in philosophy) from Georgetown University. He has been appointed and reappointed by the Governor-General of Canada to the Board of Directors of Assisted Human Reproduction Canada. He is the author of sixteen books, has edited four books, and has published over three hundred articles and reviews.

Judith Plaskow is professor of religious studies at Manhattan College and a Jewish feminist theologian who has been teaching, writing, and speaking about Jewish feminism and feminist studies in religion for over forty years. She received her B.A. from Clark University and her M.Phil. and Ph.D. from Yale University. She co-founded and for ten years co-edited the *Journal of Feminist Studies in Religion*. She is the author of over fifty articles on feminist theology and editor or author of several books, including *Womanspirit Rising: A Feminist Reader in Religion, Weaving the Visions: New Patterns in Feminist Spirituality* (both co-edited with Carol P. Christ), *Standing Again at Sinai: Judaism from a Feminist Perspective*, and *The Coming of Lilith: Essays on Feminism, Judaism, and Sexual Ethics 1972–2003*. She is the recipient of honorary doctorates from Hebrew Union College and the Reconstructionist Rabbinical College, and from 1995 through 1998 she served in the presidential line of the American Academy of Religion.

Danya Ruttenberg is the author of *Surprised By God: How I Learned to Stop Worrying and Love Religion* (Beacon Press), nominated for the 2010 Sami Rohr Prize for Jewish literature, and editor of *The Passionate Torah: Sex and Judaism* (2009) and *Yentl's Revenge: The Next Wave of Jewish Feminism*. She is also co-editor, with Rabbi Elliot Dorff, of three books for the Jewish Publication Society's *Jewish Choices/Jewish Voices* series: *Sex and Intimacy; War and National Security;* and *Social Justice*. In 2010 the *Jewish Week* named her one of the "36 Under 36" (the Jewish world's 36 most influential leaders under age 36), and the *Forward* recognized her as one of the fifty most influential women rabbis. She serves as a contributing editor or on the advisory board to four publications: *Sh'ma: A Journal of Jewish Responsibility*, Jewschool.com, *Lilith Magazine*, and the academic journal *Women and Judaism*. She received her B.A. in Religious Studies from Brown University and an M.A. in Rabbinic Studies, as well as rabbinic ordination, from the Ziegler School of Rabbinic Studies at the American Jewish University. She currently serves as Senior Jewish Educator at Tufts University's Hillel, and teaches and lectures nationwide.

David Shatz is Professor of Philosophy at Yeshiva University. He was ordained at the Rabbi Isaac Elchanan Theological Seminary and earned his Ph.D. with distinction in general philosophy from Columbia University. He has edited, co-edited, or authored fourteen books and has published over sixty articles and reviews, dealing with both general and Jewish philosophy. His work in general philosophy focuses on the theory of knowledge, free will, ethics, and the philosophy of religion, while his work in Jewish philosophy focuses on Jewish ethics, Maimonides, Judaism and science, and twentieth-century rabbinic figures. A book of his collected essays, *Jewish Thought in Dialogue*, was published in 2009. His edited and co-edited books include *Rabbi Abraham Isaac and Jewish Spirituality*; *Judaism, Science and Moral Responsibility*; and three anthologies in the philosophy of religion. He is the author of *Peer Review: A Critical Inquiry*, as well as editor of *The Torah u–Madda Journal* and editor of a book series that presents previously unpublished works of Rabbi Joseph B. Soloveitchik. He has appeared several times on PBS television. In recognition of his achievements as a scholar and teacher, he was awarded the Presidential Medallion at Yeshiva University.

Daniel B. Sinclair (LL.B. [Hons.]) [London University], LL.M. [Monash University], Ph.D. in Law [Hebrew University], Rabbi) is Professor of Jewish Law and Comparative Biomedical Law at the Striks Law School, CMAS, Israel, and Wolff Fellow in Jewish Law and Visiting Professor of Law at Fordham University Law School, New York. Formerly, Dean of Jews' College, London University, and Rabbi of the Edinburgh Hebrew Congregation, Scotland, he has published over fifty articles in the fields of Jewish law, its jurisprudence, and comparative biomedical law. His books include *Tradition and the Biological Revolution* (1989), *Law, Judicial Policy and Jewish Identity in the State of Israel* (2000), and *Jewish Biomedical Law: Legal and Extra-Legal Dimensions* (Oxford University Press, 2003). He is a member of the editorial boards of the *Jewish Law Annual* and the *Journal of Law and Religion* and has served as a member of the Ethics Committee of the Royal College of Physicians in the United Kingdom. He has testified before the Law Committee of the Israeli Knesset on the issues of cloning and germ-line genetic therapy and is a member of an advisory group to a European Union Committee on ethics and science.

Ira F. Stone has been Rabbi of Temple Beth Zion–Beth Israel in center city Philadelphia since 1988. He also runs the Mussar Leadership Programs at Beth Zion–Beth Israel. Rabbi Stone is a graduate of the University of California at Santa Barbara, where he received a B.A. in Religious Studies. He attended the University of Judaism in Los Angeles and graduated from The Jewish Theological Seminary of America in 1979 with a Masters of Hebrew Literature and rabbinic ordination. He served as the Daniel Jeremy Silver Fellow at Harvard University for the spring 2005 semester. Rabbi Stone has written articles on theology and rabbinics for various journals, including *Conservative Judaism*, *Wellspring Journal*, *Middlebury College Magazine,* and *Kerem*. He has published four books: *Seeking the Path to Life* (1992), *Reading Levinas/Reading Talmud* (1997), *A Responsible Life: Mussar as* *a Spiritual Path* (2006), and a commentary on Mordecai Kaplan's translation of *Mesillat Yesharim* (The Path of the Upright) (2010). Rabbi Stone served as lecturer in the Department of Philosophy at the Jewish Theological Seminary and presently as adjunct and visiting lecturer in Modern Jewish Thought at the Reconstructionist Rabbinical College.

David A. Teutsch is the Louis and Myra Wiener Professor of Contemporary Jewish Civilization and Director of the Levin-Lieber Program in Jewish Ethics at the Reconstructionist Rabbinical College, where he served as president for nearly a decade. He is the author or editor of dozens of articles and twenty books, including *A Guide to Jewish Practice: Everyday Living* (2011) and the *Kol Haneshamah* prayerbook series. A past president of the Society of Jewish Ethics and of the Academic Coalition for Jewish Bioethics, he is an internationally known consultant and trainer who has received three honorary degrees. He received his A.B. from Harvard University, M.A. and ordination from Hebrew Union College–Jewish Institute of Religion, and Ph.D. from the Wharton School of the University of Pennsylvania.

Arthur Waskow, Rabbi, Ph. D., founded (1983) and continues to direct The Shalom Center <www.theshalomcenter.org>. Among his seminal works on Jewish thought and practice have been the *Freedom Seder*; *Godwrestling*; *Seasons of Our Joy*; *Down-to-Earth Judaism: Food, Money, Sex, and the Rest of Life* ; *Godwrestling—Round 2: Ancient Wisdom, Future Paths*; and as co-author with Rabbi Phyllis Berman, *A Time for Every Purpose Under Heaven: The Jewish Life-Spiral as a Spiritual Path* and *Freedom Journeys: The Tale of Exodus and Wilderness across Millennia*. He co-authored *The Tent of Abraham: Stories of Hope and Peace for Jews, Christians, and Muslims* with Sr. Joan Chittister, OSB, and Murshid Saadi Shakur Chisti (Neil Douglas-Klotz). He had primary editorial responsibility for two pioneering anthologies on eco-Judaism: *Torah of the Earth: Exploring 4,000 Years of Ecology in Jewish Thought*; and (with Ari Elon and Naomi Mara Hyman) *Trees, the Earth, and Torah: A Tu B'Shvat Anthology*. In 1963 he received a Ph.D. in U.S. history from the University of Wisconsin (Madison) and was ordained to the Rabbinate in 1995 by a transdenominational *beit din* under the authority of ALEPH: Alliance for Jewish Renewal.

Laurie Zoloth is Director of the Brady Program in Ethics and Civic Life, Charles Deering McCormick Professor in Religious Studies and Jewish Studies, and Professor of Medical Humanities and Bioethics at Northwestern University, where she directed the Center for Bioethics, receiving Northwestern's Distinguished Teaching Award. She was Director of Jewish Studies at San Francisco State University. She served as President of the American Society for Bioethics and Humanities, receiving its Distinguished Service Award; as vice president of the Society for Jewish Ethics; as member of the NASA National Advisory Council, the agency's highest civilian advisory board, and its International Planetary Protection Committee, receiving the NASA National Public Service Award; as Chair of the

HHMI Bioethics Advisory Board, on the Boards of the International Society for Stem Cell Research; the Society for Women's Health Research; the NIH Asia AIDS trial group; the editorial boards of *The American Society for Law, Medicine and Ethics Journal*; *Shofar: A Journal of Jewish Studies*; *The Journal of Clinical Ethics*; *The American Journal of Bioethics*; and *Second Opinion: A Journal of Health, Faith and Ethics*. Her doctorate in Social Ethics and M.A. in Jewish Studies are from the Graduate Theological Union, where she was Alumna of the Year in 2005. She has published over 200 essays in ethics, family, feminist theory, religion and science, Judaism, and U.S. social policy, authoring *Health Care and The Ethics of Encounter: A Jewish Perspective on Justice*, and co-editing *Notes from a Narrow Ridge: Religion and Bioethics*; *Margin of Error: The Ethics of Mistakes in Medicine*; *The Human Embryonic Stem Cell Debate: Ethics, Religion and Policy*; and *Oncofertility: Religious, Ethical and Social Perspectives*.

Abbreviations

Throughout this volume, the following abbreviations will be used.

M. = Mishnah. This will be followed by the name of the specific tractate (book) of the Mishnah being referred to and the chapter and specific clause ("*mishnah*") number—e.g., M. *Sanhedrin* 4:5.

T. = Tosefta (edited c. 200 C.E. by Rabby Hiyya and Rabbi Oshaya).

J. = Jerusalem Talmud. This will be followed by the name of the tractate, the chapter and clause of the Mishnah where the quoted or intended material appears, and sometimes the page and column number (there are four columns on each page, two on the front side and two on the back) in the one-volume edition, e.g., J. *Sanhedrin* 1:1 (2a).

B. = Babylonian Talmud. This will be followed by the name of the tractate and the folio page and side (front side or back) in the standard, multivolume edition of the Talmud—e.g., B. *Sanhedrin* 32a.

M.T. = Maimonides' *Mishneh Torah*. This will be followed by the section, chapter, and clause numbers—e.g., M.T. Laws of Testimony 1:3.

S.A. = Joseph Karo's *Shulhan Arukh*. This will be followed by the name of the part of the code that is being cited (there are four parts, each with its own name), the chapter, and law number—e.g., S.A. *Hoshen Mishpat* 125:7. Where the reference is to Moses Isserles' comments, this will be followed by "(gloss)."

Acknowledgments

Theodore Calderara of Oxford University Press conceived of this project, suggested it to us, and has been our advisor and editor throughout. This project would never have seen the light of day without him. We thank him for his support, skill, perseverance, and good advice.

We especially want to thank the authors of the essays in this book. Each of them is an expert in his or her field, and each agreed to write a new essay specifically on the topic we requested. We, the editors, and you, the readers, of this volume owe them all a deep debt of gratitude.

Finally, each of us wants to thank his wife and family for their ongoing love and support. Their patience while we spent hundreds of hours on this book is a true testament of their love for us, a love that we appreciate with every fiber of our being.

INTRODUCTION

WHY STUDY JEWISH ETHICS?

ELLIOT N. DORFF AND JONATHAN K. CRANE

Many people use the terms "ethical" and "moral" synonymously, and sometimes even to reinforce each other, as when one says, "He is a very moral and ethical person." Philosophers generally distinguish the terms, with "morals" referring to judgments about specific issues (for example, is it moral to abort a fetus at any time?), while "ethics" refers to theories of morality. Still others distinguish these terms in other ways, as readers of this book will see.

However one uses these terms, ethics speaks to our judgments of right and wrong, good and bad, in our relationships with each other. It goes to the heart of what it means to be a moral human being, and thus is central to our character and identity. It is no wonder, then, that people around the world might be interested in ethics. Some are interested in the theoretical part of ethics ("metaethics"), which discusses what we mean by moral terms in the first place, who is bound by moral judgments, the grounds of authority of moral judgments, and the relationships between ethics and religion, law, custom, economics, and even art. Everyone, though, has a stake in practical ethics ("normative ethics" or "morality"), which discusses what is right or wrong, good or bad, in specific situations, for we all confront such questions throughout our lives.

Why, though, a book on *Jewish* ethics? And how is that different from "regular" ethics?

The answer lies in the fact that none of us is omniscient; nobody knows everything. As a result, even though some thinkers maintain that moral norms are absolute, applying to everyone in every time and place, we human beings cannot know for certain what those norms are. We may be very committed to our views of right and wrong, good and bad, and even to specific applications (e.g., that discriminating against others on the basis of race, gender, or religion is wrong, or, for some, that abortion is always wrong). Indeed, we may even be willing to die for some of our ethical convictions. In the end, though, all human beings perceive moral values *from their own vantage point.* That may be their own individual vantage point, or it may be that of the community to which they belong. Though our vantage points may be particular, the norms we endorse may still be universal and absolute—that is, binding on everyone in every time and place. Nevertheless, no matter how certain we may think we are, we cannot know for sure what those universal and eternal norms are.

Some philosophers maintain that the norms are not absolute, that they vary by society or even by individual. There is, indeed, a range from nihilists (who claim that there are no moral norms whatsoever) to subjectivists (who claim that what is right for me is not necessarily right for anyone else), to relativists (who claim that judgments of right and wrong are determined by, and vary by, groups or nations) to absolutists (who claim that moral norms apply to everyone at every time and place). The point, though, is that even absolutists, if they are being honest and appropriately humble about what they can know, must admit that, because they are human beings, their knowledge is inherently limited and that they inevitably perceive what is right and wrong from their own perspective. (In many ways, this idea parallels Einstein's Relativity Theory, which makes the same claim about our knowledge of objects and forces, applying it to our moral knowledge.)

What we presume is "secular" morality—or even "objective" morality—then, is actually moral norms from the vantage point of our own society. In Western societies, shaped as they were by the Western liberalism that emerged from Enlightenment philosophers such as John Locke and Jean Jacques Rousseau, what we usually mean by "secular" morality is a system of morals based on the notion of individual rights. Thomas Jefferson, in writing the U.S. Declaration of Independence, embraced this view as he quoted Locke in asserting this: "We hold these truths to be self-evident, that all men are created equal, that they are endowed by their Creator with certain unalienable rights, and that among these are life, liberty, and the pursuit of happiness."

The fact of the matter, though, is that even though individual rights as the bedrock of morality was "self-evident" to Enlightenment thinkers and the Founders of the United States, other cultures and nations see things very differently. Judaism, for example, perceives us as members of a community with duties, rather than individuals with rights. That is a bit too stark a comparison, for Americans and other Westerners also cherish family and community, and they certainly assert some duties that we have to our family and community. Conversely, Judaism maintains that every human being is created in God's image, and consequently each person is to be honored and respected. Still, the focus in American ethics is on individual autonomy, whereas the focus of Jewish ethics is on familial and communal responsibility. Even though rights and duties are sometimes reciprocal, getting up in the includes not only Reform authors such as Eugene Borowitz, who does not see the law as binding in the first place, but also some who do, including Conservative authors, such as Seymour Siegel and Robert Gordis, and even a small number of Orthodox writers, such as David Hartman.[4] In between is a host of writers in all the modern movements of Judaism who assert the integration of Jewish law with morality, with each affecting the other, but they justify and nuance this integration in a variety of ways.[5]

The omission of this last topic is representative of a larger set of omissions, for this book is a description of the field, not a set of polemical pieces arguing for one stance or another. As is stated above, some authors do argue for a particular stance after describing the lay of the land, but most do not.[6]

Despite efforts to make this volume expansive, it cannot be exhaustive. Here are some of the other theoretical and practical issues set aside for future deliberation: the ethics of Jewish historiography and the ethical sensibilities of particular Jewish communities throughout diasporic existence. More contemporary issues include the internet with its democratization of data, disintegration of privacy, and digitizing of personhood. Social media, the transformation of mass media, and the so-called demise of print media also merit ethical investigation on personal identity, civic engagement, and Jewish teaching and learning. Bioetechnologies, synthetic biology, neuroenhancers, brain imaging, cloning, genomics, and the whole realm of neuroethics both fascinate and challenge contemporary Jewish bioethicists, but with the exception of Laurie Zoloth's chapter on genetics, we were not able to address this set of issues. Corporate responsibility, safety, honesty, fiscal responsibility, environmental concerns, and more, not to mention governmental finances and systemic failures—all warrant urgent ethical attention, and the chapters in this volume on business ethics, environmental ethics, and the ethics of the treatment of animals only begin to address the many issues that arise in these areas of life. Education ethics too needs attention, especially as all education systems struggle with intellectual integrity, the tension between teaching for breadth and for depth, and the inculcation of virtues. This incomplete list of issues not fully addressed in this volume should serve only as an indication that more work in this field needs to be done, not the impoverishment of the volume. Rather, this volume may serve as a foundation and goad for those projects.

What Makes a Theory or Moral Stance Jewish?

In Part I readers will see that throughout history Jews have been embedded in a larger Western context and influenced by the ethical thought of non-Jews, and in Part II this influence will be evident in the authors' treatment of specific areas of practice. Sometimes Jews have consciously rejected what other cultures thought and did, as, for example, in the Bible's rejection of Canaanite sexual practices in Leviticus 18 and 20. To take a more contemporary example, Elliot Dorff's rabbinic ruling on violent and defamatory video games, adopted unanimously by the Conservative Movement's Committee on Jewish Law and Standards, limits the value of free speech in a way that the U.S. Supreme Court specifically does not.[7] Similarly, Jewish views on sexual relations are not as liberal as American law allows, for Jewish law forbids adultery, for example, while most Amerian states have dropped that prohibition altogether, and in some it is still on the books but is not enforced. On the other hand, Jewish law allows the use of artificial means of contraception, in contrast to Catholic doctrine.

At other times Jews have done the exact opposite, embracing what the outside world is doing and thinking deliberately and even legally, as, for example, when Jews living in northern Europe accepted Rabbenu Gershom's prohibition of polygamy, thereby adopting the Christian community's norm of monogamy. In more recent times, Jews have learned from Catholics the importance of premarital counseling and hospice care, and Jews have learned from Western liberal thought the importance of individual rights and of many norms in business ethics in the totally new contexts of corporations and modern technology.

In most times and places, though, Jews have done something in between, accepting influences from the outside only in part and in a particularly Jewish way. That response is true, for example, in how the Rabbis of the Mishnah adapted Roman family and business law when formulating Jewish laws on those topics, and it is also true for many contemporary decisions in medical ethics.

Readers will see these varying ways of responding to the surrounding culture in some essays, where authors cite non-Jewish authors or practices and respond to them in varying ways. More subtly, in other chapters authors are not as explicit about, or possibly even aware of, these influences, but readers may see their influence nevertheless.

These ways of responding to other cultures are good illustrations of what makes a particular ethical theory or moral stance recognizably Jewish. In some cases the answer will be obvious because the theory or stance extensively draws on Jewish law and thought and maintains them as they have been for centuries. In other cases, especially where the theory or moral position borrows significantly from non-Jewish perspectives or sources, the Jewish identity of the resulting theory or position will be less clear. At the same time, if the Jewish tradition will be able to thrive in ever-new circumstances, it must adapt to new conditions or sensitivities. So the fact that a theory or moral stance is new does not automatically disqualify it from being Jewish. The Jewish tradition is, after all, just that—an ongoing, evolving tradition. As a result, the religion of the Rabbis is a particular interpretation and application of the Torah (different in important ways from Christian interpretations and adaptations of the same Hebrew Bible), and the various expressions of Judaism today are all—including Orthodox ones—different in important ways from the forms of Judaism in the past. Otherwise Judaism would have fossilized and died generations ago. What makes a position that differs from the past still

Jewish, then, is that the theorist or moralist intentionally provides a pathway back to the tradition, rooting the theory or moral stance in the Jewish sources and practices of the past even if the new theory or stance is somewhat different.

Relationships of Jewish Ethics to Secular Ethical Theories and Practice

Because the Jewish tradition is evolving and because Jews themselves are as much embedded in the larger world as is Judaism itself, it should not be surprising that Jewish ethical discourse—both at the theoretical and practical levels—reflects influences from the world beyond Judaism. From as early as the Torah itself, the Jewish textual tradition incorporates words, ideas, rituals, holidays—and values—from surrounding civilizations and religions. It is not a hermetically sealed tradition. On the other hand, this is not to say that Jewish ethical deliberation incorporates what non-Jews have thought and done in a wholesale manner, or that everything non-Jews value has been brought into Judaism without some kind of vetting or reformulating. Rather, there has been a long-standing critical dialogue between Jews and non-Jews, and contemporary Jewish ethics continues this tradition.

Examples of this interreligious or religious-secular conversation abound. The Rabbis of the Talmuds wrestled vociferously with Greco-Roman and Christian worldviews, philosophies, values, and practices. Maimonides incorporated Aristotelianism in his legal and philosophical tracts, and many other medieval scholars responded to their Muslim and Christian hosts and neighbors. Arching forward into the modern period, most contemporary Jewish ethics expresses a response in some degree to the thought of Immanuel Kant. Emancipation further quickened the pace of Jewish encounters with other religious and secular systems of ethical thought, and their wake engendered various schools of Jewish thought and practice.

The more Jews became exposed to the larger world, the more they considered intellectually. This process can be seen in the last two hundred years as Jewish ethical deliberation branched out beyond the virtues, as had been championed by Maimonides and the *mussar* movement. Now, especially since Emancipation, Jews were considering with greater urgency such issues as the ethics of citizenship and the ethics of power; they found meaningful interlocutors in utilitarian, transcendental, pragmatic, and liberal philosophical schools—Mill, Thoreau, Dewey, and Rawls, to name just a few. And with the rise of technological prowess in the last century in both industry and medicine, Jews attended to the ethics of business and health alongside secular and Christian ethicists. Though they found some common ground with non-Jewish counterparts on what to do on many thorny issues, Jewish ethicists often came to these conclusions from dramatically different ways of reasoning.

Navigating this diversity of ethical thought has become a critical issue in the postmodern setting. It challenges both Jewish and other religious ethicists to justify why their religiously inspired ethics matter in religiously complex civilizations. In short, Jewish ethics has been, is, and will continue to be a dynamic conversation that both responds to and influences ethical deliberation in the larger, non-Jewish world.

Classical Literary Sources for Jewish Ethics

Readers of this volume will learn that contemporary Jews and those in recent centuries have added tremendously to the body of Jewish thinking on both ethical theory and practice. As was indicated above, though, what makes each of their theories recognizably Jewish is that they engage classical Jewish sources, sometimes confirming the views of those sources, sometimes rejecting them, and sometimes modifying their meaning or application. Readers, then, need to know what those sources are. The *literary* sources of Jewish ethics include, but are not limited to, the following:

1. The Tanakh (the Hebrew Bible). This has three parts: the Torah, Nevi'im, and Ketuvim. The Torah is the five books of Moses—Genesis, Exodus, Leviticus, Numbers, and Deuteronomy. Nevi'im (Prophets) consists of the historical books of Former Prophets—Joshua, Judges, 1 and 2 Samuel, and 1 and 2 Kings—and the literary books of Latter Prophets—Isaiah, Jeremiah, Ezekiel (the "Major Prophets" because their books are long) and the Twelve Minor Prophets (because their books are much shorter—e.g., Amos, Micah, Zekhariah [the longest of the twelve] and Obadaia [the shortest of the twelve]). Ketuvim (Writings) includes Psalms, Proverbs, and a variety of other books, including the historical books of 1 and 2 Chronicles.
2. The Mishnah, a collection of Jewish oral traditions, some undoubtedly from before the revelation at Mount Sinai and continuing to the time of the editing of the Mishnah c. 200 C.E. It is ordered by topic and was edited by Rabbi Judah Ha-nasi (president of the Sanhedrin). It is divided into six major parts (called *sedarim*, Orders), and those in turn are divided into books ("tractates," *massekhtot*), of which there are sixty-three in total.
3. The Midrash Halakhah, which consists of rabbinic commentaries on the legal sections of the Torah, edited c. 200 C.E.—namely, Mekhilta on Exodus, Sifra on Leviticus, and Sifre on Numbers and Deuteronomy.
4. The Jerusalem (or Palestinian) Talmud, a record of the discussions and expansions of the Mishnah that took place in Palestine, edited c. 400 C.E.

5. The Babylonian Talmud, a record of the discussions and expansions of the Mishnah that took place in Babylonia (modern-day Iraq), edited c. 500 C.E. When Jews talk about "the Talmud" without an adjective, they mean the Babylonian Talmud, because it was disseminated much more widely than the Jerusalem Talmud was in the centuries after their editing.
6. Midrash Aggadah—or simply "Midrash"—which consists of books of rabbinic commentaries on the nonlegal sections of the Torah, appearing in a variety of volumes edited between 425 C.E. and the twelfth century.
7. Legal codes, including especially Maimonides' *Mishneh Torah* (1177 C.E.) and Joseph Karo's *Shulhan Arukh* (1563), with glosses by Moses Isserles to indicate where the customs of Ashkenazic (northern European) Jews differed from those of Sephardic (Mediterranean) Jews, the latter being what Karo recorded.
8. Responsa (plural; *responsum* is singular)—in Hebrew, *she'elot u'teshuvot* (questions and answers) or simply *teshuvot*—which are rabbinic legal rulings, from the early Middle Ages to our own time.
9. Philosophical, literary, and liturgical works, as well as music and some art.

The Variety of Methodologies of Jewish Ethics

In addition to these literary sources, readers should be aware that the tradition offers Jews and others a wide variety of resources that influence Jewish moral thought and action through different *methodologies*. Elliot Dorff describes them in detail in the Appendix of his book *Love Your Neighbor and Yourself: A Jewish Approach to Modern Personal Ethics*.[8] What follows is an abridged version of that material. Some of the methods that Judaism uses to know and motivate the good are as follows.

Stories. For example, the core Jewish story—the Exodus from Egypt, the revelation at Mount Sinai, and the trek to the Promised Land—loudly proclaims that we can and must work together with God to redeem ourselves and others from slavery of all sorts. It also says that we must live our lives in accordance with revealed norms, and that we must continue to hope and work for the Promised Land of the Messianic age. (Note that the State of Israel's anthem is Hatikvah, "The Hope.") One way, in fact, to grasp the differences between Judaism and Christianity in moral vision is to compare the messages of their central stories, the Passion-Resurrection for Christianity and Exodus-Sinai for Judaism.[9] That same kind of comparative analysis can yield equally illuminating results when juxtaposing the central stories of other religions and secular philosophies on each other and to Judaism.[10]

Stories not only announce the norms and ideals of a religion or culture; they also give those norms and ideals a sense of reality and make them easier to apply to one's life. Moreover, because stories are concrete, they are easier to remember than rules or maxims, and, because they portray moral norms in real-life situations, stories are an effective way to educate people about moral norms (including what happens when they are broken) and to motivate people to be moral.

Because of their realia, stories also raise challenges in regard to discerning and disseminating norms. For example, insofar as contemporary Jewish norms derive in large part from precedents (see the section on law below), the details of some stories make it difficult to say with full confidence that they apply in whole or even in part to the peculiaraties of contemporary life. And there is also the problem of ambiguity: some stories are rather vague. This allows the modern reader ample room to see in them a wide range of norms. It is not uncommon, then, for a single story to inspire dramatically diverging, if not mutually exclusive, positions.[11]

History. No nation that has gone through the exile and persecution endured by Jews can possibly have an idealistic picture of human beings; the evil that people have foisted on each other must be part of the Jewish perception of reality. This is, of course, all the more true since the Holocaust, which, among other things, makes Jews wary of medical research on human subjects.

Family and Community. We first learn what is acceptable behavior and what is not from our parents. They thus make us aware of the whole realm of moral norms. They also provide the first motivation to act morally as we try to please them. Parents and, after them, siblings and other relatives are critical for the moral development of any human being. In fact, children who lack continual moral guidance from parents or some other caring adults from infancy are in serious danger of never understanding the moral dimension of life or acting morally. Judaism therefore takes care to buttress family life with very specific requirements embedded in the Torah's commands to honor and respect parents and, conversely, to require parents to teach their children the Torah and what it expects of them. Beyond these legal boundaries, Jewish family rituals are rich and pervasive, thus strengthening the family further. This emphasis on the family has been translated into Jewish consciousness through such media as popular literature and even Jewish jokes about family relationships.

As children mature, they come into contact with the larger community. While tightly knit communities can have the negative effects of squelching independent moral analysis and action, such communities can also have morally salutary effects. We learn that we cannot steal Johnnie's marbles on the playground from his and other children's reactions to such behavior. Throughout life, in fact, a strong part of our motivation to follow moral rules stems from our desire to have friends and to be part of a larger community. We also aspire to moral ideals, in part, because we crave the esteem of other people, especially those near and dear to us.

Contemporary communities in the United States, including Jewish ones, tend to be much more fractionalized and voluntary than they were in times past, and communities the world over tend to find themselves in continual interaction with other communities, thus blurring the coherence and authority of any one community's moral message. Nevertheless, communities still function to provide a shared life, including experiences and vocabulary that shape moral vision and behavior.

Leaders and Other Moral Models. Just as children learn morality first from their parents, so too adults learn to discern what is moral and gain the motivation to work for moral goals from their leaders and their other moral models. Nobody is perfect, of course, and part of the task in seeking moral leadership is to understand that specific people may be ideal in certain ways and not in others. When political and religious leaders are shown to have moral faults, this sometimes unfairly and unrealistically undermines our appreciation of their real moral leadership in other matters. Thus the leadership in civil rights shown by Presidents Kennedy and Johnson should not be forgotten just because they were each involved in morally questionable behavior in other aspects of their lives.

Similarly, Judaism uses leaders like the Patriarchs and Matriarchs, Moses, other biblical people, and rabbinic figures throughout the ages as models of ideal behavior and, importantly, also as models of what happens when you do something morally wrong. In describing what they did wrong as well as what they did right, Judaism keeps its leaders from becoming idols while still holding them up as figures to be thought of when deciding on one's own moral course.

It is not only people with specific offices in society who influence us morally. Teachers, counselors, friends, and even our children and students can show us how to behave. Although Rabbi Judah, the President of the Sanhedrin (or, in another version, Rabbi Hanina) was probably referring to the intellectual knowledge of the Jewish tradition, his famous dictum can equally apply to the moral lessons we learn from it: "Much have I learned from my teachers, more from my peers, but most from my students."[12]

General Values, Maxims, and Theories. The Torah announces some general moral values that should inform all our actions—values like formal and substantive justice, saving lives, caring for the needy, respect for parents and elders, honesty in business and in personal relations, truth telling, and education of children and adults. The Torah's laws articulate some of these general moral values, and others have found their way into books of moral maxims. The biblical Book of Proverbs and the tractate of the Mishnah (c. 200 C.E.) entitled *Ethics of the Fathers* (*Pirke Avot*) are two important ancient reservoirs of Jewish moral precepts, and medieval and modern Jewish writers have produced some others, such as Moses Hayyim Luzzato's *Paths of the Righteous* (*Mesillat Yesharim*).

Some medieval and modern Jewish thinkers formulated complete theories of morality, depicting a full conception of the good person and the good community, together with justifications for seeing them in that particular way and the modes of educating people to follow the right path. Several disparate examples of such theories, each with its own recipe for living a moral life out of the sources of Judaism, include the following: Maimonides' twelfth-century rationalist approach, borrowing heavily from Aristotle, articulated in his code (*Mishneh Torah*) and his philosophical work (*Guide for the Perplexed*); the mystical views of the thirteenth-century *Zohar* and the sixteenth-century Lurianic *kabbalah*; the behaviorist approach of the nineteenth-century figure, Israel Salanter, founder of the *musar* movement; the neo-Kantian rationalism of Hermann Cohen in the early twentieth century; and the existentialism of Emanuel Levinas in the last half of the twentieth century.

Theology. As in other Western religions, for Judaism God is central not only to defining the good and the right, but also to creating the moral person. God does that in several ways.

First, acting in God's judicial and executive functions, God helps to ensure that people will do the right thing. God is the infallible Judge, for He knows "the secrets of the world," as the High Holy Day liturgy reminds us. Nothing can be hidden from God, and God cannot be deceived. Moreover, God holds the power of ultimate reward and punishment. To do the right thing just to avoid punishment or to gain reward is clearly not acting out of a high moral motive, but such actions may nevertheless produce good results. Moreover, the Rabbis state many times over that even doing the right thing for the wrong reason has its merit, for eventually correct moral habits may create a moral person who does the right thing for the right reason.[13]

God also contributes to the creation of moral character in serving as a model for us. The underlying conviction of the Bible is that God is good, and God's actions are, as such, paradigms for us. The Bible itself raises questions about God's morality, for there are times when God appears to act arbitrarily and even cruelly; but, for all that, Jewish texts trust that God is good.[14] We, then, should aspire to be like God: "As God clothes the naked...so you should clothe the naked; as God visited the sick...so you should visit the sick; as God comforted those who mourned...so you should comfort those who mourn; as God buries the dead...so you should bury the dead."[15]

God's role as Covenant partner and as Israel's Lover probably has the greatest effect on creating moral character within us. We should abide by God's commandments, in part, because we were at Sinai, we promised to obey them there, and we should keep our promises. Thus, as the Haggadah of Passover reminds us, "In each and every generation a person is obliged to view himself as if he himself went out of Egypt" on the trek to Sinai, and God made the Covenant with all generations to come: "It is not with you alone that I create this Covenant and this oath [of obedience], but with those who are standing with us this day before the Lord, our God, and with those who are not with us today.... Secret things belong to the Lord, our God, but that which has been revealed is for us and for our children forever to carry out the words of this Torah."[16]

Ultimately, though, God serves to shape moral character by entering into a loving relationship with us. That is, the Covenant is not only a legal document, with provisions for those who abide by it and those who do not; the Covenant announces formal recognition of a *relationship* that has existed for a long while and that is intended to last, much as a covenant of marriage does. Relationships, especially intense ones like marriage, create mutual obligations that are fulfilled by the partners sometimes grudgingly but often lovingly, with no thought of a quid pro quo return. For God, as for a human marital partner,[17] we should do what the norms of morality require, and then we should go "beyond the letter of the law" (*lifnim m'shurat ha-din*) to do favors for our beloved. In moral terms, we then become the kind of people who seek to do both the right and the good, not out of hope for reward, but simply because that is the kind of people we are and the kind of relationships we have.

Prayer. Along with theology comes a life of prayer. Jews are commanded to pray three times each day, with four services on Sabbaths, Festivals, and the New Year, and five on the Day of Atonement. Aside from the spiritual nourishment, intellectual stimulation, aesthetic experience, and communal contact that Jewish prayer brings, it also serves several significant moral functions.

One of these is moral education. Until the twentieth century, most Jews could not afford to attend formal schooling beyond ten years of age. Since the printing press was not invented until 1450 or so, Jews could not learn about the Jewish tradition through reading books either. The Rabbis long ago instituted the practice of reading a section of the Torah four times each week, but that would expose Jews to the entirety of the Torah only in a year's time. As a result, the Rabbis created a framework of three biblical paragraphs constituting the *Shema* and twenty-two single-line blessings surrounding the *Shema* and constituting the *Amidah*, so that Jews would have an easily memorized formula to teach them the essence of Jewish belief. In fact, that outline is as close as Judaism ever got to a creed, an official statement of Jewish beliefs. That outline also serves to announce and rehearse some of Judaism's central values, including knowledge, forgiveness, health, justice, hope, and peace.

Moreover, the fixed liturgy reorients us to think about things from God's perspective. Even though the English word "prayer" denotes petition ("Do this, I pray"), and even though Jewish liturgy has room for asking God for things, the vast majority of the fixed liturgy praises and thanks God. This immediately tells Jews that they must get out of their egocentric concerns and think of life from God's vantage point. That alone should help them focus on the important things in life rather than the partial goods to which they may devote too much energy.

Prayer also serves as a way for people to confront what they have done wrong and to muster the courage to go through the process of *teshuvah*, return to the proper path and to the good graces of God and the community. People sometimes are stymied by their sins and by the guilt they feel. Jewish liturgy has Jews asking God to forgive our sins three times each day. Such confessional prayers enable people to relieve the guilt involved in sin so that they can repair whatever harm they have done and take steps to act better in the future.

Study. While family, community, authority figures, and even God are used by other societies to create moral character, albeit in different ways and degrees than Judaism uses those elements, study is one Jewish method for creating moral people that few other societies use. Moreover, this is an ancient Jewish method, stemming from the Torah itself. The Torah was not given to a group of elders who alone would know it; it was rather given to the entire People Israel assembled at Mount Sinai. In keeping with the public nature of revelation in Judaism, God tells Moses a number of times, "Speak to the people Israel and say to them (or command them)."[18] Moreover, every Jew is responsible to know God's commands and to teach them to their children.[19] To ensure that that would happen, the Torah institutes a public reading of the entire Torah every seven years at which "men, women, and children" were to be present.[20]

By the Second Temple period the Torah was actually read much more often than that, with small sections read on Saturday afternoons and on the mornings of the market days, Mondays and Thursdays, and larger sections read every Sabbath and Festival morning. These selections were arranged so that the entire Torah would be read once each year—or, for some communities, every three years. The reading would commonly include a translation into the vernacular and, on the Sabbath and Festivals, a lesson or homily based on the section chanted that day. This helped to ensure that the reading was not merely a mechanical act, but rather a truly educational experience. All of these public readings were part of the regular service, and so Jewish worship is characterized by the combination of prayer and study.

Moreover, the Pharisees made study an end in itself.[21]

> These are the deeds for which there is no prescribed measure: leaving crops at the corner of the field for the poor...doing deeds of lovingkindness, and studying Torah.[22]
>
> These are the deeds that yield immediate fruit and continue to yield fruit in time to come: honoring parents; doing deeds of lovingkindness; attending the house of study punctually, morning and evening; providing hospitality; visiting the sick; helping the needy bride; attending the dead; probing the meaning of prayer; making peace between one person and another, and between husband and wife. And the study of Torah is the most basic of them all.[23]

As a result, those who teach others have, in the Rabbinic view of things, special merit:

> David said: "O Lord, many groups of righteous people shall be admitted into Your presence. Which one of them is most beloved before You?" God answered: "The teachers of the youth, who perform their work in sincerity and with joy, shall sit at My right hand." [a paraphrase of Psalm 16:11][24]
>
> He who teaches his neighbor's child deserves to sit in the Heavenly Academy...and he who teaches the child of an ignoramus deserves to have God nullify a decree against him.[25]
>
> He who teaches his neighbor's child is as if he had created him.[26]

The relationship between study and morality goes in both directions: study can refine moral sensitivity and buttress the drive to act morally; conversely, morality is a prerequisite for appropriate teaching and study. Maimonides expresses this latter point explicitly:

> We teach Torah only to a student who is morally fit and pleasant in his ways, or to a student who knows nothing [and therefore may become such a person with learning]. But if the student goes in ways that are not good, we bring him back to the good path and lead him to the right way, and then we check him and [if he has corrected his ways] we bring him in to the school and teach him. The Sages said:

Anyone who teaches a student who is not morally fit is as if he is throwing a stone to Mercury [i.e., contributing to idolatry]...Similarly, a teacher who does not live a morally good life, even if he knows a great deal and the entire people need him [to teach what he knows because nobody else can], we do not learn from him until he returns to a morally good way of life.[27]

How, though, does study contribute to morality? It does so in at least four distinct ways:

(1) *Content.* The most obvious goal of text study is to inform students about what is right and wrong, good and bad.

(2) *Judgment.* In real life situations, values often clash, and so good judgment in resolving moral conflicts is a necessary asset of a moral person. Two types of text study aid the development of moral judgment: dialectic texts (e.g., the Talmud) that demonstrate moral argumentation so that those who study them sharpen their own abilities to analyze, criticize, and synthesize moral arguments; and philosophical texts that require students to stand outside the tradition and probe the justifications for its claims.

(3) *Motivation.* Text study can also help to motivate people to act morally by teaching them specifically what to do and what to avoid, by creating a community of learners who care about each other and the tradition they are studying and are thus willing to forego what they would like to do and do what they would prefer not to do in order to remain part of their community, and by presenting ideals and moral models to which to aspire.

(4) *The moral values attached to study itself.* Study can teach students such values as self-discipline, the value and pleasure of work, modesty, sociability, team spirit, caution, and exactitude. Depending on how the study is done, it can also teach students either to accept authority or to question it.

Law. Law is the other methodology to shape moral thinking and action that is employed by Judaism in ways that differ at least in degree, if not in kind, from other traditons. Judaism puts a great deal of emphasis on law as a moral tool—more than most other traditions, but with close parallels to Islam and Confucianism. Moreover, while classical Christian texts have a very negative view of law, in Judaism law is both important and sweet—indeed, as Jewish liturgy portrays it, a gift from God.

Here are some of the ways that Jewish law aids in defining and motivating morality:

Law defines and enforces minimal standards. The most obvious contribution is simply that Jewish law establishes a minimum standard of practice. This is important from a moral standpoint because many moral values can only be realized through the mutual action of a group of people, and a minimum moral standard that is enforced as law enables the society to secure the cooperation necessary for such moral attainment. Furthermore, there is an objective value to a beneficent act, whether it is done for the right reason or not. Consequently, establishing a minimum standard of moral practice through legislation provides for at least some concrete manifestations of conduct in tune with the dictates of morality, even if that conduct is not moral in the full sense of the word for lack of proper intention.

In spelling out minimal standards of moral conduct, there is always the danger that people will interpret the minimum requirements legalistically as the total extent to which they need to extend themselves for others. That, however, would involve a serious blindness to the realm of morality that would probably not be cured by removing the legal trappings from the minimum standards. Moreover, Judaism guards against such an abuse through its requirements of public and private study of the Bible and other morally enriching literature, through liturgy and sermons, and through making the minimal requirements of action rather demanding in the first place!

Law helps to actualize moral ideals. But it is not just on a minimal level that law is important for morality; law is crucial at every level of moral aspiration in order to translate moral values into concrete modes of behavior. The prophets enunciated lofty values, and we rightly feel edified and uplifted when we read their words or those of other great moral teachers in each generation. On the other end of the spectrum, when we hear "fire and brimstone" sermons or go through the painful self-examination of a confessional procedure such as Yom Kippur, we come away feeling chastened and purified. But the vast majority of life is lived between these two extremes of moral awareness as we pursue our daily tasks. Consequently, if that edification and chastening are going to contribute to a better world in any significant way, they must be translated into the realm of day-to-day activities. We ordinarily do not have sufficient time or self-awareness to think seriously about what we are doing, and hence a regimen of concrete laws that articulate what we should do in a variety of circumstances can often enable us to act morally when we would not ordinarily do so. Rabbi Morris Adler has articulated this point well:

> Religion is not a matter of living on the "peaks" of experience. That is for the saint and the mystic. More fundamentally, religion must mean transposing to a higher level of spiritual awareness and ethical sensitivity the entire plateau of daily living by the generality of men. Idolatry is defeated not by recognition of its intellectual absurdity alone, but by a life that expresses itself in service to God. Selfishness and greed are overcome not by professions of a larger view but by disciplines that direct our energies, our wills, and our actions outward and upward.[28]

Law provides a forum for weighing conflicting moral values and setting moral priorities. Until now we have spoken about areas in which the moral norm is more or less clear and the problem is one of realizing those norms. Many situations, however, present a conflict of moral values, and it must be determined which value will take precedence over which, and under what circumstances. Nonlegal moral systems usually offer some mechanism for treating moral conflicts, but they often depend on the sensitivity and analytic ability of an authority figure or each individual. By contrast, the law provides a format for deciding such issues *publicly*, thus ensuring that many minds of varying convictions will be brought to bear on the issue. This does not guarantee wisdom, but it does at least provide a greater measure of objectivity and hence a more thorough consideration of the relevant elements.

Law gives moral norms a sense of the immediate and the real. Issues are often joined more clearly in court than they are in moral treatises or announcements of policy because the realities with which the decision deals are dramatically evident in the courtroom and a decision must be reached. Moral essayists or theorists, on the other hand, do not face the immediate responsibility of having people act on their decisions, and hence they tend to be somewhat "ivory-towerish." Consensus statements on moral issues produced by denominations or other groups of people often suffer from the need to include the opinion of everyone in the group and thus lose sharpness and, sometimes, coherence. In contrast, a court ruling is specific and addressed to a real situation. In fact, much of the sheer wisdom of the Rabbinic tradition can be attributed to the fact that the Rabbis served as judges as well as scholars and teachers. Of course, how to apply a precedent to a new case is not always clear, but the legal context adds a sense of immediacy and reality to moral deliberation.

Law gives moral norms a good balance of continuity and flexibility. Because law operates on the basis of precedent, there is a greater sense of continuity in a moral tradition that is structured legally than in one that is not. After all, one of the things that people seek in creating a legal system in the first place is the security of knowing what they can expect of others and what is expected of them. This is achieved in law by the methodology of precedent, of *stare decisis*, "it stands decided." On the other hand, through legal techniques like differentiation of cases, the law preserves a reasonable amount of flexibility and adaptability. By contrast, moral decisions made on the basis of conscience often have little public effect or staying power; and moral decisions made on the basis of natural law or divine law understood in a fundamentalistic way lack sufficient malleability to retain relevance to new situations and to take advantage of new knowledge. A legal tradition, although certainly not without its problems in practice, attains the best balance that human beings can achieve between tradition and change.

Law serves as an educational tool for morality. Theories of education are numerous and diverse, but the Jewish tradition has a clear methodology for moral education.

> Rab Judah said in Rav's name: A man should always occupy himself with Torah and good deeds, though it is not for their own sake, for out of (doing good) with an ulterior motive he will come to (do good) for its own sake.[29]

This largely behavioristic approach to moral education is not totally so. As we have seen above, the study of the Tradition is also an integral part of Jewish moral education. But in the end the emphasis is on action:

> An excellent thing is the study of Torah combined with some worldly occupation, for the labor demanded by both of them causes sinful inclinations to be forgotten. All study of the Torah without work must in the end be futile and become the cause of sin.[30]

The same educational theory is applied to moral degeneracy and repentance:

> Once a man has committed a sin and repeated it, it appears to him as if it were permitted.
>
> Run to fulfill even a minor precept and flee from the slightest transgression; for precept draws precept in its train, and transgression draws transgression.

If a transgression comes to a man a first and second time without his sinning, he is immune from the sin.³¹

If one accepts this approach to moral education in whole or in part, formulating moral norms in terms of law is very important educationally; for legally *requiring* people to act in accord with moral rules is a step toward teaching them how to do the right thing for the right reason.

Law provides a way to make amends and repair moral damage. One goal of law is social peace. Legal systems therefore generally provide ways for dealing with antisocial behavior and for adjudicating disputes. A religious legal system like Jewish law also provides a way for overcoming guilt; making amends; and reconciling with God, with the aggrieved parties, and with the community as a whole. That process is *teshuvah*, return, according to which the assailant must do the following: acknowledge that he or she has sinned; experience and express remorse; apologize to the victim; compensate the victim in whatever way possible; and take steps to ensure that when a similar occasion arises again, the wrongdoer will act differently. In defining the process, Jewish law makes moral repair demanding but possible.

It goes further: it demands that when the process has been completed, the victim must respond in kind. So, for example, according to the Mishnah, if one person injures another, the assailant must pay the victim for five remedies—the injury itself, the time lost from work, pain, medical expenses, and the embarrassment the injury caused. After describing how each of these payments is to be calculated, the Mishnah says that "Even though the assailant pays the victim, God does not forgive him until he asks the victim's forgiveness;" this is the apology required in the process of return. But the Mishnah then states that if the victim refuses to pardon the assailant, the victim becomes the wrongdoer and is regarded as "cruel."³² There clearly are cases when wrongdoers should not be forgiven, but, by and large, we must forgive those who have fulfilled the requirements of the process of return and have asked for forgiveness. In the law of many American states, a felon who has been released from prison is barred from voting and from government jobs the rest of his or her life and must reveal the past felony to any potential employer. In Jewish law, by contrast, it is prohibited even to mention the person's past crime unless it has direct bearing on a practical decision, for once the person has fulfilled the requirements of the process of return, to mention the past sin is, according to the Mishnah, oppressive, slanderous speech.³³ Thus Jewish law aids and abets reconciliation and peace.³⁴

Law helps to preserve the integrity of moral intentions. We usually construe ourselves as having good intentions, but actions test, clarify, and verify our intentions. Rabbi Abraham Joshua Heschel put it this way:

> The dichotomy of faith and works which presented such an important problem in Christian theology was never a problem in Judaism. To us, the basic problem is neither what is the right action nor what is the right intention. The basic problem is: what is right living? And life is indivisible. The inner sphere is never isolated from outward activities...

It would be a device of conceit, if not presumption, to insist that purity of heart is the exclusive test of piety. Perfect purity is something we rarely know how to obtain or how to retain. No one can claim to have purged all the dross even from his finest desire. The self is finite, but selfishness is infinite.... God asks for the heart, but the heart is oppressed with uncertainty in its own twilight. God asks for faith, and the heart is not sure of its own faith. It is good that there is a dawn of decision for the night of the heart; deeds to objectify faith, definite forms to verify belief.[35]

Concretizing moral values in the form of law is thus an important method for testing the nature and seriousness of our intentions so that we may avoid hypocrisy. It also graphically shows us the effects of our intentions, so that hopefully we will alter those that are knowingly or unknowingly destructive. In other words, law brings our intentions out into the arena of action, where we can see them clearly and work with them if necessary.

In all of these ways, then, law contributes to morality. We have taken the trouble to discuss this rather thoroughly in order to demonstrate that the interaction between law and morality involves contributions in both directions. This is especially important when trying to understand Judaism, which went so far in trying to deal with morality in legal terms.

As important as law is in shaping Jewish moral vision and behavior, however, it is not the sole vehicle that Judaism uses to create a moral person and society. All of the other methods discussed earlier—stories, history, family and community, moral leaders and models, moral maxims and theories, theology, prayer, and study—play critical roles, along with law, in enabling Judaism to contribute mightily to creating moral individuals and communities. These methods do not guarantee moral character or behavior, for life does not come with guarantees, especially for something as difficult to acquire as moral sensitivity and action. Moreover, there are aspects of Judaism and of religions generally that actually function as obstacles to moral vision and behavior, and people of all religions must take steps to ensure that those factors do not lead to morally atrocious results. At the same time, we must recognize and seek to enhance the morally beneficial effects of the multiple ways in which Judaism contributes to morality.

On balance, many of us, your editors certainly included, are grateful for the moral contributions of Judaism to our lives, as we are for the many other ways it makes our lives richer. Ultimately, we might celebrate those gifts in language much like that of the Psalmist:

> The Teaching (Torah) of the Lord is perfect, renewing life.
> The decrees of the Lord are enduring, making the simple wise.
> The precepts of the Lord are just, giving the heart joy.
> The instruction of the Lord is lucid, making the eyes light up.
> The fear of the Lord is pure, enduring forever.
> The judgments of the Lord are true, completely just.
> More precious than gold, than much fine gold,
> Sweeter than honey, than drippings of the comb.[36]

Modern Movements, Modern Approaches

Finally, readers should know that modern Jews use these various literary sources and methods in very different ways. In some respects, this is nothing new: Jews have argued about moral issues with each other and even with God from the time that Abraham, the very first Jew, argued with God about the fate of the people of Sodom. Judaism is, in fact, a tradition that loves analysis and argument, one that has a remarkable tolerance for uncertainty and pluralism. There have always been differing schools of Jewish thought and practice, ranging from debates between prophets and kings in the First Temple period to the Pharisees and Saducees of the last centuries B.C.E. and the first century C.E. to the rationalists and mystics of the Middle Ages, to the modern movements of Judaism.

In other ways, though, the disputes among the modern movements are different from those of the past. The Enlightenment and its political ramifications in the late eighteenth century to our own day have made Jews living in Western countries at least theoretically and, to varying extents, legally full citizens of the nations in which they live. Their debates therefore address not only internal, Jewish issues, but how best to participate as citizens in the moral decisions of their nations. This has taken on yet another coloration in the modern State of Israel, where Jews, as a majority, have become fully responsible for the policies of the state. Furthermore, the Enlightenment provided not only freedom of religion, but freedom *from* religion, and so genuinely secular forms of Jewish expression have become both possible and actual. Thus the range of Jewish responses to moral issues has expanded immensely in the modern period. To understand the ideological background of the chapters in this volume, then, especially those in Part II, which deals with specific moral topics, it is important for readers to know how the modern movements of Judaism understand and apply the classical literature and methods of Jewish ethics described here.

In modern North and South America, and, to a lesser extent, in Europe and Israel, Jews are divided into primarily (but not exclusively) three movements: Orthodox, Conservative (Masorti), and Reform (Progressive). In the United States, the Reform movement is the largest, with 39 percent of Jews affiliated with synagogues; the Conservative Movement is next, with 33 percent; and the Orthodox is the smallest, with about 21 percent.[37] About half of American Jews, however, are not affiliated with any synagogue, so one must divide these numbers by two to see the percentage each movement represents of the Jews of the United States. Some are unaffiliated for financial or other reasons, though, so the fact that they do not belong to a synagogue does not necessarily mean that they are secular in either thought or action. Still, because it is generally the case in other religions that if you do not believe in a particular religion's central tenets or seek to abide by its ritual and moral rules, you are not a member of that religion, it is important to note that Jews can, and many do, identify as Jews culturally or ethnically but not religiously. Some self-identified secular Jews, in fact, take an active role in Jewish communal organizations such as Jewish Federation, Jewish Family Service, and Jewish Centers, for example.

Among the religious movements, Orthodox Jews believe that the Torah was given word-for-word by God at Mount Sinai and that we have an accurate record of what God said, for what God said has been unerringly transmitted from the revelation at Mount Sinai to our own day as published in modern texts of the Torah. Furthermore, in addition to this Written Torah (the Five Books of Moses), God revealed at Mount Sinai an Oral Torah, transmitted by word and action throughout the generations. The Oral Torah is at least as important and authoritative as the Written Torah. Because God is the author of both the Written and Oral Torahs, Jewish law as it has come down to us may be applied to new circumstances but otherwise must not be changed and must be obeyed as the command of God. Even Orthodox Jews, however, are not biblical fundamentalists in the way that some Christians are, for the Written Torah must always be understood and applied through the lens of the Oral Torah.

Conservative Judaism—called Masorti (Traditional) Judaism outside of the United States and Canada—is based first on the conviction that we must study the Jewish texts and practices not only through its traditional interpretations, but also by using all of the tools that scholars use to understand any other tradition. These include, but are not limited to, cross-cultural studies, linguistic studies, and archaeology. When one uses these resources, one finds evidence that the Torah consists of several documents that were composed at various times and edited together later (usually presumed by the time of Ezra c. 450 B.C.E.). This makes sense because in the ancient world writing materials were hard to come by and most people were illiterate, so all of the cultures of the ancient world were transmitted primarily in oral form—that is, literally what elders said to the young and also what people saw going on in their society. The Torah, then, represents the first written edition of these oral traditions.

How Conservative/Masorti Jews understand the role of God in the creation of the Jewish tradition, including the process of revelation, varies. Moreover, Conservative Jews generally believe that Jewish law is binding on us not only because of God's role in its creation, but also because it has been a critical identifying mark of the Jewish community. This includes what moderns call rituals, which serve to mark the transitions of time and of the life cycle and give them meaning and even artisitic expression in a uniquely Jewish way. Jewish law also includes the parts of Jewish law that moderns would call moral, giving Jews moral guidance in ways that also often differ from the guidance of other traditions. The content of Jewish law has changed in a variety of ways over time, and so Conservative/Masorti Jews believe that to be historically authentic to the Jewish tradition we as a community must be prepared to change it in our own time as well to make it relevant to new circumstances and new moral sensitivities; but in the end Jewish law is binding on us as Jews. (The communal agency within the Conservative/Masorti movement charged with applying Jewish law to modern circumstances is the Committee on Jewish Law and Standards, consisting of twenty-five rabbis chosen by a formula intended to ensure variations in expertise, experience, age, and gender, who are voting members, and five lay leaders and one cantor who serve in an advisory, but not a voting, capacity.)

The Reform movement emphasizes individual autonomy. In the nineteenth century and the first half of the twentieth, Reform leaders focused on the moral import of the Jewish tradition and rejected, or at least deemphasized, its ritual components; it saw Judaism as exclusively ethical monotheism. In the last half century, however, Reform leaders have reintroduced a concern for Jewish rituals, and they have emphasized that individual Jews should decide how they are going to express their Jewish commitments based on knowledge of the tradition and not just what they want. Reform rabbis have created a Responsa Committee to give guidance to Reform Jews in making their individual ritual and moral decisions.

As we indicated earlier, we, the editors of this volume, deliberately chose authors who reflected this diversity of modern Jewish life so that readers could understand the history of Jewish ethical thought and Jewish responses to modern issues from a variety of perspectives. At the same time, we asked authors to present their material in as objective a way as possible, indicating when they are taking their own particular approach with which other Jewish scholars might differ. In this way we hope in this volume to present our readers with a fair and accurate picture of Jewish ethical and moral thought.

Notes

1. This point was made more eloquently and convincingly by Louis E. Newman in what has by now become a classic essay in Jewish ethics, "Woodchoppers and Respirators: The Problem of Interpretation in Contemporary Jewish Ethics," *Modern Judaism* 10:2 (February 1990), 17–42; reprinted in *Contemporary Jewish Ethics and Morality: A Reader*, Elliot N. Dorff and Louis E. Newman, eds. (New York: Oxford University Press, 1995), 140–60.
2. For a description of the range of positions regarding the relationship between religion and morality, see Elliot N. Dorff, *Matter of Life and Death: A Jewish Approach to Modern Medical Ethics* (Philadelphia: Jewish Publication Society, 1998), Appendix (pp. 395–417). For a description of the issues involved in these relationships and the varying Jewish resources relevant to morality, see Elliot N. Dorff, *Love Your Neighbor and Yourself: A Jewish Approach to Modern Personal Ethics* (Philadelphia: Jewish Publication Society, 2003), Chap. One (pp. 1–32) and Appendix (pp. 311–44).
3. E.g., J. David Bleich, "Halakhah as an Absolute," *Judaism* 29:1 (Winter 1980), 30–37; J. David Bleich, "Is There an Ethic Beyond Halakhah?" in *Studies in Jewish Philosophy*, Norbert M. Samuelson, ed. (Lanham: University Press of America, 1987), pp. 527–46; and David Weiss Halivni, "Can a Religious Law Be Immoral?" in *Perspectives on Jews and Judaism*, Arthur Chiel, ed. (New York: Rabbinical Assembly, 1978), 165–70.
4. Eugene B. Borowitz, *Renewing the Covenant: A Theology for the Postmodern Jew* (Philadelphia: Jewish Publication Society, 1991), chs. 19–20, esp. pp. 280–83, 286–88. Seymour Siegel, "Ethics and Halakhah," *Conservative Judaism* 25:3 (1971), 33–40. Robert Gordis, *The Dynamics of Judaism: A Study in Jewish Law* (Bloomington:

Indiana University Press, 1990), pp. 50–68, 138–44. See also chs. 10 and 11, where he argues for changing the status of women in Jewish law on moral grounds. David Hartman, *A Living Covenant: The Innovative Spirit in Traditional Judaism* (New York: Free Press, 1985), ch. 4, esp. p. 97, where he says: "Prayer, religious awe, and the nonrational retain their place in religious life even as one makes the ethical a controlling category for the development of the *halakhah*. At the same time, however, the divine power and mystery must never be used as a justification to undermine the category of the ethical."

5. In the Conservative Movement, see, for example, Elliot N. Dorff, *For the Love of God and People: A Philosophy of Jewish Law* (Philadelphia: Jewish Publication Society, 2007), ch. 6; and, very differently, Joel Roth, *The Halakhic Process: A Systematic Analysis* (New York: Jewish Theological Seminary of America, 1986), chs. 1 and 9. Among Orthodox writers, see Aharon Lichtenstein, "Does Jewish Tradition Recognize an Ethic Independent of Halakha?" in *Modern Jewish Ethics: Theory and Practice*, Marvin Fox, ed. (Columbus: Ohio State University Press, 1975), pp. 62–88 (reprinted in *Contemporary Jewish Ethics*, Menachem Marc Kellner, ed., [New York: Sanhedrin Press, 1978], 102–23), and Shubert Spero, *Morality, Halakha, and the Jewish Tradition* (New York: Ktav and Yeshiva University Press, 1983). In the Reform movement, see Mark Washofsky, *Jewish Living: A Guide to Contemporary Reform Practice* (New York: UAHC Press, 2000), Introduction, esp. pp. xxiv–xxv.

6. For a taste of the polemics within the Jewish tradition and community, readers might consult *Contemporary Jewish Ethics and Morality: A Reader*, Elliot N. Dorff and Louis E. Newman, eds. (New York: Oxford University Press, 1995), and the *Jewish Choices/Jewish Voices* series of books, which consists of six volumes, published in 2008–2010 by the Jewish Publication Society. The first three volumes, on body, money, and power, are edited by Elliot N. Dorff and Louis E. Newman, and the last three, on sex, war, and social justice, are edited by Elliot N. Dorff and Danya Ruttenberg. Each book contains four cases that raise moral issues in the volume's area of life, some traditional and modern sources relevant to those issues, and short essays by several contemporary Jews who take differing stands on those issues, often by reading the tradition differently.

7. Elliot N. Dorff, "Violent and Defamatory Video Games," www.rabbinicalassembly.org/sites/default/files/public/halakhah/teshuvot/20052010/videogamesDorffHearshenFinal.pdf (accessed August 10, 2011). Brown v. Entertainment Merchants Association 564 U.S. (2011), www.supremecourt.gov/opinions/10pdf/08-1448.pdf (accessed August 10, 2011).

8. Elliot N. Dorff, *Love Your Neighbor and Yourself: A Jewish Approach to Modern Personal Ethics* (Philadelphia: Jewish Publication Society, 2003), Appendix.

9. For one good treatment of that, see Michael Goldberg, *Jews and Christians Getting Our Stories Straight: The Exodus and the Passion-Resurrection* (Nashville: Abingdon, 1985).

10. Dorff summarizes the differences between the Jewish, Christian, and American secular visions in Chapter One of his book *To Do the Right and the Good: A Jewish Approach to Modern Social Ethics* (Philadelphia: Jewish Publication Society, 2002).

11. See Jonathan K. Crane, *Narratives and Jewish Bioethics*. (New York: Palgrave MacMillan, forthcoming).

12. B. *Makkot* 10a, where this is quoted in the name of Rabbi (Judah, the President of the Sanhedrin); B. *Ta'anit* 7a, where it is quoted in the name of Rabbi Hanina.

13. B. *Peshahim* 50b; B. *Sanhedrin* 105a; B. *Arakhin* 16b; B. *Sotah* 22b, 47a; B. *Horayot* 10b; B. *Nazir* 23b.

14. See Elliot N. Dorff and Arthur Rosett, *A Living Tree: The Roots and Growth of Jewish Law* (Albany, NY: State University of New York Press, 1988), pp. 110–23, 249–57; and Elliot N. Dorff, *For the Love of God and People: A Philosophy of Jewish Law* (Philadelphia: Jewish Publication Society, 2007), Chapter 6.
15. B. *Sotah* 14a.
16. Deuteronomy 29:13, 28.
17. God is depicted as Israel's marital partner a number of times in the Bible, whether fondly, as in Jeremiah 2:2, or angrily when Israel proves to be an unfaithful lover, as in Hosea, chapter 2.
18. For example, Numbers 15:1–2, 17–18, 37–38; 19:1–2; 28:1–2; 34:1–2; 35:1–2, 9–10.
19. The duty for Jewish adults to learn the Torah themselves: Deuteronomy 5:1. The duty of parents to teach their children: Deuteronomy 6:7; 11:19.
20. Deuteronomy 31:9–13.
21. The Pharisees may have been influenced in this, as Moses Hadas contends, by the Greeks; cf. Moses Hadas, *Hellenistic Culture* (New York: Columbia University Press, 1959), pp. 69–71. Thanks to Rabbi Neil Gillman for this reference. The Rabbis, though, also stressed action, and so their stance toward whether study or action was more important was deeply ambivalent in a way that the Greek worship of knowledge never was. See B. *Kiddushin* 40b.
22. M. *Pe'ah* 1:1.
23. B. *Shabbat* 127a.
24. *Pesikta (Buber)*, p. 180a.
25. B. *Bava Metzia* 85a.
26. B. *Sanhedrin* 19a.
27. M. T. *Laws of Study* 4:1.
28. Morris Adler, *The World of the Talmud* (New York: Schocken, 1963), p. 64.
29. B. *Pesahim* 50b, and in parallel passages elsewhere.
30. M. *Avot (Ethics of the Fathers)* 2:1.
31. B. *Yoma* 86b; M. *Avot* 4:2; B. *Yoma* 38b.
32. M. *Bava Kamma* 8:7.
33. M. *Bava Metzia* 4:10.
34. For more on the Jewish process of return, including a discussion of when forgiveness is not appropriate, see Elliot N. Dorff, *Love Your Neighbor and Yourself: A Jewish Approach to Modern Pesonal Ethics* (Philadelphia: Jewish Publication Society, 2003), Chapter 6.
35. Abraham Joshua Heschel, *God in Search of Man* (New York: Harper and Row, 1955), pp. 296–97.
36. Psalms 19:8–10.
37. [No author stated], *The National Jewish Population Study 2000–2001* (New York: United Jewish Communities, 2003), p. 7; available at www.ujc.org/njps/pdf (accessed June 8, 2012).

PART I

JEWISH ETHICAL THEORIES

Introduction to Part I

ETHICAL THEORIES, NOT THEORY

One may rightfully ask why this volume opens with a collection of essays that examine and explain various Jewish ethical theories—and not just one essay. After all, insofar as Judaism is a monotheistic tradition, a tenet of which maintains that its truths are universal in scope, it stands to reason that the tradition should endorse just one ethical theory. This calculus of one God equals one ethic sounds attractive and, indeed, it inspired many Jews throughout the millennia to construct overarching, universal Jewish ethical theories. From such greats as Moses Maimonides in the twelfth century to Moritz Lazarus in the nineteenth, from Franz Rosenzweig in the early twentieth century to Byron Sherwin in the later part of that century, and on into the twenty-first century, many luminaries endeavored to develop unified ethical theories for Jews. For them, Judaism offers but one ethical system.

Such systems are enticing. By definition they are totalizing, which means that they understand themselves to be so encompassing that nothing could be beyond their concern. Their relevance to morally complicated practical issues need not be explained, because everything falls within their purview. It would be superfluous in such systems to justify why addressing an issue using Judaic texts and tools is important in the first place; it could not be otherwise, they assume. This certainty regarding relevance is no doubt comforting when one confronts novel situations. Such systemic theories were especially popular in the premodern period, when it was relatively difficult to relocate physically or religiously. One lived within a particular horizon or worldview that, for better and for worse, had to contend with the vagaries of existence. Alternative paradigms were either unavailable or so denigrated as to be unreasonable to consult, much less follow.

Such efforts portray the Judaic tradition as a unified whole, a system whose components fit comfortably next to each other with no contradictions or even countervailing elements. As such, these grand unified theories condensed Judaism's vast library that, undeniably, emerged over millennia and continents, into a single narrative. Like thick and rich syrups, such condensed narratives express the essence of Judaism—or at least the essence that the author sees and endorses. Some pivot on the Deuteronomic teaching to do what is right and good (*hayashar v'hatov*), while others, following the prophetic wont to single out Judaism's essence, isolate either love (*ahavah*) or righteousness (*tzedek*) as the keystone that keeps the pillars of Judaism's ethics upright. Anything in the textual tradition that might countermand these essences either is dismissed altogether through silence or suppression, or is apologetically explained away. The system's coherence and universalism are what mattered; certainty of the system's rectitude was a prerequisite.

The rise of modernity, however, shattered certainty in systemic theorizing. Since the Enlightenment and its corollary emancipation of Jews, overarching systemic theories in Jewish ethics have faced challenges they cannot explain away. The bloody twentieth century proved that systemic theories, especially of and by certain forms of government, are more dangerous than beneficial. Suspicion became necessary not only of governing regimes and of how people organize and behave, but also of the ways people think and what motivates them. That ancient and mass motivator—religion—ultimately succumbed to scrutiny. Especially in the last century, religions, in the face of skepticism, increasingly had to explain themselves both to their adherents and to non-coreligionists. Some religious communities underwent lengthy and often difficult self-critical deliberations wherein their totalizing narratives were refashioned to be more persuasive in an increasingly cynical world. The Second Vatican Council is but one prominent example of this phenomenon.

Jews, too, critically examined the Judaic tradition in ways that heretofore had been anathema if not heretical. The rise of *Wissenschaft des Judentum*, the scientific study of Judaism, in the nineteenth century entailed not only a new look at classic texts but also a new appreciation of those texts' pretexts, or assumptions, and contexts. History, and Jewish history in particular, became a field of inquiry that Jewish scholars could no longer ignore. Locating texts in their geopolitical contexts sharpened Jewish discourse and, paradoxically, muted its impact. On the one hand, Jewish scholars situated classic texts in their historical strata and thereby uncovered and highlighted the broad range of contexts and assumptions of the texts' provenance. Yet this more precise understanding of the development of the Judaic textual tradition undermined the notion of only one Jewish system of ethics, law, or theology. If the Babylonian Talmud is indeed patchwork, which *Wissenschaft* shows it is, claiming that it is all of a single cloth is disingenuous. Erecting a system based on the Talmud—or the Bible or rabbinic literature generally—seemed increasingly suspect.

Though history and historiography challenged Jews, they also pushed Jews to make a more concerted effort to justify their assertions about Jewish ethics to skeptical and pluralistic audiences of both Jews and non-Jews. Especially since the early twentieth century, Jews have used a great deal of ink to situate their notions of Jewish ethics in both history and the present—for they know that the better they explain themselves and their reasons, the more purchase they will find among co-religionists and even among sympathetic non-Jews. Justifications became an increasingly prevalent element of modern Jewish ethical writing.[1] No longer able to excommunicate deviants from the Jewish community, Jewish ethicists labored to *persuade* wayward Jews away from inappropriate behavior and toward what they understood to be the better path. In the modern Enlightenment environment, guaranteeing freedom of religion and, with it, freedom from religion, even stalwart Orthodox ethicists admit that at best they can only suggest and prod, provoke and pull Jews toward the right and the good; they cannot mandate.

Although this lean toward rhetoric has become more explicit in recent times, it has always been present in the Judaic library. From as early as the Tanakh (the Hebrew Bible), words have been the medium through which norms have been communicated and motivation expressed. Each historical layer of the Judaic library, and even different genres that developed concomitantly, articulate various ways of defining what is moral and then motivating people to choose the moral path. In so doing they simultaneously demonstrate various ways of thinking about morality, or, put differently, they manifest different ethical theories.

Hence this volume begins with a series of essays examining many of the layers of Jewish ethical theories.

Making Sense of Many Theories

The order of these theories as presented in this book warrants a brief note. Chapters 1 through 10 follow a fairly linear chronological order, starting with the Bible and ending with the Holocaust. Since this book could not give due attention to all players in Jewish ethical theorizing, editorial decisions had to be made to select the elements on which to focus, whom to include, and what to put aside. These decisions were made by the co-editors, and we added many more chapters than we initially brainstormed because others whom we consulted pointed out glaring gaps.

After this historical survey, chapters 11 through 14 describe ethical decision-making as it has developed in the largest streams of modern Jewry: Reform, Conservative, Orthodox, and Reconstructionist. To be sure, all of these streams came into being before World War II, yet their ethical theorizing matured dramatically afterward, because of, and perhaps despite, that war. Obviously this is not to say that any stream of modern Jewry has achieved a final ethical methodology—or that any could. Still, these chapters describe the considerable thought about moral issues that each stream has developed, especially as Jews confronted the meanings of the Holocaust and the State of Israel and found themselves being profoundly influenced in every aspect of life by revolutionary technological development in virtually every field.

Chapters 15 and 16, the last two chapters in this section, explore issues that pervade all streams of modern Jewry—feminism and post-modernism, respectively. The last three decades of the twentieth century witnessed the emergence and growth of these sociopolitical and philosophical concerns, which Jewish ethicists have found irresistible, irritating, or both simultaneously. A few of these ethicists have been on the forefront of these larger movements that challenge modernity's assumptions about gender, power, and moral decision-making.

With no intention to undermine the reader's enjoyment of these chapters, a brief synopsis of each follows, so that readers of Part I have an overall sense of "the forest" before they examine the individual trees.

Elaine Goodfriend opens the volume with a careful reading of biblical ethical concepts. Fear of God (*yir'at Elohim*) is perhaps the most pervasive and powerful notion inspiring social concern and behavior. It is therefore difficult to assert a strong and impermeable boundary between religion and ethics in the biblical milieu. Such a boundary does not exist between law and ethics either. For these reasons the Bible contains multiple ways to motivate people to do what is right and good, ways that are championed by later contributors to Jewish ethical theories, as subsequent chapters will demonstrate. While some of these motivating factors pertain to Israelites alone, the Bible nonetheless assumes that other nations also can and should behave according to at least some basic minimal standards. For this reason many biblical ethical texts concern relations between or among communities, including those between Jews and non-Jews, not just between or among the individuals within them.

Charlotte Fonrobert notes that speaking of ethics is rather difficult when one considers rabbinic literature. Not only does this literature lack the very notion of ethics, it also emerges from various terrains and times and perforce bespeaks not only different moral conclusions, but even differing presumptions on how to reach those positions. Hence claims that there is a single rabbinic ethic are inherently suspect. That said, the rabbis of old certainly do wrestle with ethicality, its interrelationship with both rabbinic and biblical *halakhah* (law), and the desire to balance particularist with universalist concerns.

Joseph Dan explores the medieval genre of *sifrut ha-musar*, "ethical literature," which has largely been left unanalyzed in the recent burgeoning of the field of Jewish ethics. This absence, Dan maintains, extends primarily from the fact that the genre does not call *halakhah* into question, as does Jewish ethics generally, particularly through the notion of *lifnim mi-shurat ha-din* (supererogation)—that one must act beyond the letter of the law. This does not mean, however, that *musar* is nonethical; rather its purpose is to "harmonize the spirituality of God with the values guiding his worship." This spiritualization of Jewish ritual and culture generated creativity for nearly a thousand years around the Jewish world, first in Islamic contexts and then in Christian milieus.

That the medieval period produced wide-ranging ethical thought is further demonstrated in the chapter by Warren Zev Harvey. Encyclopedic in its sweep, Harvey's chapter shows that the varieties of Jewish philosophy in the medieval period defy easy categorization, let alone condensation into a single notion of Jewish ethics. The scholars surveyed here are Saadia Gaon, Solomon ibn Gabirol, Bahya ibn Paquda, Judah Halevi, Abraham ibn Ezra, Abraham ibn Daud, Moses Maimonides, Levi Gersonides, Jedaiah Bedersi, Hesdai Crescas, Joseph Albo, and Joseph ibn Shemtov.

Baruch Spinoza's Aristotelian critique of Judaism—and of religion generally—in the seventeenth century marked the beginning of a period of intense Jewish self-evaluation that continues to this day. David Novak unpacks Spinoza's criticisms to show that the ultimate ethical existence, that is, a virtuous existence, entails attention to three interpenetrating relations: between the self and God, between the self and others, and with oneself. Obedience and love, Spinoza asserts, are the ultimate character traits that instantiate the highest forms of ethical existence in these realms.

With the increasing civic and intellectual freedoms that emancipation and the Enlightenment brought to Jews, the nineteenth century witnessed a dramatic flourishing of Jewish thought and activity. Ira Stone traces the challenges this new modernity posed to Jews and shows how they variously responded. Such scholars as Moses Mendelssohn, Samuel David Luzzato, Elijah Benamozegh, Nachman Krochmal, Samson Raphael Hirsch, Hermann Cohen, and Israel Lipkin's Mussar Movement are considered here. Though they variously retain traditionalism, their responses, Stone contends, were all reforms insofar as they each created "what might be called an indigenous Jewish response to modernity."

Early twentieth-century Jewish theologians and philosophers were no less creative than their predecessors, as Jonathan K. Crane shows in his treatment of Hermann Cohen, Franz Rosenzweig, and Martin Buber. These three German scholars, writing in the decades surrounding World War I, were both attracted to and repulsed by modernity. On the one hand, the modern drive toward nationalism inspired their commitment to Jews and Judaism, and so each plumbed the Jewish textual tradition to ground his ethical theory. Yet the destructiveness that self-centeredness can (and did) cause led each man to promote an ethic that attends to others. Crane explores this turn to others and otherness, a turn that oriented much subsequent Jewish ethical theorizing.

Matthew LaGrone engages the thought of two giants of twentieth-century American Judaism—Mordecai Kaplan and Abraham Joshua Heschel, both of whom taught at the Jewish Theological Seminary of the Conservative Movement. Emerging from the pragmatism and naturalism of the early decades of the century, Kaplan fostered a fascination with humanity that led him to eschew traditional Judaism's theocentric views of morality. For him, it would be better to understand Judaism as a civilization—no better and no worse than others—and jettison *mitzvot* (commandments) in favor of "folkways" so as to inspire social behavior, for it is through the folk themselves that morality comes into being. Heschel, by contrast, favors a more theocentric approach. For him the prophets best articulated the apocalyptic dangers of even the smallest immorality and the need to rise above human communities to root morality in God's will for us.

Lawrence Kaplan analyzes the ethical theories of Rabbis Abraham Isaac Kook and Joseph B. Soloveitchik, two luminaries in twentieth-century Orthodoxy in Israel and the United States, respectively. Kaplan shows that despite Kook's lean toward the mystical and Soloveitchik's tendency toward the rational, they nonetheless share in the perspective that ethics is central to proper Jewish living and theology. Whereas Kook views the moral impulse as already embedded in Jewish existence, Soloveitchik understands *imitatio Dei* as the central mechanism through which Jewish ethical behavior comes into being. In some ways, this difference in focus—on Jews or on God—echoes the primary difference between Kaplan and Heschel in the Conservative Movement.

Michael Berenbaum tackles the difficulties the Holocaust posed and continues to raise for Jews, Jewish theology, and specifically Jewish ethics. He identifies eight major commitments made by Jews and non-Jews that have since then inspired Jewish and global responses to such human-made atrocities as genocide and crimes against humanity.

The next several chapters turn our attention to the streams of modern Jewry. Michael Marmur traces the emergence of Reform Jewish ethical sensibility from its early days in nineteenth-century Germany through its evolution to modern America, Israel, and beyond. He identifies four major sensibilities that, while presented chronologically, are nevertheless found among contemporary Reform Jews: the notion that ethics should be the first theology of Judaism, a passion for *tikkun olam* (repairing the world from injustices), a suspicion and critique of modernity, and an ethics of authenticity.

Changing what Jews do and altering the reasons why they should do things differently was not an exclusively Reform endeavor; Conservative Judaism also instituted innovations, especially since World War II. These changes, Shai Cherry argues, are most easily apparent in Conservative liturgy as well as in *halakhic* positions vis-à-vis women, homosexuality, and *mamzerut* (bastardy). Conservative thinkers and scholars of Jewish law, however, have taken diverse approaches as to how and when to make such changes, and so one cannot articulate a single "Conservative theory" of Jewish ethics. Cherry, in fact, argues for his own approach in contrast to those of some of the other representatives of Conservative Judaism whose theories and legal rulings he discusses.

By differentiating Haredi, or ultra-Orthodoxy from Modern Orthodoxy, David Shatz focuses on the latter's wrestling with the meta-ethical issue of the interrelationship between *halakhah* and ethics. He tests four theses comprising what he calls the maximalist Modern Orthodox position to demonstrate how they go about addressing moral conundrums already embedded in the textual tradition and those that modernity poses to contemporary Jews, illustrating the strengths and weaknesses of each of them and then arguing for the approach that he thinks is best.

Though founded as a stream within Conservative Judaism in 1922 and becoming a separate movement only in 1968, the Reconstructionist Movement may be the youngest mainstream branch of modern Jewry, but its commitment to ethics has always been central to its self-understanding. David A. Teutsch demonstrates Reconstructionism's concern for ethics by identifying the movement's assumptions about how and why Jews should act in the world. Indeed, as shaping actual Jewish living has continuously been its major goal, the movement eventually developed what is now called values-based decision-making that is to guide collective as well as personal ethical deliberation and concrete action.

Judith Plaskow argues that all the many forms of Jewish feminism are "fundamentally about ethics." Across denominations, in the broader feminist movement, in academia, in Israel and North America, Jewish women have been reshaping what and how Jews and non-Jews think and act—regarding women, gender, inequality, injustice, and many other critical ethical issues, including Judaism itself. Feminist methodologies creatively critique *halakhah*, theology, liturgy, ritual, and textual interpretation, all with implications for social and political analysis and activism. In doing so, Jewish feminists—too numerous to list here—"have created both a rich literature and a legacy of activism that is ethical to its core."

Nearly concurrent with the rise of feminist criticisms in recent decades was the emergence of postmodernism that both endorsed particularity (as against the universality championed by modernity) and simultaneously critiqued the totalizing effects inhering in particularity. "To affirm Jewish tradition without affirming classical models of Jewish authority," Martin Kavka claims, "is the goal of postmodern Jewish ethics." Kavka begins by tracing the complicated interrelationship of Jewish and secular philosophy in Emmanuel Levinas's thought. He then turns to the ethical philosophy of embodiment and self-mastery by Jonathan Schofer and Chaya Halberstam, to show that postmodern Jewish ethics is simultaneously intensely personal while also procedural and communal.

ADDITIONAL THEORIES

Lest the reader assume that these chapters cover the totality of Jewish ethical theorizing, it should be stressed that it is only limited space that prevents additional Jewish ethical theories to be addressed at length here. Their exclusion is not a reflection on the sophistication of these approaches but more their prevalence relative to the other approaches included here.

For example, much more can be said about the emergence of the field of Jewish studies (*Wissenschaft des Judentums*) in the nineteenth century and its impact on how scholars think about Judaism, Jews, and Jewish ethics. Then and, truthfully, throughout Jewish history, Jews gave certain lines of inquiry privilege over others predominantly because Jews were influenced by the theoretical approaches and practical issues their Gentile colleagues were exploring. In fact, every layer of the Judaic textual library includes diverging assumptions and expectations of human agency. This is true for the Bible as it is for rabbinic literature. For example, in his study of the Talmud, Eugene Borowitz teases apart *halakhic* discourse from non-*halakhic* to show that each has its own (myriad) ethics.[2] And looking forward, there has been a resurgence of energy devoted to virtue ethics as it has been expressed in rabbinic—and postmodern—texts.[3]

With the emergence of the Society of Jewish Ethics in the early twenty-first century, a growing collection of academics, rabbis, and professional practitioners has been wrestling with Jewish ethics at practical and theoretical levels. Their annual conference, concurrent with those of the Society of Christian Ethics and the Society for the Study of Muslim Ethics, serves as a context that encourages comparative studies and cross-religious ethical theorizing.

And, of course, readers would do well to acknowledge that each chapter here offers but a summary of the theories the author addresses. Precisely because of that fact, each chapter includes a section entitled "Suggestions for Further Reading" so that readers may pursue the theories described in greater depth.

In the meantime, we hope the reader will enjoy the following chapters surveying the breadth and depth of Jewish theories of ethics.

Notes

1. See, for example, Jonathan K. Crane (2005) "Why Rights? Why Me?" *Journal of Religious Ethics*. 35/4:551–81.
2. Eugene Borowitz, *The Talmud's Theological Language-Game: A Philosophical Discourse Analysis* (Albany: State University of New York Press, 2006).
3. See, for example, Jonathan Schofer *The Making of a Sage: A Study of Rabbinic Ethics* (Madison: University of Wisconsin Press, 2005); Dov Nelkin "Virtue," in *The Cambridge History of Jewish Philosophy*, eds. Martin Kavka, Zachary Braiterman, and David Novak, 739–58 (New York: Cambridge University Press, 2012).

CHAPTER 1

ETHICAL THEORY AND PRACTICE IN THE HEBREW BIBLE

ELAINE ADLER GOODFRIEND

THIS chapter surveys the nature of ethical theory in the Hebrew Bible (Tanakh). The Tanakh's term for ethics, *yir'at Elohim*, "fear of God/gods," points to the blurred boundaries in ancient Israel between ethics and religion. A paramount element in the proper worship of Israel's God is action in the social realm to relieve the oppression of the poor and powerless and to prevent corruption of the judicial process. Further, many of God's commands are intended to deter the Israelite from acting toward his fellow with vengeance and malice. Indeed, the centrality of ethics is indicated by the placement of the command to "love one's neighbor as oneself" at the midpoint of the Torah (Lev 19:18). With its sophisticated understanding of human nature, the Torah utilizes a number of rhetorical tools to motivate ethical behavior. The second component of the Tanakh, the prophets, played a crucial role in declaring God's demand for a just and compassionate society, asserting that ethics takes precedence over ritual, in contrast to the Torah, where both are viewed as vital components of holiness. Works within the "Writings" (*Ketuvim*), the third section of the Tanakh, offer a skeptical approach to the principle of just divine retribution, thus adding a needed complexity to the Bible's view of the relationship of divine justice and ethical behavior. Further, this chapter examines the Tanakh's approach to "free will," the assumption that humans are "choosing" creatures, who can curb their impulses and thereby earn reward and punishment. Finally, the Tanakh's viewpoint regarding God's ethical demands upon the nations is examined, along with Israel's treatment of the "other," that is, slaves, foreigners, and "strangers."

The Terms for and Domain of Biblical Ethics

In the Tanakh, the expression *yir'at Elohim*, "fear of God" (also when used as a finite verb), signifies an awareness of ethical standards, the basic principles of morality. The Hebrew term later used for this concept, *mussar*, appears in the Bible in the sense of instruction or rebuke but not as an abstract term for ethics (Prov 1:7, 8, 19:20).[1] In Genesis 20:11, Abraham explains to King Abimelech of Gerar why he told the king that his beautiful wife was his sister: "I thought there is no fear of God (*'ein yir'at Elohim*) in this place and they would kill me because of my wife."[2] Here Abraham is speaking to someone who is foreign to the religion of ancient Israel, but he assumes that Abimelech would understand exactly what he meant by "fear of God"—a sense of common decency or ethical awareness which would keep Abimelech from murdering him to acquire his wife. This meaning is evident also in the case of the (probably Egyptian) midwives who refrain from killing the Israelite newborn males because "they feared God" (Exod 1:21). Conversely, in the aftermath of the Exodus, when the Amalekites attacked the Israelites who were particularly defenseless and vulnerable, Deuteronomy demands that they be wiped out because they did not "fear God" (Deut 25:18; contrast with Gen 42:18). In Leviticus 19 the command to "fear your God" is used to deter Israelites from abusing the handicapped and elderly (vv.14, 32). The Bible thus presupposes that pagan religions also taught that God/the gods punished violations of ethical principles, so that morality and decency were not dependent upon knowledge of Israel's God or its Torah.[3] Indeed, since the Hebrew *Elohim* is a plural noun in form, it would probably not be wrong to translate it as "fear of the gods." As was noted by James Kugel, "fear," an emotional state, really stands for its external expression in "acting fearful," that is, behaving with an awareness of divine expectations; this implication also applies to some degree to "love" in the Tanakh.[4]

"Fear of God" should be distinguished from "fear of the Lord," since "Lord," the Tetragram, the four-letter name of God, signifies specifically the God of Israel. "Fear of the Lord" refers in the Bible to God's minimal expectations concerning the Israelite, regarding both his state of mind and his behavior—his piety and observance of commandments.

Thus in the Tanakh the expression "fear of God" is the closest approximation to the abstract noun "ethics," if ethics is understood to be the proper treatment of others. Obviously this interpretation reflects the blurring of boundaries in the Bible between religion and ethics, as ethics occupies a central place regarding the behavior that God demands from Israel and that (the Bible assumes) other gods demanded from their worshippers as well.

Another indistinct boundary in the Bible is that between law and ethics, as the biblical God expresses Himself in commandments—that is, laws—and many of these define the proper treatment of other people. Two central collections of commandments, Exodus 20 and Leviticus 19, combine laws we would consider ethical, legal, and ritual, but the Torah considers all these equally to be the expressed will of God. Exodus 20, the Decalogue (or "Ten Commandments"), which according to the biblical narrative constitutes God's direct address to the Israelite nation, offers the basic principles of Israelite law; the first four commandments (Exod 20:2–11) deal with proper behavior to God, and the last six (Exod 20:12–17) with the Israelites' obligations toward one another. Leviticus 19, which commands the Israelites to emulate God and thus aspire to holiness, interweaves ritual, legal, and ethical obligations. The prohibitions of eating the meat of a sacrifice on the third day after its slaughter, wearing garments of linen and wool, and tattooing one's flesh (laws with no obvious moral motivation) are juxtaposed with the commands to leave portions of produce for the poor, refrain from gossip and robbery, and "love your neighbor as yourself" (v.18), certainly a powerful motivator for ethical behavior. Therefore, the Israelite God demands justice and compassion among people as a vital component in His service, and He articulates these moral demands in the form of law.

Further, Leviticus 19 provides a tantalizing indication of the centrality of ethics in the Torah when it is considered from the perspective of its position in the Torah and the order of its verses. Yehuda Radday writes that the chiasmic or inverted structure of a unit of literature (that is, A B C D C' B' A') provides a "focal concept" or "fundamental purpose." Regarding the Torah, he cites the many commonalities of the books of Exodus and Numbers and suggests reasons that Genesis and Deuteronomy "form a pair." He continues:

> There remains Leviticus. It is the central book of the Pentateuch and contains the Priestly code of law, cult, and ritual purity to the exclusion of all narrative. It occupies the central position, where, whether or not the modern reader likes it, the commandments occupy the ultimate position of preeminence.[5]

Jacob Milgrom builds on Radday's argument and adds that chapter 19 is the central turning point of Leviticus as "it is flanked by two chapters of equivalent content (18 and 20) in chiastic relation."[6] The mention of Sabbath observance and reverence for parents/elders both at the beginning and end of Leviticus 19 (vv. 3, 30, 32) suggests that we should views its central point, v. 18's "Love your fellow as yourself: I am the Lord," as the apex or climax of the chapter. Thus the verse that provides the greatest motivation for godly behavior in the social realm is situated at the focal point of the entire Pentateuch: there is no better indication than this of the centrality of ethical behavior in the Torah.

Despite the Bible's consistent emphasis on God's demand for ethical behavior, the summation of the Torah in ethical terms, such as Hillel's "that which is hateful to you, do not to the others" (B. *Shabbat* 31a) is a product of the period *after* the closing of the Bible. Exclusive fidelity to Israel's God and reverence for the holy, for example the Sabbath, were also essential and defining aspects of Israelite religion, according to the Torah and prophets.

Motivations for Ethical Behavior in the Torah

The chief motivating factor that the Torah offers for the observance of its commandments is that they are decrees of Israel's God. Both key collections of law mentioned above, Exodus 20 and Leviticus 19, contain little in the realm of punishment, because it is assumed that the authority of God, the Author, would ensure compliance. Leviticus 19 is punctuated with the declaration "I am the Lord" fifteen times. In these cases, the might and prestige conveyed by God's name were thought to be sufficient to make the hearer submit to the divine will.[7] Elsewhere, however, the Torah, with its sophisticated understanding of human nature, provides a variety of reasons one should obey its laws. Some categories of unethical behavior, such as murder, rape, robbery, or flagrant disrespect of parents, are penalized severely by courts of law. What about those prohibitions for which the Torah neglects to state an immediate judicial punishment? For example, the Torah contains admonitions against gossip (Lev 19:16), retaining a day laborer's earnings until the following day (Lev 19:13), mistreating the widow and fatherless (Deut 24:17), and taking a garment for collateral on a loan and keeping it overnight so that the debtor has nothing in which to sleep (Deut 24:10–13), but states no specific punishment for any of these actions. It is not impossible that transgressing these commandments brought prosecution in the Israelite legal system, but that is highly unlikely since many of the Torah's "ethical" commandments focus on the mistreatment of the poor and powerless, those who lack the means or knowledge to seek redress in court for injustices perpetrated against them. Others are actions that are difficult to detect, such as moving a neighbor's boundary stone (Deut 27:17) or "placing an obstacle before the blind" (Lev 19:14). Consequently, the Torah supplies reasons for obedience even when or especially when human courts do not or cannot intervene.

Other factors that motivate compliance with the Torah's ethical demands include the following:

1. *Collective reward and punishment.* The context or framework of the commandments assumes God will reward and punish on a collective, national basis. This is a consequence of the collective nature of God's covenant with Israel—that is, Israel as a nation agreed to accept its role as God's covenant partner and thereby become "a kingdom of priests and a holy nation" (Exod 19:5–6, 24:3, 7). Leviticus 26 and Deuteronomy 28 enumerate the blessings and curses that will come upon the people of Israel as a result of its observance or nonobservance of God's laws. Rewards include sufficient rains and plenteous harvests, abundant fertility for their human and animal populations, immunity from foreign invaders, and God's continual and beneficent Presence. More detailed and numerous are the penalties for flouting the commandments: affliction by disease, agricultural infertility, lethal attacks by wild animals, invasions by foreign armies and the resultant food shortages, exile from the land of Israel, and divine rejection. The collective nature of the reward

and punishment motivates individual Israelites not only to comply, but, further, to compel their fellow Israelites to observe God's laws and initiate prosecution against those who do not. Deuteronomy in particular repeats the admonition to show no toleration for evil-doers, ("show no pity" and "sweep out evil from your midst"), lest calamity engulf the nation as a whole (13:6, 17:7, 19:19, 21:21).

2. *Individual reward and punishment.* The Torah also promises retribution on an individual basis. For instance, Israelites are prohibited from oppressing the widow and fatherless, lest the cry of the abused provoke God's rage, and God "will put you to the sword and your own wives shall become widows and your children orphans" (Exod 22:23). Deuteronomy assures the Israelite that if he distributes the tithe of his produce to the widow, fatherless, stranger, and Levite (the priests), "the Lord your God may bless you in all the enterprises you undertake" (Deut 14:29). Generosity to the newly released slave similarly brings God's blessing (Deut 15:10), and he who releases a mother bird and takes only her young is rewarded with an extended life span (Deut 22:7). Honoring parents and using honest weights and measures in commercial transactions is recompensed with "enduring long on the soil that the Lord your God is giving you" (Exod 20:12, Deut 5:16, 25:15); here the reward may be individual or collective. Regarding the Decalogue's assertion that God visits "the guilt of the parents upon the children, upon the third and upon the fourth generations of those who reject Me" (Exod 20:5, Deut 5:9), Deuteronomy warns the transgressor that he cannot hope to escape punishment himself (Deut 7:10).[8]

3. *Gratitude to God.* Another powerful motivator for observance of the commandments is gratitude for God's historical role as Israel's savior and provider. The Exodus from Egypt and the conquest of a "land flowing with milk and honey," with its abundant resources for which Israel need invest little effort (e.g., Deut 6:10–11), are used to rouse Israel's appreciation and sense of obligation. God introduces Himself in the Decalogue as He who "brought Israel out of the land of Egypt, the house of bondage," to justify the following prohibition of allegiance to other gods (Exod 20:2–3). Conversely, many biblical texts assume that it is ingratitude in particular that leads to disobedience (Deut 8:11–18, 32:15; and for this idea in prophetic literature, see Isa 1:2–3, Jer 2:5–8, Ezek 16, Hos 13:4–6, Amos 2:10–12).

4. *Israel's experience as slaves and strangers.* Israel's historical experience as slaves and strangers is used to inspire ethical treatment of the landless underclass of Israelite society. On the basis of their collective memory of slavery in the land of Egypt, they are exhorted to be generous to the indentured Israelite who is freed after six years (Deut 15:13–15). Israel is warned against oppressing the stranger, "for you were strangers in the land of Egypt" (Exod 22:20, 23:9). In Deuteronomy's version of the Decalogue, the rationale for the Sabbath rest is "so that your male and female slave may rest as you do. Remember that you were a slave in the land of Egypt and the Lord your God freed you from there" (Deut 5:15). God forbids Israelites to hold their brethren as slaves, because He released them from Egyptian bondage: therefore they are to be slaves to God alone (Lev 25:42, 55).

5. *Israel's special covenant with God with its aspirations to holiness.* Israel's unique status as God's chosen covenant partner theoretically provides a national

"mission statement" that would motivate compliance with God's ethical demands. Acceptance of the Sinai covenant confers upon Israel the status of "a kingdom of priests and a holy nation" (Exod 19:6). Just as a priest adopts a distinctive lifestyle dedicated to the service of God so he can minister to the needs of the laity, so Israel's mission is to serve that role for the nations. Israel's given status as a "holy people" provides the reason they should observe the commandments (Exod 22:30, Deut 7:6, 14:2, 21), while in Leviticus 19 Israel's potential holiness is used to inspire the people to appropriate behavior as "the entire community of the people of Israel" is commanded to "be holy for I the Lord your God am Holy" (v. 2). In this case, Israel's status as a holy nation is not an assumption, but rather a goal, arrived at by performing a rich assortment of ethical demands.

6. *The inherent morality and wisdom of God and His laws.* The superiority of Israel's God and His laws are used in Deuteronomy to convince Israel that obedience is the most reasoned response to God's demands. The unprecedented nature of Israel's exodus from Egypt and their survival of the awesome, fiery theophany at Sinai provide proof of this God's astonishing singularity (4:33–35). Further, His ethical nature is preeminent as the "God supreme and Lord supreme...who shows no favor and takes no bribes, but upholds the cause of the fatherless and the widow, and befriends [literally, "loves"] the stranger, providing him with food and clothing" (Deut 10:17–18; see also Ps 146:7–9). Not surprisingly, then, the laws that Israel's moral God legislates for Israel are also ethically superior, and their observance will be proof of Israel's wisdom (Deut 4:5–8). In truth, Israel's laws were unique in the ancient Near East; in biblical law we find no vicarious punishment, no capital punishment for crimes against property, while slaves and bond-servants receive relatively generous treatment.[9]

7. *Israel's dependence on God.* The uniqueness of the land of Israel—its beauty, its bountiful resources, and its reliance on rain instead of irrigation—provide another rhetorical tool in Deuteronomy to encourage obedience (e.g., Deut 8:7–9). That Israel has no great rivers like Egypt and depends upon rainfall, itself subject to God's grace and scrutiny, indicates the importance of Israel's conduct: "It is a land that the Lord your God looks after, on which the Lord your God always keeps His eye, from year's beginning to year's end. If, then, you obey the commandments that I enjoin upon you this day...I will grant the rain for your land in season, the early rain and the late" (11:10–13).

8. *The mutual love between God and Israel.* God's relationship with Israel is grounded in mutual love, which provides a basis for covenantal loyalty. God's love for Israel is declared in Deuteronomy (4:37, 7:13, 10:15, 23:6) but also in the prophetic books (Isa 43:4, Jer 31:3, Hos 11:1). Deuteronomy exhorts Israel to love God, most notably in the passage later called the *Shema*, or Jewish profession of faith (6:5), but also elsewhere (10:12; 11:1, 13, 22; 19:9; 30:16, 20). While love that can be commanded may seem strange to moderns, biblical love (*'ahavah*), just like "fear," is an emotion that is expressed chiefly through action. Thus Deuteronomy 10:18 extols God as one who "loves the stranger, providing him with food and clothing," and v. 19 adds, "and you should love the stranger, for

you were strangers in the land of Egypt" and this is certainly a demand for generosity.[10] Therefore, Deuteronomy's command to "love" God is often understood as synonymous with fidelity and obedience, and not the heartfelt affection that the word usually connotes. However, the emotional element should probably not be minimized, as Deuteronomy 6:5 adds, "with all your heart, and with all your soul and with all your might," and God's "love" for Israel cannot be equated with fidelity. Deuteronomy's emphasis on gratitude certainly provides the basis for this love, externalized in adherence to God's ritual and ethical demands.

Ethics in the Prophets

Emphasis upon ethical behavior is also apparent in the writings of Israelite prophets, who delineate the behavior God requires from Israel. Ezekiel defines the righteous as a man who not only worships the Israelite God to the exclusion of others, but also one who "has not defiled another man's wife...has not wronged anyone...has returned the debtor's pledge to him and has taken nothing by robbery...had given bread to the hungry and clothed the naked...has abstained from wrongdoing and exacted true justice between one person and another...has followed My laws and kept My rules and acted honestly" (18:5–9). The prophet Micah reminds his Israelite audience that "He has told you, O man, what is good, and what the Lord requires of you: only to do justice and to love goodness, and to walk modestly with your God" (6:8–9). Both Hosea and Jeremiah define "knowledge of the Lord" as doing acts of kindness and justice (Jer 9:23, Hos 2:21–22). Amos likens Israel's mistreatment of the poor, a commonplace event that most people simply ignore, to horrific and infamous war crimes perpetrated by their neighbors (Amos 1:1–2:8). Isaiah tells the allegory of the vineyard which was so carefully and lovingly tended and then yielded nothing but sour, wild grapes to represent God's failed expectation that Israel would be a society based on justice and equity (5:1–7).

While the Torah affirms that ethical obligations are as vital as ritual commandments as components of holiness, the prophets assert that ethical commandments take precedence; they rebuke those Israelites who behave badly toward other people but fulfill their ritual requirements with gusto. Indeed, the prayers and sacrifices of those who oppress others are detested by God: Hosea declares that God desires "goodness, not sacrifice, obedience to God rather than burnt offerings" (6:6; see also Isa 1:10–17, 58:2–10, Jer 7:21–23, Amos 5:21–25). Early Reform writers utilized these passages to assert the primacy of ethics over ritual matters.[11] It is likely, however, that the emphasis in these passages is rhetorical and exaggerated, since it is clear that ritual matters were likewise important to the prophets (Jer 11:13, 17:21–27, Ezek 18:5–9, Hos 10:1, Amos 8:5).

Ethics in *Ketuvim*

The "Writings" section of the Bible, and in particular the three works labeled by moderns as "Wisdom Literature," add to the diversity of opinion within the biblical corpus regarding key ethical issues. These three—Proverbs, Ecclesiastes, and Job—assume that God established the world according to certain unchanging patterns, and the responsibility of the sage was to discern these underlying rules that govern not only the natural world but also human behavior.[12] The pursuit of wisdom not only was an Israelite concern, but also characterized the learned classes all over the ancient Near East. The author of 1 Kings reports that "King Solomon's wisdom was greater than the wisdom of all the Kedemites and than all the wisdom of the Egyptians" (5:10 in Hebrew, 4:30 in English), a comment suggesting that the wisdom tradition of these two peoples set a standard that was difficult to surpass.

The book of Proverbs praises the acquisition of wisdom as the basis of an ethical and successful life, in contrast to most other books of the Bible with their focus on adherence to God's commandments as enunciated in the Torah. The wise man has both practical wisdom—the means to success and a happy life—but also moral virtue. This sentiment is obvious in Proverbs 2:6–9:

> For the Lord grants wisdom;
> Knowledge and discernment are by His decree.
> He reserves ability for the upright
> And is a shield for those who live blamelessly,
> Guarding the paths of justice,
> Protecting the way of those loyal to Him.
> You will then understand what is right, just,
> And equitable—every good course.
> For wisdom will enter your mind
> And knowledge will delight you.

The terms "right," "just," "equitable," and "good" (Hebrew *tsedeq, mishpat, meysharim, tov*) are key biblical terms for ethical behavior (see also Prov 1:1–3). Thus when one gains wisdom, one will know what is right and just (compare with Deut 6:17–18). "Fear of the Lord," that is, piety—a combination of humility, trepidation before and trust in God—leads one to pursue wisdom (Prov 1:7). Conversely, evil behavior stems from ignorance, or indifference to knowledge, so "To turn away from evil is abhorrent to the stupid" (13:19) and "He who commits adultery is devoid of sense; Only one who would destroy himself does such a thing" (6:32). Such willful ignorance sets one on the path to a host of negative consequences—divine disfavor, infamy, insecurity, and the premature end of one's family line. On the other hand, the rewards for the pursuit of wisdom and righteousness are many: a long life, wealth, prosperous children, a long line of descendants, contentment and security, and community respect.[13] While the Torah assumes that people have the ability to choose adherence to some of its commandments and reject others, Proverbs takes an "all or nothing" approach and supposes that people have somewhat fixed moral characters. Either they are fools and sinners, or they are wise and righteous (e.g., Prov 10:20, 15:14). These sources point to a kind of fatalism in which choice and change are all but implausible.

The other two "wisdom" books offer less certainty regarding the rewards for ethical behavior. Ecclesiastes (in Hebrew, *Qohelet*) repeatedly emphasizes the imperative of deriving pleasure from one's life, which is God's gift to humankind (2:24–25, 3:12–13; see also 5:17–19, 8:15, 9:7–10). This hedonistic conviction is the result of Ecclesiastes' skepticism regarding divine justice—that is, that God rewards and punishes according to a person's actions, either in this world or in the afterlife; "For the same fate is in store for all: for the righteous, and for the wicked, for the good and pure and for the impure" (9:2–3; 3:19–22). He observes that "Sometimes a good man perishes in spite of his goodness, and sometimes a wicked one endures in spite of his wickedness" (7:15), and therefore he counsels the reader, "Don't overdo goodness and don't act the wise man to excess," but at the same time, "Don't overdo wickedness and don't be a fool," so "It is best that you grasp the one without letting go of the other" (7:16–18). Rather than battle against injustice as the prophets do, Ecclesiastes counsels that one accept it as a fact of life: "If you see in a province oppression of the poor and suppression of right and justice, don't wonder at the fact" (5:7). Thus, ethics are peripheral to Ecclesiastes' worldview because of his doubt regarding an ultimate reward for right behavior. For this wisdom teacher, enjoyment and living life with gusto are both the means and reward for living in accordance with God's will.

The Book of Job similarly stands in contrast to both Proverbs and the Torah regarding the principle of just retribution. Job is a prosperous and pious man whose wealth and health are destroyed by *Ha-Satan* (the Adversary), with God's acquiescence. Job's belief in a just divine order collapses as he realizes that "It is all one. Therefore I say, 'He [God] destroys the blameless and the guilty'" (9:22; see also Job 21). His friends continue to endorse the same tidy system of reward and punishment enunciated by Proverbs, a system that God Himself finally denounces as false (42:7–8).

This complicated work raises several ethical issues.[14] First, the book generally opposes the principle of just divine retribution, which is an anchor of ethical behavior according to conventional belief. (I say "generally" because this principle is restored in the epilogue, chapter 42, along with Job's wealth and family.) Further, the initial chapters of the book, where God succumbs to Satan's wager twice and destroys a blameless man (and his children) without cause, hardly present the biblical God as an ethical exemplar. The reader sees the terrible miscarriage of justice committed by Job's friends when they malign an innocent man simply because his suffering doesn't conform with their idea of divine retribution; clearly this is one of the cautionary lessons of the work. Later, in chapters 38–41, when God does respond to Job's challenge, He hardly shows compassion for the innocent man but rather ignores the issue of justice and responds with scorn and sarcasm; "The clear implication is that if you can't begin to play in God's league, then you should not have the nerve to ask questions about the rules of the game."[15] The book of Job, along with Proverbs and Ecclesiastes, all add to the complexity of the Tanakh's approach to the ethical implications of God's relationship with humankind.

Free Will

Because the Tanakh was composed by a variety of authors over the course of a millennium, it is logical that it offers diverse outlooks on human nature and free will. Its first statements about humankind confer upon them great dignity and worth, as humans are "created in God's image" (Gen 1:26–27), formed by God's hands, and animated by His breath (2:7). Thus humans have a correspondence to God that other creatures lack. That humans are "created in God's image" emphasizes the infinite value of human life (Gen 9:6), but the Torah is ambiguous regarding whether they are created "good," a judgment which is made by God in Genesis 1 concerning His other creations. God pronounces "all that He had made" in Genesis 1:31 as "very good," which could imply that humankind only amplifies the quality of goodness in creation, but this also might imply that everything is "very good" despite the presence of humankind. Genesis 3–11 depicts humankind as rebellious and prone to violence, offers negative assessments of human nature (6:5, 8:21), and includes laws as a partial remedy for their brutality (9:1–7), which certainly validates the latter possibility. The book of Judges, especially chapters 17–21, also underscores the barbarity that humans, in this case Israelites, are capable of when "there was no king in Israel; everyone did as he pleased" (21:25). Other texts depict the human potential for goodness more optimistically. Job, a non-Israelite, is depicted as wholly righteous, "blameless and upright; he feared God and shunned evil" (1:1), and evidently the widespread use of the term "righteous" in the books of Psalms and Proverbs in particular suggests that there are people capable of predominantly, if not wholly, good behavior.

The fact that God issues commands to humankind, starting with Adam in the Garden of Eden, suggests that humans are "choosing" creatures with the capacity to curb their impulses (Gen 4:7). With this "free will," humans earn their reward and punishment, because the biblical God is considered the embodiment of justice and does not issue unmerited consequences. Deuteronomy exhorts Israel, "I have put before you life and death, blessing and curse. Choose life!" (30:19). The prophet Jeremiah can justify the destruction of Judah, because God sent a series of prophets to call the people to repentance but they did not listen (Jer 7:25, 25:4–7, 26:5).

A few passages in the Bible suggest that divine prerogative occasionally requires the suspension of human free will. Most famous is the case of Pharaoh, whose heart God "hardens" in order to ensure his punishment and the multiplication of signs and wonders in Egypt (Exod 7:3–5, 10:1–2). Hophni and Phinehas, the sons of Eli the priest, persisted in their evil "for the Lord was resolved that they should die" (1 Sam 2:25). Zedekiah, the last king of Jerusalem, rebelled against Nebuchadnezzer, King of Babylonia, because of God's desire to cast sinful Judah "from out of His presence" (2 Kings 24:20), while the Judeans of Isaiah's generation have their senses dulled by the prophet lest they perceive their wrongs and repent (Isa 6:9–10). Jeremiah and Ezekiel, both of whom despaired of Israel and Judah's ability to repent and merit restoration after exile, predict that God will cure their stubborn sinful nature by implanting within them a new heart and spirit (Jer 24:7, 31:31–34, 32:39, Ezek 11:19–20, 36:26–27). These cases, however, are lonely exceptions to the importance attributed to choice.

Universality: Ethics vis-á-vis Israel and the Nations

The Tanakh assumes that there is a universal standard of ethical behavior for which God will punish nations other than Israel. As is noted above, the expression "fear of God/the gods" as the equivalent of "common decency" assumes that all nations are capable of behaving according to basic ethical standards. The Psalmist lauds God as one "who will rule the world justly, and its peoples with equity" (Ps 98:9), an idea evident in biblical narrative. God tests Abraham's worthiness by revealing to him His plan to destroy the people of Sodom and Gomorrah because of their immorality (Gen 18:17–20), not their presumed idolatry. Jeremiah is appointed as a "prophet to the nations," and several of the prophetic books include collections of oracles concerning other nations (Isaiah 13–23, Jeremiah 46–51, Ezekiel 25–32, Amos 1:3–2:3, Obadiah, Nahum 1–3). Jonah is sent to Nineveh, the capital of the Assyrian empire, to call its inhabitants to repentance: "Let everyone turn back from his evil ways and from the injustice of which he is guilty" (3:8). In Genesis 9:1–7, the aftermath of the flood, God gives laws for Noah and his family and authorizes capital punishment for homicide, but even prior to this, Genesis 1–8 presuppose a moral order that all people are expected to recognize and observe without the benefit of specific divine instruction, so that Cain and the generation of the flood can be punished for their misdeeds.[16] Abraham shows keen awareness of this universal standard and holds God accountable to it when He threatens to decimate the Cities of the Plain: "Shall not the Judge of all the earth deal justly?" (Gen 18:25). The Bible never explicitly elucidates the origins of this universal ethical consciousness, but it is logical to assume that biblical authors could hardly imagine a basis for it other than God, as noted above regarding "fear of God."

While the Tanakh assumes that all nations are expected to follow a God-based universal standard of ethical behavior, Israel's uniqueness is based on its exclusive relationship with God, its status as a "kingdom of priests" (Exod 19:6). Israel's mission is to be a "light to the nations" (Isa 49:6), and both Isaiah and Micah envision that other nations will view Zion as the source of divine instruction, which eventually will lead to universal peace (Isa 2:2–5, Mic 4:1–3; Zech 8:21–22, 14:9).

The Torah frequently acknowledges the multiethnic nature of Israelite society, using the terms *ger, zar,* and *nokhri* for strangers or foreigners. In legal texts, *ger* is the most common and refers to the non-Israelites who continued to live in the land of Israel after the conquest; they appear mostly as landless recipients of charity (Exod 22:20, Deut 10:18–19). The *nokhri* is a person who is not ethnically Israelite, perhaps visiting Israel from a foreign land (Deut 15:3, 17:15), while the term *zar* in its technical sense refers to someone who is not necessarily an ethnic stranger but is not a member of a specific category, the priesthood, for example (Exod 30:33, Num 1:51).

What are the Israelites' humanitarian obligations to these categories of people? Deuteronomy bars the ethnic foreigner from kingship (17:15), perhaps for reasons of religion or security. This two-tier approach is also evident regarding economic and ethical conduct in general. In the sabbatical year the Israelite may demand repayment of debt from a *nokhri*, but he must remit the debt for a fellow Israelite (15:3). This scheme is understandable because of the exceptional loss involved in remitting a debt, which makes sense only for one's own people or kin. The same distinction applies regarding interest on loans: "You shall not deduct interest from loans to your countrymen... But you may deduct interest from loans to foreigners" (Deut 23:20–21; see also Exod 22:24, Lev 25:35–37). In the Tanakh, loans at interest are viewed as exploitation of the indigent, since commonly the agrarian poor would be the recipients. This situation is obvious in the prohibition of taking a garment or cloak as pledge because "it is his only clothing, the sole covering for his skin. In what else shall he sleep?" (Exod 22:25–26). Further, the purpose of generosity to one's fellow Israelites is to maintain social and economic stability and prevent the emergence of an underclass encumbered by debt. The Bible mentions instances when these rules were neglected with unfortunate consequences, such as in Jerusalem during the time of Nehemiah when Judean children were distrained for their parents' debt (Neh 5; see also 2 Kings 4:1). This reason would not apply to loans for the *nokhri*, or foreigner, who perhaps was visiting the country for purposes of commerce and investment; there is no moral requirement to offer interest-free loans to him for such purposes.[17]

The most frequently mentioned non-Israelite is the *ger* or "stranger," the non-Israelite resident of the land who appears mostly in the guise of the landless poor. According to the Torah, some may have left Egypt alongside Israel (Exod 12:38, Num 11:4), but a more likely source is those who inhabited the land of Canaan before Israel's conquest and settlement (Josh 9, 1 Kings 9:20–21). For reasons of religious purity, Deuteronomy demands their extermination (7:1–4, 20:16–18). At the same time, much legal rhetoric is aimed at their protection. Thus, according to Leviticus 19:33–34, "When a stranger resides with you in your land, you shall not wrong him. The stranger who resides with you shall be to you as one of your citizens; You shall love him as yourself, for you were strangers in the land of Egypt." Admonitions against abusing the *ger* are found four more times in the Torah (Exod 22:20, 23:9, Deut 10:18–19, 24:17). Israel's God is praised as "the guardian of strangers" (Ps 146:9). They are mentioned as worthy recipients of compassionate giving, along with the poor, the widow, and the fatherless (Lev 19:10, 23:22, Deut 14:29, 16:11, 14, etc.). The Israelite is required to afford them Sabbath rest (Exod 20:10, 23:12). The stranger was afforded equal protection by Israel's laws regarding homicide and assault (Lev 24:22, Num 35:15), and he was obligated by all the same prohibitive or negative commandments as the Israelite, for violation of these endangered the purity of the land of Israel. For example, the *ger* was also required to obey the restrictions in Leviticus 18 regarding illicit sex because these "abominations" polluted the land of Israel no matter who was the perpetrator (Lev 18:26). However, he was not obligated to observe positive or performative commandments such as dwelling in booths during Sukkoth (Lev 23:42).[18] The *ger*, therefore, belongs to a distinct legal category in Israelite law: he is generally subject to the same laws as the Israelite but not required to perform the same religious duties.[19] At the same time, the Israelite is commanded to treat him according to the highest ethical standards, to "love him as yourself" (Lev 19:34).

The legal and moral distinction between Israelites and others is also made in the case of slaves. The term of service of a Hebrew slave is limited to six years, and he is manumitted in the seventh (Exod 21:2, Deut 15:12). This restriction of slavery is surely based on Israel's own experience of harsh servitude in Egypt. Leviticus 25:39–42 goes further and effectively abolishes slavery for the Israelite; his status is rather as "a hired or bound laborer" who sells his *capacity* for labor, but not his *person*, and he is manumitted in the fiftieth year of a fixed cycle, the Jubilee year. Leviticus explains Israel's immunity from slavery with their status as God's slaves (v. 42), by which they may not be enslaved by others, Israelite or stranger. With regard to non-Israelites, conversely, "it is from the nations round about you that you may acquire male and female slaves" (Lev 25:45). Thus, non-Israelites (including the *ger*) may be kept as chattel slaves and be passed down within the family as property (Lev 25:45). Israel was therefore no exception to the widespread practice of slavery in the ancient Near East, as the circumstances that generated enslavement were found throughout the region: war, self-sale and the sale of minors due to hunger or debt, and the heavy penalty for theft. Israelite legislation attempted to ameliorate the circumstances of the non-Israelite chattel slave, who was given rest on the Sabbath (Exod 20:10, 23:12) and is mentioned as participating in family religious festivals (Exod 12:44; Deut 12:12, 18; 16:11, 14). He was offered some protection from his owner's use of excessive force (Exod 21:20–21, 26–27), and those slaves who had run away from their masters were granted asylum (Deut 23:16[20], but see 1 Kings 2:39–40). Thus, while biblical Israel accepted, with some modification, the ancient Near Eastern practice of chattel slavery, regarding those of non-Israelite origins, circumstances for the Israelite sold into bondage because of debt or theft seem to have been significantly improved (but see Jer 34).

Notes

1. See Chapter 6 for more on the nineteenth-century *mussar* movement.
2. All translations, unless otherwise noted, are from *Tanakh: The Holy Scriptures* (Philadelphia: The Jewish Publication Society, 1985).
3. Moshe Greenberg, *Understanding Exodus* (New York: Behrman House, 1969), p. 31.
4. James L. Kugel, *The Great Poems of the Bible* (New York: Free Press, 1999), p. 263.
5. Yehuda T. Radday, "Chiasmus in Hebrew Biblical Narrative," from *Chiasmus in Antiquity: Structures, Analyses, Exegesis*, ed. J. H. Welch (Hildesheim: Gerstenberg, 1981), pp. 50–51, 84–86.
6. Jacob Milgrom, *Leviticus 17–22*, The Anchor Bible, Volume 3A (New York: Doubleday, 2000), p. 1364. Note that their chiastic function provides an explanation for the separation of the commandments regarding illicit sex in Leviticus 18 from the punishments thereof in Leviticus 20.
7. Milgrom, *Leviticus 17–22* (at note 6 above), p. 1612. He notes that the "most probable" reasons for the inclusion of these clauses are "to emphasize the author as God" and "as a warning of God's wrath in the wake of violating these commandments."
8. Emphasis upon individual (rather than collective or transgenerational) punishment is found in Ezek 18:2–4; Jer 31:29–30.
9. Vicarious punishment—when the penalty for a wrong is suffered by someone other than the perpetrator—is found in the Laws of Hammurabi 230 and 210, and Middle Assyrian Law A55, found in Martha T. Roth, ed., *Law Collections from Mesopotamia and Asia Minor* (Atlanta: Scholars Press, 1995). Exod 21:31 and Deut 24:16 prohibit this practice. Capital punishment for theft is absent from the Bible except for the misappropriation of goods devoted to the sanctuary, called *herem* (Deut 7:25–26; Josh 7). The Laws of Hammurabi 6–11, 21–22, 25, and Middle Assyrian Law A3 would inflict capital punishment for a variety of property crimes. Regarding slaves, according to Jeffrey Tigay, Deut 23:16–17 "treats the whole land of Israel as a sanctuary offering permanent asylum" for slaves who flee from foreign countries (*The JPS Torah Commentary: Deuteronomy* [Philadelphia: The Jewish Publication Society, 1996], p. 215). Ancient Near Eastern law collections decreed harsh penalties for harboring fugitive slaves; the Laws of Hammurabi 15–20 mandate capital punishment for giving refuge to runaway slaves. Further, Israelite law, in Exod 21:20–21, 26–27, restricts a slaveowner's abuse of his own property, while ancient Near Eastern law makes no such attempt.
10. My translation; JPS Tanakh utilizes "befriends" for Hebrew *ahav*.
11. See Chapter 11 below.
12. James L. Kugel, *How to Read the Bible: A Guide to Scripture, Then and Now* (New York: Free Press, 2007), p. 506.
13. While these ideas are scattered throughout the book, they are concentrated in Proverbs 10–12.
14. David J. A. Clines, "Job's Fifth Friend: An Ethical Critique of the Book of Job," *Biblical Interpretation* 12 (2004), pp. 233–50.
15. Robert Alter, "The Voice from the Whirlwind," *Commentary* 77 (1984), p. 33.
16. Louis E. Newman, *An Introduction to Jewish Ethics* (Englewood Cliffs, NJ: Prentice Hall, 2005), p. 40. For a larger conversation of what has become known as the Noahide Laws, see David Novak, *The Image of the Non-Jew in Judaism: The Idea of the Noahide Law*, ed. Matthew LaGrone (Oxford: The Littman Library of Jewish Civilization, 2011).

17. Jeffrey Tigay, *The JPS Torah Commentary: Deuteronomy*, 218, quoting the nineteenth-century Italian commentator Shemuel Dovid Luzzato.
18. Jacob Milgrom, *The JPS Torah Commentary: Numbers* (Philadelphia: The Jewish Publication Society, 1989), pp. 398–402.
19. The rabbis of the Roman era identify the *ger* with the convert to Judaism because of the Torah's requirement that he observe many of the same laws as Israelites do.
20. Most commentators assume that Deuteronomy 23:16–17 deals with slaves who flee from foreign countries. Jeffrey Tigay speculates on the existence of an analogous rule for Israelite slaves but suggests that the six-year limit on bondage may have been considered sufficient protection for the Israelite slave (*The JPS Torah Commentary: Deuteronomy*, p. 215).

SUGGESTIONS FOR FURTHER READING

Alter, Robert. 1984. "The Voice from the Whirlwind." *Commentary*. 77:33–41.

Barton, John. 2003. *Understanding Old Testament Ethics: Approaches and Exploration*. Louisville, KY: Westminster John Knox Press.

Clines, David J. A. 2004. "Job's Fifth Friend: An Ethical Critique of the Book of Job." *Biblical Interpretation*. 12:233–50.

Fox, Michael V. 2007. "The Epistemology of Proverbs." *Journal of Biblical Literature*. 126:669–84.

Fox, Michael V. 2007. "Ethics and Wisdom in the Book of Proverbs." *Hebrew Studies*. 48:75–88.

Friedmann, Daniel. 2003. *To Kill and Take Possession: Law, Morality, and Society in Biblical Stories*. Ada, MI: Baker Academic.

Greenberg, Moshe. 1960. "Some Postulates of Biblical Criminal Law." Pages 5–28 in *Yehezkel Kaufmann Jubilee Volume*. Edited by Menahem Haran. Jerusalem: Magnes. [Reprinted in *Studies in the Bible and Jewish Thought*. Philadelphia: Jewish Publication Society, 1995.]

Greenberg, Moshe. 1969. *Understanding Exodus*. New York: Behrman House.

Kugel, James L. 1999. *The Great Poems of the Bible*. New York: The Free Press.

Kugel, James L. 2007. *How to Read the Bible: A Guide to Scripture, Then and Now*. New York: The Free Press.

Levine, Baruch A. 1989. *The JPS Torah Commentary: Leviticus*. Philadelphia: The Jewish Publication Society.

Licht, Jacob. 1972. "Ethics." *Encyclopedia Judaica*. 6:932–39.

Mafico, Temba L. J. 1992. "Ethics (Old Testament)." *The Anchor Bible Dictionary*. 2:645–52.

Milgrom, Jacob. 1990. *The JPS Torah Commentary: Numbers*. Philadelphia: The Jewish Publication Society.

Milgrom, Jacob. 2000. *Leviticus 17–22*. The Anchor Bible. Volume 3A. New York: Doubleday.

Newman, Louis E. 2005. *An Introduction to Jewish Ethics*. Englewood Cliffs, NJ: Pearson Prentice Hall.

Niditch, Susan. 1995. *War in the Hebrew Bible: A Study in the Ethics of Violence*. Oxford: Oxford University Press.

Radday, Yehuda T. 1981. "Chiasmus in Hebrew Biblical Narrative." In *Chiasmus in Antiquity: Structures, Analyses, Exegesis*, edited by J. H. Welch. Povo, UT: Research Press. Pages 50–116.

Roth, Martha T. 1995. *Law Collections from Mesopotamia and Asia Minor.* Atlanta: Scholars Press.

Tigay, Jeffrey H. 1996. *The JPS Torah Commentary: Deuteronomy.* Philadelphia: The Jewish Publication Society.

Wenham, Gordon. 1997. "The Gap between Law and Ethics in the Bible." *Journal of Jewish Studies.* 48:17–29.

Wenham, Gordon. 2004. *Story as Torah: Reading Old Testament Narrative Ethically.* Ada, MI: Baker Academic.

CHAPTER 2

ETHICAL THEORIES IN RABBINIC LITERATURE

CHARLOTTE ELISHEVA FONROBERT

Introduction

As one sets out to explore the sources for Jewish ethics in classical rabbinic literature, one is confronted with a number of difficulties that are conditioned by the nature of the literature itself. First, there is really no term or concept in rabbinic Hebrew or Aramaic equivalent to either the Greek philosophical concepts of ethics or contemporary ones, or to related concepts such as the "self," the "subject," or even the "individual." Of course, rabbinic literature has much to offer with regard to what we would consider ethical concerns. However, constructions of ethical concepts in rabbinic literature are by necessity the product of translating rabbinic discourse into a different conceptual universe, and that act of translation itself has to remain part of any discussion of rabbinic theories.

Further, we will search in vain for a systematic or comprehensive exposition of any ethical theory in rabbinic literature, both for reasons of textual history or cultural context and of organizational principle. Much of this literature consists of large compilations, in modern scholarship often described as anthologies or collections, that are encyclopedic in scope.[1] Each compilation integrates a considerable variety of textual units and genres—legal discussions, folk narratives, didactic narratives, hagiographic tales, midrashic segments—that may or may not previously have existed independently. Not only do such individual units contribute to the multivocality within rabbinic literature, entailing a diversity of ethical sensibilities, the compilations themselves are redacted in different cultural and historical contexts, so it is near impossible to speak of a uniform rabbinic ethic. To name but one example, the Babylonian Talmud espouses a different sexual ethic than do many of the Palestinian texts, and scholars have variously attributed this disparity to the cultural context of each compilation.[2] As to organizational principle, hardly any of the rabbinic compilations are controlled or driven by a single conceptual—as opposed to formal[3]—purpose, and most compilations comprise a variety of genres.

Rabbinic "Ethical" Literature

There are exceptions to this general rule. One exception is categorized by some scholars as rabbinic "ethical" literature, including *'Avot* or *Pirkei 'Avot*, and its companion text(s), *Avot de-Rabbi Natan*.[4] The late rabbinic and early gaonic period saw the production of similar anthologies, such as *Derekh Eretz Rabbah* on general rules of conduct, that share some material with *Avot de-Rabbi Natan*, and *Derekh Eretz Zutta*, on humility and self-examination. These latter two texts are distinct in character, and they were eventually grouped together under the category of "External or Minor Tractates," along with other texts, but they nonetheless are part of the classical rabbinic library.[5]

As a foundational text for this type of rabbinic literature, *'Avot* ("Fathers") deserves some attention. It presents itself as an anthology of short, didactic maxims concerned with conduct and character formation addressed to a generic, male interlocutor.[6] The maxims are attributed to the "fathers" of the rabbinic movement reaching far back into the era of the Second Temple,[7] and forward to the last generation of sages who contributed to the making of the Mishnah.[8] Because of the universally applicable maxims in this compilation, it is often also rendered in English as "Ethics of the Fathers."[9] *Avot* became part of the Mishnah as one of its tractates, although it has a different literary and rhetorical character than much of the Mishnah, a text generally devoted to the discussion and making of rabbinic law or *halakhah*.[10] Not only did *'Avot* generate its own literary tradition, including the midrashic or homiletic exposition of *Avot de-Rabbi Natan*, it also maintained some degree of independence from the rest of the Mishnah, as it turned into a liturgical text of sorts that is included in many traditional versions of the Jewish prayer book. Thereby, it reached far beyond the talmudic study halls into popular religious Jewish culture.

By and large, *'Avot* follows in the tradition of wisdom literature emerging in later biblical and post-biblical literature, but it is adapted to the context of the rabbinic world and its Torah traditions.[11] On the one hand, the maxims are applicable to social life and philosophy of life in general; for example: "Make it a habit to judge each person ('*adam*) toward the side of merit" (M. '*Avot* 1:6); "Hold your distance from an evil neighbor, and do not fraternize with an evil person, and do not despair of the final punishment" (M. 1:7); "Which one is the straight path that a person ('*adam*) should choose for himself? The one that is the path of honor for him who does it and brings him honor from other people" (2:1); "Which one is the good path to which a person ('*adam*) should attach himself?... a generous view... a good friend... a good neighbor... a good heart" (etc., 2:13, that is, as opposed to the evil path); "The evil eye, and the evil inclination (*yetzer ha-ra*'), and hatred of his fellow creatures will drive a human being ('*adam*) from the world" (2:16). The focus in this type of literature is on the formation of a good, or virtuous person—or as scholars have called it, on self-cultivation—with no specifically Jewish reference.[12]

That cultural effort is absorbed into the talmudic literature as well, especially as the sages who compiled the Babylonian Talmud were much interested in the concept of the "evil inclination" or *yetzer ha-ra,*' sometimes merely called *yetzer,* a rabbinic concept that undergoes a complex development as it appears in various texts, from the "ethical" compendia[13] to the Babylonian Talmud.[14] It comes to play a crucial role in rabbinic conceptualizations of anthropology, of the human will, of a person's ability or failure to do good, to be compliant with the law or otherwise submit himself to the perceived will of the divine. As such, it presents a strong link between the ethical compendia and the rest of rabbinic literature. More than any other rabbinic anthropological concept, the *yetzer* has come to play a prominent role in studies of the self as the foundation for personal ethics in rabbinic literature.

The generic reflections on human nature in the "ethical" literature, however, are counterbalanced by the fact that the majority of the maxims in '*Avot* speak to conduct and character formation specifically within a scholastic culture, to a social world where the acquisition of wisdom in the form of the rabbinic Torah represents the supreme value, and where the ultimate goal is to make study one's main form of devotion; for example, "If you have studied much Torah, do not attribute that to your own merit, because for this you were created"(2:9); "He who learns in order to teach, it will be granted him, but he who learns to observe (the commandments) will be granted to learn and teach, and to observe and to practice" (4:6); "Reduce your business, and busy yourself with Torah" (4:12).[15] Here it seems that knowledge cultivation is central, and the accompanying virtues are secondary.

Embedded among these maxims are two suggestions for the three supreme ethical principles of the human world: the culturally specific "Torah, worship, and good deeds" (1:2) next to the more abstract, universal "truth, lawfulness, and peace" (1:18).[16] Without a doubt it is this combination of the universal with the culturally particular that has made this text so widely popular.

One approach toward the study of ethical concepts and theories in rabbinic literature, therefore, is to study this particular textual tradition promoting a rabbinic approach to ethics.[17] However, this approach, albeit legitimate, remains limited for two reasons. First, '*Avot* itself (and its successors) does not aim at shaping a generic good or wise person, but, as we have seen, predicates that exposition of ethics on the foundation of a Torah tradition that reigns throughout much of rabbinic literature. Thus, although the literature does follow the style of ancient Wisdom literature and could therefore be read as a rabbinic attempt at "doing ethics," doing so would ignore what the rabbinic "Torah" concretely teaches, in particular rabbinic law. It is not as if 'Avot and its successors develop an ethical discourse while the rest of rabbinic literature merely does law or *halakhah*. Rather, the premise of 'Avot remains to mold the behavior and disposition of a Jewish man such that he will allow himself to be shaped by the Torah as understood by the rabbinic sages so that he might grow as a scholar-sage.

Second, and more pertinently, rabbinic *halakhic* literature itself, in its attempt to shape Jewish lives and society according to the rabbinic understanding of the heritage of the Torah, is interwoven in complicated ways with what we would consider ethical questions. Insofar as rabbinic *halakhic* discourse does not merely aim to produce a class of scholars and sages, but also aims at shaping a Jewish society guided by *halakhic* principle, its goal is to shape Jewish conduct, if not Jewish character. Even if the answers to moral questions are solved in *halakhic* terms, using legal methods, the *halakhic* considerations are often enough driven by ethical concerns. In that sense, we may posit that all rabbinic *halakhic* literature can be read as a literature with an ethical claim on Jewish lives. Rabbinic ethics then is framed by law, by biblical tradition received and interpreted as law. But at the same time, that legal tradition also aspires to being ethical.

Law and Ethics in Rabbinic Literature

The relationship between and law and ethics in classical rabbinic literature is complex, and it has exercised the minds of scholars since medieval times. How one characterizes this relationship depends on one's understanding of the nature of rabbinic law. In addition, one's understanding today of the authority of rabbinic law and its role in defining Jewish identity further complicates this question, as later chapters of this volume will demonstrate. Even within classical rabbinic literature itself, the issue is quite difficult and will be sketched only briefly here.

The earliest and founding text of rabbinic literature is the Mishnah (c. 200 C.E.), a compendium devoted almost exclusively to organizing and developing what the early rabbinic sages considered normative Jewish law and practice, in short *halakhah*. The foregrounding of *halakhah* has characterized rabbinic Judaism as ortho*praxy* in the study of religion, in contrast to the ortho*doxy* in early Christianity, a typological juxtaposition that at times is even further reduced to ethics versus metaphysics. Problematic as such reductive typologies are, *halakhah* in the Mishnah does indeed lay claim to the shaping of human, and specifically Jewish, behavior, and it does so in a fairly comprehensive way: it circumscribes the religious practice of an individual Jew (purity, prayer, study); it defines social relations, beginning with familial to neighbor to communal; it shapes judicial traditions into a judicial system; it strengthens Jewish collectivity by fine-tuning matters relating to the Jewish calendar; and it delineates relationships with non-Jews. In its comprehensive claim to Jewish life and practice, rabbinic *halakhah* and legal discourse from the Mishnah onward incorporate whatever is meant by ethical theory, so much so that modern scholars have at times been tempted to equate rabbinic *halakhah* and ethics,[18] although such an equation ignores the apt criticisms of seeing *halakhah* as the sole *modus operandi* for Jewish behavior.

With that said, the relationship between the two is deeply entwined and difficult to disentangle even for heuristic purposes. From the Mishnah onward it is the concept of commandment (*mitzvah*)[19] that fundamentally structures human relationships as well as the relationship between people and God (e.g., M. *Yoma* 8:9), indeed that constitutes the very notion of personhood in rabbinic law. Its notion is heavily gendered: the Mishnah famously exempts women from a set of obligations, characterized as positive time-bound commandments (M. *Kiddushin* 1:7), that largely structure one's religious life (worship practices).[20] If a Jew is defined as someone who is commanded by the Torah (i.e., by biblical tradition as understood by the Rabbis), someone to whom all of the commandments apply, then the mishnaic exemption of women from the time-bound obligations raises the question of whether women are in fact considered full persons or Jews in the understanding of the Mishnah,[21] as well as beyond the Mishnah in later rabbinic legal discourse. Indeed, the recurrent talmudic dictum that "Greater is he who is commanded (*metzuveh*) and acts than he who is not commanded and acts" (B. *Kiddushin* 31a, et al.)[22] arguably articulates a fundamental ethical self-understanding of rabbinic legal discourse: the merit of observing a commandment lies in the fact that one is commanded—by the Torah and therefore by its divine author—and not in one's supererogatory piety, whether that be a Jewish woman who decides to pray as a man is commanded to do, or non-Jews studying Torah. What "greater" (*gadol mi-*) is meant to convey here remains open to discussion,[23] but it surely seeks to convey the inherent value of acting because of being subject to the law, and therefore in such a relationship with the Torah and with God, rather than acting for any other reasons. Conceptually speaking, commandments, therefore, are to be observed because they are commandments, not for any other reason.[24]

This is not to discount completely other motivating factors within rabbinic literature for acting in accordance with the commandments. The following can serve as candidates, albeit with some qualifications:

1. The biblical theology of reward and punishment (see chapter 1 of this volume) surely underwrites much of the rabbinic concept of obeying the law,[25] but talmudic texts are all too aware that that equation is anything but easy to decode,[26] and it is not generally put forward as an incentive for observance.
2. Rabbinic legal discourse upholds religious values such as love of God, infatuation with Torah, and general piety, but in general it is precisely

the observance of the commandments that is an expression thereof rather than the other way around. In fact, as independent values, these are sometimes considered to be counterproductive as far as practicing the law is concerned, or at the very least rabbinic texts remain suspicious of religious enthusiasm.[27] It is perhaps ironic that it is infatuation with study as a form of intellectual devotion, the highest value in rabbinic literature (which is, after all, the product of a scholastic movement), that is considered to rival observance and practice, so much so as to prompt extensive talmudic discussions of weighing study and theory (*talmud torah*) against deed and act (*mitzvah* and *ma'aseh*).[28]

3. Following biblical precedents,[29] midrashic texts describe the Torah as a marriage contract between the people of Israel and God and thus seem to suggest, as the Torah itself does, love of God[30] and faithfulness to God and his Torah as motivational factors for observance. At best, this idea remains implied.

4. Classical rabbinic literature does not engage much in a disciplined exercise of *ta'amei ha-mitzvot*,[31] or consideration of the "rationales for the commandments," an intellectual project that rises to prominence in the medieval period (see chapters 3 and 4 in this volume). On occasion, the Rabbis do explicate extra-*halakhic* dimensions of *halakhic* observance, especially in the midrashic literature: the commandments are said to purify people, to endow Jews with holiness, to help give the Jewish People identity, and to make life beautiful.[32] Such explications certainly add an emotive dimension to *halakhic* discourse, but generally these do not act as motivations for observance of the law as far as classical rabbinic literature is concerned but rather as descriptions of the results that the Rabbis claim obedience to the commandments produces. Thus although rabbinic literature does not completely reject or even devalue such motivations or extra-*halakhic* dispositions that might shape the relationship between law and ethics such that law would turn into a tool for ethics, it does describe some results of a moral dimension that accrue to those who obey the law.

Ethical Limits to Halakhah in Rabbinic Literature

As we have seen, an equation of rabbinic *halakhah* with ethics is inadequate and would indeed distort the rabbinic project. If anything, the considerations so far have shown that ethics are comprised within the legal discourse of the Rabbis. Rabbinic literature considers the creation of moral behavior, of the correct path to pursue in life, as one of the purposes of *halakhah* and its observance. At the same time *halakhah* has its own internal theological rationale, derived from the rabbinic understanding of Torah as a divinely authorized tradition.

However, as we shall explore in this section, we also find areas in rabbinic literature that test the limits of the law as the sole guide of Jewish behavior. First, it coins a phrase that describes behavior and disposition that go beyond the letter of the law (*lifnim meshurat ha-din*). Second, rabbinic literature, as we have already seen, does not exhaust itself in *halakhic* discourse, although the "ethical" literature discussed above more than anything poses as handmaiden to upholding Torah as the ultimate norm of human behavior. Still, midrashic and aggadic texts raise questions as to the ethical nature of *halakhah*, as to its sufficiency as a mediator of human relations, and this kind of critique would be impossible if the law were simply the same as ethics in the rabbinic mind. A third area of an intervention of ethics into legal discourse remains implicit and is the most tangential, but nonetheless deserves a brief discussion here—namely, the legal methods that the Rabbis use in interpreting biblical law that enable them to limit its applicability or to change it altogether, often for what appear to be moral reasons.

1. *Ethics beyond the requirement of the law: lifnim meshurat ha-din*. One of the classic moments in rabbinic literature that explicitly raises the question of an ethic beyond the boundaries of the law, or "independent of the *halakhah*," is the recurrent description of acts described as *lifnim meshurat ha-din*, as beyond the requirements of the law (literally "within the line of the law") and therefore supererogatory. Probably more than any other talmudic phrase, this one has been considered the pivot on which hinges the balance between law and ethics in rabbinic Judaism.[33] Depending on one's views of the authority of *halakhah* in general, for some this phrase has been raised to that of ethical or legal principle.

At the same time, we have to keep in mind that the phrase occurs only a few times within classical rabbinic literature, once in an early midrashic text and then a few times in the Babylonian Talmud, which also cites the midrashic texts twice. The early midrashic tradition presents a reading of Exodus 18:20:
Eleazar Ha-Moda'i says:

"'And you shall show them'—show them their house of life.[34]
'the way'—this means visiting the sick
'they must walk'—this means burial of the dead
'therein'—this means the practice of deeds of lovingkindness
'and the work'—this means the law
'that they shall do'—this means *lifnim mishurat ha-din*." (*Mekhilta*)[35]

The midrashic text here lists acting beyond the letter of the law as something on a par with other acts of kindness and sociability, clearly as a value that is to be aspired to. As such it is not defined or illustrated in any more detail. In the Babylonian Talmud the phrase is called upon prominently in the context of the laws of property to describe demonstrations of uncalled-for generosity by rabbinic sages toward others,[36] or to recommend acts that would entail forgoing monetary advantage.[37] It is also cited twice to describe God's merciful quality as a judge of His people.[38] The statement that is often used to demonstrate the weight of the phrase is the one attributed to Rabbi Yohanan that Jerusalem was destroyed by the Romans in 70 C.E. "because they [the Jews] established their laws in accordance with biblical law but did not act *lifnim meshurat ha-din*" (B. *Bava Metzia* 30b). However, this statement is clearly hyperbolic and is in line with a number of moral failures, such as *sin'at hinam* ("hatred without cause," B. *Yoma* 9b) to explain why God punished the people of Israel in that cataclysmic event.

From this handful of sources it remains difficult to conclude that the rabbinic sages in charge of compiling the talmudic tradition operated with a principled idea as to the legal or ethical "status" of the concept of *lifnim meshurat ha-din*.[39] None of the sources explicates that acting *lifnim meshurat ha-din* makes one a better person, a more moral person, or a superior judge. But the fact that the talmudic corpus cites this concept a few times and the suggestive nature of the phrase itself do suggest that time and again the talmudic tradition reminds its students and sage/scholars that being correct and acting correctly in accordance with the *halakhic* tradition is not necessarily sufficient, that a concern for the disadvantage to other people is something to be considered. Perhaps the sum total of these texts can be described as seeds of a corrective for absolutist legalism. *Halakhah* is what mediates human relations in rabbinic tradition, but concern for how it is implemented is part of that same tradition.

2. *Ethics between rabbinic* halakhah *and* aggadah. Another area in which the limits of *halakhah* as the ultimate regulator for human relations are tested is in the interaction between the aggadic texts that accompany the legal discussions and the discussions themselves. The texts that explore the concept of *lifnim meshurat ha-din* already presented one example of this dynamic: the narrative of a particular sage's behavior included in the talmudic tradition can serve as a corrective to a one-dimensional legalism in contemplating human relations, just as it is hoped that God is not merely acting according to what the law would allow when judging humanity. That dynamic of questioning *halakhah* as the sole regulator of human relations at times plays itself out in the interaction between *aggadic* and *halakhic* texts. That is to say, the nature of talmudic literature itself, by weaving together legal texts with *aggadic* texts, refuses the mode of apodictic law. What in later medieval and early modern Jewish literary tradition sorts itself out into distinct literary genres—*halakhic* codes and *responsa* literature (rabbinic rulings on specific cases) on the one hand, and *aggadic* and midrashic compendia on the other—remains welded together in the talmudic tradition, allowing for a complex interaction of the narrative texts with the legal discussion. This weaving together of different textual genres itself, we may suggest, turns into the foundation for negotiating law and ethics. In short, the Talmud is based on, and molds a different ethic than, the *Shulhan Arukh* does.

Some well-known examples will illustrate this point briefly:

According to the *halakhic* pretext of the Mishnah (M. *Yevamot* 6:6), a man is obligated to produce offspring.[40] Should he be married to his wife for ten years "and she bore no child, it is not permitted for him to abstain" further from his obligation to produce offspring, and he should divorce her (T. *Yevamot* 8:5), although she may remarry. This is only one of the legal traditions surrounding Jewish marriage that is deeply problematic on ethical grounds for feminist Jews, for obvious reasons. However, it is not only modern feminist Jews who find this text troubling, for the midrashic tradition tells the story of the infertile but loving couple that is initially instructed to divorce. But when the husband allows his wife to take one precious object from his house back to her father's house, she gets him drunk and has him carried over to her father's house. The story has a happy ending, as the sage in charge of doling out advice to the couple prays on their behalf, and she of course gets pregnant and bears a child.[41] The utopia of the happy ending notwithstanding, the critical intervention of the story that is preserved in the tradition opens up the possibility of ethical interrogation of the law, at the very least in the consideration of how it is to be applied.

Similarly, mishnaic *halakhah* allows the groom to claim in court that his bride was not a virgin and that either the marriage should be annulled or he should be paid back the bride price that he paid for a virgin. In the talmudic discussion, however, his right to do this is limited. In each of the various stories of the bridegroom coming to court with a claim of having found no blood or of having found an "open opening," the sage in charge undermines the claim (B. *Ketubbot* 8b–10b),[42] leaving the impression that the Rabbis wanted to limit the application of the law, perhaps to the point of extinction.[43]

As the examples demonstrate, the narratives in the talmudic discussions of the law raise questions, perhaps primarily as to how the law should be implemented. But the implications for thinking about the relationship between ethics and law are immense, as the force of the narratives is to foreground the impact of law on people's lives. By no means could we say that the interplay between narratives and legal discussions is always one of critical interrogation of the law. Narratives have all kinds of roles to play in rabbinic literature. But it is the interplay among the genres itself that provides opportunities for critical interventions in the legal treatment of moral issues.[44]

3. *Ethics between biblical and rabbinic halakhah.* While generally rabbinic *halakhic* discourse moves within the theological and legal limits laid out in the Hebrew Bible, on a few occasions it dramatically changes the parameters of biblical law. Such a situation provides us with the opportunity to observe the rabbinic sages work at putting biblical law to the test.

One of the most famous examples is perhaps the *jus talionis*. Biblical law emphatically takes a retributive approach to physical injury, summarized in the precept "an eye for an eye": "If a man maims his neighbor, as he did, so shall be done to him: fracture for fracture, eye for eye, tooth for tooth; just as he maimed a person, so shall he be" (Lev 24:19–20).[45] Almost equally famous is the early rabbinic reading of the principle as compensatory rather than retributive in nature, phrased laconically as: "An eye for an eye (means) money."[46] Earliest rabbinic law simply prescribes compensatory payment for personal injury, involving liabilities of various kinds (M. *Bava Kamma* 8:1). The midrashic acrobatics in the talmudic discussion of this law notwithstanding, this ruling clearly has no grounding in biblical reasoning and is obviously a mishnaic innovation.

The question we may ask is what may have prompted the rabbinic sages to undertake this hermeneutic and juridical intervention? Of course, there cannot be a simple answer, and the texts themselves do not offer one, because they do not ask the question in these terms. But one obvious possibility is that these rabbinic sages were driven by ethical and not merely by hermeneutic concerns. In other words, legal prescription is here circumvented and, indeed, changed for ethical reasons.

A similar question may be raised in other contexts, such as the case of the rebellious son (*ben sorer u-moreh*, Deut 21:18–21). Early rabbinic tradition had to say that rather than reading the passage as actual law to be implemented in legal practice, the biblical case had to be understood as a didactic exercise only (T. *Sanhedrin* 11:6). Subsequent interpretations of the biblical law render the biblical prescription of capital punishment for the rebellious son as inapplicable in practice (see B. *Sanhedrin* 70b–71a). Such examples can be multiplied.[47]

Each of these cases has to be evaluated carefully to consider what would have prompted such changes, whether and how changes in ethical sensitivities played a role, or whether different concerns motivated them. At the very least, however, these developments, internal to the legal discourse in rabbinic literature, offer opportunities for ethical reflections.[48]

Universality and Particularity in Rabbinic Literature

In this final section we need to consider issues of universality and particularity in rabbinic literature. Just like biblical literature, the rabbinic corpus is framed by the fundamental tension between being concerned first and foremost with a particular people, especially in the legal discourse, and between belief in a God who is not only a tribal king but is the Creator of the Universe, the "king of the world," as every rabbinically formulated blessing would have it. The same biblical God who is believed to have created humanity as a whole enters a relationship with a particular people, mediated by Torah. Thinking about ethics in rabbinic Judaism, we have to take this tension into account, as it translates ultimately into the question of the relationship between an ethic that applies to Jews only (a particularist ethic) and an ethic that would be at the least relevant to all of humanity (a universalist ethic).

How are Jews and the rest of humanity related to each other in rabbinic literature, and what is the ethical import of this question?

Purely theoretically, one might think of various ethical models by which to resolve such tension. For instance, one goal might be to resolve the tension in favor of the particular such that it is the measuring rod for the universal, and then aim to have the rest of humanity become like oneself, a model that historically many "civilizing" missions were based on. Alternately, a goal might be simply to ignore the rest of humanity and remain focused on one's own, a model that might be considered tribalist. Ethically speaking, both models are problematic for the obvious reasons: the rest of humanity is not recognized in their own right by making the particular rule the universal, at least aspirationally. The "universalism" of this first model is universal often only in claim rather than in reality. Or, alternately, the rest of humanity remains ethically irrelevant or invisible at best, with potentially detrimental consequences, as we shall see.

Arguably, rabbinic Judaism does not resolve the tension between a particularist and a universalist ethic but rather maintains it. The sages do not simply ignore the rest of humanity. First, as a whole the rabbinic project remains committed to a shared status of all humans *sub specie aeternitatis*. Furthermore, rabbinic law endows non-Jews as such with a legal status, thus sowing the seeds for what could evolve into a pluralist ethic. That is, non-Jews do not have to become Jews in order to be valued as humans. At the same time it would be naïve to claim that rabbinic Judaism is principled in its recognition of a sort of pluralist ethic, since there are many legal rulings and traditions with respect to non-Jews that have caused a stir in anti-Jewish camps from Johann Andreas Eisenmenger's days in the seventeenth century forward. The following will illustrate these thoughts.

First, the shared status of all humans derives from the basic biblical idea of human creation and is underlined in rabbinic rhetoric. That shared status is one of the ultimate value of human life. It is written into the foundational compendium of rabbinic Judaism,

> ... therefore '*adam* was created singularly ('*adam yehidi nibra*),[49] to teach you that one who destroys *a single soul* (*nefesh*) from humanity (*benei 'adam*),[50] Scripture accounts it to him as though he had destroyed an entire world; and if one saves *a single soul* of humanity, Scripture accounts it to him as though he had saved an entire world.... and to proclaim the greatness of the Holy One, blessed be He; for a human being ('*adam*) stamps many coins with one seal and they are all alike; but the King of kings, the Holy One, Blessed be He, has stamped every human being ('*adam*) with the seal of the first human being, yet not a single one of them resembles his fellow.
>
> Therefore every single person must say: For my sake was the world created.
> M. *Sanhedrin* 4:5

This powerful passage is often cited as evidence of rabbinic Judaism's support for human rights.[51] It is found in the mishnaic laws of capital punishment and the threat against false witnesses, who would be held responsible for the potential killing of an innocent suspect. In spite of this specific context, it can easily be read as a principled valuation of human life: every human being is the equivalent of an "entire world" (*olam male'*, lit., "full world"), and not merely a member of the species "humanity" (*benai 'adam*). As such every human being is irreplaceable. It is perhaps not by accident that the context of this passage is the laws of capital punishment, of presumably legitimated killing on behalf of a court, even—and this point deserves emphasis—if the ethical standard is articulated as a principle. Humanity as a whole is at least conceptually and theologically on equal footing *sub specie aeternitatis*.

At the same time, of course, the goal of the *halakhah* is to design a legal tradition not for humanity, not even aspirationally, but for a particular people referred to by the biblicizing term "Israel." Membership is first constituted ethnically, that is by birth,[52] in rabbinic law self-consciously so, and only secondarily by conversion, which makes one a member of that people.[53] By definition, the purpose of Jewish law is to mark Jewish difference from other people, and much of rabbinic legal literature is concerned with what can be considered "boundary-maintenance." The model of the *halakhic* tradition from the Mishnah onward is in many ways what we have described as tribalist above. The ethical tribalism is underlined by those legal traditions that have been variously identified as discriminatory[54] and can be found especially in the laws of dealing with so-called idolaters and in the laws of property. Suffice it to name but two examples to illustrate this: a Jewish woman may not stay alone with gentiles, because they might rape her, nor should a Jewish man stay alone with them, because they might murder him (M. *Avodah Zarah* 2:1); "An ox of a Jew that gores an ox of a gentile is exempt, but an ox of a gentile that gores an ox of a Jew...must pay the full sum of damage" (M. *Bava Kama* 4:3). How such laws are to be applied has remained subject to intense debate over the centuries.[55]

Such "tribalist" rulings notwithstanding, rabbinic *halakhah* interestingly endows non-Jews not only with legal status, but with legal obligations, thereby endowing them with a recognition that initially is retained for Jews only, namely as *halakhic* subjects. This means that at least conceptually, and much of this is on the level of concept, non-Jews as such are recognized as legal subjects, and not only on the condition of becoming Jews. The rabbinic category of non-Jews that allows us to think in this direction is the so-called Noahides (*benai Noah*). Noahides are non-Jews who observe a minimal set of laws, the seven Noahide laws, all but one of which are prohibitions—namely, the prohibition of idolatry, murder, theft, sexual immorality, blasphemy, and eating limbs of a living animal.[56] The one positive command is the establishment of courts. The development of this category and the strange idea of prescribing a set of laws to non-Jews that they must observe in order to deserve the status of Noahide remains rudimentary in its development.

The Noahide laws are perhaps as close as one can get to a recognition of an ethic with a universal claim in rabbinic legal thought and literature,[57] although it might be more precise to consider this a rudimentary pluralist ethic. This universal import may not be as universal as a post-Enlightenment ethicist might hope, for what would idolatry and blasphemy mean in an extra-Jewish context? Further, later medieval discussion of the Noahide laws add a number of rules that take on a distinctly rabbinic *halakhic* flavor and bend these toward the pole of a tribal ethic yet again.⁵⁸ Still, the important issue to be considered is that conceptually this model of universality was not based on a "civilizing" mission, a mission to allow others to become human only by making them look the same as Jews—or at least not inherently so. As Noahides, non-Jews do not have to become Jews in order to be recognized as humans.

This universalist tendency in rabbinic literature has some poignant consequences at times. For instance, according to an early tradition attributed to Rabbi Joshua, "The righteous of the nations will have a share in the World to Come."⁵⁹ That is, they can merit their eschatological share without having to become Jewish. Only Jews are subject not only to the seven Noahide laws but also to the 613 commandments of the Sinai Covenant articulated in the Torah. This is perhaps a theological reason why Jews have not sought to become missionaries for the last two thousand years. (A historian of Jewish culture would cringe at this since of course there are complex historical reasons as well, given that Jews lived as a minority under the rule of people who would not look kindly at Jewish attempts to convert Christians or Muslims.) But also, the Rabbis maintain that Jews must take care of poor, sick, and mourning non-Jews as well as Jews who suffer in those ways, "for the sake of peace"⁶⁰—admittedly a practical motivation, but one that gives concrete application to this universalist thrust among the Rabbis.

The idea that as long as humans follow a basic agreed-upon set of laws—most of which seem to support the upkeep of human society and allow for the maintenance of cultural differences—can operate as an important corrective to the exclusivist ethic that *halakhic* discourse also harbors, whether for historical or social reasons. At the same time, it can also operate as an important corrective to a kind of universalist ethic in which everyone has to be the same in order to be recognized as ethical.

This balance of exclusivist and universalist tendencies, though, is present in classical rabbinic literature only in skeletal form, and it has been left to medieval and modern Jews to build on it to articulate in their own time and place a Jewish view of the relationship between Jews and non-Jews.⁶¹

Notes

1. David Stern, *The Anthology in Jewish Literature* (Oxford University Press, 2004), especially the section on "Ancient Israel and Classical Judaism." See also Hans-Jürgen Becker, *Die grossen rabbinischen Sammelwerke Palästinas: Zur literarischen Genese von Talmud Yerushalmi und Midrash Bereshit Rabba* (Tübingen: Mohr Siebeck, 1999).
2. Daniel Boyarin, *Carnal Israel: Reading Sex in Talmudic Literature*, (Berkeley: University of California Press, 1993); Ishay Rosen-Zvi, *Demonic Desires: "Yetzer Hara" and the Problem of Evil in Late Antiquity*. Divinations: Rereading Late Ancient Religion (Philadelphia: University of Pennsylvania Press, 2011). Also Michael Satlow, *Jewish Marriage in Antiquity* (Princeton, NJ: Princeton University Press, 2001).
3. Of course, they are often organized along the lines of an easy-to-detect formal principle of collection, such that the midrashic anthologies by and large follow the

order of the text of the Torah, and the Palestinian and Babylonian Talmuds follow the Mishnah as the organizing principle for their composition.

4. *Avot de Rabbi Natan* exists in at least two manuscript versions, hence text(s). For the most authoritative text edition and critical discussion, see Hans-Jürgen Becker, ed., *Avot de-Rabbi Natan. Synoptische Edition beider Versionen* (Tübingen: Mohr Siebeck, 2006).

5. For useful introductory discussions of this literature see Jonathan Wyn Schofer, "Rabbinic Ethical Formation and the Formation of Rabbinic Ethical Compilations," in *Cambridge Companion to the Talmud and Rabbinic Literature*, C. E. Fonrobert and M. Jaffee, eds. (Cambridge University Press, 2007), pp. 313–36; as well as M. B. Lerner, "The External Tractates," in *The Literature of the Sages*, S. Safrai, ed. (Philadelphia: Fortress Press, 1987), pp. 367–403.

6. The referent is commonly *'adam*, or human being. The gendering of the addressee is not just a grammatical accident but explicitly thematized in the maxims having to do with gendered social conduct: "...do not talk excessively with a woman; they said with regard to one's wife, and even more so with the wife of one's friend" (1:5) et al.

7. The mythical "men of the great synagogue" in the opening paragraph are part of a chain of transmission of "torah" (instruction) reaching back to Mount Sinai. On the political function of the chain of transmission in its historical-cultural context, see Amram Tropper, *Wisdom, Politics and Historiography: Tractate Avot in the Context of the Graeco-Roman Near East* (New York: Oxford University Press, 2004), esp. chap. 8, "Avot's Chain of Transmission and Early Christian Parallels," pp. 208–41.

8. Rabbi Yehudah ha-Nasi, traditionally credited with the redaction of the Mishnah, and his son Rabban Gamliel. This is not to make historical claims but rather to illustrate the staging of this literature categorized as ethical.

9. E.g., R. Travers Herford, *Pirke Aboth/ The Ethics of the Talmud: Sayings of the Fathers* (New York: Schocken, 1966); Chaim Goldstein, *Ethics of the Fathers* (New York: Bloch Publishing Co., 1955).

10. See A. Tropper, *Wisdom* (at note 7 above), p. 51.

11. For a discussion of the scholarly consensus of putting *'Avot* in line with the tradition of Wisdom literature, see A. Tropper, *Wisdom*, esp. chap. 2, "Avot, Wisdom, and Artistic Prose," pp. 51–88.

12. Jonathan W. Schofer, in *The Making of a Sage: A Study in Rabbinic Ethics* (Madison: University of Wisconsin Press, 2005) focuses on *Avot de-Rabbi Natan* for its study of rabbinic ethics, specifically for its aim to shape the conduct and disposition of the scholar. Also in his *Confronting Vulnerability: The Body and the Divine in Rabbinic Ethics* (Chicago: University of Chicago Press, 2010), where he considers in more detail the applicability of virtue ethic to rabbinic texts.

13. M. *Avot* 2:16 (cited above), and further M. *Avot* 4:1 ("Who is strong? He who conquers his *yetzer*!), 4:29 ("may your *yetzer* not assuage you"). AdRN A, 16, which comments on M. *Avot* 2:16, is one of the most prominent rabbinic reflections on the *yetzer* in modern discussions of Jewish ethics. It develops the idea that a person is born with the *yetzer hara* while one acquires the good inclination upon reaching maturity, the boy at age thirteen and the girl at age twelve. Essentially it is the Torah that channels the force to combat the evil *yetzer* in AdRN. For a extensive discussion see J. Schofer, "The Redaction of Desire: Structure and Editing of Rabbinic Teachings Concerning Yeser ('Inclination')," in *Journal of Jewish Thought and Philosophy* 12/1 (2003), pp. 19–53, and Ishay Rosen-Zvi, *Demonic Desires: Yetzer Hara and the Problem of Evil in Late Antiquity* (Philadelphia: University of Pennsylvania Press, 2011), which

demonstrates the context of ancient demonology for the emergence of the concept in rabbinic texts.
14. Throughout, see Efraim E. Urbach, *The Sages: Their Concepts and Beliefs* (Cambridge, MA: Harvard University Press, 1987), pp. 417–83. But a more comprehensive discussion appears in B. *Sukkah* 51b–52b, discussed by a number of scholars for its complex notion of evil (e.g., Elisabeth S. Alexander, "Art, Argument, and Ambiguity in Talmud: Conflicting Conceptions of the Evil Impulse in B. *Sukkah* 51b–52a," *Hebrew Union College Annual* 73, pp. 97–132), and the relationship of the *yetzer* to rabbinic notions of sexuality (Daniel Boyarin, *Carnal Israel: Reading Sex in Talmudic Culture* (Berkeley: University of California Press, 1993), pp. 64–67).
15. Indeed, the entire sixth chapter, which may or may not have been added later, is an ode to the Torah and to the study of Torah.
16. On the tension between universalism and particularism in rabbinic culture, see especially M. Hirshman, *Torah for the Entire World: A Universalist School of Rabbinic Thought* (Tel Aviv: Ha-kibbutz Ha-me'uhad, 1999).
17. This is, for instance, the project of J. W. Schofer's first book, *The Making of a Sage* (at note 12 above), which focuses on *Avot de-Rabbi Natan* for its study of rabbinic ethics, specifically for its aim to shape the conduct and disposition of the scholar. In his recent book, *Confronting Vulnerability* (at note 12 above), he does however consider texts from across the classical rabbinic library.
18. This tends to be the case with modern Orthodox ethicists, such as J. D. Bleich. For a brief discussion, see David Novak, *Natural Law in Judaism* (Cambridge, UK and New York: Cambridge University Press, 1998), pp. 62–64.
19. The term does of course exist in biblical literature, but it gains in specificity in rabbinic literature, to refer to the individual commandments that are the building blocks of rabbinic law.
20. This issue became the *locus classicus* for second-wave Jewish feminism early on. See Rachel Adler's now classic "The Jew Who Wasn't There: Halakha and the Jewish Woman," first plublished in *Davka* (1972), 7–11, then republished in Susannah Heschel's equally classic anthology, *On Being a Jewish Feminist: A Reader* (New York: Schocken, 1983), pp.12–19.
21. Judith Romney Wegner, *Chattle or Person? The Status of Women in the Mishnah* (New York, Oxford: Oxford University Press, 1992). This question is further corroborated by the referent for "Jew" in the Mishnah, namely *Yisra'el*, as in "an Israel," the idealized Jewish person incorporating the sum total of the commandments. The referent for Jewish woman is *bat Yisra'el*, lit. "daughter of (an) Israel." That is, she is *per nominem* only related to or derivative of the person who incorporates the idealized subject of the Mishnah and subsequent rabbinic *halakhah*. To feminist readers of rabbinic literature, this view has raised the question whether the legal discourse of the sages is amenable to revision in order to make women subjects of *halakhah* equal to men, or whether, alternately, *halakhah* needs to be rethought altogether in order to achieve such a goal.
22. The examples of the person not commanded here are first an exemplary non-Jew who excels in the commandment of *kibbud av ve-em* (honoring one's parents), and second, a blind sage (Rav Yosef), who would be exempt from a number of commandments, also cited in cp. B. *Bava Kamma* 87a. The dictum is also called upon in considering the question of a non-Jew studying Torah, so B. *Bava Kamma* 38a and B. *Avodah Zarah* 3a.

23. See, for instance, E. Urbach, *The Sages* (at note 14 above), p. 325, who claims plausibly that the dictum in context does not state that "the deeds of one who is not commanded do not merit reward, nor is their value negated. Only their relative value is emphasized."
24. For illustration an early tradition: "Rabbi Eleazar ben Azariah said: 'From whence do we know that a man should not say "I cannot tolerate wearing *sha'atnez*, or I cannot tolerate eating pork or cannot tolerate illicit relations" but rather he should say "I am capable and willing, but what can I do [given that] my Father in Heaven decreed thus?" Therefore Scripture states: "I have separated you from the nations to be Mine" (Lev 20:24, 26), because of that he avoids the sin and accepts God's sovereignty,'" *Sifra*, Kedoshim on those verses. And according to a later talmudic hyperbolic pronouncement, attributed to Rav Nahman bar Isaac: "A transgression committed for its own sake is better than a commandment performed not for its own sake" (B. *Nazir* 23b).
25. E.g., M. *Makkot* 3:16, the homiletic end to a tractate on the application of the biblical punishment of forty lashings: "Rabbi Hananiah ben Akashiah said: The Holy One of Blessing wanted to provide the opportunity for merit to Israel, and therefore multiplied the Torah and its commandments." We may also think of the rabbinic pleasure in detecting—constructing, rather—"measure for measure" relationships between an act and its perceived consequence, displayed in M. *Sotah* 1:6-7 et al. The rabbis add the notion of earning life in "the world to come" to the biblical notion of "reward," as in M. *Pe'ah* 1:1, also added to the morning blessings in traditional prayer books, and in many other places (e.g., *Leviticus Rabbah* 35:5-6).
26. Here we may think of the famous story of Elisha ben Abuya (B. *Haggigah* 14a-15a), who was once of "us" but then turned into *Aher*, the paradigmatic "Other," by abandoning the whole idea of Torah observance after watching a boy, following his father's command to get eggs from a bird's nest, climb up and shoo away the mother bird, but then he falls off and dies in contradiction to the Torah's promise of long life for honoring one's parents (Exod 20:12) and for shooing away the mother bird (Deut 22:6-7)—all in all one of the central rabbinic narratives for the question of theodicy.
27. Consider the exceptional case of Ben Azzai, who excuses himself from the commandment of procreation—the one rabbinic exception in all of talmudic Judaism—by claiming that he is too much in love with the Torah (T. *Yevamot* 8:7, cited on B. *Yevamot* 63b; cp. *Genesis Rabbah* 34:14, *Mekhilta*, Ba-Hodesh 8), even though he himself considers the refusal to procreate as the equivalent of murder and the diminishing of the image of God. Another example would be Rabbi Shimeon bar Yohai, who in talmudic *aggadah* and *halakhic* tradition is paradigmatic for his religious extremism (*Avot d'Rabbi Natan* A41), and in his fanaticism ends up killing off his fellow Jews (B. *Shabbat* 33b-34a).
28. E.g., M. *Avot* 1:17; B. *Kiddushin* 40b.
29. E.g., Isaiah 62:4-5; Jeremiah 2:2-3; Hosea 2:21-22.
30. E.g., Deuteronomy 11:1.
31. Y. Heinemann, *Ta'amei ha-mitzvot be-sifrut Yisra'el* (Jerusalem: Ha-histadrut ha-tsiyonit: 1949).
32. That they purify people: *Genesis Rabbah*, Lekh Lekha 44:1 and *Leviticus Rabbah*, Shemini 13:3. That they endow Jews with holiness: *Mekhilta de Rabbi Yishma'el*, Massekhta de-Kaspa §20. That they contribute to Jewish identity: *Sifra* 112c and *Exodus Rabbah*, Ki Tissa 47:3. That they make life beautiful: *Song of Songs Rabbah* on Song of Songs 1:15. For more on biblical and rabbinic motivations to obey the

commandments, see Elliot N. Dorff, *For the Love of God and People: A Philosophy of Jewish Law* (Philadelphia: Jewish Publication Society, 2007), chap. 4 (pp. 173–80 for rabbinic motivations).

33. The literature on this phrase is immense and cannot possibly be cited comprehensively here. I have learned much from Louis E. Newman, listed below under further readings, who also discusses some of this literature. See also his article "Law, Virtue and Supererogation in the Halakha: The Problem of *Lifnim Mishurat Hadin* Reconsidered," *Journal of Jewish Studies* 40 (1989), pp. 61–88, and further Saul Berman, "*Lifnim Meshurat Hadin*," *Journal of Jewish Studies* 26 (1975), pp. 86–104, and 28 (1977), pp. 181–93; J. D. Bleich, "Is There an Ethic Beyond Halakhah?" in *Studies in Jewish Philosophy*, Norbert M. Samuelson, ed. (Lanham, MD 1987), pp. 498–506; Eugene Borowitz, "The Authority of the Ethical Impulse in Halakhah," ibid., 527–46; Joshua Halberstam, "Supererogation in Jewish Halakhah and Islamic Shari'a," in *Studies in Islamic and Judaic Traditions*, W. M. Brinner and S. D. Ricks, eds. (Atlanta, GA, Scholars Press 1986), pp. 85–98; Aharon Lichtenstein, "Does Jewish Tradition Recognize an Ethic Independent of Halakha?" in *Modern Jewish Ethics*, ed. Marvin Fox (Columbus, OH: Ohio State University Press, 1975), pp. 62–88.

34. In the talmudic citations of this midrashic tradition, Rashi interprets this phrase differently in the two cases, once as referring to trade and a means of income (B. *Bava Metzia* 30b) and once as referring to study of Torah (B. *Bava Kamma* 100a).

35. Found in both the *Mekhilta de Rabbi Yishm'ael*, here Tractate d'Amalek 2, and in *Mekhilta de Rabbi Shimeon bar Yohai*, Exodus 18:20.

36. B. *Bava Metzia* 30b, in the story of Rabbi Yishma'el ben R. Yossi helping the wood carrier; B. *Bava Kamma* 99b-100a, in the story of Rabbi Hiyya who misjudged a monetary case; and B. *Ketubbot* 97a, where Rav Papa returns from a field.

37. B. *Bava Metzia* 24b, with regard to returning property that one could legally keep.

38. B. *Berakhot* 7a and B. *Avodah Zarah* 4b.

39. See Louis Newman, *Past Imperatives: Studies in the History and Theory of Jewish Ethics* (Albany: State University of New York Press, 1998), p. 33: "If we were to ask the talmudic authorities whether an action performed *lifnim meshurat hadin* was a moral duty, or a legal duty, or not a duty at all but simply an act of great generosity, it appears that the answer would be unclear at best." For further analysis of the early variable meanings of the term, see Tsvi Novick, "Naming Normativity: The Early History of the Terms Shurat Ha-Din and Lifnim Mis-Surat Ha-Din," *Journal of Semitics Studies* LV/2 (Autumn 2010), pp. 391–406.

40. According to Shammai two sons as a minimum, and according to Hillel a son and a daughter. For the larger issues involved in the obligation to reproduce, see Jeremy Cohen, *Be Fertile and Increase, Fill the Earth and Master It: The Ancient and Medieval Career of a Biblical Text* (Ithaca, NY: Cornell University Press, 1989).

41. *Pesikta de Rav Kahana* 22:2. See also Judith R. Baskin's survey of the issue, "Infertile Wife in Rabbinic Judaism," in *Jewish Women: A Comprehensive Historical Encyclopedia*, accessed at jwa.org/encyclopedia/article/infertile-wife-rabbinic-judaism.

42. See also Shulamit Valler, *Woman and Womanhood in the Talmud*, Brown Judaica Series 131 (Atlanta: Scholars Press, 1999), chap. 2.

43. Whether one takes such incidents as proof for a general improvement of the legal status of women in rabbinic *halakhah* over that of biblical law and therefore the rabbinic concern for women, as Judith Hauptman does in her book *Rereading the Rabbis: A Woman's Voice* (Boulder, CO: Westview Press, 1998) remains open

to question. We also find a reverse moment of seemingly overt concern for legal disadvantage based on gender when the Mishnah rules that, in the case of a small estate, daughters are to be provided with maintenance first, even if the sons have to go begging at the doors; this provokes the question: "Because I am male, I should be disadvantaged?" attributed to a sage named Admon (M. *Ketubbot* 13:3). For the gender politics of this remarkable text, see Miriam Peskowitz, *Spinning Fantasies: Rabbis, Gender, and History* (Berkeley: University of California Press, 1997), pp. 124–26.

44. This explains at least in part the recent enormous popularity among scholars of rabbinic law of Robert Cover's essay "Nomos and Narrative," originally published in the *Harvard Law Review* 4 of 1983 and then anthologized posthumously in the collection of Cover's essays in *Narrative, Violence, and the Law: The Essays of Robert Cover* (Ann Arbor: University of Michigan, 1995), pp. 95–173.
45. Also Exodus 21:23 and Deuteronomy 19:21. The literature on this principle is immense, for obvious theological and juristic reasons. See the review in William H. Propp, *Exodus 19–40 with Introduction and Commentary*: Anchor Bible 2A (New York: Anchor Bible, 2006). See also the recent insightful discussion of the *ius talionis* by Mira Balberg, "Pricing Persons: Consecration, Compensation, and Individuality in the Mishnah," *Jewish Quarterly Review* (forthcoming, 2013).
46. Attributed to Rabbi Yishma'el in the *Mekhilta deRabbi Yishmael Mishpatim*, par. 8 (ed. Horowitz-Rabin, p. 277); also cited in the Babylonian Talmud at B. *Bava Kamma* 83b. See Menachem Kister, "Law, Morality, and Rhetoric in Some Sayings of Jesus," in *Studies in Ancient Midrash*, James Kugel, ed. (Cambridge, MA: Harvard University Press, 2001), pp. 145–55. Obviously, murder is excluded from compensation.
47. See Moshe Halbertal, *Interpretive Revolutions in the Making* (Jerusalem: Magnes Press of Hebrew University, 1997, Hebrew).
48. For some of many examples of modern philosophies of Jewish law in the Conservative/Masorti Movement that build on this issue, see Elliot N. Dorff, *For the Love of God and People: A Philosophy of Jewish Law* (at note 32 above), esp. chap. 6; Robert Gordis, *The Dynamics of Judaism: A Study in Jewish Law* (Bloomington: Indiana University Press, 1990), esp. chap. 3; and Louis Jacobs, *A Tree of Life: Diversity, Flexibility, and Creativity in Jewish Law* (Oxford, UK: Oxford University Press, 1984), esp. chap. 12. There are also a few examples in the Orthodox Movement: Eliezer Berkovits, *Not in Heaven: The Nature and Function of Halakha* (New York: Ktav, 1983); David Hartman, *A Living Covenant: The Innovative Spirit in Traditional Judaism* (New York: Free Press, 1985); and Shubert Spero, *Morality, Halakha, and the Jewish Tradition* (New York: Ktav and Yeshiva University Press, 1983).
49. Alternately: "a singular human being was created…"
50. Famously, some manuscripts have "Israel" instead of the term roughly equivalent to "humanity" (*benai 'adam*). There is no way to decide which one might be the "original" version, a philological problem that applies to much of rabbinic literature from late antiquity; we have manuscripts only from the early medieval period onward. For this problem see Peter Schäfer, "Research into Rabbinic Literature: An Attempt to Define the Status Quaestionis," *Journal of Jewish Studies* 37 (1986), pp. 139–52; Chaim Milikowsky, "The Status Quaestionis of Research in Rabbinic Literature," *Journal of Jewish Studies* 39 (1988), pp. 201–11. Another concern would be the gendering of the terminology, whether "humanity" or "Jewish people," i.e., whether the status of "'*adam*" or "Israel" can be attained fully only by men. On this question see my article "When Women Walk in the Ways of Their Fathers: On

Gendering the Rabbinic Claim for Authority," *Journal of the History of Sexuality* 10:3/4, Special Issue: Sexuality in Late Antiquity (July/October 2001), pp. 398–415.

51. David Daube, "The Rabbis and Philo on Human Rights," in *Essays on Human Rights: Contemporary Rights and Jewish Perspectives*, David Sidorsky, ed. (Philadelphia: The Jewish Publication Society of America, 1979), pp. 234–46, as well as Samuel Belkin, *In His Image: The Jewish Philosophy of Man as Expressed in Rabbinic Tradition* (Westport, CT: Greenwood Press, 1979), pp. 97–116; and Michael Fishbane, "The Image of the Human and the Rights of the Individual in Jewish Tradition," in *Human Rights and the World's Religions*, Leroy S. Rouner, ed. (Notre Dame, IN.: University of Notre Dame Press, 1988). See also Jonathan K. Crane, "Why Rights? Why Me?" *Journal of Religious Ethics* 35:4 (December 2007), pp. 559–90, for an analysis of this and other ways Jews justify supporting human rights.
52. On the emergence of the rule of matrilineality in rabbinic literature from the Mishnah onward, see Shaya J. D. Cohen, *The Beginnings of Jewishness* (Berkeley and Los Angeles: University of California Press, 1999), chap. 9, "The Matrilineal Principle," pp. 263–308.
53. Shaye Cohen seeks to capture the rabbinic institutionalization of conversion as a way to constitute membership in the people by the term "ethno-religious"; see his chapter "From *Ethnos* to Ethno-religious" in his *The Beginnings of Jewishness*, ibid., pp. 109–40.
54. Such a categorization, though, depends on political contexts. That is, as a cultural expression of a people that finds itself in a minority situation, such legal traditions have a defensive or protective character. However, if such legal traditions were to take on the role as rule of the land, they can gain discriminatory character.
55. Thus the Catalan talmudic commentator Menachem Meiri (thirteenth century) historicizes the category of idolater in rabbinic law, so that it applies to ancient times only, or at worst to people living at the far corners of the known world, exempting, for instance, the Christians of his day. See Moshe Halbertal, "'Ones Possessed of Religion': Religious Tolerance in the Teachings of the *Me'iri*," *Edah* 1:1 (2000), pp. 1–24, and more recently Gregg Stern, *Philosophy and Rabbinic Culture: Jewish Interpretation and Controversy in Medieval Languedoc* (New York: Routledge, 2009). Maimonides, on the other hand, exempts Islam and Muslims (but not Christians) from the category of idolatry. See M.T. Laws of Repentance 3:8, and M.T. Laws Relating to Idolaters 9:4, as well as his comment on M. *Avodah Zarah* 1:3 in his *Commentary to the Mishnah*.
56. The doctrine, with some variation in their lists of the seven, appears in a variety of rabbinic texts, including T. *Avodah Zarah* 8:4; B. *Sanhedrin* 56a–56b; *Genesis Rabbah* 16:6, 34:8; *Canticles (Song of Songs) Rabbah* 1:16; *Pesikta D'Rav Kahana*, Bahodesh, 202–3. For the whole question of what was commanded to Adam and what was commanded to Noah, see *Tanhuma*, ed. Buber, no. 2: 35a and, esp. n. 7 thereon. The literature on the Noahide laws and their import for Jewish ethics is immense. I cite here only David Novak, *The Image of the Non-Jew in Judaism: A Historical and Constructive Study of the Noahide Laws* (New York: E. Mellen Press, 1983).
57. Nahum Rakover, *Law and the Noahides: Law as a Universal Value* (Jerusalem: Library of Jewish Law, 1998).
58. For instance Maimonides in M.T. Laws of Kings 10:6, based on "tradition" (*kabbalah*), adds the prohibition of cross-breeding animals and grafting trees.
59. T. *Sanhedrin* 13:2.
60. T. *Gittin* 3:18; B. *Gittin* 61a.

61. For one modern example, see Elliot N. Dorff, *To Do the Right and the Good: A Jewish Approach to Modern Social Ethics* (Philadelphia: Jewish Publication Society, 2002), chap. 3.

Suggestions for Further Reading

Adler, Rachel. 1999. *Engendering Judaism: An Inclusive Theology and Ethics.* Boston: Beacon Press.

Boyarin. Daniel. 1993. *Carnal Israel: Reading Sex in Talmudic Culture.* Berkeley: University of California Press.

Dorff, Elliot N. 2007. *For the Love of God and People: A Philosophy of Jewish Law.* Philadelphia: Jewish Publication Society.

Fonrobert, Charlotte Elisheva. 2000. *Menstrual Purity: Rabbinic and Christian Reconstructions of Biblical Gender.* Stanford, CA: Stanford University Press.

Halbertal. Moshe. 1997. *Hermeneutic Revolutions in the Making: Values as Interpretive Considerations in Midrashei Halakhah* (Hebrew). Jerusalem: The Hebrew University Magnes Press.

Hauptman, Judith. 1998. *Rereading the Rabbis: A Woman's Voice.* Boulder, CO: Westview Press.

Newman, Louis E. 1998. *Past Imperatives: Studies in the History and Theory of Jewish Ethics* (SUNY Series in Jewish Philosophy). New York: State University Press of New York.

Novak, David. 1983. *The Image of the Non-Jew in Judaism: A Historical and Constructive Sutdy of the Noahide Laws.* Lampeter, UK: Edwin Mellen Press.

Rosen-Zvi, Ishay. 2011. *Demonic Desires: "Yetzer hara" and the Problem of Evil in Late Antiquity* (Divinations: Rereading Late Antique Religion). Philadelphia: University of Pennsylvania Press.

Schofer, Jon. 2005. *The Making of a Sage: A Study in Rabbinic Ethics.* Madison: University of Wisconsin Press.

Urbach, Ephraim. 1987. *The Sages: Their Concepts and Beliefs.* Cambridge, MA: Harvard University Press.

CHAPTER 3

ETHICAL THEORIES IN JEWISH MYSTICAL WRITINGS

JOSEPH DAN

Introduction

Medieval and modern Hebrew literature include a genre known as *sifrut ha-musar*, translated, literally, as "ethical literature." The contemporary boundaries and characteristics of this genre were formally fixed by Gershom Scholem, when in 1923–1924 the he edited categories of the Judaica collection of books at the just-founded Jewish National and University Library in Jerusalem. The library at that time used the Dewey decimal system, and *sifrut ha-musar* received the status of a separate category. Scholem put at the top of the list the ten best-known works in this section, including Bahya Ibn Pakuda's *Hovot ha-Levavot* (eleventh century), Rabbi Judah ben Samuel the Pious's *Sefer Hasidim* (early thirteenth century), Moshe Hayyim Luzzatto's *Mesilat Yesharim* (eighteenth century), Rabbi Hayyim Vital's *Shaarey Kedushah* (sixteenth century), and similar works.[1] In 1950 the newly appointed professor of Hebrew Literature at the Hebrew University, Simon Halkin, expanded the scope of material studied in that department and established a section dedicated mainly to *sifrut ha-musar*, and Professor Isaiah Tishby, a prominent disciple of Scholem, was appointed to teach the subject. I had the honor to be the first student to receive a Ph.D. at the Hebrew University in this section in 1964.

While Scholem should be credited as the first scholar to define the bibliographical boundaries of *sifrut ha-musar*, it seems that almost deliberately Scholem ignored this genre in his vast scholarly endeavor. In the scores of books and hundreds of articles that he published, one can hardly find the names of central figures like the MaHaRal of Prague or Moshe Hayyim Luzzatto. Even central works in kabbalistic *sifrut musar*, like *Reshit Hokhmah* by Eliyahu de Vidas or the *Shney Luhot ha-Berit* by Yeshaya ha-Levi Horowitz are absent from his studies. It is as if he said to himself when coming upon such works: "This is not mysticism, this is not *kabbalah*, this is literature, let Tishby and his department deal with it."[2]

Since the early nineteenth century, interest in Jewish ethics increased, and especially since modern trends in Judaism, notably the Reform Movement, placed Jewish ethics at the center of their redefinition of the essence of Judaism. Generations of scholars dedicated great efforts and detailed monographs to the presentation of Judaism's unique ethical message, analyzing all relevant sources—biblical, talmudic, midrashic, philosophical, *halakhic*, and, not frequently, mystical—to demonstrate Jewish creativity in this field. The emphasis was always on the presentation of social ethics, following the accepted definition of ethics since Aristotle: that ethics regulates the desired relationships among individuals and between individuals and society. The purpose of this vast endeavor in the last two centuries was to present a Jewish equivalent to the ethical systems that flourished in Western culture, based on Greek philosophy, on the one hand, and Christian norms, on the other.

It would seem that the vast treasury of Hebrew works—many of them influential in the history of Jewish culture—that are dedicated to *musar*, that is, ethics, would serve as a major source for scholars and theologians of the schools of Jewish thought dedicated to the demonstration of the importance of Jewish ethics. This did not happen. In the extensive literature concerning Jewish ethics in the last two centuries one can hardly find a reference to the major works of Jewish traditional *sifrut ha-musar*. The obvious reason for this absence is that the problems dealt with in modern analyses of Jewish ethics do not concern *sifrut ha-musar*, and vice versa. There is no meeting point between the worldview presented in the old Hebrew texts and the philosophy guiding modern thinkers. Despite the literal identity, *sifrut ha-musar* is not "ethical literature" in the European sense of the term.

An important starting point is common to both *sifrut ha-musar* and the European, Christian, Aristotelian conceptions of ethics: the sense that the Law, while very important, is not sufficient as a guide to achieving the maximal goals of human life. It lays down the minimal requirements for social survival and regulates individual behavior in a way that enables society to protect itself and its members from anarchy and chaos, yet it is not an instrument that can point the way toward perfection. The problem of the relationship between law and ethics is central in this context, and many attempts have been made to define the boundaries of each domain.

One of the most influential attempts to define the realm of ethics in traditional Jewish culture is found in the formula *lifnim me-shurat ha-din* (lit., inside the boundary of the law). This term has been used mainly in two different contexts. The first is in explaining God's behavior in several biblical contingencies, when He replaced insistence on carrying out the demands of the law (especially concerning punishment of evil-doers) with charity and mercy, mitigating his ruling, replacing justice with compassion. The second, more widely used, is the definition of a Hasid, a righteous one, as one who acts *lifnim mi-shurat ha-din*, that is, one who does more than the law requires, one who extends the demands of the *halakhah* [Jewish law] and invests more effort in the performance of the commandments. This interpretation was used in the famous tractate of the Mishnah *Avot*[3] and was codified by Maimonides in his great *halakhic* work the *Mishneh Torah*. In this sense, the term was used both in the realm of ritual, like prayer,[4] and in the realm of social behavior, like charity and caring for people in one's community.

From a religious point of view, this definition is perfect, because it does not separate the source of authority for the law from that of ethics. In fact, it subjugates the demands of ethical behavior to those of the *halakhah*. A person who wishes to study ethics must first study the law and then extend its rulings, yet always using the law as his basis. There is no independent realm of ethics; *hasidut* is just the extension of the law. Ethics, therefore, is an aspect of religious behavior and ritual; it does not require a separate or independent set of criteria, and it is impossible to differentiate between "religious" and "secular" realms within it. Giving more than the required minimum for charity, and staying an extra hour in prayer, are equally "ethical." From a theological point of view, the foundation for achieving human perfection is the law, the supreme guide. The adherence to the divine law and its extension is the only way to achieve the destiny of a human being on earth. The purpose and meaning of life are defined by the law and the law alone.

This is the reason that *sifrut ha-musar* does not deal with *lifnim mi-shurat ha-din*. The works included by tradition in the former category are not treatises that teach how one can extend the demands of the *halakhah* in order to reach the position of *hasidut*.[5] There is hardly a discussion of this subject in most of the best-known works that were written between the tenth and nineteenth centuries dedicated to *musar*. It may even be said that in many cases the scholars who wrote the treatises of the *sifrut ha-musar* wished to distance their teachings from the demands of the *halakhah* and find a different scale of values as a means for achieving perfection in both the social and religious realms.

Ethics and Intention

The concept of *lifnim mi-shurat ha-din* as the essence of ethics necessarily emphasizes the practical, the physical aspect of human life. *Halakhah* deals very little if at all with questions concerning a person's beliefs, emotions, and attitudes.[6] It deals in great detail with everything that a person does, paying meager attention to his motives. The end result of obedience to the law is apparent in the physical consequence—was a good or a bad deed done. The history of the genre *sifrut ha-musar* indicates that the Jewish teachers who developed it had a different, if not opposite, purpose: they were more concerned with what a person is than with what he does.

When Jewish religious culture reached the Middle Ages, it found itself at a disadvantage when compared with its great rivals, Islam and Christianity. The three faiths were united in the belief that the destiny of humanity is to serve the one God, who is completely spiritual. Furthermore, God's essence is present in a human being: the spiritual soul and mind represent the transcendent divinity within him. It is expected, therefore, that worship of the supreme, purely spiritual and infinite God should be spiritual, and the approach to God and fulfillment of His demands by humanity should be achieved by spiritual means. Indeed, Christian and Muslim writers of the ninth, tenth, and eleventh centuries constructed religious systems of thought and practice emphasizing the intellectual, rational, contemplative, and mystical aspects of the worship of God, marginalizing the physical expressions of adherence to Him.

Judaism faced the new ideological environment of the Middle Ages cherishing a tradition that included an enormous body of physical demands—positive and negative ones, prohibitions and commandments—that included few if any purely spiritual elements. It inherited from ancient times the question of whether the performance of the commandments should be accompanied by an emotional or intellectual intention, a question that did not receive a definite positive answer in the *halakhah*.[7] The physical adherence to the divine law seemed to be the only criterion for achieving the desired religious status. How can it be explained that the infinite, spiritual God presented the Jews with 613 commandments relating to the body, and none, or almost none, relating to the soul?

The preceding paragraph is essentially a brief summary of the questions raised by Rabbi Bahya Ibn Pakuda in the eleventh century in his Introduction to the first masterpiece of *sifrut ha-musar*, *Hovot ha-Levavot* ("The Duties of the Heart"), written in Arabic in Spain.[8] He presented "the duties of the heart" as an alternative to the "duties of the limbs," the commandments of the *halakhah*. The work is divided into ten chapters, probably parallel to the ten commandments, each of them presenting and analyzing one of the "duties of the heart": including the belief in the unity of God, the observation of God's magnificence in the creation, trusting God, spiritual self-analysis, avoiding the temptations of the world, the fear of God, and the pinnacle of religious experience—the love of God. Rabbi Bahya defined a "duty of the heart" as characterized by complete absence of any involvement of the body or the senses in its performance. Thus prayer is not included because the law demands that the words of the prayers be pronounced by the mouth, and even the study of Torah is not included because it demands participation of the eyes and the ears.[9] Concerning the need to perform the physical commandments, Rabbi Bahya explained that the religious meaning of these actions is derived from the spiritual *kavanah*, intention, that accompanies their performance, and not from the physical action itself. In this he came as near as possible as an orthodox thinker can to a denial of the religious value of the *halakhah*.[10] Rabbi Bahya expressed this attitude in the most radical way, but he was not alone. Previous Jewish thinkers who wrote the early works on ethics did not include the demands of the *halakhah* in their ethical systems.[11]

From a historical point of view, it is evident that the emergence of the *sifrut ha-musar* as a central, influential component of Jewish culture in the Middle Ages is an expression of the quest for spiritualization of Jewish religious values. It did not appear because of the need to improve social behavior or lift human relationships to a higher level of justice and fairness. It was the result of a purely religious drive: to harmonize the spirituality of God with the values guiding his worship. This quest led not only to the emphasis of the intellectual and emotional aspects of religious life, but also to a radical reinterpretation of the meaning of the physical commandments, the *halakhah*. The process is expressed by the Hebrew term *ta'amey ha-mitzvot*, "the reasons for the commandments," a subject that held a central place in the theological works of many Jewish thinkers in the Middle Ages.[12] Jewish theologians dedicated much effort to explain the meaning of the commandments within the framework of their various religious ideologies. Between the tenth and thirteenth centuries three different trends can be discerned, reflecting the worldviews of the three main Jewish theological schools of this period: Jewish rationalistic philosophy, pietism of medieval Germany ("Hasidey Ashkenaz"), and the new mystical school—the *kabbalah*.

The Jewish rationalistic philosophers had no difficulty explaining the social and ethical commandments. Saadia differentiated between "logical" commandments and "traditional" ones.[13] The former group are universal in nature and designed to regulate social behavior, and therefore their validity is confirmed by logic. The latter group are the ritualistic ones, accepted by tradition, and their reasons are unknown. We have to follow them because they are demanded by God, and we can hope that eventually their (logical) reasons will be discovered. Maimonides objected to Saadia's characterization of the ritual commandments as lacking a rationale; he defined the social commandments as laws governing society and the ritual laws as being designed to train a person to obedience and worship of God.[14] He did not hesitate to explain some of the ritualistic *mitzvot* [commandments], such as sacrifices and *shaatnez*, as divine accommodation to remnants of paganic practices that could not be completely abolished. In systems like these, the social commandments, and ethics in general, derive their power from logic rather than from revelation and are universal, having no particular Jewish characteristics. Later Jewish philosophers created elaborate allegorical systems intended to decipher the hidden rational meaning of the ritualistic commandments, an interpretation that often places them in the category of universal, logical demands. It may be said that Jewish rationalistic philosophy did not create a system of "Jewish ethics": if it is ethical, it is universal, and if it is Jewish, its ethical meaning is unknown. Explaining the commandments as having universal, logical meaning was the means by which these thinkers achieved spiritualization of the *halakhah* and Jewish religious tradition in general.

Rabbi Judah ben Shmuel ben Kalonymus, the author of the *Sefer Hasidim*, together with his father, Rabbi Shmuel, and his relative and disciple Rabbi Eleazar ben Yehudah of Worms, created a different, radical system of spiritualization of Jewish tradition in the Rhineland in the late twelfth and early thirteenth centuries. While the rationalists insisted that the commandments reflect human nature, and that following them leads a person to human perfection, the pietists of medieval Germany viewed the religious law as divine imposition that contradicts human desires and aspirations. Living under the impact of the persecutions and massacres of the period of the Crusades, their ideal was complete sacrifice to God—*kiddush ha-shem*, martyrdom, which is the expression of a denial of all that is human in order to glorify God. Each commandment—whether ritualistic, ethical, or social—is a minor reflection of that ultimate sacrifice. The religious value of any commandment, however small, is decided by the amount of spiritual effort that a person dedicates to its performance. Following the law means a continuous, unending struggle to overcome the demands of worldly life and spiritual dedication of everything to God. It is not the performance of the *halakhic* norms that is meaningful, but the pain and effort expressed in the process.[15] The commandments of the Torah are thus conceived not as a reflection of divine benevolence but rather as hurdles and trials that God presented before his worshippers in order to measure their ability to deny their human desires and devote themselves to Him. In this way, these pietists achieved a radical spiritualization of Jewish religious life: the emotional dedication is the essence of religiosity, but it cannot be achieved without the actual performance of the commandments. If a person were to say that he can reach the spiritual purpose while neglecting the practical side, he yields to the temptations of the evil inclination. Thus radical spiritualization is expressed by strict orthodoxy. The heavy price paid, however, is the denial of the benevolent, divine nature of the commandments themselves. In this system, there is no place for universal ethical norms, nor is there any distinction between ritual and ethical: every *mitzvah* is a hurdle placed before the worshipper, and he has to overcome it, both spiritually and materially. This system, unlike that of the rationalistic philosophers, is completely Jewish.[16]

From a historical point of view, the most successful solution to the problem of spiritualization was achieved by the new conception of the meaning of the commandments developed by the early kabbalists in the thirteenth century, which was forcefully expressed in the *Zohar* and which became, since the sixteenth century, the dominant theology throughout Judaism. It is a mystical interpretation of the *mitzvot*, yet it is unique to the *kabbalah* [Jewish mystical literature], and it is very difficult to find a parallel to it in other mystical systems, Jewish and non-Jewish. Various kabbalists in different periods and countries, belonging to any of the many schools of *kabbalah*, presented it in different ways with various emphases, but there is a common basic attitude that is reflected in all of them. According to this mystical conception, the commandments—all of them—have been given to Israel as a means by which the people could participate in the innermost, hidden processes within the realm of the divine powers.

The world of the *sefirot*, the ten divine hypostases, is a dynamic one, in which the various powers are moving up and down, changing their characteristics and responding to different impulses. The commandments have a theurgical power; they can influence the inner characteristics of these powers, especially the lower ones that govern and direct the universe. Most kabbalists, since the end of the thirteenth century (including the *Zohar*) believed to some extent in a dualistic conflict that divides existence between the realms of the God and that of the Satanic powers, "the other side" (*sitra ahra*). The struggle between these two camps, which takes place in the divine realms but is reflected in the affairs of the created universe, is deeply influenced by the deeds of the people of Israel. When they obey God, they strengthen the right, holy side, but when they commit sins, they encourage the evil powers. The weapons that God gave Israel by which they can take part in the cosmic conflict are the commandments. The words of the prayers, the building of a *sukkah* (a hut during the autumn Festival of Tabernacles), the giving of charity, the study of the Torah—all of them carry within them an inner power that can increase the element of justice and righteousness in the divine realm and make the good powers victorious. Sins, great ones like those of Adam and Eve or the worshippers of the golden calf, or minute ones, like neglecting to wash one's hands before a meal, carry within them the poison that strengthens the servants of Satan. The *mitzvot* were designed, according to the kabbalistic interpreters, according to the mysterious, hidden process going on within the divine world, and not according to human needs or aspirations. Human beings can never comprehend the mystical ways by which the commandments operate. A person must believe that when he worships God in the ways presented by Jewish law and ethics, he is achieving a mystical purpose, contributing to the victory of good over evil, first and foremost for the benefit of God but also to improve his personal status in this world and in the world to come, and he is enhancing the process of redemption and the coming of the messianic era. The concept of the *tikkun*, the "mending" of the universe, developed by the disciples of Isaac Luria (*ha-Ari*) in Safed in the late sixteenth century, is the most potent expression of this attitude.

The kabbalists, like the pietists in medieval Germany, thus achieved a purely spiritual conception of the commandments of Judaism, the religious as well as the social ones, and at the same time preserved and strengthened the orthodox adherence to the physical aspects of the *halakhah*. The mystical, universal endeavor in which every Jew is involved cannot succeed without the complete dedication to the performance of every minute detail of the commandments of God. It is impossible to suggest any change in the *mitzvot*, because their reasons are mystical, beyond human understanding. The kabbalistic worldview became the main pillar of Jewish orthodoxy in the modern period, and it serves to this day as the theological basis of the Hasidic movement and of its opponents, the Mitnagdim, who differ among themselves concerning many aspects of worship and leadership but are united in their faith in the kabbalistic conceptions presented in the *Zohar* and in the Lurianic *kabbalah*.[17]

Mystical Ethical Genres

Returning to our basic question, "What is *sifrut ha-musar*?" the answer is now rather clear. It is the vast body of literature in which the three ideologies described above expressed themselves in popular terms and presented their teachings to the wide Jewish public between the tenth and the nineteenth centuries. Saadia's chapter on ethical behavior, Ibn Paqudah's *Hovot ha-Levavot* (*Duties of the Heart*), Maimonides' "Eight Chapters,"[18] Rabbi Abraham bar Hijja's *Hegyon ha-Nefesh* (*The Logic of the Soul*), Rabbi Abraham Ibn Ezra's *Yesod Morah* (*Foundation of Awe*), several works by Rabbi Shem Tov Falaquera in the thirteenth century, and Jacob Anatoli's *Malmad ha-Talmidim* (*Teachings of the Talmuds*) are just a few examples of rationalistic *sifrut musar* that flourished, mainly in Spain, the Provence, and Italy, until the fourteenth century.[19] These and other rationalistic writers expanded the literary forms used in this genre to include *sifrut zavaot*, "ethical wills,"[20] brief treatises that presented the essential teachings of parents to their children. More important, the employment of the traditional Jewish literary form, the *drashah*, homiletical literature, also falls within this framework. *Hegyon ha-Nefesh* and *Malmad ha-Talmidim*, for instance, are collections of homilies. This literary form was used mainly after the writers of this ideological school began to write in Hebrew, in the twelfth century, whereas the early beginnings *sifrut ha-musar* were written in Arabic. The use of homiletical literary forms was important for the preservation of a traditional external mode of expression that mitigated sometimes the radically new ideas incorporated in these works.

Numerous works express the spiritual theology of the pietists of medieval Germany, the most important being the collection of behavioral instructions and homilies of Rabbi Judah the Pious's *Sefer Hasidim*.[21] Two treatises on spiritual ethics were written as an introduction to Rabbi Eleazar of Worms's great *halakhic* work, *Sefer ha-Rokah*, dealing, first, with *hasidut*, or piety, and second, with *teshuvah*, or repentance. Rabbi Judah and Rabbi Eleazar wrote short manuals of instructions concerning *teshuvah*.[22] *Sefer ha-Hayyim* (*The Book of Life*) is another theological-ethical work from the same period in Germany.[23] Many later works made use of sections and ideas derived from the worldview of these pietists.

The early kabbalists developed their ideas in esoteric circles and, in the first few decades, tended not to publicize their novel spiritual-mystical conception of the meaning and purpose of the commandments. However, they were dedicated to the rejection of the rationalistic views, and they expressed this in works of *sifrut ha-musar* without overtly presenting their alternative system. Thus, influential works like Rabbi Jonah Gerondi's *Shaarey Teshuvah* (*The Gates of Repentance*) and Nachmanides' Sermons do not use kabbalistic terminology; rather, they are presented as upholding traditional, talmudic-midrashic norms.[24] A popular and influential work of this genre was written at the beginning of the fourteenth century by the kabbalist Rabbi Bahya ben Asher, who presented in his *Kad ha-Kemah* (*Jug of*

Flour) a series of homilies, each dedicated to one spiritual-ethical concept, including the main subjects of faith, worship, and social behavior.

The "golden age" of *sifrut ha-musar* is undoubtedly the spurt of creativity in this genre in Safed in the sixteenth century, when it was completely identified with the *kabbalah*. In that center of Jewish culture, *kabbalah* became not only a theological and mystical subject of study and contemplation, but an actual way of life, penetrating into every realm of worship, including the *halakhah* and personal, everyday behavior. The greatest scholars and leaders of that period, including the greatest *halakhist* of modern Judaism, Rabbi Joseph Karo,[25] and the greatest homilist, Rabbi Moshe Alsheikh, included a kabbalistic aspect in their works. The two greatest kabbalistic writers of that period—Rabbi Moshe Cordovero and Rabbi Hayyim Vital, the disciple of Isaac Luria—wrote brief *musar* works: *Tomer Devorah* (*The Palm Tree of Deborah*) by Cordovero[26] and *Shaarey Kedushah* (*The Gates of Sanctity*) by Vital.[27] Both of them presented in these books the way by which a person can achieve supreme spiritual status by adopting a way of life in which the performance of the commandments is united with their kabbalistic meanings and intentions. The seminal *musar* work of this period was Rabbi Eliyahu de Vidas's *Reshit Hokhmah* (*The Beginning of Wisdom*), a detailed exposition of the spiritual norms presented by a discussion based on many different sources, including frequent use of earlier medieval works and extended quotations from the *Zohar*. This work was followed by one of the most influential works of this genre—*Shney Luhot ha-Berit* (*The Two Tables of the Covenant*), known by the acronym *Shelah*, by Isaiah ha-Levi Horowitz. These two works shaped to a very large extent the intensive creativity in this field in the emerging Jewish centers in Eastern Europe in the seventeenth and eighteenth centuries. This genre, especially in the form of homiletical literature, became the main expression of popular culture in Eastern Europe, and modern Hasidism adopted it as the almost exclusive means of its religious creativity. Thus, for instance, the *Tanya* by Rabbi Shneur Zalmon of Liadi, the founder of Habad Hasidim, is edited in the form of a *musar* work, and its chapters consist mainly of homiletical expositions.

Endowing Action with Meaning

The process of spiritualization of Jewish religious culture that began in the tenth century among Jewish thinkers in the Islamic world achieved its complete success in Eastern Europe between the sixteenth and the early eighteenth centuries. On the one hand, the domination of the *halakhah* in all aspects of Jewish life was complete, and the meaning and purpose of the practical performance of the commandments were given by the *kabbalah*. The vehicle by which this transformation was achieved was the *sifrut ha-musar*, especially in its homiletical literary form. What to do—in matters of worship, ritual, and social behavior—was decided by the *halakhah*, and the question of why we should do it was answered by the spiritualistic-mystical theology of the *kabbalah*. The laws concerning the observance of the Sabbath were formulated in the works of the *halakhah*, but the spiritual meaning of worship on that day was expressed by the belief that on the Sabbath the bride, the *Shekhinah* (the Divine Presence), is united with her husband, the bridegroom, the sixth of the divine realms (*sefirot*) portrayed by the *kabbalah*. The Sabbath thus is a day on which many things are forbidden and others are demanded, but they are enveloped by a profound spiritual experience, in which the worshipper assists and participates in a supernal mystical process that brings unity to the divine world and happiness to the righteous on earth.

It should be emphasized that throughout its history the *kabbalah* did not insist, when interpreting the spiritual meaning of the commandments, that knowledge of the detailed secret processes with which they are connected is necessary for the successful participation in the developments in the divine world. Knowledge may be helpful in achieving a higher stage in the realm of spirituality, but the main impact of worship is inherent in the very performance of the physical commandment. Kabbalistic *sifrut musar* is not intended to teach the detailed secrets of the *kabbalah*; it demands a general understanding and awareness, and it preaches spiritual dedication. But it does not insist on a systematic study of the *Zohar* and other kabbalistic works. Indeed, in many cases the kabbalists insisted that their teachings remain esoteric, despite their importance.[28] They believed in the intrinsic, theurgical power of God's commandments, so that while knowledge and intention may enhance the spiritual impact, what was crucial was the actual performance.

It is evident, therefore, that *sifrut ha-musar* cannot be regarded as "ethical literature" in the European meaning of this term. It is not intended to teach social norms nor to point out ways for a happy life on earth. Its purpose is to endow the physical requirements of religious life with profound, spiritual meaning and lead the worshipper to a high state of proximity and identification with God. Its European counterpart is not the teachings of philosophers in the realm of ethics, but rather the vast literature characterized as "spiritual" in Christianity, which is sometimes described as the literature teaching *via mystica*. Its main subject is not the mystical experience itself, *unio mystica*, but the teaching of a way of life dedicated to devotion, rejection of the temptations of the world and its pleasures, and directing one's mind and soul to the love of God. Some of these works include mystical experience as the pinnacle of such a way of life (such as the writings of Theresa of Avila or the anonymous *The Cloud of Unknowing*), but many others concentrate on leading the reader on the lower, initial road to spirituality and mysticism. Sermons are often used as a literary mode of expression in this literature. Similar writings abound also in Islam, usually associated with the various Sufi trends that express spirituality in the history of Islamic literature.

There may be some sense of disappointment in the realization that nearly a thousand years of intense Jewish discussion of spirituality and adherence to God in *sifrut ha-musar* have made hardly any contribution to the development of Jewish social ethics. This fact should be mitigated, however, by the realization that Jewish legal literature defined and governed the actions expected of and by Jews and that it encompassed every aspect and detail of Jewish life, dedicating close attention to the most minute subjects in the interactions between an individual and society, among individuals, and in family life. This vast treasure of creative and innovative ethical thought served as the main source for Jewish ethical conduct throughout the ages.

Notes

1. Concerning the history and development of this literature, see Isaiah Tishby and Joseph Dan, *Mivhar Sifrut ha-Musar* (Jerusalem: Newman, 1971); Joseph Dan, *Sifrut ha-Musar v'ha-Derush*, (Jerusalem: Keter, 1975); idem, *Jewish Mysticism and Jewish Ethics*, 2nd ed. (Northvale, NJ: Aronson, 1996); idem, *On Sanctity: Religion, Ethics and Mysticism in Judaism and Other Religions* (Jerusalem: Magnes Press, 1997), pp. 322–434 (in Hebrew).
2. In 1983, just after Scholem died, Eliezer Schweid published a book criticizing Scholem's conception of Jewish thought and mysticism, and he included in it several paragraphs dedicated to Scholem's neglect of the study of *sifrut ha-musar*. I responded to Schweid, rejecting most of the points of his critique, yet this one I accepted. I "apologized" for Scholem by pointing to the fact that though he himself did not deal with it, he was instrumental in establishing a section at the Hebrew University dedicated to this subject. See Eliezer Schweid, *Mistika ve-Yahadut lefi Gershom Scholem*, (Jerusalem: Jerusalem Studies in Jewish Thought Supplement 2, 1983); Joseph Dan, "Gershom Scholem: Between History and Historiosophy," in Joseph Dan, ed., *Binah vol. 2: Studies in Jewish Thought* (New York: Praeger, 1989), pp. 210–49.
3. M. *Avot* 6:1, B. *Bava Meziah* 30b, and many parallels.
4. See M. *Berakhot* 5:1.
5. It should be noted that even when the term *hasidut* is used in such writings, it is presented as independent of the *halakhah*. A clear example is presented in Rabbi Eleazar of Worms's chapter, *Hilkhot Hasidut* (lit., "The Laws of Pietism"), in his *halakhic* work *Rokeah*. Depite the title and context, the chapter deals with spiritual norms and does not rely on *halakhic* demands. Similarly, when authors of *sifrut musar* discsuss *hasidut*, their emphasis is clearly on spiritual values and not the extension of *halakhic* commandments.
6. Concerning the status of beliefs in Jewish law, see the recent discussion in Menachem Kellner, *Must a Jew Believe Anything?* (Oxford: Littman, 2006).
7. See, for instance, B. *Rosh ha-Shanah* 28b.
8. The work was translated into Hebrew by Rabbi Judah Ibn Tibbon in the Provence in the 1170s and became one of the most popular works in Jewish religious culture. It was first printed in 1040 and almost every decade since then, to this very day. It was very popular in the nineteenth-century *yeshivot* (study houses) of the *musar* movement, the anti-Hasidic pietist movement in Eastern Europe. On Bahya's life and thought see I. Tishby and J. Dan, *Mivhar Sifrut ha-Musar* (above, note 1), pp. 109–204; David Kaufman, *Studies in Hebrew Medieval Literature* (Jerusalem: Mosad ha-Rav Kook, 1972), pp. 11–77 (in Hebrew); J. Dan, *Sifrut ha-Musar veha-Derush* (note 1 above), pp. 47–60; George Vajda, *La Theologie ascetique de Bahya ibn Pakuda* (Paris: Imperimerie Nationale,1947); and J. Dan, *Jewish Mysticism and Jewish Ethics* (note 1 above), pp. 24–29.
9. It is meaningful that Rabbi Bahya included among the duties of the heart the practice of repentance, which he, like other thinkers in that period, viewed as being a purely spiritual process that does not demand any physical action.

10. Bahya was undoubtedly deeply influenced by Islamic Sufi thought, and examples have been presented by the scholars who studied this work. See, for instance, A. Lazaroff, "Bahya's Asceticism Against Its Rabbinic and Islamic Background," *Journal of Jewish Studies* XXI (1970), pp. 11–38. Another crucial problem that he faced was the need to explain the prevalemce of physical commandments in the Torah, compared with the minimal place of spiritual demands. He responded to this problem with a radical parable: A man comes to visit his friend, riding a horse. The friend will give the horse a large sack of fodder, and to the man—a small bowl of excellent food. The body—the horse—needs a great deal of food, while the soul—the person—can be satisfied with one plateful. See *Hovot ha-Levavot, Shaar ha-Yihud*, chapter 10.

11. Thus, Rav Saadia Gaon dedicated to this subject the tenth and last chapter in his theological work *Emunot ve-Deot* (*Book of Beliefs and Opinions*). His system demands that a person find the right harmony among thirteen spiritual values. Solomon Ibn Gabirol, the great poet and philosopher of the eleventh century, wrote a short treatise on ethics, entitled *Tikkun Middot ha-Nefesh* (*Mending the Qualities of the Soul*), in which he presented ten pairs of values, good and bad, that a person should educate himself to adopt in a harmonious way. Both Saadia and Ibn Gabirol paid no attention to the demands of the *halakhah* in their presentation of a person's quest for perfection.

12. A survey of the history and development of this subject in antiquity, the Middle Ages, and modern times is presented in the two volumes of Isaac Heinemann, *Taamey ha-Mitzot be-Sifrut Yisrael*, vols. I–II, 6th ed. (Jerusalem: Horev, 1993).

13. *Mitzvot sikhliyot* (rational commandments) and *mitzvot shim'iot* (lit., "heard ones," that is, those received from the outside).

14. He is following a talmudic distinction between *mishpatim* and *hukim*, judicial precedents and statutes. He claimed that the title of "logical" or "intellectual" commandments should be applied to a higher stratum of philosophical contemplation.

15. Rabbi Eleazar defined worship of God as what happens "where it is difficult" (*be-makom she-kasheh alav ha-davar*). Another slogan that the pietists adopted was *lefum zaara agra*—according to the effort, the reward. Rabbi Shmuel the Pious defined this in the strongest terms: A commandment that is performed while one is overcoming the evil inclination is worth more than a hundred ones when that difficulty does not exist. See *Sefer Hasidim* (below, note 21), section 2, pp. 4–5. The first sections of this work were probably written by Rabbi Shmuel, while most of the book was written by his son, Rabbi Judah the Pious.

16. An interesting example, given by Rabbi Shmuel, clearly demonstrates this point. Caring for children, he said, is not a commandment and has nothing to do with religious life. Animals also care for their offspring and may dedicate their lives to protecting them. This is a universal instinct of all creatures, and they do it of their own free will, and therefore it cannot be regarded as a part of the worship of God.

17. A major exception to this picture of kabbalistic orthodoxy can be found in the theology of the Sabbatian movement, the followers of the messiah Shabbatai Zevi in the last third of the seventeenth and during the eighteenth century. Several among the many groups of Sabbatians developed a radical antinomian theology, even declaring that the real upholding of the Torah is its annulment. Groups of Sabbatians converted to Islam, following their leader, and others converted to Christianity (the Frankists in 1760). Yet many groups remained as an underground within Judaism, and they were sometimes recognized by their extreme orthodoxy. See the classical exposition of these trends in Gershom Scholem's early study, "Redemption Through

Sin" (published in Hebrew in 1937, English translation in his collection of studies, *The Messianic Idea in Judaism and Other Essays* [New York: Schocken, 1971], pp. 78–141), and in his monograph, *Shabbatai Sevi—The Mystical Messiah*, R. J. Zwi Werblowsky, trans. (Princeton, NJ: Princeton University Press, 1973). Antinomian Sabbatianism was based on the belief that that the task of the *tikkun* has been accomplished and the messianic era has begun, and therefore a new Torah, fitting the world of the redemption, has been given by Nathan of Gaza, the prophet of Shabbatai Zevi. Some Sabbatians viewed this messianic Torah as the opposite of the old one, with the Torah's prohibitions now becoming positive commandments.

18. *Shmonah Perakim*, "Eight Chapters," Maimonides' Introduction to his Commentary on the tractate *Avot*, which was published separately and became one of the most influential treatises in this genre.
19. It should be noted that in the same period several works of this genre were written that did not have a clear philosophical message but presented traditional attitudes in contemporary terms. Among these are *Sefer ha-Yashar* (*The Book of Right Living*), which was attributed (wrongly) to Rabbenu Tam, and Rabbi Yehiel ben Yekutiel of Rome's *Ma'a lot ha-Middot* (*Elevating One's Character*).
20. A large collection of texts of this genre was assembled by Israel Abrahams and published in two volumes: *Hebrew Ethical Wills* (Philadelphia: The Jewish Publication Society, 1926).
21. The original is the Wistinezki-Freimann edition of the Parma manuscript, Frankfurt a/M 1924. In the traditional, shorter version of the work, printed in Bologna in 1538, the first 150 passages are a separate, independent work of the same genre. See Haim Soloveitchik, "Piety, Pietism and German Pietism: 'Sefer Hasidim I' and the Influence of 'Hasidei Ashkenaz,'" *Jewish Quarterly Review* 92 (2002), pp. 455–93.
22. See Ivan Marcus, "Hiburey ha-Teshuvah shel Hasidei Ashkenaz," in *Studies in Kabbalah, Philosophy and Ethics Dedicated to Isaiah Tishby*, Joseph Dan and Joseph Hacker, eds. (Jerusalem: Magnes Press, 1986), pp. 369–84.
23. Gerold Necker's edition, Tuebingen: Mohr Siebeck 2002.
24. Another Gerona kabbalist in this category is Rabbi Asher ben David, the nephew of the leader of the kabbalists in the Provence in the beginning of the thirteenth century. Rabbi Isaac the Blind wrote a treatise that combines traditional material with some kabbalistic ideas; see his *Commentary on the Thirteen Attributes*, published by Daniel Abrams in his edition of the works of Rabbi Asher (Los Angeles: Cherub Press, 1996).
25. R. J. Zwi Werblowsky, *Joseph Karo—Lawyer and Mystic* (Philadelphia: The Jewish Publication Society, 1980).
26. This was translated into English with a commentary by Louis Jacobs (New York: Hermon Press, 1960).
27. This work has four chapters, but the popular editions include only the first three. The fourth, dealing with the achievement of the *ru'ah ha-kodesh*, the holy spirit, was deemed too radical for presentation to a wide public, and it was printed only recently in Rabbi Hayyim Vital, *Ketavim Hadashim* (Jerusalem: Ahavat Shalom, 1998).
28. An example of this attitude is the fact that Rabbi Hayyim Vital demanded, after Isaac Luria's death, that the disciples do not publish or even write down the teachings of their master. See Gershom Scholem, *Major Trends in Jewish Mysticism* (New York: Schocken, 1954), p. 256. The relevant text was published by Scholem in *Zion* vol. 5 (1940), pp. 133–60.

CHAPTER 4

ETHICAL THEORIES AMONG MEDIEVAL JEWISH PHILOSOPHERS

WARREN ZEV HARVEY

MEDIEVAL Jewish philosophers engaged in the study of ethics both as Jews raised on the moral teachings of the Prophets and Rabbis, and as philosophers who had immersed themselves in those of Plato and Aristotle. Since there was not one Jewish philosophy in the Middle Ages but many different Jewish philosophies, so there was not one ethics held by all Jewish philosophers but many different varieties of ethics, as indicated in the introduction to Part I above. This chapter outlines the major views on ethics espoused by medieval Jewish philosophers.

SAADIA GAON (882–942)

Dean of the Academy of Sura, Rabbi Saadia ben Joseph of Fayyūm was the first major rabbi who was also a major philosopher. He wrote works on talmudic law, translated the Bible into Arabic and composed an Arabic commentary on some of its books, compiled the first known Hebrew dictionary and the first known Jewish prayer book, engaged in polemics against Karaites and others, penned Hebrew poetry, and composed two philosophic books: an Arabic Commentary on the mystical Hebrew classic *Sefer Yesirah* ("Book of Creation"), and a systematic dogmatic treatise, also in Arabic, *Kitāb al-Amānāt w'al-I'tiqādāt* ("The Book of Beliefs and Opinions"), known in Hebrew as *Sefer ha-Emunot ve-ha-De'ot*. His philosophic position bears Platonic, Neo-Platonic, Aristotelian, and Stoic elements but is best characterized as being representative of Kalām, the school of theology that was highly influential in Islam and also found expression in Judaism and Christianity.[1]

The Book of Beliefs and Opinions, written in Baghdad in 933, was conceived in part with a practical ethical intent. In its introduction, Saadia states that his goal is to free the reader from error, dispel doubt, and bestow wisdom, "Then thou shalt understand righteousness and justice, and equity, yea, every good path" (Prov 2:9).[2] Saadia had faith in Reason and believed his philosophical arguments could lead one to moral behavior.

In *Beliefs and Opinions*, III, 1–3, an important distinction is made between "rational" laws (Arabic: *'aqliyyāt*; Hebrew: *sikhliyyot*) and "auditory" ones (Arabic: *sam'iyyāt*; Hebrew: *shim'iyyot*). By "rational" laws, Saadia means those that, like propositions of mathematics, are required by unaided human Reason or Intellect (Arabic: *'aql*; Hebrew: *sekhel*). By "auditory" laws, he means all the other laws, which unaided human Reason does not require but which are *heard* from the Lawgiver. Rational laws include theological ones, such as the service of God and the prohibition of blasphemy, and ethical ones, such as gratitude to those who do good and the prohibitions of murder, robbery, and lying. Auditory laws include the laws of the Sabbath and holidays, the dietary laws, and the ceremonial laws. The auditory laws are not "rational" in that they are not required by unaided human Reason, but they certainly may be *reasonable*, that is, they may have good reasons; for example, the laws of the Sabbath are not rational, for unaided human Reason does not obligate us to desist from work from sundown Friday until sundown Saturday, but they have good reasons, such as giving people an opportunity to relax, study, or meet with friends.[3]

In order to understand what Saadia means by "rational" laws, let us consider some of his examples. The prohibition of murder is rational, for if it were permitted, the human race would annihilate itself and frustrate its purpose. The prohibition of theft is rational, for if everyone were to live by stealing, nobody would do the productive work necessary to preserve society, and, moreover, there ultimately would be no private property and nothing to steal. The prohibition of lying is rational, for the liar engages in a self-contradiction, knowing x but saying non-x, and this contradiction in the liar's soul is "disagreeable." In his explanations of the prohibitions of murder and theft, Saadia takes an approach similar to Kant's first formulation of the categorical imperative, according to which a moral maxim must be universalizable without contradiction (*Groundwork for the Metaphysics of Morals*, 2nd Section). In his explanation of the prohibition of lying, Saadia seems to be thinking of Socrates' view that "everyone hates a lie" since it involves deceiving the soul (*Republic*, II, 382a–b). In all these explanations, Saadia holds that ethical behavior is rational in the sense that unethical behavior is self-contradictory.

Saadia's concept of "rational" laws reflects the theory of Natural Law as set down by Greek and Roman philosophers, particularly the Stoics. This theory, as defined by

Cicero in his *De Republica*, III, 22, states that there exists a "natural law" that is (1) known by unaided human reason (*ratio*), (2) universal (i.e., valid in Athens, Rome, and everywhere else), and (3) eternal (i.e., valid in the past, present, and future). Saadia's "rational laws" are in effect "natural laws." His distinction between "rational" and "auditory" laws is a distinction between natural laws and all other ones. Although he formulated this distinction with reference to the Law of Moses, it may be applied to any legal system. Thus, in any legal system one may distinguish between those laws that are "rational" or "natural," and therefore valid in all legal systems in all places and at all times (e.g., the prohibitions of murder and robbery), and all other laws, which are distinctive of that particular system (e.g., driving on the left or right side of the road). Aristotle had made a similar distinction when he contrasted "natural" justice, which is "the same everywhere," and "legal" justice, which differs from community to community (*Nicomachean Ethics*, V, 7, 1034b; *Rhetoric*, I, 13, 1373b).

Saadia's distinction between "rational" and "auditory" laws resembles roughly the rabbinic distinction between "ordinances" (*mishpatim*) and "statutes" (*huqqim*) based on Leviticus 18:4 (see B. *Yoma* 67b; *Sifra* on Leviticus 18:4). According to this distinction, "ordinances" are laws that "had they not been written, should have been written"; and "statutes" are laws that seem to be purposeless and are subject to ridicule. The former include the prohibitions of idolatry, incest, murder, robbery, and blasphemy; the latter include the prohibition of wearing a mixed wool and linen garment (Deut 22:11), the ceremony of removing the brother-in-law's shoe (Deut 25:5), and the prohibition of eating pork (Lev 11:7). It is possible that Saadia conceived his distinction between "rational" and "auditory" laws to be a variation on the rabbinic distinction between "ordinances" and "statutes." Evidence for this conjecture is found in the fact that at the beginning of his discussion of rational and auditory laws he cites Deuteronomy 26:16, a verse mentioning "statutes and ordinances."[4] Nonetheless, there are two clear differences between his distinction and that of the Rabbis. First, his distinction is exhaustive, while that of the Rabbis is not: all laws are either "rational" or "auditory," but many, such as those concerning the Sabbath and festivals, are neither "ordinances" nor "statutes." Second, the Rabbis, unlike Saadia, did not use philosophic terms like "reason" or "intellect."

In sum, the distinction between rational and auditory laws expresses Saadia's conviction that ethics is fundamentally rational—and thus universal and eternal—and this rational ethics is at the core of the Law of Moses and should be at the core of all systems of law. Saadia's views on rational ethics had an influence on later theorists of Natural Law. In a pioneering study, Alexander Altmann concluded: "Saadya's theory...is an important milestone on the road that leads from the Stoic conception of natural Law over Justinian's *Institutes* to Hugo Grotius' *De Jure Belli et Pacis*. In its uncompromising rationalism it is a most remarkable expression of the spirit of '*Aufklärung*' [Enlightenment] with its belief in the constancy of Reason."[5]

The tenth and final treatise of *Beliefs and Opinions* is devoted to ethics. Its subject, as defined by Saadia, is "how it is most proper for a human being to behave in this world [*al-dunyā*]."[6] Saadia begins by affirming that human beings are compound entities with many different kinds of needs, desires, and purposes; and "the most proper" way to live is to strike a harmonious balance between them all.⁷ In his prescription of harmony, Saadia follows Plato (e.g., *Republic*, IV, 443d–e).

The human soul, Saadia next explains, has three faculties: (1) appetite (*shawah*), (2) impulse or anger (*ghadab*), and (3) discernment (*tamyīz*). Through the first, one desires food, drink, and sexual intercourse; through the second, one acts with courage, boldness, and vindictiveness; and through the third one controls and regulates the first two. These three faculties reflect Plato's (1) *epithumia*, (2) *thumos*, and (3) *logistikon* (*Republic*, IV, 435e–44e; IX, 580d–81a). Saadia identifies them with the biblical terms *nefesh* (e.g., Deut 12:20; Job 33:20), *ruah* (e.g., Eccles 7:9; Prov 29:11), and *neshamah* (e.g., Job 26:4; 32:8). The basis of ethical behavior is thus a harmonious soul ruled by Reason.⁸

In order to illustrate his opinion about the harmonious life, Saadia surveys thirteen human purposes that have been considered by some to be the one exclusive human ideal: (1) abstinence, (2) eating and drinking, (3) sexual intercourse, (4) eroticism, (5) accumulation of money, (6) raising children, (7) inhabiting the world (e.g., building and farming), (8) longevity, (9) dominion (i.e., politics), (10) revenge, (11) knowledge, (12) worship, and (13) rest.⁹ Saadia teaches that each is good in its right measure but harmful when pursued obsessively. The good life melodiously combines the ascetic and the erotic, creation and relaxation, theory and practice, holy and profane. Even the knowledge of the sciences and the worship of God are to be pursued only in their right measure. Here Saadia has recourse once again to the proto-Kantian premise that a moral maxim must be universalizable without contradiction: if all human beings were to devote themselves only to studying the sciences and worshipping God, no children would be born, the human race would come to an end, and there would remain no one to study science or worship God.¹⁰

Saadia, as Altmann observed, was a true *Aufklärer*, and his ethics is one of Reason, moderation, and harmony.

Solomon ibn Gabirol (c. 1022–1058)

Born in Malaga, Rabbi Solomon ben Judah ibn Gabirol was a brilliant Hebrew poet, author of the *Keter Malkhut* ("The Royal Crown"), and a profound philosopher, author of the Neo-Platonic classic *Fons Vitae* ("The Fountain of Life"), written in Arabic but surviving only in a late twelfth-century Latin translation and a thirteenth-century Hebrew abridgment. Among his other works is an ethical treatise, written in Arabic in Saragossa in 1045, *Aslāh al-Akhlāq* ("Improvement of the Qualities of the Soul"), known in Hebrew as *Tiqqun Middot ha-Nefesh*.

Like Saadia, Ibn Gabirol teaches that the ethical life requires the rule of Reason and the harmonious combination of various purposes and endeavors, but he develops these ideas in a different way. He roots ethics in psychology and physiology, and psychology and physiology in physics and metaphysics; for just as the physical world is composed of four elements (earth, water, air, and fire), so the human personality is determined by four corresponding humors (melancholy, phlegm, blood, and bile). Pursuing this psycho-physiological approach, he argues that the moral qualities are directly connected to the five senses. Each sense governs four main moral qualities. The noblest of the senses, sight, governs pride and humility, modesty and impudence. The second noblest, hearing, governs love and hate, mercy and cruelty. Third in rank, the sense of smell governs anger and favor, jealousy and diligence. The fourth, the sense of taste, governs joy and grief, confidence and remorse. Finally, the sense of touch, the grossest of the senses, governs generosity and parsimony, bravery and timidity.[11]

The relationships described by Ibn Gabirol between the five senses and the twenty moral qualities are suggestive. For example, pride and humility belong to the most abstract of the senses for they are abstract moral qualities, less material and less emotional than love and hate. By attributing love and hate to the sense of hearing, Ibn Gabirol teaches in effect that love means hearing the Other and hatred means not to hear him or her. Similarly, he cites God's words, "I will hear for I am merciful" (Exod 22:26).[12] The merciful individual hears the Other, the cruel one does not. Ibn Gabirol observes that the Bible connects the love for God with hearing: "Hear, O Israel... Thou shalt love the Lord thy God" (Deut 6:4).[13] Bravery and timidity are attributed by Ibn Gabirol to the most material sense, that of touch—as if he wanted to teach us the opinion, argued famously by Yeshayahu Leibowitz, that military heroism reveals nothing about one's intellectual, spiritual, or ethical level.[14]

The thought-provoking analogues Ibn Gabirol draws between the five senses and the twenty moral qualities do not have an explicit antecedent in the philosophic literature. It seems that he derived many (or all?) of them from Hebrew idioms. Thus the expression "high eyes" (e.g., Prov 6:17; 21:4) refers in Hebrew to pride[15]; "inclining" one's ear (e.g., Ps 31:3; 88:3) or "stopping" it (e.g., Isa 33:15; Prov 21:13) reflects mercy or cruelty[16]; "fire in the nose" (e.g., Gen 30:2; Exod 4:14) means anger[17]; "meat" and "wine" define "joy" (Deut 27:7; Ps 104:15; see B. *Sanhedrin* 109a)[18]; and "an open hand" (Deut 15:8; Ps 145:16) or "a closed fist" (Deut 15:7; Prov 13:11) indicates generosity or parsimony.[19] Ibn Gabirol, the masterful Hebraist, seems to have taken the Hebrew language as his guide to the purported connections between physiology and ethics. He must have presumed that ancient Hebrew idioms reliably reflect human physiology and psychology and therefore may be used to construct a theory of moral qualities. That there exist connections between physiology and ethics and that they are encrypted in Hebrew idioms is a controversial thesis, but fascinating.[20]

Bahya ibn Paquda (fl. 1050–1090)

Rabbi Bahya ben Joseph ibn Paquda was a younger contemporary of Ibn Gabirol. He was an eclectic philosopher influenced by Sūfism. His masterwork, *Al-Hidāyah ilā Farā'id al-Qulūb* ("The Guide to the Duties of the Heart"), was written in Saragossa around 1080, and known in Hebrew as *Sefer Hovot ha-Levavot*. The book preaches the importance of inner spirituality as opposed to external behavior ("the duties of the limbs").

From Saadia, Bahya borrowed the distinction between "rational" and "auditory" laws. The duties of the limbs, he taught, are partly rational (e.g., the prohibitions of murder and theft) and partly auditory (e.g., the dietary laws), but those of the heart are all rational (e.g., love of God and love of neighbor).[21] Ethical deeds, like helping one's neighbor, are duties of the limbs but depend on duties of the heart, like loving and respecting one's neighbor. Ethical acts depend on moral sensitivity. The limbs depend on the heart.

Although a mystic, Bahya was a stalwart believer in Reason. In *Duties of the Heart*, III, 5–10, he presents a fascinating philosophic dialogue between the Intellect (*'aql*) and the Soul (*nafs*) in which the former tries to convince the latter to abandon her love for the fleeting sensual pleasures of this world and devote herself to the service of God. It is thus the Intellect, according to Bahya, that causes one to live a pious and moral life.[22]

In *Duties of the Heart*, III, 10, Bahya presents a list of twenty moral qualities, largely borrowed from Ibn Gabirol's similar list. His list, like Ibn Gabirol's, contains ten pairs, but his pairs are all examples of contraries: (1) joy and sorrow, (2) fear and hope, (3) bravery and timidity, (4) modesty and impudence, (5) favor and anger, (6) mercy and cruelty, (7) pride and humility, (8) love and hate, (9) generosity and parsimony, and (10) idleness and diligence.[23] Of Bahya's twenty moral qualities, seventeen had appeared on Ibn Gabirol's list. Eight pairs are identical with those on Ibn Gabirol's list (although Bahya gives a different antonym for "joy"). Bahya has furthermore "corrected" the two pairs in Ibn Gabirol's list that were not apparent contraries ("jealousy and diligence" and "confidence and remorse"): "jealousy" is replaced by a proper antonym of "diligence," and "confidence and remorse" are replaced by a new pair: "fear and hope." Whereas Ibn Gabirol had ordered his twenty moral qualities under the rubrics of the five senses, Bahya remarks that he has not set down his moral qualities in any special order, but simply as they "occur to me now."[24] If Ibn Gabirol gave the moral qualities psycho-physiological explanations, Bahya gives them pietistic ones. Thus, he states that "bravery" is to be shown when one is fighting the enemies of God, while "timidity" is to be shown when one is rebuked by friends of God. Similarly, "idleness" is appropriate in pursuit of this-worldly pleasures, while "diligence" is appropriate in pursuit of the eternal spiritual delights.[25] Ibn Gabirol's ethics was part of his physics, whereas Bahya's is part of his theology.

Judah Halevi (before 1075–1141)

Like Ibn Gabirol, Rabbi Judah ben Samuel Halevi was both a preeminent Hebrew poet and an original philosopher. Born in Tudela, he is the author of the *Ode to Zion* and the anti-Aristotelian dialogue, *The Kuzari*, written in Arabic. The *Kuzari* is a fictional reconstruction of discussions that led to the conversion of the king of the Khazars and his kingdom.

In *Kuzari*, II, 47–48 (cf. III, 11), Halevi develops Saadia's distinction between "rational" and "auditory" laws, giving it a new twist. He defines the auditory laws as "divine" (*ilāhiyyāt*) and the rational ones as merely "social" (*siyāsiyyāt*). He explains that the ritual and ceremonial laws, which are auditory or divine, lead one to true spiritual felicity, while the moral ones, which are rational or social, do not presuppose spiritual excellence. He approvingly cites Plato's remark that even members of a gang of robbers observe rules of justice among themselves (*Republic*, I, 351c). Moral behavior is thus natural and requires neither science nor religion. When Micah taught that God asks nothing but justice, mercy, and humility (Micah 6:8), he referred not to the ultimate spiritual goals, but to the moral minimum that must be achieved before one can attain those goals.[26]

The Parable of the King of India illustrates Halevi's attitude toward ethics. In *Kuzari*, I, 19–25, the rabbi who converts the Khazar king asks him: If we knew that the inhabitants of India were just and righteous, would it prove they have a king? The Khazar replies: No, for they might be just and righteous by their own nature.[27] In other words, human beings have the natural ability to live morally, and government is not a necessary condition for a moral society.

In Halevi's view, the rational moral laws do not provide spiritual felicity, but one cannot attain it without them. Morality can do without religion, but religion cannot do without morality.

Abraham ibn Ezra (1089–1164)

Rabbi Abraham ibn Ezra was born in Tudela, like his elder friend (and according to some sources father-in-law), Judah Halevi. He was a philosopher, grammarian, mathematician, astronomer, astrologer, poet, and Bible commentator. He fled Spain in 1140 because of the Almohad persecutions and wandered from community to community in Europe, supporting himself by writing biblical commentaries, Hebrew grammars, and scientific works. Among his writings is a philosophic book written in Hebrew in London in 1158 entitled *Yesod Mora* ("Foundation of Awe").

Liberty is at the center of Ibn Ezra's ethics. Although he believed in astrological influences, he held that human beings have the ability to choose between good and bad, and the future is not strictly determined.

In his Commentary on Exodus 2:3, he remarks on the significance of Moses' having grown up in freedom in the house of Pharaoh and not as a slave in the house of bondage: owing to the education he received in the palace and the habits he acquired there, his soul was "on the highest rank" and not "lowly" as are the souls of slaves. Moses' noble morality is already exemplified at a young age, when on two occasions (Exod 2:11–12, 15–17) he physically interceded against those who were acting with violence [*hamas*]. Similarly, Ibn Ezra remarks, Moses' verbal intervention in the fight between the two Hebrews (Exod 2:13) was motivated by his desire to prevent violence. These comments about Moses' "high soul" and bold actions bring to mind Nietzsche's views on master morality versus slave morality in his *Genealogy of Morals*. However, while Nietzsche's master acts egocentrically on the basis of values he has created by his own will, Ibn Ezra's Moses acts altruistically in order to prevent oppressors from doing violence to others. It is Moses' determination to save victims from the violence of their oppressors that, according to Ibn Ezra, qualified him to liberate the people of Israel from slavery in Egypt.[28]

In his Commentary on Exodus 14:13, Ibn Ezra asks why the Israelites fleeing Egypt did not fight their Egyptian pursuers, but instead waited passively for God to perform a miracle for them at the Red Sea. "The answer," he writes, is that "the generation that went forth from Egypt had learned from its youth to suffer the yoke of Egypt, and its soul was lowly—so how could it now fight with its masters?" With this mentality, continues Ibn Ezra, the Israelites could not conquer the Land of Canaan, and so the conquest had to wait until the generation that went forth from Egypt had died and were replaced by one born free.[29]

In his Commentary on Leviticus 25:10 (cf. on Ps 84:4), Ibn Ezra discusses the word *deror* ("liberty") used in the decree, "Proclaim *liberty* throughout the Land." He explains that it refers to a small bird, the swallow, and by extension to liberty (cf. Prov 26:2), for the swallow sings when free "but if in human captivity it will not eat until it dies."

Abraham ibn Daud (c. 1110–1180)

Rabbi Abraham ibn Daud was born in Andalusia, probably in Cordoba, moved to Toledo in the wake of the Almohad conquest in 1148, and died a martyr. He was the author of two major works, both completed around 1160: a historical book, *Sefer ha-Qabbalah* ("The Book of Tradition"), written in Hebrew; and the first systematic Aristotelian book in Jewish philosophy, *Al-'Aqīdah al-Rafī'ah* ("The Exalted Faith"), written in Arabic but surviving only in two late fourteenth-century Hebrew translations, *Ha-Emunah ha-Ramah* and *Ha-Emunah ha-Nisa'ah*. The *Exalted Faith* concludes with a discussion of ethics, comprising the short Book III, subtitled "Cure of the Soul."[30] This discussion is indebted to the Muslim Aristotelians Alfarabi and Avicenna, as well as to Saadia, Halevi, and Ibn Ezra.

Like Saadia, Ibn Daud accepts Plato's tripartite division of the soul. In his formulation, the soul has three faculties: (1) the vegetative or appetitive; (2) the vital, spirited, or angry; and (3) the rational. It is the task of the rational faculty to ensure that the other two faculties observe the golden mean: desire, yes, but neither too much nor too little; bravery, yes, but not rashness or cowardice (cf. Aristotle, *Nicomachean Ethics*, III, 10–12, 1117b–119b). The rational faculty, explains Ibn Daud, must maintain justice among the other two faculties, as justice is "giving each his due" (cf. Plato, *Republic*, I, 331e; Aristotle, *Nicomachean Ethics*, V, 1131a).³¹ Justice, moreover, is the "head of all virtues." Influenced by Ibn Ezra, he remarks that Moses was chosen for his mission because he possessed the virtue of justice, as evidenced by his interventions on behalf of the oppressed (Exod 2:11–17). Ibn Daud quotes the prophet: "what doth the Lord require of thee, only to do justice" (Micah 6:8). If Halevi had minimized this verse, Ibn Daud maximizes it.³²

Ibn Daud differs with Halevi with regard to the "rational" and "auditory" laws. The rational ones, he holds, are the most important, for they concern faith and ethics, whereas the auditory ones have "a very weak rank in the Law." Although he calls the ethical laws "rational," he notes that they are not so in the strict sense but are better called "generally accepted opinions" (Arabic: *mashhūrāt*; Hebrew: *mefursamot*; cf. Greek: *endoxa*; see Aristotle, *Nicomachean Ethics*, I, 3, 1094b).³³ Having deprecated the auditory laws as "very weak in rank," he concludes his book with a good word about them: they inculcate reverence.³⁴

Moses Maimonides (1138–1204)

Most renowned of medieval Jewish philosophers, Rabbi Moses ben Maimon or Maimonides was also the leading ethical philosopher among them. He was born in Cordoba, where Ibn Daud had probably been born a generation earlier and where the Muslim philosopher Averroes had been born a dozen years earlier. Averroes and he were the last two great representatives of the Arabic Aristotelian school founded by Alfarabi. His family fled Cordoba after the Almohad conquest, arriving in Morocco. He visited the land of Israel and finally settled in Egypt in about 1165, where he served as physician in Saladin's court. In Rabbinics, he completed a Commentary on the Mishnah in 1168 and the *Book of the Commandments* shortly afterwards, both in Arabic; and during the 1170s he wrote in Hebrew the Mishneh Torah, a fourteen-volume code of Jewish Law. In medicine he wrote many treatises in Arabic. In philosophy he wrote two books in Arabic: an Introduction to Logic, written in his youth, and the extraordinary *Dalālat al-Hā'irīn* ("The Guide of the Perplexed"), known in Hebrew as *Moreh ha-Nevukhim*, completed in the early 1190s.

Maimonides' Commentary on the Mishnah includes a treatise on ethics known as "The Eight Chapters," written as an introduction to the tractate *Avot*. In this treatise, he develops his version of the theory of the golden mean, based largely on Aristotle, Alfarabi, and Ibn Daud. The virtues that lead one to intellectual perfection and the knowledge of God are designated by him as the mean, while the deviations from that path are the extremes: thus temperance is the mean, and lustfulness and insensibility the extremes; bravery is the mean, and rashness and cowardice the extremes; generosity is the mean, and extravagance and parsimony the extremes. A life of temperance, bravery, and generosity will enable one to achieve the intellectual knowledge of God better than one of lust, rashness, and extravagance, or insensibility, cowardice, and parsimony. Maimonides teaches that one must in general follow the mean, but for therapeutic reasons one may sometimes tilt toward an extreme (cf. Aristotle, *Nicomachean Ethics*, II, 9, 1109b). Leaning toward the deficient extreme can cure one of addiction to the excessive extreme, and vice versa. For example, a lustful person may be cured by being required to abstain temporarily from all pleasure until the mean virtue of temperance is attained; a miser may be cured by being required to act temporarily with extravagance until the mean virtue of generosity is attained; or a coward may be cured by being required to act temporarily with rashness until the mean virtue of bravery is attained. Maimonides thus posits a strictly behavioral method for shaping moral virtues. This moral psychotherapy follows the Aristotelian doctrine that repeated actions create habits and habits are hard to break (cf. Aristotle, ibid., II, 1, 1103a–b). Maimonides' teaching that the *telos* of moral behavior is intellectual excellence and the knowledge of God accords with Aristotle's view that ethics is a precondition of the contemplative life (Aristotle, ibid., X, 7–8, 1177a–79a).[35]

Although his ethics is profoundly Aristotelian, Maimonides gives a privileged place in it to the biblical term *hesed*, translated as "love," "kindness," or "lovingkindness." "All the commandments between human beings," he wrote, "are included in *gemilut hasadim*" (Commentary on Pe'ah 1:1), that is, in doing acts of *hesed*.[36]

Maimonides' Mishneh Torah begins with *The Book of Knowledge*.[37] Its first section, *Hilkhot Yesode ha-Torah* ("Laws concerning the Foundations of the Law"), contains laws relating to our knowledge of God and includes a summary of the sciences, since the Creator is known through the study of creation. Its second section, *Hilkhot De'ot* ("Laws of Character Traits"), contains ethical laws. The order is surprising. Doesn't Maimonides hold that ethics precedes our knowledge of God and is a means to it? Maimonides, in fact, recognizes two kinds of ethics: (1) a routine ethics that is a means to intellectual perfection, in accordance with Aristotle's view that the *vita activa* is a precondition of the *vita contemplativa*; and (2) a higher ethics that is a by-product of intellectual perfection. While the former precedes knowledge of God, the latter is preceded by it. The former is an ethics based on rules and habit and does not require intellectual excellence. The latter is a teleological ethics that cannot be reduced to rules but is based on a rational analysis of the given situation with an eye to attaining intended goals, and since it involves rational analysis, it requires intellectual excellence. The two kinds of ethics thus differ regarding the reasons given for the moral act. For example, two individuals who find themselves in identical predicaments may both decide to tell the truth: one may do so because there is a moral rule prohibiting lying, while the other may do so because an analysis of the given situation shows that telling the truth would more likely advance peace. In ordinary situations, the difference between the two kinds of ethics may have no practical consequences. The ethics based on rules works adequately almost all of the time, but not in hard situations. In such situations, it may be immoral to follow the moral rules; for example, it was moral for Christians during World War II to lie to Nazi police officers in order to save the lives of Jews hiding nearby. Judges and governors are frequently faced with situations in which the moral rules conflict and an appeal to them is futile; and they must then turn to the higher teleological ethics that is a by-product of intellectual perfection. Given that judges and governors are frequently faced with hard situations, Maimonides requires of them intellectual excellence and broad knowledge (*Hilkhot Sanhedrin* 2:1; cf. *Hilkhot Teshubah* 9:2).

In *Hilkhot De'ot* 1–3, Maimonides expounds the Aristotelian virtues (e.g., temperance, generosity, bravery), legislating them under the rubric of the commandment, "Thou shalt walk in His ways" (Deut 28:9). The general ethical commandment of *Hilkhot De'ot* is thus a commandment of *imitatio Dei*. Now, since only one who knows God's ways can walk in them, it is clear that the general ethical commandment of *Hilkhot De'ot* is predicated not on the ethics of rules, but on that based on Reason. In *Hilkhot Yesode ha-Torah* we are commanded to study the sciences in order to fulfill the commandments relating to the knowledge of God; and in *Hilkhot De'ot* we are commanded to act morally as a result of that knowledge. The Law, as codified by Maimonides, is not content with an ethics based on habit, but commands an ethics based on Reason. The commandment to walk in God's ways is also a charge to do acts of *hesed*, since God's ways are those of *hesed* (Exod 34:6).

Ethics is discussed often in the *Guide of the Perplexed*. Developing Ibn Daud's hint, Maimonides argues that the moral rules, including the prohibitions of murder and theft, are not "rational" but merely "generally accepted opinions."[38] He thus rejects the theory of Natural Law. Unaided Reason, he explains, knows the objective concepts of "true" and "false," but not the subjective ones of "good" and "bad." "True" and "false" designate that which does or does not correspond to reality, while "good" and "bad" designate that which does or does not correspond to one's intent or purpose. There is no "good" and "bad" in the absolute, but only good for *me*, for *you*, for *him* or *her*, and so on. Moral rules, contra Cicero and Saadia, are thus fundamentally different from mathematical propositions. "2+2=4" is always valid, but "Lying is bad" is not—for example, in the case of the Christians and the Nazi police officers.

A main theme in the *Guide* is *hesed*. An act of *hesed*, Maimonides explains, is one of beneficence done neither to repay a debt nor for the sake of gain, but solely out of love. The universe is the paradigmatic act of *hesed*, for it exists only by virtue of God's beneficence (cf. Ps 83:9). As the universe, which constitutes God's "ways," is an act of *hesed*, so the moral deeds of those who know God and walk in His ways—that is, the ways of Nature—are acts of *hesed*.[39]

At the conclusion of the *Guide*, Maimonides resourcefully interprets Jeremiah 9:22–23, "Let not the wise man glory in his wisdom, neither let the mighty man glory in his might, let not the rich man glory in his riches; but let him that glorieth glory in this, that he understandeth and knoweth Me, that I am the Lord who exercise lovingkindness [*hesed*], judgment, and righteousness on earth, for in these things I delight." He explains that the true human perfection is not wealth ("riches"), nor physical strength ("might"), nor the observance of the generally accepted moral rules ("wisdom"), but the intellectual knowledge of God ("that he understandeth and knoweth Me"); and God delights when those who know Him imitate His attributes of *hesed*, judgment, and righteousness. Jeremiah, according to this exegesis, distinguishes between the two kinds of ethics: the ethics based on rules ("wisdom") and the higher ethics ("*hesed*, judgment, and righteousness") that is a by-product of the intellectual knowledge of God and is *imitatio Dei*.[40]

LEVI GERSONIDES (1288–1344)

The premier Jewish Aristotelian after Maimonides was Rabbi Levi ben Gershom, or Gersonides. He was born apparently in Bagnols-sur-Cèze, lived in Orange, and did astronomical research at the papal court in Avignon. He wrote Hebrew commentaries on the Bible, supercommentaries on Averroes' Aristotelian commentaries, scientific books, and a book of Jewish philosophy, *Milhamot Adonai* ("The Wars of the Lord"), completed in 1329.

Gersonides considered ethics unscientific. Our knowledge of ethics is "defective," he writes, because the subject is "defective." Ethics does not treat of *intelligibilia* but merely "generally accepted propositions."[41] He argues that knowledge of good and bad, as opposed to scientific knowledge, is not specifically human. Many animals, he explains, distinguish between the pleasant and unpleasant; some distinguish between the useful and harmful (e.g., the sheep knows to flee the wolf), and others distinguish between the noble and base (e.g., camels do not have sex in public). Moreover, while human beings agree about the proofs of science, they have differing views about "good" and "bad," such that "the good for some is the bad for others" (cf. Aristotle, *Nicomachean Ethics*, I, 5, 1095b–1096a).[42]

The Law, Gersonides observes, teaches ethics primarily by means of stories, not commandments. "If the Law were to command us not to get angry except at that for which it is worth becoming angry...all people would be in sin always, except a negligible few." The Law, he continues, does not command people to do what they deem impossible, but teaches the virtues by means of stories about good deeds, and warns against the vices by means of stories about bad deeds. Ethics, he maintains, is not to be compelled by law, but taught by example and through narrative.[43]

JEDAIAH BEDERSI (1280–1340)

Rabbi Jedaiah ben Abraham Bedersi, born perhaps in Béziers, was a younger colleague of Gersonides and corresponded with him on problems in physics.[44] He was a poet-philosopher and author of the most popular philosophic book ever written in Hebrew, *Behinat 'Olam* ("Contemplation of the World"). This little book, written in lyric prose, has been printed more than seventy-five times, has had about thirty commentaries written on it, and has been translated into at least seven languages. Moses Mendelssohn translated two of its chapters into German.

The *Contemplation of the World* presents an existentialist ethics—ironic, pessimistic, but pious. It begins with a statement about the uniqueness of the human mind: "The heavens have height, the earth depth, but the width of the wise person's heart has no bounds." However, laments Bedersi, our limitless human potential is wasted. He feels shame as a human being: "When I see violence and strife in the city, I despise my image."[45] The source of this calamity is lust for this world.[46] "The world," he writes, "is an angry sea, deep and wide, and time is a rickety bridge built over it." It is a frighteningly narrow bridge, beginning in Nothingness and ending in Bliss. Those who adhere to the moral virtues will successfully traverse it, while those immersed in vices will fall to their spiritual deaths.[47]

Hasdai Crescas (c. 1340–1410/11)

The foremost anti-Maimonidean Jewish philosopher was Rabbi Hasdai ben Judah ben Hasdai Crescas. He was born in Barcelona, died in Saragossa, was leader of the Jewish community of Aragon and advisor to the Crown. His *Or Adonai* ("The Light of the Lord"), completed in Hebrew in 1410, is known for its critique of Aristotelian physics and its metaphysics of love. Like the modern Pragmatists, but contrary to Aristotle, he argued that *praxis* is not a means to *theoria*, but *theoria* a means to *praxis*. "The practical element," he wrote, "is the final cause of the theoretical."[48] In the following unforgettable 250-plus-word sentence, quoted here in abridged form, he explains how the Law promotes the moral virtues:

> [I]n addition to that which [the Law] has directed us by means of particular commandments and the stories of the Patriarchs regarding moral qualities, like [1] *righteousness and equity*, in saying "Keep thee far from a false matter" [Exodus 23:7]…; and like [2] *courage*, in saying "Ye shall not be afraid of the face of any man, for the judgment is God's" [Deuteronomy 1:17]…; and like [3] *generosity*, in the obligation of charities [Deuteronomy 15:17 et al.] and gifts to the poor [Leviticus 19:9–10, et al.]…; and like [4] *humility*, with which was characterized the Master of the prophets [Moses], peace be upon him [Numbers 12:3]…; and like [5] *the prohibition of flattery*, as we were commanded concerning rebuke, "Thou shalt surely rebuke thy neighbor" [Leviticus 19:17]; and like [6] *the prohibition of hate, revenge, and grudge-bearing*, in its saying "Thou shalt not hate thy brother in thy heart…thou shalt not take vengeance, nor bear any grudge…" [Leviticus 19:17:18]—and in addition to all this, [the Law] directed us with a commandment embracing all the affairs of human beings with one another, to wit, *love*, saying "Thou shalt love thy neighbor as thyself!" [Leviticus 19:18]; and indeed, Hillel the Elder replied to the man who came to become proselytized on the condition he teach him the entire Law on one foot, and said to him: Thou shalt love thy neighbor as thyself—"What is hateful to your fellow, do not do…Everything else is its commentary. Go forth and learn!" [B. *Shabbat* 31a].[49]

Disagreeing with Gersonides, Crescas argues that the Law teaches virtues by means of *both* commandments and narratives; and the greatest of all commandments concerning virtues is the all-encompassing *Love thy neighbor as thyself!*

Joseph Albo (c. 1380–1444)

Rabbi Joseph Albo studied under Hasdai Crescas in Saragossa, participated in the Disputation of Tortosa (1413–1414), and wrote in Hebrew in about 1425 the popular *Sefer ha-'Iqqarim* ("The Book of Principles"). His ethics was influenced by Crescas' pragmatic critique of Aristotelianism.

In *Principles*, III, 5, Albo interprets Jeremiah 9:22–23, the verses Maimonides had expounded at the conclusion of the *Guide of the Perplexed*. Praise, Albo explains, is due only with a view to the purpose of a thing. A race horse is praised for its speed, and if we praise it for its color or shape, we do so because those are indications of its speed. Jeremiah, continues Albo, mentions three human excellences—wisdom, might, and wealth—but adds that these are not praiseworthy, unless complemented by practice [*ma'aseh*], that is, unless the wisdom, might, and riches are used for the sake of "lovingkindness, judgment, and righteousness." The true human purpose, which is *imitatio Dei*, is doing acts that benefit others.[50]

Joseph ibn Shemtov (c. 1400–1460)

Son of the anti-Maimonidean kabbalist, Rabbi Shemtov ibn Shemtov, and father of the loyal Maimonidean, Rabbi Shemtov ben Joseph ibn Shemtov, the Castilian Rabbi Joseph ben Shemtov ibn Shemtov wrote more than a dozen theological books. His *Kevod Elohim* ("The Glory of God"), written in Hebrew in 1442, examines the concord between Aristotle's *Nicomachean Ethics* and Judaism, and it is remembered in the history of philosophy for having been ridiculed by Spinoza in his *Theological-Political Treatise*, Chapter 5.

Toward the end of the *Glory of God*, Ibn Shemtov cites a ruling of Maimonides regarding the seven "Noahide laws," that is, the minimal laws required of non-Jews: the duty to establish courts of law and the prohibitions of blasphemy, idolatry, incest, murder, robbery, and eating a limb from a live animal (Gen 9:1–7; B. *Sanhedrin* 56a). Maimonides rules: "Anyone who accepts the seven laws...is among the pious of the nations of the world and has a portion in the world-to-come...if one accepts them because God has commanded them in the Law...; but if one observed them because of a rational decision, one is...not one of the pious of the nations of the world, but one of their wise" (M.T. *Hilkhot Melakhim* 8:11). Ibn Shemtov comments that all the Noahide laws except one (the prohibition of eating a limb from a live animal) are "rational," and thus "the wise of the nations of the world" may be presumed to observe them, and the "excellent" Aristotle certainly did. Nonetheless, he adds, Aristotle did not according to Maimonides' text merit a portion in the world-to-come since he observed them out of wisdom, not piety.[51] Spinoza mocks Ibn Shemtov for lauding Aristotle but denying him immortality, and he censures Maimonides' text.

Clearly, however, Maimonides has been gravely misinterpreted by Ibn Shemtov. It is hard to imagine how someone like Ibn Shemtov, a serious reader of Maimonides, could suppose that he held the "pious" to be more worthy of immortality than the "wise." Maimonides, it should have gone without saying, valued intellectual knowledge more than pious obedience, and he considered the wise more worthy of eternal life than the pious.[52] Spinoza understandably derided Ibn Shemtov, but he himself deserves reproof for uncritically accepting Ibn Shemtov's blatant misreading of Maimonides.[53]

With his misinterpretation of Maimonides' text, Ibn Shemtov poignantly raised the question of universalism versus particularism in Jewish ethics—a question that would occupy modern Jewish philosophers from Spinoza and Mendelssohn until today.

Conclusion

Our discussion of Rabbi Joseph ibn Shemtov has taken us deep into the fifteenth century, and this is a convenient place to conclude our survey of a half-millennium of ethical views among the medieval Jewish philosophers.

Notes

1. See Sarah Stroumsa, "Saadya and Jewish *Kalam*," in *The Cambridge Companion to Medieval Jewish Philosophy*, ed. D. H. Frank and O. Leaman (New York: Cambridge University Press, 2003), pp. 71–90.
2. Saadia Gaon, *The Book of Beliefs and Opinions*, trans. S. Rosenblatt (New Haven, CT: Yale University Press, 1948), p. 4. Arabic text and Hebrew translation by J. D. Kafih (Jerusalem: Makhon Sura, 1970). Medieval Hebrew translation: Rabbi Judah ibn Tibbon (1186).
3. *Beliefs and Opinions* (at note 2 above), pp. 138–47.
4. Ibid., p. 138.
5. Alexander Altmann, "Saadya's Conception of the Law," *Bulletin of the John Rylands Library* 28 (1944), p. 333.
6. *Beliefs and Opinions*, (at note 2 above), X, p. 357.
7. Ibid., X, exordium-1, pp. 357–59.
8. Ibid., X, 2, p. 360; cf. VI, 3, pp. 243–44. See Steven Harvey, "A New Islamic Source of the *Guide of the Perplexed*," *Maimonidean Studies* 2 (1991), pp. 5–57.
9. *Beliefs and Opinions* (at note 2 above), X, 4–16, pp. 364–99.
10. Ibid., X, 14–15, pp. 394–95.
11. Ibn Gabirol, *The Improvement of Moral Qualities*, Arabic text and English translation by Stephen S. Wise (New York: Columbia University Press, 1902), intro, pp. 29–51 (Arabic, 59b–73b).
12. *Improvement* (at note 11 above), intro., p. 39 (Arabic, 66a).

13. Ibid. (Arabic, 65b).
14. See Yeshayahu Leibowitz, "Heroism," in A. A. Cohen and P. Mendes-Flohr, eds., *Contemporary Jewish Religious Thought* (New York: Scribner, 1987), p. 365.
15. Cf. *Improvement* (at note 11 above), intro., p. 38 (Arabic, 64b), where Isaiah 2:11 and 5:15 are cited; and also I, 1, p. 57 (Arabic, 76b), where Proverbs 21:4 is cited.
16. Ibid., p. 36 (Arabic, 63b), where Isaiah 33:15 is cited.
17. Ibid., p. 40 (Arabic, 66a), where Judges 14:19 and Daniel 3:19 are cited.
18. Ibid., p. 40 (Arabic, 66b), where Ruth 3:7 is cited.
19. Ibid., p. 41 (Arabic, 67a), where Psalms 13:11 is cited.
20. On facial and other nonverbal expressions of joy, anger, etc. in ancient Hebrew, see Mayer I. Gruber, *Aspects of Nonverbal Communication in the Ancient Near East* (Rome: Biblical Institute Press, 1980).
21. Bahya ibn Paquda, *The Book of Direction to the Duties of the Heart*, trans. M. Mansoor (London: Routledge and Kegan Paul, 1973), intro., pp. 87–90. Arabic text and Hebrew translation by J. D. Kafih (Jerusalem: Central Committee of Yemenite Jews, 1973). Medieval Hebrew translation: Rabbi Judah ibn Tibbon (1161).
22. *Duties of the Heart* (at note 21 above), III, 5, pp. 198–99.
23. Ibid., III, 10, pp. 218–20. Cf. Diana Lobel, *A Sufi-Jewish Dialogue* (Philadelphia: University of Pennsylvania Press, 2007), pp. 3–4, 247.
24. *Duties of the Heart*, (at note 21 above), III, 10, p. 218.
25. Ibid., pp. 218, 220.
26. Judah Halevi, *The Kuzari*, trans. H. Hirschfeld (London: Routledge, 1904; New York: Schocken, 1963), II, 48, pp. 111–12. Arabic text, ed., D. H. Baneth and H. Ben-Shammai (Jerusalem: Magnes, 1977). Medieval Hebrew translation: Rabbi Judah ibn Tibbon (1167). See my "Judah Halevi's Political Philosophy and Its Relevance for the State of Israel Today," Schwarcz Memorial Lecture, *Occasional Papers*, Center for Jewish Studies, Queens College, New York 2005.
27. *Kuzari*, pp. 45–47.
28. Ibn Ezra's Commentary on the Bible is found in standard Rabbinic Bibles. Cf. *Perushe ha-Torah*, ed. A. Weiser, 3 vols. (Jerusalem: Mosad Ha-Rav Kook, 1976). In his Commentary on Genesis 6:11, Ibn Ezra defines *hamas* as referring to acts of violent oppression such as robbery and rape.
29. See also his comments on Exodus 21:2, 5–6.
30. Ibn Daud, *The Exalted Faith*, trans. N. M. Samuelson and G. Weiss (Rutherford, NJ: Fairleigh Dickinson University Press, 1986), pp. 259–67; *Sefer ha-Emunah ha-Ramah*, ed. S. Weil (Frankfurt am Main: Typografische Anstalt, 1852), pp. 98–104; *Emunah Ramah* (II, 5-III), ed. Y. Eisenberg (Jerusalem: Jerusalem College, 1987), pp. 122–45. Rabbi Solomon ibn Labi translated the book as *Ha-Emunah ha-Ramah* and Rabbi Samuel Motot as *Ha-Emunah ha-Nisa'ah*. Weil's edition contains Ibn Labi's translation and Eisenberg's contains both. See also Resianne Fontaine, *In Defense of Judaism: Abraham ibn Daud* (Assen: Van Gorcum, 1990), and Amira Eran, *Me-Emunah Tamah le-Emunah Ramah* (Tel Aviv: Ha-Kibbutz Ha-Me'uchad, 1998).
31. Samuelson, *The Exalted Faith* (at note 30 above), p. 259; Weil, *Sefer ha-Emunah ha-Ramah* (at note 30 above), pp. 98–99; Eisenberg, *Emunah Ramah* (at note 30 above), pp. 122–25.
32. Samuelson, *The Exalted Faith* (at note 30 above), pp. 259–60; Weil, *Sefer ha-Emunah ha-Ramah* (at note 30 above), p. 99; Eisenberg, *Emunah Ramah* (at note 30 above), pp. 124–27.

33. Samuelson, *The Exalted Faith* (at note 30 above), pp. 262–64; Weil, *Sefer ha-Emunah ha-Ramah* (at note 30 above), pp. 101–2; Eisenberg, *Emunah Ramah* (at note 30 above), pp. 134–41. Cf. Samuelson, *The Exalted Faith* (at note 30 above), II, 5, 2, pp. 204–5; Weil, *Sefer ha-Emunah ha-Ramah* (at note 30 above), pp. 75–76; Eisenberg, *Emunah Ramah* (at note 30 above), pp. 29–33.
34. Samuelson, *The Exalted Faith* (at note 30 above), pp. 265–66; Weil, *Sefer ha-Emunah ha-Ramah* (at note 30 above), pp. 103–4; Eisenberg, *Emunah Ramah* (at note 30 above), pp. 143–45.
35. *The Eight Chapters of Maimonides on Ethics*, trans. J. I. Gorfinkle (New York: Columbia University Press, 1912), chaps. 4–5, pp. 54–74. Arabic text, ed. I. Shailat (Maaleh Adummim: Me'aliyyot, 1992). Medieval Hebrew translation: Rabbi Samuel ibn Tibbon (1202).
36. See my "Grace or Loving-kindness," in Cohen and Mendes-Flohr, *Contemporary Jewish Religious Thought* (at note 14 above), pp. 299–303.
37. The Hebrew text of the Mishneh Torah is found in standard editions. Thirteen of its fourteen volumes have been published in English translation by Yale University Press, New Haven 1949–present. *The Book of Knowledge*, translated by B. Septimus, has been announced. Previous English translation: M. Hyamson (New York: Bloch, 1937).
38. Maimonides, *The Guide of the Perplexed*, trans. S. Pines (Chicago: University of Chicago Press, 1963), I, 2, pp. 24–25; II, 33, p. 453; cf. III, 13, p. 453. Arabic text: S. Munk and I. Joel, eds. (Jerusalem: Junovitch, 1929). Medieval Hebrew translations: Rabbis Samuel ibn Tibbon (1204) and Judah Alharizi (c. 1205).
39. *Guide* (at note 38 above), I, 54, pp. 123–28; III, 53, pp. 630–32. Cf. III, 12, pp. 446–48.
40. Ibid., III, 54, pp. 636–38.
41. Gersonides, *The Wars of the Lord*, 3 vols., trans. S. Feldman (Philadelphia: Jewish Publication Society, 1984–1999), I, 7, p. 169. Hebrew text: Riva di Trento 1560. *Perushe Ralbag 'al ha-Megillot*, ed. Y. L. Levi (Jerusalem: Mosad Ha-Rav Kook, 2003), Ecclesiastes, preface, pp. 15–16. Cf. Charles Touati, *La Pensée philosophique et théologique de Gersonide* (Paris: Éditions de Minuit, 1973), pp. 514–19.
42. *Be'ur ha-Ralbag*, Genesis, ed. B. Braner and E. Freiman (Maaleh Adummim: Me'aliyyot, 1995), on Genesis 2:4–3:24, pp. 85–86; cf. on Genesis 2:9, p. 91. Cf. *Genesis Rabbah* 76:7.
43. *Be'ur ha-Ralbag* (at note 42 above), Genesis, preface, pp. 2–3.
44. See Ruth Glasner, *Vikkuah Madda'i Filosofi be-Me'ah ha-14* (Jerusalem: World Union of Jewish Studies, 1999).
45. *An Investigation... of the World*, Hebrew text and English translation by Tobias Goodman (London: London Rabbinate, 1806), 2, p. 2. Cf. Psalms 73:20. The Hebrew word here for "image" (*selem*) is the same one used to designate the divine image (Genesis 1:26–27).
46. Ibid., 4, p. 6.
47. Ibid., 8, pp. 11–13.
48. *Or Adonai*, ed. S. Fisher (Jerusalem: Ramot, 1990), II, 6, 1, p. 235. Cf. my "The Philosopher and Politics: Gersonides and Crescas," in Leo Landman, ed., *Scholars and Scholarship* (New York: Yeshiva University Press, 1990), pp. 59–60.
49. *Or Adonai* (at note 48 above), II, 6, 1, pp. 229–30.
50. Albo, *Book of Principles*, ed. and trans. I. Husik (Philadelphia: Jewish Publication Society of America, 1946), III, 5, pp. 48–49. Cf. my "The Philosopher and Politics" (above, note 48) pp. 63–64.

51. Joseph ibn Shemtov, *Kevod Elohim*, Ferrara 1555, quarto page 8a. Cf. Ruth Birnbaum, *An Exposition of Joseph ibn Shem Tov's* Kevod Elohim (Lewiston: Edwin Mellen, 2001), pp. 85–86, 124–25.
52. Maimonides identified immortality with intellectual cognition (M.T. *Hilkhot Teshuvah* 8:1–2). He seems to have held that the "pious of the nations of the world" have a portion in the world-to-come only in the sense that they have a portion in the Law of Moses, which educates people to knowledge (ibid., 9:1). On the superiority of the "wise" to the "pious" in Maimonides' text, see Rabbi Abraham Isaac Kook, *Iggerot*, vol. 1 (Jerusalem: Mosad Ha-Rav Kook, 1962), no. 89, pp. 99–100.
53. It may be said in Spinoza's defense that he had a corrupt version of Maimonides' text—reading "nor one of their wise" instead of "but one of their wise." This corruption is found in the *editio princeps* of the Mishneh Torah (Rome 1480) and some other editions. The defense is limited, however, since Spinoza also had before him Ibn Shemtov's *Kevod Elohim*, which reads "but one of their wise."

Suggestions for Further Reading

Guttmann, Julius. (1964) *Philosophies of Judaism.* Translated by D. W. Silverman. New York: Doubleday. 2nd ed., New York: Schocken, 1973.

Harvey, Warren Zev. (1986) "Ethics and Meta-Ethics, Aesthetics and Meta-Aesthetics in Maimonides." In *Maimonides and Philosophy*, edited by S. Pines and Y. Yovel, pp. 131–38. Dordrecht: Martinus Nijhoff.

Husik, Isaac. (1916) *A History of Mediaeval Jewish Philosophy.* New York: Macmillan, 1916. New edition, Mineola: Dover, 2002.

Safran, Bezalel. (2007–2008) "Maimonides on Pride and Anger." In *Turim: Studies Presented to Bernard Lander*, edited by M. A. Shmidman, vol. 1, pp. 185–232, vol. 2, pp. 137-69. New York: Touro College Press.

Sirat, Colette. (1985) *A History of Jewish Philosophy in the Middle Ages.* Translated by M. Reich. Cambridge: Cambridge University Press.

Weiss, Raymond. (1991) *Maimonides' Ethics.* Chicago: University of Chicago Press.

CHAPTER 5

SPINOZA AND JEWISH ETHICS

DAVID NOVAK

THE THREE SPHERES OF HUMAN ACTION

Writing shortly before Baruch Spinoza's birth in 1632, the Polish-Jewish commentator Rabbi Samuel Edels, better known as Maharsha (whose work Spinoza might have encountered during his years as a student in the Ets Hayyim Yeshivah of Amsterdam's Portuguese-Jewish community), defined what could be seen as the superlative virtue in the Jewish tradition. Synthesizing apparently differing views of three rabbis recorded in the Babylonian Talmud as to what constitutes a person of superlative virtue, Edels interprets their respective views to be about three different, yet complementary types of virtue. "Superlative virtuous action [*ha-yoter tov*]," he wrote, "is threefold: involving what is good regarding God, what is good regarding other humans, and what is good regarding oneself."[1] Whether Spinoza ever read this comment of Edels, or whether he was actually influenced by it, cannot be ascertained; nevertheless, it represents a view of virtue ethics (*middot* in Hebrew) that earlier Jewish thinkers such as Maimonides had worked into the Jewish tradition through their reading of Aristotle's *Nicomachean Ethics*.[2] Spinoza certainly comes out of that tradition.

For Aristotle, virtue or what might be called "personal excellence" (*aretē*) is of two kinds: ethical excellence and intellectual excellence.[3] Ethical excellence, moreover, is of two kinds: justice, which concerns our relations with other persons in society, and the other ethical excellences such as courage and temperance, which concern an individual's relation to himself. Intellectual excellence is concerned with the relation of the universe to God and the individual human's role therein.[4]

The threefold ethical scheme noted by Edels above involves three types of human relationship. (1) There is the relation of a human to God, which, for Spinoza, is an internal relation within God per se, where the human part directly participates in the divine whole. This relationship is the subject of philosophical ethics, and it cultivates in those who can engage in it what Aristotle took to be intellectual excellence. (2) There is the relation or interrelation of humans with each other that in Spinoza's view, means the external relations between humans who are physically separate from each other and who come together only as parties to a contract that institutes and maintains a polity. This relationship is the subject of political ethics, and it cultivates in those who engage in it what Aristotle took to be ethical excellence.[5] (3) There is a relation of an individual human being with himself, which Spinoza represents as the constant drive (what Spinoza calls *conatus*) of an individual human being to survive in a basically amoral environment.[6] This relation is the subject of no ethic at all. Aristotle regarded those who live at this level either subhuman or superhuman, that is, they are humans who have no need for external relations *with* other persons and have no need to find their place *within* the internal relations of God.

From Biology to Politics

Human experience begins at the biological level and then necessarily moves into the political level of being human, but it is the experience of only a few humans to necessarily move into the philosophical level. Nevertheless, this philosophical, level of human development is what the fullest human striving aspires to. In Spinoza's words, these rare few felicitous minds view all that is beneath them, even if not antithetical to them, *sub aeternitatis specie*, that is, "from the perspective of eternity" or what we might call *seeing along with the infinite view from God's eye on God's universal parts*.[7]

Spinoza assumes there is a real pre-political human condition where morality is simply absent because it would have no meaning there. To even speak of something like a "right" in this context is at best to employ but a metaphor, since a right is a claim upon another that is justified by the polity of which they are both citizens. Thus "the natural right of the individual person... extends as far as his desire [*cupiditas*] and power extend."[8] This innate power (*conatus*) is "natural" because human nature is part of Nature as a whole, and "Nature" is God's only other name (*deus sive natura*).[9] Thus the "natural" in "natural right" is used not metaphorically but literally. Furthermore, since "nature certainly does not create peoples, individuals do," only the power of individuals can be considered natural. So Spinoza elaborates:

> Nature has a sovereign right [*ius summum*] to do everything it can do, i.e., the right of nature extends as far as its power extends [*quae potest*]... the right of each thing extends so far as its determined power extends. And since it is the supreme

law of nature [*lex summa naturae*] that each thing strives [*conetur*] to persist in its own state so far as it can, taking no account of another but only of its own, it follows that each individual has a sovereign right to do this.[10]

Elsewhere, Spinoza argues that "Nature's bounds are set not by the laws of human reason, whose aim is only man's true interest and preservation, but by infinite other laws which have regard to the eternal order of the whole, of which nature of man is but a tiny part [*particula est*]."[11] Hence, "sin cannot be conceived except in a state, that is, where what is good and bad is decided by the common law of the entire state."[12]

Unlike some recent social contract thinkers, Spinoza does not regard the pre-political "state of nature" to be a hypothetical construct.[13] For him it is a historical reality. As a result, the move from the state of nature to the civil state becomes more than a mere thought experiment. In other words, the move of some humans from the state of nature to the political realm via the social contract actually *occurred* in past history. Spinoza invokes Jewish history to make this point.

> Thus, now that their state [*imperium*] is dissolved, there is no doubt that the Jews are no more bound by the Law [*lege*] of Moses than they were before the commencement of their community and state [*respublica*]. For while they dwelt among other peoples...they had no special laws and were bound only by the natural law [*iure naturalis*] and, indubitably, the law of the state in which they were living, so far as it did not conflict with the natural divine law.[14]

The question now is: What motivates humans to move from the state of natural anarchy to the state of civil society?

Like Hobbes, Spinoza thinks the move from the state of nature to civil society is done in order to save oneself from the kind of jungle where one's constant precarious struggle is merely to survive.[15] Along these lines Spinoza writes: "To help us live in safety and to avoid injury from other people and from animals...reason and experience have taught us no surer means than to establish a society with fixed laws, to occupy a determinate region of our earth, and to bring everyone's resources into...the body [*quasi corpus*] of a society."[16] That social body is a society governed by its own law. It is what modern political theorists would call a *Rechtstaat*, or a "constitutional polity." But by what kind of law is this polity governed?

There are three kinds of law governing human life: (1) natural law; (2) the law of one's own polity, wherein one enjoys the rights of a full citizen; (3) the law of a polity under whose alien rule one lives as a slave. Clearly, the law of one's own polity is, for the Jews, Mosaic law or the Torah. Just as clearly, "the law of the state in which they were living" is Egypt, from where the Jews escaped from enslavement into the Wilderness.[17] Spinoza regards natural law to be *law* in the same sense that the necessary interactions of physical entities designated by physics are called "laws," but not "norms." They are not commanded, and they are called "decrees" only metaphorically.[18] Humans discover these laws of nature and need to take them seriously in their regular struggle to survive in the pre-political state of nature. But at Sinai the Jews contracted with God to become their Sovereign, and God gives them a new kind of law by which to govern their public lives. And when they enter the land of Israel, this law becomes the civil law of their country.

Distinguishing between natural law and civil law, Spinoza writes that "the word "law" [*lex*] in an absolute sense signifies... [what] necessarily follows from the very nature or definition of a thing.... [But] a law that depends upon a human decision [*ab hominum placito*], which is more properly called a decree [*ius*], is one that men prescribe to themselves and to others in order to achieve a better and safer life."[19] Unlike natural law, civil law is made for a definite purpose (*finem praescribit*).[20] Natural law, or "laws of nature," are not norms legislated *by* nature or *for* nature; instead, they are the necessary patterns of interaction *of* entities *within* nature.[21]

The political "purpose" or "end" is a necessity for human survival in a world where cooperation is the only means of protection from dangerous destabilizing forces: both from external physical threats and, especially, from the internal political threat of anarchy. Even the purpose of a lawfully constituted polity is a means to another end: protection from politically destabilizing forces. Thus Spinoza says that "no society can subsist without government [*imperium*] and compulsion, and hence laws."[22] Indeed, "the constitution [*iura*] is the very soul of the state [*anima enim imperii*]."[23] That is why "our [human] mind, so far as it perceives what is true or false, can very clearly be conceived without these decrees, but not without the necessary law of nature."[24]

These man-made laws, however, though enunciated by humans, were inspired by God, at least in ancient Israel. In no way does Spinoza dispute the fact of revelation. (How can anyone argue that a historical event didn't happen?) Spinoza denied only that biblical revelation teaches any ontologically valid truth. That can be done only by philosophy. Biblical revelation's meaning and value are confined to the practical-political concern with the good and the just. On this question, both Spinoza and Maimonides before him accept Aristotle's differentiation between the theoretical realm and the practical-political realm, making the former ontologically prior to the latter.[25] And like Aristotle, the practical realm stands above the world of the experience of animal drives, but beneath the world of concern with divine eternity.[26]

Obedience: The Chief Political Virtue

The question now is this: How are the realms of the political (*ius*) and the physical (*conatus*) related to each other? Spinoza addresses himself to that question as follows:

> There is no one who does not wish to live in security and so far as that is possible without fear; but this is very unlikely to be the case so long as everyone is allowed to do whatever they want... [hence] it was necessary for people to combine together in order to live in security and prosperity... [nevertheless] the right [*ius*] to all

things that each individual had from nature...would no longer be determined by the force [*ex vi*] and appetite of each individual.[27]

The polity and its law protect its individual citizens by limiting the range of their *conatus* by giving it realistic and realizable goals. But how does divinely revealed law that is properly conceived function better politically than merely human law?

An answer to that question might emerge if we look closely at what Spinoza considers to be the chief character trait that should be inculcated in the citizens of a constitutionally structured polity. That chief character trait is *obedience*, which is dutiful submission to the commands of an external authority. Obedience, then, is the prime political virtue. The object of "revealed knowledge"—which Spinoza thinks provides the best source of political governance—"is simply obedience."[28] Yet most moderns committed to a democratic public life are liberals of one stripe or another and are put off when they hear (rarely anymore) the word "obedience." The very mention of that seemingly archaic word conjures up images of glassy-eyed troops, marching in lockstep, blindly following a leader who issues orders as if he were God and they his slaves. Moreover, for many moderns, the very notion of a demanding God seems to be the ontological foundation of tyranny, and tyranny seems to create great political inequality. Nevertheless, perhaps we can discern in Spinoza's concept of obedience a way to avoid these negative connotations and therefore be able to see his concept of obedience in a more positive light. In other words, is all obedience necessarily obedience to tyrants and therefore necessarily bad? And, aren't obedience and equality two unrelated species, each being a member of a different genus? Nevertheless, let us try to understand how Spinoza correlates obedience and equality—and, indeed, hope that this will bring us to the heart of his theological-political ethic.

Let us begin by enquiring of Spinoza: *To whom* do we reasonably give our obedience and thus benefit ourselves when we do so? And, *to whom* do we do unreasonably give our obedience and thus harm ourselves? Only by differentiating good from bad obedience can we appreciate the difference between obedience to divine law and obedience to human tyrants.

In what seems to be an expression of how a purely secular social contract requires obedience to the polity as a whole which it has founded—as opposed to monarchy as the arbitrary and alien rule of one man—Spinoza writes that "there is nothing that people find less tolerable than to be ruled by their equals and serve them...[so therefore] the whole society...should hold power [*imperium*] together, collegially, so that all are subject to themselves, and nobody must serve their equal."[29] Furthermore, "Democracy...is properly defined as a united gathering of people which collectively has the sovereign power to do all that it has the power to do....For they must all have made this agreement [*pactum*], tacitly or explicitly, when they transferred their whole power [*potentiam*] of defending themselves."[30] But what makes one citizen the equal of the other and, accordingly, have the civil right not to obey that other because he is his equal? What is the source of this civil equality?

It would seem that equality does not come from the pre-political, natural realm of *conatus*, since everyone's power there is different from everyone else's. Yet Spinoza asserts that "in a democracy...one transfers their natural right...to the majority of the whole," and thus "all remain equal as they had been previously in the state of nature [*in statu naturali*]."[31] Nevertheless, how can there be any such "natural" equality when the very concept of equality is essentially mathematical and mathematics is not involved in the way *conatus*-bearing individuals are self-conscious in the state of nature? For that reason, I do not think Spinoza means "equality" literally in this pre-political context, since the concept of equality is irrelevant there. Perhaps it could be said that the only equality there is the equality of difference, that is, each being there is "equally" different from every other dissimilar being. Moreover, what makes the polity as a collection of individual citizens superior to the very citizens who make it up, and thus entitled to require their obedience? How can what is *made* require obedience from its *makers*?

At this point we can better appreciate why Spinoza represents the ancient Hebrew polity of the Bible as the paradigm that any future democracy might well emulate, even though it would be a dangerous antiquarianism that attempted to actually replicate that long lost polity.[32] Nevertheless, that polity did function like a democracy politically, even though its ultimate warrant is theological, thus making it a *theocracy*.[33] That can be seen when we examine more closely what Spinoza means by "divine law."

> Divine law [*ius divinum*] began from the time when men promised to obey God in all things by an explicit agreement [*pactum*]. With this agreement they surrendered their natural liberty...transferring their right to God, and this occurred...in the civil state....For the civil law [*ius civile*] derives from his own decree...which is concerned solely with human good [*humanum utile*]. [34]

It is only in civil society, especially as presaged by the ancient Hebrew polity, where divine revealed law pertains to real, equal subjects. And their political equality was theologically based because "the Hebrews [at Sinai] did not transfer their right to any other person, but rather all gave up their right, equally, as in a democracy."[35] In this way, "they all remained perfectly equal as a result of this agreement [*ab hoc pacto*]. The right to consult God, receive laws, and interpret them remained equal for all, and all equally without exception retained the whole administration of the state."[36]

We now can see why real equality can only be spoken of, and can only speak to citizens in the ongoing process of democratic governance. Spinoza seems to be saying that the citizens of this theocratically founded and democratically governed polity are *equal because of their inequality before God*—and God alone deserves their full obedience. Accordingly, each and every citizen is an equal subject of the revealed law of God, and each and every citizen can equally consult that law, that is, each and every citizen could equally refer to the revealed law when justifying the exercise of their political rights and duties. This is their public ethic, which is essentially superior to their simply deferring to the collective power of the polity. In fact, that collective power without the restraints of divinely revealed law often creates greater inequality among the citizens of the polity than they experienced as individuals in the state of nature. It is only with the introduction of this crucial theological foundation of the polity that real political equality can be maintained.[37] That is why "they [the Hebrews]...resolved [originally]...to transfer their right to no mortal man, but to God alone."[38]

Although Spinoza (like Maimonides) does not believe in the literally verbal character of biblical revelation, nonetheless he does not dispute that the prophets were, in effect, reading the mind of God.[39] In a state of what might be called "inspired exaltation" or "moral imagination," the prophets—first and foremost Moses—gave the people of Israel commandments that would clearly enable the Jews to live a life of security, justice, and peace. That seems to be what God wills from eternity for this little human part of the infinite universe, that is, intelligent order rather than unintelligent chaotic anarchy.[40] And the law governing this theological-political order is practical, being solely concerned with deeds to be done in public. This law is the warrant for all morality governing interhuman relations: "Justice, therefore, and all the doctrines of true reason...receive the force of law and command [*imperii iure*] from the authority of the state alone."[41] Nevertheless, the state is not the true source of that law; it is only the means for that law to have political effect.

"Obedience to God," which is the chief political virtue, as we have seen, "consists solely in loving our neighbour."[42] That love of neighbor is practical. It means benefitting our neighbor who is our fellow citizen.[43] Conversely, "all other philosophical concerns that do not directly lead to this goal [viz., obedience], whether concerned with knowledge of God or of natural things, are irrelevant to Scripture and must therefore be set aside from revealed religion."[44]

From Politics to Philosophy

What, then, is the relation of this philosophical concern with God and Nature to the type of polity ordered constitutionally (i.e., by *ius*), especially a polity ordered theologically by law that is taken to issue from divine revelation as mediated by the prophets? And how does philosophy call for a different ethic than that called for by revealed religion? The answer is best sought in discerning how Spinoza sees the proper relation between theology and philosophy.

Spinoza states that "by theology here I mean revelation insofar as it proclaims the purpose [*scopum*] which we said Scripture intends [viz., simple obedience]...the dogmas of true piety and faith...that it agrees with reason, and if you look at its intent and purpose [*finem*]...it does not conflict with reason in anything."[45] Now, when Spinoza speaks of theology's agreement with reason, he does not mean that morality can be simply invented by humans. Rather, he means that there is nothing patently irrational in biblical morality that deals with interhuman relations, notwithstanding that its adherents have always accepted it as God's law. Thus it is acceptable as such. Moreover, the only religious beliefs that are needed in a polity with a proper theological-political constitution are those that reinforce "obedience to God [which] consists solely in love of our neighbour."[46] The same applies to religious rituals; their only value is when they serve moral ends.[47] And when a good polity sticks to its practical-political mandate from the social contract, simultaneously avoiding either theological or philosophical dogmatism, "it can very rarely happen that sovereigns issue totally absurd commands. To protect their position and retain power, they are very much obliged to work for the common good [*commune bono*] and direct all things by the dictate of reason...so that they may dwell in peace and harmony."[48]

It is important to note that Spinoza is using the word "theology" differently than how it was used by previous philosophers. "Theology" was coined by Aristotle to denote what we would call "metaphysical" speculation about the nature of God.[49] Indeed, the term (*logos tou theou*) might be translated as what we now call "God-talk." But for Spinoza, this kind of speculation is the proper business of philosophy, not the type of religious speculation that confuses the separate domains of ontology and revelation. Therefore, it seems that Spinoza is not using the word "theology" in its Greek philosophical sense but, rather, in its Hebraic sense of "the word of God" (*d'var adonai*).[50] And, contrary to the Jewish theologians, first and foremost Maimonides, who would have biblical revelation talk philosophy, Spinoza thinks that he is saving both theology and philosophy from each other by keeping them apart.[51] In other words, theologians make bad philosophers and philosophers make bad theologians.[52]

In fact, keeping theology and philosophy apart is a political-ethical imperative so that a good polity not be dominated either by theologians or by philosophers. Theologians function best when they provide religious background for proper political rule. When they overstep their proper role and exercise political power, they impose irrational religious dogmas rather than piously teaching moral norms which are at least consistent with reason.[53] And when philosophers attempt to come down from the heights of speculation to rule in a human polity (as Plato wanted), they inevitably will look to the polity to enforce the theories that they think the polity must endorse as official policy.[54] Thus Spinoza warns that "alleged subversion for ostensibly religious reasons undoubtedly arises because laws are enacted about doctrinal matters"; but "if the laws of the state 'proscribed' only wrongful deeds [*facta*] and left words [*dicta*] free...intellectual disputes could not be turned into sedition."[55] Therefore, it is in the best interest of the state's government not to overstep its bounds by proscribing the right of each individual "to think what they wish and to say what they think."[56] In fact, that right is not an entitlement from the state; instead, it is a natural right that the individual did not hand over to the state when agreeing to the social contract.

Restraint on the part of the government regarding individual liberty of conscience means that the right of every individual thinker to write what he thinks should have government protection. That is, as Spinoza prudently notes, as long as the thought that an intellectual like himself expresses what "entirely accords with the laws of my country, with piety, and with morality."[57] And, contrary to a widely accepted view that Spinoza lived the life of a hermit after leaving the Jewish community of Amsterdam, we know that he was even politically active in the Netherlands, the society *where* he did his thinking.[58] In other words, even a philosopher is a political being, a fact that may have prompted Spinoza to write "though men, therefore, generally direct everything according to their own lust, nevertheless, more advantages than disadvantages follow from their forming a common society."[59] And none of that should be a problem in a polity that does not engage in what we call "thought-control" by greatly limiting freedom of speech and freedom of assembly, that is, the freedom to assemble other citizens to listen to what an individual thinker has to say, not only about practical-political questions but, even more important, about truly theoretical questions. In those polities Spinoza disapproves of, one is allowed to speak only what we now call "politically correct speech" (i.e., what is approved by government officials), and one is not allowed to say anything that goes against the official dogmatic theology of the religious body from whom the state takes its fundamental warrant.

Nevertheless, theology and philosophy must have some sort of connection inasmuch as even philosophers have to live in some sort of polity, and even philosophers do not become philosophers *ex nihilo*. Instead, philosophers like Spinoza himself grow up in theologically constituted and saturated societies where they first learn to speak the word "God" as the most common name of the Absolute. Also, it is hoped that under the best political conditions, "the purpose of the state [is] to...allow their [viz., its citizens'] minds and bodies to develop in their own ways in security and enjoy the free use of reason."[60] That is the politically sanctioned freedom to philosophize [*libertatus philosophandi*].[61]

To be sure, in a well-ordered polity, the work of philosophers in their thought, their speech, and their writing has a beneficial effect on the conduct of the polity by limiting its pretensions to theoretically based tyranny by drawing a proper boundary between philosophy and theology. It is thereby suggested that freedom of thought and expression can lead some citizens not to lower licentiousness but rather to knowledge of higher truth. But what do philosophers do and not do within the realm of thought itself, which seems to be a realm having no boundary above it? For philosophy is unlike theology, which has philosophy limiting its range from above.

The Philosopher's Ethic

At first glance, it would seem that Spinoza regards the quest of the lone philosopher to be quite similar to the quest of the lone *conatus*-bearing individual in the state of nature when he writes: "the more each one strives, and is able, to seek his own advantage, that is, to preserve his being, the more he is endowed with virtue."[62]

Moreover, "no one strives to preserve his being [*conatur*] for the sake of anything else."⁶³ But then isn't the philosopher's transcendence of the limits of social and political life not a progression to a higher level of human life—as political life is a progression from the state of nature—but regression to a pre-political life absorbed in the all-consuming struggle for physical survival? After all, isn't our political concern with others—our fellow citizens—an improvement over our concern with ourselves alone in the state of nature?

The key to understanding why a philosopher's state of mind when thinking and acting ontologically is higher than both the mind of a *conatus*-bearing individual in the state of nature, and even higher than that of a perceptive citizen in a justly governed polity, is to understand Spinoza's differentiation between active and passive emotions. The way a philosopher deals with his emotions gives him a different—yet not contradictory—ethic from the ethic of the person who might be termed a "political man" (*homo politicus*).⁶⁴ (Unlike almost all other philosophers, Spinoza does not underestimate the role emotions play in everybody's life, including the life of a philosopher like himself.)

Spinoza writes: "An affect which is a passion ceases to be a passion as soon as we form a clear and distinct idea of it"; and "in so far as the mind understands all things as necessary, it has greater power over the affects, or is less acted on by them."⁶⁵ Now this understanding of the emotions should be contrasted with what Spinoza in one place says about love, which is certainly the strongest of our emotions. About it Spinoza writes: "Love is joy accompanied by the idea of an external cause."⁶⁶ Yet there are two kinds of emotions, and two kinds of love as the strongest of the emotions. There is love that is an affective reaction or response to someone outside itself, and there is love that acts effectively within One greater than oneself.

Clearly, this first kind of political love is very much like Aristotle's notion of *philia*, which is the mutual and reciprocal love of friends *one for the other* in a society that encourages such love, its being the factor that makes sociality itself desirable for human happiness and not just necessary for human survival.⁶⁷ This is a good society's *raison d'être*, or as Spinoza puts it: "The entire Law consists in just one thing, namely love of one's neighbour."⁶⁸ What makes political love, when properly understood, much more than the exercise of *conatus* in the state of nature, is that it is accompanied by joy. In the state of nature, however, there is no joy and there is no love, but only the grim struggle to survive in a world where one is but an isolated being. There one's struggle to survive is most often a struggle *against* the constant *negative* impediments to that very survival. It is in the transition from the state of nature to the political realm that one first learns to recognize others *positively* and thus attempts to cooperate with them for one's own good, which in turn becomes their good as well. Here one can balance being *affected by others* (i.e., when they act causally on us) with *effecting them* (i.e., when we act causally on them). Here we see mutual and reciprocal love.

But Spinoza envisions a realm where there is almost pure effect—where oneself is not affected by any other, neither by positive others as in the political realm nor by negative others as in the state of nature. This realm is where "knowledge of God is the mind's greatest good [*summum bonum*], and its greatest virtue is to know God."[69] Yet how does the pursuit or love of this good differ from the pursuit of the good as profit in the state of nature, and the good of sociality itself in the political realm? Spinoza's answer is: "He who understands himself and his affects clearly and distinctly loves God, and does so the more he understands himself and his affects."[70] Here we see that this is not the individual looking upon his own will as the first cause, a notion that becomes more and more absurd when a person sees his own individual insignificance in the infinite universe. Instead, at this ontological level, one loves himself—and all others—as God as the whole loves all his individual parts. The true philosopher, then, does not *react* to this love but rather he *acts* or *effects* along with it. This is the true imitation of God, since God is essentially *the efficient cause* of the universe.[71] The true philosopher *participates* in this love, which is within the life of God because there is nothing outside the love of God (*amor sui*). At this point the philosopher knows that he is not just a finite part of an infinite whole but rather that he is an active participant in divine causality working not *on* him but *through* him. As such, this love is neither responsive nor reactive.[72] "The intellectual love of God is the very love of God which God loves himself... [is] part of the infinite love by which God loves himself... it follows that insofar as God loves himself, he loves men, and consequently that love of God of men and the mind's intellectual love of God are one and the same thing."[73] Those rare humans who truly participate in this divine love, like God, activate or effect it toward their fellow humans, yet in no way do they desire that this love be reciprocated. This love is proactive, never reactive.[74] This love lies at the heart of Spinoza's philosophical ethic.

The ethics this contemplative life requires its true adherents to live is considerably simpler than the ethics required by political life, inasmuch as it has only two components: God and the human mind.[75] Political life, though, involves many bodies and their respective minds with all their many interactions. As such, the contemplative life is beyond politics, and that is why Spinoza insists that "people are not obliged by commandment [*ex mandato*] to know God's attributes; this is a peculiar gift bestowed on certain of the faithful... no one can be wise by command any more than he can love or exist by command."[76] Nevertheless, that philosophical ethics, though, does not contradict the ethics prescribed in a good polity, that is, a polity that respects philosophy precisely by, minimally, leaving philosophers alone to contemplate God and imitate God, plus maximally, encouraging the type of public education that makes the activity of philosophy attractive to those few minds who are up to it.

This contemplative ethic entails what we might call "acts-to-be-done" rather than deeds commanded by an external cause. They are *virtues*, which are not so much character traits as they are acts whose intelligibility is immediately evident. When so understood, how could any rational person go against them? These acts, then, are causes themselves (*causa sui*); and when one acts for them for their sake, what could compete with them? Thus vice is easily overcome. Accordingly, the last proposition of Spinoza's *Ethics* (a work that contains very little of what we would call "ethics" until its very end) reads: "Blessedness [*beatitudo*] is not the reward [*praemium*] of virtue, but virtue itself; nor do we enjoy it because we restrain our lusts; on the contrary, because we enjoy it, we are able to restrain them."[77]

A Final Thought About Spinoza

The simple elegance and persistent coherence of Spinoza's conception of ethics is an intellectual joy to behold. Whether or not it is adequate to the Jewish ethical tradition, though, is the subject of some other studies of mine.[78] Nevertheless, the continued influence of the Jewish tradition on the life and thought of Baruch Spinoza and his continuing influence on Jewish thought are beyond dispute. Despite his own choice to live apart from any Jewish community, he is still of great interest to Jews—and that is the case even for those of us who still live in the community Spinoza himself left: a community that is both sustained by and that itself sustains the divinely revealed Torah and its tradition, still teaching us what is true and what is good and just.

Notes

1. Maharsha, *Hiddushei Aggadot* on B. *Baba Kama* 30a.
2. For the Aristotelian flavor of Maimonides' virtue ethics (as distinct from his more legally formulated ethics), see his *Commentary on the Mishnah*: Avot, intro. (*Shemonah Peraqim*); and M.T. *Deot*. See Chapter 4 above for other medieval Jewish philosophers and theologians who incorporated or wrestled with Aristotle's notions of the virtues.
3. See *Nicomachean Ethics*, 1.13/1103a5–10.
4. See ibid., 2.1/1103a15–20; 5.1/1129a1–5.
5. Spinoza would agree with Aristotle that individual ethics and politics are two sides of the same coin. See Aristotle, *Nicomachean Ethics*, 1.2/1093b20–4a10.
6. Since Spinoza hardly ever speaks of women when discussing human beings, I have used the noun "man" and the pronouns "he" or "him" or "himself" when analyzing his anthropology. Yet that does not mean, I think, that female readers have to reject his thought in toto because of any inherent misogyny.
7. See *Ethics* V: P30, Demonstration, in *A Spinoza Reader* (Princeton, NJ: Princeton University Press, 1994), trans. and ed. E. Curley, p. 258. Latin text [hereafter "L"] from *Spinoza: Opera*, 4 vols., ed. C. Gebhardt (Heidelberg: C. Winter, 1924), II:299.
8. *Tractatus Theologico-Politicus* [hereafter "TTP"], pref., trans. M. Silverthorne and J. Israel (Cambridge: Cambridge University Press, 2002), p. 11 (=L/III:11). For more on the notion of rights in Judaism, see my *Covenantal Rights: A Study in Jewish Political Theory* (Princeton, NJ: Princeton University Press, 2000).
9. See esp. *Ethics* IV: pref., p. 198 (=L/II:206).

10. TTP XVI, pp. 195–96 (=L/III:189). See *Tractatus Politicus* II, trans. S. Shirley (Indianapolis/Cambridge: Hackett Publishing Co., 2000), p. 38.
11. *Tractatus Politicus* II, p. 41 (=L/III:279).
12. Ibid., II, p. 45. Cf. Maimonides, *Guide of the Perplexed*, 1.2.
13. Cf. John Rawls, *A Theory of Justice* (Cambridge, MA: Harvard University Press, 1971), 11–13.
14. TTP V, p. 71 (=L/III:72). See also ibid. XVII, p. 213.
15. See Hobbes, *Leviathan*, chap. 13.
16. TTP III, p. 46 (=L/III:47).
17. TTP V, p. 71.
18. Note Richard Mason, *The God of Spinoza* (Cambridge: Cambridge University Press, 1997), 76–77: "*Law* and *nature* are the same—*leges, sive natura*: the way in which something exists and acts is its nature…how things are and how they act, not in any set of rules explaining how and why they behave as they do."
19. TTP IV, p. 57 (=L/III:57).
20. Ibid., p. 58 (=L/III:58).
21. Cf. Maimonides, M.T. *Melakhim*, 8.11; Thomas Aquinas, *Summa Theologiae*, 2/1, q. 90, a. 4—for whom both universally valid divine law is God's explicit legislation. For Spinoza's critique of what he sees as Maimonides' confusion on this point, viz., confusing natural law and revealed law, see TTP V, p. 79.
22. TTP V, p. 73 (=L/III:74).
23. *Tractatus Poliitcus* X, p. 132 (=L/III:357). Here Spinoza might have been virtually translating into Latin the dictum of the ninth-century Jewish theologian Saadiah Gaon: "our nation is only a nation because of its laws [*be-sha'ariha*]" (my translation) in his *Book of Beliefs and Opinions* III, Judaeo-Arabic text, 3rd ed., ed. Y. Kafih (Jerusalem: n.p., 1970), p. 132.
24. TTP IV, pp. 57–58; see also ibid. XV, pp. 193–94.
25. See Maimonides, *Guide of the Perplexed*, 1.2; 2.40; 3.27.
26. See *Nicomachean Ethics*, 6.7/1141a20–22; 7.1/1145a25–30.
27. TTP XVI, p. 197 (=L/III:191).
28. TTP, pref., p. 10.
29. TTP V, p. 73 (=L/III:74).
30. TTP XVI, p. 200 (=L/III:193). See also *Tractatus Politicus* XI, p. 385.
31. TTP XVI, p. 202 (=L/III:195).
32. See TTP XVIII, p. 230.
33. TTP XVII, p. 255. Like "obedience," the word "theocracy" also scares modern liberals, who equate "theocracy" with "clerisy," viz., a dictatorship of clerics. But Spinoza is quite explicit in his revulsion at this kind of "theocracy," which he expresses anachronistically in his critique of the political power of the ancient Israelite priesthood (*kehunah*) and monarchy (*melukhah*) in TTP XVIII, pp. 235–38; see also ibid., pref., pp. 7–8. Instead, by invoking the term *theocracy*, Spinoza is going back to its original meaning, given by the first-century Jewish historian Josephus (*Contra Apionem*, II.165), who coined the very term *theokratia*, viz., the rule of God (*kratos tou theou*) through God's law revealed to all the people and which is regularly made known to all the people.
34. TTP XVI, pp. 205–6 (=L/III:198–99). "Natural right [*ius naturale*]," conversely, "derives from the laws of nature [*a legibus naturae*]" (ibid.).
35. TTP XVI, p. 214 (=L/III:206).
36. Ibid.; see also ibid., p. 224.

37. Yet ancient Israel moved away from this true theocracy in the direction of monarch or clerisy (see TTP XVII, pp. 211–13). Nevertheless, Spinoza thinks that theocracy might be "imitated," i.e., at least restored in principle, even in his own time (see ibid. XVIII, p. 230).
38. TTP XVII, p. 213. Here Spinoza is clearly rejecting Hobbes' notion that in the social contract the monarch to whom the people turn over all their rights is "this mortal god" (*Leviathan*, chap. 17, ed. M. Oakeshott [New York: Collier Books, 1962], p. 132).
39. See Maimonides, *Guide of the Perplexed*, 1.65; TTP XII, p. 167.
40. By "God's will" (*voluntas*) Spinoza means God's eternal plan for the universe in all its parts (*natura naturata*). See *Ethics* I: P29–33, pp. 104–9 (=L/II:70–76). But God does not make choices, since God is essentially eternal; choices are made in mutable time (see ibid. I:P8, pp. 88–89; ibid. V:P30, p. 258). God's eternally willed plan is discovered by perceptive humans on various historical occasions. This discovery is a *novum* for them from their temporal perspective; it is not for God, since from God's eternal perspective there is nothing new or old.
41. TTP XIX, p. 240 (=L/III:230).
42. TTP XIII, p. 213.
43. The exact content of that neighbour-love is determined by the state. See TTP XIX, p. 242.
44. TTP XIII, p. 173. For more on Spinoza's notions of obedience, see Jonathan K. Crane "On Obedience in Spinoza's *Theological-Political Treatise*." ARC. The Journal of the Faculty of Religious Studies, McGill University. 34 (2006): 239–50.
45. TTP XV, pp. 190–91 (=L/III:184–85).
46. TTP XIII, p. 173. Nevertheless, for Spinoza, the true love of God per se is immediately directed to God alone, and only therefrom does that love extend to one's neighbor. But that is the prerogative of the philosopher, who alone can truly love God intellectually (*amor dei intellectualis*). Cf. *Ethics* V:P32, p. 259.
47. TTP V, pp. 74–75. Cf. Maimonides, *Guide of the Perplexed*, 3.38–39.
48. TTP XVI, pp. 200–201 (=L/III:194).
49. Aristotle, *Metaphysics*, 6.1/1026a15–21. Actually, the term "metaphysics" is not a term used by Aristotle himself. What subsequent Aristotelians called "metaphysics," Aristotle himself called "wisdom" (*sophia*) or "the science of divine things." See ibid., 1.2/982a15–983a10. Hence the subject matter of Aristotle's "theology" is the subject matter of Spinoza's "philosophy."
50. See e.g. Zech 4:6.
51. See TTP XIV, pp. 178–85.
52. For a more recent statement of this position, from a twentieth-century Jewish thinker very much beholden to Spinoza, see Leo Strauss, "The Mutual Influence of Theology and Philosophy," *Independent Journal of Philosophy* 3 (1979), 111–18. For a critique of Strauss (and, indirectly, of Spinoza) on this interrelation, see David Novak, "Philosophy and the Possibility of Revelation: A Theological Response to the Challenge of Leo Strauss," in *Leo Strauss and Judaism*, ed. D. Novak (Lanham, MD: Rowman and Littlefield, 1996), 173–92.
53. Perhaps Spinoza had learned in the Amsterdam *yeshivah* the dictum in J. *Horayot* 3.2 (47c) re Gen. 49:10, viz., "priests are not to be anointed as kings."
54. Cf. Plato, *Republic* 519D–520C; also David Novak, *Suicide and Morality* (New York: Scholars Studies Press, 1975), 21–24.
55. TTP, pref., p. 6 (=L/III:7), quoting Tacitus, *Annals*, 1.72.
56. TTP XX, p. 259.

57. TTP, pref., p. 12.
58. See Steven Nadler, *Spinoza: A Life* (Cambridge: Cambridge University Press, 1999), 303–19.
59. *Ethics* IV, Appendix, XIV, p. 241.
60. TTP XX, p. 252.
61. Ibid., p. 254 (=L/III:243).
62. *Ethics* IV: P20, p. 210.
63. Ibid.: P25, p. 212 (=L/II:226).
64. For a profound treatment of the difference between *vita contemplativa* as the philosopher's life and *vita activa* as the citizen's life, see Hannah Arendt, *The Human Condition* (Chicago: University of Chicago Press, 1958).
65. *Ethics* V: P3, p. 247; ibid.: P6, p. 249.
66. *Ethics* IV: P44, demonstration, p. 223.
67. See *Nicomachean Ethics*, 8.1/1153a3–30.
68. TTP XIV, p. 179.
69. *Ethics* IV: P28, p. 213 (=L/II:228).
70. *Ethics* V: P15, p. 253.
71. See *Ethics* I: P16, cor. 1, p. 97.
72. See *Ethics* V: P19, p. 253.
73. Ibid.: P36 and corollary, p. 260.
74. Cf. Maimonides, *Guide of the Perplexed*, 3.54 re Jer 9:22–23.
75. See Augustine, *Soliloquies*, I, 2.7 in *Basic Writings of Saint Augustine* I, ed. W. J. Oates (New York: Random House, 1948), p. 262.
76. TTP XIII, p. 175 (=L/III:169).
77. Ibid.: P42, p. 264 (=L/II:307).
78. See David Novak, *The Election of Israel: The Idea of the Chosen People* (Cambridge, MA: Cambridge University Press, 1995), pp. 22–49 (chap. 1: "Spinoza and His Challenge"); and idem., "The Enlightenment Project, Spinoza, and the Jews" in *Religion, the Enlightenment, and the New Global Order*, ed. J. M. Owen IV and J. J. Owen (New York: Columbia University Press, 2010), 109–39. I am grateful to the University of Toronto students who have worked with me in a course on Spinoza (PHL2051) in the 2010 fall semester; and in a course on Philosophy of Religion (PHL335) in the 2011 spring semester (where Spinoza's notion of God was extensively discussed). From working with them, my appreciation of Spinoza has increased, without, however, lessening my differences from him on both philosophical and theological grounds.

References

Garrett, Don (ed.). 1996. *The Cambridge Companion to Spinoza*. Cambridge: Cambridge University Press.
Goetschel, Willi. 2004. *Spinoza's Modernity*. Madison: University of Wisconsin Press.
Mason, Richard. 1997. *The God of Spinoza*. Cambridge: Cambridge University Press.
McShea, Robert J. 1968. *The Political Philosophy of Spinoza*. New York: Columbia University Press.
Nadler, Steven. 1999. *Spinoza: A Life*. Cambridge: Cambridge University Press.
Nadler, Steven. 2003. *Spinoza's Book of Life*. New Haven and London: Yale University Press.

Nadler, Steven. 2006. *Spinoza's Ethics: An Introduction*. Cambridge: Cambridge University Press.
Nadler, Steven. 2001. *Spinoza's Heresy*. Oxford: Clarendon Press.
Smith, Steven B. 1997. *Spinoza and the Question of Jewish Identity*. New Haven and London: Yale University Press.
Wolfson, Harry A. 1934. *The Philosophy of Spinoza*, 2 vols. Cambridge, MA: Harvard University Press.

CHAPTER 6

MUSSAR ETHICS AND OTHER NINETEENTH-CENTURY JEWISH ETHICAL THEORIES

IRA F. STONE

Varying Ways to Make Judaism Modern or to Make Modernity Jewish

It is taken as common knowledge that the nineteenth century was the century of rationalism par excellence, with the students of Kant and Hegel taking center stage. From a Jewish point of view it was preeminently the century of *Haskalah* (the Enlightenment), which embodied an attack on the foundations of traditional Judaism; the century of Reform, of social ferment resulting in Jewish affiliation with revolutionary movements, nationalism, and assimilation.

Indeed, all of this is true. And yet it was also a time of extraordinary efforts to understand the traditional elements of Jewish life in new ways that would sometimes confront and sometimes conform to these currents of radically changing thought and cultural conditions. In the course of preparing this chapter, what struck me most was not the presence of the usual suspects of reform and radicalism, only some of whom I have included below for reasons of both space and subject matter, but the fact that many of the most important thinkers, even if not necessarily best known in the contemporary milieu, advocated a "modern" reading of Judaism that maintained the traditional lifestyle of the Jew and reinterpreted the traditional theological underpinnings of Judaism so that they could continued to be used in a contemporary discourse. Torah, *halakhah* (Jewish law), *aggadah* (Jewish lore), and, it turns out, especially *kabbalah* (Jewish mysticism) surface among nineteenth-century thinkers as a means to interpret the "new" that deepened and enriched the "old," rather than discard it.

The least successful and least interesting of these means was offered in the eighteenth century by Moses Mendelssohn. Mendelssohn's adoption of the rationalism of his century and his defense of Judaism as a religion of law as opposed to a religion of the spirit would resonate with neither those interested in living harmoniously among their non-Jewish neighbors nor with those interested in critiquing the traditional reliance on Jewish Law to define the spiritual content of Judaism. The nineteenth century would create, in the shadow of Mendelssohn, alternatives for thinking and living Jewishly that would have (may actually have) created what we would today call a vibrant, modern traditionalism that is at home in the "modern" world, sometimes critical of it, sometimes embracing its new insights, but never at the expense of the ongoing perceived truth of the Jewish historical and intellectual experience.

In the end, this might be called Orthodoxy, but I believe it would be wrong to do so. Despite the fact that we will explore some of the thought of Samson Raphael Hirsch, the "father" of Neo-Orthodoxy, the term "orthodox" does not do justice to the phenomenon I am describing. In this regard, even Hirsch's orthodoxy can be understood as a reform, and the almost ultra-orthodox associations of Israel Lipkin's *Mussar* movement must also be understood as a reform, in the sense that reform indicates not what it has come to mean conventionally, but rather what might be called an indigenous Jewish response to modernity. "Traditionalism" here means a response that absorbs and transforms modernity and reimagines it as if it were a seamless continuation of traditional Judaism. This process, it can be argued, describes the way in which Judaism has evolved over the centuries, unself-consciously.

It turns out that when looked at anew, the history of nineteenth-century Judaism contained a variety of candidates for such an evolution. They were more similar to one another than they themselves might have thought, and they may well have been expected to result in a synthesis of sorts by the early twentieth century that would have gone forward carrying the rubric of "modern Judaism" when viewed by future historians. That this did not happen may be attributed to the particularly radical nature of modernity and its shock to the system of traditional thought. Many would, I think, explain it this way.

I am more inclined to suggest that the force of modern thought, of rationalism and science, secularism and the sovereignty of the self, might all have been either withstood or absorbed creatively absent the traumas of the latter part of the nineteenth century and their centrality to the twentieth century. Though it does not belong in this discussion per se, one might suggest that the efforts of contemporary Judaism in the twenty-first century to recover both the tradition and the critique of tradition that will allow for a regeneration of a living Judaism might be a long-delayed continuation of the project that is the subject of this chapter. It is from this perspective—the attempt to find the core value and experience of Jewish existence and express it against the seeming onslaught of modernity—that I will view the larger issues of Jewish thought within the period. Rather than applying the lens of those who see Judaism as problematized by modernity and defining that lens as the *sine qua non* of nineteenth-century Jewish thought, I will try on the lens of those who see modernity as needing to be problematized by traditional Judaism and the ways, successful and not, that these thinkers attempted to do this.

Moses Mendelssohn (1729–1786) Sets the Stage for Nineteenth-Century Jewish Ethics

"Enlightenment" and "emancipation," the by-words of modernity, describe the arena of intellectual, social, and religious struggle for the Jewish people of Europe during the nineteenth century. A civilization had to rethink itself, self-consciously keeping a watchful eye on the larger society whose approbation was necessary for this process ultimately to succeed. The contours of this process of rethinking would remain remarkably the same for the entire period: the relation between religion and reason; the significance of history; and the impact of both of these on individual ethics. The effect of the Napoleonic reforms that provided Jews with the possibility of emancipation and the impact of modern rationalism stemming from the thought of Descartes and Spinoza mediated through the influential work of Moses Mendelssohn, provided the basis upon which the major thinkers of the Jewish nineteenth century would build. At the beginning of the century this building would take place first among Italian scholars, be taken up by German scholars, and by the end of the century would also begin to emerge among figures closer to the great Jewish communities in Russia and Poland. The thinkers involved in this process would without exception come out of the traditional Jewish community. They would all have traditional Jewish religious educations and would all be exposed both formally and informally to the great philosophical traditions of the West.

The emergence of the sovereign self, the breakdown of religious authority under the critique of scientific reason, the expansion of the idea of individual rights, and the view that history could reveal the conditions that gave rise to a variety of human institutions indebted to those historical conditions rather than to objective or universal truths can suffice as a definition of the modernity that continued to shape the general culture of the eighteenth and then the nineteenth century. These factors that together we call "modernity" raised the issues with which both Jewish and non-Jewish thinkers wrestled.

The question that was at the heart of Jewish thought throughout the nineteenth century (and beyond) was the question of ethics. On a philosophical level the question concerned the origin of ethics, that is, whether or not ethics is self-generated, autonomously present in consciousness, or imposed from without, either naturally or supernaturally. On a culture level the question concerned the evolution of ethics, that is, the criteria by which ethical norms are to be determined. Similarly, the question of the efficacy of religious practice to ensure both the appropriate evolution of ethics and, more important, the instantiation of ethical behavior received scrutiny.

The nineteenth century begins, as it were, under the sway of Mendelssohn's exposition of Jewish life. It is Mendelssohn's description of Judaism as a religion of revealed law separate from revealed belief that allows him to use rationalism as the arbiter of a universal ethical practice without having to jettison Jewish ritual and therefore communal norms. Mendelssohn essentially disconnects ethics from the sphere of religion in general and from Judaism specifically. For Mendelssohn, ethics is a subset of reason; moral norms are the tool for bringing our behavior into harmony with the intellect and its rational discovery of the foundations of human happiness. On the other hand, the Revealed Law delineates the sphere into which rational speculation can legitimately be applied. Judaism as a particular religion is but one way of structuring the community such that Reason can be allowed to do its universal work.[1]

The centrality of this ethical concern is not unconnected from the historical situation of the Jews in this century. The ethical question hid a deeper concern: how was the anti-Semitic caricature of the Jew to be viewed while Jews began to enter general European society? The isolation of the Jewish community and the ongoing enmity between Jews and Christians would hold the social norms of the Jewish community up to inspection in a way that it had not been before. How Jews *behaved* would become more important *in the minds of Jews*; or more correctly: how Jewish behavior was viewed from the vantage point of the emerging Christian and Jewish middle class became Jews' ultimate concern. Mendelssohn's "Jew in the world" raised for Jews the need to ask themselves the extent to which their Jewish heritage provided the ethical/behavioral standards that "the world" appeared to expect of them. More critically, it also raised the question whether the life of the Jew "at home," that is, the rituals of Jewish religious culture, contributed positively to the formation of the values expected of the Jew "in the world."

SAMUEL DAVID LUZZATO (1800–1865)

It is in the shadow of Mendelssohn's work that the nineteenth century unfolds. Writing in his *Lezioni di Teologia Dogmatica Israelitica (Lessons in Israelite Dogmatic Theology)*, Samuel David Luzzatto refers to Mendelssohn as the starting point for his own work.[2] Luzzatto (Shadal), who was born in Trieste, Italy, in 1800 and died in Padua in 1865, received an intense Jewish education that came to an end because of illness at the age of thirteen. Thereafter he attended only the talmudic lectures of Abraham Eliezer Ha-Levi and continued to read voraciously in every subject, Jewish and general. In his youth he published a pamphlet proving that the *Zohar* could not have been written by Rabbi Yohanon ben Zakkai because it used Hebrew vowels and musical cantillations for interpretive purposes, and those dated from the post-talmudic period. He also wrote books of poems and an unfinished philosophic-theological work, *Torah Nidreshet*. In 1829 he was appointed professor at the rabbinical collage of Padua, where he could further expand the scope of his work. He is viewed as one of the earliest Jewish practitioners of Bible criticism, studying Syriac among other ancient languages and suggesting emendations to the biblical text, and the same critical tools helped him understand the origins of the *Zohar*, the thirteenth-century cornerstone of medieval Jewish mysticism.

On the basis of his debunking of the antiquity of the *Zohar*, Luzzatto argued against the emerging interest among early scientific scholars of *kabbalah* as a philosophy of Judaism. This scholarship was already well underway during the first half of the nineteenth century. Beginning with the work of Meier H. Landauer and Adolph Jellinek, the field of Jewish mysticism had opened amid the general flowering of Jewish scholarship in the wake of Leopold Zunz's early Jewish studies. In France Adolphe Franck, a professor of philosophy, contributed a monograph, *Le Kabbale* (1842), that identified *kabbalah* as the essential philosophy of Judaism. ("The Religious Philosophy of the Hebrews" was the subtitle of Franck's monograph.) In Luzzatto's 1852 work, printed in French, *Dialogues sur la Kabbale et le Zohar et sur l'antiquité de la ponctuation et l' accentuation dans la langue hebraïque*, he called those who viewed *kabbalah* as Franck had as "ignorant." It was at most *one* rendering of Jewish tradition and certainly not the dominant philosophy of Judaism, let alone the religion of the Hebrews of antiquity.

Scholars' lively academic interest in *kabbalah* rarely indicated an equal religious interest in it.[3] But the level of the interest and the critiques taken together indicate at the very least a passion to derive both a philosophic and ethical road map through modernity drawn from the indigenous sources of Judaism. The larger work of Jewish historians during this period—by Zunz, Abraham Geiger, and Heinrich Graetz—also made available a growing body of classical Jewish sources for the construction of this road map.

Despite the modernism of his biblical work, Luzzatto identified Rationalism as a threat to the survival of Judaism. Philosophical Judaism, which he called "Atticism," was opposed in his mind to "Abrahamism," which denoted the "Revelation" of ethical consciousness to human beings through the engagement of the faculty of pity. In his *Tzelem Elohim* (1828), he explains that, like God, man has comprehensive powers. Man also possesses freedom to act according to his will and a rational faculty. But more important is man's ability to feel the pain and pleasure of others as well as his own. It is to these emotions that Torah's supernaturally rooted divine imperatives are directed. The innate existence of the faculty of pity is the source of love and compassion in humans and is divinely given. The Divine lawgiver then supports this initial call to Abraham with the second Revelation, given to Moses, to specifically direct the natural compassion of man. "Ethics, then, is the essence of Judaism, and speculative judgments do not apply to it."[4]

For Shadal, then, nineteenth-century Jewish thought under the impact of eighteenth-century Jewish thought had created what we could call a category error. While rationalism had led to breathtaking advances in many fields of human endeavor, it could not simply on that basis be assumed to become the only criteria for judging all aspects of human endeavor. Most important, it could not supplant the rationale for the ethical to which Judaism testified—namely, to live a life in accordance with the God-given human faculties of pity, compassion, and love.

What then do we make of this acknowledged "modernist," an early advocate of the principles that would inform the scholarship of the nineteenth-century school of Jewish thought called *Wisenschaft* (The Science of Judaism), who rejects as pernicious to Jewish civilization, and ultimately to general society, the growth of philosophic rationalism in particular and philosophy in general? We might be tempted to call him an exception, until we turn our attention to others of a similar bent that begin to fill the roster of Jewish thinkers in the period.

Elijah (or Elia) Benamozegh (1822–1900)

We turn to the Italian scholar Elijah Benamozegh and his great work *Israël et l'Humanité (Israel and Humanity)*. Born in 1822 at Leghorn, Italy, of native Moroccan parents, he lived in one of the most longstanding communities of Jews in the world, Jews who had been at home in Italian culture from before the advent of Christianity.

The security of this community may be considered among the reasons for Benamozegh's fearless exploration of the entire range of philosophic and scientific thought of the age.[5] In his introduction to *Israel and Humanity*, Benamozegh wrote:

> Two great lessons will emerge, we hope, from our labor. On the one hand, we shall demonstrate, contrary to the allegations of the rationalist critic, that Judaism, far from being a purely ethnic religion, has a universalist character, and that it has not ceased to concern itself with mankind and its destinies. On the other hand, we shall show that the ideal that Hebraism has evolved of man and of social organization not only has never been surpassed, but has not even been approached, except from a distance; and that it is in accepting this ideal, in reforming Christianity on this model, that mankind, without disavowing its dearest principles, will be able to have a reasonable faith in God and in his Revelation.[6]

In language that closely mirrors the views of Luzzatto, Benamozegh will use and apply the historical and critical methodologies of his day, as well as the breadth of general learning permitted to him as a quintessential nineteenth-century Jew, to critique the critique of the rationalist and to put forth Judaism as an *evolving* religious civilization! Near the beginning of *Israel and Humanity* Benamozegh reveals the fundamental role that a kabbalistic reading of Jewish thought will play in the development of his work. He wrote:

> The theory of emanation is particularly interesting because it contains a double concept: polymorphism (or the pluralist element in Divinity) and immanence. Let us see if Hebraism does not contain something of the sort, and if the Pentateuch itself does not furnish us with solid foundations for constructing such a system. This at least is what kabbalistic theology affirms; for despite denials from all sides, Kabbalism has the merit of being the first school to declare that the theory of emanation can be found in the Bible.[7]

Benamozegh's interest in a theory of emanation only served to form the basis of his more important goal: to describe a truly universalist religious vision that would embrace Judaism, Christianity, and Islam in a coming together where each maintained its particularity but each saw the other as equal. He resurrected the classical rabbinic idea of the Noahide laws to describe a universal ethic that undergirded this eventual mutual embrace. For Benmozegh, the foundations of social life, the possibility of civil peace, were borne on the commitment of the three biblical religions to the commandment of ethical consciousness. The textual, ritual, and national characteristics of the three religious traditions were all in support of this abiding ethical consciousness. Benmozegh derives his ethical vision in part from the elements of kabbalistic thought that support a theory of universal distribution of ethical vision. The combination of *kabbalah* and ethics will become even more important when we turn to the work of Israel Salanter below.

Nachman Krochmal (1785–1840)

Another voice among Jewish scholars of the century whose work bears on our subject was Nachman Krochmal. Born in Brody, Galicia, in 1785, Krochmal began the study of Talmud at an early age. He proceeded to study German and the German philosophers, especially Kant and including Fichte, Schelling, and finally Hegel, whose theory of historical periodization greatly influenced Krochmal's great and only publication, *Moreh Nevukhey Ha-Zman* (*The Guide for the Perplexed of This Time*). The lack of these assimilationist pressures resulted in Krochmal's more sympathetic reading of earlier stages in Jewish philosophical development as being appropriate to the goal of what he called *Netzah Yisrael*, "Eternal Israel," to describe the curious relation between historical periodization and the project of Jewish history. His goal was to establish the eternal relevance of Judaism as it underwent historical evolution. Each period of Jewish history, rather than needing to be rejected as being somehow primitive, could be embraced for its contribution to this ongoing process.

While Jews were subject to the same rise and fall throughout history, a particular "truth" guaranteed that they would eternally rise again. This was their encounter with God at Sinai. Given that context, the Jews of each generation used their powers of reason and imagination to articulate this truth for their generation. Those articulations were, of course, historically conditioned and were not necessarily useful to subsequent generations, but they could very well be studied by future generations in order to locate whatever part of them might still deserve to be carried forward. In this context David Biale, in his essay *The Kabbala in Nachman Krochmal's Philosophy of History*, asks:

> Why did a modern philosopher of Judaism devote so much of his work to examining earlier "sciences of faith" when they were only inadequate representations of Absolute Spirit? Why are there lengthy chapters in the *Guide* on the Kabbala, Gnosticism, Neoplatonism, Maimonides, and Ibn Ezra? The answer is that, for Krochmal, the modern "science of faith" is historical criticism: the modern philosopher is obligated to investigate older "sciences" as part of his own historical "science."[8]

While Biale's conclusion is that Krochmal saw the historical method of the nineteenth century to be the highest form of intellectual achievement and scrutinized early "sciences" of Judaism only for hints of this as well as for hints of the "Absolute Spirit" behind all of "Jewish science," nevertheless this is an expression of a nineteenth-century rationalism. As Moshe Idel writes: "It is only in the tone of the critiques that a greater involvement is felt. [Gustav] Landauer, [Adolph] Jellinek, [Nachman] Krochmal, or [Adolph] Franck should not be regarded as immersed in any deep belief in the concepts characteristic of *kabbalah*, though they expressed sympathy toward some of these concepts."[9] For Krochmal, the identification of a secret "science of faith" extending all the way back to the rabbinic period and hidden from the masses, including *kabbalah*, are preliminary to the explications his work reveals "at the end of many days." Thus esoteric doctrines of the past contain within them the seeds of the truths to be revealed by the historical method.

It is not my intent to suggest that Krochmal was a secret *kabbalist*. Rather it is to highlight his clear interest in *kabbalah* to touch on the larger issue of the persistence of a response to radical rationalism among Jewish thinkers of the period that looked toward what can only be called a "reconstruction" of Judaism after the assault of assimilationist rationalism. That is to suggest that more common to the thinkers of this century was their intent to preserve the integrity of Jewish thought and Jewish life rather than to abandon it, while being fully conversant with the elements of modernity that challenged it.

Samson Raphael Hirsch (1808–1888)

In this framework, the life and work of Rabbi Samson Raphael Hirsch can be viewed in a different light than they often are. Born in 1808 in Hamburg, Germany, Hirsch is universally considered the founder of "Neo-Orthodoxy," the attempt to maintain the lifestyle and intellectual framework of "premodern" Judaism while making necessary accommodations to modernity. Hirsch's so-called defense of traditional Judaism can more appropriately be read as a critique of it.

His critique—much like that of other thinkers of his century—focused on two areas, ethics and historical-critical thinking. In the face of the assimilationist pressures at work in the German-Jewish community mentioned above, Hirsch rejected the idea of "reforming" Judaism. However, he did recognize that by focusing on the core ethical values of Jewish tradition, Jews could better defend the particularity of their ritual observances in terms that their non-Jewish neighbors might appreciate. In his earliest important work, *Neunzehn Briefe über Judenthum* (*Nineteen Letters on Judaism*), published in 1836, he offered an uncompromising defense of traditional Judaism in the face of the growing movement to reform it. He wrote:

> There is but one road that leads to salvation; amends must be made precisely where the wrong was done. We must forget the views and prejudices that we inherited about Judaism and, instead, turn to the sources of Judaism, the Tanakh (Scriptures), the Talmud and the Midrash. We must read, study, and comprehend them in order to live by them and to draw from them Judaism's views about God, the world, mankind, and [the People] Israel. Thus Judaism must be studied and understood out of itself and be elevated, all by itself, to a science of wise living.[10]

This Judaism as the "science of wise living" showcases Hirsch's formula for a Jewish renewal. In arguing for a return to the sources of Judaism unencumbered by the prejudices of the non-Jewish world, Hirsch argues for the relevance of the traditional sources themselves in leading the way to such a renewal. Against the charge of Jewish isolationism and the fact that it leads to ethical insensitivity Hirsch wrote:

> You wrote that the Torah isolates us. True! If it did not, Israel would long since have lost its identity. Look what struggles are required to preserve the purity of Israel's spirit within our people despite this isolation! But does this spell enmity? Or pride? As if God were not the Lord of all creatures, all men? An unfortunate misinterpretation indeed! After all, Israel has no other task than to acknowledge as its God the One Who calls and educates all human beings to His service, and to make Him known as such through its destiny and way of life![11]

And further he asserts: "Judaism, correctly conceived and conveyed, constitutes a bond of love and justice encompassing all creatures."[12]

In his other great work, *Horeb, oder Versuche über Jissroel's Pflichten in der Zerstreuung* (A Philosophy of Jewish Law), a textbook on Judaism for educated Jewish youths, he focused in large degree on finding the possible symbolic meanings of Jewish religious precepts. Hirsch's focus on the "bond of love and justice" signaled to his readers a response to the same charge of ethically empty ritualism to which nineteenth-century Jewish thinkers had to respond and which they themselves had internalized. Mendelssohn's exposition of Judaism as revealed law with no connection to ethics provided both Jewish and non-Jewish critics of Judaism with ammunition to abandon it. To dispute the claim that Judaism had no direct access to ethics emerges more and more as the goal of Hirsch as well as other nineteenth-century Jewish thinkers.

Hermann Cohen (1842–1918)

It is impossible to do justice to the life and work of Hermann Cohen in this section. Born in 1842, he was one of the founders of the Marburg School of Neo-Kantianism and one of the most important Jewish philosophers of the nineteenth century. Cohen was educated at the Jewish Theological Seminary of Breslau and at the Universities of Breslau, Berlin, and Halle. In 1875 he was elected Professor at Marburg.

Cohen's *"Religion der Vernuft aud den Quellen des Judentums"* (*The Religion of Reason Out of the Sources of Judaism*), in 1919, articulates the centrality of ethical thought to Jewish identity. In this work Cohen argues for the persistence of Judaism as the source for the universal idea of ethics and therefore the persistence of the Jewish people and their religious practice. For this reason it goes without saying that Cohen's influence significantly supported the general movement of Reform and provided a philosophic rationale for Jews' embracing of German culture as long as they focused their religious view on ethics and social justice. Yet the profound universality of his religious vision coupled with its ascribed source in Jewish historical experience would serve as the basis for some Jews' abandonment of Jewish tradition. More important, it would serve as the springboard for the later, twentieth-century revival of Judaic philosophy in that both Martin Buber and Franz Rosenzweig would be inspired by Cohen to articulate competing views of Jewish tradition (see the following chapter for evidence of this inspiration and disagreement). That Rosenzweig, in fact, could indirectly derive from his grounding in Cohen a system of religious thought that combined both mystical and ethical elements suggests that the conventional reading of Cohen as a pure rationalist should be reevaluated.[13]

Israel Lipkin of Salant (a.k.a. Israel Salanter, 1810–1883) and the Mussar Movement

Nineteenth-century Jewish thought thus reveals a combination of streams, not unexpectedly, combining a consciousness of the power of reason, a strong distrust of the power of reason, and a concomitant interest in the power of nonrational forms, namely *kabbalah*, to provide what reason by itself does not unequivocally provide, that is, an imperative for ethics. Arguably the thinker who most holistically embodied these streams and created the most influential popular movement within traditional Jewish life was Rabbi Israel Lipkin. Born in Zhagory, Lithuania, in 1810, Lipkin studied as a youth with Rabbi Tzvi Hirsh Braude of Salant, and under Rabbi Yosef Zundel of Salant, a direct disciple of Rabbi Hayyim of Volozhin, in turn a student of the great Gaon of Vilna. Lipkin is commonly known as the

Salanter Rav (Rabbi) or often Rabbi Israel Salanter. A prodigious Talmud scholar, Lipkin was appointed head of the Meile Yeshiva in Vilna in 1842. However, the scandal of his achieving this position over the heads of older, more established rabbis caused him to resign and move to a small town outside of Vilna, where he established a new *yeshiva* (rabbinical seminary) in which he began to implement the ideas and practices that would soon become associated with the "Mussar Movement," which would be his lasting contribution to Jewish religious culture.[14]

At his *yeshiva*, Lipkin instituted the study of classical works of Jewish ethical piety, especially *Mesillat Yesharim (Paths of Uprightness)* by Rabbi Moshe Hayyim Luzzatto, and Menahem Mendel Lefin's *Heshbon Ha-Nefesh (Accounting of the Soul)*. A specific genre of literature had developed over the course of nearly a thousand years of a type of ethical, exhortative book to which Luzzatto's and Lefin's belonged. From its inception this literature developed side by side with the development of *halakhic* (legal) literature, especially codes of Jewish law, as though to assert that the growing identification of Jewish religious life with the performance of legal obligations should not obscure the fact that the goal of this intricate web of commandments was the achievement of "holiness" defined by the concern for justice and compassion. This literature was vast, well-known, and yet, in the mainstream *yeshivot* [seminaries] of Lithuania and Eastern Europe, viewed as decidedly secondary.[15] In fact, the entire body of non-*halakhic* literature, including the aggadic or narrative tradition within the Talmud itself, was viewed as by and large secondary. Ethics was subsumed as a branch of *aggadah* and treated as such.

Nevertheless, what struck Lipkin was not merely the need to reappropriate this literary tradition, which he did by making it a central part of the curriculum at his *yeshivot*, but the inefficacy of this literature alone to affect behavior. We can paraphrase the question he must have asked himself: "If there is so much textual material teaching us how and why to be good, why is it so hard to be good? Why is there so much evil in the world? And why does so much of that evil begin in the very nature of the relationships with those closest to us, our friends and neighbors?" The answer that he gave resulted in this new movement in Jewish life.

The social forces at work on the Lithuanian community in which Salanter worked were similar to those in Western Europe. On the one hand, the forces of Enlightenment that had both emancipated Western European Jews and undermined their attachments to Judaism earlier in the nineteenth century had begun to make inroads in the Eastern European Jewish world as well. The attempts of the Czarist government to establish "official" *yeshivot*, and their support by *haskalah* (Enlightenment) Jewish leaders, were seen as a serious threat to the Jewish establishment. More important, the blandishments of secular education and the rise of socialist and other worker organizations not only threatened the rabbinic establishment but critiqued that establishment precisely on the issue of Jewish behavior, that is, ethics, both within the community and outside it.

The impact of this threat of secularization has often been noted in discussions of Salanter's work, but I believe its importance has sometimes been minimized.[16] Instead, the inroads of Hasidism into Lithuania, with its challenge to the so-called "dry" approach to talmudic texts and *pilpul*, the concern with textual minutia, has been cited as a major factor in Salanter's desire to create a more enthusiastic brand of Jewish religiosity. While there is no doubt truth in this view, the perceived disaffection of young Jews with mainstream Jewish life not only was real, but was, to a large extent, predicated on a critique of the ethical norms of the community.[17]

How then did Salanter answer the question we have rhetorically put in his mouth? The intense study of Mussar literature was part of his answer, but in addition Salanter understood classical rabbinic and Kabalistic analysis of the "soul" or self to reveal an internal, unconscious arena that ultimately controlled behavior and was not easily amenable to improvement based merely on intellectual means. Study by itself could not guarantee ethical behavior. Rather, a method had to be found for breaking through the rational surface of consciousness in order to intervene on the level of the subconscious ("soul root"[18]) of the individual. The method that he developed began with putting Mussar texts at the center of *yeshiva* education, but the method of studying those texts, borrowing indeed from traditional forms of Jewish pedagogy but with new emphasis, he called "studying with lips aflame." That is, he advocated using the Mussar text as a type of "mantra" to be repeated over and over until the intellectual resistance to its import, until all of the rationalizations that we use to protect ourselves against ethical self-critique, were worn down, and the student was reduced to pure openness at the level of the unconscious. This process was accompanied and supported by the organization of the students into *va'adim*, peer group cells, in which students would critique one another's behavior and push one another to greater awareness about their behavior.

Salanter's concept of the soul as the unconscious anticipates later nineteenth-century thought, but it is predicated on nineteenth-century ideas regarding the integrity of the individual. Certainly his concern with embracing and then critiquing the central *haskalah* ideas becomes evident in his work. His own peripatetic life adds to the body of evidence for this view. Likening the onslaught of *haskalah* in Russia and Lithuania to a team of runaway horses racing downhill, he despaired of halting the flight of Jews to emancipation. Instead, he moved to Prussia, at first for medical reasons, and sensing that among German Jews the "stampede" had reached level ground, he chose to remain and work among that community of Jews. There he championed the inclusion of Jewish Studies in the university, began (but did not complete) a translation of the Talmud into German, and otherwise participated in strengthening the traditional Jewish community with a method of study that potentially responded positively to the ongoing critique aimed at that community.

The process of understanding the sources of Lipkin's thought has only just begun. Neither of the two great scholarly works on his thought, one by Hillel Goldberg and the other by Immanuel Etkes,[19] have adequately accounted for its genesis. Was he a *sui generis* genius? Was he influenced by secular sources other than the ones of which we are aware? Both of these are real possibilities. But an important source for the development of his thought and work may also be found in the role *kabbalah* played in the development of his ethics.

While Lipkin's knowledge and involvement in kabbalistic learning constitutes a point of controversy between Goldberg and Etkes, there is *prima facie* evidence that this involvement may well have been profound and significant. Aside from the obvious fact that *kabbalah* essentially functioned as Jewish theology within the Eastern European traditional community,[20] there is the fact of Salanter's educational heritage. Lithuanian Jewry is known as consisting preeminently of *mitnagdim*, that is, "opponents" of *Hasidim*. This has resulted in the erroneous perception that this *mitnagdic* community was opposed to *kabbalah*. Nothing could be further from the truth.[21] The lineage of learning that produced Lipkin began with Rabbi Elijah ben Yosef, the Gaon of Vilna and one of the great kabbalists of the age. His student, Rav Hayyim of Volozhin, continued this tradition, as did Lipkin's teacher, Rav Yosef Zundel. It is simply inconceivable that Lipkin was not well versed in kabbalistic learning. It is also inconceivable that he would make such knowledge public and available, the precise "sin" of the Hasidim.[22]

Moreover, his choice of *Mesillat Yesharim* as the central text of *mussar* instruction supports this thesis. For indeed Moshe Hayyim Luzzatto, the author of that book, was one of the consummate kabbalists of his day. *Mesillat Yesharim*, however, contains not a single direct kabbalistic reference. One reason is the fact that fears of incipient Shabbatianism caused the rabbinic authorities of Amsterdam to elicit from Luzzatto a promise not to produce kabbalistic texts. Another motivation for Salanter's choice of *Mesillat Yesharim* was Luzzatto's own belief, long held among some kabbalists, that one could not begin to study and appreciate kabbalistic wisdom before one had perfected one's ethical character![23] For him, ethics preceded and lay the groundwork for the advance into *kabbalah*. Thus Lipkin's *mussar* precisely grounded the return to indigenous resources of philosophy latent within traditional Jewish learning on the achievement of a level of ethical behavior that answered both the internal and external perceptions of Judaism as lacking in ethical consciousness.

The full impact of the *mussar* movement, however, would not be felt as a result of Rabbi Lipkin's groundbreaking thought. His three main students, Rav Naftali Amsterdam, Rabbi Jacob Joseph, and Rabbi Simhah Zissel Ziv, would institutionalize and spread *mussar* teaching in three distinct schools of practice. The cataclysm of World War One would severely disrupt the spread of the movement, and the Second World War would relegate it to the margins of Jewish life only to await a resurrection of interest in the twenty-first century.[24]

Notes

1. Moses Mendelssohn, *Jerusalem or On Religious Power and Judaism*, Allan Arkush, trans. (Hanover, NH: University Press of New England, 1983), pp. 89–90.
2. Nathan Rosenstreich, *Jewish Philosophy in Modern Times* (New York: Holt, Rinehart, and Winston, 1968), p. 30.
3. Moshe Idel, "Appendix," in Elia Benamozegh, *Israel and Humanity*, Maxwell Luria, trans. (New York: Paulist Press, 1995), p. 381.

4. Rosenstreich, *Jewish Philosophy in Modern Times* (see note 2 above), p. 33.
5. Benamozegh, *Israel and Humanity* (see note 3 above), p. 10.
6. Ibid., p. 58.
7. Ibid., p. 69.
8. David Biale, The Kabalah in Nachman Krochmal's Philosophy of History, *Journal of Jewish Studies*, v32 n1.
9. Benamozegh, *Israel and Humanity* (at note 3 above), p. 381.
10. Samson Raphael Hirsch, *The Nineteen Letters of Ben Uzziel*, Bernard Drachman, trans. (New York: Feldheim, 1969), p. 210.
11. Ibid., Letter Fifteen, p. 198.
12. Ibid., Letter Nineteen, pp. 333–34.
13. See Robert Gibbs, *Correlations in Rosenazweig and Levinas* (Princeton, NJ: Princeton University Press. 1992), pp. 18–19.
14. The word *mussar* means "discipline" and/or "instruction" or "correction." More properly, it means all of these at once. It was at that time, and continues to be, used as the common Hebrew term for ethics.
15. Among the many works in this category are *Duties of the Heart* by Bahya ibn Pekuda; *Kav V'Yashar* by Rzvy Hirsch Kaidanover; *Tomar Devorah* by Moshe Cordevero; and *Orot Zadikim*, whose author is unknown.
16. Immanuel Etkes, *Rabbi Israel Salanter and the Mussar Movement* (Philadelphia: Jewish Publication Society, 1993), pp. 120–21.
17. Ibid., p. 11.
18. Hillel Goldberg, *Israel Salanter, Text, Structure, Idea: The Ethics and Theology of an Early Psychologist of the Unconscious* (New York: KTAV, 1982), p. 105.
19. Goldberg, *Israel Salanter*, ibid., and Etkes, *Rabbi Israel Salanter* (at note 16 and 18 above).
20. Benamozegh, *Israel and Humanity* (at note 3 above), pp. 14–15.
21. Allan Nadler, *The Faith of the Mitnagdim* (Baltimore: Johns Hopkins University Press, 1997), pp. 1–4.
22. The sin of Hasidism is not that it studies *kabbalah* but that it disseminates it to the masses.
23. See, for example: Moshe Hayyim Luzzato, *The Path of the Upright*, Mordecai Menahem Kaplan, trans. (Philadelphia: Jewish Publication Society, 1936, 2010), p.16.
24. For contemporary approaches to Mussar see: Alan Morinis, *Everyday Holiness* (Boston, MA: Trumpeter, 2007); Ira Stone, *A Responsible Life* (New York: Aviv Press, 2006); Elyakim Krumbein, *Mussar for Moderns* (Jersey City, NJ: KTAV, 2005); and Zvi Miller, *Ohr Yisrael* (New York: Targum/Feldheim, 2004).

Suggestions for Further Reading

On Nineteenth-Century Jewish Thought Generally

Cohen, Arthur A. 1962. *The Natural and the Supernatural Jew: An Historical and Theological Introduction*. New York: Pantheon Books. 2nd rev. ed.: New York: Behrman House, 1979.

Guttman, Julius. 1964. *Philosophies of Judaism: The History of Jewish Philosophy from Biblical Times to Franz Rosenzweig*. David W. Silverman, trans. New York: Holt, Reinhart, and Winston.

Katz, Steven T. 1975. *Jewish Philosophers*. New York: Bloch.

Rotenstreich, Nathan. 1984. *Jews and German Philosophy: The Polemics of Emancipation*. New York: Schocken.

On Moses Mendelssohn

Altman, Alexander. 1973, 1986. *Moses Mendelssohn: A Biographical Study*. London: Routeledge and Kegan Paul.

Arkush, Allan. 1994. *Moses Mendelssohn and the Enlightenment*. Albany: State University of New York Press.

Sorkin, David J. 1996. *Moses Mendelssohn and the Religious Enlightenment*. Berkeley: University of California Press.

On Samuel David Luzzato

Baron, Salo. 1952/53. "Samuel David Luzzato." In *Sefer Asaf*. Umberto Cassuto, ed. Jerusalem: Magnes Press of Hebrew University, pp. 40–63.

Rosenbloom, Noah H. 1965. *Luzzatto's Ethico-Psychological Interpretation of Judaism*. New York: Yeshiva University.

On Elijah Benamozegh

Dayan, Menahem. 1986. *Universal Elements in the Jewish Thoughts of Elia Benamozegh*. Ann Arbor, MI: University Microfilms International.

Eidelberg, Paul. 2009. *Toward a Renaissance of Israel and America: The Political Theology of Rabbi Elijah Benamozegh*. Springdale, AK: Lightcatcher Books.

Guetta, Allessandro. 2009. *Philosophy and Kabbalah: Elijah Benamozegh and the Reconciliation of Western Thought and Jewish Escotericism*. Albany: State University of New York Press.

Idel, Moshe. 1998. *"Al ha-Kabbalah ezel ha-Rav Elijah Benamozegh"* (Hebrew). In *Pe'amim* 74: 87–96.

On Nachman Krochmal

Harris, Jay Michael. 1991. *Nachman Krochmal: Guiding the Perplexed of the Modern Age*. New York: New York University Press.

Katsh, Abraham Isaac. 1946. *Nachman Krochmal and the German Idealists*. New York: Conference on Jewish Relations.

Schechter, Solomon. 1911. *Studies in Judaism, First Series*. Philadelphia: Jewish Publication Society of America (repr. in *Studies in Judaism: A Selection*. New York, Meridian, 1958).

Taubes, Jacob, Charlotte Elisheva Fontrobert, and Amir Engel. 2010. *From Cult to Culture: Fragments Towards a Critique of Historical Reason*. Stanford, CA: Stanford University Press.

On Samson Raphael Hirsch

Breuer, Mordecai. 1970. *The Torah im Derekh Eretz of Samson Raphael Hirsch*. New York: Feldheim.

Ellenson, David. 2004. *After Emancipation: Jewish Religious Responses to Modernity*. Cincinnati: Hebew Union College.

Hildesheimer, Meir. 2008. *Historical Perspectives on Samson Raphael Hirsch*. New York: Rabbinical Council of America.

Jakobovits, Immanuel. 1970. *Samson Raphael Hirsch: A Reappraisal of His Teaching and Influence in the Light of Our Times*. London: Office of the Chief Rabbi.

Rosenbloom, Noah H. 1976. *Tradition in an Age of Reform: The Religious Philosophy of Samson Raphael Hirsch*. Philadelphia: Jewish Publication Society.

On Israel Likpin Salanter

Etkes, Immanuel. 1993. *Rabbi Israel Salanter and the Mussar Movement*. Philadelphia: Jewish Publication Society.

Goldberg, Hillel. 1982. *Israel Salanter: Text, Structure, Idea*. New York: KTAV.

On the Mussar Movement

Krumbein, Elyakim. 2005. *Mussar for Moderns*. Jersey City, NJ: KTAV.

Miller, Zvi. 2004. *Ohr Yisrael*. Southfield, MI: Targum/Feldheim.

Morinis, Alan. 2007. *Everyday Holiness*. Boston: Trumpeter.

Stone, Ira. 2006. *A Responsible Life*. New York, NY: Aviv Press.

CHAPTER 7

ETHICAL THEORIES OF HERMANN COHEN, FRANZ ROSENZWEIG, AND MARTIN BUBER

JONATHAN K. CRANE

INTRODUCTION

Early twentieth-century German Jewish thinkers were increasingly swept up with fin-de-siècle broader philosophical and political trends, especially the pursuit of rationalism as well as the drive toward nationalism. Influenced by the resurgent interest in Kantian rationalism, these Jews sought to demonstrate to themselves and to their gentile hosts that Judaism is and has always been a rational, or at least a reasonable, tradition, and its ethics are both intelligible and appropriate for the modern age. In a fashion mimicking *Euthyphro*, Moritz Lazarus, for example, asserted in his *Ethiks des Judentum* (1903) that God's commandments are moral precisely because their morality antedated God's commanding them (§79).[1]

Even though Lazarus claimed that Jewish ethics was not confined to a theological backwater out of touch with modernity, other Jewish scholars, especially Hermann Cohen, found Lazarus's stance still too beholden to God to be universally reasonable. Rather, as Cohen and others after him argued, the search for a theory of reasonable religious ethics needed to lean even more heavily on Kant, just as contemporary Christian ethics did. With keen interest in, and intimate engagement with, the thought of their gentile neighbors and hosts, early twentieth-century

Jewish ethicists began to develop Judaic ethics that claimed to be both universally reasonable and reasonably universal. Through their efforts, modern Jewish ethics both took seriously and could be taken seriously in return by those not beholden to the narrow strictures of Jewish law. In many ways these early twentieth-century German Jewish thinkers demonstrated that the other—gentile, fellow Jew, or both—is quintessential to Jewish ethics, and that loving the other is the only reasonable orientation. As will be shown, this turn to loving the other is, in many ways, one of the signature moves of modern Jewish ethical thought, especially in the works of Hermann Cohen, Franz Rosenzweig, and Martin Buber.

Hermann Cohen (1842–1918)

Trained in Kantian ethics at Breslau, Berlin, and Halle, Hermann Cohen taught at the University of Marburg department of philosophy, where, along with Paul Natrop and Ernst Cassirer, he founded the Marburg school of Neo-Kantianism. Like Kant, Cohen examined reason and its role in shaping reality, but unlike his muse, he maintained a passionate concern for the well-being of minorities in Germany. He argued for universal suffrage, for worker collective mobilization, and for protecting Jews from unwarranted persecution. As is articulated in his *Ethics of Pure Will* (1904, 1907), ethics could not be divorced from history, especially if ethics was to be reasonable. It was this dual perspective—looking at ideas as well as at reality—that informed Cohen's Jewish ethics, especially in his major opus published posthumously, *Religion of Reason: Out of the Sources of Judaism* (1919).

For Cohen, as for many other nineteenth-century German idealist philosophers, ideas are the primary origin of all things. Ideas, or more precisely the *thinking* of ideas, creates what *is*.[2] Just as the Good is both an idea and *is*, so too for God: God is an idea and also is; and the concept of the Good ultimately converges into the idea of God.[3] God's unique *is*-ness, or being (*Dasein*), is not merely the idea of divine unicity (*Einzigkeit*); it founds the very possibility of difference both in the realm of ideas and in reality. As such, the idea of God therefore grounds the possibility both of human diversity and of change; it inspires and demands moral improvement.[4]

Ethics is also an idea, a notion famously championed by Kant. It is an idea about morally improving civilization and the philosophical system that shapes that upbringing. Insofar as ethics focuses on the *ought*, its attention is on change. Or, in Cohen's terms, ethics attends to human becoming and to becoming ever more good and more holy in particular. Because the Good is always idealized—as in Plato's idealized forms—and God is the ultimate Good, the ethical task of increasingly embodying the Good must necessarily be holy and eternal. For this reason, Cohen emphasizes "*there is no distinction in the Jewish consciousness between religion and morals.*"[5]

The fact that becoming perfectly moral or holy is achievable only in the eternally distant future does not deter Cohen, for he understands that the idea of the ideal moral future, the messianic future itself, is intelligible only to the degree that ethics retains one foot in the real world of here and now.[6] And this is where Cohen departs some from Kant's notions of pure reason and monological—that is, heady and not fleshy, or enacted—ethics. For Cohen, ethics must function not only in the realm of ideas but also in nature and time, in history itself, if they are to be ethics at all. Only if ethics can be actualized can the notion of the messianic future have any meaningful pull.[7]

Since ethics functions both in the world of nature and in the world of ideas, it perforce pertains to society as a whole. But whereas philosophical ethics sought to fashion individuals alike and thus create a homogenous society, Cohen asserts that diversity and otherness are necessary for humanity's well-being. For him, the other can never be sublated (*aufgehoben*) or subsumed, as traditional ethics supposes; the unique other is never obliterated as such.[8] The self and other always remain isolated, for only then can the individual other be recognized, honored, and protected, according to his or her particular needs. In theory, I, this individual here, become individualized through thinking about you, the other over there.

Cohen is careful to insist that the others one considers are not correlative concepts of the I, much less correlative realities. While some ethicists of his day preferred to think of the ordinary and generic other (*Nebensmensch*), his Jewish philosophy focuses on the peculiarity of the fellow, needy person immediately facing me (*Mitmensch*). Acknowledging the uniqueness of this person next to me—this recognition of her idiosyncratic suffering—is what ultimately individuates me.

Cohen further says, as does Leo Tolstoy, that not all sufferings are alike, such as impoverishment and being a stranger. Whereas witnessing another's poverty induces pity, a response championed by secular philosophical ethics, religion in general and Judaism in particular notice the other's strangerliness, a quality that necessarily prompts love.[9] By loving the other, my self becomes a truly individuated and special I. (To my own suffering, Cohen suggests that I can and perhaps should be indifferent, a position that seemingly anticipates Emmanuel Levinas.[10])

This new orientation faces difficulty when God is brought back into the picture. Insofar as every human being is created *betzelem elohim*, in God's image, each is—at least from God's perspective—equal: we are all equally human. So it is from a liberal government's perspective too: all citizens are equal before the law.[11] A similar claim can be made about secular philosophy's view of humanity. In Cohen's view, religion's contribution therefore is its humanizing effect. Religion generally and Judaism in particular inculcate ways of thinking and acting that honor the uniqueness of each human being actually encountered. It should not be thought, however, that God does not relate to each human being in the throes of his or her own peculiar condition. On the contrary, God loves the stranger in all her strangerliness.[12] In this way, the idea of "the idea of God" loving each person uniquely is simultaneously the ground and goal of moral improvement for both society as a whole and each individual. Insofar as God is best understood as the moral archetype, *imitatio dei* or behaving Godly thus becomes intelligible for creatures who are *imago dei*, created in the divine image.[13]

Yet each person's emulation of God is not the same. Each person's pursuit of moral perfection is an idiosyncratic and eternal approach toward (the idea of) God. In this way Cohen insists that humankind's love for each other, which itself is a love for morality, is essentially and in actuality love for God. About this claim he says in a Kantian fashion, "This thesis means for religion what the following thesis means for ethics: action does not result from an extraneous and foreign motive, nor from an extraneous command. It is the result of the will, to which autonomy belongs. Love has to exclude every extraneous and foreign motivation."[14] Morality therefore is an internally driven pursuit to ever more perfectly manifest love (broadly construed) toward distinct and unique others. Put differently, it is not so much that God commands me to love my neighbor that inspires my moral behavior; rather, my conceptualization of idealized love, which itself is God, pulls me toward greater moral behavior.[15]

In this way Cohen promotes the notion of ethical monotheism. As the (idea of a) singular God grounds and guides (ever more perfect) morality, it also is a process of removing human action from the constraints of history. This is so because morality, perfectly conceived and hence messianic, is eternal and perforce must exist beyond history. An individual and society that improve their morality step ever closer toward this idealized ahistorical or eternal existence. Though Cohen soberly acknowledges that this pursuit remains an infinite task for such finite creatures as humans, he maintains with his fellow German nineteenth-century neighbors a fundamental optimism that people singularly and collectively can nonetheless ever improve morally as long as they reason clearly and keep an idea of God in mind.

This is the source of one of the major criticisms lobbied against Cohen: the ethical monotheism he endorses is so universalist in scope and method that its Jewishness is hardly perceptible and its "idea of God" not personal. In his drive to present Judaism as reasonable as Christianity, he urges fellow Jews to assimilate so as to contribute to civilization scientifically, politically, and socially. And yet, Cohen claims, Jews should retain their distinctiveness in religion, in holding onto "our idea of the One God"—but even this concept of God is nothing but ethics, an attendance to the other.[16]

Franz Rosenzweig (1886–1929)

Though he is acknowledged as one of Cohen's greatest prodigies, Franz Rosenzweig suggests that it was his cousin Hans Ehrenberg who had a greater influence on his thinking. Both Rosenzweig and Ehrenberg, born into liberal Jewish homes and encouraged to pursue education at German institutions, were enamored with

Hegelian political philosophy. This shared interest fueled a strong friendship, to which Ehrenberg's baptism to Protestantism added sparks for heated conversations about the interrelationships between religion and history, subjectivity and objectivity, self and world. Together they explored these themes with Eugen Rosenstock-Huessy, a sociologist fascinated with spoken language, in an all-night midsummer 1913 conversation from which Rosenzweig emerged all but convinced that Christianity indeed had a this-worldly enterprise that was the best way of unifying self and world.[17] Despite the temptation to leave Judaism altogether for Christianity, Rosenzweig experienced a revelation at the next Yom Kippur that convinced him not to abandon Judaism but rather to immerse himself in its study. He now saw that Judaism, no less than Christianity, had a role in the world's redemption, and his task was to elucidate it.

His rededication to Judaism led him to study at the Higher Institute for Jewish Studies in Berlin, where Cohen was then teaching after his retirement from Marburg. Together they established the Lehrhaus, a school devoted to both scholarly investigations of Judaism and community education. It was through reading Cohen's *Religion of Reason* that Rosenzweig began to identify God, World, and Self as three interlocking elementary facets of existence that warranted further study. Rosenzweig wrote his reflections about these themes on postcards sent home while he served at the Balkan front during World War I. After the war he compiled these thoughts into what became his *magnum opus, The Star of Redemption*. This book, he later claimed, is not a Jewish book or a rethinking of religion generally but a system of philosophy whose intention is to model and bring about a renewal of thinking broadly speaking.[18] Indeed, the new thinking he champions is a speech-thinking (*Sprachdenken*) wherein narration, and not reason per se, functions as the organon through which human grasping of the world in time and space plays out.[19]

While this novel speech-thinking requires both time and space, philosophers of other schools of thought abstracted themselves from time so as to identify and explain universal truths. Such temporal disembodiment undermined their philosophies' abilities to speak of what things actually are in their necessarily interrelatedness to other things. What Rosenzweig called philosophy's abstraction from time corresponded to its reduction of particulars into generalities.[20] By subsuming idiosyncratic particulars into the generic All, with nothing remaining unexplained, such philosophies obliterate the peculiarities of each individual in favor of an idealized world that has no corresponding reality. And in so doing, they pursue an absolute abstraction that is simultaneously timeless and displaced or place-less. It is as *ou*topic, without place, as it is generic, without specifics. In short, such philosophies construe things as they are not.[21]

Rosenzweig's speech-thinking, on the other hand, acknowledges time as indispensable for human reasoning and existence generally.[22] Indeed, narration itself requires time and tenses, for through them the ability to speak of people and things and eras becomes possible. Past, present, and future are not merely grammatical forms but paradigms for both thought and experience.[23] History itself warrants confronting, for the world already existed before the individual came into being.

Taking history seriously thereby enables the individual to recognize her temporal and spatial uniqueness in the present, and from this embedded perspective she is able to consider potential relations in the future. In this way speech-thinking places the human back into temporal and spatial history so as to better grapple with the messiness of relatedness. Only after philosophy ends its obsession with thinking, Rosenzweig claims, can experiential philosophy, the philosophy of *lived* experience, begin.[24]

Relations thus come to the fore in Rosenzweig's *Star* system. Taking his cue from Cohen, Rosenzweig stipulates that the basic elements of existence—God, Humankind, and World—bespeak critical relations. God creates the world, God reveals to humans, and humans redeem the world.[25] These relations can be articulated well in a now famous visual (figure 7.1).

These elemental relations, as much as speech-thinking itself, presuppose others and otherness. Moreover, like all relations, creation, revelation, and redemption are not static, one-time events rupturing history or future. They are ongoing relations, ever adjusting to the open-ended vicissitudes of present human existence. In this way, Rosenzweig's religio-philosophy better reflected the reality of human experience than idealism to the degree that it took otherness, relations, and change seriously.

The realization of the inexorability of change sparked a controversy with Rosenzweig's friend and colleague Martin Buber. Over the years of their correspondence they pondered, among other themes, the nature of revelation.[26] As will be discussed more fully below, Buber held that revelation could never rightfully be formulated as law per se, because law is humanly manufactured. Buber could not fathom letting law cloud his will lest he be distracted from God's unmediated word that is, by definition, directed for the needs of the moment.[27] As he explained in his letters and in a brief essay entitled "The Builders," Rosenzweig did not wholly disagree with his friend, because for him revelation is also not a moment of law-giving, though the law remains central to Jewish living.[28] Rather, God reveals by revelation revealing itself. If Rosenzweig were pressed to ascribe to revelation some particular content—and this is one of the major critiques of his approach—he would say that revelation reveals command—an as yet ambiguous content and notion.[29]

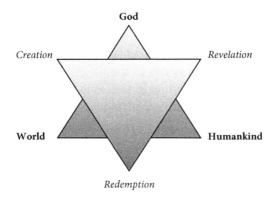

FIGURE 7.1

Though both command and law are imperatives, their temporal foci differ. Law deals with duration insofar as it seeks to stitch together time, past and future into the present.[30] Command, by contrast, conceives no future, only the immediacy of this moment's obligations. There is but one command: the command to love. Unpremeditated and with no desire for the next moment, this audible divine command "Love me!" is urgency itself.[31] Because this command integrates consciousness, expression, and waiting for fulfillment in this very moment, it lacks all temporality and can never become law. All other commandments, however, can become law, that is, embedded in time.[32]

The urgency of the command to love is not yet ethics, however. What the revelation of this command demonstrates is love itself. It expresses God's attention and care for humanity by awakening humankind to the need to attend and care, though as yet its concern is God and not fellow humans. It is here that Rosenzweig brings in his existentialist bent. Insofar as humans are embodied beings and dwell in the world, it is impossible for humankind to love only God in this very moment. Rather, the commandment to love is embodied in the command to "Love your neighbor." With this commandment, the mature soul leaves the safety of divine love and journeys forth into the world.[33]

The commands to love God and to love your neighbor are inextricably linked. The latter presupposes the former, and the former can be externalized only through the latter. Put differently, only the soul already loved by God can receive the command to love neighbors and thereby fulfill it; only the already beloved can manifest God's will, or love another. In this way both God and the human soul need the neighbor, the other.

This other is not uniform, to be sure. The commandment in its full reads, *v'ahavtah l're'ekha kamokha*, "love your neighbor as yourself" (Lev 19:18). Rosenzweig understands this last phrase, "as yourself," to mean "not 'you'": your neighbor is not the Self, but rather, like you, is also a Self, an I, a distinct soul.[34] This command thereby confirms the Self as a self in and through juxtaposition to a different Self. And because each Self is unique and embodies distinct needs, no encounter between Selves, and thus no two moments, can be the same. Hence Rosenzweig says, "this fulfillment of God's love in the world is not a singular act, but a whole series of acts; love of the neighbor always newly arises; it is always a new beginning."[35] For this reason fulfillment of this other's momentary needs must therefore be free of any encumbrances like law. For only in absolute freedom can one truly respond to the unique needs of the neighbor. Hence, embedded in the center of his reflections on redemption, Rosenzweig discovers that the divine command to love requires complete and free surrender.

> This can be nothing other than the love for the neighbor. Love for the neighbor is that which at every moment surmounts and yet always presupposes that pure surrender. For without this presupposition, it could not be that which according to its essence it must be: necessary, despite—yes, despite!—its self-renewing at every moment. It would be only "freedom," for its origin would only reside in the will alone; but man can only externalize himself in the act of love, once the

soul has been awakened by God. Only the love received from God makes the act of love on the soul's part more than a mere act, namely the fulfillment of a commandment of love.[36]

Ethics is not only an eternal set of unique, momentary purposive acts of care; it is redemptive insofar as it fulfills the divine command. Redemption emerges precisely in this moment when one soul turns to the next in caring attention, and this loving act instantiates eternity itself. For unlike Cohen's forever retreating eternity, Rosenzweig's understanding of eternity is tangible by "touching and grasping the individual [neighbor] with a strong hand."[37] Distinct, momentary acts of love between others thereby manifest eternally the Kingdom of God; or put pithily, ethics manifests redemption in the here and now both always and, paradoxically, not yet, insofar as the Kingdom of God remains incomplete. Redemption *of* the world can, for Rosenzweig, occur *in* the world. In this way humankind redeems the world that God re-creates in every moment by receiving and fulfilling revelation's command to love God and neighbor.

Martin Buber (1878–1965)

Born in Vienna to a devout family, Martin Buber grew up at the feet of the great *haskalah* (Enlightenment) scholar of *midrash*, Solomon Buber, his grandfather, and at the home-schooling table of Adele, his grandmother. An early polyglot and autodidact, Buber read widely, inspired by the richness of fin-de-siècle Viennese heady and emotional cosmopolitanism. Very much a part of the late romantic justification efforts for nationalist movements, Buber supported the nascent Zionist drive, first aligning with Theodore Herzl at *Die Welt*, the movement's newspaper, and then supporting Chaim Weizmann's more democratic wing, where he could meditate more clearly on why Jews warranted a distinct homeland. His focus on social psychology led him away from his early studies of *hasidut*, Taoism, and Nietzsche, and more toward Kant and the philosophy of dialogue.[38]

These intellectual shifts paralleled his move in 1916 to Frankfurt, where he met Rosenzweig, who recruited him to teach at both the Lehrhaus and the university. Together they forged a strong friendship, began a new German translation of the Bible, and fostered a regeneration of adult Jewish learning in Germany.[39] Despite Rosenzweig's influence, Buber's utter dismay at the carnage of World War I and the degeneracy of bourgeois society in general fueled his skepticism of systemic thinking and acting. He preferred existentialism, or lived experience (*Erlebnis*).[40] For him, human existence is neither systemic and perforce generic, nor is it so completely idiosyncratic that each person exists in utter isolation as if in a vacuum, contra Kierkegaard.[41] Rather, existence is a series of encounters, and it is upon such experiences that Buber reflected for the rest of his career, first in Germany until 1938 and thereafter at Hebrew University in Jerusalem.

His initial book-length existentialist foray into the human situation of encounters was *I and Thou* in 1923. This slim volume on the dialogic principle (*das dialogische Prinzip*) spoke volumes to such fields as education, philosophy, anthropology, psychology, and religion.[42] The dialogic principle views human existence as a series of encounters in which verbal, and more often nonverbal, communication fosters relationships.

The dialogic principle entails two primary relationships between the self and others, regardless if the others are human, animate, or inanimate.[43] The first is I–Thou (*Ich–Du*), a relationship of full mutuality, wherein attention and care are reciprocated and authenticity is realized and not idealized.

> The relation to the You [Thou] is unmediated. Nothing conceptual intervenes between I and You, no prior knowledge and no imagination; and memory itself is changed as it plunges from particularity into wholeness. No purpose intervenes between I and You, no greed and no anticipation; and longing itself is changed as it plunges from the dream into appearance. Every means is an obstacle. Only where all means have disintegrated encounters occur.[44]

Because the I–Thou relation countenances no intellection, it can be imagined no more than it can be legislated beforehand. For Buber, this intense, fully encompassing moment of relation requires neither content nor command but only sincere presence.[45] This therefore leads him to resist Rosenzweig's insistence (in "The Builders") that revelation's content was command that became legislation. In his June 24, 1924, letter to Rosenzweig, Buber explains: "I do not believe that revelation is ever a formulation of law. It is only through man in his self-contradiction that revelation becomes legislation."[46] Indeed, if revelation had content, it would be only that which he, the individual recipient, discerns.[47]

The other primary relation is I–It (*Ich–Es*). Whereas I–Thou is spontaneous and reciprocal mutuality, this relation is more plodding and lopsided insofar as it is more intellectual and instrumental. Here the self cogitates: it conceives itself in relation. Self-consciousness emerges to the degree that the object of relation is conceptualized. The very process of conceiving objects orders the world, that is, it manipulates the world and thus uses it for the self's purposes. Because this kind of relation is conceived, literally and phenomenologically, it is bounded and can be directed. Being thought beforehand, the I–It relation can be pre-scribed: law is conceivable here.[48]

Human relations fluctuate between these two primary modes of relating. For the most part human relations function according to I–It. This is readily visible in the classroom, where students use the teacher as a source of knowledge and a goad toward wisdom.[49] The transfer of data and skills would not occur were students and teacher to relate according to the intensity and intimacy of I–Thou. Throughout every aspect of every society, humans treat each other as tools to achieve ends; this is necessary for civilization. Yet this is not the totality of human interaction; if it were, humankind would not be human. Some relationships, Buber asserts, can transform into I–Thou relations wherein the parties thereto rid themselves of preconceived notions and goals and *just are*. Such moments of raw meeting between concrete others are rare and fleeting; indeed, nearly every I–Thou relation reverts back to I–It at some point.[50]

The one exception to this pattern is the relation between humankind and God.[51] Buber critiques Cohen's God-idea for being dangerously heady. Instead of relying (solely) on ideas and words to bespeak and foster this human-divine relation, it would be better to be silent, as God's incomprehensibility is better experienced than thought.[52] Unmediated by mere human thought, this eternal I–Thou relation now, in this very moment, enables one to receive revelation's presence, through which meaning emerges and is borne into the world via one's actions.[53]

Buber thereby translates revelation as response. "To endure revelation is to endure this moment full of possible decisions, to respond to and to be responsible for every moment."[54] Responsibility presupposes an independent addressor to whom the self is answerable. Every I–Thou encounter is, at base and at most, a moment of revelation wherein the ontic other warrants attention.[55] But the attention and response given to God and those given to a fellow human differ fundamentally. Like Cohen and Rosenzweig, Buber acknowledges the command to love as indispensable.[56] In his essay about Kierkegaard, Buber notes that the biblical command to love God reads, "Love God with all your heart, with all your soul, and with all your might" (Deuteronomy 6:5), and the command to love humans says, "Love your neighbor as one like yourself" (Leviticus 19:18). The neighbor—the one encountered fairly regularly—is to be loved "as I wish it may be shown to me."[57] That this love given to the unique other is to a certain degree self-serving does not revert this I–Thou relationship back to an I–It relation automatically. Rather, this idiosyncratic expression of love expresses both the concrete uniqueness of the loved and the lover. Love among humans thus differs in degree.[58] Love between humans and God, however, is a different kind: it is to be done with all one's heart, soul, and might.[59]

This is not to say that Buber's notion of love among humans is as radically individualized as might be found among later scholars, such as Emmanuel Levinas.[60] Rather, Buber speaks in terms of reciprocity and equal responsibility and mutuality—terms that reflect modernist notions of fundamental human similarity and common duty. Yet this does not mean Buber endorses Rosenzweig's systemic project. Human meetings, in Buber's view, are encounters with real others in *Erlebnis*—in concrete experience of lived life, not in the ether of existentialism.[61] When he says, "Man becomes an I through a You," he suggests that it is here, in every concrete encounter, that humans instantiate responsibility and individuate into distinct persons.[62] In this moment of real meeting, "We find the ethical in its purity only there where the person confronts himself with his own potentiality and distinguishes and decides in this confrontation without asking anything other than what is right and what is wrong in this, his own situation."[63] In this way genuine responsibility ultimately devolves into, and is fulfilled by, the ascertaining person embedded in the peculiarities of the particular encounter.[64]

It is precisely this devolution of moral discernment to the individual that is problematic. Buber's is a subjectivist ethics wherein the single person is the best arbiter of what is good and bad in a particular moment—a notion modern Christians celebrate with gusto. And yet for all his antinomianism, Buber cannot conceive of himself as the "ultimate source of moral approval or disapproval of myself."[65] He still understands that human encounters occur within larger historical and cultural contexts that cannot be completely ignored.[66] For it is only in the peculiarities of these larger social contexts that the idiosyncratic needs of a concrete neighbor can actually be met. This situational ethics thus presupposes that what *ought* to be done in this moment *can* be done. Contrary to Cohen's notion that the ethical is ultimately messianic and not fully realizable in this moment, Buber's notion of the ethical is eminently achievable here and now.

The Turn to the Other in Jewish Ethics

In distinct ways, each of these three scholars orients Jewish ethics around the other. For Cohen the other emerges from intellection; in Rosenzweig's view the other is an existential reality distinct from oneself; for Buber the other is a concrete, living human being who cannot be fully fathomed regardless of an encounter's intimacy. It could be said that this turn to the other is these scholars' singular contribution to modern Jewish philosophy, theology, and ethics, as well as to general, secular ethics, including existential, phenomenological, and relational philosophical schools.[67]

Moreover, all agree that the proper relation to this other is best articulated in the biblical command to love one's neighbor. Perhaps, as intimated by the challenges to *au courant* thinking as expressed in Rosenzweig's *Star of Redemption*, this emphasis on love was to counter Christian claims that Christianity was the (or, if it must be said, a) religion of love whereas Judaism was a religion of law (Islam is one too). That love is the proper relation Jews should manifest toward others is not a point to be glossed over, even though modern practical Jewish ethics pays scant attention to it. Rather, as Lenn Goodman remarks in his Gifford Lectures, the command to love one's neighbor is so essential to Judaism's covenantal theology that it is unfathomable to think of Judaism or its ethics without it. As Goodman says, "Just as we should love God for what He [*sic*] is, so should we love human beings for what they are: beings whose subjecthood places them on a plane of moral worth," and "We learn about God through our ethical understanding, and we learn about ethics through our understanding of God."[68] Neighbors, love, theology, and ethics are inextricably intertwined, and Jewish ethics cannot but trace these threads through the knots of modern conundrums.

One of the threads of this turn to the other/neighbor is a turn away from normative law. Though each was steeped in the Judaic textual tradition and knowledgeable of its substantial legal corpus, Cohen, Rosenzweig, and Buber nonetheless viewed that genre with suspicion. The lengthy history of Jewish legal deliberation secured their respect, no doubt, but it failed to garner their commitment—philosophically or personally. They could not fathom meaningful Jewish life or ethics being confined to *halakhah* alone. On the other hand, they could not endorse a Jewish life completely devoid of *halakhah* either. Nor were they willing to say that secular human reason by itself should shape Jewish life and ethics. Instead, both reason *and* revelation, tradition *and* modernity, needed to be accounted for when constructing the foundations and applications of contemporary Jewish ethics. (It should also be noted that each scholar reached this hybrid position through early intellectual journeys well beyond the confines of traditional Jewish learning. Each of these scholars investigated secular philosophy as well as other religious traditions before turning their sights more narrowly to Jewish concerns.)

Their turn from law was not a radical *hiddush*, a novelty in Jewish normative deliberation; it was novel more in its degree than its kind. For throughout the Judaic textual tradition, other normative genres have accompanied law, including *midrash* (interpretation) or *aggadah* (lore), liturgy and, more recently, *responsa* and sermons. The coexistence of these various normative genres reinforces the ongoing and complex interrelationships among them, making it all but impossible to consider one in complete isolation of the others. So the turn from law in Cohen, Rosenzweig, and Buber is less a new way of conceiving and constructing Jewish ethics than it is an honest assessment of what is already extant in the Judaic normative tradition. Their dual turn both to nonlegal sources and experiences for normative insight and to the neighbor as the locus of Jewish ethical concern is at base a clarification of the other: the other is beyond law and self. Modern Jewish ethics continues these scholars' exploration of duties to others—be they Jews or not—and the contours of what substantiates love of neighbors.[69]

Notes

1. Much appreciation to Elliot Dorff and Aaron Gross for comments on earlier drafts. See Socrates' famous proposed dilemma in Plato's *Euthyphro*, 10a. Chief Rabbi Jonathan Sacks contends that Judaism does not countenance this dilemma. See Jonathan Sacks, *To Heal a Fractured World: The Ethics of Responsibility* (New York: Schocken Books, 2005), in particular p. 164.
2. This kind of idealism follows Plato's notion of forms. Gottfried Leibniz, Immanuel Kant, and Georg Hegel brought idealism firmly into the center of German philosophical thought, and it is to them that Cohen is indebted, even as he argues for a more nuanced, religiously sensitive kind of idealism.
3. Cohen speaks regularly of the "concept of God" in chapter 1 of *Religion of Reason*, and throughout the rest of the work. See Hermann Cohen, *Religion of Reason Out of the Sources of Judaism*, Simon Kaplan, trans. (Atlanta: Scholars Press, 1995). See also p. 353.
4. Cohen uses the trope of archetype and correlation to flesh out this complicated relationship. For example: "God is in truth 'beyond me,' for He is the Holy One, the archetype of all human morality. This archetype serves not merely as an exemplar; rather, it represents the ground of all law, and is as such the basis for both morality and natural science." Ibid., p. 58.
5. See Cohen's Introduction to *Religion of Reason*, p. 33. Emphasis in the original. Later on he says, "Holiness is through and through only morality" (ibid., p. 110).

6. Ibid., chap. 13, "The Idea of the Messiah and Mankind." Cohen also comments on messianism in *Reason and Hope: Selections from the Jewish Writings of Hermann Cohen*, Eva Jospe, trans. (Cincinnati: Hebrew Union College Press. 1971), pp. 119–27.
7. See *Religion of Reason* (at note 3 above), pp. 206–7; *Reason and Hope* (at note 6 above), pp. 60ff. In 1908 Cohen summarized his view that ethics cannot be only thought: "The ethical self must be engaged in action." See *Reason and Hope*, p. 218.
8. Sublation is a major theory championed by Hegel. See Cohen's challenge to this notion in chap. 8, "The Discovery of Man as Fellowman," in *Religion of Reason* (at note 3 above). See also the note on p. 15 in his introductory essay there.
9. Ibid., chap. 8, esp. pp. 132–43.
10. Ibid., p. 134. On Levinas, see chap. 16 below.
11. Ibid., p. 119. At least in regard to Jews, this line of reasoning draws from both Baruch Spinoza and Moses Mendelssohn.
12. Ibid., p. 127.
13. Instead of imitating (*Nachahmung*) God, Cohen would rather humans emulate (*Nacheiferung*) the divine. See ibid., p. 160. See also Michael Zank, "The Ethics in Hermann Cohen's Philosophical System," in *Herman Cohen's Ethics*, Robert Gibbs, ed. (Leiden: Brill, 2006), pp. 1–15.
14. Cohen, *Religion of Reason* (at note 3 above), p. 164. See Dana Hollander, "Some Remarks on Love and Law in Herman Cohen's Ethics of the Neighbor," *The Journal of Textual Reasoning* 4/1(November 2005). http://etext.lib.virginia.edu/journals/tr/volume4/TR_04_01_E03.html.
15. Cohen also stresses that the very possibility of atonement (*teshuvah*) presupposes immorality or sin, which, in his ethical monotheistic worldview, is a failure of ethicality. Self-improvement, a primal goal of Judaism and especially of Yom Kippur, is nothing but a turn away from sinfulness and toward greater ethicality, which, in turn, constitutes "the individual as an I" and enables the I to correlate even more with God. See Cohen's discussion of atonement in *Religion of Reason* (at note 3 above), chap. 11, esp. p. 193. See also pp. 20–22. See Steven Kepnes, "Liturgical Ethics in Cohen's Religion of Reason," *The Journal of Textual Reasoning* 5/1(December 2007). http://etext.lib.virginia.edu/journals/tr/volume5/number1/TR05_01_kepnes.html.
16. See his 1907 essay, "Religious Postulates" in *Reason and Hope* (at note 6 above), esp. p. 47.
17. It seems Rosenzweig had been considering Gnostic views that the best way to integrate selfhood and God was through denying the world. Rosenstock-Huessy countered that Christianity was not as anti-worldly as Rosenzweig heretofore held but was very much concerned with the world as evidenced through the long history of Christian redemptive efforts—or neighborly love.
18. Though his essay entitled "The New Thinking" (in Franz Rosenzweig, *Philosophical and Theological Writings*, trans. and ed. by Paul W. Franks and Michael L. Morgan [Indianapolis: Hackett Publishing Company, Inc. pp. 109–39]) functions as a summary and introduction of his *Star of Redemption*, he staunchly refused both to view it as the book's introduction per se and to publish it within the same covers as the book.
19. See Leora Batnitzky, "Dialogue as Judgment, Not Mutual Affirmation: A New Look at Franz Rosenzweig's Dialogical Philosophy," *The Journal of Religion* 79/4 (October 1999), pp. 523ff.
20. Franz Rosenzweig, *Star of Redemption*, Barbara E. Galli, trans. (Madison: Wisconsin University Press, 2005), p. 12. The Introduction of Part One deals Rosenzweig's most scathing blows against generally philosophy, especially Hegel's.

21. Rosenzweig dismantles idealism's prioritization of thinking over all else, especially language, as it erects a kind of idolatry that misdirects human endeavors. See his discussion of Creation in ibid., Part II, Book One, esp. pp. 151–57.
22. In the Introduction to Part III in his *Star of Redemption*, he examines how Christianity and Judaism construe time differently. The primacy of language can be found at the end of the Introduction to Part II, ibid., esp. 118ff.
23. In a 1917 letter to Hermann Cohen, Rosenzweig writes about the importance of language, and grammar in particular, to adult Jewish education. See Franz Rosenzweig, *On Jewish Learning*, Nahum N. Glatzer, ed. (New York: Schocken Books, 1955), pp. 27–54. And it is only after Revelation is situated in the center of time that before and after, time itself, become comprehendible to humankind. See *Star of Redemption*, ibid., pp. 382ff. Such lines of "the new thinking" led Rosenzweig to recognize in Martin Heidegger a philosophical cousin insofar as they both take inspiration from Hermann Cohen. See Peter Eli Gordon, *Rosenzweig and Heidegger: Between Judaism and German Philosophy* (Berkeley: University of California Press, 2005).
24. "The New Thinking" (see note 18 above), p. 117.
25. Part Two in his *Star of Redemption* meditates on these primordial relations.
26. Indeed, not only were they friends, they were collaborators. Together they sought to translate the Hebrew Bible into a German idiom that would speak volumes to the contemporary German, as had Luther centuries before them. Rosenzweig did not survive to complete the project; Buber finished it after World War II. They wrote of their theoretical and methodological challenges in their *Scripture and Translation* (Bloomington: Indiana University Press, 1994).
27. See Buber's letters in Rosenzweig's *On Jewish Learning* (at note 23 above), esp. pp. 109–18.
28. "The Builders" is found in *On Jewish Learning* (at note 23 above), pp. 72–92, and see Rosenzweig's responses to Buber there, pp. 109–18.
29. See Part II, Book Two, in *Star of Redemption* (at note 20 above). See critique by Eugene Borowitz, *Choices in Modern Jewish Thought: A Partisan Guide*, 2nd ed. (West Orange, NJ: Behrman House,1995), pp. 134–42.
30. In the *Star*, Part III, Rosenzweig meditates on this stitching in State Law, Jewish Law, and Islamic Law. See Robert Gibbs, "Gesetz in *The Star of Redemption*," in *Rosenzweig als Leser. Kontextuelle Kommentare zum "Stern der Erlösung"* Max Niemeyer von Martin Brasser, ed. (Tubingen: Verlag Tubinger, 2004), pp. 395–410.
31. See *Star of Redemption* (at note 20 above), p. 192.
32. See "The Builders" (at note 28 above), esp. p. 85. Compare with *Star of Redemption*, (at note 20 above), p. 191, and his letter of June 29, 1924 to Buber, in *On Jewish Learning* (at note 23 above), pp. 112–13.
33. The divine command cannot but obligate revelation's recipient to respond, negatively or positively, a response that itself manifests or expresses what Martin Kavka and Randi Rashkover call theological eros. This eros reflects the tension between existential homelessness in the world and a sense of internal redemption insofar as one acknowledges the revealed divine command. Loving one's neighbor is therefore an externalization or expression of this internal experience. It is a way of treating others "like myself" who have also, in their idiosyncratic ways, experienced the internal divine command. See Martin Kavka and Randi Rashkover, "A Jewish Modified Divine Command Theory," *Journal of Religious Ethics* 32/2 (2004), pp. 387–414.

34. See *Star of Redemption* (at note 20 above), p. 257.
35. Ibid., p. 231.
36. Ibid., p. 230; see also p. 258.
37. Ibid., p. 344; see also pp. 257–59.
38. In 1910 Buber translated into German Chuang Chou's mystical tract, *Chuang Tzu*, which has since been brought into English by Jonathan Herman, *I and Tao: Martin Buber's Encounter with Chuang Tzu*, (Albany: State University of New York, 1996). In scrutinizing Buber's translation's infidelities and curious interpretations, Herman argues that Buber's dialogicalism was already nascent in his early Eastern intellectual adventures.
39. On their Bible project, see note 26 above.
40. See Michael Gardiner, "Alterity and Ethics: A Dialogical Perspective," *Theory, Culture & Society* 13/2 (1996), pp. 121–43.
41. See Buber's 1936 essay, "The Question to the Single One," in his *Between Man and Man*, Ronald G. Smith, trans. (Boston: Beacon Press, 1947), pp 40–82.
42. This book is divided into three parts that examined the two primary relations in regard to the world, people, and the divine—a trinity echoing Cohen's and Rosenzweig's. Buber takes up this theme again in his 1938 essay, "What Is Man?" when he says, "man's threefold living relation is, first, his relation to the world and to things, second, his relation to men—both individuals and to the many—third, his relation to the mystery of being—which is dimly apparent through all this but infinitely transcends it—which the philosopher calls the Absolute and the believer calls God, and which cannot in fact be eliminated from the situation even by a man who rejects both designations." See *Between Man and Man* (at note 41 above), p. 177.
43. Buber demonstrates these relationships even with trees (*I and Thou*, Walter Kaufmann, trans. [New York: Simon & Schuster, 1970]), pp. 57–59; *Meetings*, Maurice Friedman, ed. [La Salle: Open Court Publishing Company], pp. 41–42), with horses (*Meetings*, pp. 26–27), and with cats (*I and Thou*, p. 145). He revisits whether it is truly possible to experience profound I-Thou relations with animals in his post-script, *I and Thou*, pp. 172–73. See Jacques Derrida, "The Animal That Therefore I Am (More to Follow)," *Critical Inquiry* 28/2 (Winter 2002), pp. 369–418.
44. *I and Thou*, pp. 62–63.
45. Ibid., pp. 157–60. See Kenneth Seeskin's discussion of Buber's theonomy in his *Autonomy in Jewish Philosophy* (New York: Cambridge University Press, 2001), pp. 190–200.
46. This letter is found in Rosenzweig's *On Jewish Learning* (at note 23 above), pp. 111–12.
47. See his letters of July 5 and July 13, 1924, to Rosenzweig, in ibid., pp. 114–15. Buber reinforces the individuality of revelation in his theories of covenant, as articulated in *Moses: The Revelation and the Covenant* (Atlantic Highlands, NJ: Humanities Press International, 1988). He explores these themes as well in "The Question to the Single One," (at note 41 above), esp. pp. 68–71.
48. Whereas I–Thou relations are pure present, I–It are rooted in the past. This temporal disjunction allows for cognition (reflection) and categorization—both necessary for human existence. See ibid., pp. 73–75, 82–85, 88.
49. Ibid., p. 178. Compare with *Between Man and Man* (at note 41 above), pp. 99–100.
50. Ibid., p. 68, *ad loc.*
51. See ibid., Part Three.
52. For Buber's critique of Cohen, see his *Eclipse of God* (Atlantic Highlands, NJ: Humanities Press International), pp. 53–62, esp. p. 58. On the incomprehensibility of God and the impossibility of subsuming the divine, see ibid., pp. 88–89.

53. Hence his insistence on deeds rather than law or commandment as being essential to righteousness. See Buber's exchanges with Rosenzweig in *On Jewish Learning* (at note 23 above).
54. This is from Buber's 1936 essay, "The Man of Today and the Jewish Bible," reprinted in *The Martin Buber Reader*, Asher D. Beimann, ed. (New York: Palgrave Macmillan, 2002), p. 54.
55. See *Between Man and Man* (at note 41 above), p. 45.
56. See, for example, *I and Thou* (at note 43 above), p. 66.
57. *Between Man and Man* (at note 41 above), p. 51.
58. On the concreteness of neighbors and persons for such love to come about, see *Eclipse of God* (at note 52 above), p. 58.
59. See Deuteronomy 6:5. This verse and the following five verses constitute the first of the three paragraphs of the *Shema*, the watchword of Jewish liturgy and faith.
60. See, for example, "Martin Buber and Emmanuel Levinas: An Ethical Query," in Maurice Friedman, *Martin Buber: The Life of Dialogue* (London: Routledge. 2002), 4th ed., pp. 337–52. See also *Levinas and Buber: Dialogue and Difference*, Peter Atterton, Matthew Calarco, and Maurice Friedman, eds. (Pittsburgh: Duquesne University Press, 2004).
61. See *Eclipse of God* (at note 52 above), p. 59.
62. *I and Thou* (at note 43 above), p. 80.
63. *Eclipse of God* (at note 52 above), p. 95.
64. *Between Man and Man* (at note 41 above), p. 16. See the chapter, "Ethics" in Friedman, *Martin Buber* (at note 60 above), pp 233–44.
65. *Eclipse of God* (at note 52 above), p. 18. See Borowitz, *Choices in Modern Jewish Thought* (at note 29 above), pp 163–65; Charles Kegley, "Martin Buber's Ethics and the Problem of Norms," *Religious Studies* 5/2(December 1969), pp. 181–94.
66. See, for example, Part Two in *I and Thou* (at note 43 above); *Between Man and Man* (at note 41 above), pp. 63–65.
67. The concept of "the other" is considered "a core concept" to contemporary continental and critical philosophy. See Aaron Gross, "The Other," in *Encyclopedia of Global Religion*, Mark Juergensmeyer and Wade Clark Roof, eds. (Thousand Oaks, CA: Sage, 2011) [forthcoming].
68. Lenn Goodman, *Love Thy Neighbor as Thyself* (New York: Oxford University Press, 2007), pp. 26, ix.
69. See Kenneth Reinhard, "The Ethics of the Neighbor: Universalism, Particularism, Exceptionalism," *The Journal of Textual Reasoning* 4/1(November 2005), http://etext.lib.virginia.edu/journals/tr/volume4/TR_04_01_E01.html.

Suggestions for Further Reading

Gibbs, Robert. (2000) *Why Ethics? Signs of Responsibility*. Princeton, NJ: Princeton University Press.

Munk, Reiner. (1997) "The Self and the Other in Cohen's Ethics and Works on Religion." *Herman Cohen's Philosophy of Religion*, 161–81. Edited by Stéphane Moses and Hartwig Wiedebach. Hildesheim: Georg Olms Verlag.

Rosenzweig, Franz. (1999a) *Franz Rosenzweig's "The New Thinking."* Translated by Alan Udoff and Barbara E. Galli. Syracuse, NY: Syracuse University Press.

Rosenzweig, Franz. (1999b) *Understanding the Sick and the Healthy: A View of World, Man, and God.* Translated by Nahum Glatzer. Cambridge, MA: Harvard University Press.

Rosenzweig, Franz. (2000) *Franz Rosenzweig: Philosophical and Theological Writings,* 109–39. Translated by Paul W. Franks and Michael L. Forman. Indianapolis, IN: Hackett Publishers.

Schwarzschild, Steven S. (1970) "The Personal Messiah." *Arguments and Doctrines: A Reader of Jewish Thinking in the Aftermath of the Holocaust,* 521–37. Edited by Arthur A. Cohen. New York: Harper & Row, Publishers.

Yaffe, Martin D. (1979) "Liturgy and Ethics: Hermann Cohen and Franz Rosenzweig on the Day of Atonement." *The Journal of Religious Ethics.* 7/2 (Fall):215–28.

CHAPTER 8

ETHICAL THEORIES OF MORDECAI KAPLAN AND ABRAHAM JOSHUA HESCHEL

MATTHEW LAGRONE

Introduction

Along with Joseph Soloveitchik, Mordecai Kaplan (1881–1983) and Abraham Joshua Heschel (1907–1972) were and continue to be the most significant and influential theologians in American Jewish religious life. Both Kaplan and Heschel were on the faculty of the Jewish Theological Seminary—the midcentury staff of that institution likely will never be surpassed in its intellectual status and accumulated wisdom—during their most creative years, but it would be difficult to match a pair of thinkers more contrasting than Kaplan and Heschel. Except for their joint support for Zionism, which was political as well as religious, they diverged on almost every serious religious issue: the nature of God; the relationship between God, the world, and the People Israel; and the meaning of fundamental Jewish concepts such as commandment, covenant, and chosenness. They held some things in common, since both nurtured their own disciples and were instrumental in the denominationalization of American Jewish life, and their outsized personalities often obscured their writings.

Kaplan and Heschel's personal relationship was cordial, if not particularly deep. However, in his diaries, Kaplan confided that the Seminary elevated Heschel as a counterbalance to the former's perceived radicalism. He viewed his younger rival as a competitor, but this recognition did not seem to lead to any long-term hostility. Nevertheless, some of their profound differences can be seen in some of Kaplan's private musings. Identifying Heschel properly as a "romantic-mystic,"[1] and personally scorning both romanticism and mysticism, Kaplan described his feelings when Heschel took over teaching responsibility for some of his courses: "With virtually no students in any of those classes in any way troubled by religious doubts, and with all of them blinded by a passionate chauvinism, I was unable to make any headway in my attempt to reorient them into an evolutionary conception of the Jewish religion.... It did not take me long to realize that he [Heschel] would only confirm the students in their obscurantist views."[2] The latter's indifference to biblical criticism in particular galled Kaplan. Kaplan would be relegated to teaching a social science curriculum and removed from teaching courses that directly affect religious belief and choice. In a fit of pique, he accused his junior colleague of "stuff[ing students] with the specious kind of buberized Hasidism" and creating a "yarmulke and minyan kind of piety"[3] at the Seminary.

Kaplan and Heschel did not establish their reputations because of their respective expositions of Jewish ethics. Neither developed a fully dressed theory of ethics, nor are their legacies pegged to any one ethical insight. Kaplan's scholarly strength rested in keen sociological awareness, whereas the phenomenological approach of Heschel resisted any easy systematic presentation of ethical practice. (Kaplan's scholarship illustrated the lived religious life of American Jews, the way they actually chose and acted; Heschel's work, on the other hand, offered a vision of what many American Jews wished to be.) But the absence of a developed ethical theory did not by extension mean that either ignored ethical choices in their writings. This chapter will explore their contributions to Jewish ethics, how they integrated moral intuition and moral reasoning into their theories of Judaism, the role of prophetic morality in their thought, the development of ethical humanity, and, most important, the deep divergence between Kaplan's humanism and Heschel's theocentricity.

Mordecai Kaplan

Both as a work of sociology and a prescriptive manual, if not for its workmanlike prose, Kaplan's *Judaism as a Civilization* (1934) has retained its status as an essential document about the future of American Jewish community. It is a rare work of sociology that has withstood the passage of time and the advance of knowledge. The theoretical approaches of *Judaism as a Civilization* were not novel—a functionalist amalgam of Dewey, Durkheim, James, and Matthew Arnold—but its application to American Jews was unparalleled.

Kaplan maintained that Jews needed a renewal of purpose, because they were losing group cohesion in the libertarian ethos of America. Continuing a tradition that stretches back to the patriarchal narratives, he fretted about the future group existence of Judaism: "It is by no means a foregone conclusion that Judaism in America is destined to live."[4] According to Kaplan, American Jews were manic for assimilation, eager to rid themselves of the burden of their ancient pedigree, with its demands of separation from full participation in general culture. They wished as well to smooth away their European background: Anti-Jewish sentiment was present in the United States, but its slights were not usually political, as they had been in Europe, but social.

He argues that the collapse of collective identity is due to the loss of belief in otherworldly salvation, an option that educated Jews can no longer rationally accept in the face of comparative religion, higher criticism, evolutionary theory, moral experience, and so on. What, then, can replace doctrine that consoled so many generations? For Kaplan, the answer resided in reframing Judaism as a civilization rather than as a supernatural religion or a chosen people. Jews merely constituted one civilization among others, neither superior nor inferior. He explained that "a civilization is not a deliberate creation. It is as spontaneous a growth as any living organism."[5] Civilizations have their own internal dynamic, and while they are of human design, their trajectory is not subject to individual whim but to a rather nebulous collective consciousness. Consequently, for Kaplan, the challenge of being Jewish in the modern world melts away. If Judaism is a civilization, with its own mores, habits, language, and history, then it is a "unique experience, need[ing] no further justification."[6]

This civilization would retain traditional Jewish concepts in repackaged form. Most famously, Kaplan designated *mitzvot* as "folkways"[7]—the rooted practices of a people—in contradistinction to its traditional meaning as divinely revealed commandments and the preeminent source of all later Jewish ethics. In terms of theology, he opposed the formulation of *mitzvah* as "command" because it presumed an active Commander, and because he judged that the tradition had raised the ritual commandments over the moral commandments.[8] In any case, he kicks the bottom out of the entire edifice of traditional Jewish belief: belief in a supernatural revelation was childish, and the Scriptures of Judaism had human fingerprints upon them. If revelation was untrue, then so too was the idea of chosenness ("the aura of divine election has departed"[9]), a doctrine rejected by Kaplan because of its separationist tendency and because he believed that chosenness represented a Jewish claim to superiority, despite the paucity of classical sources that make such a claim. Particularly germane to modern Jewish life, chosenness has a deleterious effect. This doctrine, so central to Jewish self-understanding over the centuries, barred Jews from "complete self-identification with the state.... Competition between the Jewish people and the state for the Jew's active participation in public undertakings is inevitable."[10] Such a line of reasoning has a significant effect on ethical choices and outcomes: the demands of a particular religious community are sacrificed to the demands of citizenship, the internal moral norms of a revealed tradition supplanted by a more universal ethic (this is not, however, the hoary distinction between positive and natural law), and the question of ultimate authority is ceded to the state rather than to divine law. This challenge, and it has certainly challenged almost all morally sensitive Jews in modernity, offers no easy resolution. It remains the great liberal Jewish dilemma.

As a religion of revelation—however we may understand this term—Judaism has constituted its ethics with reference to a divine source. At the beginning of modernity, and especially in some of the more extreme possibilities of Mendelssohn's thought, grounding an ethics whose origins are imputed to a transcendent but providentially involved God increasingly fell into, if not disfavor, at least dubiety. And before the postmodern reclamation of traditional Jewish vocabulary and symbols, often translated into ideas and images remote from their origins, Kaplan, who rejected supernatural revelation and a transcendent divinity, described God not as a personality but as a force, internally felt but not externally present. Although God was removed as an active, independent reality in Kaplan's theology, this removal did not mean that the idea of God was altogether immaterial to his ethical imagination.

In his *The Meaning of God in Modern Jewish Religion*, Kaplan defines God thusly: "God may therefore be defined as the Power that endorses what we believe ought to be, and that guarantees that it will be. Viewed thus, the belief in God is just as indispensable on the ethical level of human thinking as on the authoritative and moral."[11] The consequence is this: we make, and are responsible for, our own moral frameworks; and these frameworks are ex post facto rubber-stamped by God. Kaplan here feathers himself in Spinoza's reversal of the covenantal norm: God did not choose Israel, Israel chose God, and thus the God who commands becomes the God who is commanded. He goes on to argue for a dynamic conception of God, one that sheds the extremes of traditional faith in a commanding Presence and the total rejection of the God-idea as Hermann Cohen once articulated it. Although the God-idea is necessarily abstract because "God" as such does not exist, the idea has practical effects, mainly moral. Faith in God converts into faith in humanity: God is "the totality of all those forces in life that render human life worthwhile. The term "worthwhile," in modern parlance, is the equivalent of the more traditional term, holy."[12] Holiness, of course, refers to something or someone set apart; it touches on the transcendent. "Worthwhile," on the other hand, is thoroughly secular, a Taylorian immanent frame.[13] Kaplan, like Spinoza, reverses the traditional order of the God–human relationship: "To attain this faith in man, in the latent possibilities of his nature, is to accept the kingship of God."[14] We recognize God only through humanity, and God is found, known, and completed only in humanity.

Kaplan is probably the most important "predicate" theologian in Judaism. As a predicate theologian, Kaplan's God happens or occurs naturally in human life and is best described through active verb forms. His God idea allows us to actualize our highest self, encouraging and nurturing our truly good ethical self: "If we recognize the sovereignty of God in the creative and regenerative forces at work in human society, it follows that that society most clearly manifests God's sovereignty in which human personality has the fullest opportunity for self-realization."[15]

"Self-realization" is a key word in the construction of Kaplan's moral universe. Today, of course, this key word has the crass ring of a particular kind of popular psychology that emphasizes fulfillment of the self, often to the exclusion of externally imposed burdens, as the apogee of individual achievement. Kaplan eschewed such simplicities.[16] For him, self-realization is how the individual situates herself within the larger community:

> Such self-realization has nothing in common with egotism or selfishness, for it is based on a recognition that the ego can fulfill itself only by being an efficient unity of a social organism. We can enhance the value of our own life only by bringing into play all our human instincts, including those which have reference to the interests of the society in which we live.[17]

Self-realization, then, ultimately intends social ends. As an optimist about human nature, in contradistinction with the darker view of Heschel, Kaplan maintains that the removal of economic inequalities, poor public policy, and inefficient social planning—that is, a dramatic change in environment through a great deal of "positive liberty"[18]—will bring us closer to the (secular) messianic future. Every evil is in theory capable of correction if we only allowed true human nature to flourish:

> For there is something in the human being that craves giving itself to others in selfless devotion, some objective to live far beyond one's self, whereby one's life becomes integrated into the context of universal human life. The suppression of this phase of human nature is more truly the cause of the sense of frustration and unhappiness than the suppression of one's physical hungers. Hence, if we do not want life to appear fatuous and useless, we must live for some goal which is linked with the good of humanity.[19]

The takeaway is this: the means and ends of individual self-realization match and enhance the means and ends of society, creating the social glue necessary for ethical community. Like a feedback mechanism, he ties all of the foregoing together with his religious vision. Although his religious ideals are, in the end, this-worldly, he argues that Jews "must be governed by our devotion to the Kingdom of God, to a social order in which universal peace, justice and enlightenment make possible the maximum development of every individual's personality."[20] It is the obligation of all Jews to serve humanity in order to create this ideal society. We are forbidden "to delegate to others alive or dead the responsibility for our own ethical decisions."[21]

Ethically, then, we are on our own. Judaism's sacred texts—sacred because the people have declared them so—offer guidance, moral suasion, and general behavioral norms, but we are not bound to them. While Heschel believes that we are very poor judges of our moral choices and, consequently, need the Torah's commandments and their subsequent interpretation by the rabbis, Kaplan's God is a God that affirms the self, and therefore texts can be used or discarded according to a person's innermost moral convictions. Modern Jews must look forward to the future they create together rather than to a shared past, and, in any case, the historical facticity of a shared past is gossamer-thin.

This idea plays out most completely in Kaplan's discussion of royal metaphors during Rosh Hashanah. He writes: "Obedience to a code, no matter how ancient and sanctified it may be, is not enough. This is the clear implication of faith in the kingship of God, when we give to that metaphor the only meaning that it can have in the light of our modern attitude to kingship."[22] In an important passage, he continues:

> The main inference to be drawn from the "sovereignty of God" must henceforth be the duty which that sovereignty imposes upon man to transform the conditions of life so as to make the world liveable physically, socially, and spiritually. This inference is in keeping with that growth of the conception of God which has led to the emphasis upon divine immanence in human life. The tendency is now to view man's initiative and active striving in transforming the conditions under which he lives as the way in which God manifests Himself or becomes sovereign in human life. This more recent conception of God's sovereignty is, in a sense, a return to the mood of earlier prophecy, when the dominant stress was upon righteousness as a means of immediate salvation rather than of salvation at some remote future.[23]

God's sovereignty (*malkhuyot*) is, of course, the controlling image of the New Year. This sovereignty traditionally is imagined as absolute and final, but in Kaplan's hand it is translated from the divine to the human, the supernatural to the natural, the transcendent to the immanent. Kaplan's view here is also remote from the view of Jewish mysticism—which he despised as darkened medievalism—that considers our actions in this world as affecting the world above and vice versa. He was, as Scult's biography gracefully demonstrates, a genuinely religious person, but his worldview, including his ethics, was humanistic. The idea of divine sovereignty, for Kaplan, drives social progress. It is an ethically robust concept, found in the prophets—giving it the highest moral imprimatur—and applicable to the practical desire of modern Jews to repair the world. From the Enlightenment forward, both in America and Europe, the majority of Jews had discarded the long-transmitted assumption that the New Year refers to our standing in literal judgment before a king, where our lives hang in the balance. Rather, Rosh Hashanah is a moment of moral self-examination and self-correction. Discover the problem, find its root causes, develop a solution and implement it. This heavily psychologizing tendency is now dominant in all strands of modern Jewish life. As in the passage below, once an ethical dilemma has been identified, it is possible to mend it:

> But for the modern Jew to whom the conception of Rosh Ha-Shanah as a day of judgment is a poetic figure of speech, the meaning which that figure conveys is that Rosh Ha-Shanah should help us discern in the very suffering that proceeds from our shortcomings the evidence of a divine law which shows us the way to overcome them. Where there is a flaw in a bridge and it breaks under its own weight, the engineer learns to appreciate all the more keenly the law of gravitation upon which he must depend for the security of the bridge he wishes to build.[24]

This passage is remarkable: ethics is presented here as a science, and the gap with Heschel could not be more abysmal. Just as an engineer detects and corrects design flaws prior to the construction of a bridge, so too an ethical actor will find that her afflictions need only consult a "divine law," which is internal and natural, in order to heal herself. This metaphor can be extended beyond an individual's ethical approach to the wider social world.

Finally, and as we will see with Heschel later, Kaplan reflected on the roles of the prophet and the philosopher. Kaplan sided with the prophets, extolling them as upholders of the best of the Jewish ethical tradition. They are "practical revolutionaries," whereas philosophers are "dreamers and creators of Utopias."[25] He praised the particularity of Israel's prods, contrasting it with the ethical ideals of the philosophers, who did not anchor their thought to any one civilization:

> The ethical teacher who promulgates his intuitions and experiences as though they belonged to man or mankind in the abstract, may develop a system of formal but not living ethics. The ethical teachers who left the deepest impress upon mankind were those who came to save their own peoples, not mankind in general. By addressing themselves to their own civilization, their message had a concreteness and dynamic character which compelled attention. This explains why prophets have succeeded where ethical philosophers have failed.[26]

It should be noted that the lionizing of the prophets and prophetic morality in non-Orthodox Jewish discourse had been, at least from the time of Geiger to the mid-twentieth century, to contrast with and consequently diminish the authors of the Pentateuch's legal sections; the former were often framed as universalists, the latter as obscurantists. Kaplan was certainly a religious liberal, but he also criticized classical Reform for abandoning a distinctive Jewish ethical stance. In any case, the prophets are presented by Kaplan as social reformers, seeking to correct social ills by moral persuasion. But the sense of sin, of violating a divine norm by allowing the most vulnerable members of society to suffer most keenly, is absent in his major works. The fiery hand of sin and the sunshine promise of repentance and redemption, however, touch every page of Abraham Joshua Heschel's work.

Abraham Joshua Heschel

As with Kaplan, Heschel's oeuvre lacks a comprehensive ethical theory. But, like Kaplan again, ethical considerations pervade his work. With Heschel, it is difficult to get past the practical ethical action of his life: his social and political activism—vocal opposition to racism and segregation, his pacifism, and his support for Soviet Jewry—threaten to eclipse his writings. His moral example as a man of action rather than a man of thought dominates the public image of him, exclusive of being seen as a representative of the lost culture of East European Jewry.

Despite the popularity of books such as *The Sabbath*, *God in Search of Man*, and *Man Is Not Alone*, perhaps the best place to uncover the core ideas of Heschel's ethical thought is The Prophets. While The Prophets considers all of Israel's messengers, it is not a work of historical criticism, placing, for example, Isaiah in the larger ancient Near Eastern context. Rather it is phenomenological, reflecting on the inner experiences and moral torments of Israel and her prophets. Unlike Kaplan's religious humanism, Heschel centers our ethical worth on the fact that we are created in the image of God: "The basis of the claim of human dignity is the divine image. It was asserted in the *Aggadah* that one should not distinguish between the honor due God and the honor due human beings. Since the Holy and Blessed One cares for human dignity, how much more so should mortals take care."[27] This approach is theocentric and borders on divine command morality (though at quite a distance from someone like Yeshayahu Leibowitz, who argues that morality is a human invention): our moral worth—most important, our right not to be harmed by others—emerges from our similarity to God.[28] The prophets, unlike the philosophers,[29] "did not conceive of the ethos as an autonomous idea, as a sovereign essence, higher in the scale of reality than God Himself, standing above Him like a supreme force. God to them was more than a moral principle or a moral exemplar."[30]

Though we do this fitfully at best, we ought to value what God values: justice and righteousness. According to Heschel, this pair of concepts was "deeply ingrained in the mind of biblical man.... It [was] not an inference, but an a priori of biblical faith, self-evident; not an added attribute to His essence, but given with the very thought of God. It is inherent in His essence and identified with His ways."[31] Clearly rejecting the medieval rationalist insistence that we cannot truly know God's essence but only His attributes, Heschel argues passionately that God's personality is defined by justice and righteousness and that we should seek to identify with His moral qualities rather than aspire only to a frigid, intellectual connection. And for Heschel, revelation is an ongoing process throughout Israel's history, and her prophets deliver, wittingly or not, this continuing moral revelation.

Unlike the rather conventional and certainly earth-bound ethics of Kaplan, Heschel's ethical thought, framed by his discourses on the prophets, are almost apocalyptically extreme. The majority of humanity ignores, whether through indifference or some lesser ethical infraction, the moral rot that surrounds them daily. Heschel writes: "To us a single act of injustice—cheating in business, exploitation of the poor—is slight; to the prophets, a disaster. To us injustice is injurious to the welfare of the people; to the prophets it is a deathblow to existence: to us, an episode; to them, a catastrophe, a threat to the world."[32] For us, acts of injustice are individual, discrete; for the prophet, indicative of a world in decay. It is the charge of the prophet, then, to speak for the voiceless, the powerless, and the fearful. Keenly and intuitively, the prophet in his bones experiences the afflictions of humanity: "Prophecy is the voice that God has lent to the silent agony, a voice to the plundered poor, to the profaned riches of the world. It is a form of living, a crossing point of God and man. God is raging in the prophet's word."[33] Although *The Prophets* contains a great deal of comparative material with prophecy in other religions, it is only in Israel that prophecy takes on a meaning that affects history and transcends Israel itself. Israel alone in the ancient world, according to Heschel, produced opponents of the state, its power and its shibboleth of "might makes right." He suggests that Mesopotamians were moral cowards: "'The command of the palace, like the command of Anu, cannot be altered. The king's word is right; his utterance, like that of a god, cannot be changed!' The prophets repudiated the work as well as the power of man as an object of supreme adoration."[34]

God's providence, His active role in the drama of history, is for the whole world, but His special concern is with this small people. (Contrary to Kaplan, the doctrine of chosenness is viewed warmly by Heschel and manifests itself fully in *God in Search of Man*.) The moral necessity of prophecy is that "God's kingship and man's hope were at stake in Jerusalem. God was alone in the world, unknown or discarded. The countries of the world were full of abominations, violence, falsehood. Here was one land, one people, cherished and chosen for the purpose of transforming the world. This people's failure was most serious."[35] The burden placed on Israel was almost too much to bear, and the prophets usually failed to elevate the people's behavior. But the demand remained: as Israel was God's chosen people, its moral life would be placed under greater scrutiny than that of the other nations of the world.

All of the foregoing ties together two of the most interesting threads about Heschel's ethical thought: in terms of the classical doctrines of Judaism—commandment, covenant, and chosenness—Heschel was in general an arch-traditionalist, but these traditionalist means did not by extension lead to, for want of a better term, "conservative" ends. His politics could loosely be defined as liberal, and he maintained, similar to the classical position in Reform, that Israel's divine mission was to be a moral light to the nations. His thought, like his life, was a rare combination of disparate elements. He argued that the prophets "remind us of the moral state of a people: Few are guilty, but all are responsible."[36] We are not just ourselves, atoms freely floating and unaffected. We come from somewhere, and are products of our environment. Because we emerge out of and are responsible to a particular cultural matrix, he continued, moral failures at the communal level reflect, even if indirectly, on the individual. He writes: "In a community not indifferent to suffering, uncompromisingly impatient with cruelty and falsehood, continually concerned for God and every man, crime would be infrequent rather than common."[37] What we are not supplied with, however, is a mechanism to determine where we are as a community—how does one judge community, and who has the authority to judge? This is part of the problem of joining one's ethical thinking to prophecy. Prophetic discourse is rarely explicit, and telling a true from a false prophet was not always easy. Nevertheless, Heschel's attachment to prophetic morality as the authoritative source of Jewish ethics grounds his perspective more deeply than Kaplan's within both the tradition's sacred literature and its lived reality.

Heschel's ethical thought ultimately is wrapped up in what he sees as the connection between God and humanity. God is actively involved in the world, cares for us, and suffers when we sin. God is, above all, not impartial. This idea, of course, runs contrary to a great tradition of medieval Jewish philosophy that argued for

God's impassivity. But an active God gives moral meaning to history. In a long passage, Heschel continues:

> [T]he central achievement of biblical religion was to remove the veil of anonymity from the workings of history. There are no ultimate laws, no eternal ideas. The Lord alone is ultimate and eternal. The laws are His creation, and the moral ideas are not entities apart from Him; they are His concern. Indeed, the personalization of the moral idea is the indispensable assumption of prophetic theology. Mercy, grace, repentance, forgiveness, all would be impossible if the moral principle were held to be superior to God. To identify God with the moral idea would be contrary to the very meaning of prophetic theology. God is not the mere guardian of the moral order. He is not an intermediary between a transcendental idea of the good and man. The prophet does not think of Him as a being whose function it is to supervise the moral order and to bring about the realization of an autonomous morality.[38]

This text reflects a repudiation both of the theological coolness of Maimonidean ethics and the liberal Jewish insistence that ethics is unconstrained by a direct divine hand (and that ethical actors do best when they are self-governing). God's concern for humanity burns intensely, and Heschel wishes for us to duplicate it: as God practices righteousness, so too should we, and as he despises injustice, so too should we.

One of Heschel's lesser known but finest and most transparent writings was a contribution to a work devoted to Reinhold Niebuhr, who, like Heschel, was a theologian whose reputation transcended his community, a thinker of universal importance. While his essay presumptively acts as a Jewish response to Niebuhr, it is more of a presentation of Heschel's own views, which were quite proximate to Niebuhr's. Writing a few years after the Holocaust, Heschel emphasized that "the present generation, which has witnessed the most unspeakable horrors committed by man and sponsored by an extremely civilized nation, is beginning to realize how monstrous an illusion it was to substitute faith in man for faith in God."[39] Faith in human progress, so prominent in an optimist like Kaplan, is, in Heschel's view, unjustified. Belief in amoral science, in the state and its power, in utilitarian ethics, and in an efficient economic calculus that did not take into account human cost, had replaced faith in the redeeming God. Secularism, as a comprehensive ideology, had won, and the world was chastened for this sin.[40] Ideally, humanity actively helps in the world's redemption from sin, hatred, and terror, but this can be done only through God's guiding hand and the words of His law and His prophets.

The theocentricity of Heschel's ethics is remarkable. Like Niebuhr, he believes that the self is radically free and that reason rarely drives our choices, ethical or otherwise. In this polemic against secularism as a worldview, he insists that human nature is in general evil, unable by itself to determine right and wrong: "If the nature of man were all we had, then surely there would be no hope for us left. But we also have the word of God, the commandment, the *mitzvah*."[41] Jewish ethical life turns on commitment to commandment. Although, as Nahmanides famously said, one can be a scoundrel while observing the law,[42] the commandments present a bright-line test for good and evil. Heschel maintains that the challenge is not distinguishing between good and evil, but "His commandment to love good and hate evil. The central issue is not the sinfulness but the obligations of man.... Our tradition does not believe that good deeds alone will redeem history; it is the obedience to God that will make us worthy of being redeemed by God."[43] Good and evil are theological, not humanly created categories, and thus it is the charge of the Jew to adjust her ethical perspective and ethical choices to the mitzvot rather than to transform them into humanistic "folkways."

Conclusion

Steven Katz contends that Kaplan "was a near total failure as a philosopher,"[44] and I believe that assessment is accurate. He was not a first-rate thinker, and he was never considered even in his time an important philosopher, but rather a public intellectual with an acute, almost intuitive, sociological sense of the trajectory of American Jewish life. Still, Katz's point is germane to this chapter. Kaplan's sense of evil is impoverished: evil is a social phenomenon capable of correction once we get the incentives right, or alter the environmental conditions that allow poverty, for instance, to flourish, or align public policy more efficiently and more proximately with the needs of society. His ethical thought seems to work at changing voting patterns rather than at the level of hearts and minds. The question for Kaplan is not, why is there evil, but rather, what can be done about it and how can we nurture human nature to make better choices? Certainly social evil haunts all societies, but the reality of evil, whether at a communal or a personal level, does not detain Kaplan. Even his biographer admits that Kaplan did not have a fully fleshed-out theory of evil, and this point is relevant because it affects his ethical thought. As Katz notes, "Some standard, involving some theory, is required for moral action and moral activism, and here the Kaplanian values of 'self-fulfillment,' 'human happiness,' and 'realizing our potential' are insufficient bases for authentic ethical choices."[45]

Expanding on Katz's comment, and particularly relevant in a book on Jewish ethics, Kaplan's sense of personal sin is feeble, reduced to easy psychologizing, and morally colorless: "Repentance is part of the normal functioning of our personality in its efforts at progressive self-realization."[46] Through no fault of his own, Kaplan's kind of reflection on repentance as self-awareness has been diluted to the level of daytime talk shows and the fodder of so many Rosh Hashanah sermons.[47]

The main problem with Heschel's ethical thought lies in the opposite direction of Kaplan's. Rather than not being sufficiently deep, his moral intuitions can be suffocating: all is evil, the world colored in moral stain. The combination of

Heschel's pessimism and mysticism can be dangerous: it can lead to hatred of the world and, by extension, of its Creator. Heschel by and large avoids this tendency, but he could have used some of Kaplan's optimism and sense of progress: the idea of *yeridat ha-dorot*, that the generations from Sinai are always in decline, does not hold up well under investigation. But Heschel's vision did contain moments of redemption, especially *The Sabbath*, with its insistence on the beauty of time and our participation in it.

Kaplan and Heschel marked out two distinct ethical frameworks. On most social issues—from racism to Zionism—their views were similar, but how they arrived at their conclusions was completely divergent. Kaplan's theological naturalism and religious humanism left no role for traditional Jewish beliefs, but he recast Judaism as a civilization and shaped his ethical thought by drawing on the great functionalists of the early twentieth century. Heschel excluded humanistic considerations in ethics: we do not know good and evil independently of divine revelation.

What, then, of Kaplan and Heschel's ethical thought for the future of Jews and Judaism? What endures? In non-Orthodox Judaism, the legacy of both men has been profound. In Kaplan's case, his prescription for American Judaism has become largely descriptive. Most American Jews—and this designation is limited here to those for whom Jewish identity is relevant if not always paramount—live their Judaism in a Kaplanian manner. Judaism is not a religion, and it is certainly not supernatural, but rather an ethnic impulse, a gathering of nostalgia, self-selected familial and group history, with an emphasis on measured difference from the dominant culture (though today there is no dominant culture as such). So, Kaplan's larger vision has been borne out, but his ethical ideas offer no advance in our understanding of how Jews ought to think, believe, feel, and act. His moral thinking was conventional, lacking both depth and definition. It might help inform public policy, but it does not provide a meaningful path forward.

Heschel's ethics, on the other hand, appear more promising for non-Orthodox Jews. His life and his choices match well with the liberalism of most nontraditionalist American Jews. While the ends are the same, the means diverge. Heschel's theocentricity rattles in the ears of the theologically tone-deaf American Jewish community. His language about the individual's relationship to God, our distance from God through moral sin, the absence of a metaphorical framework regarding God's activity in the world, his contempt for pure secularism, and his claim that humans have value only because we were created in the image of God echoes the discourse of Evangelical Christianity more than it does contemporary Judaism. Unlike most Evangelicals, of course, the conclusions drawn by Heschel line up more proximately with liberal ends. But to accept Heschel's ethical judgments without the theology that underwrites it is to trim it so gratuitously that it simply disappears. His example of moral courage will not disappear, but for most Jews the bottom has already been kicked out of his theological ethics.

Notes

1. Mel Scult. "Kaplan's Heschel: A View from Kaplan Diary," *Conservative Judaism* 54:4 (2010), p. 10.
2. Ibid., pp. 10–11.
3. Ibid., p. 11.
4. Mordecai Kaplan. *Judaism as a Civilization* (New York: Schocken, 1967), p. 81.
5. Ibid., p. 180.
6. Ibid., p. 182.
7. Ibid., p. 431.
8. Ibid., p. 159.
9. Ibid., p. 15.
10. Ibid., p. 23.
11. Mordecai Kaplan. *The Meaning of God in Modern Jewish Religion* (New York: Reconsructionist Press, 1962), pp. 323–24
12. Ibid., p. 133.
13. Charles Taylor, *A Secular Age* (Cambridge, MA: Harvard University Press, 2007), pp. 539ff.
14. Kaplan, *The Meaning of God* (at note 11 above), p. 135.
15. Ibid., pp. 114–15.
16. Sometimes, though, it does appear that he let his inner Ayn Rand loose. For instance: "Every individual must be for himself. A parasitic dependence on others is allowed only to the immature, the insane, the physically handicapped, and those criminals whom society has not the heart to destroy but cannot trust as cooperating members." Ibid., p. 112.
17. Ibid., p. 115
18. See Isaiah Berlin, "Two Concepts of Liberty," in *Four Essays on Liberty* (Oxford: Oxford University Press, 1969).
19. *The Meaning of God* (at note 11 above), pp. 115–16.
20. Ibid., p. 112.
21. Ibid., p. 119.
22. *The Meaning of God* (at note 11 above), p. 119.
23. Ibid., pp. 120–21.
24. Ibid., p. 144.
25. Kaplan, *Judaism as a Civilization* (at note 4 above), p. 462.
26. Ibid.
27. Abraham Joshua Heschel. *Heavenly Torah: As Refracted Through the Generations*, Gordon Tucker, ed. and trans. (New York: Continuum, 2006), p. 787.
28. See Avi Sagi and Daniel Statman's *Religion and Morality*, Batya Stein, trans. (Atlanta: Rodopi, 1995) for a primer on the spectrum of natural law theory and positivism/ divine command theory in Judaism. For a more recent treatment of these themes, see Martin Kavka and Randi Rashkover, "A Jewish Modified Divine Command Theory," *Journal of Religious Ethics* 32/2(June 2004), 387–414.
29. Additionally, the philosophers worked in the "mansions of the mind," and the prophets "in the slums." See Heschel's *The Prophets* (New York: Harper & Row, 1969), p. 3.
30. Ibid., pp, 16–17.
31. Ibid., pp. 199–200.
32. Ibid., p. 4.

33. Ibid., p. 5.
34. Ibid., p. 159.
35. Ibid,, p. 14.
36. Ibid., p. 16.
37. Ibid.
38. Ibid.,p. 217.
39. Heschel, "A Hebrew Evaluation of Reinhold Niebuhr," in *Reinhold Niebuhr: His Religious, Social and Political Thought*, Charles Kegley, ed. (New York: Pilgrim, 1952), p. 398.
40. For an important examination of Heschel's "theoconservatism," see Martin Kavka, "The Meaning of that Hour: Prophecy, Phenomenology, and the Public Sphere in Heschel's Early Writings," in *Religion and Violence in a Secular World: Toward a New Political Theology*, Clayton Crockett, ed. (Charlottesville: University of Virginia Press, 2006), pp. 108–36.
41. Heschel, "A Hebrew Evaluation of Reinhold Niebuhr" (at note 39 above), p. 407.
42. See Nahmanides' comment to Lev. 19:2 in *Commentary on the Torah*, v. 3, C. Chavel, trans. (New York: Shilo Publishing House, 1971–1976).
43. Heschel, "A Hebrew Evaluation of Reinhold Niebuhr" (at note 39 above), p. 407.
44. Steven Katz, "Mordecai Kaplan's Theology and the Problem of Evil," *Jewish Social Studies* 12.2 (2006), p. 116.
45. Ibid., p. 124.
46. Kaplan, *The Meaning of God in Modern Jewish Religion* (at note 11 above), p. 182.
47. See Kathyrn Lofton's excellent *Oprah: Gospel of an Icon* (Berkeley: University of California Press, 2011).

Suggestions for Further Reading

Mordecai Kaplan

Kaplan's Own Works

Judaism as a Civilization. 1934. New York: Reconstructionist Press; repr. New York: Schocken, 1967.

The Meaning of God in Modern Jewish Religion. 1937. New York: Reconstructionist Press; repr. 1962.

The Future of the American Jew. 1948. New York: MacMillan.

Judaism without Supernaturalism. 1958. New York: Reconstructionist Press.

Secondary Literature on Kaplan

Ben-Horin, Meir. 1981. "Defining God: Arnoldian Elements in Kaplan's Theology." *Jewish Social Studies* 43 3/4, pp. 189–214.

Breslauer, Daniel. 1994. *Mordecai Kaplan's Thought in a Post-Modern Age*. Atlanta: Scholars Press.

Breslauer, Daniel. 1994. "Mordecai Kaplan's Approach to Jewish Mysticism." *Journal of Jewish Thought and Philosophy* 4,1 (1994), pp. 39–54.

Gurock, Jeffery, and Jacob J. Schacter. 1997. *A Modern Heretic and a Traditional Community: Mordecai M. Kaplan, Orthodoxy, and American Judaism*. New York: Columbia University Press.

Jewish Social Studies 12.2 (2006). Entire volume devoted to Kaplan.

Novak, David. 1995. "Mordecai Kaplan's Rejection of Election." *Modern Judaism* 15.1, pp. 1–19.
Scult, Mel. 1976. "The Sociologist as Theologian: The Fundamental Assumptions of Mordecai Kaplan's Thought." *Judaism* 25, pp. 345–52.
Scult, Mel. 1993. *Judaism Faces the Twentieth Century: A Biography of Mordecai Kaplan*. Detroit: Wayne State University Press.
Scult, Mel. 2003. "Kaplan's Heschel: A View from the Diaries." *Conservative Judaism* 54.4, pp. 3–14.

Abraham Joshua Heschel:

Heschel's Own Writings

Man Is Not Alone: A Philosophy of Religion. 1951. New York: Jewish Publication Society.
The Sabbath: Its Meaning for Modern Man. 1952. New York: Farrar, Straus and Giroux.
Man's Quest for God. 1954. New York: Scribner.
God in Search of Man: A Philosophy of Judaism. 1956. New York: Harper & Row.
Between God and Man: An Introduction to Judaism. 1959. Fritz Rothschild, ed. New York: Harper.
The Prophets. 1962. Philadelphia: Jewish Publication Society; repr., New York: Harper & Row, 1969.
Heavenly Torah as Refracted through the Generations. 2006. Gordon Tucker, trans. and ed. New York: Continuum.

Secondary Literature on Heschel

Chester, Michael. 2005. *Divine Pathos and Human Being: The Theology of Abraham Joshua Heschel*. Portland, OR: Vallentine Mitchell.
Conservative Judaism (50.2) 1998. Entire issue devoted to Heschel.
Dresner, Samuel. 2002. *Heschel, Hasidism, and Halakha*. New York: Fordham University Press.
Erlewine, Robert. 2009. "Reclaiming the Prophets: Cohen, Heschel, and Crossing the Theocentric/Neo-Humanist Divide." *Journal of Jewish Thought & Philosophy* 17.2, pp. 177–206.
Kaplan, Edward. 1972. *Spiritual Radical: Abraham Joshua Heschel in America, 1907–1972*. New Haven, CT: Yale University Press.
Kavka, Martin. 2006. "The Meaning of That Hour: Prophecy, Phenomenology, and the Public Sphere in the Early Writings of Abraham Joshua Heschel." In *Religion and Violence in a Secular World*. Clayton Crockett, ed. Charlottesville, VA: University of Virginia Press, pp. 108–36.
Magid, Shaul. 2009. "The Role of the Secular in Abraham Joshua Heschel's Theology: (Re)reading Heschel after 9/11." *Modern Judaism* 29.1, pp. 138–60.
Merkle, John. 2009. *Approaching God: The Way of Abraham Joshua Heschel*. Collegeville, MN: Liturgical Press.
Moore, Donald. 1989. *The Human and the Holy: The Spirituality of Abraham Joshua Heschel*. New York: Fordham University Press.
Novak, David. 2009. "The Theopolitics of Abraham Joshua Heschel." *Modern Judaism* 29.1, pp. 106–16.
Sherwin, Byron L. 2006. "The Assimilation of Judaism: Heschel and the 'Category Mistake.'" *Judaism* 55:3–4, pp. 40–50.

CHAPTER 9

ETHICAL THEORIES OF ABRAHAM ISAAC KOOK AND JOSEPH B. SOLOVEITCHIK

LAWRENCE KAPLAN

Some Broad Comparisons of Rabbis Kook and Soloveitchik

Rabbis Abraham Isaac Kook (1865–1935) and Joseph B. Soloveitchik (1903–1993) were two of the most outstanding rabbinic scholars and creative theologians of the twentieth century. Indeed, Kook and Soloveitchik may be unique in their combination of first-rank talmudic scholarship with profound theological and philosophical reflection that sought to come to grips in a thoughtful and serious, if critical, way with the challenges and opportunities posed by modern Western culture. Not surprisingly, they are generally viewed as the two leading exemplars of and spokesmen for Modern Orthodoxy, that stream of Judaism that combines fidelity to the rabbinic tradition with critical openness to and a positive evaluation of Western culture. But beyond their iconic standing in the Modern Orthodox community, their writings are of interest to both Jews and non-Jews who are concerned with the place of religious tradition in the contemporary world.

One might describe Kook and Soloveitchik in contrasting terms. Kook functioned as a communal rabbi, holding several important positions, first in the Diaspora and later in the land of Israel, culminating in his serving as the first Chief

Rabbi of the *Yishuv* in Mandatory Palestine from 1920 until his death in 1935; in contrast, Soloveitchik served for over forty years as Rosh Yeshiva of the Rabbi Isaac Elhanan Theological School of Yeshiva University in New York City. Kook's main field of activity was in the land of Israel, Soloveitchik's in the Diaspora.

Following from this, Kook's thought, while not neglecting to examine the religious experience of the individual, focused primarily on the religious significance of the communal and historical aspects of Jewish peoplehood, in particular on the religious significance of the Jewish national revival in the land of Israel. Soloveitchik's thought, by contrast, while not neglecting to examine the religious significance of the communal and historical aspects of Jewish peoplehood, especially the religious significance of the Jewish national revival in the land of Israel, focused primarily on the religious experience of the individual. Kook had a romantic, lyrical, poetic soul that perceived the harmony pervading all existence and uniting the individual, the nation, the cosmos, and the divine. Soloveitchik was of a more restrained classical temperament, and his thought often explored the tragic, conflicted nature of human existence and the individual's encounter with the divine.

Neither Kook nor Soloveitchik was a systematic thinker. The literary unit favored by Kook was the brief reflection, consisting of a paragraph or at most two or three pages. It is no surprise then that his major work was a mystical journal, in eight notebooks (only published recently in full), written over a period of some fifteen years, from 1904, shortly after he made *'aliyah* [moved to Israel] to become the Chief Rabbi of Jaffa, until 1919, when he returned to Israel after having spent the war years in Europe. Soloveitchik favored the extended essay or short monograph, which provided room to develop a long and often complex argument. The major intellectual influence on Kook was the *Kabbalah*, the Jewish mystical tradition, interestingly enough with a historicized Hegelian inflection; Soloveitchik's early writings, particularly his classic essay *Halakhic Man*, display the influence of neo-Kantianism, and his later writings, especially his popular essay *The Lonely Man of Faith*, the influence of Existentialism, while Maimonides serves throughout his writings as a significant presence, most notably in his essay *And from There You Shall Seek*.

Notwithstanding these dissimilarities between Kook and Soloveitchik, there are a number of important points of convergence between them in their reflections on ethics. That said, it is precisely at these points of convergence that significant divergences come to light, perhaps, at least in part, as a result of the above noted dissimilarities.

Neither Kook nor Soloveitchik made ethics, as such, a subject for sustained philosophical inquiry. Kook's one work apparently devoted to ethics, *Middot ha-Reayah*, is a series of brief reflections on ethical and religious virtues—and vices—such as *ahavah* (love of God and humanity), *emunah* (faith), *yirah* (fear of God), *ga'avah* (pride), *'anavah* (humility), and the like. A recent posthumously published, untitled monograph by Soloveitchik is entitled by its editor, Michael Berger, *The Emergence of Ethical Man*. But the monograph's theme, as indicated by Soloveitchik himself in the work's conclusion, is the "different phases through which the emergent human personality passes," and ethics is only one of those phases, albeit a critical one, insofar as "man acquir[es a] personality by experiencing the ethical norm and getting involved in sympathetic co-existence with the Thou."[1] On the whole, as we shall see, Soloveitchik reflects more on the foundations of ethics than does Kook.

While for both Kook and Soloveitchik, ethics stands at the center of Judaism, for the former, and at times for the latter as well, Judaism's uniqueness is ultimately to be found in a realm that transcends the ethical. As to what that realm is, however, Kook and Soloveitchik differ radically—that is, when Soloveitchik maintains that there *is* such a realm.

Regarding the centrality of ethics to Judaism, which I will understand as referring to social ethics—the normative principles of righteousness, justice, lovingkindness, mercy, and generosity and the many specific commandments they generate—Kook writes:

> The soul of the Jewish people is absolute justice which, in its realization encompasses all actualized ethical virtue.[2]

In a similar vein Soloveitchik states:

> It is well known that Judaism contributed to the world the belief in a supreme God, monotheism... (although sparks of belief in a supreme deity appeared here and there among other religions). Judaism can also pride itself in an additional great contribution to mankind and that is the connection between religious experience and ethical action. Judaism was the first religion to place the service of God at the center of its concern, and it took care to emphasize that the service of God included social ethics. The ritual and cultic service of God must always be accompanied by one's cultivating ethical inter-human relationships.[3]

From this point on, however, their paths diverge. Kook in writing of his mystical yearning for God—"Expanses expanses/ Expanses divine my soul craves"—exclaims that this yearning leads his soul to soar far beyond "Walls of heart and walls of deed/... Morality, logic [and] custom."[4] Or again: "My life's joy consists of a profound faith in God without any natural, logical, conventional, or ethical barriers."[5]

But if, for Kook, at the very heart of Judaism stands the subjective, inner, mystical religious experience, for Soloveitchik—that is, for the Soloveitchik of *Halakhic Mind*—to the contrary, at its heart stands the *objectification* of the subjective religious experience as represented by "concrete deeds, psycho-physical acts, prayer, worship, rituals, cult."[6] Therefore, Soloveitchik maintains in that essay, despite the significance accorded by Judaism to ethics, "religion is typified and described not so much by its ethos as by its ritual and cult," and "the unique character of a particular religion appears only in the ritual," while "the existence of an ethical norm is a common denominator in all religious systems."[7] Thus ethics occupies a middle ground, falling between the subjective inward religious experience, which for Kook comprises the heart of Judaism, and the concrete, objective, cultic, and ritual deed, which for Soloveitchik constitutes the "highest" expression of religion and the divine spirit.

As was indicated, Soloveitchik's position on this matter is not consistent. For both in his essay "On Man's Religious Nature," cited above, and more important, in *Halakhic Man* Soloveitchik eloquently, indeed passionately, argues that ethical behavior takes clear precedence over ritual and the cult.

> Neither ritual decisions nor political leadership constitute the main task of halakhic man.... The actualization of the ideals of justice and righteousness is the pillar of fire which halakhic man follows.... More, through the implementation of the principles of righteousness man fulfills the task of creation imposed upon him: the perfection of the world under the dominion of Halakhah.... The ideal of righteousness is the guiding light of this world view. Halakhic man's most fervent desire is the perfection of the world under the dominion of righteousness and lovingkindness.... The Halakhah is not hermetically enclosed within the confines of the cult sanctuaries, but penetrates into every nook and cranny of life.[8]

We will return later to the ground of Soloveitchik's assertion of the centrality of ethics.

Mystical Unification and Ethics

Both Kook and Soloveitchik unify ethics and ontology and consequently reject the is/ought distinction so prevalent in both secular and religious discussions of ethics. But again, the grounds for their doing so differ. For Kook this unification flows naturally—almost immediately—from his mystical harmonizing perspective. It should not, after all, be surprising that Kook, consistently rejecting all dichotomies—whether between sacred and profane, body and spirit, deed and intent, law and lore, exoteric and esoteric—should also reject any distinction between ethics and ontology.

Thus in one passage he writes:

> Scholastic philosophy tends to regard morality and reason as distinctive dimensions separate from each other, which can be joined only in an instrumental way .... Not so states the Torah. The light of Israel shines with a supernal and equitable strength. It recognizes the all-encompassing and harmonious unity. Morality and reason are not distinctive dimensions that can be joined together only through one [morality] being the means to the attainment of the other [reason], but both constitute one soul, one essence.[9]

Placing the issue in a broader frame, he argues in another passage:

> Morality is a component part of the orders of existence and is rooted in the totality of existence to the extent that existence in its totality requires it. This establishes a significant relationship between the spirit of a person who has reached a high level of moral development and existence in its entirety .... The source of morality is the divine guidance that established existence and directs it towards its unfolding.[10]

Even in passages where Kook, to begin with, appears to view morality as an independent value alongside other values, he always concludes by viewing morality as part of a larger divine whole. Thus in a famous brief essay he speaks of "three basic demands of which our life and the life of all individuals are comprised of: the holy, the nation, and humanity."[11] Each of these three demands has its advocates among the Jewish people.

> Orthodoxy champions the cause of the holy; it speaks with vigor...on behalf of the Torah and commandments [and] religious faith .... The new nationalism battles for all the aspirations of the nationalist tendency.... Liberalism...demands general human enlightenment, culture, morality.and much else.[12]

Kook goes on to say that "we must always seek to reach a healthy state where these forces will act in our lives jointly...in harmonious integration.... Then the holy, the nation, and humanity will cleave together in a practical and spiritual love."[13]

We seem to have here three separate forces that need to join together. At the essay's end, however, Kook significantly modifies or, better, clarifies this contention.

> It is obvious that by having included the holy among the three forces...we referred only to the technical and practical (the institutional) aspect of the holy .... But holiness, in its essence, is a comprehensive ideal...free of all confinement .... When a person or nation walks in the way of justice...peace is sure to reach out to the widest domain of the spiritual life.[14]

Ethics, then, on both an individual and national level is an integral part of the holy, which itself is identified with the one true reality.

It is precisely this intrinsic link between ethics and holiness as a "comprehensive ideal" that is at the root of Kook's famous assertion, often made in the face of strong criticism from those on his ideological right, that the irreligious pioneers in early twentieth-century Palestine were acting in a fundamentally religious manner. They were doing God's work, he maintained, by virtue of their fierce determination to establish a society based on justice and righteousness, despite their irreligiosity and, at times, antireligiosity. For their ethical urge was an expression on one level of a deep-seated religious urge.

It follows that, for Kook, ethics is a given. Both the individual and even more so the Jewish people as a collectivity possess a natural desire for the good, for justice and social harmony, as part of the individual's and the Jewish people's yearning for that true ideal reality.

> We are pervaded by a moral sensibility; we yearn to live a life of purity. Our imagination excites in our hearts a deep desire that conjures up images of the most exalted, the most beautiful, the purest, and the noblest. Our inner desire is that our permanently established will should be pure and holy, that our entire life's goal be clearly focused on life's most exalted ideal.[15]

In a famous passage Kook writes:

> It is forbidden for piety to override man's natural morality, for then it is no longer pure piety. The sign of pure piety is that it elevates man's natural morality to higher levels than it would have attained without it. However, if we could imagine a type of piety that...as a result of its influence on life, diminishes the ability of life to serve as a force for the good and for bringing forth matters useful for the individual and the community, then this piety is an invalid piety.[16]

Kook's ethical views thus reflect a harmonious picture of a harmonious reality, of "the 'world of unity,' where all is woven into one entity."[17] Morality and reason "constitute one essence," ethics is subsumed under holiness as "a comprehensive ideal," while natural morality serves as a base for piety, which piety, in turn, elevates that natural morality.[18]

TRANSCENDENT ETHICS

Soloveitchik, with his more realistic and, we may say, more critical view of man, does not appear to place much credence in this type of natural morality. To be sure, in a recently published letter he refers to "natural feelings of justice and mercy."[19] However, he is suspicious of making these natural feelings the basis of a binding ethical system.

Thus, in *Lonely Man of Faith* he speaks about majestic, creative Adam the first "legislating for himself norms and laws."[20] Soloveitchik raises two problems, however, with such self-legislation. First, he suggests that the motivation for such legislation is not a profound ethical concern for the other or a sense of *hesed*, lovingkindness, but rather the attaining of a dignified existence, though that motivation in itself, while limited, is praiseworthy.[21] More fundamentally, later in the essay he argues that "the worth and validity of the ethical norm, if it is born of the finite creative-social gesture of Adam the first, cannot be upheld. Only the sanctioning by a higher moral will is capable of lending to the norm fixity, permanence, and worth."[22]

In his essay "Catharsis" Soloveitchik, in a rather extreme statement, takes an even more jaundiced view of man "legislating for himself norms and laws":

> The moral law cannot be legislated in ultimate terms by the human mind. Any attempt on the part of scientific research...to replace the moral law engraved by the divine hand on the two stone tables with man-made rules of behavior is illegitimate. Adam tried to legislate the moral norm; he was driven from paradise. In our age modern man is engaged in a similar undertaking, which demonstrates pride and arrogance, and is doomed to failure.[23]

Here man's attempt to "legislate the moral norm" is not just invalid, but reenacts Adam's original sin[24] and "demonstrates pride and arrogance."

In both these passages Soloveitchik is tacitly rejecting Kant's view that reason is the foundation of morality, and more specifically, that it is man's rational will which legislates the moral law in universal and objective terms. Soloveitchik explicitly addresses Kant's view in a much discussed passage in *Halakhic Man*. In the text of the book, Soloveitchik asserts that *halakhic* man "is free and independent in his normative understanding."[25] In a note to the text[26] he clarifies:

> This concept of freedom should not be confused with the principle of ethical autonomy propounded by Kant and his followers. The freedom of the pure will in Kant's teachings refers essentially to the creation of the ethical norm. The freedom of halakhic man refers not to the creation of the law itself, for it was given to him by the Almighty, but to the realization of the norm in the concrete world. The freedom

which is rooted in the creation of the norm has brought chaos and disorder to the world. The freedom of realizing the norm brings holiness to the world.

Soloveitchik here does not set forth any substantive grounds for his rejection of Kant's view.[27] My own—admittedly impressionistic—sense is that Soloveitchik's conception of man's free will is not as metaphysically robust as that of Kant. The human being, for Soloveitchik, is too immersed in time, history, and finitude, to possess the transcendental freedom of will necessary to self-legislate the moral law. Moreover, in this note Soloveitchik refers to Kant's doctrine of "the creation of the ethical norm," while in truth Kant refers to the self-legislation of the moral law. The substitution of creation for legislation introduces a note of subjectivity and perhaps even instability not found in Kant's moral teaching.

On other occasions Soloveitchik takes an approach somewhat similar to that of Saadya Gaon (882–942) with regard to man's attempt to legislate moral norms. In his *Book of Beliefs and Opinions*, Saadya argues that while reason does indeed legislate moral norms, revelation is needed to determine their concrete application.[28] Thus, for example, "although reason considers stealing objectionable, there is nothing in it to inform us how a person acquires property so that it becomes his possession."[29] This role is played by revelation.

Similarly, Soloveitchik argues that even assuming, like Saadya, that man's intellect can legislate general moral norms, such legislation could not provide guidance for problematic, boundary cases. Thus, for example, even if reason can determine that murder is forbidden, it may hesitate in the case described in *Crime and Punishment* regarding Raskolnikov's murder of the old grasping pawnbroker. Or it may hesitate when confronting the issue of abortion.[30] On this point, Soloveitchik follows Saadya's lead.

In other ways, however, Soloveitchik differs from Saadya significantly. For Saadya, the issue is revelation providing concrete, almost conventional, particulars making possible the practical application of moral norms. For Soloveitchik, in contrast, revelation goes beyond reason by providing definitive moral guidance for difficult boundary cases where reason may go astray.

Some scholars have criticized this contention of Soloveitchik by noting that *halakhah* also has to deal with boundary cases, and halakhists often disagree as to whether the standard law does or does not apply in such cases.[31] A good example would be precisely that chosen by Soloveitchik, namely, abortion. Granted that the *halakhah* forbids abortion on demand, but what of abortion, say, of a Tay-Sachs fetus in the second trimester of pregnancy? This, as is well known, is the subject of a rather fierce debate between two eminent twentieth-century *halakhists*, Rabbi Moses Feinstein, who forbids such an abortion, and Rabbi Eliezer Waldenburg, who permits it.[32] Perhaps Soloveitchik might reply that while *halakhah* cannot definitively and noncontroversially resolve all boundary cases, it can provide guidance in more such cases than can be provided by man's unaided intellect. To defend his claim, however, one would have to look more closely at the claims, say, of natural-law Catholic moralists to infer detailed moral norms from reason.

IMITATIO DEI AND CREATION

Soloveitchik's objections to natural morality lead him to ground ethics in "a higher moral will." There are, however, two different ways in which he does this: Imitation of God and direct divine revelation of the moral law.[33]

First he grounds the ethical life in the Maimonidean doctrine of the divine attributes of action and man's duty to imitate those attributes. Two key texts that Soloveitchik often cites are *Laws of Moral Dispositions* 1:5–6 and *Book of Commandments*, Positive Commandment 8.[34]

In *Laws of Moral Dispositions* 1:5 Maimonides states:

> We are commanded to walk in these middle ways, which are the good and right ways. As it is said: "And you shall walk in His ways" (Deut 28:9). Thus they taught in explaining this commandment: Just as He is called gracious, you too should be gracious; just as He is called merciful, you too should be merciful; just as He is called holy, you too should be holy.

In *Book of Commandments*, Positive Commandment 8, Maimonides states:

> We are commanded to imitate Him according to our ability. As it is said: "And you shall walk in His ways" (Deut 28:9) .... They taught in explaining this: Just as He is called gracious, you too should be gracious; just as He is called merciful, you too should be merciful .... This is the text of the *Sifre*. This commandment is repeated in a different fashion: "You shall walk after the Lord your God" (Deut 13:5). They taught in explaining this that its intent is that we should imitate the good deeds and noble virtues used allegorically to describe God, may He be blessed, Who is greatly elevated above all this.

Note that in *Laws of Moral Dispositions* 1:5, Maimonides, basing himself on the *Sifre*, maintains that it is through the acquisition of moral virtues that man imitates God, while in *Book of Commandments*, Positive Commandment 8, Maimonides, basing himself not only on the *Sifre* but on B. *Sotah* 14a, maintains that it is both through the performance of deeds of lovingkindness and the acquisition of moral virtues that man imitates God.

The centrality of *imitatio Dei* accounts for Soloveitchik's assertion, discussed earlier, that ethical behavior takes precedence over ritual and the cult. For while man serves God through the performance of ritual and the cult, it is only through living the ethical life, thorough the performance of deeds of lovingkindness and the acquisition of moral virtues, that man imitates God, that is, becomes God-like.[35]

Of special importance is Soloveitchik's reliance upon the Maimonidean doctrine of the divine attributes of action as presented in the latter's *Guide of the Perplexed* 1:54. Soloveitchik not only grounds the source of ethical life in the cognition of these attributes, but from a perspective very different from that of Kook, breaks down the is/ought distinction.

In an important but somewhat enigmatic passage in *Halakhic Man*, Soloveitchik cites the verse, "The heavens declare the glory of God, and the firmament recites His handiwork" (Ps. 19:2), and comments as follows:

But what is the tale of the heavens if not the proclamation of the norm? What is the recitation of the firmament if not the declaration of the commandment?...The principle of "And you shall walk in His ways" (Deut 28:9) (*imitatio Dei*) flows from halakhic man's normative relationship to the world. We can know God's ways only through studying the cosmos, for it is in the cosmos that there stand revealed before us the glorious and resplendent attributes of action. And, as Maimonides already taught in the *Guide* (1:54), the cognition of the attributes of action is the source of ethical life. In order to implement the ethical ideal we must fix upon the whole of being and cognize it. This cognition is teleological in essence—it aims to reveal the traces of the norm hidden in reality.[36]

What does Soloveitchik mean when he states that "the cognition of the attributes of action...aims to reveal the traces of the norm hidden in reality"? In *Halakhic Man*, Soloveitchik does not elaborate upon this important claim. But his meaning becomes clearer when we turn to his discussion of the attributes of action and *imitatio Dei* in *And from There You Shall Seek*. There he states:

> The idea that the creation of the world is a moral act and that man is obligated to imitate God by devoting himself to acts of creation is the basis of Maimonides' doctrine of the attributes of action....[All these] attributes of divine action whereby God created and governs the world...are ethical actions—characteristics that obligate man to assimilate his acts to them.[37]

And again:

> The source of ethics is God and its revelation is creation. The fact of being is an embodiment of the ethical will....The highest ethical good is perfected being ....Imitation of God, the foundation of Israelite morality, expresses itself in imitation of His creative acts. The entire cosmic process is the revelation of divine ethics.[38]

As Aviezer Ravitzky has noted, we have here the "far-reaching [assertion that] creation is a combination of fact and value: the norm is rooted in being itself, the 'ought' in the 'is.'...Not only are the Creator and the Commander one, but also creation and commandment are unified."[39] Ravitzky goes on to maintain that Soloveitchik *unifies* creation, the ontological law, and commandment, the revealed law. And, in this connection, Ravitzky cites a passage from Soloveitchik that makes this point explicitly. "Judaism declares that there is no difference between the revealed law and the ontological law but by [human] perception. The ontological law, demonstrated in the existence of creation, makes itself known to man as a revealed commandment."[40]

In his unpublished lectures on the *Guide of the Perplexed*, Soloveitchik argues that, looking at matters from man's standpoint, unification of creation and commandment, ontology and moral law, constitutes the ultimate goal of a person's religious development. Basing himself on Maimonides' famous palace parable in *Guide* 3:51, he argues that there are three sequential stages in man's experiential approach to God: (1) Normative-Halakhic; (2) Cosmic-Intellectual; and (3) Mystical-Ecstatic. Particularly relevant for our purposes here is Soloveitchik's conclusion.

> The Normative-Halakhic experience must lead to the Mystical-Ecstatic experience. For both the Normative-Halakhic experience and the Mystical-Ecstatic experience,

unlike the Cosmic-Intellectual experience, are normative experiences, both are experiences of the service of God. The Philosophical experience is a transition between the two. One begins and ends with the normative.

What is the difference between the Normative-Halakhic experience and the Mystical-Ecstatic experience, if both are normative experiences? ... The Normative-Halakhic experience is a categorical imperative imposed by God, while in the Mystical-Ecstatic experience the normative and the intellectual blend; the norm is converted into part of my personality, into a principle of existence.[41]

Soloveitchik considerably broadens the traditional rabbinic and Maimonidean notion of *imitatio* to extend beyond the imitation of the ethical attributes. He goes back to God's creation of the world and argues that man is obligated to imitate that creative act.[42] However, he views that creative act in two ways. At times, following the plain sense of the biblical text as well as the rabbinic and philosophical understanding of creation, he understands creation as creation pure and simple. *Imitatio* consequently means: As God was creative, so you should be creative. At other times, following the Kabbalistic doctrine of *tzimtzum*, namely, that God's first act in creating the world was an act of withdrawal to make room for finitude to exist alongside Him, he understands creation as sacrifice. *Imitatio* here consequently means: As God sacrificed, so you should sacrifice. Indeed, in some essays—namely, *The Lonely Man of Faith*, "Majesty and Humility," and "Catharsis"—he develops what he refers to as a dual morality, a morality of majesty or creativity and a morality of humility or sacrifice.[43] In general, we may say that creativity involves an expansive movement, sacrifice a restrictive one. But exactly what creation and sacrifice on the human level mean appear to vary from essay to essay, and the relation of both concepts to ethics in the interpersonal social sense, therefore, varies as well.

In *Halakhic Man*, in which God's creation of the world serves to obligate man to engage in creation,[44] creation has a dual meaning. First, Soloveitchik establishes the following equation: "the realization of the *halakhah* = contraction = holiness = creation."[45] Obviously, both the realization, that is, performance, of the *halakhah* and holiness subsume ethics, but they are not identical with it. Immediately following this equation, man's obligation to engage in creation is understood as referring first and foremost to self-creation. But while Soloveitchik develops at great length the meaning, significance, and importance of self-creation,[46] he is careful to emphasize that "the whole process of self-creation [must] proceed in an ethical direction."[47] Self-creation, then, is intimately bound up with ethical behavior, but not identical with it.

Taking up an earlier theme, in *The Lonely Man of Faith* majestic Adam the first "engages in creative work trying to imitate his Maker (*imitatio Dei*)."[48] But there, as opposed to *Halakhic Man*, creation refers neither to the performance or realization of the *halakhah* nor to self-creation, but primarily to gaining limited mastery of nature and thereby attaining a dignified existence.[49] To be sure, as was noted earlier, Soloveitchik states that Adam the first "legislates for himself norms and laws," which is another form of creativity, but, as we have seen, this self-legislation on Adam the first's part has exactly the same purpose as his gaining limited control and mastery of nature, namely, attaining a dignified existence.

Similarly, the concept of sacrifice in *The Lonely Man of Faith* and "The Community" differs from that found in "Majesty and Humility" and "Catharsis." In *The Lonely Man of Faith* sacrifice is essentially connected with withdrawal in order to recognize and make room for the other, both human and divine. Limiting ourselves to the human other, sacrifice means that Adam the second must withdraw in order to make room for the other, in order to listen to and hear what the other has to say in his or her otherness, for only thereby are true communication and consequently true community possible.[50] In "The Community," in like manner, the recognition of another's existence is "*eo ipso*, a sacrificial act, since the mere admission that a Thou exists in addition to the I is tantamount to *tzimtzum*, self–limitation and self-contraction."[51] Here the connection between sacrifice and ethics is clear and immediate, for by sacrifice Soloveitchik means withdrawal for the purpose of recognition of the other—and more precisely, of the other's needs.

In "Majesty and Humility" and "Catharsis," however, sacrifice means that "at every level of [one's] total existential experience,"[52] the individual gives up, withdraws from, if only temporarily, whatever he "desires the most."[53] This act of withdrawal, of self-defeat is, for Soloveitchik, the true heroic act. Man, whenever "victory is within reach ... stop[s], turn[s] around, and retreats.'"[54] Defeat here is an intra-psychic category, one essentially unconnected with the presence of an other, whether human or divine. It is an *akedah* experience in the precise sense of the term, as man sacrifices that which is most precious to him only to re-acquire it once again. Given the intra-psychic nature of sacrifice here, its connection with social ethics is at best only indirect. R. Soloveitchik argues that such self-defeat is a heroic, cathartic act, a "divine dialectical discipline,"[55] whereby man purges himself of pride and arrogance and develops a sense of humility and critical self-awareness. Presumably, such refinement of character can have only positive ethical consequences. On the other hand, as we shall see, this concept of sacrifice as retreat and self-defeat lends itself to potentially ethically troubling consequences.[56]

Worthy of note is that only in "The Community"[57] and "Majesty and Humility"[58] is sacrifice grounded in *imitatio*, in God's act of *tzimtzum* in order to create the world. In *The Lonely Man of Faith* and "Catharsis," however, the ethic of sacrifice is grounded not in *imitatio*, but in the direct divine revelation of the moral law. This emerges with particular clarity in *The Lonely Man of Faith*. In a key passage Soloveitchik writes:

> Only when God emerged from the transcendent darkness of He-anonymity to the illumined spaces of community knowability *and charged man with an ethical-moral mission* did Adam *absconditus* and Eve *abscondita*, while revealing themselves to God in prayer and unqualified commitment—also reveal themselves to each other in sympathy and love on the one hand and common action on the other.[59]

The first part of the passage, "Only when God emerged from the transcendent darkness of He-anonymity to the illumined spaces of community," sounds like a variation on the theme of *tzimtzum*, and one can easily imagine Soloveitchik rewriting the passage along the lines of *imitatio*. It might read: "Only when God emerged from the transcendent darkness of He-anonymity to the illumined spaces of community knowability, did Adam *absconditus* and Eve *abscondita*, in imitation of God, emerge from their hiddenness and reveal themselves to each other in sympathy and love on the one hand and common action on the other." Soloveitchik, however, does not take this route, specifically referring to God's charging man with an ethical-moral mission.

Note that this difference between the essays cuts across their differing conceptions of sacrifice. Both "The Community" and *The Lonely Man of Faith* view sacrifice as an interpersonal category, yet the former grounds it in *imitatio*, while the latter grounds it in the direct divine revelation of the moral law. Similarly, both "Majesty and Humility" and "Catharsis," view sacrifice as an intra-psychic category, yet again, the former grounds it in *imitatio* while the latter grounds it in the direct divine revelation of the moral law.

One might suggest that *The Lonely Man of Faith* and "Catharsis," unlike "The Community" and "Majesty and Humility," engage in direct critiques of human legislation of moral norms—*The Lonely Man of Faith* in more moderate terms, "Catharsis" in more extreme ones. Perhaps his leveling of this critique in these essays leads Soloveitchik to emphasize in them the need for direct divine revelation of the moral law. Indeed, it is striking that whereas in *Halakhic Man* Soloveitchik understands the verse "The heavens declare the glory of God" to mean that the heavens proclaim the norm, in *The Lonely Man of Faith* he appears to deny this claim and argues that while "The heavens declare the glory of God," their tale is not a "personal one" and their "message...is at best equivocal," and precisely because of this "God...arranged for the apocalyptic-covenantal meeting with man."[60] Soloveitchik here appears to be cutting the ground from under the cosmic conception of *imitatio* that plays such a critical role in both *Halakhic Man* and *And from There You Shall Seek*.

In a public address in 1972 Soloveitchik grounded his view regarding the importance of submission to the divine moral law in a voluntaristic conception of man.

> The human center is to be understood in volitional, not rational categories. If I am a man, it is because I will, not because I understand. To understand is very important, but it comes after willing. The will blazes and illumines a path for the logos to follow.[61]

Because man is a volitional being, it follows, for Soloveitchik, that he finds fulfillment in submitting his will to the higher divine will. We have traveled very far here from Soloveitchik's view in *Halakhic Man*, where the ethical life founded in man's intellectual understanding of "the glorious and resplendent attributes of action" was attained "through studying the cosmos."

In *The Emergence of Ethical Man* Soloveitchik also speaks of the direct divine revelation of the ethical norm which, indeed, he identifies with the divine command to Adam not to eat of the fruit of the tree of knowledge of good and evil.[62] But in this essay the emphasis is not on sacrifice, self-defeat, and submission, but on the ethical command as a means whereby man begins "to experience his selfhood, his personalistic existence."[63]

In what sense is this command not to eat of the fruit of the tree of knowledge of good and evil ethical? Soloveitchik appears to suggest that one has to view the command in context, namely, Adam's meeting with Eve. Precisely this command, which symbolizes a norm "completely alien to the biological impulse,"[64] enables man to "raise his sex-experience from the natural-factual to the ethical-ideal level. The erotic love of *zakhar–nekevah* [male–female] becomes the ethical love of *ish ve-ishto* [man and his wife] steeped in ethical dynamism and activism."[65] This ethical community between lover and beloved forms, in turn, the basis for the larger ethical community, "contributes to the stirring of a sense of fellowship between human beings."[66]

Were it not for this command, then, the sexual relationship would remain purely biological and inevitably degraded and exploitative, and, by extension, relationships between persons in general would be similarly exploitative. In this connection, it is striking that in "Majesty and Humility" and "Catharsis" as well the sexual relationship acquires broader symbolic significance, and Soloveitchik offers as a prime example of the need for self-defeat, for withdrawal from, if only temporarily, whatever one "desires the most," the "strict *halakhic* rules of [sexual] segregation."[67]

Primacy of *Halakhah*

Soloveitchik's emphasis on submission in so many of his essays leads—in an interesting if disturbing way—to the last important point of convergence between Kook and Soloveitchik. While both, particularly Kook, were often critical of the religious ethos and attitudes of Orthodox Jewry of their day, from both a generally religious and more specifically ethical standpoint, neither, unlike other prominent twentieth-century Orthodox rabbis and scholars such as Rabbis Yehiel Yaakov Weinberg,[68] Eliezer Berkovits,[69] and Emanuel Rackman,[70] leveled any ethical critique of the *halakhah* in its contemporary form. To the contrary, both used their ethical positions to defend contemporary *halakhic* practice.

Thus Soloveitchik's emphasis on the religious and moral significance of sacrifice as self-defeat and renunciation, as an intrapsychic category, allows him to take some—by no means all, perhaps not even most—of the edge off the inability of halakhists to find solutions for situations in which *halakah* imposes hardship on individuals.[71] In a famous speech in 1975,[72] in response to a controversial suggestion regarding broadening the grounds for annulling marriages, Soloveitchik referred to the hardship caused by the law forbidding a *kohen* (a male of priestly descent) to marry a convert. He told the story of a gentile girl who became a convert not for the sake of marriage. Later she met a young Jewish man from an alienated background who had no knowledge of Judaism. She brought him closer to Judaism, and as a result he looked into his family background and discovered that his grandfather was a *kohen*. Soloveitchik notes that his eminent grandfather Rabbi Hayyim Soloveitchik always tried to find leniencies in such situations. However, he goes on to say:

> There are limits even to Reb Hayyim's leniencies. When you reach the boundary line you have to say "I submit to the will of the Almighty." With sadness in my heart, I shared in the suffering of the poor girl. She was instrumental in bringing him back to the fold, and then she had to lose him. She lost him. She walked away.

Soloveitchik describes the young woman's renunciation as heroic. Note, however, that while Soloveitchik defines heroic defeat as man withdrawing *temporarily* from whatever one "desires the most," here the renunciation was permanent. There is also some confusion as to just who is heroically submitting to the divine will: The young woman who gave up her fiancée or the rabbi who was unable to issue a lenient ruling. Finally, there is the danger that the praise of the heroic submission here might overshadow the tragedy of the outcome and the need for halakhists to work even harder to find solutions in such situations.

Kook, as well, invokes his ethical views in order to uphold what appear to be ethically problematic rulings. Thus in 1919–1920, with the establishment of the mandate in Palestine and the organization of the Jewish community there, the question of women's suffrage arose. Many eminent rabbis supported a woman's right to vote, but Kook, to the surprise and consternation of many, opposed it. We cannot enter into his reasons here. What is significant is that, with slight variations, he argues his case in terms of the three overarching forces discussed above: "the Torah and commandments, [and] religious faith"; "the aspirations of the nationalist tendency"; and "general human enlightenment, culture, [and] morality."[73] For Kook, traditional Judaism as embodied in *halakhah* and *aggadah*, nationalism, and modern ethical concerns reasonably discourage supporting women's suffrage; or to put it more precisely, Kook's understanding of these considerations led him to this position.

Even more troubling, Kook defends as ethically ideal all *halakhic* institutions, even those no longer in force. In a letter to a disciple he goes so far as to maintain, making use of Aristotelian arguments regarding slavery, that the institution of the non-Jewish slave was not just a reflection of and concession to premodern social and economic conditions—the view of the vast majority of Modern Orthodox scholars and thinkers—but is based on natural morality and embodies an ethical ideal and consequently will be re-instituted in messianic times![74]

There appears to be a conservative streak in both thinkers' approaches to controversial *halakhic* issues—almost reactionary in the case of Rav Kook[75]—particularly issues dealing with women's place in Judaism,[76] that seems at odds with or perhaps serve as a counterbalance to their often bold theological and ethical reflections as well as their genuine openness to the revolutionary changes of their day, whether it be the renewal of Jewish national life in the land of Israel in the case of Kook, or the integration of the American modern Orthodox community into the surrounding society in the case of Soloveitchik. Perhaps, in classic rabbinic fashion, we should conclude with *ve-tzarikh 'iyyun*: the matter requires further examination.

Notes

1. *The Emergence of Ethical Man*, Michael Berger, ed. (Jersey City, NJ: Ktav, 2005), p. 203.
2. *Lights of Penitence* in *Abraham Isaac Kook*, translation and introduction by Ben-Zion Bokser (New York: Paulist Press, 1978), p. 50. Note the national motif here.
3. "Al Hagdarato ha-Datit shel ha-Adam" ["On Man's Religious Nature"], in *Ha-Adam ve-Olamo* (Jerusalem: Sifriyyat Eliner, 1998), pp. 31–32.
4. "Expanses, Expanses," in *Abraham Isaac Kook* (above, note 2), p. 379.
5. *Shemonah Kevatzim* [*Eight Notebooks*], 2nd ed., Vol. 1 (Jerusalem: n.p., 2004), p. 427.
6. *Halakhic Mind* (New York and London: Seth Press, 1986), pp. 68–69
7. Ibid., pp. 69–70. Cf. *Kuzari* 2:48.
8. *Halakhic Man*, Lawrence Kaplan, trans. (Philadelphia: Jewish Publication Society, 1983), pp. 91, 94.
9. *Shemonah Kevatzim*, Vol. 2 (above, note 5), p. 317.
10. Ibid., Vol.1, p. 40.
11. Ibid., Vol. 1, p. 355.
12. Ibid., Vol.1, pp. 355–56.
13. Ibid., Vol.1, p. 356.
14. Ibid., Vol.1, pp. 356–57.
15. Ibid., Vol.1, p. 424.
16. Ibid., Vol.1, p. 21. To be sure, Kook often speaks of "divine morality." But it seems that the divine morality is the institutionalization of natural morality in the form of commandments. For the continuity between natural and divine morality, see *Kevatzim mi-Ktav Yad Kadsho*, Boaz Ofen, ed. (Jerusalem: Makhon le-Hotzaat Ginzei ha-Reayah, 2006), pp. 119, 145. Note also Kook's striking statement in *Shemonah Kevatzim*, Vol. 1 (above, note 5), p. 128, that the natural morality of the untutored masses is often superior to that of the rabbinically learned elite. (I am indebted to Marc Shapiro for this citation.) Speaking in Kabbalistic terms, we might suggest that, for Kook, Natural Morality = *Shekhinah*; Divine Morality = *Tiferet*; Expanses = *Binah*; and Profound Faith = *Hokhmah*.
17. Ibid., Vol.1, p. 279.
18. Of course, this is on the ideal level. But, as the passage about the three contending groups indicates, on the social-political level there is much conflict and strife.
19. "Letter of August 6, 1964, to S. Z. Shragai," in *Community, Covenant, and Commitment: Selected Letters and Communications*, Nathaniel Helfgot, ed. (Jersey City, NJ: Ktav, 2005), p. 333. Soloveitchik here appears to be adopting the perspective of the Scottish moralists, like Hume and Hutcheson, that only "natural feelings of justice and mercy" and, as he states later in the letter, "psychological instincts and predilections" (pp. 333–34) can be the basis of a natural morality.
20. *The Lonely Man of Faith* (New York: OU Press, 2011), p. 12.
21. Ibid., p. 12.
22. Ibid., p. 66.
23. "Catharsis," *Tradition* (Spring 1978), p. 52.
24. See *Emergence of Ethical Man* (above, note 1). p. 93, where Soloveitchik speaks of "the focal problem of the story of man: to borrow a Christological term for our purposes, the Original Sin."
25. *Halakhic Man* (above note 8), p. 66.
26. Ibid., n. 80, p.153.

27. This has already been noted by Dani Statman and Moshe Sokol in their essays in *Emunah bi-Zemanim Mishtanim*, Avi Sagi, ed. (Jerusalem: Sifriyyat Eliner, 1996). See Statman, "*Hebeitim bi-Tefisato ha-Musarit shel ha-Rav Soloveitchik*" ["Perspectives on Rabbi Soloveitchik's Ethical Views"], pp. 252–53; and Sokol, "'*Al Autonomiyyah ha-Enoshit Nochach ha-El be-Haguto shel ha-Rav Soloveitchik*" ["Human Autonomy in the Presence of God in R. Soloveitchik's Thought"], pp. 410–13.
28. Saadya Gaon, *The Book of Beliefs and Opinion*, Treatise Three: Concerning Commands and Prohibitions, Chapter 3, Samuel Rosenblatt, trans. (New Haven, CT: Yale University Press, 1948), pp. 145–47.
29. Ibid., p. 146.
30. See Soloveitchik's lecture at Yeshiva University on March, 25, 1972 (*Yahrzeit Shiur*), www.heartherav.com.
31. See Statman, "Perspectives on R. Soloveitchik's Ethical Views," *Emunah bi-Zemanim Mishtanim* (above, note 27), p. 253. Much of Statman's article is devoted to a critique of Soloveitchik's attempts to demonstrate the inability of human reason to legislate the moral norm and the consequent need for a revealed ethic.
32. The relevant *responsa* in English translation can be found in *Jewish Law* (*Mishpat Ivri*): *Cases and Materials*, M. Elon, B. Auerbach, D. Chazin, and M. Sykes, eds. (New York: Matthew Bender, 1999), pp. 610–20.
33. Of course, the imitation of God is also a divine commandment; nevertheless, it makes a significant difference if the moral law is revealed through the mediation of imitation of God, particularly if such imitation requires cognition of the cosmos, or if it is revealed directly.
34. See, for example, "*Be-'Inyan Mehikat Ha-Shem*," *Shi'urim le-Zekher Abba Mari, Z"L*, Vol. 2 (Jerusalem: Makhon Yerushalayyim, 1985), pp. 170–73.
35. Cf. Yehezkel Kaufmann, *The History of the Religion of Israel* (in Hebrew), Vols. 6–7 (Tel-Aviv: Mossad Bialik, 1967), pp. 80–81.
36. *Halakhic Man* (above, note 8), p. 64.
37. *And From There You Shall Seek*, Naomi Goldblum, trans. (Jersey City, NJ: Ktav, 2008), p 185, note 16.
38. Ibid., p. 233.
39. Aviezer Ravitzky, "Rabbi Joseph B. Soloveitchik on Human Knowledge: Between Maimonideanism and Neo-Kantian Philosophy," *Modern Judaism* 6:2 (1986), p. 177.
40. *And From There You Shall Seek* (above, note 33), p. 225. Shubert Spero, "The Role of the Ethical," *Aspects of Rabbi Joseph Soloveitchik's Philosophy of \Judaism* (Jersey City, NJ: Ktav, 2009), pp. 69–71, finds it difficult to take these statements of Soloveitchik at face value, arguing that "At least since David Hume philosophy has been cognizant of the gap between...the 'is' and the 'ought'" (p. 70). In truth, however, the existence or nonexistence of this gap is a matter of serious and intense debate in modern philosophy.
41. Soloveitchik delivered lectures on the *Guide* at the Bernard Revel Graduate School in 1950–1951. We have very full notes of these lectures taken by Rabbi Gerald (Yaakov) Homnick, a student in the course. I am currently editing these notes for publication.
42. A leading twentieth-century Haredi theologian, R. Isaac Hutner, however, basing himself on a midrash (*Genesis Rabbah* 9:1) that speaks of the hiddenness of creation, argues that "the obligation of *Imitatio* applies only to the divine attributes that were revealed after the creation of the world, ... but all the divine attributes expressed in the process of creation are not included in the obligation of *Imitatio*." See *Mamarei Pahad Yitzhak*, # 110 (Brooklyn, NY: Gur Aryeh, 2008), pp. 283–84. But

note *Y. Hagigah* 2:1, which asserts that it is permitted to inquire into the six days of creation.
43. For a discussion of this dual morality, see Shalom Carmy, "Pluralism and the Category of the Ethical," *Exploring the Thought of R. Joseph Soloveitchik*, Marc Angel, ed. (Hoboken NJ: Ktav, 1997), pp. 344–46.
44. *Halakhic Man* (above, note 8), pp. 100–101.
45. Ibid., p. 109.
46. Ibid., pp. 109–37.
47. Ibid., p. 137.
48. *Lonely Man of Faith* (above, note 20), p. 11.
49. Ibid., pp. 8–13.
50. See Lawrence Kaplan, "Rav Soloveitchik's *The Lonely Man of Faith* in Contemporary Modern Orthodox Jewish Thought" (in Hebrew), *Rabbi in the New World: The Influence of Rabbi J. B Soloveitchik on Culture, Education, and Jewish Thought*, Avinoam Rosenak and Naftali Rothenberg, eds. (Jerusalem: Magnes Press and Van Leer Institute, 2011), pp. 147–76, where I analyze the concept of sacrifice as found in *Lonely Man of Faith*.
51. "The Community," *Tradition* (Spring 1978), p. 15.
52. "Catharsis" (at note 23 above), p. 44.
53. "Majesty and Humility," *Tradition* (Spring 1978), p. 36.
54. "Catharsis" (at note 23 above), p. 43.
55. Ibid., p. 46.
56. Both "Majesty and Humility" and "Catharsis" were originally delivered as lectures on university campuses under the aegis of the Bnai Brith Hillel Foundation. Could Soloveitchik's college audiences be at least partially responsible for his emphasis in these essays on the need for retreat and self-defeat?
57. "The Community" (at note 51 above), p. 15.
58. "Majesty and Humility" (at note 53 above), pp. 35–36.
59. *Lonely Man of Faith* (above, note 20), pp. 50–51. [Emphasis added: L. K.]
60. Ibid., pp. 35–36. Ravitzky, "Rabbi Joseph B. Soloveitchik on Human Knowledge," (above, note 39), p. 187, n. 109; and Spero, "The Role of the Ethical" (above, note 40), pp. 70–71, have noted this discrepancy between these two passages. Their ways of accounting for it differ from my own, however.
61. Lecture, 1972 (see above, note 30).
62. *The Emergence of Ethical Man* (at note 1 above), pp. 76–88.
63. Ibid., pp. 87–88.
64. Ibid., p. 87. Again, Soloveitchik is tacitly rejecting the Kantian view that man's rational will can self-legislate such a norm.
65. Ibid., pp. 114–15.
66. Ibid., p. 115.
67. "Majesty and Humility" (at note 53 above), pp. 35–37; and "Catharsis" (at note 51 above), pp. 45–46. One should not forget that these two essays were originally delivered as lectures before college audiences. See above, note 56.
68. See Marc Shapiro, "Scholars and Friends: Rabbi Jehiel Jacob Weinberg and Professor Samuel Atlas," *Torah U-Maddda Journal* 7 (1997), pp. 112, 118.
69. See Eliezer Berkovits, *Not in Heaven: The Nature and Function of Halakhah* (Hoboken, NJ: Ktav, 1983); and *Jewish Women in Time and Torah* (Hoboken, NJ, Ktav, 1990).

70. See Emanuel Rackman, *One Man's Judaism* (New York: Gefen, 2000).
71. See David Hartman, "Judaism as an Interpretive Tradition" in *A Heart of Many Rooms: Celebrating the Many Voices within Judaism* (Woodstock, VT: Jewish Lights Publishing, 1999), p. 14.
72. Lecture on June 19 to the Yeshiva University Rabbinic Alumni," cited in Aaron Rakeffet-Rothkoff, *The Rav: The World of Rabbi Joseph Soloveitchik*, Vol. 2 (Hoboken NJ: Ktav, 1999), pp. 35–36.
73. See Rabbi Abraham Isaac Kook, "On the Election of Women" and "On Women's Voting;" and for a dissenting view supporting a woman's right to vote and hold office, Rabbi Ben-Zion Uziel, "Women's Rights in Elections to Public Institutions;" in *Jewish Political Tradition*, Vol. 2 *Membership*, M. Walzer, N. Zohar, and M. Loberbaum, eds. (New Haven, CT: Yale University Press, 2006), pp. 198–202 (Kook) and 202–208 (Uziel).
74. *Iggerot ha-Reayah* (Letters), Vol.1 (Jerusalem: Mossad ha-Rav Kook, 1962), pp. 95–97 (letter of 1904 to R. Moshe Seidel). Kook allows that slavery as practiced in the non-Jewish world was a moral and social evil and deserved to be abolished. I should note, however, that in his very next letter to Seidel (pp. 103–4) Kook raises the possibility that once the ultimate redemption and concomitant reestablishment of the Great Court take place—but not before!—if a particular Torah law does not seem to accord with that generation's moral concepts and needs to be understood in a way different from the standard understanding, the Great Court can decide that this law applied only in limited circumstances that are no longer in force and find a source in the Torah upon which to base that decision. It is unclear why this suggestion cannot not be applied to the issue of slavery. Cf. Chapter 13 of *Li-Nevuchai ha-Dor*, an early work of Rav Kook only recently made available on the internet at http://kavvanah.files.wordpress.com/2010/05/kook-nevuchai.pdf.
75. Of course, as is well known, Kook often issued lenient *halakhic* rulings where an overriding national need seemed to call for it, most famously in his defense of the *heter mekhirah*, the selling of land to a non-Jew during the Sabbatical year to allow Jewish farmers to work it. Moreover, in many *responsa* he opposes in principle being stringent where the law does not require so, such as his responsum regarding the permissibility of sesame seed oil on Passover. At the same time, he could be very restrictive, even where the development of the *yishuv* [the Jewish community in Palestine] might seem to call for a more lenient approach, such as his stringent ruling regarding milking on the Sabbath by a Jew. The matter is very complex. For a full discussion of these rulings and others, with complete references, see Avinoam Rosenak, *The Prophetic Halakhah: R. Kook's Philosophy of Halakhah* [in Hebrew] (Jerusalem: Magnes, 2007), pp. 259–81.
76. Note though that Soloveitchik lent the full weight of his enormous *halakhic* authority to supporting the then revolutionary idea—at least in Orthodox circles—of teaching Talmud to girls and young women, and thus giving them access, along with men, to "the inner halls of *Torah she-beal peh*" [oral Torah]. See "Letter of May 27, 1953, to Rabbi Leonard Rosenfeld," *Community, Covenant, and Commitment* (above, note 19), p. 83. This is in contrast to Kook, who allowed for only minor changes in the traditional patterns of Jewish education for woman, which provided very limited, almost nonexistent, exposure to classical Jewish texts. See Rosenak, *Rav Kook's Philosophy of Halakhah* (above, note 75), pp. 250–52.

Suggestions for Further Reading

Primary Sources

Kook, Abraham Isaac. 1961. *Iggerot ha-Reayah* [*Letters*] Vol.1. Jerusalem: Mossad ha-Rav Kook.

Kook, Abraham Isaac. 1978. *Abraham Isaac Kook: The Lights of Penitence, The Moral Principles, Lights of Holiness, Essays, Letters, and Poems*, Translation and Introduction by Ben- Zion Bokser. New York: Paulist Press.

Kook, Abraham Isaac. 2004. *Shemonah Kevatzim* [*Eight Notebooks*], 2nd ed., 2 Volumes. Jerusalem, n.p.

Kook, Abraham Isaac. 2006. "On the Election of Women" and "On Women's Voting"; *Jewish Political Tradition*, Vol. 2 *Membership*, M. Walzer, N. Zohar, and M. Loberbaum, eds. New Haven, CT: Yale University Press, pp. 198–202.

Soloveitchik, Joseph B. 1978a. "The Community." *Tradition* 17:2, pp. 7–24.

Soloveitchik, Joseph B.1978b. "Majesty and Humility." *Tradition* 17:2, pp. 25–37.

Soloveitchik, Joseph B. 1978c. "Catharsis," *Tradition* 17:2, pp. 38–54.

Soloveitchik, Joseph B. 1983. *Halakhic Man*, translated by Lawrence Kaplan. Philadelphia: Publication Society.

Soloveitchik, Joseph B. 1985. *Shi'urim le-Zekher Abba Mari, Z"L*, Vol. 2. Jerusalem: Makhon Yerushalayyim.

Soloveitchik, Joseph B. 1986. *The Halakhic Mind*. New York and London: Seth Press.

Soloveitchik, Joseph B. 1998. "*Al Hagdarato ha-Datit shel ha-Adam*" ["On Man's Religious Nature"], *Ha-Adam ve-'Olamo*. Jerusalem: Sifriyyat Eliner, pp. 31–32.

Soloveitchik, Joseph B. 2005a. *Community, Covenant, and Commitment: Selected Letters and Communications*, Nathaniel Helfgot, ed. Jersey City, NJ: Ktav.

Soloveitchik, Joseph B. 2005b. *The Emergence of Ethical Man*. Michael Berger, ed. Jersey City, NJ: Ktav.

Soloveitchik, Joseph B. 2008. *And from There You Shall Seek*, translated by Naomi Goldlblum. Jersey City, NJ: Ktav.

Soloveitchik, Joseph B. 2011. *The Lonely Man of Faith*. Reuven Ziegler, ed. New York: OU Press.

Secondary Sources:

Carmy, Shalom. 1997. "Pluralism and the Category of the Ethical," *Exploring the Thought of Rabbi Joseph Soloveitchik*, ed. Marc Angel (Hoboken NJ: Ktav), pp. 325–46.

Hutner, Isaac. 2008. *Mamarei Pahad Yitzhak*. Brooklyn, NY: Gur Aryeh.

Kaplan, Lawrence. 2011. "Rav Soloveitchik's *The Lonely Man of Faith* in Contemporary Modern Orthodox Jewish Thought" (in Hebrew), *Rabbi in the New World: The Influence of Rabbi J. B. Soloveitchik on Culture, Education, and Jewish Thought*, Avinoam Rosenak and Naftali Rothenberg, eds. (Jerusalem: Magnes Press and Van Leer Institute), pp. 147–76.

Ravitzky, Aviezer. 1986. "Rabbi Joseph B. Soloveitchik on Human Knowledge: Between Maimonideanism and Neo-Kantian Philosophy," *Modern Judaism* 6:2, pp. 157–88.

Rosenak, Avinoam. 2007. *The Prophetic Halakhah, Rabbi Kook's Philosophy of Halakhah* [in Hebrew]. Jerusalem: Magnes.

Saadya Gaon. 1948. *Book of Beliefs and Opinion*, translated from the Arabic and Hebrew by Samuel Rosenblatt. New Haven, CT: Yale University Press.

Sokol, Moshe. 1996. "'*Al Autonomiyyah ha-Enoshit Nochach ha-El be-Haguto shel ha-Rav Soloveitchik*" ["Human Autonomy in the Presence of God in Rabbi Soloveitchik's Thought"], *Emunah bi-Zemanim Mishtanim*, Avi Sagi, ed. Jerusalem: Sifriyyat Eliner, pp. 403–43.

Spero, Shubert. 2009. "The Role of the Ethical," *Aspects of Rabbi Joseph Soloveitchik's Philosophy of Judaism*. Jersey City, NJ: Ktav, pp. 65–92.

Statman, Dani. 1996. "*Hebeitim bi-Tefisato ha-Musarit shel ha-Rav Soloveitchik*" ["Perspectives on Rabbi Soloveitchik's Ethical Views"], In *Emunah bi-Zemanim Mishtanim*, Avi Sagi, ed. (Merkaz Ya'akov Herzog: Hakibbutz Ha-Dati, 1996), pp. 249–64.

CHAPTER 10

ETHICAL IMPLICATIONS OF THE HOLOCAUST

MICHAEL BERENBAUM

"In their deaths, they commanded us to life."
"Never Again."
"Remember, do not let the world forget!"

In the aftermath of what survivors experienced, they made six profound commitments: they decided (1) to survive; (2) to perpetuate the memory of what happened; (3) to survive *as Jews*; (4) to set the moral bar high such that people are expected to be "upstanders," not bystanders, in the face of evil; (5) to re-create relationships with people of other faiths; and (6) to combat discrimination and genocide. None of these decisions was self-evident, and the determination to re-create life was a dramatic and perhaps unjustified resolve to have faith in the future. They were, as Abraham Joshua Heschel once noted, "optimists against their better judgment."[1] Their decision to reengage Jewish history has reinvigorated the Jewish future.

In addition, the evil perpetrated in the Holocaust has moved professional and governmental bodies (7) to define and demand humane standards for medical research and (8) to learn how to attain both justice and reconciliation after genocidal atrocities. Thus the Holocaust has taught moral lessons not only to Jews, but to society as a whole. In what follows, we shall examine each of these moral lessons.

The Imperative to Survive

Perhaps the survivors' motives were not as exalted as one might imagine; many married out of loneliness and desperation. It is also not surprising that they had children, often quite soon after their liberation. Many women in the camp had feared that the loss of their periods in the camps—which they incorrectly presumed was the result of something that the Nazis put in their food—would make them unable to bear children forever. Having a child meant that there was someone to love and in turn someone who loved you—unconditionally, innocently.

What is more surprising and far less appreciated is that survivors instinctively made a decision to circumcise their newborn sons and also to circumcise those boys who were born during the war years, when the act of circumcision was potentially lethal and nearly impossible. Rabbi Arnold Weider, a Holocaust survivor and a *mohel* [a Jewish ritual circumciser], testified that after the war he and his father went from Displaced Persons Camp to Displaced Persons Camp circumcising the boys.[2] For six long years, the mark of the covenant imperiled all Jewish men. Within months, before their future was either known or secure, and while their circumstances were still precarious though not quite perilous, they dared to make an indelible mark of Jewishness on the flesh of their sons.

Some learned a different lesson from the Holocaust. The parents of Madelyn Albright, Katie Marton,[3] and many others, whose numbers we will never know, learned that being Jewish was potentially lethal, and given conditions in the world and the tenuous nature of their own commitment to that Jewishness, they felt it might just not be worth the risk. So they concealed their identity and assimilated.

Yet for the overwhelming majority of survivors the decision was to re-create life, manifestly Jewish life. And the form that public Jewish life took in the Displaced Persons Camps was primarily Zionism. Yehuda Bauer, a distinguished Israeli historian of the Holocaust and of Zionism, put it simply: "The reason why Holocaust survivors turned to Zionism is not hard to understand. The murder of the European Jews seemed to vindicate the Zionist argument that there was no future for Jews in Europe."[4] After World War I, Jews could imagine that they could find their future by appealing for the protection of minority rights within majority cultures. After World War II such a position was untenable.

Though Israel may not be the answer to the Holocaust, the foundation of the State of Israel is the most manifest Jewish response to the conditions that brought about the Holocaust, an attempt to change the situation of the Jewish people and the world's perception of Jews. It was also a significant consolation for post-World War II Jews.

In addition to a state and a flag, the Jewish people learned from the Holocaust that powerlessness invites victimization.[5] Hence Israel and the American Jewish community have not been apologetic about seeking power. Jews now understand that people must have the means to defend themselves.[6]

Israelis had also learned from the Holocaust to despise the Jews' dependence. They could not rely on the help of others. Dependent Jews were murdered seemingly at will, abandoned by the world, betrayed by Allies and even by neighbors. The clear solution was to become independent, fully capable of determining their destiny.

The narrative of Jewish history was thought to be simple. From Auschwitz to Jerusalem, from homelessness to our own homeland; from borders that were slammed shut to fleeing Jews, to gates that were open to receive all Jews; from powerlessness to *Tzahal*, the Israel Defense Forces, that could defeat armies poised for Israel's destruction, that could reach even into Uganda and Ethiopia to rescue Jews; from dependence to independence; and from vulnerability to security. Those Jews who lived through the first generation of Israel's independence were raised on these expectations. This became their ethical imperative: survival and dignity through independence and strength.

Yet the Jewish narrative is never simple. The Jewish reality is ever more complex.

Israel became independent precisely as the world became interdependent—politically, militarily, and economically—and it is becoming increasingly interdependent. Even an empowered Israel—in possession of nuclear weapons—found itself replicating the dependence of exilic Jews, whose fate was determined by the good will of gentiles and also of Jews of dubious Jewish commitments as intercessors. For 72 hours during the Yom Kippur War the fate of Israel was dependent on the good will of an American president who was pro-Israel yet antisemitic, on an American Secretary of Defense who had converted from Judaism to Lutheranism during his college years, and on an American Secretary of State who described himself in those days as being "of Jewish origin," as President Richard Nixon, Secretary of Defense James Schlesinger, and Secretary of State Henry Kissinger had to decide on the re-supply of arms to Israel, which had run dangerously low. Many have learned—painfully so—that Israel cannot quench the fires of antisemitism, that it can instead fuel its flames. In many ways Israel's power is its weakness, and its weakness is its power. In the battle between the powerful and the powerless, people tend to side with, and believe that justice lies with, the powerless. Jews still imagine themselves as David fighting Goliath, but others now see Jews and Israel itself as Goliath. And this perception has only grown as power in the last part of the twentieth and first part of the twenty-first century became primarily located in the management of information and the education of the population. And in this, Israel—and the Jewish people generally—is a superpower and growing stronger.

Yet power has not alleviated the Jewish sense of vulnerability. As of this writing, Israel portrays itself and is portrayed by its most ardent supporters as facing three existential threats to its own existence: a nuclearized Iran, the establishment of a Palestinian State, and its own delegitimization. The passage of generations and the amassing of significant political, military, cultural, and economic power have not allowed large segments of the Jewish people to shed the self-perception of victimization.

If the amassing of power is morally necessary to deter victimization, the use of power is not ethically neutral. If the Holocaust teaches us anything, it is that the unrestrained use of power is morally dangerous. Professors Hammer and Kasher, in this volume, will deal with political ethics in Israel and Jewish military ethics, respectively; suffice it to say that power imposes responsibility, and the moral use of such power, especially when there is considerable imbalance between the power one possesses and the relative powerlessness of one's adversary, is problematic.

THE IMPERATIVE TO REMEMBER

There is a second significant long-term response by Holocaust survivors. Under the leadership of survivors, the Shoah has been moved into the forefront of contemporary political and ethical consciousness. It has become the negative absolute, a cornerstone for consideration of values. In a world beset by ethical relativism, the Holocaust has become the "gold standard" of evil and all too frequently invoked by people who want to call attention to an evil that is being perpetrated.

To function in that way, the Holocaust must be remembered by generations still to come. Toward that end, museums and memorials teaching and commemorating the Holocaust have been created throughout the world. Holocaust remembrance has become a basic part of the Jewish calendar and increasingly a part of the calendars of many nations affected by the Holocaust, including the United States, Germany, Poland, and Great Britain—as well as the United Nations. Because of Holocaust denial and antisemitism, these countries have intensified the emphasis on Holocaust commemoration. The International Task Force on Holocaust Education has led a large-scale effort to teach tolerance, to promote pluralism, to foster respect for human rights and dignity, and to remember the past in order to transform the future.

Testimony has been gathered on an unprecedented scale, in the most contemporary technologies. In addition, many memoirs have been written. Both of these forms will provide living voices of their witness far beyond their lifetimes. Their stories will form cornerstones for films and educational programs for generations.

Holocaust survivors, who were a small minority of the victims, were faced with the question of what to do with the random "accident" of their survival: "Why did I survive?" Over time they found meaning in how they lived their lives in the aftermath, especially how they bore witness and transmitted the legacy. Because they have faced death, many have learned what is most important in life is life itself, love, family, and community. They have found value even in what survivor Gerda Klein called "a boring evening at home."[7] They transformed victimization into witness, dehumanization into a plea to deepen our humanity. And in recent years, especially in response to the passage of time and the occurrence of other genocides, they have expanded what sociologists have termed "the universe of moral obligation" beyond Jews to encompass other victims of genocide.

Holocaust survivors have thus responded to survival in the most biblical of ways possible: by remembering evil and suffering to deepen conscience, by enlarging memory and broadening responsibility. It is thus that the ancient Israelites responded to slavery and the Exodus. It is thus that its survivors responded to the Shoah.

The Imperative to Survive as Jews

Emil Fackenheim

Post-Holocaust Jewish philosophers struggled with the ethical and religious implications of the Holocaust. On Purim preceding the June 1967 war, Emil Fackenheim, the preeminent Canadian-Jewish philosopher, made his most influential statement:

> The Commanding Voice of Auschwitz said: Jews are forbidden to hand Hitler posthumous victories. They are commanded to survive as Jews, lest the Jewish people perish. They are commanded to remember the victims of Auschwitz, lest their memory perish. They are forbidden to despair of man and his world, and to escape into either cynicism or otherworldliness, lest they cooperate in delivering the world over to the forces of Auschwitz. Finally, they are forbidden to despair of the God of Israel, lest Judaism perish. A secularist Jew cannot make himself believe by a mere act of will, nor can he be commanded to do so... And a religious Jew who has stayed with his God may be forced into new, possibly revolutionary relationships with Him. One possibility, however, is wholly unthinkable. A Jew may not respond to Hitler's attempt to destroy Judaism by himself cooperating in its destruction. In ancient times, the unthinkable Jewish sin was idolatry. Today, it is to respond to Hitler by doing his work.[8]

Fackenheim called this the 614th commandment, uttered from the ashes of the symbolic death camp that had become shorthand for the Holocaust and for the Shoah. His use of the term the "Commanding Voice of Auschwitz" was intended to solve a theological problem. How can one speak of God in the aftermath of the Holocaust? Responding to the absence of the Saving God at Auschwitz, he maintained that in the two paradigmatic historical experiences of the Jewish people— the Exodus and Sinai—there were two different manifestations of the Divine, the saving God of the Exodus and the Commanding God of Sinai. Fackenheim could not speak of the Saving God at Auschwitz, but in its ashes he discerned the Commanding Voice.

For Fackenheim and for many Jews of his generation, the central Jewish imperative of the post-Holocaust world is that Hitler cannot win, the Nazis cannot have the final word, which he defines as a fourfold obligation: Survival, Remembrance, Engagement with the World, and Maintaining Judaism even if in a transformed form. Fackenheim never argued that the God of Israel or the world created by God was worthy of the Jewish people's faith, but merely said that the consequences of such loss of faith were so devastating—the self-willed demise of Judaism or cooperation in delivering the world over to the forces of Auschwitz—that he—and the Jewish people—simply could not go there. He backed away from the void that shattered faith in God and creation.[9]

Fackenheim was later not satisfied with this iteration of the theological and ethical implications of the Holocaust, and so he wrote a major work on the post-Holocaust task of the world, *To Mend the World*, in which he argued that the Holocaust was a rupture but not a complete dissolution of Western civilization.[10] Because there was mending in isolated moments within the Holocaust itself, the rupture was not complete. Thus, for Fackenheim the task of the post-Holocaust world is to mend, in Hebrew *Tikkun*.

Israel, for Fackenheim, was the great mending, the great restoration. In his autobiography, which he presents as a series of journeys, the fourth and final journey of his life was from Toronto to Jerusalem. Yet nowhere does he indicate why a commitment to the Jewish State, not only to the right of the Jewish people to such a state, but also of the urgency of the state as a mending for a broken nation and for a broken world, should result in right-wing politics.

Irving Greenberg

Irving Greenberg presented a much more radical view of Jewish theology but a similar view of Jewish ethics after the Holocaust. In an article that still stands as a landmark in Holocaust theology, "Clouds of Fire, Pillar of Smoke," Irving Greenberg established the principle for authenticity in post-Holocaust scholarship: "No statement, theological or otherwise, can be made which cannot be said in the presence of burning children."[11] Thus Greenberg was reluctant to speak aloud of God's mercy or justice but was prepared to create such mercy and justice, what Harold Schulweis termed "predicate theology."[12] He spoke boldly of the theological challenge the Holocaust posed to Jewish and Christian theology, but equally boldly he spoke of the challenge it represented to secular values and to the romance with modernity.

Greenberg argued that the Holocaust and the rise of the State of Israel have initiated the third great era of Jewish history. According to Greenberg, in the biblical era God was the active partner in His Covenant with Israel. Divine intervention included commandment and historical reward. The human role was essentially passive, obedient. The symbol of the covenant, circumcision, was "sealed into Jewish physical existence and thus is experienced in part as involuntary."[13]

In the rabbinic era, the second era, God called the Jews to a new level of covenantal existence. "God had 'constricted' or imposed self-limitation to allow the Jews to take on true partnership in the covenant." Direct revelation ceased, Greenberg argues, "yet even as Divine Presence becomes more hidden, it becomes more present; the widening of ritual contact with the Divine goes hand in hand with the increased hiding." The Divine presence is to be found in Torah study and in deeds of kindness and graciousness; God is not only in the Temple, but in a seemingly secular environment.

In our era, the third era of Jewish existence, the Covenant was shattered in the Holocaust. Following Elie Wiesel and the Yiddish poet Jacob Gladstein, who wrote that "the Torah was given at Sinai and returned at Lublin" [the site of the death camp Majdanek],[14] Greenberg recognized that the Holocaust had altered our perceptions of God and humanity. Greenberg argues that the authority of the covenant was broken in the Holocaust, but the Jewish people—released from its obligations—chose voluntarily to renew the covenant. "We are in the age of the renewal of the covenant. God was no longer in a position to command, but the Jewish people were so in love with the dream of redemption that they volunteered to carry on the mission." Our choice to remain Jews, Greenberg argues, is our response to the covenant with God and the restatement of the response to Sinai: "We will do and we will hear."[15] The ethical task of Jewish existence is to re-create the divine image and the human image defiled during the Holocaust, to respond to death by creating life, and to continue the journey of the Jewish people in history—in short, to bring the redemption.

Greenberg established several ethical imperatives that emerged from the Holocaust: The first is to confront evil, for not to confront it is to repeat it. He applies this maxim both to the religious antagonism of Christianity toward Judaism and to the denial of their complicity in the Holocaust by secular states and institutions—banking, insurance, and industry.

Second, the Holocaust may not be used for triumphalism: "Those Jews who feel no guilt for the Holocaust are also tempted to moral apathy. Religious Jews who use the Holocaust to morally impugn every other religious group but their own are the ones who are tempted thereby into indifference at the Holocaust of others.... Israelis...are tempted to use Israeli strength indiscriminately."[16]

Elie Wiesel

Elie Wiesel, the bard of the Holocaust, continues to occupy a unique role as survivor witness. A Nobel Laureate for peace, his citation reads: "[Through] his own personal experience of total humiliation and of the utter contempt for humanity shown in Hitler's death camps"...and his "practical work in the cause of peace," Wiesel had delivered a powerful message "of peace, atonement, and human dignity." Forty-five years ago, the late Steven Schwarzschild, a scholar not easily given to compliments, spoke of Wiesel as the "de facto high priest of our generation."[17] Leonard Fein was no less laudatory when he called Wiesel "the Conscience Laureate of the Jewish people."

His classic work *Night*, which describes his experience as a boy of fifteen being transported to Auschwitz from Sighet in German-occupied Hungary is now an essential part of the Holocaust cannon. The key to Wiesel's understanding of suffering and response, though, is presented in his most important novel, *The Town Beyond the Wall*. Pedro, an existentialist Spaniard (and one of the very few non-Jewish masters in Wiesel's work), who is the protagonist Michael's mentor, says:

> You frighten me. You want to eliminate suffering by pushing it to its extreme: to madness. To say "I suffer, therefore I am" is to become the enemy of man. What

you must say is "I suffer, therefore you are." Camus wrote somewhere that to protest against a universe of unhappiness, you had to create happiness. That is the arrow pointing the way: it leads to another human being and not via absurdity.[18]

Tentative truths are also represented in Pedro's response to death. "Man may not have the last word, but he has the last cry. That moment marks the birth of art."[19] For Pedro, life is a duel between man and God. Man seeks to create and to build, and God reminds all creation of its finitude. Pedro sees that art may endure but only as a challenge or a question in the face of an all-consuming absurdity.

Michael applies the lessons that Pedro taught him in prison and in the process discovers the possibility of finding meaning in living for another and in helping another. His soliloquy with Menachem—the name means "he who consoles," and he is Michael's young cellmate—is a lesson in living with tentative truths. It is a discovery that the memory of suffering can be used to heal, to reach out to someone else. Wiesel shows that suffering need not tear us apart but can bring us together into a discovery of our common humanity and our common fragility.

Wiesel's entire public career is built on this understanding of suffering and how suffering can be used as a warning, as a lesson, and as a means of healing. Suffering may not make cosmic sense as an integral part of God's justice, but it can be used to help others and to heal others. The answer to absurdity is to create reason; to ugliness, beauty; to death, life.

In his service as a public voice, especially after being awarded the Nobel Prize, he has sought to speak from the Holocaust to the totality of the human experience. "Never again" became for him a double-edged pledge. "Never again" for the Jewish people—from Soviet Jewry to the Israelis—but also "Never again" for other people, from Cambodia to Rwanda to Bosnia to Darfur. He sees a kinship among all suffering people and the obligation to bear witness to suffering.

The Imperative to Be an Upstander, Not a Bystander, in the Face of Evil

The Holocaust has clearly provided us with vivid illustrations of anti-ethical behavior and, with them, new models—perhaps more urgently needed models—of the ethical behavior needed to avoid or respond to evil.

On one side were the rescuers. When the Israeli Parliament, the Knesset, passed legislation creating Yad Vashem, Israel's and the Jewish People's Memorial to the Holocaust, it defined its basic functions to include recognition of the "Righteous Among the Nations." To date, more than 22,000 people have been so honored by Yad Vashem and the State of Israel, people from each of the countries of German occupation or allied with Germany as well as from neutral and Allied countries.

Yad Vashem bestows the title of *"righteous among the nations"* on the rescuers. Elsewhere I have argued that it transforms the behavior of the rescuer into a religious sphere, which often misrepresents the motivation of many rescuers, who were guided not by religious aspirations but by common decency, which they were prepared to exercise even in the most precarious situation. Furthermore, that designation does not allow us to account for other rescuers, including someone of the stature of Oskar Schindler, a Nazi war profiteer, who enjoyed a life of wine, women, and song even as he worked to save those Jews who worked for him. Above all, it provides a misleading model of what is required in order to assist those in need, even those in dire need: the designation indicates that one needs to be genuinely righteous, beyond the level of morality that most people attain, to act nobly.

Yad Vashem has honored non-Jews, but significantly less attention has been devoted to the important efforts of self-help and individual ingenuity of Jews themselves, which enabled some to survive and save others and many more to forestall death. This is a serious omission, for those people too are morally praiseworthy, all the more praiseworthy when conditions make self-help, assisting others, and basic survival difficult.

On the other side were perpetrators and bystanders. The role of the bystander has received considerable attention in recent years. One often hears a quote attributed to Edmund Burke: "All it takes for evil to triumph is for men of good will to do nothing." Elie Wiesel has said: "Indifference is always the friend of the enemy, for it benefits the aggressor—never his victim."[20] Similarly, Yehuda Bauer has listed three commandments as stemming from the Holocaust. In a speech on Holocaust Remembrance Day to the German Bundestag, Bauer said:

> You, your children and your children's children shall never become a perpetrator.
> You, your children, and your children's children shall never, ever allow yourselves to become victims.
> You, your children, and your children's children shall never ever, never, be passive onlookers to mass murder, genocide or (may it never be repeated) a Holocaust-like tragedy.[21]

Elsewhere, he has been more succinct:

> Thou shalt not be a perpetrator;
> Thou shalt not be a victim;
> And above all, thou shalt not be a bystander.

One may quarrel with Bauer's emphasis on the bystander. After all, the perpetrator is far more morally culpable than the bystander, but his emphasis, morally proper or not, focuses attention on the role of the bystander, the enabler of the perpetrators.

Conversely, Holocaust educators and moralists are increasingly focusing on the role of the upstander—that is, those who stood up both within the areas where slaughter was taking place, those who risked their lives and their careers to call attention to what was happening and took steps, however unpopular or far fetched, to rescue. Examples of those who stood up in opposition to the genocide include Jan Karski, a Polish courier who brought word of the fate of the Jews to the West. Randolph Paul, Josiah Dubois, and John Pehle wrote the famous memo "On the Acquiescence of the American Government to the Murder of European Jews" and were thus whistle-blowers risking their careers and implicating the State Department in a cover-up, in lying and misrepresentation, but they created and implemented a concrete program of rescue with the War Refugee Board. These and many other upstanders provide role models for appropriate ethical behavior in response to genocide.[22]

Institutions have also been created as a response to genocide, including Genocide Watch and Jewish World Watch, all insisting that indifference is the silent accomplice to killing. This reaction is probably a direct result of the failure to respond not only personally, but institutionally, during the Holocaust, because of either despair or fear.

The rescue of Soviet Jewry in the 1970s and 1980s is a concrete illustration that Jews learned from the Holocaust that they dare not be passive. The idea that the Jewish community could succeed in rescuing Soviet Jewry from the assimilationist and anti-Judaic, openly antisemitic, throes of Soviet Communism seemed far-fetched, implausible, if not impossible, and for a long period of time such accepted "wisdom" prevented the Jewish community from taking serious action. Over time, the small gestures that American Jewry took gained momentum and spurred a great movement of liberation.

The Imperative to Re-create Relationships with People of Other Faiths

The Holocaust has had a profound impact on Jewish-Christian relations and interreligious ethics for both Christians and Jews. It led to totally new ways of perceiving each other and interacting with each other.

The Roman Catholic Church under Pope John XXIII and Pope John Paul II transformed its teachings regarding Jews. Pope John XXIII initiated Vatican II (1962–1965), which significantly reversed two millennia of Roman Catholic teaching on the Jews. *Nostra Aetate*, a document promulgated by the Council and, as such, the most authoritative voice of the Church, reinterpreted Christian Scripture to broaden responsibility for the crucifixion. It changed Scriptural readings and modified the liturgy for Good Friday so that Jews are portrayed neither as Christ-killers nor as accepting of themselves and their children the responsibility for his death. *Nostra Aetate* recognized the religious legitimacy of continuing Jewish life and thus reversed major anti-Judaic components of Christian teaching. After *Nostra Aetate*, the Church held the sins of all humanity responsible for the death of Jesus, and the Jews were not portrayed as cursed by God for Jesus' murder. Antisemitism was condemned. Perhaps most important, the Church addressed Jews respectfully as the sons of Abraham, bearers of a covenantal tradition. These steps, and the further developments in Vatican documents that followed, completely revolutionized Catholic perceptions of Jews and interactions with them.

Pope John XXIII had come to terms with 1,878 years of Jewish life—the years of Jewish exile from 70 CE to 1948—yet neither he nor his immediate predecessor or successor accepted the renascent State of Israel, the very form of Jewish life since 1948. Pope John Paul II recognized the State of Israel. He visited a synagogue for prayer and treated the rabbi and the congregation of Rome with every religious courtesy. Instead of dividing the world between Christians and Jews, he spoke of the commonality of the religious traditions and he spoke with reverence of the Torah. He spoke out against antisemitism again and again. He visited the sites of Jewish death and acknowledged on numerous occasions the centrality of the Shoah.

In March 2000 Pope John Paul II visited Israel. From the moment he arrived at Ben-Gurion Airport near Tel Aviv to the moment he departed, it was clear to Roman Catholics and Jews, and to the international media, that this was an extraordinary gesture of reconciliation in the shadow not only of two millennia of Christian antisemitism but in the massive shadow of the Holocaust. Even if Pope John Paul II did not say everything that could be said, his bowed head at Yad Vashem and his note of apology that he personally inserted into the Western Wall said more than could be said by words alone. In the Third Millennia, The Pontiff was determined that Roman Catholics act differently, behave differently, and believe differently. An eyewitness to the Holocaust, he had come to make amends. He took all-important steps to make certain that the full authority of the papacy was brought to bear against antisemitism. His theology was quite simple: antisemitism is a sin against God. It is anti-Christian. These are welcome words to every Jew, and one could sense their power by the manner in which the Israelis received Pope John Paul II. Even ultra-Orthodox Rabbis, opposed by conviction to anything ecumenical and raised on the stories transmitted through the generations of confrontations between priests and rabbis, were deeply impressed by the Papal visit to the offices of the Israel's Chief Rabbis.

There are at least two important ethical insights that must be derived from the impact of the guilt of innocent Catholics—since both Popes John XXIII and John Paul II had exemplary records of friendship for Jews during the Holocaust—for what their fellow religionists did and failed to do through the generations and especially during the Holocaust. First, *no religious ethic is acceptable if it demonizes another religion and disparages the right of any religion to hold their faith and worship God as they see fit*. The innocent ones who felt guilty have led contemporary Roman Catholicism to renounce antisemitism and to accept the integrity of the ongoing religious life of Jews. This behavior should serve as a model for Jews and Muslims as well as for other religious leaders as to the ethical requirements of religious doctrine. The tools to reinterpret traditional texts were used by Roman Catholics to shape a new theology of ecumenism that has resulted in perhaps the most important era of Jewish-Catholic relations since the Roman Catholic Church was established.

In a world where religious extremism is present in diverse faiths, this second important ethical insight must be emphasized again and again: *Jews may not celebrate the efforts of Christians to renounce antisemitism without at the same time accepting the collateral obligation to reformulate religious doctrine to eliminate religious demonization of the other within their own tradition.* The same is also true for Jewish behavior regarding Islam, where political tensions fuel such demonization. In contemporary religious discourse, Jewish, Christian, and Moslem, we can each cite example after example of demonization, and even in intradenominational discourse among people of the same faith. Quite often—far too often—headlines are made in Israel and in the United States by a rabbi who proclaims that Jewish teaching permits certain acts of aggression against non-Jews or that the Arabs have the status of Amalek, who should be driven off the earth, as if Jewish teaching should be unmediated by Jewish experience and as if reciprocity of expectations from one community to another is not required when Jews press for compassionate and respectful treatment from other traditions, and as if there are no other means to understand our interreligious obligations.

The Imperative to Combat Discrimination and Genocide

Almost forty years ago my teacher, Richard L. Rubenstein, wrote a slim but important volume, *The Cunning of History: Mass Death and the American Future*.[23] Rubenstein was wrong about several issues in the book, especially about some horrific scenarios for the American future. And yet he was right about so much more. Rubenstein argued that the Holocaust was an expression in the extreme of what is common to the mainstream of Western civilization. In demographics and political bureaucracy, in economics and the treatment of superfluous populations, the Holocaust represented not an aberration but an extreme manifestation of what is present in our society. This is not the occasion to revisit all of Rubenstein's points. I will confine myself to the concept of superfluous population.

Rubenstein highlighted the issue of superfluous populations, those who have no rightful place in the societies in which they live. By choice and by ideology, the Nazis defined the Jews as a superfluous population, those who had no right to live among them and demonized them to the extent that ethnic cleansing, what Daniel Goldhagen termed "eliminationist antisemitism," was insufficient. Annihilation, extermination, eradication became the chosen means of being rid of this superfluous and "cancerous" population.[24] Rubenstein shows that the presence of what are perceived by the majority as superfluous populations is manifest throughout our society. What he did not adequately consider then was the covenant among the generations inherent in the American experience. Those who are productive are responsible for those who are no longer productive, not yet productive, or unable to be productive. Those who are no longer productive are taken care of by Social Security and Medicare, those who are not yet productive are offered the opportunity of an education, and while the amount and the form of assistance to those who cannot work within our society is debatable, the responsibility to provide for them is generally accepted as shared.

Contemporary debates on domestic policy have centered on the issue of superfluous populations, including the aged, the young, the disabled, immigrants, those on welfare, and those caught in the spiral of multigenerational poverty and/or crime. The strains of the current economic crisis in America have placed the issue of superfluous populations into the center of national discourse. Do we reduce the national debt by eliminating support for the elderly, the poor, undocumented immigrants, and children? All these issues are now center stage as the ethics of how to deal with such populations is the central political issue of our time. Is it to be every person for him/herself, or is there a covenant that binds the members of the nation together now and across the generations, that shares the burden with government, and that assumes the responsibility for some equitable distribution that provides for those who cannot provide for themselves? Seen in this light, the strengthening of covenant, as Rubenstein stressed in the second edition of *After Auschwitz*[25] (but not almost two decades earlier when he wrote the first edition of *After Auschwitz: Radical Theology and Contemporary Judaism* and *The Cunning of History*) is essential to combating the ethics that would lead to destruction. Helen Fein would also add that the expansion of the universe of common obligation, those bound within the covenant, is essential.[26]

The Imperative to Legislate Against Genocide

There is no disagreement that a major impact of the Holocaust was the drafting of *A Convention for the Prevention of Crimes of Genocide*, which was adopted by the United Nations on December 9, 1948, and belatedly ratified by the U.S. Senate almost forty years later. Raphael Lemkin first introduced the term "genocide" in 1933 when he submitted a draft proposal to the League of Nations for an international convention on barbaric crimes and vandalism. He had a major hand in drafting the Genocide Convention, which was designed to overcome the claims of Nuremberg defendants that they had violated no law. The Convention specifically defines the various aspects of Nazi genocide as criminal. It prohibits the killing of persons belonging to a specific group (the Final Solution); causing grievous bodily or spiritual harm to members of a group; deliberately enforcing upon the group living conditions that could lead to complete or partial extermination (ghettoization and starvation); enforcing measures to prevent births among the group (sterilization); and forcibly removing children from the group and transferring them to another group (the "Aryanization" of Polish children).

This Convention enunciated new standards of behavior on the international community, standards that more often than not have been violated without consequences, but standards that are reiterated in the aftermath of mass murder. The Nuremberg trials also indicated a standard of responsibility and have been invoked as the model for the trials of war criminals from Rwanda and Bosnia and even, however belatedly, Cambodia.

American presidents from Ford to Obama restated this record of indifference and made the solemn pledge of "Never Again." One powerful example of how the Holocaust forces even U.S. presidents to rise to that standard occurred when President Clinton appeared at the dedication of the U.S. Holocaust Memorial Museum in April 1993. I can verify that his speechwriters were reluctant to repeat the familiar lines against indifference to genocide for fear that the president would be asked the obvious questions about Bosnia. The gathering of European leaders for the dedication of the museum spurred the president into round after round of diplomatic meetings that were described as grappling with the problem of Bosnia. Clearly, a consciousness of the Holocaust—intensified by the dedication of the museum—would not permit indifference to other genocides, or at least the appearance of such indifference.

The failure to bomb Auschwitz lurked in the shadows of the decision regarding the bombing of Kosovo. Surely, one cannot compare the two situations. Precision bombing today is substantially different from what was considered precision bombing more than a half century ago. And the conditions in Kosovo, however bad, did not remotely resemble Auschwitz. Still, the failure to bomb Auschwitz set the stage for responses to the bombing of Kosovo. Without the precedent of Auschwitz, opponents might have said: "There was nothing the Allies could have done. Therefore, not doing anything was justified." It would have provided moral legitimacy for a policy of inaction.

The Holocaust does not always work to prompt action against genocide. Rwanda is but one tragic example. Somalia is another. Regimes killing their own citizens in Libya and Syria are yet another. Still, Samantha Power, a Harvard Professor and now a member of the National Security Council staff in the Obama White House, and scholar of genocide who wrote a Pulitzer-Prize-winning book on it, *A Problem from Hell*,[27] was instrumental in the White House announcement on August 4, 2011, of the creation of an Interagency Atrocities Prevention Board and Corresponding Interagency Review. The opening line of the White House statement begins: "Preventing mass atrocities and genocide is a core national security interest and a core moral responsibility of the United States."

Israel also sees itself as bound to offer a political response to genocide, sometimes actively so, sometimes in a confused manner. The recurring debate over the offer of asylum to genocide victims in Darfur raises the question of whether "never again" is intended for the Jewish people or for all people. And Israel sees its own power and the Israel Defense Forces as a tool preventing genocide and fulfilling the imperative of Never Again. Ehud Barak said it most eloquently and succinctly when he first entered Auschwitz in 1994 as chief of staff of the Israel Defense Forces: "We have come fifty years too late."

The Imperative to Define and Demand Humane Standards for Medical Research

Few nonspecialists realize the impact of the Holocaust on medical ethics. At the conclusion of the International Military Tribunal Trials at Nuremberg of twenty-two major Nazi leaders, a series of other trials were held by the United States. One hundred eighty five defendants in all were divided into twelve groups. Mobile killing unit leaders and camp commandants, judges and corporate leaders were tried. Doctors were tried for their participation in selection, murder, and medical experimentation. In response to the trial of German physicians, in 1947 the judges declared what is known as the Nuremberg Code, consisting of ten principles of legitimate medical experimentation, principles that will sound quite familiar even to those casually concerned with medical ethics and with only limited interest in the Holocaust, for they have become standard in medical ethics today:

1. The *voluntary consent* of the human subject is absolutely essential...
2. The experiment should be such as to yield fruitful results for the good of society, unprocurable by other methods... The anticipated results will justify the performance of the experiment.
3. The experiment should be... based on the results of animal experimentation and a knowledge of the natural history of the disease or other problem under study [so] that the anticipated results will justify the performance of the experiment.
4. The experiment should be so conducted as to avoid all unnecessary physical and mental suffering and injury.
5. No experiment should be conducted where there is an *a priori* reason to believe that death or disabling injury will occur, except perhaps in those experiments where the experimenting physicians also serve as subjects.
6. The degree of risk to be taken should never exceed the humanitarian importance of the problem to be solved by the experiment.
7. Proper preparations should be made and adequate facilities provided to protect the experimental subject against even remote possibilities of injury, disability, or death.
8. The experiment should be conducted only by scientifically qualified persons. Through all stages of the experiment, the highest degree of

skill and care should be required of those who conduct or engage in the experiment.
9. During the course of the experiment the human subject should be at liberty to bring the experiment to an end if he has reached the physical or mental state where continuation of the experiment seems to him to be too onerous or risky.
10. During the course of the experiment the scientist in charge must be prepared to terminate the experiment at any stage if he has probable cause to believe, in the exercise of the good faith, superior skill, and careful judgment required of him, that a continuation of the experiment is likely to result in injury, disability, or death to the experimental subject.[28]

Subsequently, these standards were refined and expanded by the World Medical Association's Declaration of Helsinki in 1964, and that document has been revised six times since (most recently in 2008) and has served as the basis for the Common Rule for medical experimentation and the Good Clinical Practice guidelines that are enforced by the U.S. government.

The Imperative to Attain Both Justice and Reconciliation

The Holocaust has taught other societies to attain both justice and reconciliation after genocidal atrocities. It has played that role in Argentina after the overthrow of the military regime in the late 1970s and early 1980s that simply kidnapped people and killed them secretly (the "Desperados"), in Uganda after Idi Amin, in South Africa after apartheid; and, belatedly, even in Cambodia some thirty years after "the killing fields."

Historians seek understanding of such genocidal atrocities. Lawyers ask what is to be done with the perpetrators? Politicians ask yet another question: How do we reconcile and rebuild society? All three of these questions are often complicated by the fact that those who were left in positions of power often were part of the abusive system—judges, lawyers, and the police.

The Holocaust served as a model for responding to all three types of questions. There is a major difference between gathering legal evidence and gathering historical evidence, but the trials at Nuremberg provided the first understanding of the scope of German crimes, the first definition of what happened, as has the testimony before the Truth Commission in South Africa.

The Nuremberg trials served as one model for post-genocide justice that has been emulated in Bosnia, Rwanda, and even Cambodia—albeit at a distance of three decades. The limitations of the Holocaust model have also become evident in situations where total victory against the perpetrators was not achieved and some are still in power. Such people would obviously prefer to hold on to the office and to the relative safety that their political power can provide rather than to give up that office and face an international tribunal and possibly life in prison. Thus, in places where the dictators are still in power, one wonders whether it is politically helpful to initiate proceedings against them or whether those places would not be better off with a negotiated agreement for their tyrant's departure that grants them unmerited amnesty. Still, there must be some insistence on accountability, for future genocides can be deterred only if perpetrators are brought to justice. So, for example, Israelis are fearful that their behavior in Gaza or Lebanon might subject them to the jurisdiction of national or international courts, and even American officials worry about being tried for torturing captured "enemy combatants."

The Holocaust itself was a manifestation of the rule of law—Rubenstein, among others, have argued that the Nazis committed no crime,[29] for they violated no existing laws—but we must be concerned with the values underlying the law. We must reemphasize the notion of rights that the state cannot take away, of constraints on the power of the state, of international law that can define "crimes against humanity," of the idea that the Creator endows human equality and human rights. The Holocaust has demonstrated that these rights are far from self-evident or assured, that they must be continually reaffirmed and enforced.

THE HOLOCAUST AS ABSOLUTE

Decades after it occurred, the Holocaust has taken its place as a defining moment of human history. It was the moment when we learned something about what we are as individuals and communities, about human capacity for good and evil. We have learned also about the power of states and institutions to shape the world and to accomplish so much, even the annihilation of a people.

In a world of relativism, it has taken its place as the Absolute. On many issues, we may disagree as to what is good or bad. The Holocaust, though, is clearly evil, absolute evil. It is for this reason that many different groups use the word to call attention to their suffering—the Black Holocaust, the Holocaust of the American Indians, the Holocaust in Armenia, Kosovo, Rwanda, Bosnia. The Holocaust is the nuclear bomb of moral epithets. It is an event of such magnitude that the more we sense the relativism of values, the more we require the Holocaust as the foundation for a negative absolute—absolute evil.

I suspect that this is the reason why the leaders of European nations have rediscovered the importance of the Holocaust for contemporary moral education. I also suspect that this is the reason why it becomes the focal point for Papal visits to Israel, for German society, and for American society. Moreover, this is the reason that Holocaust deniers are perceived as so perverse, for they are denying an event that all standards of rationality and morality recognize and condemn.[30] It is in this function as negative absolute that the Holocaust may loom largest in the coming years.

For Jews the question may be totally different: can we stop seeing our current condition through the prism of the Holocaust, or is the event so catastrophic and so dominating that it will not allow us to perceive the distance we have traveled from the world of Auschwitz? Can we remember and be faithful to the implications of that memory, but can we also forget long enough to understand where we were, where we are, and where we must go?

Notes

1. See Steven Brand's Film, "Praying with My Feet," in production.
2. Personal communication with the author.
3. It was only while serving as Secretary of State that Madelyn Albright acknowledged her Jewish ancestry, even though the names of her grandparents were on the wall of the Prague synagogue listed among the deportees who were murdered, and her own description of her family as Czechoslovakian patriots and social democrats would have described Jews in her native land. While many others were surprised and presumed that she was lying, I found her story credible. I believe that she had learned almost instinctively as a child that things Jewish were dangerous and so she repressed such familiar knowledge. Katie Marton, who has written movingly about the Holocaust and her own story, learned only as an adult that her parents were of Hungarian Jewish ancestry.
4. Yehuda Bauer. in, Menachem Rosensaft, ed., *Life Reborn: Jewish Displaced Persons 1945–1951* (Washington, DC: United States Holocaust Memorial Museum, 2000) p. 25.
5. See Irving Greenberg, "Clouds of Fire, Pillar of Smoke," in Eva Fleischner, ed., *Auschwitz Beginning of a New Era: Reflections on the Holocaust* (New York: KTAV, 1977); repr. in part in *Contemporary Jewish Theology: A Reader*, Elliot N. Dorff and Louis E. Newman, eds. (New York: Oxford, 1999), pp. 396–416.
6. See Tom Segev, *The Seventh Million: The Israelis and the Holocaust* (New York: Hill and Wang, 1993). See also J. J. Goldberg, *Jewish Power: Inside the Jewish Establishment* (Reading, MA: Addison-Wesley Publishing Company, Inc. 1996), pp. 133–62.
7. Gerda Klein, *A Boring Evening at Home* (Washington, DC: Leading Authorities, 2007). See also her speech when *One Survivor Remembers* won the Academy Award for the best documentary of 1995.
8. Emil Fackenheim, "On Jewish Values in the Post-Holocaust Future: A Judaism Symposium," *Judaism* 16:3 (Summer 1967), pp. 266–67. The symposium was held on Purim 5727. Fackenheim elaborated on these seminal remarks in his book *God's Presence in History* (New York: New York University Press, 1969).
9. For a critique of Fackenheim see Michael Berenbaum, *The Vision of the Void: Theological Reflections on the Works of Elie Wiesel* (Middletown, CT: Wesleyan University Press, 1979), pp. 154–60.
10. Emil Fackenheim, *To Mend the World: Foundations of Future Jewish Thought* (New York: Schocken Books, 1982).
11. Greenberg, (at note 5 above)., p. 23 (in Dorff and Newman, at note 5 above, p. 406).
12. Harold Schulweis, "From God to Godliness: Proposal for a Predicate Theology," *The Reconstructionist* 41:1 (1975), pp. 16–26; reprinted in Dorff and Newman, *Contemporary Jewish Theology* (at note 5 above), pp. 122–30. See also his work *Evil and the Morality of God* (Cincinnati: Hebrew Union College, 1984).

13. Irving Greenberg, "Voluntary Covenant" (a pamphlet of the National Jewish Resource Center [now CLAL] 1982), p. 4.
14. Jacob Gladstein, (1946) *Nisht di meysim loybn got from Shtralndike yidn* [Dead Men Don't Praise God], Ruth Whitman, trans., in *Modern Poems on the Bible*, David Curzon, ed. (Philadelphia: Jewish Publication Society, 1994/5754), pp. 165–67.
15. Exodus 24:4.
16. Greenberg, "Clouds of Fire," p. 22.
17. Steven Schwarzschild, "Toward Jewish Unity," *Judaism* 15:2 (Spring 1966), p. 157.
18. Elie Wiesel, *The Town Beyond the Wall* (New York: Holt, Rinehart and Winston, 1964), p. 118.
19. Ibid., p. 96.
20. Wiesel, White House Speech, April 12, 1999.
21. Yehuda Bauer, *Rethinking the Holocaust* (New Haven and London: Yale University Press, 2001), p. 273.
22. See, for example, the educational material developed by Facing History and Ourselves (www.facinghistory.org).
23. Richard L. Rubenstein, *The Cunning of History: Mass Death and the American Future* (New York and San Francisco: Harper and Row, 1972).
24. Daniel Jonah Goldhagen, *Hitler's Willing Executioners: Ordinary Germans and the Holocaust* (New York: Alfred A. Knopf, 1996), pp. 81–126.
25. Richard L. Rubenstein, *After Auschwitz: History, Theology and Contemporary Judaism*, 2nd ed. (Baltimore and London: Johns Hopkins University Press, 1992). The subtitle of the original edition was *Radical Theology and Contemporary Judaism*. Written twenty-five years after the original, the second edition has two major chapters devoted to the concept of Covenant and Divinity.
26. See Helen Fein, *Accounting for Genocide: National Responses and Jewish Victimization During the Holocaust* (New York: The Free Press, 1979).
27. Samantha Power, *"A Problem from Hell:" America and the Age of Genocide* (New York: Basic Books. 2002).
28. *Trials of War Criminals before the Nuremberg Military Tribunals under Control, Council Law No. 10, Vol. 2* (Washington, DC: U.S. Government Printing Office, 1949), vol. 2, pp. 181–82; available at http://ohsr.od.nih.gov/guidelines/nuremberg.html (accessed August 8, 2011).
29. Richard L. Rubenstein, *The Cunning of History: The Holocaust and the American Future* (New York: Harper and Row, 1978), p. 33.
30. See, for example, Deborah Lipstadt's *Denying the Holocaust: The Growing Assault on Truth and Memory* (New York: Plume, 1993), and *History on Trial: My Day in Court with David Irving* (New York: ECCO, 2005).

Suggestions for Further Reading

Bauer, Yehuda, 2001. *Rethinking the Holocaust*. New Haven and London; Yale University Press.
Berenbaum, Michael. 1990. *After Tragedy and Triumph: Modern Jewish Thought and the American Experience*. New York: Cambridge University Press.
Blumenthal, David R. 1999. *The Banality of the Good and Evil: Moral Lessons from the Shoah and Jewish Tradition*. Washington, DC; Georgetown University Press.

Burg, Avraham. 2008. *The Holocaust Is Over, We Must Rise from Its Ashes*. New York: Palgrave Macmillan.

Burleigh, Michael. 1997. *Ethics and Extermination: Reflection on Nazi Genocide*. Cambridge: Cambridge University Press.

Roth, John K. 2007. *Ethics During and After the Holocaust: The Shadow of Birkenau*. New York: Palgrave Macmillan.

Rubenstein, Richard L. 1972. *The Cunning of History: Mass Death and the American Future*. New York and San Francisco: Harper and Row.

Segev, Tom. 1993. *The Seventh Million: The Israelis and the Holocaust*. New York: Hill and Wang.

CHAPTER 11

ETHICAL THEORIES IN THE REFORM MOVEMENT

MICHAEL MARMUR

Four Sensibilities

Reform places ethics at the very heart of its conception of Judaism. Choirs proclaim the primacy of the ethical from the pulpit, and Reform campers intone its centrality around the campfire. The ethical imperative of *Tikkun Olam* (repairing the world) is affirmed by Reform Jews in Minsk and Melbourne, Sao Paolo, Brazil, and St. Paul, Minnesota.

Practitioners of Reform Judaism have imbued the notion of ethics with a broad range of meanings and emphases. Why is it, then, that across continents and historical periods, the ethical has maintained its centrality and sanctity in the lexicon of Reform?

Perhaps the core tension at the heart of Reform since its earliest stirrings is between that which its leaders and followers can no longer accept, and that which they refuse to give up. The theological assertions of premodern Judaism seemed impossible to accept at face value. The philosophical and scientific axioms upon which modernity was founded seemed undeniable. At the same time, the prospect of abandoning Judaism was rejected. Reform Judaism was born at the nexus of these insights.

It may prove helpful to identify four distinct sensibilities in Reform ethics. I have called the first of these "Ethics as First Theology," adapting a term from Emanuel Levinas. It relates to the privileged role given to ethics in Reform theology, particularly in its first century.

I have termed the second great phase of engagement with ethics in Reform Judaism "*Tikkun Olam*," referring to the turn from theology to activist ideology. Here Reform Judaism comes to epitomize a commitment to mending the world as a fulfillment of the highest goals of Judaism and humanity. The heroes of this aspect of Reform Judaism are not renowned for the originality of their theological insights, but rather for their tenacity and efficacy in the promotion of various social causes.

The third sensibility is "A Critique of Modernity," in which postwar American Reform Jews provided both a trenchant critique of some of the excesses and miscalculations of their predecessors, and a defense (no less trenchant) of the enterprise of an engaged liberal Judaism.

For the fourth sensibility I have employed Charles Taylor's phrase, "The Ethics of Authenticity." This involves a number of mostly new directions that help describe the current state of Reform ethics.

In North America today classical Reform voices can be heard among neo-traditionalists of various hues. Having made the observation that these four sensibilities co-exist, it is true that history plays its part. Ethics moves from being first theology to an activist ideology for effecting social change under the influence of American Protestantism in the late nineteenth century. The tumultuous events of the late thirties through the late sixties of the twentieth century challenge the assumptions held by Reform Jews in earlier times. Postmodern winds now blow strongly through institutions and attitudes of Reform Judaism. In some sense, then, these four sections describe a historical development. As attitudes or sensibilities, however, there is evidence that each is alive and well in contemporary Reform Judaism.

Ethics as First Theology

The world built by the founders of Reform was disenchanted, disabused of the literal veracity of ancient myths. Yet it was reenchanted by modernity, convinced that the march of Progress would lead to a more perfected world. In the early writings of Reform thinkers and in statements promulgated by Reform institutions, the enthusiasm for the modern project of Enlightenment shines through.

Two aspects of Kantian ethics were particularly significant in Reform theology in its first century. In his *Groundwork for the Metaphysics of Morals*, Kant emphasized that "all moral concepts have their seat and origin completely *a priori* in reason... they cannot be obtained by abstraction from any empirical, and therefore merely contingent, cognitions."[1] Second, Kant "rejects any moral philosophy which incorporates the attainment of happiness in its doctrines."[2] It is obedience to duty rather than eudaemonism that must motivate ethical action.

For Liberal Jews eager to align themselves with the legacy of Kant, the questions of reason and duty had to be addressed. The first attempt to do this in a systematic way was Moritz Lazarus's *Die Ethik des Judenthums* [*The Ethics of Judaism*]

(1898–1899), which suggested a way of accommodating the notion of God with the concept of radical individual autonomy. In Lazarus's presentation of Judaism, "the moral principle, without suffering change or losing aught of its peculiarity and independence, finds its archetypal expression in God. To recognize and lay hold of the good, without compulsion, without external command, without hope of profit, without any sort of ulterior motive, solely and alone by reason of man's moral nature—that surely is to be autonomous and autonomously moral!"[3]

Lazarus insisted that "the intimate connection with religion does not annul the independence of the ethical idea. The reference to God is made, not to establish, but to urge the claims of the moral" [§89; see also §79]. For Lazarus, "autonomy implies the absence of every extraneous will in the creation of morality," but it does not preclude the use of theistic terminology. Indeed, "the fool who avoids theistic views by supposing himself the creator of his own nature is the last to whom we may look to fix the basis of the purely moral" [§102]. He preserves the centrality of the Jewish textual tradition itself when he says it is to "the prominent Jewish thinkers of all epochs" to whom one should look to find "safeguarding of the immaculate honor of the moral" [§103].

In a similar vein, Kaufmann Kohler strove to harmonize Mosaic monotheism with Kantian ethics:

> The soul of the Jewish religion is its ethics. Its God is the fountainhead and Ideal of morality....
>
> Jewish ethics...derives its sanction from God...and sees its purpose in the hallowing of all life, individual and social. Its motive is the splendid conception that man, with his finite ends, is linked to the infinite God with His infinite ends.[4]

There can be little doubt that there was an apologetic dimension to this insistence that the dictates of a disembodied universal rational morality would coincide with revealed law from an ancient and ostensibly particularistic tradition. Samson Hochfeld averred that "[t]he ethics of Judaism is dominated by the principle of universalism, that is, it knows no difference in its requirements and regulations between Jew and non-Jew. What it commands applies universally. Any separation of men according to descent and belief into classes or nationalities or races or religions is meaningless for it." Any attempt to argue differently would be "not only to defame, but completely to misconstrue" the true spirit of Judaism.[5] Such statements hardly reflect a dispassionate consideration of attitudes to universalism in the biblical, rabbinic, and medieval periods, which are frankly much less universalistic than these early Reform leaders claimed.

This apologetic tendency in the presentation of Judaism's ethical core was undoubtedly linked to the social aspirations and political concerns of modernist Jews in Europe and America. In 1885 the Deutsch-Israelitische Gemeindebund published a pamphlet, *Principles of Jewish Morality*. These fifteen principles included the unity of the human race, respect for private property, and concern for the material welfare of non-Jews. It mandated giving honor to governmental authority and forbade financial dishonesty. Authored by Lazarus, signed by 350 rabbis and scholars, and a further 270 Austrian and German Jewish jurists, it represented the apotheosis of ethics as apologetics.

Unlike later exponents of Reform, the founders of the movement were not always adherents of what today would be termed pluralism. The claim that Judaism is devoid of national distinctions could be found alongside the assertion that Judaism had brought ethics to its most perfect expression. In a sermon published in 1881, Isaac Mayer Wise described the God of Israel as "Ethics' Primeval Rock." He continued:

> In this point Israel's theology and faith are superior to all religious systems known in history. Morality is the offspring of truth. Corruption and degeneration are the children of error and fiction. Truth redeems and unites; error enslaves and sows discord among brethren. Neither the God nor the gods of the Gentiles are represented as free, wise, just, benevolent and merciful. Slavery and fatalism were characteristics of all Pagan theology; because their gods were natural forces and natural objects deified and fantastically magnified; and their one and most high God is an abstraction, a collective idea of their gods. Their lords are no God, but their God is an ideal abstraction of their lords. There is no foundation of ethics in their theology. Neither their God nor their gods are types of holiness.
> In Israel, God is and always was the most sublime ideal of moral perfection.[6]

This championing of Jewish uniqueness, or primacy, or pedigree, is one of the chief characteristics of Reform theology in its classic phase.

The philosophical engagement with Kant reached its apogee in the work of Hermann Cohen. As a neo-Kantian philosopher and Jewish thinker, Cohen occupies a unique position in the development of Reform ethics. His formulations do more than provide Liberal Jews with an accommodation between two worlds: they represent a profound attempt to argue for a "substantive similarity between the ethics of the Kantian system and the basic idea of Judaism."[7]

Cohen grappled with the relation of philosophy to religion, and he found a role for the latter in providing a basis for individuality. While ethics operates at the level of a general law, religion is able to help the individual find a place in the world by encouraging the transition from self-centeredness to love of God.

Many of the key characteristics of the thought of Rosenzweig, Buber, and others can be traced to ideas developed by Hermann Cohen.[8] His reading of Jewish sources in keeping with his general philosophical outlook went beyond apologetics and offered a remarkable re-understanding of Judaism. Maimonides, for example, is singled out for "his basic tendency to ground the entire religion of Israel in ethics and, insofar as it can be carried out, to dissolve religion into ethics."[9] His core concept of correlation "between the spiritual domain of ideas and the spatial domain of nature,"[10] between the divine and the human, is read out of Maimonides and other medieval philosophers, for whom, in Cohen's reading, "reason is made the root of the content of revelation."[11]

Cohen was by no means the first Reform thinker to engage with the question of Jewish sources and their validity in the discerning of Jewish ethics. In the early years of the Reform movement, Samuel Holdheim had attacked attempts to cite the

Talmud as a source of morality, declaring: "The Talmud speaks with the ideology of its own time, and for that time it was right. I speak from the higher ideology of my time, and for this time I am right."[12] In 1913 Jacob Lauterbach argued that the teachers of the *halakhah* "interpreted the Torah in such a manner as to make all its laws the expression of ethical ideals, conducive to the promotion of righteousness, peace and love among men."[13] From early in the nineteenth century, some leading exponents of Reform saw the discourse of the *halakhah*, and most particularly *responsa* literature, as a means of expressing modern ethical commitments in a profoundly Jewish way. Reform *responsa* have continued to be a genre of Reform creativity ever since, although there has been considerable debate within the movement regarding both the validity and relevance of this approach.[14] Although the literature of the rabbis was seen in different ways, all of the early Reform thinkers asserted that the sources of Judaism, certainly the Bible, could be trawled for evidence of sublime moral instruction.

The Pittsburgh Platform of 1885 provides a clear and systematic description of this classic phase of Reform Judaism's development. The third of its eight brief statements stated that Mosaic legislation was "a system of training the Jewish people for its mission during its national life in Palestine" and as such it is now defunct. "[T]oday we accept as binding only the moral laws, and maintain only such ceremonies as elevate and sanctify our lives, but reject all such as are not adapted to the views and habits of modern civilization."[15]

Once the husk of an outmoded historical context had been discarded, only the ethical core remained. As the fourth article maintains, laws relating to diet, priestly purity, and dress are deemed to be "altogether foreign to our present mental and spiritual state...their observance in our days is apt rather to obstruct than to further modern spiritual elevation."

The fifth statement makes explicit the spirit with which the entire document is infused: "We recognize in the modern era of universal culture of heart and intellect the approaching of Israel's great Messianic hope for the establishment of the kingdom of truth, justice and peace among all men." Modernity is not to be perceived as a threat to the religion of Israel, but rather as an intimation of its most sublime values and a conduit to their fulfillment.

Conscious that it may be inferred from such a view that affiliation with Judaism may now be eschewed, the next clause in the statement affirms the authors' conviction of "the utmost necessity of preserving the historical identity with our great past." As proud heirs to Jewish tradition (now interpreted in new ways), these Reform Jews pledged to "extend the hand of fellowship to all who cooperate with us in the establishment of the reign of truth and righteousness among men."

Early Reform was either deconstructionist or minimalist with regard to many of the staples of Rabbinic and medieval Jewish life. Ethics fared much better than most of these other concepts and practices in the transition to modernity. *Halakhah* was often rejected as obscurantist and archaic: ethnic solidarity as tribalism. It is the ethical core that persists as the shells peel away.

In his *Jewish Theology* Kaufmann Kohler decried Zionism, declaring that "[w]e require a regeneration, not of the nation, but of the faith of Israel, which is its soul." As for Jewish law, Kohler expressed admiration for the edifying lessons in sobriety, moderation, and self-mastery that the *halakhic* system had engendered in earlier times. The modern Orthodox Jew, who does not inquire into the purpose of the law, may be consistent in following all the minutiae of Jewish law. However,

> Reform Judaism has a different view, as it sees in the humanitarianism of the present a mode of realizing the Messianic hope of Israel. Therefore it cannot afford to encourage the separation of the Jew from his environment in any way except through the maintenance of his religion, and cannot encourage the dietary laws as a means of separatism. Its great problem is to find other methods to inculcate the spirit of holiness in the modern Jew, to render him conscious of his priestly mission, while he lives in unison and fellowship of his fellow-citizens.[16]

The impulse to do good is understood as the original foundation of Judaism, which is later overlaid by elaboration and ornament, much of which is no longer necessary or desirable.

For a final word on ethics as first theology, we can look to Leo Baeck, who in the circumstances of his life provides a bridge to the second sensibility of Reform Judaism. In the 1920s Baeck declared:

> The insistence upon morality, as a principle of religion, is the very core and backbone of Judaism. In it, ethics does not need to be added to religion because it is already an essential part of it; without ethics there can be no belief in its judgment, in the meaning of this life, nor in that which pertains to the life beyond. This definite ethical character, which is peculiar to it, is the root of the new thing that the faith of Israel has contributed to the world.[17]

Tikkun Olam

Leo Baeck was forced to confront in his own experience the most profound undermining of Judaism understood as "the religion of ethical optimism."[18] His behavior in the Nazi era demonstrated his willingness to translate his views on the primacy of the ethical into practice. In this sense, Baeck can be seen as an exemplar of the second sensibility, a transition from theology and apologetics to ethical activism.

However, Leo Baeck remained until his last days a symbol and exponent of a European Reform Judaism. In America a different strain of the movement had emerged, one that was more activist, more political, and more practical. As Meyer and Plaut have noted, "although the Reform movement in Germany identified strongly with prophetic Judaism, its environment militated against independent activity in the area of social action. Only in America, where it was influenced by Protestant activism, did social justice become an integral part of Reform Judaism."[19]

There seems little doubt that the Social Gospel movement and progressivism pervading the American landscape of the second half of the nineteenth century provided the backdrop for this development. The early career of Stephen S. Wise is informative in charting this development. At one point we find him comparing his own hero of American Reform with leading figures in the Social Gospel movement, averring that "what Washington Gladden and Graham Taylor and Walter Rauschenbusch...have done in their churches, Emil G. Hirsch has done for the Synagogue of Israel."[20] Hirsch himself noted in 1893 that the religion of the future "will be impatient of men who claim that they have the right to be saved...while not stirring a foot or lifting a hand to redeem brother men from hunger and wretchedness."[21]

The final clause of the 1885 Pittsburgh platform was authored by Hirsch, and it turned the spotlight on society: "In full accordance with the spirit of Mosaic legislation...we deem it our duty to participate in the great task of modern times, to solve, on the basis of justice and righteousness, the problems presented by the contrasts and evils of the present organization of society."

Bolstered by a uniquely American confidence in the possibility of effecting social change, liberated to a great degree from the concern that voluble support for social causes might provoke an anti-Semitic response, American Reform Judaism moved from a theological concern with ethics to a practical program of involvement in some of the most pressing social concerns of the day. Abraham Cronbach, professor of social studies at Hebrew Union College, the Reform seminary, expressed this new sensibility thus: "Social justice is Jewish. Even if it were not Jewish, it would behoove us to espouse social justice. For social justice is right, and the right must be done whether it is Jewish or not."[22]

In 1918 the Committee on Synagogue and Industrial Relations of the Central Conference of American Rabbis (the organization of Reform rabbis) issued its first report. The fourteen principles adumbrated in that brief document include equitable distribution of profits, universal workers' insurance, and recognition of the right of labor to organize. The 1928 Report of the Commission on Social Justice prefaced its expanded list of social principles with a preamble noting that "our inspiration for social justice" was derived "from the great teachings of the prophets of Israel and other great traditions of our faith" that were then applied "concretely to the economic and social problems of today."[23] The list of issues in the 1928 report included prisons and penal laws, women in industry, child labor, lynching, civil liberties, and a final section entitled "Social Justice in International Relations," denouncing economic imperialism and warmongering, and insisting that a popular referendum precede any future declaration of war by Congress. The Reform movement had become fully engaged in the political process.

In the years following the Second World War, this new approach reached new heights. In the late 1950s Albert Vorspan and others began penning a series of books. The first of these, co-authored with Eugene L. Lipman, was tellingly entitled *Justice and Judaism: The Work of Social Action*. Its opening chapter relates to the foundations of social action in Judaism. The leading statement, namely that "[a] passionate belief in and concern for justice for all men is inherent in Judaism,"[24] would not have been out of place in a German tract decades before. The authors go on to describe the nature of synagogues in America, which, in their view, had deferred to nonreligious Jewish institutions and pulled away from their historic role in advancing social justice. This backdrop accentuates all the more the courageous stand of certain rabbis who chose to develop the platform afforded them to advance causes they held dear.

Justice and Judaism then lists a litany of rabbinic heroism. For example, David Einhorn attacks the institution of slavery in 1861, and he is forced to leave Baltimore after threats are made to his life. Samuel Goldenson's sermon in Pittsburgh in 1928 is quoted, in which he supports the miners' strike despite the prominence of leading coal producers in his congregation, declaring that "no man in the entire world has as much right" as the clergyman to speak about these issues, and that "there is no man upon whom the responsibility to speak about such questions is so great as upon the one who raises his voice in the name of ethics and religion."[25]

The examples Vorspan and Lipman provide of rabbis prepared to run the gauntlet of lay disapproval are many, including rabbis from Chicago to Texas, from Cincinnati to San Francisco. A common theme in the speeches quoted by these rabbis, sometimes at the expense of their pulpit, is the imperative to match lofty rhetoric with focused action and the willingness to take a stand. In 1955 Maurice Eisendrath, the president of the Union of American Hebrew Congregations, the organization of Reform synagogues (later renamed the Union of Reform Judaism), declared that a guide for Reform Judaism would have to cover more than ritual, "not merely a minimal code for liturgical worship but a minimal code of moral conduct incumbent upon anyone who calls himself a Reform Jew presuming to be the heir of Hebrew prophet and sage."[26]

This was the atmosphere in some of the pulpits and at the helm of the Reform movement at the dawn of the 1960s. Social action committees were established in several Reform congregations as early as the 1950s. It is striking to note how often the key actors in this emergent social justice caucus presented their passion for social justice as an imperative on a par with and even superseding prayer and study. The prophetic heritage was cited as a basis for this approach, exemplified in the 1962 dedication address of the first director of the movement's Religious Action Center, a social justice advocacy organization in Washington, DC, Richard G. Hirsch:

> Is there to be a Reform Jewish viewpoint on breaking the glass at weddings and not a Reform Jewish viewpoint on breaking the pattern of racial prejudice? Shall our congregations devote their energies to increasing membership dues and not to increasing concern for world peace?[27]

The events of the civil rights campaign in North America brought this social ethics trend within Reform Judaism to unprecedented levels. In a sermon delivered in Nashville in March 1958, Rabbi William B. Silverman held up the examples of the prophets of Israel in ancient times, and the life of Isaac Mayer Wise in more recent days, as evidence of the Jewish imperative to side with the cause of civil rights. He declared:

> "WE WILL NOT YIELD TO EVIL. We will not capitulate to fear. We will not surrender to violence. We will not submit to intimidation but, as Reform Jews, we will continue to speak for truth; we shall continue to dedicate ourselves to social

justice and to the brotherhood of ALL men, knowing and believing that all men are created in the divine image."[28]

A number of Reform rabbis and institutions were at the forefront of campaigns and struggles that came to define that decade of tumult. Indeed, the Civil Rights Act of 1964 and the Voting Rights Act of 1965 were drafted in the conference room of the movement's Religious Action Center because the Leadership Conference on Civil Rights was housed there.

The leading actors in this drama were often at pains to stress that there was more than one way of responding to the complex social challenges of the day, and that no monopoly on the truth was being claimed. The enemy to be faced was *anomie* and apathy, the unwillingness to take a stand. Social values are understood as being crucial to the Jewish enterprise. In the words of David Saperstein, the current director of the Religious Action Center and an embodiment of this transition from theology to activist ideology and practice:

> To be a Jew means to be involved in testing those values. To be a Jew means to speak out on those issues. To be a Jew means to be bound up with the struggle for social justice.[29]

This second sensibility represents a kind of Reform imperative, capable of engendering passionate adherence and personal sacrifice. It finds expression in educational materials designed to engender commitment among new generations of Reform Jews born and bred in North America.[30] In youth groups and camps, these young people were educated to believe that the ethical is at the heart of Judaism in general, and Reform Judaism in particular. Eugene Borowitz summarizes the peak expression of this second sensibility thus: "By the late 1960s most American Jews took it for granted that the most important thing about Judaism was its ethics and that Jewish ethics meant liberal politics."[31]

The Critique of Modernity

The events of the mid-twentieth century were enough to shake some of these assumptions to their core. Liberals were forced to reexamine their primary commitments. Notions such as the belief that radical changes in understanding science, society, and the individual would all lead to the amelioration of ills and the promotion of tolerance; that reason would prevail and moderation become the norm; that today's enlightenment would cancel out the ignorance of yesterday; that outmoded rituals could now give way to pure intentions; indeed, that an ancient tradition could coincide precisely with a contemporary political platform—these could no longer be taken for granted.

It took time for many of the leading figures of Reform thought to give voice to this new postwar sensibility. To some degree it was a European voice, contrasted with the sunny can-do approach of postwar America. An outstanding case of this voice can be found in the thought of Emil Fackenheim, the German-trained philosopher and Reform rabbi who rose to prominence in Canada and ended his days in Jerusalem. Fackenheim attacked the naïve suppositions of a liberalism that in his view had become radically compromised by the events of the twentieth century. In his *To Mend the World* he discussed Adolf Eichmann's evocation of Kant's categorical imperative at his 1961 trial, and while clearing Kant of any proto-Nazi intentions, he concludes that "Kant's own principle is not immune to this unheard of, unprecedented, unique assault."[32]

Among American-born Reform thinkers, some were also turning back to the roots of classical Reform with a critical eye. In characteristically forthright fashion, Arnold Jacob Wolf described the promulgators of the 1885 Pittsburgh Platform as "fine scholars in the noble tradition of Abraham Geiger, but...very poor theologians." He then proceeded to catalogue their shortcomings, which included a god-idea instead of God, absolute personal autonomy instead of heteronomy under God, anthropocentrism instead of theocentrism, an emphasis on what *mitzvot not* to keep rather than obedience to Torah, Judaism as a religion instead of the faith of a people, individualism over solidarity, prophetic rather than rabbinic texts, the centrality of the Reform Temple rather than home and school, freedom above responsibility, *aggadah* to the exclusion of *halakhah*, aesthetics over authenticity, rabbis rather than communities in power, the primacy of reason to the exclusion of all else, a rhetoric involving a faceless humanity rather than concrete people in real situations, timeless principles over specific situations and practices, self-confidence over humility, and more.[33] This is nothing less than a frontal assault on the ethical and religious assumptions of nineteenth-century Reform from within the twentieth-century Reform movement.

In Eugene Borowitz Reform Judaism finds its single most prolific and significant exponent of Jewish ethics. In the postwar era, the writing and teaching of Borowitz have defined and transformed the field of Reform ethics. He has surveyed the history of the field, offered a critique of earlier trends in Reform ethics, pointed the way to new areas of challenge, and inspired students to take Reform ethics into new directions.

In his *Renewing the Covenant*, Borowitz describes modernity as a betrayer. His rejection of some of the bedrock assumptions of modernist liberalism led him to a renewed interest in religion and belief, although not from a traditionalist stance:

> With the demise of the generative Kantian premise of liberal religion—that ethics was more certain than belief—the converse of the liberal axiom now asserted itself: If ethics rightly deserves a substance and power that rationalism can no longer provide, then faith must now once again provide its foundation and standard.[34]

While it is tempting to regard this review of the excesses of modernity as a later development, it should be recalled that "the critique of modernity has been part of the modern spirit since its very inception."[35] It is true, however, that in Jewish circles the Holocaust was a watershed, and many committed to a Reform approach came to seek something other than an unquestioning faith in the inexorable path of progress.

The ways in which Borowitz mounts an assault on some of the ethical presuppositions of his Reform forerunners while defending others have developed over decades of creativity.[36] Unlike another of his generation of Reform thinkers, Steven Schwarzschild,[37] he made a definitive break with the rationalism and neo-Kantianism of Cohen and set off in search of a new basis for a "thick" non-Orthodox Judaism, centered around the image of the covenant:

> In contrast to contemporary privatistic notions of selfhood, the Jewish self, responding to God in Covenant, acknowledges its essential historicity and sociality....
>
> With heritage and folk essential to Jewishness, with the Jewish service of God directed to historic continuity lasting until messianic days, the Covenanted self knows that Jewish existence must be structured. Yet as long as we honor each Jew's selfhood with a contextually delimited measure of autonomy, this need for communal forms cannot lead us back to law as a required, corporately determined regimen. Instead, we must think in terms of a *self-discipline* that, because of the sociality of the Jewish self, becomes communally focused and shaped. The result is a dialectical autonomy, a life of freedom-exercised-in-Covenant."[38]

Ethics of Authenticity

Although Borowitz associated with institutions of Reform Judaism throughout his long career, he himself eschewed the title of a Reform ideologue. He pointed out that his models—Cohen, Baeck, Kaplan, Buber, Rosenzweig, and Heschel—tended to operate outside denominations or on their edges, and that he has tried to emulate them. He is a Jew of a particular time and place trying to think through the truth of Judaism as best he can.[39] The strengthening of transdenominational trends have made it more difficult to identify a discernibly Reform ethics, and it has called into question the need for such distinctions.

The tension between movement-specific and transdenominational pressures is only one of a number of tensions that characterize contemporary Reform ethics. Another could be described as the tension between *ethical clarity* and *competing values*. The culture of pluralism has certainly made a mark on contemporary Reform ethics. Where earlier generations were likely to set down ethical statements as self-evident truths issued from on high, the ethical dilemmas presented by Vorspan and Saperstein are presented as "tough choices," for which "[t]here is no specific Jewish "right" answer."[40]

This openness to differing narratives certainly provides a challenge to the fervor of certainty that has often accompanied effective social activism. Ironically, there is evidence of a resurgence of grass roots social organizing, mobilizing individuals to form coalitions and effect change.[41] It remains to be seen, within Reform

Judaism and throughout the developed world, how ethical activism will fare in a postmodern context. The possibility of advancing a committed and engaged moderate Judaism has major implications for the Jewish future.

A connected tension is that between the *radical* and the *conventional*. From its inception, the Reform movement was a bourgeois phenomenon. It is true that some of its European pioneers had socialist leanings, and the 1937 Columbus Platform, with its "promotion of harmonious relations between warring classes on the basis of equity and justice," shows that something of this spirit crossed the Atlantic.[42] Nonetheless, in the main the ethics of the movement were solidly and conventionally middle class. The prophets of Israel are quoted, but few Reform Jews adopted their lifestyle. As Roland Gittlesohn noted in 1965, it is actually remarkable to note not how many Reform rabbis behaved as martyrs in the service of a high cause, but how few. Many rabbis worked intensively with their congregations to bring them to accept more radical positions than they may have otherwise done: only a few rabbis were dismissed "because of their serious effort to apply the teachings of Judaism to the problems of society."[43]

Another key tension is that between *duty* and *happiness*. We have noted that one of the most attractive aspects of Kantian ethics for the early Reformers was its excoriation of the pleasure principle. Commitment to duty has been subject to psychological and anthropological critique, and in twentieth-century Reform ethical discourse, ethical demands are framed differently: each section of the 1999 Pittsburgh Principles concludes with the statement that the principle in question "gives meaning and purpose to our lives."[44] The cultural shift which Charles Taylor has called "the ethic of authenticity"[45] has brought an unprecedented individualism and a form of instrumental reasoning that hardly seems to encourage altruism. Taylor's claim, by which I am convinced, is that behind a thirst for personal meaning and fulfillment, a quest for authenticity can be discerned. For a liberal religious movement such as Reform, a key question is: can serious ethical demands be expressed in a culture of self-expression and self-fulfillment? Can such standards be identified in such an era in the first place, and in the end, how can individuals rightfully be held accountable to them?

The perennial tension between *universal* and *particular* is certainly to be found in current Reform ethics. Lawrence Hoffman has written on this theme, perhaps most poignantly in a piece relating to the illness of his daughter. In that article he reflects that for the founders of Reform, healing was messianic and on a global scale: "Focused macrocosmically, they preached the prophets but did not make house calls." Deliberately employing an oxymoron, he calls for a "local universalism, saving the world one local life at a time." Such a local universalism "does not displace the global social justice mandate of early Reform; it completes it."[46]

How does a contemporary Reform ethic in search of authenticity and defined by these tensions and others come to expression? It is in the area of feminist thought that Reform ethics has been most significantly transformed over the last decades. At first, the call to include women as full partners in the ritual, intellectual, and spiritual life of Judaism may have been understood as a matter of equality. In time, however, it has become apparent that an "engendered" approach to Judaism is more than simply the cooption of women into the existing stable structure: it involves a questioning and perhaps also an undermining of many of the assumptions upon which the existing traditions have been based. Feminist voices not only have been appreciative of the Reform movement: they have also taken aspects of its structure and theology to task. Borowitz's covenant imagery and his stance on issues related to the family and sexual identity have not been immune to this critique.[47]

Feminist theology advances "a Judaism that honors completely the prophetic ideal of a broken society renewed and made whole though the vision and action of humanity in partnership with God."[48] The publication of Rachel Adler's *Engendering Judaism* was a landmark in feminist Jewish theology. Based on the notion that Judaism is greater than any particular manifestation, and that it is only penultimately patriarchal, Adler's work includes "An Ethics of Sexuality and Relationship." If the fathers of modernity read their own assumptions into the fabric of reality, Adler's task is to offer different metaphors and approaches that can allow women to have a voice as something other than honorary men.

Adler's work is subtitled "An Inclusive Theology and Ethics." She argues that the progressive branches of Judaism "are not yet fully attentive to the impact of gender on the texts and lived experiences of the people Israel."[49] The challenge of evolving and enunciating an ethic of inclusion is certain to feature high on the agenda of Reform Judaism in the coming years. The voices of LGBT Jews, the voices of those who are not in conventional Jewish family structures—these and other voices demand their place in the discourse of Reform ethics.

There have been attempts to develop an ethics of the body, healing, and wellness. In Hoffman's terms, Reform Jewish ethics has begun to make house calls. This does not mean, however, that Reform Judaism has lost sight of global concerns. Along with others in the liberal camp, the movement has become highly engaged with issues relating to ethical consumption and environmental issues. Enthusiasm for the consumer paradise offered by modernity has been tempered by consciousness of impending ecological meltdown. Ethical eating is the order of the day.[50]

Spirituality, too, has recently become a major concern of many Reform Jews. While Arnold Jacob Wolf decried this tendency, suggesting that it would pull attention away from the great ethical and religious challenges,[51] aspects of Jewish spirituality have become increasingly central concerns for at least a section of the Reform movement.[52] Rather than being feared as a distraction from ethical concerns, many of those most involved with these concerns root their moral commitments in spiritual search.

As part of the move away from disembodied universalist claims, there has been interest in some parts in plumbing traditional Jewish sources of different kinds—*halakhah*, the Musar literature, philosophy, the Talmud, the literature of *kabbalah* and *Hasidism*—in search of a grounding for contemporary Reform ethics. A number of such attempts have been undertaken in recent years. To cite Rachel Sabath Beit-Halachmi's felicitous phrase, Reform Judaism is in search of "textual grounding and ethical vigilance."[53]

From theological reflection to engaged activism and beyond, the question of the provenance of Jewish ethics has been discussed in Reform circles. William B. Silverman, noted above for his Nashville sermon, had written a work to be used in religious school settings. In that work he presents different voices that have combined to form Jewish ethics. The list begins with the voice of Jacob (contrasted in a remarkable way with the brutish hands of Esau). It goes on to include the voice of Jewish Law (biblical legislation), the voice of Sinai (the Decalogue), the voice of the Prophets, the voice of the Psalmist, the voice of Wisdom (highlighting the Book of Proverbs), the voice of the Fathers (tractate *Avot*), the voice of the Rabbis, and finally, the still, small voice.[54] The omissions from this list are as informative as is what has been included, and a new generation of Reform learners is studying from a much broader curriculum.

There is also growing interest in what might be referred to as applied ethics. This term covers fields as diverse as discussions of the application of traditional Jewish moral virtues to contemporary settings[55] to discussions of business and bioethics by leading Reform *halakhists*[56] to ethical challenges arising within the synagogue,[57] and (as was mentioned above) to new approaches to community organizing. In all these cases the principal aim is to provide Jews with guidelines by which they may make practical decisions.

Another area of ethical debate is Israel. Founders of Reform Zionism saw facing up to the realities of sovereignty as an ethical imperative. Opponents of Israeli government policy are no less keen to cite the ethical foundations of Reform Judaism in their arguments. Richard Hirsch, founder of the movement's Religious Action Center, came to Israel in the 1970s at the helm of the World Union for Progressive Judaism. In a 1995 paper he declared that the apparent dichotomy between the universal and the particular is illusory: "We cannot repair the world, if we do not repair the Jewish people. We cannot repair the Jewish people, unless we are committed to repairing the world."[58]

In the early twenty-first century some around the Reform world see the efforts of the Israel Movement for Progressive Judaism as a vehicle for the advancement of their most cherished values. Others, however, seek an ethical Reform Judaism that is either removed from, or cool to, Israel. For some Reform Jews today, Israel is not the fulfillment of their ethical ambitions, but an immense challenge to their conception of Jewish ethics. Some choose to grapple with this challenge by devoting their energies to defending Israel and promoting their vision of a pluralistic and tolerant society, while others keep their distance from Israel and Zionism.

Beyond the specifics of the debate within Reform Judaism over Israel, there are significant processes at work. A generation of Reform Jews for whom the events of 1938–1948 do not represent the fulcrum of their Jewish consciousness is being attracted in some ways to a postmodern variant of the classical Reform posture: an interest in Judaism as a religious ethical system, rather than in Jewish peoplehood as a primary commitment. It remains a challenge to demonstrate to such Jews that engagement with Israel is more than an atavistic chore. The question of whether a local universalism can extend to include *'am olam*, a universal people, hangs in the balance.

Conclusion: An Ethics of the Future

This chapter has presented four sensibilities that inform ethics discourse in Reform Jewish circles. Taken sequentially, they tell a story, albeit stylized and simplistic. The founders of the movement, imbued with ethical optimism, placed ethics at the heart of their system. Their American heirs, inspired by New World confidence, took on the role of world changers. A third wave looked askance at some of the certainties of their predecessors, and a new generation is striving for "local universalism" in an age of authenticity. The ethical lauded in choirs and around campfires around the Reform world means different things to adherents of these different sensibilities.

Michael Meyer has described the problems facing a Reform Jew seeking moral guidance from a religiously based Jewish ethics. This individual "seeks an ethic grounded in God, but cannot accept Torah as verbal revelation," "seeks a religious moral imperative, but wants to remain open to the demands of each new situation," "seeks to link…moral acts with the morality of Jewish tradition, but finds that Jewish history has spawned varying, even conflicting moral points of view."[59]

These problems apply to all four of these nuances within Reform Judaism. Looking to the past, the movement can take a modicum of pride in its contribution to the moral debate within the Jewish world. Surveying the present, the ethical challenges confronting the Reform Jew are daunting in their range and intensity. For a synthesis between these contrasting approaches, and for the next development in the unfolding drama of Reform Jewish ethics, it is imperative to turn to the future. To return to Hermann Cohen: "[T]he past is predicated upon the future that is anticipated. It is not the past that is prior to one's thinking, but rather the future."[60]

Notes

1. Immanuel Kant, *Groundwork for the Metaphysics of Morals* [1785] (Toronto: Broadview Press, 2005), p. 72.
2. Felix Grayeff, *A Short Treatise on Ethics* (London: Duckworth, 1980), p. 27.
3. Moritz Lazarus, *The Ethics of Judaism*, trans. Henrietta Szold (Philadelphia: Jewish Publication Society of America, 1900), vol. 1, pp. 131–32, § 99.
4. Kaufmann Kohler, *Jewish Theology* [1918] (New York, Macmillan, 1928), p. 477.
5. Samson Hochfeld, "Equality of All Human Beings," in ed. Simon Bernfeld, *The Foundations of Jewish Ethics*, trans. Armin Koller [1929] (New York: Ktav, 1968), p. 150.
6. Isaac Mayer Wise, "Hebrew Monotheism," in *The American Jewish Pulpit: A Collection of Sermons* (Cincinnati: Bloch & Co., 1881), p. 204, http://americanjewisharchives.org/wise/attachment/5244/HebrewMonotheism.pdf, accessed October 1, 2011. For a later example of a similar strain within Reform Judaism, see Abba Hillel Silver, *Where Judaism Differed: An Inquiry into the Distinctiveness of Judaism* (Philadelphia: Jewish Publication Society of America, 1957).
7. "Affinities Betweeen the Philosophy of Kant and Judaism," in *Reason and Hope: Selections from the Jewish Writings of Hermann Cohen*, trans. and ed. Eva Jospe (Cincinnati: Hebrew Union College Press, 1993), p. 77.

8. See, for example, the chapter on these three thinkers by Jonathan K. Crane in this volume (#7).
9. Hermann Cohen, *Ethics of Maimonides*, trans. with a commentary by Almut Sh. Bruckstein (Madison: University of Wisconsin Press, 2004), p. 105.
10. Eva Jospe: "Hermann Cohen's Judaism: A Reassessment," *Judaism* 25.4 (Fall 1976), p. 468.
11. Hermann Cohen, *Religion of Reason Out of the Sources of Judaism*, trans. Simon Kaplan (New York: Frederick Ungar, 1972), p. 82.
12. Quoted in David Ellenson, "Autonomy and Norms in Reform Judaism," *CCAR Journal* (Spring 1999), p. 22.
13. Jacob Z. Lauterbach, "The Ethics of the Halakhah," in *Rabbinic Essays* (Cincinnati: Hebrew Union College Press, 1951), p. 266.
14. See Mark Washofsky, "Responsa and the Reform Rabbinate," in *Teshuvot for the Nineties: Reform Judaism's Answers for Today's Dilemmas*, eds. W. Gunther Plaut and Mark Washofsky (New York: CCAR Press, 1997), pp.xiii–xxx. See also Eugene B. Borowitz, "*Halakhah* in Reform Jewish Usage: Historic Background and Current Discourse", in Eugene B. Borowitz, *Studies in the Meaning of Judaism* (Philadelphia: Jewish Publication Society, 2002), pp. 415–33.
15. Quoted in Richard N. Levy, *A Vision of Holiness: The Future of Reform Judaism* (New York: URJ Press, 2005), pp. 259–61.
16. Kaufmann Kohler, *Jewish Theology*, at note 4 above, p. 453.
17. Leo Baeck, "Morality as a Basic Requirement of Judaism," *The Foundations of Jewish Ethics*, at note 5 above, p. 17.
18. Leo Baeck, *The Essence of Judaism* (New York: Schocken, 1948), p. 84.
19. Michael A. Meyer and W. Gunther Plaut, *The Reform Judaism Reader: North American Documents* (New York: UAHC Press, 2001), p. 145.
20. Robert D. Shapiro, *A Reform Rabbi in the Progressive Era: The Early Career of Stephen S. Wise* (New York and London: Garland, 1988), p. 82.
21. Quoted in Egal Feldman, "The Social Gospel and the Jews," *American Jewish Historical Quarterly* 58 (1969), pp. 311–12.
22. Quoted in W. Gunther Plaut, *The Growth of Reform Judaism: American and European Sources until 1948* (New York: World Union for Progressive Judaism, 1965), p. 118.
23. Quoted in Albert Vorspan and Eugene J. Lipman, *Justice and Judaism: The Work of Social Action* (New York: Union of American Hebrew Congregations, 1959), p. 255.
24. Albert Vorspan and Eugene J. Lipman, *Justice and Judaism: The Work of Social Action*, 1959, p. 6.
25. Ibid., p. 15.
26. Ibid., p. 21.
27. Richard G. Hirsch, *From the Hill to the Mount* (Jerusalem: Geffen, 2000), p. 38.
28. Quoted in David J. Meyer, "Fighting Segregation, Threats and Dynamite: Rabbi William B. Silverman's Nashville Battle," *American Jewish Archives Journal* 60, 1–2 (2008), p. 109. The article mentions a number of the other Reform rabbis engaged in this struggle.
29. David Saperstein, "Mandate for Social Justice," in Allan L. Smith, ed., *Where We Stand: Jewish Consciousness on Campus* (New York: UAHC Press, 1997), p. 388.
30. See, for example, Lillian S. Freehof, *The Right Way: Ethics for Youth* (New York: Union of American Hebrew Congregations, 1957); Helen Fine, *At Camp Kee Tov: Ethics for Jewish Juniors* (New York: Union of American Hebrew Congregations, 1961); Albert Vorspan, *To Do Justly: A Junior Casebook for Social Action* (New York:

Union of American Hebrew Congregations, 1969); Balfour Brickner and Albert Vorspan, *Searching the Prophets for Values* (New York: Union of American Hebrew Congregations, 1981).

31. Eugene B. Borowitz, "'Jewish?' 'Ethics?' 'Jewish Ethics?'—The New Problems," *Exploring Jewish Ethics: Papers on Covenant Responsibility* (Detroit: Wayne State University Press, 1990), p. 30.
32. Emil L. Fackenheim, *To Mend the World: Foundations of Post-Holocaust Jewish Thought* (New York: Schocken Books, 1982), p. 272. It is interesting to contrast this comment with the anecdote told by Hans Jonas of visiting a former teacher who had resisted Nazism, who told him that "[w]ithout Kant's teaching I couldn't have done it." Hans Jonas, "Contemporary Problems in Ethics from a Jewish Perspective," in Daniel Jeremy Silver, ed., *Judaism and Ethics* (no location stated: Ktav/Central Conference of American Rabbis, 1970), p. 113.
33. Arnold Jacob Wolf, "Reform's Original Sin," in Dana Evan Kaplan, ed. *Contemporary Debates in American Reform Judaism: Conflicting Visions* (New York: Routledge, 2001), pp. 90–91.
34. Eugene B. Borowitz, *Renewing the Covenant: A Theology for the Postmodern Jew* (Philadelphia: The Jewish Publication Society, 1991), p. 23.
35. Albrecht Wellmer, *The Persistence of Modernity* (Cambridge: Polity, 2007), p. vi.
36. See in particular Eugene B. Borowitz, *Choosing a Sex Ethic: A Jewish Inquiry* (no place stated: Schocken/B'nai B'rith Hillel, 1969); *Exploring Jewish Ethics* (1990), at note 30 above; *Renewing the Covenant* (1991), at note 33 above; *Judaism After Modernity: Papers from a Decade of Fruition* (Lanham, MD: University Press of America, 1999), esp. pp. 233–48; *Studies in the Meaning of Judaism*, at note 14 above, esp. pp. 133–48, 179–92, 275–88.
37. See Steven Schwarzchild, "The Question of Jewish Ethics Today," in Menachem Kellner, ed., *The Pursuit of the Ideal: Jewish Writings of Steven Schwarzchild* (Albany: SUNY Press, 1990), pp. 117–36.
38. *Renewing the Covenant*, at note 34 above, p. 288.
39. Eugene B. Borowitz, "'Im ba'et, eyma*—Since You Object, Let Me Put It This Way,*" in Peter Ochs, ed., *Reviewing the Covenant: Eugene B. Borowitz and the Postmodern Renewal of Jewish Theology* (Albany: SUNY Press, 2000), p. 148. See also his response to Elliot Dorff's review of *Renewing the Covenant* (in *Conservative Judaism* 48:2 [Winter 1996], pp. 64–68), in which Dorff portrays him as a Reform thinker, and a published response, "The Reform Judaism of *Renewing the Covenant*: An Open Letter to Elliot Dorff," in which Borowitz objects that he intended to articulate his own theory, not a Reform theory: *Conservative Judaism* 50:1 (Fall 1997), pp. 61–65. Dorff then responds to his letter in the same issue. Borowitz liked the exchange so much that he had it published as a separate pamphlet distributed to every member of the Central Conference of American Rabbis, and Dorff republished the exchange in Elliot N. Dorff, *The Unfolding Tradition: Jewish Law After Sinai* (New York: Aviv Press [Rabbinical Assembly, 2005], pp. 464–80.
40. Albert Vorspan and David Saperstein, *Tough Choices: Jewish Perspectives on Social Justice* (New York: UAHC Press, 1992), p. 290. The series of books that came after *Justice and Judaism* constitutes a guide of applied social ethics in the North American Reform movement over the last decades. See Albert Vorspan, *Jewish Values and Social Crisis: A Casebook for Social Action* (New York: Union of American Hebrew Congregations), 1968; Albert Vorspan, *Great Jewish Debates and Dilemmas: Jewish Perspectives on Moral Issues and Conflict in the Eighties* (New York: Union

of American Hebrew Congregations, 1980); Albert Vorspan and David Saperstein, *Jewish Dimensions of Social Justice: Tough Moral Choices of Our Time* (New York: UAHC Press, 1998).

41. See, for example, Jonah Dov Pesner, "Redemption for Radicals: Jewish Congregation-Based Community Organizing," in Or N. Rose, Jo Ellen Green Kaiser, Margie Klein, eds., *Righteous Indignation: A Jewish Call for Justice* (Woodstock VT: Jewish Lights, 2008), pp. 87–93; Jonah Dov Pesner and Lila Foldes, "Building the Power for Redemption: An Introduction to and Theology of Congregation-Based Community Organizing," *CCAR Journal* 55.2 (2008), pp. 57–66.
42. Quoted in Richard N. Levy, *A Vision of Holiness*, at note 15 above, p. 265.
43. Roland B. Gittelsohn, "The Conference Stance on Social Justice and Civil Rights," in Bertram Wallace Korn, ed., *Retrospect and Prospect* (New York: Central Conference of American Rabbis, 1965), p. 110.
44. Quoted in Richard N. Levy, *A Vision of Holiness*, at note 15 above, pp. xv–xx.
45. Charles Taylor, *The Ethics of Authenticity* (Cambridge, MA: Harvard University Press, 1992). See also Charles Taylor, *A Secular Age* (Cambridge: Belknap, 2007), esp. pp. 473–504.
46. Lawrence A. Hoffman, "Post-Colonial Healing in the Land of the Sick," *CCAR Journal* 53.1–2 (2006), pp. 27, 29, 30. See also William Cutter, ed., *Midrash and Medicine: Healing Body and Soul in the Jewish Interpretive Tradition* (Woodstock, VT: Jewish Lights, 2010). Approximately one half of the articles in that work are authored by individuals affiliated in some way with the Reform movement.
47. See Laura Levitt, *Jews and Feminism: The Ambivalent Search for Home* (New York and London: Routledge, 1997), esp. pp. 75–90. For important insights, see also, Elyse Goldstein, ed., *New Jewish Feminism: Probing the Past, Forging the Future* (Woodstock, VT: Jewish Lights, 2009). Karla Goldman, "Women in Reform Judaism: Between Rhetoric and Reality," in Riv-Ellen Prell, ed., *Women Remaking American Judaism* (Detroit: Wayne State University Press, 2007), pp. 109–34; Pamela S. Nadell, "Bridges to 'A Judaism Transformed by Women's Wisdom': The First Generation of Women Rabbis," Riv-Ellen Prell, ed., *Women Remaking American Judaism*, pp. 211–28.
48. Alexandra Wright, "An Approach to Feminist Jewish Theology," in Sybil Sheridan, ed., *Hear Our Voice: Women Rabbis Tell Their Stories* (London: SCM Press, 1994), pp. 160–61.
49. Rachel Adler, *Engendering Judaism: An Inclusive Theology and Ethics* (Boston: Beacon Press, 1998), p. 24.
50. See Mary Zamore, ed., *The Sacred Table: Creating a Jewish Food Ethic* (New York: CCAR Press, 2011); *Jewish Dimensions of Social Justice*, at note 39 above, pp. 109–35. See also Hans Küng and Walter Homolka, eds., *How to Do Good and Avoid Evil: A Global Ethic from the Sources of Judaism* (Woodstock VT: Skylight Paths, 2009), esp. pp. 19–39, where the basis for the global ethic is read straight out of Hermann Cohen and Abraham Geiger. See also Aaron Saul Gross, "Continuity and Change in Reform Views of Kashrut 1883–2002: From the treifah banquet to eco-kashrut." *CCAR Journal* (Winter 2004), pp. 6–28.
51. Arnold Jacob Wolf, "Against Spirituality," *Judaism* 50.3 (2001), pp. 362–66.
52. For the term, see Niles E. Goldstein and Steven S. Mason, *Judaism and Spiritual Ethics* (New York: UAHC Press, 1996); for evidence of this new emphasis on spirituality within the Reform movement, see Richard N. Levy, *A Vision of Holiness*, at note 15 above.

53. Rachel Sabath Beit-Halachmi, "The Changing Status of Women in Liberal Judaism," *New Jewish Feminism*, at note 47 above, p. 208.
54. William B. Silverman, *The Still Small Voice: The Story of Jewish Ethics* (New York: Behrman House, 1955), pp. 207–8.
55. See Kerry M. Olitzky and Rachel T. Sabath, *Striving Toward Virtue: A Contemporary Guide for Jewish Ethical Behavior* (Hoboken, NJ: Ktav, 1996); Eugene B. Borowitz and Frances Weinman Schwartz, *The Jewish Moral Virtues* (Philadelphia: The Jewish Publication Society, 1999).
56. Reform halakhists such as Walter Jacob, Daniel Schiff, and Moshe Zemer have all grappled with a range of ethical issues in their work. See, for example, Mark Washofsky, "AIDS and Ethical Responsibility: Some Halachic Considerations," *Journal of Reform Judaism*, 36.1 (1989), pp. 53–65; "Halachah, Aggadah and Reform Jewish Bioethics: A Response," *CCAR Journal* 53.3 (2006), pp. 81–100. Reform engagement with *halakhah* has been part of every stage of the movement's history. The Freehof Institute of Progressive Halakhah also produces periodic volumes of Reform *responsa* and scholarship on pressing biomedical, social, religious, and political issues.
57. In 1989 the Union of American Hebrew Congregations published a manual on synagogue ethics. The work of Arthur Gross Schaefer has been of particular significance in this field. See, for example, "Teshuvah and Rabbinic Sexual Misconduct," *CCAR Journal* 42.2 (1995), pp. 75–80.
58. Richard G. Hirsch, *From the Hill to the Mount*, at note 26 above, p. 118.
59. Michael A. Meyer, "Problematics of Jewish Ethics," *CCAR Journal* 15.3 (1968), p. 63.
60. Quoted from *Logik der reinen Erkenntnis* in *Ethics of Maimonides*, at note 9 above, p. xxxvi.

Suggestions for Further Reading

Adler, Rachel. 1998. *Engendering Judaism: An Inclusive Theology and Ethics*. Boston: Beacon Press.

Borowitz, Eugene B. 1990. *Exploring Jewish Ethics: Papers on Covenant Responsibility*. Detroit: Wayne State University Press.

Cohen, Hermann. 2004. *Ethics of Maimonides*. Translated with commentary by Almut Sh. Bruckstein. Madison: University of Wisconsin Press.

Kaplan, Dana Evan, ed. 2001. *Contemporary Debates in American Reform Judaism: Conflicting Visions*. New York: Routledge.

Martin, Bernard, ed. 1968. *Contemporary Reform Jewish Thought*. Chicago: Quadrangle.

Silver, Daniel Jeremy, ed. 1970. *Judaism and Ethics*. Jersey City, NJ: Ktav.

CHAPTER 12

ETHICAL THEORIES IN THE CONSERVATIVE MOVEMENT

SHAI CHERRY

To know about the ethics of an institution, do not look just at its mission statement; look at its budget. *Mutatis mutandis,* to understand the ethics of the Conservative Movement, do not look just at its ethical theories; look at its liturgical and *halakhic* [legal] idiosyncrasies.[1] Individual rabbis, often the leaders of the movement, have made varying and contradictory pronouncements—much like the venerable sages of the Talmud. But, if one seeks something of a consensus concerning the Conservative Movement and its relationship to ethics, one is better served by analyzing those documents that speak louder than any single legal theorist, as important as theory is. Thus this examination of Conservative Judaism and ethics begins not with theory, to which we will eventually arrive, but with the liturgical and *halakhic* innovations implemented since the end of World War II.[2]

LITURGICAL MODIFICATIONS

The first morning blessings of the traditional prayer book thank God for making the male pray-er (1) not a gentile, (2) not a slave, and (3) not a woman. The Rabbinical Assembly and the United Synagogue of Conservative Judaism—the rabbinic and congregational arms of the Conservative Movement, respectively—published the

Sabbath and Festival Prayer Book in 1946 that boldly began by modifying these blessings. The Conservative worshipper thanks God for making him *or her* in the divine image, a Jew, and a free person. These shifts, with varying degrees of precedence in liturgical history, foreshadow the universalism and egalitarianism of subsequent liturgical changes while remaining faithful to the traditional liturgy as much as possible.

Next, and more significant (although more subtle), is the change of texts prior to the first recitation of *Kaddish d'Rabbanan*. In traditional prayer books there had been rabbinic passages concerning animal sacrifices and the listing of Rabbi Ishmael's thirteen principles of expounding the Torah. In both the 1946 *Prayer Book* and the 1985 *Siddur Sim Shalom*, the sacrificial passages were replaced by rabbinic teachings concerning ethics. Rabban Yohanan ben Zakkai, for example, is cited as saying that, in the wake of the Temple's destruction and our resulting inability to engage in animal sacrifice, acts of lovingkindness serve to provide atonement. Alongside of Rabbi Ishmael's thirteen principles is Rabbi Simlai's claim that the Torah begins and ends with acts of lovingkindness. The message to the worshipper is that just as sacrifices atoned for Israel's transgressions in the ancient past, today deeds of lovingkindness both atone for our transgressions *and* inform how we read the Torah.

Within the *Amidah* itself, we see the changes from the preliminary blessings reinforced. The 1946 *Prayer Book* inserts a plea for universal peace in the climactic final blessing rather than restricting peace geographically and ethnically to Israel. In both the later, separate editions of *Sim Shalom* for Sabbaths and Festivals (1998) and weekdays (2002) and in the Israeli Masorti prayer book, *Va'ani Tefilatti* (1999), the matriarchs have been included as an optional addition to the first blessing. More subtly, but grammatically necessary to maintain ideological consistency with egalitarianism, the Israeli *Va'ani Tefilatti* changes the word *redeemer* (*go'el*), which in Hebrew is exclusively masculine, to *redemption* (*ge'ulah*) in the first blessing. Rather than beseeching God to bring a male redeemer, Israelis now look toward a gender-neutral redemption. The chairman of the 1946 prayer book, Rabbi Robert Gordis, refrained from making such explicit changes because, he averred, the prayer book is poetry, not prose. "Thus, the emphasis in the prayer book upon the Messiah need not mean for us the belief in a personal redeemer."[3] Such poetic ambiguity is easier to maintain with the ungendered English *messiah* than with the gendered Hebrew *go'el*, in distinction to *go'elet*.

Finally, the concern with universalism, egalitarianism, and lovingkindness explicit in Conservative liturgy is reflected not only in what the prayer books have replaced (the preliminary blessings and the study sections before *Kaddish d'Rabbanan*) and inserted (references to the matriarchs and a plea for universal peace in the *Amidah*), but also in what they have consciously chosen to exclude. The 1984 *Artscroll Siddur*, an Orthodox prayer book, for example, returned to the *Aleinu* a passage that had been edited out centuries earlier because it was deemed to be offensive to Christianity. The Conservative Movement refrained from restoring the polemical passage to the *Aleinu*.

Halakhic Decisions

Since the end of World War II, there have been at least three major *halakhic* issues that have both polarized Conservative Rabbis and distinguished Conservative Judaism from Orthodoxy. Those issues are driving an automobile/using electricity on the Sabbath, allowing women into the rabbinate, and legitimizing homosexual relations. The last two issues are particularly valuable for this investigation because they represent ethical issues explicitly dealt with as such by the *nonhalakhic* movements within Judaism. Reform and Reconstructionist seminaries began ordaining women in 1972 and 1974, respectively, as a matter of fairness and gender equality.[4] Similarly, with regard to homosexuality, the Reform and Reconstructionist movements officially welcomed homosexuals into their congregations and onto their pulpits as a matter of fairness, without any significant *halakhic* argumentation, well before the Conservative Movement took these steps.[5] However, as we examine the *halakhic* discussions, we will see that on both issues, gender equality and acceptance of homosexual behavior, the Conservative Movement's legal reasoning involves qualifications and restrictions that significantly vitiate women's and gay rights. The liturgy's poetic emphases on egalitarianism and lovingkindness have been far more difficult to effect within the world of *halakhah*.

Rabbi Joel Roth's legal analysis concerning the ordination of women is largely regarded as the Jewish Theological Seminary's justification for doing so beginning in 1985. What is most interesting for our present purposes is Roth's insistence that "the issue of male-female equality plays no part in my thinking on the subject."[6] Roth asserts that he is attempting to provide an avenue for women to express their own sense of being commanded by God without yoking all women to the *mitzvot* from which they had traditionally been exempt. Roth "dread(s) the thought" of creating a new class of sinners.[7] He argues that there is no *halakhic* impediment for women voluntarily to accept as binding the commandments that traditionally obligated only men. If and only if a woman has imposed upon herself all the commandments that oblige a man (clearly excluding circumcision but including the duty to don *tefillin* during daily morning prayer and possibly the duty to procreate, both of which traditionally apply only to men) may she then assume the privileges inherent in the *halakhic* system necessary to become a rabbi.[8] Although there is a general (mis)perception that Conservative Judaism is egalitarian, Roth's strategy does not rely on issues of fairness or comprehensive equality between genders. Mixed seating (men and women) has characterized Conservative congregations from the early twentieth century, but it is difficult to define Conservative Judaism as *ideologically* (as opposed to aesthetically or practically) egalitarian.[9] The default attitude of Conservative *halakhah* toward women remains the same as that of Orthodoxy: women are exempt from most time-sensitive prescriptions, which precludes them from some essential rabbinic duties.

In Roth's eagerness to prevent creating a new class of sinners, his legal reasoning may have turned women's participation in synagogue life into a farce. There was a strong temptation by many who claimed to follow Roth's ruling to engage in a "don't ask, don't tell" policy that allows women to lead prayers even though the vast majority of Conservative women, like Conservative men (!), do not consider themselves obligated to prayer thrice daily. According to Roth's logic, when a brother and sister commit to saying *Kaddish* once a day for the eleven months following their father's death, and to further honor their father's memory they commit to leading the prayer service but do not otherwise live a *halakhic* life, only the brother should be eligible to lead prayers.[10] But, the reality is that no one asks the sister if she has committed to praying three times daily. Thus she will be warmly greeted as the prayer leader. According to Roth, however, she should be ineligible to serve in that role. What, then, is the *halakhic* status of a rabbi who knowingly allows such a woman to lead services? Is he or she a sinner? What about the other members of the prayer quorum—have they fulfilled their obligation to pray?

Although the mechanism that Roth used was relatively narrow in its legal scope, the practical effect was far reaching. Rabbi Roth himself taught me that the Interstate Commerce Clause was used by the U.S. Supreme Court to prohibit restaurants from racial discrimination against customers.[11] His point was that when working within a legal system, one uses the tools available to accomplish the desired goal while preserving the integrity of the system. But in our case, the method seems to rely on a wink and nod that impugns the entire *halakhic* system.

The other issue that has exercised the Conservative Movement relates to its posture toward homosexuals. In December 2006 there were two mutually exclusive legal rulings approved by the Jewish Committee on Laws and Standards (more on this body and its function later in the chapter). The first, authored by Rabbi Joel Roth, expressed sympathy for the plight of homosexuals but preserved the tradition's opposition to all homosexual behavior. The second paper, authored by Rabbis Elliot Dorff, David Nevins, and Avram Reisner, offered a much more innovative approach that promoted ethical concerns without allowing ethics to trump biblical law as understood by the Rabbis. In doing so, one sees a striking parallel with the method of Rabbi Joel Roth in his approach to women in the rabbinate. Depending on one's perspective, the Dorff et al. *responsum* was as much a legal fiction as was Roth's *responsum* on women and the rabbinate.

The Dorff et al. *responsum* hinges on the rabbinic principle that a person's dignity is so important that it supersedes biblical prohibitions (see, e.g., B. *Shabbat* 81b). The Talmud, however, immediately qualifies that statement to refer only to the biblical commandment in Deuteronomy 17 to obey the judges of each generation. The authors of the Dorff et al. *responsum* therefore argue that this *halakhic* principle allows them to suspend rabbinic, although not biblical, prohibitions that would prevent homosexuals from enjoying loving, committed relationships. The authors contend that although the biblical prohibition of anal intercourse remains in place (Lev 18:22), in the name of preserving the dignity of homosexuals contemporary rabbis should use their authority to suspend the rabbinic restrictions involving other acts of same-sex physical intimacy. (The *responsum* makes clear that bisexuals who are able to have fulfilling sexual relationships with members of the opposite gender are not permitted to engage in homosexual activity.) The conclusion of the *responsum* is that homosexuals may engage in acts of physical intimacy, although not biblically prohibited anal intercourse, and be eligible for all honors and privileges available in the community. Shortly after the Committee on Jewish Law and Standards passed this *responsum*, both American Conservative seminaries declared homosexuals welcome to apply to rabbinical school. In 2012, the Israeli Conservative/Masorti seminary made a similar shift. (To date, the Hungarian and Argentinean seminaries are still closed to openly gay students.)

Dorff later acknowledged that he is bothered by maintaining the restriction against anal intercourse, since he knows full well that such a condition is likely to be widely ignored.[12] Indeed, much earlier in Dorff's career he wrote that "we should not engage in overdoses of legal fictions, as we have been wont to do in the past."[13] Nevertheless, since Dorff feared (correctly) that he would not have had the necessary votes from the Committee on Jewish Laws and Standards were he and his co-authors to argue for nullifying the biblical prohibition, he did "what [could] be done and [took] satisfaction from the progress that a partial step in the right direction [achieved]."[14] This strategy is similar to Roth's vis-à-vis women in the rabbinate: both achieved their goal by legal means that then allowed others to employ what Dorff refers to as "wise silence" in order to obviate the *halakhic* restrictions that allowed the *responsa* to be passed in the first place.[15] Wisely silent rabbis would refrain from asking invasive questions about a woman's *halakhic* observance or gay men's sexual activity, thus conniving in the *halakhic* charade.[16]

A third *halakhic* issue, that of bastardy (*mamzerut*), throws into relief the tension between ethics and the Conservative Movement's general approach to *halakhah*. Rabbi Elie Spitz argues that the *halakhah* should not punish a bastard because of the deeds of his or her parents. Spitz cited both Dorff and the Modern Orthodox thinker Eliezer Berkovits to argue that the *halakhah* must respond to what the judges of the day perceive to be unethical. On the issue of *mamzerut*, Spitz advocates rendering the law procedurally inoperative. In the event that a congregant should reveal to his rabbi that he is a *mamzer*, according to Spitz, the rabbi's response should take the following form: "I did not hear and will not hear anything that you say regarding your possible status as a *mamzer*. You are a full Jew. In the Conservative Movement, we do not consider the category of *mamzerut* as operative, because we are committed to judging each person on his or her own merits as a result of the moral teachings of our tradition."[17]

If the category of *mamzerut* is inoperative, then why must the rabbi in the example claim to "not hear" anything in regard to *mamzerut*? Why not hear and acknowledge the voice of the congregant, and respond that the status of *mamzerut* is no longer operative in the Conservative Movement? Neither Rabbis Joel Roth nor Avram Reisner, a co-author with Dorff concerning homosexuality, were willing to render the biblical law of bastardy inoperative. In this case, Dorff's "wise silence" has morphed into wise deafness. There is talmudic precedent for such self-imposed deafness. In the Talmud, one rabbi ordered witnesses to stuff their ears with gourds to prevent them from hearing a recalcitrant husband cancel a writ of divorce that the rabbi had forced him to provide his wife (B. *Gittin* 34a). The rabbis of the talmudic period were also loath to admit uprooting a biblical law.[18] Nevertheless, in my opinion, some methods, even if precedented, are unworthy of perpetuating.

The Latest *Halakhic* Initiatives and *Hekhsher Tzedek*

Lest one imagine that Conservative Judaism is dedicated exclusively to lightening the yoke of the law,[19] there have been a number of recent decisions leaning in the opposite direction. Rabbi Seymour Siegel, a staunch advocate that "the *aggadah* [Jewish lore and theology] should control the *halakhah*—not vice-versa," argued that smoking should be forbidden because it is dangerous to both the smoker and those around the smoker.[20] In addition to this prohibition, there has also been a prescription mandated in the field of health, namely, post-mortem organ donation. Rabbi Joseph H. Prouser contends that it is obligatory for Jews to donate their organs upon their own death, and arrangements should be made while one is still alive to that effect.[21] Furthermore, the family that refuses to allow the deceased's organs to be harvested is in violation of "Do not stand idly by the blood of your neighbor" (Lev 19:16).

Shifting from the personal to the commercial, the Conservative Movement and the United Synagogue of Conservative Judaism have recently launched an initiative that brings business ethics into the realm of religion. Rabbi Morris Allen, outraged by a national scandal involving a kosher meat packing plant in Iowa, formulated a process by which kosher foods could earn a seal of approval (*hekhsher*) for their business methods. This new seal, *Magen Tzedek*, guarantees to the consumer public that the company is conscientiously providing for the health and safety of their employees through proper work conditions, training, wages, and benefits.[22] Furthermore, *Magen Tzedek* takes into account the environmental impact of the production process as well as the transparency of the company's finances. Not insignificantly, this move within the Conservative Movement has inspired rabbis within Orthodoxy to devise a similar initiative, *Tav HaYosher*.

Jill Jacobs has been instrumental in bringing these issues of labor management back to the *halakhic* agenda. Not only has Jacobs authored a far-reaching *responsum* on how Jewish-owned businesses and Jewish institutions should relate to the laborers who sustain their operations;[23] she has also penned a more popular work to bring these issues to a wider audience.[24] One hundred years after the tragic Triangle Shirtwaist fire of 1911, in which Jews were both owners and victims, the Conservative Movement is jockeying for a position of moral authority in the workplace. More and more contemporary rabbis, like Jacobs and Rabbis Aryeh Cohen and Sharon Brous of Los Angeles, are putting social justice at the very center of their rabbinate.[25] As Jacobs writes, "Ritual commandments are *useless* unless they sharpen our awareness of the condition of the world, increase access to the divine pathos, and engage us in working toward the biblical vision of a redeemed world."[26]

Ethical Theories

In the appendix to Rabbi Elliot N. Dorff's *Matters of Life and Death: A Jewish Approach to Modern Medical Ethics*, he presents four different relationships that may obtain between religion and ethics.[27] Although Dorff advocates (1) a mutually reinforcing dialogue between religion and ethics, others argue that (2) religion and ethics are independent spheres, (3) what religion says or demands is, *ipso facto*, moral, and (4) morality is a logical prerequisite for religion. Consistent with his rejection of these last three positions, Dorff is committed to changing the *halakhah* that the rabbis of each generation consider immoral.[28]

Rabbi Joel Roth, on the other hand, while recognizing the role of ethics in the *halakhic* process, rejects the notion that ethics, by itself, can justify *halakhic* change.[29] In his 2006 statement on homosexuality, he insists that allowing ethics or theology to determine the movement's *halakhic* positions represents a clear violation of the rules of the *halakhic* system as evidenced throughout the history of Jewish legal development. (Moreover, in both his 1992 and 2006 *responsa* on homosexuality, Roth claimed that the prohibition on homosexual behavior was *not* immoral.)

In a book review of Rabbi Moshe Zemer's *Evolving Halakhah: A Progressive Approach to Traditional Jewish Law*, Roth offers a critique of this Reform rabbi's thinking that applies equally well to Conservative legists like Dorff and Rabbi Gordon Tucker, who reject Roth's brand of legal positivism. Zemer cites Rabbi Seymour Siegel, who, as we have seen, argued that the *halakhah* must submit itself to our understanding of ethics. Roth may sympathize with the end, but he cannot abide by the means.

> If the classical sources of the law can support the view which the modern "knows" must be the law, there is no need to deal with such side issues as the weight of precedent or *hilkheta ke-vatra'ei* (the law follows the latest authorities) because they do not really matter. The modern is certain what the law must be, and finding support for it is sufficient. Accepted decision-making principles are not relevant because conscience and moral certainty are determinative. And, if the classical sources of the law cannot support the desired conclusion, that too is no problem. After all, modern scholarship has demonstrated conclusively that *halakhah* has a history and has always evolved.[30]

Roth, subsequent to resigning from the Committee on Jewish Law and Standards following the split decision on homosexual behavior, charged that rabbis who adjudicate predicated exclusively on their own conscience and moral certainty are playing God.[31]

Recently, Rabbi Tucker has cited an eighteenth-century rabbi, Yehezkel Landau, in a striking formulation that asserts, much like Roth, that *aggadah*/ethics have no determinative *halakhic* force.³² Tucker laments this legal posture and argues that a religious legal system hides its face from its collective understanding of God's will by hamstringing itself to the posited rules and precedents of a legal system (*à la* legal positivism) rather than adopting a more self-consciously Dworkinian posture that incorporates principles/ethics/*aggadah* in legal decision-making. In particular, Tucker argues that *agaddah*, especially in hard cases, should enhance traditional *halakhic* methodology.³³

It is worthwhile to examine a particular *halakhic* decision rendered by Yehezkel Landau to appreciate how his own practice undermined his theory. When asked if Jews were allowed to hunt for sport, his intuitive response was, "Barbaric! How can a Jew justify taking the life of one of God's creatures for recreational pleasure?! It's immoral." But, as Tucker has pointed out, morality is not a *halakhic* category for Landau, so he is unable to prohibit the practice on the basis of that criterion.

Landau proceeds to recount the story (*aggadah*!) of Esau's encounter with Jacob upon returning famished from the hunt. When Jacob offers to exchange his lentil stew for Esau's birthright, Esau responds, "I'm going to die—what good to me is the birthright?" (Gen 25:32) Although there are medieval commentators who interpret this statement as the hyperbole of an impetuous and myopic boor, there is another stream of biblical commentary that argues for the literal sense. Commentators like Abraham ibn Ezra suggest that Esau understands that hunting is dangerous business and that he is likely to predecease his father, thereby rendering his birthright worthless. Better, Esau shrewdly reasons, to get something for the birthright now. Landau uses this commentary on an *aggadic* passage in Genesis to conclude that hunting is dangerous for the hunter,³⁴ and placing oneself unnecessarily in a dangerous situation is a clear violation of the *halakhah*! Thus, sport hunting is prohibited not because of the senseless murder of the hunted animal, but because of the potential danger to the hunter.³⁵ One wonders how Landau would argue the issue today, given hunters with high-powered telescopic rifles riding in jeeps akin to armored personnel carriers.

Rabbi Tucker, in his contribution to the homosexuality dialogue, notes that previous watershed decisions used a similar methodology to the one Landau employed to prohibit hunting.³⁶ But there is something deeply dissatisfying and disingenuous about the use of such legal contortions in a religious legal system. There may have been a place for wise silence, Maimonidean duplicity, and *halakhic* contortions in the premodern era, Tucker maintains, but not today. According to the National Jewish Population Survey of 2000–2001, of those Americans who identify their religion as Jewish, 44 percent describe their outlook as secular or somewhat secular. (The figure is 16 percent among non-Jewish adults.)³⁷ *Halakhic* gymnastics often alienate those secular Jews—and many religious Jews, too!—who long for ethical inspiration from Jewish leadership but reject premodern assumptions, outlooks, and methodologies. Tucker argues that we should be both honest and consistent in our approach to Torah and *halakhah*. The academic study of the Bible, which the Conservative Movement long ago adopted, rejects any qualitative distinction between biblical and rabbinic law.³⁸ By and large, so does the American Jewish community. The traditional *halakhic* distinction between these two realms, precisely the distinction upon which the Dorff et al, *responsum* turns, is, therefore, problematic.

Both the Torah and its rabbinic literary successors (midrash and Talmud) represent human attempts to reflect the divine will. Ontologically, the status of both texts and genres is equal. The Torah does not necessarily represent a more transparent or reliable path to God's will than does later rabbinic literature. Tucker's critique of current *halakhic* methodology includes a plea for showing mercy to all God's creatures (an *aggadic* principle with *halakhic* force),[39] including homosexuals, even if doing so involves uprooting a biblical prohibition that is determined to no longer embody God's will as understood by fallible humans. It was precisely that deep resistance to uprooting a biblical prohibition that resulted in Tucker's *responsum*'s failing to garner enough votes for passage.

Aside from the fact that the *responsum* by Dorff et al. was officially approved by the Conservative Movement's Committee on Jewish Law and Standard and the one by Tucker was not, practically, the difference between them is that Tucker's approach allows for anal intercourse between gay men because it dispenses with the traditional distinction of biblical versus rabbinic prohibitions and uproots them both. Thus, not only is his approach more consistent with the way in which the Conservative Movement teaches about the Torah; it is more honest about gay sex. Indeed, it might be argued that by allowing homosexual physical intimacy while retaining the prohibition on anal intercourse, the *responsum* by Dorff et al. is in violation of the *halakhic* prohibition against placing a stumbling block before the blind.[40]

The dividing line among Conservative theorists is whether or not rabbis' moral sensibilities are sufficient to uproot a traditionally understood biblical prohibition. (Within traditional *halakhah*, it is much easier to prohibit what was permitted than to permit what was prohibited.) Rabbi Roth remains the most articulate, though increasingly isolated, legal theorist in the Conservative Movement to reject such a possibility. There are different approaches utilized by those who are willing to give their own sense of morality a trump card over biblical prohibitions. Some, like Dorff and Spitz, rely on legal fictions while preserving the biblical/rabbinic distinction; others, like Tucker, promote *aggadah* and reject the biblical/rabbinic distinction. I would like to suggest a third approach that also rejects the biblical/rabbinic distinction but that preserves and rehabilitates the classical *halakhic* method of midrash.

Many literary theorists see parallels between rabbinic midrash and modern literary theory. As Moshe Greenberg wrote citing James D. Smart, "the meaning and significance of a passage (an event, an utterance) may not be realized until activated by later circumstances or contemplation."[41] In the imagery of the Talmud, the Torah is like a fig tree that has multiple crops. Each time one returns to the tree, one finds new fruit (B. *Eruvin* 54 a–b). Rabbi Abraham Joshua Heschel gives this botanical metaphor an evolutionary edge. "The Bible is a seed, God is the sun, but we are the soil. Every generation is expected to bring forth new understanding and new realization."[42] When the soil changes, it affects the fruit, which means that the seed inside the fruit, responsible for the next generation, also changes. In Heschel's image, we are the soil, and we have changed both by virtue of our acceptance of biblical criticism and our recognition of the immorality of denying homosexuals a legitimate avenue for intimate partnership. The change in the soil affects the fruit and its seed. We have a different Torah than our ancestors had, or, more precisely, the Torah means something different to us than it did to our ancestors.

I understand "Do not lie with a male as one lies with a female" (Lev 18:22) to mean that a man who *does* have sex with females, namely heterosexuals and bisexuals, is prohibited from having sex with males. *This verse is not, however, addressing gay men.* What is my logic? If the text were addressing gay men, what would be the force of the otherwise superfluous verbiage "as one lies with a female" in the prohibition? The text could have just said, "Do not lie with a male."[43] Do I believe that this reading reflects the conscious intention of the author/s or editor/s? No. But I do believe that such a reading is consistent with what literary theory has helped us understand about the nature of literature in general *and*, more importantly, how the classical Jewish sages read the Torah in particular.

There are four advantages to my reading over Dorff's and Tucker's: (1) I do not rely on the intellectually problematic distinction between biblical and rabbinic law as does the *responsum* by Dorff et al.; (2) my reading argues that there is not a prohibition on gay anal intercourse—and thus my reading does not uproot a biblical prohibition as does the suggestion by Tucker—since this verse is not to be read as directed toward homosexuals;[44] (3) the traditional bias toward heterosexism is preserved by claiming that this prohibition is directed toward bisexuals. (Tucker does not address this point.) (4) Another virtue of this reading is that it employs traditional *halakhic* methodology by making an *ukimta*, a legally restrictive interpretation, from seemingly superfluous words. Many *halakhists* may point to this use of *halakhic* midrash as a fatal disadvantage because I sideline two thousand years of interpretive consensus in favor of an innovative and idiosyncratic reading. One response to that critique can be found in the Committee on Jewish Law and Standards.

Committee on Jewish Law and Standards

Since 1927, the Conservative Movement has helped guide the *halakhic* decisions of its members. In the published *responsa* since World War II, the following disclaimer regularly appears: "The Committee on Jewish Law and Standards provides guidance in matters of *halakhah* for the Conservative Movement. The individual rabbi, however, is the authority for the interpretation and application of all matters of *halakhah*." In other words, the Committee gets a vote, not a veto, on the actual application of legal rulings.

Decisions of the committee are not binding; they are advisory. Because they have only advisory capacity to the rabbis in the Rabbinical Assembly, there is no need for a majority of the committee members to vote in favor of a *responsum* for it to be considered a viable option. Currently, if six of the twenty-five voting members of the committee vote for a given *responsum*, that is sufficient to provide institutional endorsement upon which an individual rabbi may rely. Rabbi Tucker describes this situation as "modified majoritarianism without authoritarianism."[45] This communal mechanism provides a significant measure of control over idiosyncratic readings such as the one I offered above. *Aharei rabbim l'hatot*—incline after many rabbis, in this case six. The committee's work also distinguishes Conservative Judaism from Reform, where individual Jews, as opposed to trained rabbis, are free to determine their own religious practice.[46]

This modified majoritarianism leads to the possibility that mutually exclusive *halakhic* positions will simultaneously be endorsed by the committee, as indeed happened during the 2006 vote on homosexuals.[47] Tucker, writing in 1993, explains the virtues of this artifact of the post-prophetic and pre-messianic era. "[Rabbinic majoritarianism] is the interpretation under which [modified] majority decisions are a best approximation to a truth which God has decided to leave indeterminate to humans, and are thus both the culminations of rounds of debate and dissension, and the preludes to further such rounds."[48] (The Conservative Movement has nothing like a doctrine of Papal Infallibility, although there is an uncomfortable similarity between that doctrine and the Daas Torah of certain Orthodox sages.) The Committee recognizes that an individual rabbi may still rely on his own reasoning, as has been the case for much of Jewish history. There is no tyranny of the modified majority since not even a majority of the Committee "should be granted a monopoly on legal competence and authority."[49]

Richard L. Claman, a Jewishly educated attorney who participates in the discussion of Conservative Judaism's legal philosophy, pushes Tucker's principled defense of the committee further. Tucker's argument is based on the epistemological indeterminacy of the divine will. Claman argues, following Sir Isaiah Berlin, that some values are incommensurate with one another and hence incapable of being exhaustively compared—for example, the stability of a legal system versus the dignity of the human being. Thus, there is a philosophical basis for a value-pluralism that is not necessarily relativistic. (Not *all* values are equal or commensurate.) According to Claman, within Conservative Judaism there exists a value pluralism that becomes concretized in mutually exclusive *halakhic* opinions. "Value-pluralism in *halakhah* requires, I suggest, not just an acceptance of pluralism in outcomes, but also a pluralism in reasoning and discussion."[50]

The Road to the Future

Value-pluralism combined with modified majoritarianism without authoritarianism *allows for the Conservative Movement to shelter and nourish competing ethical theories, halakhic methodologies, and legal decisions.* In the Talmud, value-pluralism was reflected in the statement that "These and those are words of the living God" (B. *Eruvin* 13b). But, at least in the case of Hillel and Shammai, the law was decided according to one side. In the expansive, democratic landscape of American Judaism, there is no need to retain that limitation. The philosophy of the committee resonates deeply with the value-pluralism of the Talmud, *halakhic* practices in the far-flung Jewish communities of the Diaspora, and American culture.

Judaism by committee creates a movement where the interplay between *halakhah* and ethics will continue to be an open question. The inclusion of the matriarchs in the *Amidah* is optional, mutually exclusive *responsa* are approved, and desired *halakhic* outcomes are attained by what some see as methodologically dubious means. In the secular soil of American Judaism, the honesty and integrity with which the movement approaches future ethical question will, in some measure, determine Conservative Judaism's viability in the twenty-first century. Will the leaders of the movement be able to embrace both the Tree of Knowledge, which tells us that the Torah is neither uniquely divine nor authoritative, and the Tree of Life, which insists on the preeminence of ethics? Or, will we grow gourds and cultivate silence?

Notes

1. In this case, Conservative Judaism's consensus document, *Emet Ve'Emunah*, predictably posits that Judaism embodies "the highest moral principles," but then proceeds to equivocate on how to effect those principles. *Emet Ve'Emunah* (New York: Jewish Theological Seminary of America, 1988), p. 22.
2. My comments are largely restricted to Conservative Judaism in the United States.
3. Robert Gordis, "A Jewish Prayer Book for the Modern Age," in *Understanding Conservative Judaism,* Max Gelb, ed. (New York: Rabbinical Assembly, 1978), p. 146.
4. Jonathan D. Sarna, *American Judaism: A History* (New Haven, CT: Yale University Press, 2004), pp. 339–44.
5. The history of the Reform movement and homosexuality can be traced by viewing the resolutions adopted by the Central Conference of American Rabbis at http://ccarnet.org/rabbis-speak/resolutions/. For the Reconstructionist position, see http://jrf.org/GLBT-Inclusion.
6. Joel Roth, "On the Ordination of Women as Rabbis," in *The Ordination of Women as Rabbis: Studies and Responsa*, Simon Greenberg, ed. (New York: Jewish Theological Seminary of America, 1988), p. 170.
7. Ibid., pp. 166f.
8. Ibid., p. 172.
9. Indeed, in no circumstances are women allowed to initiate divorce proceedings against their husbands, a rule that again undermines any claim toward complete egalitarianism.
10. Roth acknowledges this problem—Roth, "On the Ordination of Women" (at note 6 above), pp. 168f.—but insists his primary concern is for the "*halakhic* status of behaviors" (p. 169).
11. *Katzenbach* v. *McClung*, 379 U.S. 294 (1964).
12. Elliot N. Dorff, *For the Love of God and People: A Philosophy of Jewish Law* (Philadelphia: Jewish Publication Society of America, 2007), p. 235. Dorff cites studies that suggest a significant percentage of homosexual men do not engage in anal intercourse. He concludes that "this means that our position is not a legal fiction." I disagree with his conclusion.

13. "Towards a Legal Theory of the Conservative Movement," *Conservative Judaism* 27:3 (1973), p. 75.
14. Dorff, *For the Love of God and People* (at note 12 above), p. 235.
15. Ibid.
16. Rabbi Joel Roth, in a private communication (1/9/2011), assures me that not only was this not his intention but that Rabbi Gerson Cohen at Camp Ramah *did* ask women if they should be counted in the *minyan* based on the Roth *responsum*. Nevertheless, it seems to me a predictable consequence of the Roth *responsum* that it would be widely exploited as an indiscriminate invitation for synagogue egalitarianism, which it has indeed become.
17. Elie Spitz, "Mamzerut," *Responsa of the Committee on Jewish Law and Standards*, 1991–2000 (New York: Rabbinical Assembly 2002), p. 585.
18. B. *Yevamot* 89b.
19. There is a well-reasoned theory for this posture. See Richard L. Claman, "Vinegar and Wine, Leniency and Piety: Justifying a Bias Toward Lightening the Yoke," *Conservative Judaism* 56:3 (Spring 2004), pp. 63–80.
20. Seymour Siegel, "Ethics and the Halakhah," in *Conservative Judaism and Jewish Law*, Seymour Siegel and Elliot Gertel, eds. (New York: Ktav Publishing House, 1977), p. 127. The *teshuvah* can be found at http://www.rabbinicalassembly.org/sites/default/files/public/halakhah/teshuvot/19861990/siegel_smoking.pdf?phpMyAdmin=GoIs7ZE%2CH7O%2Ct%2CZ1sDHpI8UAVD6.
21. http://www.rabbinicalassembly.org/sites/default/files/public/halakhah/teshuvot/19912000/prouser_chesed.pdf. ; http://www.rabbinicalassembly.org/sites/default/files/public/halakhah/teshuvot/19912000/prouser_organ.pdf.
22. http://magentzedek.org/.
23. http://www.rabbinicalassembly.org/sites/default/files/public/halakhah/teshuvot/20052010/jacobs-living-wage.pdf?phpMyAdmin=GoIs7ZE%2CH7O%2Ct%2CZ1sDHpI8UAVD6.
24. Jill Jacobs, *There Shall Be No Needy: Pursuing Social Justice through Jewish Law and Tradition* (Woodstock, VT: Jewish Lights Publishing, 2009).
25. These rabbis all contributed to *Righteous Indignation: A Jewish Call for Justice*, ed. Or N. Rose, Jo Ellen Green Kaiser, and Margie Klein (Woodstock, VT: Jewish Lights Publishing, 2008). See also Aryeh Cohen, *Justice in the City: an Argument from the Sources of Rabbinic Judaism* (Boston: Academic Studies Press, 2012).
26. Jacobs, *There Shall Be No Needy* (at note 24 above), p. 48. Italics added.
27. Elliot N. Dorff, *Matters of Life and Death: A Jewish Approach to Modern Medical Ethics* (Philadelphia: Jewish Publication Society of America, 1998), pp. 395–417. See also his *Love Your Neighbor and Yourself: A Jewish Approach to Modern Personal Ethics* (Philadelphia: Jewish Publication Society, 2003), Appendix, pp. 311–44, and his *For the Love of God and People* (at note 12 above), chap. 6 for further articulations of his view on the relationships between Judaism and morality.
28. Dorff, *Matters* (ibid.), p. 399. Dorff is one of many rabbis who holds this position. For example, see also Bradley Shavit Artson, "Halakhah and Ethics: The Holy and the Good," *Conservative Judaism* 46:3 (Spring 1994), pp. 70–88.
29. Joel Roth, *The Halakhic Process: A Systemic Analysis* (New York: Jewish Theological Seminary of America, 1986), p. 301. He makes the same point in http://www.rabbinicalassembly.org/sites/default/files/public/halakhah/teshuvot/20052010/roth_revisited.pdf, p. 27. See also Israel Francus, p. 35 and Joel Roth, pp. 170f., in Greenberg, ed. *The Ordination of Women as Rabbis* (at note 6 above).

30. Joel Roth, "Review of Moshe Zemer's *Evolving Halakhah: A Progressive Approach to Traditional Jewish Law,*"*Conservative Judaism* 54:1 (Fall 2001), p. 113.
31. Joel Roth, "Musings Toward a Personal Theology of Revelation," in *Edut BeYhosef: Rabbi Dr. Yosef Green: Essays Presented to Rabbi Dr. Yosef Green on the occasion of his eightieth birthday* (Jerusalem, 2008).
32. "Can a People of the Book Also Be a People of God?" *Conservative Judaism* 60:1–2 (Fall/Winter 2007–2008), p. 11, citing *Noda Biyehudah* (latter edition), *Yoreh Deah* 161.
33. http://www.rabbinicalassembly.org/sites/default/files/public/halakhah/teshuvot/20052010/tucker_homosexuality.pdf.
34. Landau incorrectly attributes this comment to Moses Nahmanides.
35. *Noda Biyehudah* (latter edition), *Yoreh Deah* 10.
36. http://www.rabbinicalassembly.org/sites/default/files/public/halakhah/teshuvot/20052010/tucker_homosexuality.pdf, p. 22.
37. New York: United Jewish Communities, 2001, p. 12.
38. Nevertheless, *Emet Ve'Emunah*, the Conservative Movement's statement of principles, posits that "the single greatest event in the history of God's revelation took place at Sinai" (p. 19) Even Reform theologians, such as Eugene Borowitz and Naomi Patz, have great difficulty escaping from under the shadow of Sinai; see their *Explaining Reform Judaism* (West Orange, NJ: Behrman House, 1985), p. 102.
39. *Sifre Pinchas* 133, cited in http://www.rabbinicalassembly.org/sites/default/files/public/halakhah/teshuvot/20052010/tucker_homosexuality.pdf, p. 21.
40. Cf. http://www.rabbinicalassembly.org/sites/default/files/public/halakhah/teshuvot/20052010/dorff_nevins_reisner_dignity.pdf. Roth also points this out in his 2006 responsum.
41. "To Whom and for What Should a Bible Commentator Be Responsible?" in *Studies in the Bible and Jewish Thought* (Philadelphia: Jewish Publication Society of America, 1995), p. 239. Cited and discussed in Shai Cherry, *Torah through Time: Understanding Bible Commentary form the Rabbinic Period to Modern Times* (Philadelphia: Jewish Publication Society of America, 2007), p. 32.
42. Abraham Joshua Heschel, *God in Search of Man: A Philosophy of Judaism* (New York: Farrar, Strauss, and Giroux, 1956), p. 274. Cited and discussed in Cherry, *Torah through Time* (at note 41 above), p. 189.
43. Although Elliot Dorff graciously included my reading in his book, *For the Love of God and People* (at note 12 above), p. 242, n. 39, he mistakenly believed that I claimed this was the *peshat*, or contextual meaning. My reading is midrashic and, I argue, should have just as much claim to *halakhic* status as the midrashim of the ancient rabbis.
44. As Tucker explains, even if there is not a qualitative or ontological distinction between biblical and rabbibic law, biblical law is the *first* sacred expression of law within our tradition and thus has a special place. http://www.rabbinicalassembly.org/sites/default/files/public/halakhah/teshuvot/20052010/tucker_homosexuality.pdf, 6.
45. Gordon Tucker, "A Principled Defense of the Structure and Status of the CJLS," http://www.rabbinicalassembly.org/sites/default/files/public/halakhah/teshuvot/19912000/tucker_defense.pdf?phpMyAdmin=GoIs7ZE%2CH7O%2Ct%2CZ1sDHpI8UAVD6. Rabbi Dorff frequently would say in class, "The vote in the CJLS helps us determine if this is just another one of Dorff's crazy ideas, or if it is the will of God."
46. Elliot Dorff and Eugene Borowitz, a leading Reform theologian, engage in a contemporary version of the Buber-Rosenzweig letters on this issue. These letters are published in Elliot N. Dorff, *The Unfolding Tradition: Jewish Law After Sinai* (New

York: Aviv Press, 2005), pp. 464–80. On this exchange, see discussion by Michael Marmur in chapter 11 above in this volume.
47. Rabbi Adam Kligfeld voted for both the Roth and Dorff *responsa*. Clearly, Kligfeld was not endorsing the conclusions of both *responsa*; he was acknowledging that both *responsa* were legitimate expressions of Conservative *halakhah*.
48. Tucker, "A Principled Defense" (at n. 45 above), p. 765.
49. Ibid., pp. 771f.
50. Richard L. Claman, "A Philosophical Basis for Halakhic Pluralism," *Conservative Judaism* 54:1 (Fall 2001), p. 78. Joel Roth has recently focused attention on the borders of his own *halakhic* pluralism. "*Gufei Torah*: The Limit to Halakhic Pluralism," in *Tiferet Le-Yisrael: Jubilee Volume in Honor of Israel Francus*, Joel Roth, Menahem Schmelzer, and Yaacov Francus, eds. (New York and Jerusalem: JTS Publications, 2010).

Suggestions for Further Reading

Conservative Writers Treating Specific Moral Issues

Dorff, Elliot N. 1998. *Matters of Life and Death: A Jewish Approach to Modern Medical Ethics*. Philadelphia: Jewish Publication Society.

Dorff, Elliot N. 2002. *To Do the Right and the Good: A Jewish Approach to Modern Social Ethics*. Philadelphia: Jewish Publication Society.

Dorff, Elliot N. 2003. *Love Your Neighbor and Yourself: A Jewish Approach to Modern Personal Ethics*. Philadelphia: Jewish Publication Society.

Dorff, Elliot N. 2005. *The Way into Tikkun Olam (Repairing the World)*. Woodstock, VT: Jewish Lights.

Dorff, Elliot N., and Louis E. Newman. 1995. *Contemporary Jewish Ethics and Morality: A Reader*. New York: Oxford University Press, chaps. 22–24, 26–27, and 32.

Dorff, Elliot N., and Louis E. Newman. 2008. *Jewish Choices, Jewish Voices: Body, Money, Power*. Philadelphia: Jewish Publication Society, 3 vols.

Dorff, Elliot N., and Danya Ruttenberg. 2010. *Jewish Choices, Jewish Voices: Sex and Intimacy, War and National Security, Social Justice*. Philadelphia: Jewish Publication Society, 3 vols.

Feldman, David. 1968. *Birth Control in Jewish Law*. New York: New York University Press. Subsequently republished as *Marital Relations, Birth Control, and Abortion in Jewish Law*. 1974. New York: Schocken.

Gold, Michael. 1988. *And Hannah Wept: Infertility, Adoption, and the Jewish Couple*. Philadelphia: Jewish Publication Society.

Gold, Michael. 1992. *Does God Belong in the Bedroom?* Philadelphia: Jewish Publication Society.

Jacobs, Jill. 2009. *There Shall Be No Needy: Pursuing Social Justice through Jewish Law and Tradition*. Woodstock, VT: Jewish Lights.

Mackler, Aaron. 2000. *Life and Death Responsibilities in Jewish Biomedical Ethics*. New York: Jewish Theological Seminary of America.

Many of the *responsa* of the Conservative Movement on specific issues, many of them moral issues, can be accessed at: http://www.rabbinicalassembly.org/law/teshuvot_public.html.

On the Rabbinical Assembly website, there is also a link to more information about social action policies and, under "Kashrut," there is more information on Hekhsher Tzedek.

Responsa of the Israeli Conservative Movement can be found at: http://www.responsafortoday.com/eng_index.html.

Conservative Writers on the Relationship between Jewish Law and Ethics:

Cherry, Shai. 2007. "The Daughters of Zelophehad," in *Torah through Time: Understanding Bible Commentary from the Rabbinic Period to Modern Times.* Philadelphia: Jewish Publication Society, pp. 161–88.

Cosgrove, Elliot. 2007. "Conservative Judaism's 'Consistent Inconsistency.'" *Conservative Judaism* 59:3 (Spring), pp. 3–26.

Dorff, Elliot N. 2007. *For the Love of God and People: A Philosophy of Jewish Law.* Philadelphia: Jewish Publication Society. See also the appendicies to his books, *To Do the Right and the Good* and *Love Your Neighbor and Yourself,* both of which are listed above.

Dorff, Elliot N., and Louis E. Newman. 1995. *Contemporary Jewish Ethics and Morality: A Reader.* New York: Oxford University Press, chaps. 2–5 and 9–12.

Greenberg, Simon, ed. 1987. *The Ordination of Women as Rabbis: Studies and Responsa.* New York: Jewish Theological Seminary of America.

Roth, Joel. 1986. *The Halakhic Process: A Systematic Analysis.* New York: Jewish Theological Seminary of America.

Tucker, Gordon. 2007–2008. "Can a People of the Book Also Be a People of God?" *Conservative Judaism* 60:1–2 (Fall/Winter), pp. 4–25.

CHAPTER 13

ETHICAL THEORIES IN THE ORTHODOX MOVEMENT

DAVID SHATZ

OBSERVERS often divide adherents of Orthodox Judaism, no doubt simplistically, into two main subgroups: Modern Orthodox and *haredi* (ultra-Orthodox). The differences between them lie somewhat in behavior, but more so in ideology.[1] Both groups affirm a contentful revelation in which God communicated laws to Moses, laws that the prophet then passed on to the Jewish people fully and accurately and that we today possess. Both further believe that the consensus interpretations and legal decisions of rabbis of the talmudic, medieval, and modern periods—components of what is known as *Torah she-be-al Peh*, The Oral Law—are binding for Jews today. Both also affirm that Torah laws are—in some sense admittedly in need of explication—immutable because they are divine. And both adopt an approach to *halakhic* decision-making that is to a large degree formalistic and casuistic. That is, Orthodox Jews believe that *halakhah* is determined at least mostly by rules, precedents, and analogies—and only by legitimate rabbinic authorities. Crucially, however, Modern Orthodoxy's ideology affirms the value of the modern world and seeks to engage it, whereas *haredi* Orthodoxy rejects most features of that world, at least in theory.

This distinction between the groups has numerous ramifications, and salient among them is their respective attitudes to modern ethical values and the role of those values in making *halakhic* decisions (*pesak*). Modern Orthodox thinkers as a rule affirm, within limits, the values of equality, autonomy, tolerance, and pluralism that inform the modern Western world, and they grapple with conflicts between *halakhah* and these values with respect to issues like the status of gentiles and secular Jews, homosexuality, and the role of women in synagogue and community life.[2] The Modern Orthodox, more than *haredim*, tend to be outspoken about preventing the deaths of innocent Arab civilians during Israel's war on terrorism, reflecting a Western sensibility that is more stringent, some would say, than *halakhic* rules governing war.[3] They also tend to espouse and practice *tikkun olam*, "repair of the world"; that is, they are more likely to involve themselves in problems facing humanity at large, such as world hunger, genocide, and natural disasters.[4]

Of primary importance for our purposes are the groups' differing attitudes toward three major issues in Jewish meta-ethics: (1) whether there exists a *standard* of ethics that is valid independently of God's will and of *halakhah*, and/or *individual ethical truths* that are true independently of His will and of *halakhah*; (2) whether human beings are able to form, independently of God and *halakhah*, correct moral judgments about this independent standard and/or about individual ethical assertions; and finally, (3) whether an authority should integrate his independently formed ethical values into his *halakhic* decision-making.[5] (In what follows, I will at times compress judgments about moral standards and ethical judgments about individual situations into one category, "independent ethical judgments" or "external ethical judgments" or simply "ethical judgments.")

The aim of this chapter is to explore critically the treatments of these issues in Orthodox writing, but primarily the writings of *Modern* Orthodox thinkers. (Disputes between *haredi* and Modern Orthodox thinkers over substantive values will be referenced only indirectly but must be kept in mind.) To frame the discussion, I will focus on what I will call the *maximalist* Modern Orthodox position. It consists of four assertions:

1. *The validity thesis*: There are ethical truths that are true independent of God's will and *halakhah* (again, some are truths about a valid standard of ethics outside of *halakhah*, and some are about the independent rightness/wrongness of particular acts). The validity thesis rejects divine command theories, which define right as what accords with God's will or command and wrong as what diverges from God's will or command—thus denying the very idea of a valid secular ethics. Modern Orthodox thinking disputes Dostoevsky's character Ivan Karamazov, who declared, "If there is no God, everything is permitted."[6]
2. *The knowledge thesis*: Human beings can know ethical truths and standards even without divine revelation, and can know how to apply the standards correctly, although of course they will on occasion err.
3. *The jurisprudential thesis*: Posekim (*halakhic* decisors, i. e. authorities who issue rulings) should at times use an external ethical standard in *halakhic* decision-making, and have done so in the past. They should not be "strict constructionists" and "formalists" who believe that judges have to set aside their subjective moral judgments when they render decisions. This is not to say that ethical judgments simply override laws. For example, although the

rabbis adopted certain leniencies in the cases of *mamzerut* and *agunah*,[7] no Orthodox decisor has found a way to dispose of *mamzerut* altogether, and it is no easy matter to legitimize forcing a husband to give a *get* or to annul marriages—notwithstanding the moral unease and deep anguish that many *posekim* feel over the plight of *mamzerim* and *agunot*.[8] Likewise Orthodox authorities do not nullify the biblical prohibition against homosexuality, but they call for sensitivity and compassion, distinguishing between one's view of the act and one's view of the agent.[9] Still, the Modern Orthodox *halakhist* has a fairly expansive view about when he may introduce moral judgments into decision-making.[10] In this same vein, Modern Orthodox thinkers stress that Jewish law encourages and in some cases even mandates acting *lifnim mi-shurat ha-din*, going beyond the strict law,[11] and that *halakhah* at times regards acting beyond the rules as a *middat hasidut* (the way of the pious). These thinkers tend to understand such categories as predicated on external, independent ethical judgments or natural morality. Likewise their understanding of Jewish ethics is such that they tend to call for the exercise of virtues like compassion even when the letter of the law does not require such judgments—a form of *imitatio Dei*; and they highlight sources that suggest this stance.[12] Some see *lifnim mi-shurat ha-din* and a concern for virtue as an escape from formalism; others see acting *lifnim mi-shurat ha-din* and the pursuit of virtue as included within a system of rules.[13] Either way, these categories, for Modern Orthodox thinkers, reflect some form of interplay between formal rules and ethical and/or religious values and aspirations. In addition, the Modern Orthodox urge perhaps more than *haredim* the application of principles such as "her [The Torah's] ways are the ways of pleasantness," *kevod ha-beriyyot* (human dignity) and *darkhei shalom* ("the ways of peace," understanding that principle as expressing an inherent value, peace, rather than a prudential idea of reciprocity for mutual benefit). All these views are manifestations of the same thesis: that independent ethical judgments play a role in *halakhic* decision-making.

4. *The reconciliation thesis*: The existence of ethically troubling biblical practices such as slavery and the destruction of Amalek, and of troubling rabbinic pronouncements as well, may be reconciled with the fact that contemporary morality deems these practices and positions immoral.

I call the conjunction of (1)–(4) the *maximalist* Modern Orthodox position in order to indicate that there can be minimalist and intermediate positions. A significant number of thinkers blend Modern Orthodox and *haredi* elements, and a small number who self-identify as Modern Orthodox reject one or more of the above theses,[14] but the "tendencies" described here (or their rejection) do capture the "maximalist" position within each camp.[15]

How do maximalist Modern Orthodox thinkers defend their claims? They may proceed in two ways. First, they may argue that positions (1)–(4) inherently make more sense—that is, are philosophically more compelling—than the opposite theses maintained in *haredi* ideology. Second, the thinkers may say that traditional authorities support their positions (i. e., [1–4]). Because Modern Orthodox thinkers believe in the integration of Torah with good philosophical thought, a Modern Orthodox thinker would hope that the two methods lead to the same place.

What follows is a candid attempt to articulate and grapple with issues that confront a Modern Orthodox orientation toward *halakhah*. Not all the problems are solved, but they are defined, and the options are laid out.

THE VALIDITY THESIS

To establish thesis (1), the validity thesis, a thinker must reject divine command theories of ethics. There are good grounds for rejecting such theories, and these include both philosophical reasoning and authoritative texts that contravene the theories. To be sure, contrary to both *haredi* and "liberal" Orthodox writers, the sources are not monolithic, and many are ambiguous.[16] Ironically, some of the same Modern Orthodox writers who stress that the tradition is pluralistic and includes multiple, competing voices, maintain a monolithic view of sources regarding the question of independent ethical truths and standards. That picture needs correction.

Notwithstanding these caveats, the validity thesis has, as Modern Orthodox theorists assert, a firm foot in tradition. We find, for example, a category of laws called *mishpatim*, defined thus: laws such that "had they not been written, they should have been written," such as laws against killing and stealing (B. *Yoma* 67b).[17] Furthermore, the Bible itself calls God's laws "just" (Deut 4:8). Like the verse "And God saw that it [the world] was good" (the steady refrain in Genesis 1), Deuteronomy 4:8 would be a tautology were there no independent standard of goodness and justice. In addition, when the prophets and talmudic sages wonder—as they frequently do—how God could allow evil, or the Patriarch Abraham prevails upon God not to destroy the righteous inhabitants of Sodom with the wicked, arguing "Will the judge of all the earth not do justice?" (Gen 18: 23–25), they tacitly reject the notion that there is no valid standard of ethics independent of God's will.[18] The validity thesis, then, has textual support in addition to the philosophical support furnished by standard refutations of divine command theories.[19] (Due to space limitations, I will not review more texts[20] or present philosophical refutations of divine command theories.) To be clear, the texts are not being adduced to establish a philosophical theory in meta-ethics—the sages may not have thought in those terms—but rather the sages' acceptance of an independent standard shows that such an approach is not religiously out of bounds and was not offensive to the sages' sensibilities.

The Knowledge Thesis

The text in B. *Yoma* that defines *mishpatim* in a way that suggests the existence of a valid independent ethic (thesis 1) does not say that we could have arrived at *misphatim* on our own (thesis 2), though this is a natural interpretation. Perhaps the rabbis' thought is only that once the *mishpatim* have been revealed, we can appreciate their value, just as we can appreciate a theory in physics or a mathematical proof after it is promulgated even though we could not have arrived at it on our own.

Nevertheless, prominent thinkers in medieval and modern times invoke notions like *mitzvot sikhliyyot* (rational laws) and natural morality, suggesting the knowability thesis. Although it is no simple matter to transplant such assertions to a philosophical climate populated by sundry forms of relativism and skepticism,[21] it is plain that this stream of thought endorses the independent knowability of ethical truths.

How might this knowability thesis be supported? To begin with, there is a large degree of correspondence between divine commands and human moral judgments, as in the cases of paying workers on time, aiding the poor, not bearing grudges, and loving one's neighbor. So we human beings who see ethical bases for those laws have *some* ability to think correctly about ethics. However, the Hebrew people has helped shape moral intuitions over the course of history, so the "match" between the Bible and morality, one might object, is not surprising and may be explained without reference to the knowability of independent ethical truths.

Whatever the cogency of this response, there is another reason for accepting thesis (2)—it is presupposed in much monotheistic discourse. For example, the Psalmist declares, in a verse incorporated in the liturgy, "Give thanks to the Lord because He is good (*hodu la-Shem ki tov*)" (Ps. 118:1, 136:1). This verse makes no sense unless we posit a moral duty to thank a benefactor—a duty that is independent of divine command. In addition, it is disingenuous to assert the unknowability of ethical truth yet at the same time be troubled by the existence of evil—by the Temple's destruction, by the Holocaust, by 9/11. After all, the many religious people who *are* thus troubled impose moral judgments such as "It is wrong to let innocent people suffer or die" and do not give them up; and when theologians respond with a theodicy, they are accepting the moral judgments in that theodicy, such as that the value of human free will, up to a point, outweighs the disvalue of evil. Of course these questioners and responders may be wrong in their judgments, but the fact that religious people make them on so large a scale suggests that a wholesale distrust of human judgments is inconsistent with time-hallowed religious discourse.

Granted, however, that we human beings can know *some* moral truths on our own, it is not assured that we can know *all* moral truths on our own. Indeed, given the foundational belief that God is infallible, and in particular morally infallible, we apparently cannot. What, for example, is the moral justification for the *mitzvah* of destroying Amalek, or of laws allowing slavery,[22] or laws that create the status of *mamzerut*, or laws that create or reinforce certain inequalities? Likewise, if destroying an entire people—innocent men, women, and children, as in the case of Amalek—is not morally wrong, how can we who believe that such behavior is wrong by "independent" moral standards trust ourselves with regard to any of our other judgments? Would you persist in using a calculator to solve complex multiplication problems if, by consulting a superior source, you previously have found the calculator to give wildly wrong answers to what seem like elementary questions (in the moral case: questions about genocide and fairness)? Thus, if God has good independent moral reasons for issuing the troubling commandments, but we don't fathom them, then human beings should not trust their own moral judgments.[23] People then have only one adequate basis for acting one way rather than another—namely, divine commands. If, as well, we do not fathom God's reasons for allowing evil, then our moral judgments or our ability to apply correct ethical standards must be flawed. In a word, we will need divine commands.[24]

But so what, you might ask? Why can't Modern Orthodox thinkers concede that human beings are bad at doing ethics but know how to act by following divine commands? What difference does it make how they answer thesis (2), as long as divine commands provide a short-cut to knowing how to act, like learning the answer to a math problem by viewing the answers in the back of the book? The answer—the reason this approach will not serve here—is that skepticism about our capacity for correct moral judgment impairs the Modern Orthodox thinker's ability to sustain an affirmative answer to thesis (3), the jurisprudential question. Skepticism about moral judgments *prima facie* dictates that a *posek* has tenuous grounds if he incorporates his moral judgments into *pesak* (*halakhic* rulings).

To defend thesis (2), then, Modern Orthodox thinkers must either:

- Supply a morally satisfying explanation for the commandment about Amalek, the permission of slavery, inequalities and so on (as thesis [4] demands anyway);
- Prove that the ethically problematic parts of the system were never meant to be applied (or are highly limited in their application);[25]
- Show that, whatever God's reasons may be for the ethically problematic parts of the system, they do not preclude ethical knowledge in the sorts of situations *posekim* address, nor even the majority of ethical judgments; for the most part we (and *posekim*) are able to "get ethics right";
- Show that *posekim*, perhaps even by divine fiat, are permitted to rely on their ethical judgments even though they are fallible; "A judge has only what his eyes see" (B. *Niddah* 20b).[26]

None of these responses *establishes* thesis (2); they merely either rebut skepticism about thesis (2),[27] or else reconcile skepticism about thesis (2) with thesis (3), the jurisprudential thesis[28]—to which we now turn.

The Jurisprudential Thesis

Orthodoxy at one time shrank from comparing *halakhah* to other legal systems, reasoning that divine law and human law are incommensurable. But Modern Orthodoxy now sometimes draws its understanding of *halakhah* from such comparisons and the writings of influential legal theorists such as Ronald Dworkin. From the literature on jurisprudence and philosophy of law, it is clear that every legal system has to confront two sorts of problems, which we may call the problem of indeterminacy and the problem of untoward (and sometimes even repugnant) results. Indeterminacy may arise from several sources: lack of a close precedent for the case at hand (put another way: "the rules run out" in certain cases), ambiguity in crucial terms (such as "cruel and unusual punishment" in the Eighth Amendment to the U.S. Constitution), and conflicts between rules. "Untoward results" means results (applications of the law) that will strike people either as presenting socially undesirable consequences or as yielding immoral results when applied to particular cases.

These problems face Jewish law as well. In fact Jewish law addresses one type of untoward result that does not affect secular judges: it worries that certain technically permissible behaviors create or reflect bad character traits.[29] Judaism's concern with virtue is reflected in a comment attributed to Rabbi Joseph B. Soloveitchik: "*Halakhah* is not a ceiling but a floor."[30]

Thesis (3), then, as I am construing it, allows or mandates the use of ethical judgments to respond to both challenges—indeterminacy and untoward results. Now, the existence of indeterminacy in the law, while undermining formalism, does not *by itself* mandate that jurists appeal to independent ethics to resolve the indeterminacy; they might use other considerations—social consequences, for example. The Modern Orthodox thinker will argue for thesis (3) differently: namely, by citing real-life rabbinic decision-making over the millennia and arguing that the fact that the rabbis used ethics in *pesak* (assuming they did) establishes a norm for how *halakhic* decision-making should proceed.[31] We must consider, therefore, the historical question of whether *posekim* have been influenced in their *pesak*, consciously or subconsciously, by externally acquired ethical beliefs.

Perhaps the best answer to this question, and for that matter about whether *posekim* implicitly or explicitly accepted theses (1) and (2), is "Some did, some didn't." Whom one selects as a model—will it be those for whom external ethical beliefs ostensibly have an influence on *pesak* or those for whom they ostensibly don't?—might depend on one's viewpoint about thesis (3) itself. However, Modern Orthodox thinkers have sometimes argued that even *haredi* decisors do not develop rulings in a completely formalistic fashion, but rather are subtly influenced by moral positions of their own in the process of arriving at *halakhic* decisions regarding, say, abortion, end-of-life issues, and conduct toward gentiles. And, the argument continues, what is sauce for the goose is sauce for the gander.

Having identified the Modern Orthodox proposal to look at the history of *halakhic* decision-making as corroborating thesis (3), we come now to a widely aired objection to the conclusion that the Modern Orthodox draw from that history—an objection that has formed perhaps the crux of the debate within Orthodoxy. The objection is that even if *posekim* appear to invoke values and not rules alone, there is no guarantee that those values are external to *halakhah*. They may be internal, drawn from Jewish sources in *halakhah, aggadah*, or Jewish thought.[32] Thus, for example, if Rabbi Akiva and Rabbi Tarfon declared "had we been in the Sanhedrin, no one ever would have been executed" (B. *Makkot* 7a)—a text often used to show that external ethical values influence rabbinic decision-making—this statement need not reflect the influence of external values but rather may reflect the "internal" value of human life, a value that, to be sure, coincides with a universal, external value but can be derived internally.[33] The celebrated case of *prosbul* (B. *Gittin* 36a)[34] easily lends itself to explanation in terms of internal values that coincide with universal ones (the passage cites the biblically declared value of people being willing to lend money [Deut 15:9]). Likewise, laws whose stated rationale is *tikkun olam, darkhei shalom* (the ways of peace), *kevod ha-beriyyot* (human dignity), *derakhehah darkhei no'am* (ways of pleasantness)—these are based on certain *Jewish* values, even if the latter coincide with universal values and serve as a "conduit for moral considerations."[35] Once armed with the distinction between internal and external values, we can declare also that the impetus behind limitations that authorities impose, based on their interpretations of the relevant laws, upon *mamzerut*, the stubborn and rebellious son, and Amalek, and their hesitation about applying certain laws altogether, was not external values but rather internal ones such as the value of life and the principle of just desert.[36]

Yet, that said, there are two arguments for thinking that, in dealing with cases that involve indeterminacy or untoward results, *posekim* use not only internal but also external values. The first argument is that sometimes when we search for internal values in *halakhic, aggadic*, or Jewish philosophical texts, we end up with competing and irreconcilable values. Now in such cases each authority nonetheless ends up with some conclusion, and these authorities may disagree—because some prioritize one value, while others prioritize another value. Hence, it may be argued, in order to choose between conflicting values, each disputant *must have been* influenced by *external* values that determined which internal value deserves greater weight.[37] This view is reminiscent of a central claim of the eminent legal theorist Ronald Dworkin—that morality should guide a jurist's interpretation of the law and in particular the identification of "principles" that underlie the system's set of rules, in order to deal with indeterminacy and untoward results.

But the conclusion that the rabbis must have used independent morality does not follow from the premise that different rabbis selected between conflicting values in opposing ways. People can differ over how to interpret a stanza of Tennyson or a Civil War document without moral considerations shaping their views. Further, many disputes in Judaism revolve around ritual law, where external morality does not have to be used in order to choose between conflicting values.

Thus, while differing external values *might* have been what produced differing rabbinic decisions about ethically charged matters, it has not yet been shown that this is indeed the case—in other words, that we *must* impute external moral values to disputants in order to explain why two rabbis disagree about the ranking of certain internal moral values.

The second objection to the "authorities use only internal values" approach runs as follows. Sometimes it is clear that certain rules are from a formalistic standpoint less weighty than certain other rules (e. g., they are endorsed only by a minority), and that, as we look at the total corpus of biblical and rabbinic texts, certain values are less weighty than certain other values. Yet some *posekim* rule that the former (less weighty) set of rules and the former set of values prevail. Therefore, so goes the argument, the *posek* must be drawing on his own *external* values—precedents and internal values do not support his rulings.

And indeed, for the advocate of thesis (3), it strains credulity to think that external morality is never an element in *pesak*. Consider Orthodox attitudes to slavery, various inequalities, and polygamy (which in the early Middle Ages was banned by Rabbi Gershom, living in a Christian society). On the view that only internal values operate, "externally derived" ethical objections to these practices are not admissible in the *halakhic* process. But if no such external objections were on the minds of any rabbis who in later times came to look negatively upon these practices, what could have propelled this change in attitude in Orthodox society? Why didn't the rabbis accept the existing laws? Isn't a changed moral sensibility the most plausible explanation? Why else, to take another example, do few rabbis today oppose women's voting, even though prominent authorities opposed it strongly when the concept was first introduced circa 1920?

This, at least, is the externalist's "story" of what produced *pesak* on certain issues. This is not to say that, for externalists, it is always obvious whether we are dealing with an internal rather than external value. At least through the eighteenth century, rabbinic authorities who discussed triage cases maintained that we follow the *mishnah* in tractate *Horayot* (3:7-8) that places a priest (*kohen*) before a levite, a Torah scholar before an ignoramus, and formulates other such hierarchies. In the twentieth and twenty-first centuries, major authorities are very reluctant to apply these laws, and they restrict their scope to instances such as one in which two people arrive at a hospital at exactly the same time. Did the democratic climate have an influence on these attempts to limit the *mishnah*'s application? It is hard to tell.[38]

To be fair, we need not saddle "internalists" with denying *any* causal role to external ethical truths in the process of making *halakhic* decisions. For example, internalists need not take the implausible position that it is a *coincidence* that, as the years went on, major *posekim* did not oppose women's voting. Rather, internalists might hold that although *halakhic* positions ultimately taken in these areas (either expressly or tacitly, that is, by not objecting) may coincide with democratic values, those external values serve but a *causal* role. In particular, they stimulate authorities to focus on certain internal Jewish values that otherwise would have been neglected or demoted in importance, and in fact were neglected or demoted in previous eras, at least with regard to the issue at hand. Nevertheless, internalists will insist, the external values were not *appropriated* before being judged to be internal Torah values as well.[39] Thinkers who advocate this account have a twofold challenge: to specify which internal values in Jewish tradition lend support to women's suffrage and other positions that seem to have been stimulated by the advent of certain external values, and second, to show that the weight and salience that contemporary authorities ascribe to those values is correct from an *internal* standpoint even though previous authorities did not assign that degree of weight and salience. That task, I suggest, is no small order, though it may be doable.

To sum up this assessment of thesis (3), it is plausible to claim that rabbis who make *halakhic* decisions *sometimes* use an external, independent ethic in addition to values that may be derived internally. I have not sought to explain what justifies a rabbi in letting external morality have this weight—especially what justifies the first rabbi who ever used external morality in this way. As was noted earlier, the *halakhic* process might simply dictate that one may or must draw on one's ethical judgments in one's place and time. The rationale for such latitude is not clear, other than that it is the best the jurist can reasonably do.[40]

An outstanding issue is whether the existence of *subconscious* influence of independent ethical judgments on previous *pesak* (assuming it existed) can provide grounds for legitimizing *conscious* influence today. On the one hand, there seems to be a leap here. On the other hand, disallowing conscious use of ethical judgments might seem to place a taint on the rulings of earlier authorities. Of course the rulings themselves stand. But if the *halakhic* record shows many instances of unconscious external influence, especially in important cases, it may be more satisfying to accept the *conscious* importation of external ethics today than to feel that the community is saddled with rulings that were based on considerations that it would have been wrong to invoke on the conscious level.

THE RECONCILIATION THESIS

The final component of the Modern Orthodox position is the reconciliation thesis: The existence of ethically troubling biblical practices such as slavery and the destruction of Amalek, and of troubling rabbinic pronouncements as well, may be reconciled with the fact that contemporary morality deems these practices immoral. This reconciliation may be achieved either by justifying the law in general ethical terms, or by reinterpreting the law in a way that renders it inapplicable or greatly reduces its scope, or in some other way. I will consider two of those "other" ways.

An aretaic (virtue) approach: Normally a virtue-centered approach to Jewish ethics is directed toward virtues like kindness and compassion, which are grounded in *imitatio dei*. Thus, even if the technical law allows for certain harsh or discriminatory conduct toward gentiles, one must develop compassion and kindness too, which militates against such conduct.[41] But a contrasting aretaic approach focuses on the virtue of *yir'at shamayim*, fear of Heaven, expressed through submission to God's will.[42] On this approach, our moral judgments are correct *qua* moral judgments. However, a religious personality needs two contrasting virtues: on the one hand, a developed moral sense, but on the other *yir'at Shamayim* (fear of Heaven). Judaism aims at cultivating a personality that is both autonomous and heteronomous.[43] Someone who insists that a moral virtue should always trump *yir'at Shamayim* is simply begging the question.

But why must this virtue of *yir'at Shamayim* require submission specifically to immoral commands? Cannot the virtue of *yir'at Shamayim* be developed by one's submitting to ritual laws that seem pointless and outmoded, or geared to a different civilization, or are difficult emotionally and psychologically rather than morally? And would God care more about obedience to Him than about, say, human life (the Amalek case)? Would He demand that people act contrary to morality if He had other ways of eliciting *yir'at Shamayim*? Advocates of the aretaic approach might answer yes, since perhaps the virtue of *yir'at shamayim* must be cultivated in a variety of ways, and prioritizing it over morality and not just over "difficult" ritual commandments gives the virtue its highest expression.[44] We humans may not be able to determine "how much" submission is needed. So would go the response.

Another problem looms for the aretaic approach, however. Introducing heteronomous submission as a virtue makes it difficult to know whether a particular morally problematic command is one that is simply to be accepted, or one that should be subjected to reinterpretation. Perhaps advocates of the aretaic approach will reply that if a decisor has struggled to find a rationale and has come up empty, this is a case where God wants heteronomous obedience.[45]

Accommodationism: In *Guide of the Perplexed* III:32, Maimonides states that God allowed (indeed, commanded) the Israelites to bring sacrifices, a lower form of worship, only as a concession or accommodation to their being psychologically unable to abandon the practices of the Egyptian society in which they had formerly been enslaved. In like fashion, one way of understanding slavery, polygamy, and the brutal treatment of other nations (e.g., Amalek) is to say that in allowing these practices, the Torah made concessions to the moral sense and societal structure prevalent at an earlier time in history. When society and the moral sense change—that is, mature—the concession is withdrawn and a norm closer to the ideal, one reflecting "true" Torah values, is implemented. "The time was not yet ripe, and people were not yet ready, for the full realization of that [The Torah's] vision. Only over time...were people's hearts made ready."[46] Thus, external values play a role in altering approaches and sensibilities, but the values do not come into focus until particular post-biblical or post-talmudic eras in history.

The accommodationist approach answers the question that was the Achilles heel of the theories we considered previously, namely, why can a *posek* let moral considerations override a rule, if those who formulated the rule did not let the values in question determine the law?[47] But how far can an Orthodox accommodationist go? Slavery and polygamy are merely once-exercised options that there can be no moral objection to *not* exercising today. By contrast, in the case of Amalek, the Torah *mandates* war and destruction rather than present them as options. Again, to distribute an inheritance equally among children, rather than give two-thirds to the eldest son and disinherit daughters unless there are no sons, goes against a Torah *mandate*. Is an accommodationist willing to go so far as to affirm that moral sense or society may evolve to the point of making a Torah *requirement* unacceptable (as opposed to not exercising a mere option)? (I suspect that in fact an accommodationist would *frown* on someone who used the *Torah* method of distribution.) This is one matter that accommodationists must address if they are to align *halakhah* with current moral sensibilities.[48]

Indeed, accommodationism opens a Pandora's box for Orthodox thinkers. For, given a particularly strong societal trend that conflicts with biblical law, how would the accommodationist know that society's moral sensibility was not progressing and that the Bible was not simply accommodating a lower sensibility? Once the horse is out of the barn, there seems to be no way of stopping it. And so, Orthodox thinkers are likely to be wary of the accommodationist strategy and to adopt instead other appoaches to the problem of reconciliation.

Conclusion

The four components of the maximalist Modern Orthodox positions have varying degrees of textual, philosophical, and empirical support. Perhaps the deepest problem confronting a Modern Orthodox thinker is how a decisor can trust his ethical judgments, as thesis (3) requires; for given that some of God's commands and permissions strike people as immoral and yet He is assumed to be infallible, human judgment appears to be deeply flawed. In order to resolve this tension, the Orthodox thinker has several options. One is to supply morally satisfying explanations for the problematic commands and permissions; another is to argue that certain laws were not meant to be applied in practice; a third is to claim that decisors have *enough* moral knowledge to issue rulings; and a fourth is to hold that God simply declares that a *posek* must do his best, even if his moral judgments are fallible. The accommodationist perspective is a variant of the first option. The aretaic approach may be viewed in this way as well, albeit perhaps not as naturally.

For all its complexity, the preceding discussion is but the tip of an iceberg. A full discussion of how Jewish law relates to morality would not only consider a far larger array of ethical values and *halakhic* issues, but would address a host of elements identified in secular legal theory besides rules and principles. As identified by Suzanne Last Stone, these include slippery slopes, the stretching of legal categories, localized decision-making, *ad hoc* solutions, legal fictions, creative analogies, the dialectic between stability and flexibility, and finally the diverse aims of laws, which sometimes sit in tension.[49] Defining and assessing the role of these concepts in *halakhic* decision-making is an immensely exciting endeavor, and a natural next step in exploring how *halakhah* engages human morality and human society.

Acknowledgment

The author thanks Yitzchak Blau, Yoel Finkelman, Daniel Rynhold, and Aaron Segal, along with the editors of this volume, Jonathan K. Crane and Elliot Dorff, for their comments on an earlier draft.

Notes

1. As is to be expected, the dichotomy is way too sharp and, as I said, simplistic, since many Orthodox Jews exhibit both *haredi* and Modern Orthodox elements, depending on the issue. But for our purposes the dichotomy is useful and appropriate, at the very least heuristically. Note as well that my forthcoming characterization of Orthodoxy yields necessary conditions, not sufficient ones, because it leaves out adherence to principles of faith. Rather than agonize over such complications, in what follows I will use a simple criterion for "Orthodox thinker"—self-identification.
2. See the essays in Marc Stern (ed.), *Formulating Responses in an Egalitarian Age* (Lanham, MD: Rowman & Littlefield, 2005). This book and a few others I cite are proceedings of the Orthodox Forum, a think tank that meets annually and generally addresses ethical, political, social, and intellectual challenges facing Modern Orthodoxy.
3. See Michael J. Broyde, "Just Wars, Just Battles and Just Conduct in Jewish Law: Jewish Law Is Not a Suicide Pact!" in *War and Peace in the Jewish Tradition*, ed. Lawrence Schiffman and Joel B. Wolowelsky (New York: Yeshiva University Press, 2007; Orthodox Forum Series), pp. 1–43. Cf. Yitzchak Blau, "Biblical Narratives and the Status of Enemy Civilians in Wartime," *Tradition* 39:4 (2006), pp. 8–28, who cites midrashic voices that protect innocent lives in a time of war.
4. See the essays in David Shatz, Chaim Waxman, and Nathan Diament (eds.), *Tikkun Olam: Social Responsibility in Jewish Thought and Law.* (Northvale, NJ: Jason Aronson, 1997; Orthodox Forum Series). See also Jacob J. Schacter, "*Tikkun Olam*: Defining the Jewish Obligation," In *Rav Chesed: Essays in Honor of Rabbi Dr. Haskel Lookstein*, ed. Rafael Medoff, vol. 2 (Jersey City, NJ: Ktav, 2009), pp. 183–204.
5. I use the masculine pronoun because Orthodoxy almost uniformly opposes women's ordination, notwithstanding significant strides in creating programs and positions for women that require *halakhic* expertise.
6. The validity thesis does not entail that a person ought to do "independently ethical" actions *for* independent ethical reasons; the thesis is compatible with an insistence on acting out of submission to divine or rabbinic authority.
7. A *mamzer/mamzeret* is a child born from adultery or incest, or the descendant of such a child (except when the mother and hence the child are not Jewish). The *mamzer/mamzeret*, while not subjected to a general stigma or exclusion, is restricted in whom he/she can marry. The moral problem is why the child must suffer for

parents' (or ancestors') sins. An *agunah* is a woman "chained" in a marriage either because it is uncertain whether her husband has died, or because her husband is mentally incapacitated and unable to give her a *get* (writ of divorce), or because her husband *refuses* to give her a *get*—a valid *get* requires the husband's consent. Without a *get*, a woman is considered to have committed adultery if she has relations with another man (for example, someone with whom she enters a civil marriage), and any children born from such a union are *mamzerim*. The fact that a woman may be "chained" because of a husband's recalcitrance about giving a *get* has aroused much outrage and frustration, especially since the recalcitrance may be due to vindictiveness, a desire to extract a favorable divorce settlement, and similarly deplorable motives. Among the Modern Orthodox, prenuptial agreements have become a standard and often effective means of legitimizing economic sanctions against a recalcitrant husband in order to induce him to give a *get*.

8. See the Rabbis' anguish about the plight of *mamzerim* in *Ecclesiastes Rabbah* 4:1.
9. See, for example, Chaim Rapoport, *Judaism and Homosexuality: An Authentic Orthodox View* (London and Portland: Vallentine Mitchell, 2004).
10. In addition, while insisting on some form of the immutability thesis, many Modern Orthodox Jews allow that social and economic factors have at times influenced *halakhic* decision-making.
11. See especially Aharon Lichtenstein, "Does Jewish Tradition Recognize an Ethic Independent of Halakhah?" in *Modern Jewish Ethics: Theory and Practice*, ed. Marvin Fox (Columbus: Ohio State University Press, 1975), pp. 62–88. This, I suspect, is the single most cited article in Modern Orthodox writings on how *halakhah* relates to ethics.
12. See Yitzchak Blau, "The Implications of a Jewish Virtue Ethic," *The Torah u-Madda Journal* 9 (2000), pp. 19–41.
13. Samuel Morrell notes, however, that "In almost all of the major categories of equity discussed [by Aaron Kirschenbaum, the author of a book under review] in volume 1, post-talmudic developments curtailed the flexibility which [Kirschenbaum] has so painstakingly documented." See Samuel Morrell, "The Religious Dimension of Civil Law," *AJS Review* 18 (1993), p. 267.
14. Striking and surprising exceptions include Marvin Fox, "The Philosophical Foundations of Jewish Ethics: Some Initial Reflections," in Fox, *Collected Essays on Philosophy and on Judaism* (Lanham, MD: University Press of America, 2003), vol. 3, pp. 51–74 (Fox denies theses [1]–[3] explicitly); and Eliezer Berkovits, *Not in Heaven: The Nature and Function of Halakha* (Jersey City, NJ: Ktav Publishing, 1983). Despite his reputation as a maverick and radical relative to other Modern Orthodox thinkers, Berkovits denies thesis (3) and possibly even (1)–(2). Focusing on talmudic sages, he claims instead that halakhic judgments are derived internally from Jewish sources, a view discussed later. Berkovits's stress on internally based judgments may grow out of his dismay over what he calls "the collapse of values" in modern society, though one can readily argue that in truth certain modern values have influenced him.
15. Divisions between *haredim* and the Modern Orthodox about these questions are reflected in their respective biblical exegeses. Modern Orthodox interpretations of the *akedah* sometimes see Abraham's *not* sacrificing Isaac—his *adhering* to morality when he withdraws the knife—as the story's true punchline, while *haredim* tend overwhelmingly to stress Abraham's submission to an immoral command in the first part of the story. Mystical/kabbalistic thought contains fascinating treatments of the *halakhah*/morality question, but I cannot address them here.

16. See Michael J. Harris, *Divine Command Ethics: Jewish and Christian Perspectives*. (London and New York: Routledge Curzon, 2003).
17. Some might argue that the *Yoma* passage conveys only the pragmatic value of the laws, not their ethical value. But arguably, in order for us to value laws that lead to social order, social order must be an ethical value. (The legal positivist H. L. A. Hart addressed this issue in the context of general legal positivism.)
18. Perhaps one will say by way of retort, "The prophets are not asking how God violates *our* standards, they're asking how He violates His *own*," or "They're asking how God violates His own promises to His people." But they would then be endorsing the judgment, "It is wrong for one to violate one's own standards," or the judgment "It is wrong to break promises." Hence, in advancing the problem of evil, they are *still* using a standard of ethics that is independent of God's will.
19. On the philosophical issues, see Avi Sagi and Daniel Statman, *Religion and Morality*, trans. Batya Stein (Amsterdam and Atlanta: Rodopi, 1995).
20. A particularly significant omission is B. *Sanhedrin* 56a, which derives the laws that govern Noahides. Most of those laws *seem* like "rational" laws, but the rabbis derive them from biblical texts by means of *midreshei Halakhah* (legal derivations that are removed from the plain meaning of the biblical texts they utilize).
21. Cf. Walter Wurzburger, *Ethics of Responsibility* (Philadelphia: Jewish Publication Society, 1994), chaps. 1–2.
22. On nineteenth- and twentieth-century Orthodox approaches to slavery, see Gamliel Shmalo, "Orthodox Approaches to Biblical Slavery," *The Torah u-Madda Journal* 16 (2011–2012), forthcoming.
23. That the Bible's moral judgments are correct follows from the Orthodox principles that the Torah is God's actual word and that God is infallible. Non-Orthodox thinkers might reverse the argument as follows: since God's judgments are infallible, and the Bible's moral judgments are incorrect, therefore the Bible's judgments are human judgments, even if they are judgments about what God was saying.
24. In addition, as Saadyah Gaon noted in his *Sefer Emunot ve-De'ot* III:3, even if a general law (e.g., "Do not steal") is *sikhli* (can be known by reason), we might need revelation or rabbinic authority to inform us about *details* of those same laws (e.g., "How does one come to own an object?"). See also Rabbi Joseph B. Soloveitchik, "Surrendering Our Minds to God," in *Reflections of the Rav*, adapted by Abraham R. Besdin (Jerusalem: The Jewish Agency, 1979), 99–106.
25. For this and other options *vis-à-vis* the Amalek commandment, see Avi Sagi, "The Punishment of Amalek in Jewish Tradition: Coping with the Moral Problem." *Harvard Theological Review* 87:3 (1994), pp. 323–46; Shalom Carmy, "The Origin of Nations and the Shadow of Violence: Theological Perspectives on Canaan and Amalek," in Schiffman and Wolowelsky (eds.) (at note 3 above), pp. 163–99; Eugene B. Korn, "Moralization in Jewish Law: Genocide, Divine Commands, and Rabbinic Reasoning," *Edah Journal* 5:2 (2006), http://www.edah.org/backend/JournalArticle/KORN_5_2.pdf.
26. One possibility that has been raised is that the sages, like literary theorists today, thought that a biblical text does not have a meaning until they interpret it. See Moshe Halbertal, *Interpretative Revolutions in the Making: Values as Interpretative Considerations in Midreshei Halakhah* [Hebrew] (Jerusalem: Magnes Press, 1999), chap. 8.
27. As in the case of the first two solutions.
28. As in the case of the last two solutions.

29. See Blau, "The Implications of a Jewish Virtue Ethic" (at note 12 above).
30. Quoted by Wurzburger, *Ethics of Responsibility* (at note 21 above), p. 32.
31. See Daniel Statman, "Halakhah and Morality: A Few Methodological Considerations," *Journal of Textual Reasoning* 6, 1 (December 2010). http://etext.virginia.edu/journals/tr/volume6/number1/TR06_01_statman.html, along with the other articles in that issue.
32. See especially Fox, "Philosophical Foundations" (at note 14 above), pp. 67–71.
33. See Gerald J. Blidstein, "Capital Punishment: The Classic Jewish Discussion," *Judaism* 14:2 (1966), pp. 164–70.
34. Normally, a sabbatical year cancels debts, but when Hillel saw that people were not lending, thus violating a biblical imperative, he created a system known as *prosbul* by which loans are transferred to the court for collection.
35. See Mark D. Rosen, "Reframing Professor Statman's Inquiry: From History to Culture," *Journal of Textual Reasoning* 6:1 (2010). See also Devora Schoenfeld, "Formalism, Morality and Ovadia Yosef: A Response to Daniel Statman." *Journal of Textual Reasoning* 6:1. http://etext.virginia.edu/journals/tr/volume6/number1/TR06_01_schoenfeld.html; and Suzanne Last Stone (2010), "Halakhah and Legal Theory." *Journal of Textual Reasoning* 6:1. http://etext.virginia.edu/journals/tr/volume6/number1/TR06_01_stone.html. I thank Jonathan K. Crane for stressing the qualification, "even if they coincide with and express universal values." This formulation concedes that a *posek* who introduces internal values may *ultimately* be using independent values, but not *qua* independent values. The issue at hand, however, is whether a *posek* is licensed to introduce independent values even if there is no corresponding internal value, or if the weight of the internal values point in a different direction than independent ethical judgment would.
36. See also Harris, *Divine Command Ethics* (at note 16 above), chaps. 4–5. Even Nahmanides' comments on "be holy" (Lev 19:2) and "do the straight and the good" (Deut 6: 18)—cited in many or most Modern Orthodox essays on how *halakhah* relates to ethics—refer to a standard that is inferred from *other laws of the Torah*, not from an independent standard. (Nahmanides interprets these verses, respectively, as "do more than the law requires" [which prevents untoward results] and "when approaching cases that have no precedents, use ethical reasoning" [which covers cases where the rules run out]). Indeed, he draws a parallel between "be holy," "do the straight and the good," and the general law *tishbot* (rest) on Shabbat. The latter's applications are extrapolated from other laws of the Shabbat and clearly do not come from an independent ethic. Interestingly, as Yitzchak Blau pointed out to me, when he labels drunkenness as inconsistent with "be holy," Nahmanides cites biblical texts. To be sure, in other parts of his commentary, such as his treatment of the sin that led to the Flood, Nahmanides affirmed an independent ethic. (See his commentary to Gen 6:2). In Ronald Dworkin's theory, too, the jurist infers principles of law from the total body of rulings. The "internalist" view resembles a haredi-associated notion known as *Da 'at Torah*—roughly, the idea that rabbinic authorities have a unique ability to derive the "right" answer to all cases by drawing upon the larger corpus of *internal* Torah values. Wurzburger, *Ethics of Responsibility* (at note 21 above), 31–33, tries to differentiate the approaches. Cf. David Shatz, "Beyond Obedience: The Ethical Theory of Rabbi Walter Wurzburger," in Shatz, *Jewish Thought in Dialogue: Essays on Thinkers, Theologies, and Moral Theories* (Boston: Academic Studies Press, 2009), 374–75.
37. See Moshe Halbertal, "Halakhah and Morality: The Case of the Apostate City," *S'vara* 3:1 (1993), pp. 67–72.

38. See Moshe Z. Sokol. "The Allocation of Scarce Medical Resources: A Philosophical Analysis of the Halakhic Sources," *AJS Review* 15 (1990), pp. 63–93.
39. David Berger (in correspondence) suggested this formulation of the view I am describing.
40. This contention generates an interesting question: Does the permission for a *posek* to follow his own moral sense fit best in a relativist framework for external ethics?
41. See Blau, "The Implications of a Jewish Virtue Ethic."
42. Cf. Aharon Lichtenstein, "Being Frum and Being Good: On the Relationship between Religion and Morality," in Lichtenstein, *By His Light: Character and Values in the Service of God*, Adapted by Rabbi Reuven Ziegler (Jersey City, NJ: Ktav, 2003), pp. 101–33; Wurzburger, *Ethics of Responsibility* (at note 21 above).
43. "Hark, the Lord is in strength, the Lord is in splendor" (Ps. 29:4) can be used to express this twofold duty. "Strength" refers to commands that reflect sheer imposition of divine will, "splendor" to commands that appeal to our ethical sense. So suggests Lichtenstein, "Being Frum and Being Good" (at note 42 above), 107.
44. I thank Aaron Segal for these two points.
45. Cf. Lichtenstein, "Being Frum and Being Good" (at note 42 above); Wurzburger, *Ethics of Responsibility* (at note 21 above).
46. "The Way of Torah." *Edah Journal* 3:1 (1993). (Translated from Hebrew.) See also Eliezer Berkovits, *Jewish Women in Time and Torah* (Hoboken, NJ: Ktav, 1990), pp. 27–37; Norman Lamm, "Amalek and the Seven Nations: A Case of War vs. Morality," in *War and Peace in the Jewish Tradition* (at note 3 above), pp. 201–38.
47. Rabbi Kook nuances the approach to war by saying that if Jews were to have implemented an ideal ethic when they entered Canaan under Joshua, they would have lost their battles. Thus the concession has a pragmatic thrust and is not strictly an outgrowth of moral relativism. See *Iggerot ha-Reayah* (Jerusalem: Mossad HaRav Kook, 1985), vol. 1, p. 100.
48. In the case of wills, many Orthodox Jews have adopted the practice (one with precedents) of using technical legal devices to write wills that in effect distribute an inheritance equally, but are halakhically valid. The use of a technical device to create an equal distribution acknowledges a shift in values and implements the new values while not changing the *technical* law. This is an interesting compromise between laws and values that helps accommodationists handle the case of wills.
49. Suzanne Last Stone,"Formulating Responses in an Egalitarian Age: An Overview," in *Formulating Responses in an Egalitarian Age* (at note 2 above), pp. 76–77.

Suggestions for Further Reading

Bleich, J. David. 1977–2005. *Contemporary Halakhic Problems*. Five volumes. Hoboken, NJ: Ktav [vols. 1–4] and Southfield, MI: Targum/Feldheim [vol. 5].

Herring, Basil. 1981. *Jewish Ethics and Halakhah for Our Time*. Two volumes. Hoboken, NJ: Ktav.

Kirschenbaum, Aaron. 1991. *Equity in Jewish Law*. Two volumes. Hoboken, NJ: Ktav Press and New York: Yeshiva University Press.

Korn, Eugene. 1997. "*Tselem Elokim* and the Dialectic of Jewish Morality." *Tradition* 31:2, pp. 5–30.

Levy, Yamin (ed.). 2010. *Mishpetei Shalom: A Jubilee Volume in Honor of Rabbi Saul (Shalom) Berman*. New York: Chovevei Torah Rabbinical School.

Lichtenstein, Aharon. 2006–2007. "'*Mah Enosh*': Reflections on the Relation between Judaism and Humanism." *The Torah u-Madda Journal*. 14: 1–61.

Sagi, Avi, and Daniel Statman. 1995. "Divine Command Morality and the Jewish Tradition." *Journal of Religious Ethics* 23: 49–68.

Sokol, Moshe (ed.). 1992. *Rabbinic Authority and Personal Autonomy*. Northvale, NJ: Jason Aronson. Orthodox Forum Series.

Sokol, Moshe (ed.). 2002. *Tolerance, Dissent and Democracy: Philosophical, Historical, and Halakhic Perspectives*. Northvale, NJ: Jason Aronson. Orthodox Forum Series.

Spero, Shubert. 1983. *Morality, Halakhah, and the Jewish Tradition*. New York: Ktav and Yeshiva University Press.

CHAPTER 14

ETHICAL THEORIES IN THE RECONSTRUCTIONIST MOVEMENT

DAVID A. TEUTSCH

THE Reconstructionist movement, which understands Judaism as the evolving religious civilization of the Jewish people, is the only Jewish denomination founded in America. Despite the fact that it is a young movement, it is hard to determine a single date for its beginning. The Society for the Advancement of Judaism, its first congregation, was founded in 1922. Mordecai Kaplan's *Judaism as a Civilization*, which contains a chapter on ethics, is its 1934 manifesto. *The Reconstructionist*, its magazine that often addresses moral questions, began publication in 1935. Its first national organization, the Jewish Reconstructionist Foundation, founded in 1940, ran a major conference on ethics chaired by famed social psychologist Kurt Lewin in 1944. By that time the commitment of the movement's leaders to ethics had clearly and strongly emerged. Indeed the logo of the movement (see Figure 14.1), introduced in 1944, places a triad of ethics, religion, and culture in a central position.[1] While not uniformly pursued in the latter half of the twentieth century, Reconstructionist work on ethical issues accelerated in the last years of that period and into the next century.

FIGURE 14.1

Underlying Assumptions

Five basic trends within Reconstructionist thought have shaped the movement's approach to ethics.

1. The movement has a deep commitment to a social-scientific approach to Judaism. Kaplan's famous dictum, "Judaism is the evolving religious civilization of the Jewish people,"² understands the Jewish people across history and geography to be a self-identifying group anchored in its own culture. Torah is the result of the Jewish people's search for God, rather than the result of supernatural intervention. Jewish peoplehood is transmitted by Jewish communities, which share a calendar, folkways, language, and all the other trappings of culture. Jewish ethics is rooted in that culture. Thus ethics is perceived not primarily as a matter of individual conscience, but rather as an important strand within the fabric of a community's culture.

2. The Reconstructionist movement, which emerged in the first half of the twentieth century, understandably has a long-standing commitment to pragmatism, which sees the meaning of an action or proposition in terms of its observable consequences. The Reconstructionist *functional* understanding of Judaism followed the kind of analysis favored by Harvard psychologist William James in his ground-breaking work, *The Varieties of Religious Experience* (1902). In emphasizing how its approach applies to *practice*, Reconstructionist understanding reflects the thought and primary focus of American philosopher and educator John Dewey, who saw practical analysis as a precursor to a decision based

on "valuation." (See, for example, *Democracy and Education* [1916] and *Human Nature and Conduct* [1922].) From this perspective, its concern with ethics is not so much as a field for specialists who can justify assumptions and procedures at the meta-level of moral philosophy, but rather leaders capable of analyzing and shaping the conduct of real people and the choices that people face in their daily lives. Mordecai Kaplan described this approach approvingly as an ethical movement "of the prophetic type and not of the philosophic type."[3] This is a criterion by which the success of work in ethics can be judged. Just as Kaplan took a functionalist approach to theology and religion, he took a functionalist approach to ethics that remains central to the movement.

3. The Reconstructionist movement has commitments to Zionism and to progressive social values. This combination resulted in an early involvement with Labor Zionism. In the 1930s the wholehearted commitment of Reconstructionists to Zionism, rooted in their focus on Jewish peoplehood, differentiated them from Reform Jews, and the outspoken commitment to a progressive stand on social justice issues, also rooted in their communal and pragmatic foci, differentiated Reconstructionists from Conservative and Orthodox Jews. In later times these twin commitments have manifested as leadership in a broad variety of social justice issues in Israel, America, and around the world.[4] The values used by Reconstructionists, such as inclusion, egalitarianism, democracy, and pluralism, reflect this progressive perspective. Reconstructionists start from the particular of Jewish culture but move from there to universalism and concern for all peoples.

4. Kaplan and his followers recognized that the traditional understanding made no distinction between ritually based *mitzvot* (literally, commandments; required actions) and ethically based *mitzvot*. Jewish tradition understands them as all equally God's will. A transnaturalist rather than a supernaturalist, Kaplan regarded the ritually based practices to be folkways particular to the Jewish people and described only ethically based practices—which he regarded as universal—as *mitzvot*. One advantage of this equation is that it allows the inclusion of ethical actions that were defined by tradition as being *lifnim mi-shurat ha-din* (beyond what the law can require) in the category of *mitzvot*. Subsequent Reconstructionist writers have argued that the distinction between ritual and ethics that Kaplan used, which is so common in Western thought, is not necessarily a black-and-white distinction. As Kaplan himself argued in *The Meaning of God in Modern Jewish Religion*, Shabbat and the holidays carry values, as does liturgy. Furthermore, a shared calendar, conversation, and study help to shape the shared life of the community, which is a primary determinant of individuals' conduct. If folkways convey moral content, then the elements of culture are not as easily divided into rituals and ethics as was once thought. Of course Kaplan believed in preserving folkways where doing so did not raise ethical problems, because he understood that folkways carry Jewish culture, which in turn preserves Jewish community and Jewish ethics. His intellectual interest in clarity about what is particular and what is universal should not be understood to undermine his critically important insight that

ethics has a cultural context; ethical living can be easily sustained only when it is supported by culture and community.

5. The Kaplanian understanding of *mitzvot* depends in part on his theory regarding the development of the *halakhah* (Jewish law). He sees it as having undergone natural evolution as long as Jews lived in self-governing, organic, Jewish communities. With the advent of emancipation, which made Jews citizens of modern nations, those organic communities ceased to function. Anyone who was sufficiently unhappy with the *halakhah* could simply stop practicing it and create a meaningful life outside the traditionally observant community. As a result, the dynamics of the community that drove the evolution of the *halakhah* ceased to exist. The *halakhah* became the property of Jewish subgroups composed of people who chose not to leave. These were the people who experienced the *halakhah* as neither too onerous nor wrongheaded. The Kaplanian definition of *mitzvot* rests on an analysis of the *halakhah* as being no longer fully functional.

Later Reconstructionist thinkers have come to describe themselves as post-*halakhic*, meaning that they take the *halakhah* seriously as a resource but do not consider it binding. Kaplan's dictum regarding inherited Jewish practice, that "tradition has a vote but not a veto,"[5] continues to shape Reconstructionist action.

When the authority of rabbis interpreting *halakhah* is not automatic, serious questions are raised about the sources and legitimation of authority. One alternative is to emphasize the sovereignty of individual conscience, but this strategy has received two major objections in Reconstructionist circles. The first is that morality is shaped by language, culture, and experience. It therefore does not make sense to talk about individual conscience as if it could function in a moral vacuum. The context for moral life is the community. Second, even though the Jewish people in a post-*halakhic* world does not accept the binding authority of the *halakhah*, Jewish authenticity depends in part on continuity with previous Jewish experience and practice. The carrier of that experience and practice is the community, so the rightful location for decisions about Jewish ethics is the community, which is a legitimate decision-maker when it adopts suitable decision-making processes and is sufficiently steeped in the broad range of inherited Jewish texts and practices.

This way of doing things, of course, shifts the role of rabbis as teachers of Torah from authoritative judges to communal resources and advisors. In a *halakhic* system, the official decision-makers are rabbis. In traditional Jewish communities non-rabbis participated in the decision-making through unofficial communication and social pressure regarding the issues; their most extreme prerogative was to dismiss and replace the rabbi. The role of judge made sense for the rabbi in this dynamic situation. In the current voluntary community, however, a near-consensus is needed if the decisions are to be obeyed; for example, the decision to tithe and put money jointly in a charitable fund can be enforced only by a near-unanimous group. This requires democratic decision-making, with the rabbi and other available intellectual resources providing education and clarification of the issues and the implications of particular outcomes. This reality partly explains the Reconstructionist movement's commitment to democratic decision-making.

This commitment also represents the movement's belief that democracy is the best of the known forms of governance. Of course ignorance and apathy destroy the effectiveness of democratic decision-making, so ensuring suitable education and engagement is critical for legitimating the outcome. Because of this position, Reconstructionists have generally avoided using the *responsa* format, which utilizes *halakhic* methodology to answer *she'elot*, questions about what Judaism requires in a particular situation. Reconstructionist leaders have instead chosen to address questions through journal articles, books, and resolutions that draw on the *halakhah* without giving it final authority or using legalistic reasoning. By relying on principles, values, and reasoning that usually come to be shared with the movement's members, leaders can influence local and movement-wide democratic processes in a way parallel to the sway that *halakhic* reasoning can have only among those with commitment to the *halakhah* and substantial knowledge of it.

The Reform movement, no less than the Orthodox and Conservative Movements, makes extensive use of *responsa*. (See, for example, *American Reform Responsa* [CCAR, 1983]). This literature reflects a broad and deep understanding of earlier Jewish legal thinking, but it has often reached conclusions that are discontinuous with that literature without providing sufficiently substantial explanations that justify them. Furthermore, the Reform *responsa* seem to have had little influence on the conduct of Reform Jews, perhaps partly because the *responsa* are overwhelmingly aimed at providing guidance to rabbis, and partly because the *responsa* process itself is isolated from most people in the Reform movement.

The Conservative Movement, primarily through the Rabbinical Assembly Committee on Jewish Law and Standards, regularly produces authoritative *responsa* that embody the *halakhic* positions of the Conservative Movement. This substantial and intellectually serious body of work shapes the policy of most Conservative synagogues, but at least until the early 1990s, the questions it addressed and the way it responded to those questions had relatively little impact on the lives of most Conservative Jews. While over the last twenty years the Committee on Jewish Law and Standards has addressed such issues as contraception, infertility, removing life support during the dying process, tattooing, intellectual property, and whistle blowing, the methods of its *responsa* do not seem to have commanding authority for most American Jews, and the actual writing is not in a form that most Jews find compelling.[6]

One critical test for work in ethics is whether it has a real impact on real people—something that matters considerably to Reconstructionists given their pragmatic orientation. In the judgment of Reconstructionist leaders, neither the Reform nor the Conservative approaches to *responsa* are successful by that criterion. Reconstructionist efforts both at providing detailed written guidance in ethical matters and at strengthening community-based decision-making are still too young to do a meaningful accurate assessment of their effectiveness in shaping the behavior of Jewish communities and individuals, but in the long term that is what they are intended to accomplish.

The Foundation in Moral Philosophy

Many moral philosophers have attempted to derive full-blown moral guidance from a very few moral principles. The utilitarian "greatest good for the greatest number" and Kant's categorical imperative, to name but two, suffer from the same difficulties as other such efforts: the logical deductions needed to move from these principles to judgments in specific cases are so complex that it is hard to imagine a non-philosopher functioning in this way. It is even harder to imagine philosophers starting with the same principles and methods, avoiding their own biases and judgments, and arriving at the same conclusions. John Rawls's brilliant contribution to this genre, *A Theory of Justice*, demonstrates that for very narrow questions of justice for society as a whole, an outstanding thinker can apply such techniques successfully. Ordinary people faced with problems that have many more variables cannot do for their issues what Rawls did with a more abstract question. His very success underlines the unlikelihood of such a method's providing concrete, everyday guidance.

Effective everyday ethical guidance must be sufficiently specific and must fit with the way ordinary people think about ethical issues. People are not all the same. They are shaped by the cultures of which they are a part, and they are responsive to the political, economic, social, and techno-scientific situations in which they live. Naturally their ethics reflect such factors as their professions, the institutions with which they are engaged, and their religious outlooks. As Jeffrey Stout puts it:

> The languages of morals...are embedded in specific practices and institutions—religious, political, artistic, scientific, athletic, and so on. We need many different moral concepts because there are many different linguistic threads woven into any fabric of practices and institutions as rich as ours. It is a motley: not a building in need of new foundations, but a coat of many colors, one constantly in need of mending and patching, sometimes even recutting and restyling.[7]

This is particularly the case for Reconstructionists, who think in terms of incorporating the best of Jewish and American cultures into their moral framework. But even people not undertaking anything so complex have moral frameworks that are not based on a single element or even a few. People operate in what Alasdair MacIntyre (in his discussion of *eudaemonia* in *A Short History of Ethics*) calls a moral thicket—a tangle consisting of virtues, values, ideals, norms, principles, concepts, beliefs, and so on. Individuals intuitively weigh the parts of the moral thicket differently according to their situation. The elements that compose the moral thicket are passed on as cultural elements through example, vocabulary, stories, policies, and all the other elements of shared life.

The powerful assimilatory forces operating in North America and throughout the post-industrial world have resulted in significant erosion of shared Jewish life for most Jews (though not of the academic study of Judaism or production of Jewish resources), and hence the weakening of shared Jewish culture, and with it, Jewish ethics as lived by most Jews. Of course no community ever fully lives up to its own ethical standards. Even the finest human beings occasionally struggle and even stumble ethically. But any community can be stronger or weaker in terms of ethics. For those who would like to see the presence of Jewish ethics among Jews strengthened, the challenge is to build a shared life that teaches moral vocabulary, adapts the content and application of the moral thicket, and creates the interlocking relationships that sustain moral behavior. For that to occur, the shared life that moral leaders work to create must build on the culture and moral lives with which the people they are trying to reach are engaged.

Toward a Reconstructionist Approach to Ethics

The group process by which decisions are made needs to have a strong educational component and a reliable method for legitimation and, where possible, for building consensus. This theory was applied at the Society for the Advancement of Judaism, where important changes were studied and voted upon by the board, and at times by the whole congregation. These discussions were limited, however, to major issues of synagogue practice, such as giving women *aliyot* (calling women to the Torah). Of course the issue of who can have an *aliyah* has a strong ethical component, and that is reflected in the minutes of the SAJ meetings when the issue was discussed over several years in the early 1950s.

The fundamentals of Reconstructionist thought clearly indicate that a thorough approach to ethical decision-making is needed, but this issue was not systematically undertaken for a very long time. Some major issues were addressed through convention resolutions, such as the 1969 movement resolution recognizing ambilineal (usually erroneously described as patrilineal) descent in deciding who is a Jew—that a child of either a Jewish father or a Jewish mother is to be identified as a Jew if the child is raised as a Jew, contrary to *halakhah*, which passes on Jewish identity only through the matrilineal line. The systematic tackling of this issue did not begin until the 1980s, by which time there were reasonable numbers of graduates of the Reconstructionist Rabbinical College and of congregations in the Federation of Reconstructionist Congregations and Havurot (now JRF).[8]

The initial shifts in thinking occurred around the role of the rabbi. Moving away from the model of the rabbi as decision-maker and toward the rabbi as teacher and guide required thinking about who would then take on the decision-making burden. The notion of democracy within congregations and *havurot* (small ongoing groups for prayer, socializing, social action, celebration, and other activities) emerged broadly. However, what was to guide congregations away from making relatively shallow decisions that did not reflect the thinking and practices of inherited Jewish tradition? And what would help people to explore the nature of their conflicts in a constructive way?

Part of the answer came in the development of processes for important decisions that involve serious study, careful exploration of alternatives and their implications, and building toward consensus. The 1980s discussion of *kashrut* policy at Congregation Mishkan Torah in Greenbelt, Maryland, for example, included a series of adult learning sessions and required attendance at these sessions in order for one to vote on the congregational policy. This approach had the advantage of providing serious education, engagement, and important steps toward consensus, but it did not provide a regularized process that would be easy to utilize on a broad range of issues. Furthermore, the process would work only when the question was one of congregational policy.

The major methodological advance was the development of values-based decision-making (VBDM). That was the method used by the Reconstructionist commission on homosexuality that published its then ground-breaking report in 1989. I described VBDM formally in 2001.[9] While the name is somewhat misleading, the multiple steps of VBDM lead participants through investigation, education, and clarification prior to their making a decision. The steps are suitable for use both by an individual and by a group. And they encourage the explication of concepts, definitions, and precedents so that the past can "have a vote." Participants in the process gain insights and vocabulary that can guide subsequent decisions. The steps of VBDM are:[10]

1. Determine facts, alternative actions, and their outcomes.
2. Examine relevant scientific and social scientific approaches to understanding these.
3. Consider the historical and contemporary context, including the history and rationales of Jewish practice.
4. Look for norms that might exclude some actions.
5. Assemble and weigh relevant attitudes, beliefs, and values.
6. Formulate decision alternatives.
7. Seek consensus (if a group is deciding).
8. Make the decision.

Anecdotal evidence indicates that this method has been used effectively by families and individuals to make end-of-life decisions such as whether to use a ventilator and when to proceed with a "Do Not Resuscitate" (DNR) order. VBDM has been used to think through other bioethical decisions as well, including whether to use a surrogate mother and whether to abort at least one fetus when there was to be a multiple birth. Congregations have used VBDM to decide matters of policy such as *kashrut*, the role of non-Jews in synagogue life, and how to assess dues.

The educational component in VBDM provides vocabulary, concepts, and methods that increase the literacy of participants regarding Jewish ethics. VBDM is often also a group experience, thereby strengthening the commitment of the group to Jewish ethics and strengthening the knowledge and values carried in the culture of the group. Some individuals who have experienced VBDM in a synagogue decision-making process have reported carrying what they have learned into their personal lives. Given the Reconstructionist commitment to promoting a lived Jewish ethics, its effectiveness in spreading ethical thinking and action is one important criterion by which its success can be evaluated, though a formal evaluation process has not yet been undertaken.

The usefulness of VBDM has very real limits because the inputs to it can easily be insufficient. Unless thoughtful analysis of the ethical question is available, it may be too difficult for the individual to access the perspectives of traditional Jewish texts and practice and to blend them with insights from contemporary life and scholarship. This recognition led to producing the volumes of *A Guide to Jewish Practice*, which uses a values-based approach. I wrote the first book in the series in 2000. In addition to providing a guide to *kashrut*, it lists Jewish values, beliefs, and attitudes with definitions reflecting the Reconstructionist understanding of Jewish tradition. This list is broadly used as an aid to the VBDM process. The guides are unusual in that they all include commentary from a diverse group of rabbis and experts who amplify the main text, disagree with it, provide practical advice, and cite traditional texts. This commentary challenges the reader to develop a personal view in dialogue with the voices on the page. At the time of this writing, ten small books and a full-sized volume are available (see the bibliography below). Eventually they will cover the full range of everyday ethical and ritual practice, practice of the Shabbat and holiday cycles, and the life cycle.

The commitment of the RRC Center for Jewish Ethics to the *Guide* project represents the belief that providing clear choices in values-based contemporary language will be valuable to Jews, particularly those who would like their lives to be informed by their Judaism without abandoning their values but who lack the skills or time to do extensive original work in traditional texts and moral philosophy. The guides are designed for them and are used in education, training programs, and committee work as well as for advice in individual and group decision-making. Of course, the guides' suggestions are not always followed, but creating currency for the vocabulary of Jewish values and concepts is critical if they are to be preserved in the cultures of Jewish communities.

Again, the guide effort is too new to be judged by its long-term impact. Insofar as what is involved is the reinvigoration of a minority culture—and given that general American values are often in tension with Jewish values, Judaism is at least to some extent a counterculture, the success that can be hoped for in pragmatic terms will be uneven at best.

The idea that individuals and congregations can engage in Jewish decision-making with integrity has broad support. Even where a community does not follow VBDM or study a *Guide* volume, the Reconstructionist commitment to community decision-making does result in processes that are sensitive to the needs of individuals, to Jewish tradition, and to contemporary science and social science. Other methods for decision-making that draw on narrative ethics or are case-based are certainly compatible with the Reconstructionist approach described above.[11]

CRITIQUES OF VALUES-BASED DECISION MAKING

The most obvious criticism of the VBDM approach comes from those with a commitment to *halakhah* and the *halakhic* process. Switching entirely to a values-based approach requires a commitment not to approach decisions about Jewish ethics and practice from a *halakhic* perspective. All those who recognize the *halakhah* as the hallmark of legitimacy must necessarily reject VBDM except, perhaps, for those areas that are *lifnim mi-shurat ha-din* (beyond the requirement of the law) or not addressed by *halakhah*.

A second criticism involves the form of VBDM. It argues that the intellectual leaders who share Reconstructionist values should use a more *responsa*-like form to flesh out texts. This lengthier, deeper analysis could produce more nuanced positions that are tightly anchored in thorough text citations. While such *responsa* might be a helpful resource to rabbis and other learned Jews, it is doubtful that they would be broadly used—they are not very helpful for teaching most people because their language is so technical. Furthermore, the genre of *responsa* is limited to experts in rabbinics, whereas contemporary ethical decision-making needs a much broader array of areas of expertise to shape best outcomes.

A third criticism lies in the capacity to engage in a VBDM process without sufficiently consulting primary Jewish texts. The texts introduce terminology, analogies, historical parallels, and nuances that can affect thinking about a broad variety of issues. Anyone who has observed VBDM in practice has seen that some who use it omit such textual inputs in ways that weaken the process, reduce the level of education for participants, and sometimes affect the final decision. Stage 3 of VBDM is meant to include such examination of Jewish resources, but sadly it often does not. This omission frequently reflects a lack of textual skill or of the commitment to textual exploration; if a rabbi functions as educator or advisor in the process, it is sometimes the rabbi's error as well. Sometimes the lack of textual engagement seems to result from people's taking the approach that generates the least work or from an overemphasis on contemporary, American values without sufficient thoughtful struggle with more traditional Jewish values that are often in tension with the contemporary ones. Mordecai Kaplan pointed out the danger in insufficient engagement with Jewish texts and tradition. This frequent lack of engagement is not a failure of VBDM theory, but it is an all too frequent failure of VBDM in practice.

A fourth criticism of VBDM is that people in a community often place such great value on keeping peace in the community that the decision-making process is distorted. If the issue to be decided creates very strong feelings in a subgroup, the community sometimes acquiesces to their feelings, arriving at a decision different from the one that would otherwise have been reached through VBDM. Avoiding this outcome requires ongoing training of leaders. The challenge of meeting the needs of minorities while supporting the will of the majority is a complex process that depends upon the judicious leadership of rabbis and lay leaders. In Reconstructionist communities, which need and want to retain their members, a healthy dynamic usually characterizes public VBDM processes.

A fifth criticism is that VBDM does nothing to strengthen the virtues in its participants. After group pressure and rewards, individuals' virtue plays one of the most important roles in encouraging people to be ethical when their immediate environment does not. Virtue, of course, plays a major role in Jewish thought. A Yiddish proverb declares, *Sei a mensch*, "Be a mensch." *Menschlichkeit* (the state of being a *mensch*) requires such virtues as integrity, caring, strength, compassion, empathy, courage, sensitivity, and humility. Of course it is true that the inculcation of virtue has great moral importance and that different cultures emphasize different virtues. (Think, for example, of the Christian virtues of faith, hope, and charity.) And it is true that VBDM has relatively little effect on developing virtues. That, though, is not its purpose.

No single approach to ethics can be expected to do everything that is needed to create a morally vigorous culture. Jewish virtue inculcation requires the partnership of home, Jewish schools, synagogues, and other Jewish institutions. It is aided by the support of peer groups, particularly *musar* (the approach championed by Rabbi Israel Salanter that has recently undergone revival) groups. There is increasing attention to developing curricula that strengthen virtue. This is a critically important educational and societal activity that goes beyond the capacity of ethicists to provide.

Efforts within congregations to develop their own ethical guidelines are important both because of what is accomplished for participants who formulate the guidelines and because of the influence wielded by the guidelines themselves. Adat Shalom in Bethesda, Maryland, is an example of a congregation that has constructed some specific guidelines in areas such as Shabbat observance and giving *tzedakah*, though the development of such guidelines has not yet become widespread.

Contemporary American Jews live in a technologically, socially, and economically turbulent society. As Judaism adapts to that turbulence, the culture of Judaism thins as an inevitable result of rapid adaptation. As that occurs, the capacity of its ethical component to influence Jews wanes even as the changes make it more relevant to the moral issues Jews face. If Judaism is to be preserved as a way of life and Jews are to remain true to a heritage that strives for ethical vigor, Jewish ethical life will need attention from a number of fronts in an ongoing and intensive way to support adaptation and rethickening of Jewish moral life.

Notes

The author wishes to express his thanks for providing comments on an earlier draft to Galen DeGraf and to Rabbis Dan Ehrenkrantz, Jacob Staub, and Deborah Waxman. All remaining errors are my own.

1. I am grateful to Rabbi Deborah Waxman, who generously shared the portion of her doctoral research on the history of ethics in the movement. She pointed out the logo as an example of the movement's unusually integral approach to ethics.

2. See Mordecai Kaplan, *Judaism as a Civilization* (New York: Macmillan, 1934; Reconstructionist Press, 1957, 1967; Jewish Publication Society, 1994) Also *Religion of Ethical Nationhood* (Jenkintown, PA: Reconstructionist Press, 1970), pp. 4–5. For more on Kaplan's notions of ethics, see Chapter 8 above by Matthew LaGrone.
3. Mordecai M. Kaplan, *Judaism as a Civilization: Toward a Reconstruction of American-Jewish Life* (New York: Schocken Books, 1972), p. 462.
4. David Teutsch, "Reconstructionism in the Public Square: A Multicultural Approach to Judaism in America" in Licht, Mittleman, and Sarna, eds. *Jewish Polity and American Civil Society* (Lanham, MD: Rowman and Littlefield, 2002), pp. 337–62.
5. See Jacob Staub and Rebecca Alpert, *Exploring Judaism: A Reconstructionist Approach* (expanded edition, Jenkintown, PA: Reconstructionist Press, 2000), p. 39.
6. The CJLS itself wrestles with this sociological reality. See discussion by Shai Cherry in Chapter 12 above in this volume.
7. Jeffrey Stout, *Ethics after Babel* (Boston: Beacon Press, 1988), pp. 291–92.
8. For a thorough discussion of the history and reasoning regarding the Reconstructionist position on patrilineal descent, see Jacob Staub, "A Reconstructionist View on Patrilineal Descent," *Judaism* 34.1 (Winter 1985), pp. 97–106. Also available at http://jrf.org/showres&rid=764.
9. David A. Teutsch, "Values-Based Decision Making," *The Reconstructionist* 65.2, (Spring 2001), pp. 22–28.
10. The steps in VBDM are quoted from the article above.
11. Case and narrative methods are common in bioethics. Literary examples can also play a role in narrative ethics, as discussed in Adam Z. Newton's *Narrative Ethics* (Cambridge, MA: Harvard University Press, 1997).

Bibliography

Alpert, Rebecca. 1985. "Ethical Decision Making: A Reconstructionist Framework," *The Reconstructionist* 50.7 (June 1985), pp. 15–20.

Behoref Hayamim: A Values-Based Jewish Guide to Decision Making at the End of Life. 2002. Wyncote, PA: RRC [Reconstructionist Rabbinical College] Press.

Cedarbaum, Dan. 2001. "The Role of *Halakha* in Reconstructionist Decision Making." *The Reconstructionist* 65.2 (Spring), pp. 25–38.

Hirsh, Barbara. 2005. "Values-Based Decision Making: Some Second Thoughts." *The Reconstructionist* 70:1 (Fall), pp. 107–10.

Hirsh, Richard. 2006. *A Guide to Jewish Practice: The Journey of Mourning.* Wyncote PA: RRC Press,

Hirsh, Richard. 2008. *A Guide to Jewish Practice: Welcoming Children.* Wyncote PA: RRC Press.

Kaplan, Mordecai. 1934, 1972. *Judaism as a Civilization: Toward a Reconstruction of American-Jewish Life.* New York: Reconstructionist Press (1934 edition); New York: Schocken Books (1967 edition).

Kaplan, Mordecai. 1945, 1967. *The Future of the American Jew.* New York: Reconstructionist Press.

Macintyre, Alasdair. 1966. *A Short History of Ethics*. New York: Collier Books.

Macintyre, Alasdair. 1981. *After Virtue*. Notre Dame, IN: University of Notre Dame Press.

Rawls, John. 1971. *A Theory of Justice*. Boston: Belknap Press.

Schwarz, Sidney. 1985. "A Synagogue with Principles." *The Reconstructionist* 50.7 (June), pp. 21–25.

Schwarz, Sidney. 1988. "Operating Principles for Reconstructionist Synagogues." *The Reconstructionist* 53.4 (January), pp. 28–31.

Stout, Jeffrey. 1988. *Ethics after Babel*. Boston: Beacon Press.

Teutsch, David A. 2000. *A Guide to Jewish Practice: Kashrut: The Jewish Dietary Laws & Attitudes, Values and Beliefs*. Wyncote, PA: RRC Press.

Teutsch, David A. 2005. *A Guide to Jewish Practice: Bioethics & Reinvigorating the Practice of Contemporary Jewish Ethics*. Wyncote, PA: RRC Press.

Teutsch, David A. 2005. *A Guide to Jewish Practice: Tzedaka*. Wyncote, PA: RRC Press.

Teutsch, David A. 2006. *A Guide to Jewish Practice: Ethics of Speech*. Wyncote, PA: RRC Press.

Teutsch, David A. 2007. *A Guide to Jewish Practice: Organizational Ethics and Economic Justice*. Wyncote, PA: RRC Press.

Teutsch, David A. 2009. *A Guide to Jewish Practice: Community, Gemilut Hesed and Tikun Olam*. Wyncote, PA: RRC Press.

Teutsch, David A. 2010. *A Guide to Jewish Practice: Family and Sexual Ethics*. Wyncote, PA: RRC Press.

Teutsch, David A. 2011. *A Guide to Jewish Practice: Everyday Spirituality*. Wyncote, PA: RRC Press.

Teutsch, David A. 2011. *A Guide to Jewish Practice: Everyday Living*. Wyncote, PA: RRC Press.

Teutsch, David A. 2005. "A Reply to Barbara Hirsh." *The Reconstructionist* 70:1 (Fall), pp. 110–13.

Teutsch, David A. 2005. *Spiritual Community: The Power to Restore Hope, Commitment and Joy*. Woodstock, VT: Jewish Lights.

CHAPTER 15

FEMINIST JEWISH ETHICAL THEORIES

JUDITH PLASKOW

VERY little Jewish feminist work comes with the label "ethics." A search for formal feminist Jewish ethical theories yields only a handful of results. Yet Jewish feminism, for all its internal diversity, is fundamentally about ethics. Feminists' insistence that women's subordination in Judaism and the larger society are real and unjust and that change is urgent and necessary are the common threads that unite them and that define Jewish feminism's ethical core. But Jewish feminists differ greatly in their analyses of gender and other injustices, in the settings in which they seek justice, and in their views of what might constitute repair.

This chapter highlights some key contexts in which feminist ethical discourses emerge and describes some important methods that Jewish feminists employ in order to address gender and other inequalities. The categories used to describe feminist approaches are not mutually exclusive but overlapping and cross-cutting, and the examples given within each category are meant to be suggestive rather than exhaustive. My hope is that this structure will capture more of the richness and complexity of feminist Jewish ethical thinking than would a chronological or issue-oriented framework and that it will convey the great variety of approaches to ethical questions embraced by different Jewish feminists.

CONTEXTS

Denominations. The ethical claims at the heart of Jewish feminism were first articulated in the context of the denominational movements within American Judaism, beginning in the early 1970s. Framing their criticisms in the sharpest ethical terms, Jewish feminists ringingly denounced the exclusion of women from public prayer and study and demanded access to all the rights and responsibilities of Jewish life. In one of the first articles on Jewish feminism, published in 1972, Rachel Adler argued that the problem of Jewish women "stems from the fact that we are viewed in Jewish law and practice as peripheral Jews" and are "educated and socialized toward a peripheral commitment" to Judaism. Affirming Adler's analysis, Esther Ticktin claimed in 1973 that a significant group of Jewish women feel like "strangers in the house of Israel." They "are begging, asking, demanding, or screaming (depending on their temperament and tolerance for injustice)" for "full and equal participation in the spiritual and intellectual life of Judaism." The purpose of the precepts of Torah, argued Cynthia Ozick in 1979, is to call the Jewish people to justice in opposition to "the-way-the-world-ordinarily-is." Against the common impulses to steal or commit adultery come the commandments prohibiting theft and adultery. Only with regard to the status of women, Ozick said, is the Torah missing an immutable moral principle opposing the world's widespread tendency to perceive women as less than men. "There is no mighty 'Thou shalt not lessen the humanity of women' to echo downward from age to age."[1]

Initially, feminist rhetoric in all the denominational movements was a rhetoric of equality. Women should have access to forms of religious participation and leadership formerly enjoyed only by men because women are equal to men in intellectual, spiritual, and leadership capacities.[2] But as access was achieved within the liberal movements, feminists found themselves confronting deeper contradictions between women's participation in public religious life and the *content* of tradition. A woman reading from the Torah might find herself chanting a passage on selling daughters as slaves. A woman wanting to celebrate some life passage might discover that there are few Jewish forms for marking important moments in women's lives. At this point, feminists began to disagree about their ultimate goals, and a range of Jewish feminisms emerged. While some liberal Jews were content with access as an end point, others saw it as only a first step. Most Orthodox feminists sought fuller access within the boundaries of *halakhah* (Jewish law) while many non-Orthodox feminists envisioned a more thorough transformation of Judaism that would incorporate women's voices and perspectives.

The Feminist Movement. Jewish feminism did not magically spring up within Judaism as a sudden reaction to the accumulated insults of many centuries. It emerged out of the movement for women's liberation of the late 1960s and early 1970s as Jewish women began to apply a feminist critique of women's traditional socialization and roles to their Jewish lives. While the exclusion or marginalization of women in study and public worship was a central item on some feminists' agendas, other Jewish feminists were concerned about issues that were not tied to denominational structures. These included the subordination of women in Jewish communal organizations, negative images of Jewish mothers in literature and the media, the myths surrounding women's status in Israel, and the unacknowledged reality of family violence in the Jewish community.[3] Thus Jewish feminist ethical concerns were always broader than just religious participation.

Moreover, in the 1980s, as Jewish feminists struggled with Jewish invisibility and anti-Semitism within the feminist movement, the movement itself became an object of Jewish feminist critique.[4] This willingness to be critical of a movement with which they strongly identified came out of an intersectional analysis of gendered power relations that is an important model for Jewish ethics more broadly: it was not enough to talk about "women's subordination" as if women were an undifferentiated group. Gender subordination intersected with, and took on different forms depending on religion, culture, race, class, and sexuality. If feminists addressed only one dimension of subordination while ignoring other axes of inequality, they might end up reinforcing anti-Semitism or other forms of oppression even while deploring sexism. In the hands of such Jewish feminists as Melanie Kaye/Kantrowitz, Irena Klepfisz, and Marla Brettschneider, intersectional analysis became a powerful tool both for ongoing self-criticism and for addressing social issues well beyond the borders of the Jewish community. They and other writers and activists ground their ethical commitments in Jewish history and culture but express their Jewish feminist identities through critiquing and seeking to transform hierarchies of gender, sexuality, religion, nationality, race, and class.[5]

Academia. The feminist movement has had a profound impact not only on women in religious institutions but also on academia. Jewish feminist scholars have taken their places alongside many others in the academic world who have critiqued the ways that traditional scholarship has reinforced the invisibility of women and who have employed gender as a category of analysis that can illuminate both texts and historical processes. The rich and nuanced histories; sociological, anthropological, and literary studies; and explorations of canonical Jewish texts produced by Jewish feminist scholars may seem far afield from Jewish ethical theories. Yet, even where ethical concerns are not made explicit, the desire to right the inequities of past scholarship and to produce accounts of Jewish history and Jewish life that fully incorporate women's presence provides a powerful motive for Jewish feminist work. As Miriam Peskowitz and Laura Levitt comment in their anthology *Judaism Since Gender*, published in 1997, even as feminist theory and gender analysis are becoming increasingly professionalized, it is important that "critiques of patriarchy and the structural inequities of women's lives in a male-dominated society" remain visible "as at least a partial rationale" for feminist scholarship.[6]

Jewish Lesbians. Jewish lesbians are not a context in the same sense as the academy or feminist movement; yet they have been centrally involved in all aspects of Jewish feminism and have made distinctive contributions to Jewish feminist ethics in all spheres. Evelyn Torten Beck's *Nice Jewish Girls*, the first Jewish lesbian anthology, challenged both lesbian invisibility in the Jewish community and Jewish invisibility within the feminist movement. An early example of intersectional analysis, it highlighted many issues often neglected by the Jewish community: among them, sexuality, race, ethnicity, class, and conversion.[7] Lesbians have been at the forefront of those who have brought a Jewish feminist perspective to issues of social justice in the larger society, using their own complex social positions as a foundation for multilayered analyses of social inequalities. They have held leadership positions in Jewish social justice organizations and have forged links with Palestinian women to work toward a just peace in the Middle East. Jewish lesbians have also made important contributions in the religious arena, deepening the critique of women's religious marginality as well as participating in the transformation of Judaism. Rebecca Alpert's *Like Bread on the Seder Plate*, for example, examines those aspects of Jewish tradition that are particularly hurtful to lesbians and also explores "what would make it possible for lesbians to participate fully, as lesbians, in Jewish life."[8]

Israel. Feminists in Israel face their own distinctive set of issues, beginning with the persistent myth of women's equality in the founding of the state. Books such as Lesley Hazelton's *Israeli Women* and Barbara Swirski and Marilyn Safir's collection *Calling the Equality Bluff* debunk the notion that Israeli women have achieved many of the goals of women's liberation. Images of female pioneers working side by side with men to build the land and female soldiers serving as equals in the Israeli army disguise the reality that women have at no time played a full and equal part in Israel's public life. On the contrary, the state has failed to ensure women's economic or political equality, and pressure toward marriage and motherhood to the exclusion of other roles is a defining aspect of Israeli women's lives.[9] Israeli feminists tend to be much less interested in the equality of women within Judaism than with the ways in which the power of the Orthodox religious establishment over matters of personal status results in profound disadvantages to women in marriage and divorce. Moreover, they are deeply concerned with the ways in which living in a society under siege affects every aspect of women's experience from the prevalence of rape, to the constant anxiety about losing husbands and sons, to the construction of female bodies as requiring protection.[10]

METHODS

Cutting across these contexts are a wide variety of methods used by Jewish feminists to address gender and other injustices within both Judaism and the larger society. As Rachel Adler points out in her introduction to *Engendering Judaism*, Jewish feminists must be flexible, imaginative, and multidisciplinary in analyzing the workings of gender in Jewish life. Confronted by legal sources that disadvantage women, historical and textual materials that obscure their experiences, and a spiritual tradition that makes it difficult for women to see themselves as created in the image of God, feminists require all the methodological tools at their disposal if they are to articulate an alternative vision of what Judaism might be.[11] Just as any given Jewish feminist may find herself working in multiple contexts, so she might use a variety of methods to address a particular issue, even within the space of a single article or book. As was noted above, therefore, the categories that follow are neither mutually exclusive nor comprehensive. Rather, they suggest the range and creativity of feminist ethical engagement as well as some significant disagreements that characterize feminist work.

Halakhah. Because *halakhah* has been both central to Jewish self-understanding and a key factor in women's subordination, it has also been an important object of feminist critique, and, for some feminists, a crucial medium for repair. The earliest articles on Jewish feminism focused on the ways in which *halakhah* disadvantages women because feminists saw *halakhah* as the source of women's marginalization in public religious life. Feminists in the liberal movements have generally broadened their critiques of Judaism beyond *halakhah*, but for Orthodox feminists, it defines the parameters within which any expansion of women's roles must take place. For the last several decades, Orthodox women have engaged in a difficult dance between respecting the boundaries of the *halakhic* system and pressing for maximal change within it. In *On Women and Judaism*, the first full-length work by an Orthodox feminist, Blu Greenberg maintained that "where there is a rabbinic will, there is a *halakhic* way": *halakhah* is sufficiently flexible and sensitive to ethical concerns that it can respond to the desire among women for greater equality with men. In Greenberg's view, the concept of equality has functioned in *halakhah* both as principle and as process, so that the trajectory of *halakhic* development over the centuries has been toward greater equality in both the ethical and ritual spheres.[12] Tamar Ross disagrees with Greenberg, claiming that in depicting the *halakhic* process as a vehicle for achieving any goal one might choose, Greenberg manifests an insufficient appreciation of the fine points of *halakhic* deliberation from an insider's perspective. But Ross too believes that *halakhah* has always evolved and is open to continuing evolution. In fact, she is convinced that Orthodox women with feminist sensibilities constitute an ideal group for bringing about the development and renewal of *halakhah* in that they provide a broad constituency for creative *halakhic* change and can play an instrumental role in determining the direction of future *halakhic* interpretation.[13]

Not all feminists who are interested in *halakhah* understand that term as denoting the classic rabbinic system. In her extended discussion of renewing *halakhah* in *Engendering Judaism*, Rachel Adler defines "*halakhah* not as a closed system of obsolete and unjust rules, but as a way for communities of Jews to generate and embody their Jewish moral visions." In her view, it is imperative that feminists repair *halakhah* both because it is critical to Jewish self-definition and because it is the vehicle for *enacting* feminist commitments. The problems with traditional *halakhah*, however, are in her view too systemic to allow for the patchwork changes envisioned by Orthodox feminists. Because the presuppositions and categories of classical *halakhah* shape the very questions that it can even consider, Torah, Mishnah, Gemara, codes, and *responsa* amass huge bodies of data on such problems as women's status in marriage, divorce, and desertion, while completely neglecting other subjects of deep interest to women. Orthodox women have been able to take advantage of the places where *halakhah* has nothing to say to create independent women's prayer groups or take on certain leadership roles in the synagogue. But a progressive feminist *halakhah* would be proactive, dynamic, and visionary, beginning not with content and principles that need to be preserved or adapted but with revisioning the very meaning of *halakhah*. Drawing on the legal theory of Robert Cover, Adler defines law as a bridge between our current world of norms and behaviors and future normative worlds that might emerge from foundational Jewish stories. As feminists claim a place within multiple Jewish interpretive communities, they have the power to resist the law or reject it as it stands "in order to live out some alternative legal vision."[14]

Theology. Adler's revisioning of *halakhah*, and Ross's as well, stand on the boundary between *halakhah* and theology. *Halakhah* can furnish the context and vehicle for living a Jewish life and/or enacting feminist commitments, but if a feminist scholar wishes to raise fundamental questions about the significance and purpose of law, she requires a framework broader than *halakhah* can provide. Theology offers conceptual tools for describing the place of *halakhah* in a feminist Judaism, exploring the meta-*halakhic* assumptions that often guide *halakhic* decision-making, and addressing a host of other vital feminist issues from the nature of God to the sources of religious authority and the meaning of revelation.

In *Engendering Judaism*, Rachel Adler uses the term "theology" as the overarching category within which feminists can address the *"ethical task"* of reexamining "the values and priorities enunciated by Jewish tradition in...light of current needs, injuries, [and] aspirations."[15] While she believes that Jewish feminists must move fluidly among halakhah, theology, ethics, liturgy, and textual exegesis in addressing the "moral wrong" of women's subordination, theology provides the largest umbrella for doing the critical and constructive work necessary to engender a Judaism in which women and men are equals.

Tamar Ross agrees with Adler that the specific ethical and *halakhic* problems posed by feminism inevitably open up into broader theological questions concerning the relationship between *halakhah* and the values that it is meant to embody. As she points out in her preface to *Expanding the Palace of Torah*, questions concerning the status of women in *halakhah* "often relate to moral sensibilities that are pivotal to human experience, touching upon religious attitudes and principles that define our total vision of ourselves." How crucial is gender differentiation to Judaism, she asks, and does the expansion of women's independence and self-expression come at the cost of minimizing valuable gender differences? When women enter into the Jewish public sphere, does the gain of a vast pool of spiritual talents and energies compensate for the loss of a specifically female contribution to Jewish culture? The charged nature of women's issues combined with the urgency of women's demands for greater participation means that "changing the fundamental *halakhic* status of women has profound implications for the entire system." On the most basic level, feminism forces the Orthodox community to reexamine the relationship between divine revelation and human interpretation and to reflect on whether and how a tradition rooted in the notion of revelation at Sinai can accommodate the changing moral sensibilities of its adherents.[16]

I have been an outspoken champion of the view that the status of women in Judaism is ultimately a theological question and have pressed the non-Orthodox community to confront the radical implications of a feminist critique. We cannot assume, I argue, that if women become equal shapers of Jewish tradition, *halakhah* will be our medium of expression and repair, because *halakhah* is a key part of the system that women had no hand in creating. Since women have not been full participants in the more-than-three-thousand-year-old conversation through which Judaism has evolved, full inclusion of women's voices and perspectives would require a thorough reconceptualization of the fundamental categories of Jewish thought. In *Standing Again at Sinai*, I undertake such a reconceptualization, offering a feminist interpretation of Torah, Israel, and God, sexuality, and repair of the world. While I agree with Adler that thought and praxis are inseparable in a feminist Judaism, I understand theology itself as always having implications for Jewish practice, and ethical questions as being at base theological. Imaging God as male, for example, reinforces the subordination of women in Jewish ritual and law. Conversely, ethical problems such as *agunot*—women whose marriages have ended but whose lives are put on hold because they cannot obtain a Jewish bill of divorce—point both to the meaning of Jewish marriage as a husband's acquisition of his wife's sexual function and the difficulties of resolving crucial issues of justice for women within a *halakhic* framework.[17] For me, then, theology is a sufficient framework for considering those issues of deepest concern to Jewish feminists, without recourse to *halakhah*.

Liturgy and ritual. Creative and imaginative work has been just as central to Jewish feminist ethics as have various modes of intellectual reflection. It would require a separate essay to begin to do justice to the outpouring of poetry, literature, music, and the visual arts through which writers and artists have imagined a Jewish culture transformed by feminism. But two important creative vehicles through which feminists have expressed their ethical commitments, and ones that complement *halakhah* and theology, are liturgy and ritual. Because these are central modalities for remembering and passing on Jewish history and values, they allow feminists to enact their visions of an egalitarian Judaism, bring distinctly female voices into the liturgical arena, and convey new theological understandings in accessible form.

Marcia Falk's *The Book of Blessings*, a feminist reworking of Jewish prayer, is a rich example of the fusion of theology and ethics with feminist liturgy. In Falk's view, the traditional male images of God promulgated through Bible stories, midrash, and prayer communicate that maleness is primary and femaleness secondary. Such images inculcate an acceptance of male authority in society and the Jewish community that she sees as being in conflict with the Jewish imperative to pursue justice. "If we are all created in the image of divinity," she says, "the images with which we point to divinity must reflect us all." For her, the search for imagery that is effective and meaningful is identical with the search for imagery that is just. Her blessings, which for the most part make no use of gendered language, are meant to capture the presence of God in the whole of creation and to express the "deepest longings and best dreams" of those who seek God in prayer.[18]

The creation of new rituals has been another particularly fertile area of feminist inventiveness and one of the signal contributions of Jewish feminism. Using new rituals both to critique the gaps in traditional ritual practice and to develop innovative ways to celebrate significant turning points in women's lives, feminists have created new Jewish ways to mark an extraordinary range of occasions. Naming ceremonies for girls, for example, pioneered in the early 1970s, allow new parents to publicly celebrate the birth of daughters with the seriousness traditionally reserved for *brit milah* (the covenant of circumcision) used for boys. Feminist Seders bring the significant but neglected history of women's involvement in the Exodus into the observance of Passover. Rituals for divorce help women to heal after being subjected to the profound inequities of Jewish divorce law. Not all feminist rituals are deliberately compensatory; many revolve around individual experiences or life-cycle events simply not envisioned by the tradition. But they are all reparative in that they allow women to function as creators and shapers of a tradition that has often marginalized them.[19]

Orthodox feminists have been less involved than feminists in the liberal denominations in creating new rituals and liturgy, but they have been centrally concerned with expanding women's ritual participation. They have created a women's *tefillah* (prayer) network that builds on the separation of women and men in prayer in the Orthodox community and is comprised of women-only prayer groups that have sprung up around the country since the 1970s. While participants in these groups do not consider them *minyanim* (congregations that fulfill the quorum for prayer), they nonetheless provide contexts for women to learn to lead prayer and read from the Torah.[20] Partnership congregations, a more recent innovation, allow for maximal participation by women within the framework of traditional worship. Tova Hartman, a co-founder of the partnership synagogue Shirah Hadashah in Jerusalem, describes wanting to "create a traditional prayer space that respect[s] and embodie[s] feminist religious values." Convinced of the dignity of women's religious needs and filled with a sense that it is time to repair the dissonance between their feminist sensibilities and religious practices, Hartman set out to create a congregation that would respect yet push on the boundaries of *halakhah* in order to nurture the religious lives of all members. Her book *Feminism Encounters Traditional Judaism* conveys clearly and forcefully the power of ritual space to provide women access to formerly male religious behaviors and also invite their ways of doing and being into the public religious sphere.[21]

Textual interpretation. Not surprisingly, given the centrality of textual interpretation in Judaism, rereading Jewish texts—both traditional and nontraditional—has been a crucial mode of Jewish feminist ethical engagement. Seeking to fill what British feminists have called the "half-empty bookcase" of Jewish textual commentaries, feminists have offered new readings of canonical sources and also expanded the canon to include modern texts by Jewish women. They have produced Torah and Haftorah commentaries, critical analyses of biblical and rabbinic texts, as well as readings of contemporary feminist literature.[22] Textual interpretation is the arena in which we find "feminist Jewish ethical theories" in a formal sense, in that several Jewish feminists who define themselves as doing ethics employ textual reinterpretation as a central method. This is also a place where we see significant differences among feminists in the focus of their ethical concerns and in their attitudes toward Jewish tradition.

Rachel Adler believes that Jewish feminist theologians have paid insufficient attention to the hermeneutics of classical texts. Because, in her view, God is present precisely in the interaction between traditional texts and the lived experiences of communities, feminists must "interrogate [the] moral universe" of the texts they read, holding them accountable for their androcentric categories and motifs, but at the same time redeeming them by learning Torah from them. When she encounters texts that are clearly not addressed to her and that distort her reality as a woman, she refuses to let them go until she receives a blessing from them. As she puts it, "I will not abandon traditional texts, and I will not absolve them of moral responsibility." Using this approach, Adler rereads a range of texts that have been important in the construction of gender relationships within Judaism, both analyzing the ways in which they have perpetuated injustice and highlighting insights that nonetheless speak to contemporary aspirations and needs. Since in her view *halakhah* is rooted in and legitimated by foundational Jewish narratives, retelling the tradition's stories from a feminist perspective has the power not just to create new meanings but to resist and revitalize the law as it stands, creating a bridge toward a different legal future.[23]

Laurie Zoloth, who defines herself as a feminist Jewish bioethicist, also develops a methodology for doing feminist ethics that begins with engagement with classical Jewish sources. As she puts it, "The central claim of Jewish ethics is that truth is found in the house of... study."[24] The conversational encounter created through face-to-face argument about the relevance and meaning of Jewish texts both exemplifies and provides the context for forging a language of ethical values grounded in community. Because the core of any ethical discourse must be a radical meeting with the other, Zoloth argues, discussion of the applicability and implications of Jewish texts offers a starting point for framing public policy on a range of issues. She affirms the traditional Jewish approach to moral decision-making, but as a feminist, she also critiques and seeks to repair its inattention to the lived reality of women's lives. Her book *Health Care and the Ethics of Encounter* uses the Book of Ruth as the entry point for developing an ethical language appropriate to the health care debate—not the usual locus for Jewish discussion of this topic. In her view, Ruth richly depicts both the feminist claim that the personal is the political, and the Jewish insight that persons are always embedded in community. This vantage point provides principles for thinking about health care that emerge from the details of a text in which women are very much at the center. Whereas Adler rereads Jewish texts in order to engender Judaism, transforming Judaism is not Zoloth's primary project. Rather, her readings of Ruth and other narratives are meant to bring a Jewish feminist perspective to important questions of public policy that she believes can benefit much from a distinctively Jewish feminist voice.[25] Reshaping Jewish tradition is secondary to this larger purpose.

Rebecca Alpert writes from a distinctively lesbian perspective and approaches Jewish texts very differently than does either Adler or Zoloth. Although she agrees with them that it is important to engage with classical sources, she feels no need to find blessings in them where, in her view, there are none to be had. She rereads canonical texts because they continue to affect the lives of lesbian and gay people, and often in negative ways. She freely criticizes texts that lesbians experience as alienating, arguing that passages such as Leviticus 18:22 (which outlaws sex between men) need to be confronted in their oppressiveness as well as reinterpreted.

At the same time, she tries to broaden and complicate the notion of sacred text both by offering lesbian readings of classical narratives such as the Book of Ruth and by expanding the canon to include modern Jewish texts on gender nonconformity and contemporary Jewish lesbian fiction. Alpert's interpretation of Micah 6:8 ("Do justice; love well; and walk modestly with God"), to which she devotes three chapters of *Like Bread on the Seder Plate*, is particularly interesting from an ethical perspective. Appealing to Jewish commentators' common practice of taking some verse as a prooftext for contemporary ideas, she uses Micah 6:8 as a template for exploring some of the issues confronting Jewish lesbians today. "Walking modestly with God" she sees as pointing to the importance of self-acceptance and the ability to be honest with others about one's sexuality. "Love well" entails reflection on the special issues raised by lesbian relationships. The injunction to "Do justice" reminds individuals and couples to look beyond issues that affect them personally to work actively for a more just world.[26]

The fullest discussion of feminist Jewish ethical theory is found in Donna Berman's unpublished dissertation *Nashiut Ethics: Articulating a Jewish Feminist Ethics of Safekeeping*. Although Berman also draws on Jewish texts, she, unlike Adler, Alpert, and Zoloth, explicitly does *not* root herself in classical sources. *Nashiut* ethics (from the Hebrew for women, *nashim*) "begins with the critique and repudiation of those aspects of traditional Judaism that are oppressive to women" and then "seeks to create something altogether new from the voices of Jewish women." Berman shares Alpert's commitment to expanding the feminist/lesbian canon, but she retrieves the ethical insights embedded in normative texts only as a last step in creating a feminist ethic. For her, women's voices, rather than traditional narratives, stand at the center of ethical discourse and provide the hermeneutic through which to read and evaluate traditional texts. Thus, while in her view Jewish tradition offers few stories that highlight women's moral agency, the writings of radical Jewish women—Emma Goldman in particular—provide a rich moral vocabulary on which feminists can draw. Goldman's autobiography, *Living My Life*, and also her other writings become Berman's texts of choice as the foundation for a *nashiut* ethics because they have much to say to Jewish women about the oppressive ideologies at work in their lives.[27]

Berman does not limit herself to Goldman as a source of women's moral wisdom, however. She also conducts group ethnographic interviews with women who are angry at and frustrated with mainstream Judaism but nonetheless feel a continued connection with Jewish tradition. It is these women's voices that become her foundational "texts" as she sketches the contours of a *nashiut* ethics. Such an ethics "seeks not to redeem oppressive texts, but to redeem Jewish women—and men—*from* oppressive texts" by rejecting those that justify the exploitation of any group or assert the superiority of some persons over others. It also draws on the moral wisdom of women as a source of guidance in addressing urgent contemporary moral issues. Berman ends her dissertation with a discussion of how Goldman and her informants shed light on the ethical problems involved in globalization. Thus—like Alpert and Zoloth—she looks beyond the Jewish context even as she roots herself in (new) Jewish sources.[28]

Social/political analysis. Feminists have articulated their ethical visions not just through traditional Jewish modalities such as *halakhah* and ritual but also through social and political analysis. Whether focusing on the dearth of women's leadership in Jewish communal organizations, the barriers to women's equality in Israeli society, denominational resistance to liturgical innovation, or a host of other issues, they have exposed the power relations at work in Jewish and larger social institutions in ways that challenge long-standing norms and values. Feminists who locate themselves within the women's movement, for example, have led the way in bringing Jewish cultural and ethical resources to bear on questions ranging from anti-Arab racism and Palestinian rights, to complex issues of Jews and race, to definitions of family and the place of lesbians in the Jewish community.

Irena Klepfisz's essay collection, *Dreams of an Insomniac*, for example, tries to articulate a progressive Jewish identity that does not simply equate Jewish identity with political activism but draws on the rich history of Yiddish culture as a resource for struggles against injustice. Whether she is discussing the Israeli/Palestinian conflict or office work and the politics of class, she comes at issues with a strong sense of secular Jewish identity with deep historical roots.[29]

Marla Brettschneider's *The Family Flamboyant* considers the relationship among contemporary constructions of family; racial transformation; Jewish, sexual, and gender identities; adoption, marriage, and monogamy; and class and economic justice. In bringing together multiple modes of identity-based critical analysis within a Jewish framework, she tries to address both academics who ignore the contributions of Jews to multiculturalism and critical theory and a Jewish community generally unaware of the ways in which larger social forces shape the Jewish family.[30]

Melanie Kaye/Kantrowitz's book, *The Colors of Jews*, focuses on the changing relationship between Jews and whiteness. She argues that Jews of color can help the hegemonic Ashkenazi community to fight more effectively against racism and anti-Semitism and to build more powerful social justice coalitions.[31]

Social and political analysis is certainly not the exclusive province of secular feminists, however—as the work of Zoloth, Alpert, and Berman clearly shows. Such analysis is also found, for example, in the work of Orthodox feminists who want to understand their community's profound resistance to feminist efforts at change, even when such efforts respect the boundaries of *halakhah*. The Orthodox community has made little progress over the past forty years on the most pressing ethical issue for feminists, that of *agunot* (women chained by Jewish law to failed marriages). Despite the existence of several *halakhic* solutions to the problem proposed by prominent rabbis, the number of women held hostage by men who refuse to write bills of divorce continues to grow.[32] The profound injustice of this situation has caused a crisis for many Orthodox feminists, who have begun to question the institution of Jewish marriage, the fairness of Jewish courts, and the integrity of the halakhic system. Feminists such as Rivka Haut, Susan Aranoff, and Norma Joseph have written impassioned analyses of the religious and political obstacles to solving this problem and have called both for a thorough overhaul of a *beit din* (court) system that is inherently prejudicial to women and for creative and courageous *halakhic* change.[33]

Activism. Finally, all Jewish feminist ethical discourse is characterized by a continuing relationship between reflection and praxis that repeatedly finds expression in a variety of modes of direct action. One of the founding moments of Jewish feminism was the trip of the fledgling feminist organization, Ezrat Nashim, to the convention of the Rabbinical Assembly (the Conservative Rabbinic Organization) in 1972, where they demanded full and equal participation for women in all aspects of Jewish life.

In very a different vein, Jewish feminists vigorously protested against the anti-Semitism they experienced at the UN Decade for Women conferences in the 1970s and 1980s and organized dialogue groups to foster more constructive relationships between Jews and Arabs at the meetings.[34] Another feminist initiative was to found Women in Black in 1988, an originally Israeli women's peace group that opposed the occupation of Palestine. Women dressed in black gathered weekly in a central area of Jerusalem, standing silently with signs reading "End the Occupation." The vigils quickly spread to other sites within Israel and around the world, where they have continued for over twenty years.[35]

In yet another key, several *agunah* rights organizations within the Orthodox community guide individual *agunot* through the difficult process of getting a *get* (bill of divorce) and/or pressure the Orthodox community to come up with overarching solutions. *Agunah* activists have demonstrated at rabbinic conventions, collected signatures on petitions, picketed the homes and businesses of recalcitrant husbands, and exerted pressure on synagogues not to call to the Torah men guilty of *get* refusal. [36]

But even when Jewish feminists are not founding new organizations, organizing conferences, or participating in demonstrations, all the methods discussed here have activist components in that they emerge out of direct engagement with concrete issues in women's lives and include both analysis and substantive proposals for repair.

Conclusion

Understanding Jewish feminist ethical theories thus requires attending to the rich tapestry of contexts and methods within and through which Jewish feminists have expressed their ethical commitments. There is no one Jewish feminism nor any one Jewish feminist approach to ethics. Grounding themselves in a wide range of conceptions of both Jewish identity and feminism, feminists have criticized inequalities of power within both the Jewish community and the larger society. They have also sought to redress the historical subordination of women in Jewish tradition and the absence of distinctively Jewish and female voices addressing wider issues of public concern. In doing so, they have only rarely treated ethics as a distinct category, but they have created both a rich literature and a legacy of activism that is ethical to its core.

Notes

1. Rachel Adler, "The Jew Who Wasn't There: Halacha and the Jewish Woman" and Esther Ticktin, "A Modest Beginning," both in *Response: The Jewish Woman: An Anthology* 18 (Summer 1973), pp. 77, 79, and 84; Cynthia Ozick, "Notes Toward Finding the Right Question," in *On Being a Jewish Feminist: A Reader*, ed. Susannah Heschel (New York: Schocken Books, 1983), p. 149. Adler's article initially appeared a year earlier in the summer issue of *Davka*. Many other feminists wrote in a similar vein during this period.
2. It is interesting to note the similarities in rhetoric between Orthodox Blu Greenberg's *On Women and Judaism: A View from Tradition* (Philadelphia: The Jewish Publication Society, 1981), pp. 39–40 and liberal Ezrat Nashim's "Call for Change," http://jwa.org/feminism/_html/JWA039.htm.
3. See Elizabeth Koltun, ed., *The Jewish Woman: New Perspectives* (New York: Schocken Books, 1976); Susannah Heschel, *On Being a Jewish Feminist* (at note 1 above); and Naomi Graetz, *Silence Is Deadly: Judaism Confronts Wifebeating* (Northvale, NJ: Jason Aronson, 1998).
4. This is a central theme of Evelyn Torten Beck, ed., *Nice Jewish Girls: A Lesbian Anthology*, Rev. and Updated Ed. (Boston: Beacon Press, 1989), and Melanie Kaye/Kantrowitz and Irena Klepfisz, eds., *The Tribe of Dina* (Boston: Beacon Press, 1986).
5. Melanie Kaye/Kantrowitz, *The Issue Is Power* (San Francisco: Aunt Lute Books, 1992); Irena Klepfisz, *Dreams of an Insomniac: Jewish Feminist Essays, Speeches and Diatribes* (Portland, OR: The Eighth Mountain Press, 1990); Marla Brettschneider, *The Family Flamboyant: Race Politics, Queer Families, Jewish Lives* (Albany: SUNY Press, 2006). The Jewish feminist journal *Bridges* was founded precisely to foster such analyses.
6. Miriam Peskowitz and Laura Levitt, *Judaism Since Gender* (New York: Routledge, 1997), p. 7.
7. Beck, *Nice Jewish Girls* (at note 4 above). Cf. Kaye/Kantrowitz and Klepfisz, *The Tribe of Dina* (at note 4 above).
8. Rebecca Alpert, *Like Bread on the Seder Plate: Jewish Lesbians and the Transformation of Tradition* (New York: Columbia University Presss, 1997), p. 7. Cf. Rebecca Alpert, Sue Levi Elwell, and Shirley Idelson, eds., *Lesbian Rabbis: The First Generation* (New Brunswick, NJ: Rutgers University Press, 2001), and my *The Coming of Lilith: Essays on Feminism, Judaism and Sexual Ethics, 1972–2003* (Boston: Beacon Press, 2005), part 4.
9. Lesley Hazelton, *Israeli Women: The Reality Behind the Myths* (New York: Simon and Schuster, 1977); Barbara Swirski and Marilyn Safir, *Calling the Equality Bluff: Women in Israel* (Elmsford, NY.: Pergamon Press, 1991).
10. Hazelton, *Israeli Women*, chaps. 4 and 5; Swirski and Safir, *Calling the Equality Bluff*, chap. 3; Susan Sered, *What Makes Women Sick? Maternity, Modesty, and Militarism in Israeli Society* (Waltham, MA: Brandeis University Press, 2000), p. 3.
11. Rachel Adler, *Engendering Judaism: An Inclusive Theology and Ethics* (Philadelphia: The Jewish Publication Society, 1998), pp. xxiii, xxiv.
12. Blu Greenberg, *On Women and Judaism* (at note 2 above), pp. 44, 45. Conservative Jewish feminist scholar Judith Hauptmann agrees with this analysis. See her *Rereading the Rabbis: A Woman's Voice* (Boulder, CO: Westview Press, 1998).
13. Tamar Ross, *Expanding the Palace of Torah: Orthodoxy and Feminism* (Waltham, MA: Brandeis University Press, 2004), pp. xi, 172.
14. Adler, *Engendering Judaism* (at note 11 above), chap. 2; quotations on pp. 21 and 35. Cf. "'I've Had Nothing Yet So I Can't Take More," *Moment* 8 (September 1983), pp. 22–26.
15. Adler, *Engendering Judaism* (at note 11 above), p. xv.

16. Ross, *Expanding the Palace of Torah* (at note 13 above), pp. xiv–xvi; quotations on p. xv.
17. Judith Plaskow, "The Right Question Is Theological," in Heschel, *On Being a Jewish Feminist* (at note 1 above), pp. 223–33; and *Standing Again at Sinai: Judaism from a Feminist Perspective* (San Francisco: Harper San Francisco, 1990), esp. chap. 1; Plaskow, *The Coming of Lilith* (at note 8 above), p. 16.
18. Marcia Falk, *The Book of Blessings: New Jewish Prayers for Daily Life, the Sabbath, and the New Moon Festival* (San Francisco: Harper San Francisco, 1996); "What About God?" *Moment* (March 1985), pp. 32–36; the quotations are on pp. 34 and 36.
19. For some examples of feminist rituals, see Debra Orenstein, ed., *Lifecycles: Jewish Women on Life Passages and Personal Milestones*, vol. I (Woodstock, VT: Jewish Lights, 1994); Debra Orenstein, and Jane Rachel Litman, eds., *Lifecycles: Jewish Women on Biblical Themes in Contemporary Life*, vol. II (Woodstock, VT: Jewish Lights, 1997); Elizabeth Resnick Levine, ed., *A Ceremonies Sampler: New Rites, Celebrations, and Observances of Jewish Women* (San Diego: Woman's Institute for Continuing Jewish Education, 1991); Nina Beth Cardin, *Seeds of Sorrow, Seeds of Hope: A Jewish Spiritual Companion for Infertility and Pregnancy Loss* (Woodstock, VT: Jewish Lights, 1999); and http://ritualwell.org.
20. Rivka Haut, "Women's Prayer Groups and the Orthodox Synagogue," in Susan Grossman and Rivka Haut, eds., *Daughters of the King: Women and the Synagogue* (Philadelphia: The Jewish Publication Society, 1992), pp. 135–57.
21. Tova Hartman, *Feminism Encounters Traditional Judaism: Resistance and Accommodation* (Waltham, MA: Brandeis University Press, 2007).
22. The literature is much too extensive to cite here but includes Ellen Frankel's *The Five Books of Miriam: A Woman's Commentary on the Torah* (New York: Grossett/Putnum, 1996), and Elyse Goldstein, ed., *The Women's Torah Commentary* and *The Women's Haftorah Commentary* (Woodstock, VT: Jewish Lights, 2000 and 2004); Tamar Cohn Eskenazi and Andrea L. Weiss, eds., *The Torah: A Women's Commentary* (New York: URJ Press and Women of Reform Judaism, 2008) is a particularly fine example of women's Torah commentary that represents the fruition of years of feminist scholarship in many areas.
23. Adler, *Engendering Judaism* (at note 11 above), quotations on pp. xxv, 1.
24. Laurie Zoloth, "The Promises of Exiles: A Jewish Theology of Responsibility," in *Visions of a New Earth: Religious Perspectives on Population, Consumption, and Ecology*, Harold Coward and Daniel C. Maguire, eds. (Albany: SUNY Press, 2000), p. 102.
25. Laurie Zoloth, *Health Care and the Ethics of Encounter* (Chapel Hill: University of North Carolina Press, 1999), chap. 8. See also her essay "An Ethics of Encounter: Public Choices and Private Acts," in *Contemporary Jewish Ethics and Morality: A Reader*, Elliot N. Dorff and Louis E. Newman, eds. (New York and Oxford: Oxford University Press, 1995), pp. 219–45.
26. Alpert, *Like Bread on the Seder Plate* (at note 8 above), chaps. 4–6.
27. Donna Berman, "Nashiut Ethics: Articulating a Jewish Feminist Ethics of Safekeeping" (Ph.D. Dissertation, Drew University, 2001), pp. 5–6; chap. 4; quotation, p. 5.
28. Ibid., pp. 180, 202, 204, 215–32; quotation, p. 202.
29. Klepfisz, *Dreams of an Insomniac* (at note 5 above), esp. p. 182.
30. Brettschneider, *The Family Flamboyant* (at note 5 above), introduction.
31. Melanie Kaye/Kantrowitz, *The Colors of Jews: Racial Politics and Radical Diasporism* (Bloomington and Indianapolis: Indiana University Press, 2007), p. xi.
32. Rachel Levmore, "Recognizing Shame on International Agunah Day," (2011) http://67.199.16.63/pageroute.do/47522.

33. Rivka Haut, "The *Agunah* and Divorce," in Orenstein, *Lifecycles* I (at note 20 above), pp. 188–200; Aranoff, "Two Views of Marriage—Two Views of Women: Reconsidering *Tav Lemetav Tan Du Milemetav Armelu*," *Nashim* 3 (Spring/Summer 5760/2000), pp. 199–227; Norma Josesph, "The Feminist Challenge to Judaism: Critique and Transformation," in *Gender, Genre, and Religion: Feminist Reflections*, Morny Joy and Eva K. Neumaier-Dargyay, eds. (Waterloo, Ont: Wilfred Laurier University Press, 1995), pp. 58–59.
34. Sherry Gorelick, "Peace Movement," in *Jewish Women in America: An Historical Encyclopedia*, vol. II, Paul E. Hyman and Deborah Dash Moore, eds. (New York: Routledge, 1997), pp. 1035–36.
35. Gila Svirsky, *Standing for Peace: A History of Women in Black in Israel* (1996), at http://www.gilasvirsky.com/wib_book.html.
36. Haut, "The *Agunah* and Divorce" (at note 33 above).

Suggestions for Further Reading

Adler, Rachel. 1998. *Engendering Judaism: An Inclusive Theology and Ethics.* Philadelphia: The Jewish Publication Society.

Alpert, Rebecca. 1997. *Like Bread on the Seder Plate: Jewish Lesbians and the Transformation of Tradition.* New York: Columbia University Press.

Berman, Donna. 2001. "Nashiut Ethics: Articulating a Jewish Feminist Ethics of Safekeeping," Ph.D. Dissertation, Drew University.

Graetz, Naomi. 1998. *Silence Is Deadly: Judaism Confronts Wifebeating.* Northvale, NJ: Jason Aronson.

Greenberg, Blu. 1981. *On Women and Judaism: A View from Tradition.* Philadelphia: The Jewish Publication Society.

Heschel, Susannah, ed. 1983. *On Being a Jewish Feminist: A Reader.* New York: Schocken Books.

JOFA [Jewish Orthodox Feminist Alliance] Journal V/4 (Summer 2005). The entire issue is on *agunot*.

Kaye/Kantrowitz, Melanie. 1992. *The Issue Is Power.* San Francisco: Aunt Lute Books.

Klepfisz, Irena. 1990. *Dreams of an Insomniac: Jewish Feminist Essays, Speeches and Diatribes.* Portland, OR: The Eighth Mountain Press.

Koltun, Elizabeth, ed. 1976. *The Jewish Woman: New Perspectives.* New York: Schocken Books.

Plaskow, Judith. 2005. *The Coming of Lilith: Essays on Feminism, Judaism and Sexual Ethics, 1972–2003.* Boston: Beacon Press.

Zoloth, Laurie. 1999. *Health Care and the Ethics of Encounter.* Chapel Hill: University of North Carolina Press.

CHAPTER 16

POSTMODERN JEWISH ETHICAL THEORIES

MARTIN KAVKA

WHEN the University of Minnesota Press first published Jean-François Lyotard's *The Postmodern Condition* in 1984—assembling between two covers translations of both Lyotard's 1979 *La condition postmoderne* and the 1981 article "*Réponse à la question: qu'est-ce que le postmoderne?*"—readers interested in theology could have one of two responses. On one hand, they could seize on the last sentence of "Answering the Question: What Is Postmodernism?"—"let us wage a war on totality; let us be witnesses to the unpresentable; let us activate the differences and save the honor of the name"[1]—and infer that postmodernism was a movement that supported the validity of theological discourse, and specifically the theological discourse of minority communities. What could be more unpresentable than God, who, as Moses told the Israelites in Deuteronomy (4:15), was invisible when the covenant at Sinai occurred? How better to activate differences than for professors of Jewish studies to leave behind the constraints embedded in the hyphen in "Judaeo-Christian"? How better to honor God than to say that the theologies that scholars promulgated from behind their podia at lectures and conferences were just ideologies? In short, what could be more legitimating to Judaism than postmodernism?

On the other hand, they could seize on the Lyotard's introduction to *The Postmodern Condition*, where Lyotard defined "postmodern" as "incredulity toward metanarratives,"[2] that is, "grand narratives" that served to legitimate varying authority structures and ideologies (whether Enlightenment philosophy, Marxism, or capitalism). They could then infer that postmodernism was at its base a movement that would delegitimize religious authorities along with secular ones and undermine the authoritative texts and bodies of majority religious traditions as well as minority ones.

The field of Jewish ethics has, for the most part, followed the first of these paths, predominantly insofar as the work of the French Jewish philosopher Emmanuel Levinas became theoretically dominant in Jewish ethics at the end of the twentieth century.[3] This chapter will register discontent and incredulity at this move—lest it congeal into an ideology that would instantly be as *démodé* as aspic—and show how the work of young scholars in rabbinics at the beginning of the twenty-first century can point the way to an articulation of a postmodern Jewish ethics that is theologically and philosophically sophisticated *and* that expresses incredulity with the very metanarratives that establish it as Jewish. Their work shows that postmodern Jewish ethics is a viable field. It does not fall apart by claiming *both* antifoundationalist status *and* knowledge of divine norms, or knowledge that the West is in need of norms that the Jewish tradition could provide.

Postmodernism contains two strands: a war on totality, and a war on authority. Postmodern Jewish ethicists cannot know the good; this is what their postmodern commitments entail. Yet postmodern Jewish ethicists can *do* good when they articulate the reasons why such foundational knowledge is lacking, and they can show how Jewish communities in previous ages have both acknowledged and coped with this lack. If there is a postmodern turn in Jewish ethics, it is a shift away from trying to determine what the right decision is by applying right principles, and toward an awareness that authority is not the fruit of self-reliance, or an individual's quest for knowledge that (once an individual believes he or she has achieved that knowledge) can then be lorded over others.

To affirm Jewish tradition without affirming classical models of Jewish authority is the second goal of postmodern Jewish ethics. It legitimates ordinary people in Jewish communities, who are just as epistemically finite as (but no more epistemically finite than) their rabbis, and it does so by showing how previous authorities, such as the classical rabbis, saw value in accepting the limits of human knowledge.

Ethics as Confronting the Other

To critique a metanarrative is to critique an individual's ability to justify the claim that such a foundational narrative is in fact known (or perhaps even knowable) by that individual. As such, postmodernism is a critique of egoism. It overlaps the various formulations of the argument that philosophy begins in ethics ("ethics is first philosophy") in the work of Emmanuel Levinas (1906–1995).

In various essays of the 1950s, and in his first magnum opus, *Totality and Infinity* (published in 1961), Levinas argued that propositional language was not neutral. Because language is at its core conversational, embedded in the give-and-take of a responsive scene—we do not speak in order to speak monologues—communication at any moment is always communication *to someone else*. The fact of self-expression is exterior to any semantic analysis of the content of a speech-act. To say that "it is raining" refers to a world in which it is raining at this place is to omit the fact that it also refers to a dialogical scene (between two people, or between a weatherman and his audience).

Self-expression or self-attestation, necessary to have a system of significant meaning, is what Levinas famously termed "face." Thus, in the classic 1957 article "Philosophy and the Idea of Infinity," Levinas wrote that "in a face, the expressed [content of language] is a witness to [*assiste à*] its expression, expresses its very expression... it resists identification, does not go back to the already known."[4] And later, in *Totality and Infinity*, he says: "The event proper to expression consists in bearing witness to oneself.... This attestation of oneself is possible only as a face, that is, as speech. It produces the commencement of intelligibility."[5]

Why is this apparently picayune point about language ethical? Because self-expression is exterior to intelligibility, we can say that the other person with whom I am in conversation transcends me. The other person, in his or her face, introduces something to the scene that I am powerless to introduce myself. I cannot be, or produce, the other's face; I cannot conjure it up. (If I dream of someone else speaking to me, it is *my* dream, the result of *my* imaginative power.)

If we customarily think of transcendence as that which outstrips my own powers, then the face of the other person is something that transcends. As Levinas wrote in "Philosophy and the Idea of Infinity," the other person's "gaze must come to me from a dimension of the ideal. The other must be closer to God than I."[6] The other person has priority—authority—over me; and this heteronomous situation is one that Levinas frequently described as being commanded by the other.[7] To live in accordance with this fact—to live in accordance with the law of what it is to be human—is to acknowledge that a life of egoism, or a life lived in accordance with a set of abstract and universal norms (what Levinas and Lyotard meant by "totality"—for example, those of science, or of calculative economics in which quality of life is reduced to a nation's gross domestic product and persons themselves are elided[8]), is a life of false consciousness. Instead, one works on behalf of others to promote their flourishing and to produce justice. Thus, from an analysis of our language-use as engaging in an ability to respond (to put it inelegantly, our response-ability), Levinas deduced an ethics of responsibility. To be responsible to others is to make explicit the fact that the constraint of response-ability is implicit in (or the transcendental condition of) every conversation.

It will be clear from the sentence quoted just above from "Philosophy and the Idea of Infinity" that Levinasian ethics is also a philosophy of religion. Other texts show that it is also biblical. In Levinas's second magnum opus, *Otherwise than Being* (1974), he described our responsibility to others with reference to Isaiah's acceptance of his mission by uttering *hineni* (Isaiah 6:8), "here I am" (or, in Levinas's French, *me voici*). Indeed, Levinas wrote that *hineni* is synonymous with the following word in the Hebrew Bible, *shelaḥeni* ("send me"); to become a subject is already to obey a command from outside oneself.[9]

Of course, stating that a way of thinking is biblical is not the same as stating that it is Jewish. After all, the Hebrew Bible is part of the Christian canon too. As a result, in order to affirm that Levinas is not just a postmodern ethicist, but a postmodern *Jewish* ethicist, scholars often point to a series of commentaries on varying talmudic *sugyot* that Levinas gave at annual colloquia of French Jewish intellectuals between 1959 and 1989, for it is in these essays that Levinas's ethics appears to have been developed out of a reading of the Talmud, one important rabbinic work that defines the Jewish tradition as distinct from the Christian one. His postmodernism seems to lead to Judaism.[10]

The most accessible of these essays is a commentary on B. *Shabbat* 88a that was originally delivered in 1964, published under the title "The Temptation of Temptation." In this essay Levinas claims two things, as Annette Aronowicz has argued.[11] On the one hand, he shows that Judaism marks the reversal of the Western way of life. When Moses reads the content of the Israelites' covenant with YHWH in Exodus 24, the people respond by saying "*kol asher dibber YHWH na'aseh ve-nishma*'"—"All that YHWH has spoken we will do and we will hear" (24:7). In the Talmud, this notion of "doing before hearing" is a reversal of the normal reflective process, for usually one listens to an idea, one deliberates on it, and only then does one decide whether to act on it. He therefore describes the commitment to action before hearing what is involved as a "secret of the angels." (The rabbi into whose mouth the Talmud places this description, R. Eleazar, has deduced this because Psalms 103:20 describes the angels as doing the divine word [*'osey devaro*] before it describes them as hearing the divine word [*lishmo'a beqol devaro*]. The structure of doing before hearing is analogous to that of Exodus 24:7.) Levinas endorsed this understanding of the covenant[12]: the reversal of the primacy of subjective rationality, the account of the self as being always already oriented toward that which transcends, the association of transcendence with command, all could be found—for him—in this talmudic *sugya*. The Western self is self-reliant and self-grounding; the Jewish self is for the other. Yet at the same time, as Aronowicz points out, Levinas insisted in this essay that Judaism was not eternally foreign to the West; "Jewish" values could be translated into "Greek" as a critique of sedimented Western practices and ideas. (Levinas, after all, was most likely the first person to use the word "ontology" when commenting on the Talmud!)

From this point, it was easy to import this understanding of Levinas as somehow essentially Jewish back into his philosophical writings, and therefore to describe him, as Richard A. Cohen has recently done, as a figure who "defends and renews a specifically Jewish vision, driven by Torah, Talmud, and rabbinic commentary, which is at once faithful to *halakhic* Judaism and relevant to all humanity."[13] Such a claim might be an accurate description of Levinas's intent; but if one were to take it as an accurate description of Levinas's philosophy regardless of his intent—as a philosophy that has Judaism as its *content* (as if Judaism were somehow smooth and consistent over the centuries), and as legitimated by a revelatory discourse that is correct because God has spoken it—one would be mistaken. For it is in such claims that metanarratives about Levinas begin to take root. There are two possible critiques of such a claim: one rooted in Levinas's writings on the Talmud, and one rooted in Levinas's philosophical writings.

First, it is not clear to me that Levinas's reading of the *sugya* at B. *Shabbat* 88a can be said to be representative of something that is simply "Jewish." It is a report on the meaning of one text, to be sure. Yet Levinas's attachment to a notion that "doing before hearing" is a transcendent value, a "secret of the angels," belies his own Platonic approach to philosophy, in which capital-T truth resides in a beyond and this world is always constituted by lack, more than it does an appropriation of a unitary Jewish tradition. In other words, what this talmudic reading shows is that Levinas constructed as "Jewish" a set of values that he had derived from "Greek" thinking. (Levinas's abstract of *Totality and Infinity*, written when it was submitted as a thesis toward a doctorate from the University of Paris, described the book as a "return to Platonism."[14] One could describe several of Levinas's talmudic commentaries in the same fashion.)

For while Levinas endorsed R. Eleazar's view of "doing before hearing" as a secret of the angels, the Talmud as a whole does not endorse such a view. As Peter Schäfer has made clear in his discussion of over seventy talmudic passages,[15] angels in the Talmud are not smarter than humans. Their existence gives them no secrets of truth. They are marked primarily by their jealousness of human beings; they are mischievous imps. One of the most notable passages in the Talmud that supports Schäfer's view occurs on the very next folio page of B. *Shabbat*, almost directly after the *sugya* that serves as the focus for Levinas's "The Temptation of Temptation." In this *aggadah* ascribed to R. Yehoshua b. Levi, the angels complain to God as soon as they see Moses coming up Mount Sinai; they want the Torah for themselves. They say to God, "Precious and hidden, saved by you for 974 generations before the world was created...and you seek to give it [the Torah] to flesh and blood?!" They then quote Psalms 8:5f. to remind God that humans were created as lesser beings than the angels. But when Moses arrives at the top of Mount Sinai, he proves to the angels that the Ten Commandments could not possibly apply to them:

> Moses said before Him, "Master of the Universe, what is written in the Torah you are giving me? 'I am the Lord your God who brought you out of the land of Egypt. (Exod 20:2)." Moses [then] said to them [the angels], "Did you go down to Egypt? Were you enslaved to Pharaoh? Why should the Torah be yours? What else is written in the Torah? 'You shall have no other gods besides me' (Exod 20:3). Do you live among nations who worship idols? What else is written in it? 'Remember the Sabbath day and keep it holy' (Exod 20:8). Do you engage in any labor from which you would need to rest? What else is written in it? 'You shall not bear false witness' (Exod 20:13). Are there business transactions among you [that would require oath-taking]? What else is written in it? 'Honor your father and mother' (Exod 20:12). Do you have a father and mother? What else is written in it? 'You shall not murder; you shall not commit adultery; you shall not steal' (Exod 20:13). Is there envy among you? Does the evil inclination exist among you? (B. *Shabbat* 88b–89a)

On the basis of this *sugya*, one could infer that the Torah—like Aristotelian ethics—offers as its subject matter not the good that transcends being, but the specifically human good.[16] If one were to take this *sugya* as central to the tradition, there would be no need to translate a Jewish way of being into Greek philosophy, for Judaism would not be opposed to the deliberative model of philosophy that characterizes the West. The difference between the "Jew" and the "Greek" would be nothing more than a difference between two cultures' vocabularies of the good life.

So it seems that if Levinas is driven by the Jewish tradition, he has a partial take on it, one that reflects his own position as a Jew in twentieth-century France (to be sure, one who was deeply impacted by the Holocaust, which took his entire family in Lithuania, where he was born and lived until the age of eight, as well as from 1920 to 1923). Likewise, Levinas's philosophy provides no account of morality that one could describe as Jewish; indeed, it proves no account of morality that has any normative content whatsoever. His analysis of language shows that I am not, at bottom, constituted by freedom or spontaneity, for language is fundamentally discourse, "the relation with the other person."[17] This interpretation puts into question my own freedom, for it poses a call to respond to which I must react (even if my reaction is to ignore the other person).

Once I acknowledge this point, I acknowledge that freedom's ambit is *granted* to it. Freedom is "invested," as Levinas wrote[18]; it is installed in its position of power by another agency.

Levinas did indeed write that the cardinal ethical act of "welcoming the other person"—an act that is also associated with "placing my freedom into question"[19]—is welcoming "the Almighty [*le Très-Haut*]."[20] Levinas's language here might suggest to the reader that the investiture of freedom proves the existence of God, and perhaps a commanding God. Yet elsewhere in *Totality and Infinity*, Levinas explicitly denies the validity of such an inference: "One does not prove God thus because this is a situation that precedes proof."[21]

Yet what might the argument prove, if not God? It seems to me that Levinas could prove from his analysis of language only that we exist in a normative space in which the norms of a community are not grounded in knowledge; that a community's norms are not right once and for all. Levinas did not prove that transcendence has revealed itself directly to anyone, or to any community, in language; he did not prove that a supernatural agent established concrete norms in a code; he did not direct his readers to a true and correct morality system, and certainly not to Torah. He did show that we are naturally embedded in normative space.

Nevertheless, to be ensconced in normativity is not the same as having firm norms. In this situation of "normativity without norms,"[22] in a situation where norms do not come with proof of their eternally binding validity, communities have the ability to alter their norm-systems—to unmake them, remake them, test them, and remake them further and further—in accordance with whatever a community's needs might be at a particular historical juncture.[23]

Ethics as a Set of Practices

Levinas was a postmodern ethicist. And he was indeed a Jewish ethicist, insofar as his writings are inflected by the Jewish tradition. But we cannot discern from his writings whether Judaism determined, or was determined by, his philosophical positions. If there is to be an articulation of a postmodern Jewish ethics in which the two adjectives do not exist side-by-side by mere coincidence, it must start elsewhere.

Although postmodernism suggests that knowledge cannot be legitimated through some purely mental set of practices—either one that uncovers the right, or one that uncovers the meaning of history—a postmodern ethics need not simply be one that points to a conversational scene as the site of the making of meaning. To say that meaning arises from linguistic practices is not to uncover the full array of meaning-making practices in which humans engage. For humans are more than merely thinking beings, and more than merely speaking beings. We are also embodied beings; the turn to language must also be a turn to a whole set of bodily comportments that accompany discourse. (Philosophy does not improve when philosophers give brains in vats the ability to speak.)

In the canon of postmodern thought, the turn to an account of *ēthos* as a set of practices of self-cultivation is most readily found in the work of Michel Foucault and Pierre Hadot. Drawing on Hadot's work on spiritual exercises, which was originally published in the early 1980s,[24] Foucault turned to the ethos of "care of the self" (*epimēleia heautou*) as a set of nonintellectual exercises geared toward self-mastery.[25] In various writings and lecture courses from the last years of Foucault's life, in which he took up the theme of self-knowledge in ancient texts, Foucault showed that for the ancients, according to Edward McGushin, "knowledge of the self was worked out as a practical matter and not in a theoretical way. In other words, we might say that knowledge of the self was developed in purely 'regional ontologies' that were defined in a pragmatic way—as areas in need of work, as questions calling for answers."[26] The meaning of selfhood is not understood in terms of various principles, but through the use of the self in various practices. Existence is an art, not a science. The life that sees the truth about the self as being uncovered through practices is, for Foucault, a spiritual life. "Spirituality," on this definition:

> postulates that the subject as such does not have right of access to the truth and is not capable of having access to the truth. It postulates that the truth is not given to the subject by a simple act of knowledge [*connaissance*], which would be founded and justified simply by the fact that he is the subject and because he possesses this or that structure of subjectivity. It postulates that for the subject to have right of access to the truth he must be changed, transformed, shifted, and become, to some extent and up to a certain point, other than himself.[27]

Spirituality would thus be the dimension of those practical exercises and experiences in which a self relates to itself by transforming itself so that it comes to know the truth, otherwise and hitherto unknowable and unknown.

Since this is a form of postmodernism—something that delimits the subject's claims to self-sufficient knowledge—a postmodern Jewish ethics would show how the various principles of the life of Torah would have been seen by the talmudic sages as techniques for self-mastery. Jonathan Schofer, a scholar of rabbinics, has made this issue the hallmark of his work. In his study of the antique text *Avot de-Rabbi Natan*, a commentary on Mishnah *Avot* that may date as early as the tannaitic period (no rabbis from the third century onward are quoted in it), Schofer shows how the text positions the student in a particular way for a particular end. It institutes a curriculum that Schofer helpfully describes as "an interpersonal homosocial spirituality."[28] In commenting on M. Avot 1:6 ("Acquire for yourself a fellow [*ḥaver*]"), *Avot de-Rabbi Natan* states that "a man should acquire a fellow for himself, that he will eat with him, drink with him, study Scripture with him, study Oral Torah with him, sleep with him, and reveal to him all his secrets—secrets of Torah and secrets of *derekh 'eretz*."[29] Self-transformation requires this bond and its requisite renunciation or modification of other bonds (to women, to Romans, to ordinary Jews who are not part of the rabbinic collegium) in order for learning to take place. As Schofer writes, bolstering the analogy between this rabbinic text and the ancient texts analyzed by Foucault and others, "the voices of *Rabbi Nathan* call out not to a universal subject but to one who locates himself as a student in a particular set of relationships and distinctions."[30] Through the practices associated with rabbinic study and the life of Torah, a student is able to transform himself so that his negative impulses (the "bad *yetzer*") can be worn down, or conquered, or otherwise transformed so that the student can increase control over those impulses, train his impulses to do the good (create, or give power to, the "good *yetzer*") and, over time, gain the self-mastery that his teacher in the collegium already exhibits.[31]

At this point, it might seem to the reader that any approach to Jewish ethics that takes the perspective of virtue ethics or character ethics, as Schofer's Foucault-inspired approach does, should be described as postmodern. Nevertheless, for many readers this characterization would be undesirable. For Schofer's account of rabbinic ethics cannot make any end runs around authority structures, so that the agent of self-care is the self and *only* the self. To leave modernity and its knowledge regime behind, one might think, is to turn to tradition as a viable source of an account of the good. Postmodernism, in effect, means never having to say you're sorry for adhering to tradition, no matter how antimodern it appears. (Tradition is a place from which to declare a "war on totality," which would declare some or all religious traditions to be obsolete.)

Ethics as Recognition of the Limits of One's Moral Knowledge

For me, this cluster of issues about authority arises out of Schofer's very precise description of the position that the member of the rabbinic collegium and the student take: "chosen subjection."[32] Just as Foucault describes the care of the self as a "mode of action that an individual exercises upon himself,"[33] so one can see *Avot de-Rabbi Natan* as a text in which a student chooses a certain way of life for the sake of the self-mastery that that way of life promises, at the same time that one subjects oneself to the authority of the teacher, and to Torah. To move from theory to practice, Schofer implicitly shows, is simply *to transpose the seat of authority* from the scientist to the master of arts (the rabbinic teacher). What this kind of postmodern Jewish ethics suggests is simply that truth is available in other forms of life besides the scientific (or the modern philosophical) one. Yet in this Jewish form of life, the path to truth is not to be contested.[34] And in this respect, a Jewish ethic such as Schofer's is not fully postmodern. Despite its broadening the horizon of ethics to include character-forming practices that lie outside of the mental deduction of principles and their prudent application, Schofer ends up presenting a set of texts that express incredulity toward only some metanarratives and not others.

This is not Schofer's fault. After all, *Avot de-Rabbi Natan* is the text that it is. But Jewish ethicists should ask whether this relation of power, in which the teacher governs the student, might meet its limit in other rabbinic texts. To answer such questions, one would have to find those texts in which the rabbinic teacher is not described as having already reached the telos of self-transformation, in possession of the truth.[35]

Schofer himself implicitly points to a limit in a few places in his work. In his catalogue of the various metaphors in *Avot de-Rabbi Natan* that describe how the student's subjection to Torah transforms his impulses into good ones, Schofer does point to one set of passages in *Avot de-Rabbi Natan* that describes one sage, R. Yose ha-Gelili, as deferring the telos of the rabbinic student's curriculum. The vast majority of us are ruled by both the "bad *yetzer*" and the "good *yetzer*," in perpetual contest with each other.[36] The final decision in this contest is not made until the act of divine judgment that takes place at the eschaton; as a result, one can infer from this text that "Torah is not sufficient to discipline, reform, conquer, or govern their transgressive impulses."[37] Whether one can give a unitary reading of *Avot de-Rabbi Natan* starting with this passage is an open question, but at this moment in the text, a modern reader sees how the authority of the teacher is finite, for if the teacher indeed knew the truth, there would be no need for the rabbis to describe the heart as beset by a contest between impulses. For the truth in *Avot de-Rabbi Natan* is not simply a list of normative principles; they are also, as Schofer shows, promises of self-mastery. Yet if R. Yose ha-Gelili is correct, and transgression is necessary, then self-mastery becomes a Sisyphean endeavor—the process of caring for the self, in this passage, extends all the way up to the moment of death. However, as opposed to threatening the worthiness of the life of Torah, the limits of self-mastery generate ethical norms. This process is clear in Schofer's more recent work, in which he shows both that the rabbis saw their vulnerability to aging and early death (whether or not this death was the chosen death of a martyr) as generative of ethical ideals, and that contemporary readers can take this attitude as an implicit sign that the life of Torah does not lift the sage above such vulnerabilities or historical contingencies.[38]

Yet the finitude of the rabbinic life is clearest in the Talmud's accounts of lawmaking. In a recent book on the disjunction between ethics in the Hebrew Bible and ethics in the Talmud, Chaya Halberstam has reminded us to take care not to confuse a rabbinic court's issuing a *legal* verdict with its issuing a *true* verdict. These adjectives are not synonymous. For example, in M. *Sanhedrin* 6, the Mishnah "casually" raises the possibility that a person convicted of a capital crime might have been innocent. This is not to say that the convict was *wrongfully* convicted; the evidence has dictated what the evidence has dictated, and the court's ruling was procedurally correct. But the Mishnah does not invoke the category of truth here. As Halberstam writes,

> [T]he closest the Mishnah comes to the notion of objective truth, the use of the word *'emet*, is in stipulating the reaction of the convict's family after the execution. The relatives are required to ask after the welfare of the judges and the witnesses, "as if to say that we have nothing against you in our hearts, that you have judged a true judgment" (6:6). The word "truth" is never applied...to describe the legal decision, but such a validation of the work of the court is placed in the mouths of the convict's family, thus requiring not that the judgment *be* true but that it be *said* to be so.³⁹

In this passage, the life of Torah does not give the rabbinic collegium access to the truth, regardless of the varying spiritual exercises that the members of the collegium have engaged in during their lives. The selfhood constructed by spirituality cannot block out the world, and possibilities in the world—that an exculpatory witness will not come forward, that improper inferences will be made from physical evidence—cannot simply block such access once and for all. For Halberstam, the disjunction in this mishnah between truth and procedural correctness is both acknowledged and repressed by the text. For the mishnah has the court bolster its own authority by *demanding* that it be recognized as having made a true decision by the convict's family, whether or not its decision was actually true or just. What she calls the "messy world of uncertain reality"⁴⁰ recedes as soon as the convict's family speaks. One hesitates to describe their words as spoken out of free consent.

But if the court bolsters its own authority, whether or not it is in actuality just, it does this only in imitation of how it envisions God. In her account of rabbinic martyrdom narratives, Halberstam quotes the following text from another rabbinic text with tannaitic strata, the *Mekhilta de-Rabbi Ishmael*:

> At the time when R. Simeon and R. Ishmael were led out to be killed [by the Romans for teaching Torah], R. Simeon said to R. Ishmael, "Master, my heart fails me, for I do not know why I am to be killed." R. Ishmael said to him, "Did it never happen in your life that a man came to you for a judgment or with a question and you let him wait until you had sipped your cup, or had tied your sandals, or had put on your cloak? And the Torah has said, 'If you abuse in any way ['*im 'anneh te'anneh*]...' (Exod 22:22), whether it be a severe affliction or a light affliction. Whereupon R. Simeon said to him, "You have comforted me, Master."⁴¹

In this passage, the doubling of the verb for "abuse" in Exodus 22:22 leads R. Ishmael to affirm that the world of divine authority allows God to punish sages severely even for small sins with respect to others. But whereas R. Simeon is comforted by R. Ishmael's midrashic reading of Exodus 22, Halberstam is deeply discomfited by the text's wanton throwing of proportionality to the wind. For this text does not affirm that God's ways are not our ways (as other texts in the rabbinic corpus do indeed affirm⁴²). Rather, it affirms that God's ways are known, and they violate our contemporary sense of proportionate reason. Divine authority in this text is not—and cannot be—just authority.

Nevertheless, perhaps there is a slim thread by which a deeply troubling text such as this can be saved.[43] For what R. Ishmael does is chastise R. Simeon for having turned his chosen subjection into mastery, for having persuaded himself that he had reached the telos of the spiritual life. When a person in need came to him, R. Simeon may have ignored the pressing nature of that person's needs, glorying in his own mastery of Torah instead.[44] Whatever the purpose of this story about R. Simeon was for the rabbis of late antiquity, for us today (who are not at risk of being martyred for our commitment to the Jewish tradition) the story does serve as a warning against the arrogance that comes with having mastered a wide array of scriptural interpretations and their legal applications. A sage's knowledge is never justified, for he or she is always and already subject to someone else. Yet what R. Ishmael reminds R. Simeon is that that "someone else" is not only God, but also the person in need who (like the sage) is aiming at the freedom that comes with self-mastery, a person whom R. Ishmael classifies with other vulnerable people in the community, the widow and the orphan of Exodus 22:21.

In other words, even a sage can acknowledge that another person, in expressing his or her desires or questions, introduces something into the sage's life and reasoning process that he could not have introduced himself. The sage is constituted by his ability to respond to another. There are other such warnings against autocratic and arrogant behavior in rabbinic literature, especially when it involves the humiliation of others.[45] It is in these stories, where authority meets its limit, that an ethic that is truly both Jewish and postmodern, affirming tradition and circumscribing authority, not only becomes viable, but enacts a robustly grounded reading of the traditional past.[46]

Notes

1. Jean-François Lyotard, "Answering the Question: What Is Postmodernism?" Régis Durand, trans., in Lyotard, *The Postmodern Condition* (Minneapolis: University of Minnesota Press, 1984), p. 82.
2. Ibid., p. xxiv.
3. There is a school of Jewish philosophy that has produced a movement known as "textual reasoning" (or, in environments of interreligious discussion, "scriptural reasoning"), that has also been understood as exemplifying a postmodern Jewish ethic. See Steven Kepnes, Peter Ochs, and Robert Gibbs, *Reasoning after Revelation: Dialogues in Postmodern Jewish Philosophy* (Boulder, CO: Westview, 1998); the first issue of the *Textual Reasonings* e-journal (http://etext.lib.virginia.edu/journals/tr/volume1/index.html; 2002); *Textual Reasonings: Jewish Philosophy and Text Study at the End of the Twentieth Century*, Peter Ochs and Nancy Levene, eds. (Grand Rapids, MI: Eerdmans, 2003); Steven Kepnes, *Jewish Liturgical Reasoning* (Oxford: Oxford University Press, 2007), pp. 193–200. I have not analyzed this movement here, because its philosophical influences amalgamate postmodern European philosophers with the classical American

pragmatists. (For the latter, see Peter Ochs, *Peirce, Pragmatism, and the Logic of Scripture* [Cambridge: Cambridge University Press, 1998].) To claim that both of these strands are equally postmodern would entail a long narrative that reconciles the relationship to Hegelian philosophy in the post–WWII French context with that in the late nineteenth-century American context. Sources for beginning such a narrative are Stefanos Geroulanos, *An Atheism that Is Not Humanist Emerges in French Thought* (Stanford, CA: Stanford University Press, 2010), and Italo Testa, "Hegelian Pragmatism and Social Emancipation: An Interview with Robert Brandom," *Constellations* 10 (2003), pp. 554–70, esp. pp. 554–56. I see both Levinasian ethics and the textual-reasoning movement as arguing that pragmatics—the discursive art in which meaning is made, assessed, unmade, and remade—is prior to, and therefore more basic than, semantic systems in which (allegedly eternally valid and binding) meaning is represented.

4. Emmanuel Levinas, "La philosophie et l'idée de l'infini," in *En découvrant l'existence avec Husserl et Heidegger*, 2nd ed. (Paris: Vrin, 1967), p. 173; Levinas, "Philosophy and the Idea of Infinity," Alphonso Lingis, trans., in *Collected Philosophical Papers* (Dordrecht: Martinus Nijhoff, 1987), p. 55.

5. Emmanuel Levinas, *Totalité et infini* (The Hague: Martinus Nijhoff, 1961), p. 175; Levinas, *Totality and Infinity*, Alphonso Lingis, trans. (Pittsburgh: Duquesne University Press, 1969), p. 201.

6. Levinas, "Philosophie" (at note 4 above), p. 174; Levinas, "Philosophy" (at note 4 above), p. 56.

7. For example, see the same page in *Totality and Infinity* (at note 5 above). See also Levinas, "Liberté et commandement," in *Liberté et commandement* (Montpellier: Fata Morgana, 1994), pp. 25–48; Levinas, "Freedom and Command," Alphonso Lingis, trans., in *Collected Philosophical Papers* (at note 4 above), pp. 15–23.

8. See, in this regard (but without allusion to Levinas), Martha C. Nussbaum, *Creating Capabilities: The Human Development Approach* (Cambridge, MA: Belknap, 2011). For a treatment of Nussbaum and Judaism, see Martin Kavka, "Judaism and Theology in Martha Nussbaum's Ethics," *Journal of Religious Ethics* 31:2 (2003), pp. 343–59.

9. Levinas, *Autrement qu'être* (The Hague: Martinus Nijhoff, 1974), p. 181 and n. 11; Levinas, *Otherwise than Being*, Alphonso Lingis, trans. (Dordrecht: Kluwer, 1981), p. 146 and p. 199, n. 11.

10. Such a claim about postmodernity and Judaism, often centering on the polysemy of rabbinic midrashic interpretation, was made most notably in Susan Handelman, *The Slayers of Moses: The Emergence of Rabbinic Interpretation in Modern Literary Theory* (Albany: State University of New York Press, 1982). It was disassembled with fierce panache by David Stern in "Moses-cide: Midrash and Contemporary Literary Criticism," *Prooftexts* 4:2 (1984), pp. 193–204.

11. Annette Aronowicz, "Emmanuel Lévinas's Talmudic Commentaries: The Relation of the Jewish Tradition to the Non-Jewish World," in *Contemporary Jewish Ethics and Morality: A Reader*, Elliot N. Dorff and Louis E. Newman, eds. (New York: Oxford University Press, 2005), pp. 112–19.

12. Levinas, "La tentation de la tentation," in *Quatre lectures talmudiques* (Paris: Minuit, 1968), pp. 98ff; Levinas, "The Temptation of Temptation," Annette Aronowicz, trans., in *Nine Talmudic Readings* (Bloomington: Indiana University Press, 1990), p. 45ff.

13. Richard A. Cohen, "Emmanuel Levinas: Philosopher and Jew," in *Levinasian Meditations* (Pittsburgh: Duquesne University Press, 2010), p. 228.

14. See Adriaan T. Peperzak, "The Platonism of Emmanuel Levinas," in *Platonic Transformations: With and After Hegel, Heidegger and Levinas* (Lanham, MD: Rowman & Littlefield, 1997), pp. 113–21.

15. Peter Schäfer, *Rivalität zwischen Engeln und Menschen: Untersuchungen zu rabbinische Engelvorstellung* (Berlin: de Gruyter, 1975).
16. I owe this insight to Martha Nussbaum. My discussion of "Temptation of Temptation" is drawn from Martin Kavka, "Is There a Warrant for Levinas's Talmudic Readings?" *Journal of Jewish Thought and Philosophy* 14 (2006), pp. 153–73.
17. Levinas, *Totalité et infini* (at note 5 above), p. 188; Levinas, *Totality and Infinity* (at note 5 above), p. 213.
18. Levinas, *Totalité et infini* (at note 5 above), p. 278; Levinas, *Totality and Infinity* (at note 5 above), p. 302.
19. Levinas, *Totalité et infini* (at note 5 above), p. 58; Levinas, *Totality and Infinity* (at note 5 above), p. 85.
20. Levinas, *Totalité et infini* (at note 5 above), p. 276; Levinas, *Totality and Infinity* (at note 5 above), p. 300.
21. Levinas, *Totalité et infini* (at note 5 above), p. 281; Levinas, *Totality and Infinity* (at note 5 above), p. 304.
22. I borrow this language from Diane Perpich's excellent *The Ethics of Emmanuel Levinas* (Stanford, CA: Stanford University Press, 2008), pp. 124ff.
23. It is in this manner that the account of normativity in Levinasian philosophy nears the account of triadic signs in the work of Charles Sanders Peirce, so influential for Peter Ochs and the textual-reasoning movement described briefly in note 3 above. See Ochs, *Peirce, Pragmatism, and the Logic of Scripture* (at note 3 above), esp. pp. 7, 246–325. Meaning for both Levinas and Peirce is communal, but I find Levinas to have a more robust commitment to fallibilism about norms than that produced by Peirce's scientific teleology. See Peirce, "The First Rule of Logic," in *The Essential Peirce. Selected Philosophical Writings, Vol. 2 (1893–1913)*, Peirce Edition Project, ed. (Bloomington: Indiana University Press, 1998), pp. 44f. On pragmatism and truth more generally, see Jeffrey Stout, "On Our Interest in Getting Things Right: Pragmatism Without Narcissism," in *New Pragmatists*, Cheryl Misak, ed. (Cambridge: Cambridge University Press, 2007), pp. 7–31.
24. See Pierre Hadot, *Exercices spirituels et philosophie antique* (Paris: Etudes Augustiniennes, 1981); Hadot, *Philosophy as a Way of Life*, Arnold Davidson, ed., Michael Chase, trans. (Cambridge, MA: Blackwell, 1995); Pierre Hadot, "Philosophical Discourse as Spiritual Exercise" and "Philosophy as Life and as Quest for Wisdom," Marc Djaballah, trans., in *The Present Alone Is Our Happiness* (Stanford, CA: Stanford University Press, 2009), pp. 87–120.
25. See Michel Foucault, *The Care of The Self*, Robert Hurley, trans. (New York: Random House, 1986); Michel Foucault, *Hermeneutics of the Subject: Lectures at the Collège de France 1981–1982*, Graham Burchell, trans. (New York: Picador, 2005); Michel Foucault, "Technologies of the Self," in *Ethics: Subjectivity and Truth*, Paul Rabinow, ed. (New York: The New Press, 1997), pp. 223–51. For a helpful discussion of Foucault's later work, see James W. Bernauer, *Michel Foucault's Force of Flight: Toward an Ethics for Thought* (Atlantic Highlands, NJ: Humanities Press, 1990), pp. 158–84, and Edward F. McGushin, *Foucault's Askēsis: An Introduction to the Philosophical Life* (Evanston, IL: Northwestern University Press, 2007), pp. 5–172. For an application of Foucault's later work to religious studies, see Ivan Strenski, "Religion, Power, and Final Foucault," *Journal of the American Academy of Religion* 66:2 (1998), pp. 345–67. McGushin reads Foucault as not having made a turn in his thinking, and so he reads Foucault's earlier texts through his later ones.
26. McGushin (at note 25 above.), p. 35.
27. Foucault, *Hermeneutics of the Subject* (at note 25 above), p. 15.

28. Jonathan Wyn Schofer, *The Making of a Sage: A Study in Rabbinic Ethics* (Madison: University of Wisconsin Press, 2005), p. 33.
29. *Avot de-Rabbi Natan*, version A, chapter 8; version B, chapter 18.
30. Schofer (at note 28 above), p. 65.
31. This sentence is a very compact summary of Schofer's second chapter (pp. 67–119) (at note 28 above).
32. For more on this, see Schofer, "Self, Subject, and Chosen Subjection: Rabbinic Ethics and Comparative Possibilities," *Journal of Religious Ethics* 33:2 (2005), pp. 255–91.
33. Foucault, "Technologies of the Self" (at note 25 above), p. 225.
34. In other words, it is possible to critique a Jewish ethic inspired by Foucault and/or Hadot from two contrary positions. The first would charge it with egoism, for it seeks to transform the self (and not the self's community, or the world at large), and it mis-describes the self as abstracted from larger social and political currents. (See, for example, John Kelsay, "Response to Papers for 'Ethnography, Anthropology, and Comparative Religious Ethics' Focus," *Journal of Religious Ethics* 38 [2010]: pp. 485–93, esp. pp. 490ff.) The second would charge it with masochism, because it gives institutions too much power in dictating the kind of being that an ego should become. Both of these charges end up settling, in my opinion, into a series of debates that do not move anywhere without more thoroughgoing accounts of the various dynamics by which individual selves come to be portrayed as in need of institutions, as well as those by which institutions come to be portrayed as responsible to individual selves. As the next pages show, I see the beginnings of one such account in the work of Chaya Halberstam.
35. For a wonderful treatment of teacher-student contestation in the Talmud, see Barry Wimpfheimer, "'But It Is Not So': Towards a Poetics of Legal Narrative in the Talmud," *Prooftexts* 24, pp. 51–86, esp. pp. 53–61. My thanks to Jonathan Crane for providing me with this reference.
36. See *Avot de-Rabbi Natan*, version A chap. 32; see also B. *Berakhot* 61b and *Genesis Rabbah* 9:7–8.
37. Schofer, *Making of a Sage* (at note 28 above), p. 105.
38. Jonathan Schofer, *Confronting Vulnerability: The Body and the Divine in Rabbinic Ethics* (Chicago: University of Chicago Press, 2010), esp. p. 184.
39. Chaya T. Halberstam, *Law and Truth in Biblical and Rabbinic Literature* (Bloomington: Indiana University Press, 210), p. 90.
40. Ibid.
41. *Mekhilta*, Neziqin 18, quoted at Halberstam (at note 39 above), p. 132.
42. See Halberstam (at note 39 above), pp. 141ff., and Zachary Braiterman, *(God) After Auschwitz: Tradition and Change in Post-Holocaust Jewish Thought* (Princeton, NJ: Princeton University Press, 1998), pp. 35–59.
43. There will, of course, be those who do not care to save it, or are happy to jettison it. While that stance may be legitimate, it is not the only legitimate stance.
44. See Schofer's interpretation of varying rabbinic stories about R. Simeon in *Confronting Vulnerability* (at note 38 above), p. 106. Here, Schofer seems to depart from a line of interpretation in a 2003 article that seeks to justify God in these texts, against which Halberstam protested in her book. See Schofer, "Protest or Pedagogy? Trivial Sin and Divine Justice in Rabbinic Narrative," *Hebrew Union College Annual* 74 (2003): 243–78.
45. See, most notably, the set of narratives detailing R. Gamaliel's deposition as head of the collegium after his humiliating treatment of R. Joshua, and other stories about members of the collegium shaming their colleagues. See M. *Rosh Hashanah* 2:9–11; B.

Berakhot 27b–28a; Y. *Berakhot* 4:1; B. *Rosh Hashanah* 25a; B. *Bekhorot* 36a; Menachem Fisch, *Rational Rabbis: Science and Talmudic Culture* (Bloomington: Indiana University Press, 1997), pp. 63–71; Jeffrey L. Rubenstein, *The Culture of the Babylonian Talmud* (Baltimore: Johns Hopkins University Press, 2003), pp. 54–79. For another set of traditional references, see Jonathan Crane, "Shameful Ambivalences: Dimensions of Rabbinic Shame," *Association for Jewish Studies Review* 35 (2011), pp. 61–84, esp. those discussed at pp. 74–78, as well as the list of references at p. 64, n. 16.
46. My thanks to both Jonathan Crane and my colleague John Kelsay for feedback on previous drafts of this chapter, as well as to spirited discussions with Jon Schofer over the last decade in which he taught me much about the multifaceted nature of Jewish ethics.

Suggestions for Further Reading

Ajzenstat (Eisenstadt), Oona. 2001. *Driven Back to the Text: The Premodern Sources of Levinas's Postmodernism*. Pittsburgh: Duquesne University Press.

Borowitz, Eugene B. 1991. *Renewing the Covenant: A Theology for the Postmodern Jew*. Philadelphia: Jewish Publication Society.

Gibbs, Robert. 2000. *Why Ethics? Signs of Responsibilities*. Princeton, NJ: Princeton University Press.

Schofer, Jonathan W. 2007. "Rabbinical Ethical Formation and the Formation of Rabbinical Ethical Compilations." In Charlotte E. Fonrobert and Martin S. Jaffee, eds., *The Cambridge Companion to the Talmud and Rabbinic Literature*. Cambridge: Cambridge University Press, pp. 113–35.

Wyschogrod, Edith, Peter Ochs, José Faur, Robert Gibbs, and Jacob E. Meskin. 1993. "A Symposium on Jewish Postmodernism." *Soundings* 76, pp. 129–96.

Zoloth, Laurie. 2002. "Seeing the Doubting Judge: Jewish Ethics and the Postmodern Project." In Peter Ochs and Nancy K. Levene, eds., *Textual Reasonings: Jewish Philosophy and Text Study at the End of the Twentieth Century*. London: SCM Press, pp. 214–28.

PART II

TOPICS IN JEWISH MORALS

Introduction to Part II

DIVERSITY IN BELIEF, RELATIVE UNITY IN ACTION

After reading the multiple Jewish approaches to ethics in Part I, readers may have concluded that Judaism is so fractious that it is incoherent, that it has so many voices approaching issues in so many different ways that nothing can safely be called "Judaism's view on *x*" or "*the* Jewish view of *x*." This is indeed true. As was indicated in the Introduction to this volume, "Why Study Jewish Ethics?" Louis Newman has definitively demonstrated that at most one can speak of "*a* Jewish approach" to a given topic and then demonstrate how what one is describing has pathways back to Jewish sources and can therefore be called "Jewish" with some warrant.¹ Thus Judaism is not a happy home for those who like things neat and certain. Jews instead must cultivate great tolerance for debate and diversity while simultaneously maintaining a strong attachment to the Jewish tradition and the Jewish people despite—and some would say, precisely because of!—such disagreements.

That said, when we turn now to specific moral topics, readers will find that there is remarkable coherence among Jews about a host of issues. It is true that Jews cannot be pinned down to only one view on most matters, but that fact does not prevent our authors here from identifying the predominant streams of thought among Jews and then noting that some Jews think differently.

In many ways, this wide diversity of thought yet comparatively harmonious agreement on action has ancient roots in the Jewish tradition. "The interpretation is not the crucial thing, but the action," says Rabbi Shimon ben Gamliel in the first chapter of a popular tractate of the Mishnah, *Avot (Ethics of the*

Fathers).[2] Jews, of course, disagree among themselves also about what is the appropriate action—virtually every page of the Talmud records such debates. In the end, though, the Rabbis had to come to some decision about what the law would be so that Jews would know what to do. In contrast, biblical and rabbinic Judaism does not insist that adherents affirm a specific list of beliefs. Thus methodologies and beliefs could be multiple and varied as long as Jews did what God wanted of them.

This stance, of course, differs from that of Christianity, which defines itself through creeds of belief. Judaism certainly has beliefs, and its core beliefs could be defined relatively easily. Even so, all the medieval attempts to articulate an official list of beliefs, created largely in response to the creedal assertions of Christianity and Islam, suffered from a distinctly Jewish fate—they were debated! Louis Jacobs, a British twentieth-century Conservative rabbi and scholar, examines each of the beliefs on Maimonides' list of thirteen and demonstrates that every one of them had multiple interpretations among later rabbis and Jewish thinkers. Even something as central to Judaism as the assertion in the *Shema*, the central Jewish prayer, that God is one (Deut. 6:4) is interpreted by Jewish thinkers in thirty different ways, according to Jacobs's count.[3] When it comes to action, however, with all the feisty debates and with continual evolving customs and practices, by and large one can describe what the Jewish tradition commands us to do with regard to specific issues, and one can also describe the extent to which Jews follow what that tradition bids them do. Hence readers of Part II will probably find more coherence and unity than they might have expected from the diverse approaches described in Part I.

Applying an Ancient Tradition to Modern Settings

One problem that will appear in virtually every chapter in Part II is that of applying an ancient tradition like Judaism to modern circumstances. Modern technology—including contraceptive devices and, conversely, techniques to assist reproduction; surgeries, medicines, and machines as well as public health measures that enable us to live longer; new modes of communication and transportation—have significantly transformed our world and our capacities for changing it.

These developments immediately raise three methodological problems. First, why would one look to an ancient tradition for moral guidance in the first place? This issue requires the kind of meta-ethical discussions seen in Part I, particularly of the sort that have taken place in the last century and up to today, when Jews have the freedom to affirm their Jewish identity or ignore it, and they also have the freedom to choose how they will be Jewish, if they choose to be Jewish at all.

Second, assuming that one has one or more reasons to be committed to the Jewish tradition, how can one reasonably apply that tradition to modern circumstances? In most cases, a simple reading of an ancient text—or even many of them—will not do because the question either did not exist in the past or existed in settings so substantially different from our own that it makes little sense to expect sound guidance from any use of ancient texts. After all, if our ancestors could not even have anticipated a world in which business transactions are made worldwide in seconds, how can what they wrote guide us in such transactions now? And what does it mean for sexual ethics if people now attend graduate school in large numbers and therefore postpone marriage to their late twenties or thirties? After all, the Mishnah, which says that a man should marry by age eighteen[4] to a woman who was probably a year or two younger, presumed that people were earning their own living by that time, that life expectancy was considerably shorter than it is today, and that no effective forms of birth control existed.

Third, the philosopher Immanuel Kant pointed out in the late eighteenth century that "can implies ought." That is, if one cannot do x, then no moral questions about doing x arise, for doing x never happens. If one can do x, though, then one does have to ask whether one should do x, for there are all kinds of things that one can do that one should not do. One can, for example, abuse drugs or alcohol, but one should not. One can spend all day on the internet, but one should not. One can eat a half gallon of ice cream every night, but one should not. So the mere fact that we can stay wired to each other every moment of every day does not mean that we should, and the fact that we can sustain a person's bodily functions almost interminably does not mean that we should. Thus the new abilities that we now have, most of which were intended for very good purposes, raise moral problems that our grandparents and in some cases even our parents never faced. This capability exacerbates the difficulty of deriving moral guidance from a tradition that presumed much less human capacity to adjust the world to our purposes.

All these factors, though, also vastly increase our need to derive moral guidance from the ancient traditions that can provide it. For if we do not look to those reservoirs of experience and values, where should we turn to decide what to do? We may know from science much more than our ancestors did about how the world works, and we may be able to manipulate it in far more ways than they ever imagined, but, as David Hume and Kant pointed out, one cannot derive "ought" statements from "is" statements. That is, science can and should be called on to help us understand the implications of our various options, but those outcomes will not in and of themselves determine what we should do. For that kind of decision, we need a lens through which to look at the world, a viewpoint that describes who we are as individuals and as communities, what the goals of life should be, and what values we should strive to incorporate into our lives. We need, in other words, a way of defining what we mean by good in the first place, including the goals we are trying to achieve. Of course, the views we adopt might be totally of our own making, but then they lack the experience and wisdom of the ages. At the same time, we need to exercise *judgment* in using ancient traditions to guide us morally in the modern world, for our views and values need to evolve as our knowledge increases and our circumstances change. The one thing that is clearly not wise is to make moral decisions simply by citing chapter and verse from some ancient source written in a vastly different world, and ascribing to that old source absolute authority for this novel circumstance it could not conceive.

The Essays in Part II

Because we are keenly aware of these issues, we, the editors, deliberately chose as the authors of the essays in Part II men and women with very different connections to Judaism. They include people who describe themselves variously as Orthodox, Conservative, Reconstructionist, Reform, and secular. The biographies at the beginning of this volume indicate the authors' wide range of academic and Jewish backgrounds. What they share is deep knowledge of their subject matter and a willingness to describe not only how they interpret Judaism's import for the topic, but what other serious Jews have written about it from other viewpoints.

The topics in this section include a wide selection of moral issues, but they inevitably do not include everything that we, the editors, or our readers may have wanted. Space limitations forced us to make some choices about what to include. As in Part I, though, each essay offers Suggestions for Further Reading, covering related topics.

Beginning with medical ethics, Elliot Dorff discusses issues at the beginning of life. He first describes Judaism's fundamental convictions that affect its views of medical matters. He then discusses Jewish views about preventing pregnancy through contraception and abortion, and, conversely, assisting those with infertility problems. He also uses this analysis to discuss embryonic stem cell research and genetic testing.

Daniel Sinclair discusses issues at the end of life. After describing how the Jewish tradition views the stages of the end of life and how the categories it uses are interpreted differently by Orthodox and Conservative rabbis, he then discusses the degree to which patients have autonomy to decide what treatments they will accept or reject, including the question of withholding medications, machines, and artificial nutrition and hydration and even the question of killing a terminally ill patient in order to save a viable life. He closes with a description of the new law in Israel that governs treatment of patients at the end of life.

Aaron Mackler discusses the distribution of health care, an issue that has become particularly urgent and controversial in recent years. Because the median age in most English-speaking countries has risen, more people need more extensive medical care. This is happening, though, just as people have come to expect new but often expensive interventions. As a result of these and other factors, health care costs have risen dramatically. Mackler discusses the Jewish principles that might guide the discussion of who gets what in medical care, and who pays for it.

Laurie Zoloth explores one of the most important new frontiers in medicine—the new genetics. She addresses the issues of identity and free will that genetics raises in new ways, and she uses the case of a woman with one of "the breast cancer genes" as an example of how genetic testing poses excruciating new questions. Aside from the practical questions of what to do when faced with such a diagnosis, does this and the other Ashkenazi Jewish genetic diseases serve as a basis for "discrimination, stigmatization, and marginalization" of Jews generally? Should Jews be thought of as a "sick" people? For Jews, of course, such discussion of eugenics has a painful past both in the United States and in Nazi Germany. This is complicated yet further by the fact that in some cases, as with the breast cancer genes, the presence of one of these genes does not guarantee that the woman will have cancer but only adds to the probability of that happening. What, then, if anything, should be done with such a diagnosis? Will financial considerations lead to the decision that it is simply futile to care for such people because they are going to die anyway, that we cannot afford to do so? Furthermore, the availability of prenatal testing for genetic diseases could easily create expectations that families with a history of a particular genetic disease be tested for it, and if they bear a child with the disease, they may be seen as morally delinquent to both the child and society. Zoloth brings Jewish concepts and values to bear on these questions.

With Barry Leff's article, we turn to Jewish business ethics. Leff notes that Jews have developed three primary approaches to how the Jewish tradition should be applied to modern circumstances. He identifies several fundamental principles of Jewish business ethics and then applies them to various common issues in business ethics: fraud, anticompetitive behavior, theft (including theft of intellectual property), deception, kickbacks, and contract negotiation and interpretation. He then discusses more briefly a number of concrete examples where Jewish sources have much to tell us about how to conduct business morally.

Danya Ruttenberg addresses Jewish sexual ethics. She discusses extramarital sex and marriage, consent, and pleasure in contrast to the duty of both partners to satisfy each other sexually, the traditional requirement that a couple refrain from sexual relations during the woman's menstrual period, masturbation, procreation, same-sex relationships, and gender identity and sexuality—all from her unique vantage point as both a Conservative rabbi and a feminist. As a Conservative rabbi, she is committed to the Jewish tradition and aware that it has changed in the past and must be adjusted to respond to new scientific findings about sexual orientation and sexual practices as well as new social conditions and moral sensitivities. As a feminist, she probes that tradition for its biases against women, homosexuals, and transgender people.

Arthur Waskow discusses Jewish environmental ethics. Most essays in this volume base themselves primarily on Jewish law, for it is in that form that much of Jewish moral thinking has taken place. Waskow brings Jewish law into his exposition of Jewish environmental ethics, but he focuses on another source for Jewish ethics—namely, Jewish lore (*aggadah*), the stories in the Bible and Rabbinic literature that shape the Jewish frame of mind. Using three primary biblical stories—the Garden of Eden, the Flood, and the Plagues with which God afflicts the Egyptians—Waskow describes what a Jewish approach to the environment entails in carrying out the biblical mandate "to work it and to preserve it" (Gen. 2:15).

Aaron Gross focuses on one subset of Jewish environmental ethics—namely, Jewish animal ethics. He first identifies the central concept in this area of Jewish ethics, *tza'ar ba'alei hayyim*, the ban on causing undue pain to animals, and he describes the varying justifications for that ban. Some of them focus on how compassion for animals will benefit human beings, including human moral character, and others assert the inherent value of animals in and of themselves. He also discusses how the prohibition against causing animals pain is balanced in Jewish sources by human need. This balance affects not only our use of animals, but also Jewish rules regarding eating their flesh, with a persistent minority urging vegetarianism. He then turns to two responsibilities that humans have to animals according to the Jewish tradition—to preserve compassion toward them and to guard them from abuse produced by economic motives. In general, as Gross demonstrates, Jews are required to provide animals with both a good life and a good death. This requirement, in Gross's view, argues against many modern factory farming methods.

Alyssa Gray describes a Jewish ethic of speech. American law, in particular, has very few limitations about what one can say to or about another without incurring legal sanctions for libel, slander, or endangering others. That is because of the First Amendment's guarantee of free speech, which, especially in recent U.S. Supreme Court decisions, has been expanded immensely. Jewish law is much more detailed and demanding in defining what people are not supposed to say. The list includes foul language, slander, and lies, as one might expect, but also oppressive speech, gossip, and even true but negative speech about others when the hearer had no practical need to know such things. On the other hand, Judaism also defines categories of speech that are holy, including vigorous debate of Jewish law, blessings, and plans for raising funds for charitable purposes. Jewish law also commands reproof of others and other forms of speech that are deemed beneficial for society, and it defines exactly when and how to engage in such speech.

The political situations in the United States and Israel raise such different questions for Jews that we have included two chapters on political ethics, one for each of those contexts. Jill Jacobs examines Jewish political ethics as it has emerged in the American setting. Unlike virtually all the places where Jews have lived throughout history, American Jews are full-fledged citizens, and some have taken leadership roles in both local and national politics, to say nothing of the professions, academia, and business. Jacobs describes four different approaches that Jews have taken to respond to this new reality: "(1) Jews should participate in American politics in service of Jewish self-interest; (2) Political participation replaces religion; (3) The United States is a step in the march toward messianic redemption; and (4) Jews should involve themselves in American politics, as Jews, for the betterment of all."

She describes each of these positions, quotes some representative spokespersons for each, and shows how each has influenced Jewish political ethics in America. She then illustrates how varying Jewish prayers for the nation articulate each of these approaches.

In Reuven Hammer's essay the focus shifts to Israel. Because the modern State of Israel is the first Jewish state in close to two thousand years, it presents a whole new gamut of moral issues that Jews have not had to confront for centuries. Some of these concern the ethics of war, with which, unfortunately, Israel has had a plethora of experience. Asa Kasher addresses those issues in a later chapter of this volume. Hammer instead looks at the following issues: Who is a Jew to qualify for immediate citizenship under Israel's Law of Return? Who may be married or buried as a Jew? How can Israel be both a Jewish state and a democratic state open to both Jews and non-Jews? What authority, if any, should classical Jewish law have in the Jewish state in contrast to laws legislated by the Knesset (the Israeli Parliament) and precedents used by judges (based largely on British Common Law together with decisions of Israeli courts from 1948 on)? How should Israel respond to the Palestinians claiming to be refugees driven from their lands in 1948, and what should it do with the large Arab population living in the West Bank that Israel conquered in the 1967 war? Can it remain a Jewish state and also a democracy if it retains the West Bank and then, in the not-too-distant future, the majority of the population is no longer Jewish?

Laurie Levenson explores Jewish criminal justice. She first discusses the rationales that make punishment moral and not just an exercise of sovereign power. She then addresses capital punishment, decreed for thirty-six different offenses in the Torah but made virtually inoperative by the Rabbis. She then turns to what makes a defendant criminally liable, describing the conceptions of causation, joint offenders, criminal intent, and defenses in Jewish law, and, with that foundation, she asks whether there is anything like a victimless crime in Jewish law. Finally, she points out the lessons that Western criminal justice today can learn from both the content and the processes of Jewish criminal law.

Asa Kasher addresses the situation in which all of the usual laws of society are obliterated—namely, war. Author of the Code of Ethics of the Israeli Defense Forces, he first describes what ancient and medieval Jewish sources tell us about the ethics of going to war (*jus ad bellum*) and of waging war (*jus in bello*)—especially Deuteronomy 20–21 and Maimonides' code of Jewish law, the *Mishneh Torah*. Recognizing that until the founding of the modern State of Israel, Jews fought in armies governed by non-Jewish rulers, he then examines a nineteenth-century book intended to instruct Jews about how to act in military service. The overriding principle in that book as well as the few other Jewish treatments of the ethics of war during the last two thousand years, though, was "the law of the land is the law," and that law was determined by the non-Jewish ruler. What happens, though, when Jews determine the law of the land? Kasher examines some Jewish writings published just before and after the establishment of the State of Israel that anticipate this issue. He then discusses the doctrine of "purity of arms" that has shaped

Israeli military ethics, the role of the military rabbinate, the Code of Ethics that now governs Israel's military actions, the ethics of fighting terrorism, and the ethics of seeking peace.

As was indicated in the Introduction to this volume, the specific topics included here in Part II surely do not exhaust the field of Jewish ethics. We can assure readers, however, that this volume gives them a good sense of some of the most prominent topics discussed in the field as well as the methodological tools for understanding the varying ways in which Jews gain guidance from their tradition with regard to both long-standing and completely new moral issues.

Notes

1. Louis E. Newman, "Woodchoppers and Respirators: The Problem of Interpretation in Contemporary Jewish Ethics, *Modern Judaism* 10:2 (February 1990), 17–42. Reprinted in Elliot N. Dorff and Louis E. Newman, *Contemporary Jewish Ethics and Morality: A Reader* (New York: Oxford University Press, 1995), 140–60.
2. M. *Avot* 1:17.
3. Louis Jacobs, *Principles of the Jewish Faith* (New York: Basic Books, 1964; republished, Northvale, NJ: Jason Aronson, 1988), ch. 3.
4. M. *Avot* 5:21.

CHAPTER 17

JEWISH BIOETHICS
THE BEGINNING OF LIFE

ELLIOT N. DORFF

Fundamental Convictions

A number of Judaism's fundamental convictions affect Jewish approaches to the moral issues at the beginning of life:

1. *The body belongs to God*. Unlike American secular ethics, in which each person's body belongs to him- or herself, Jewish classical texts assert that God, as Creator of the universe, owns everything in it, including our bodies.[1] Therefore God can and does make certain demands of us as to how we use our bodies, demands articulated in Jewish law. It is as if we were renting an apartment: we have fair use of the apartment during our lease—and, in the biological analogue, during our lease on life—but we do not have the right to destroy the apartment (commit suicide) or harm it unnecessarily, because it is not ours. What constitutes "fair use"—that is, the risks that we may take—depends, according to Jewish law, on whether most people assume the risk.[2] So, for example, one may drive a car, even though it clearly raises the possibility of injury or even death, but whether one may engage in experimental medical procedures depends on the degree to which they have a chance of preserving one's life or curing an illness or disability.

2. *Humans may and should use medicine to prevent, mitigate, or cure illnesses.* The Torah maintains that God imposes illness as punishment for sin[3]—although the biblical Book of Job strongly challenges this belief—and that God is our healer.[4] That idea might lead some to conclude that medicine is an improper human intervention in God's decision to inflict illness, indeed, an act of human hubris.

The Rabbis of the Talmud and Midrash were aware of this line of reasoning, but they counteracted it by pointing out that God Himself authorizes us to heal. In fact, the Rabbis maintained, God *requires* us to heal. They found that authorization and that imperative in several biblical verses. Exodus 21:19–20 requires that an assailant must provide for his victim to be "thoroughly healed," thus presuming that physicians have *permission* to cure. Deuteronomy 22:2 ("And you shall restore the lost property to him"), in their interpretation, imposes an *obligation* to restore another person's body as well as his/her property. On the basis of Leviticus 19:16 ("Nor shall you stand idly by the blood of your fellow"), the Talmud expands the obligation to provide medical aid to encompass expenditure of financial resources for this purpose. And Rabbi Moses ben Nahman ("Nahmanides," thirteenth century) understands the obligation to care for others through medicine as one of many applications of the Torah's principle, "And you shall love your neighbor as yourself" (Lev 19:18).[5] God is still our ultimate Healer, and hence Jewish liturgy has Jews pray to God for healing of body and soul three times each day; but the physician, in Jewish theology, is God's agent in accomplishing that task, and so use of the medical arts is not only permissible, but required. Jews, in fact, may not live in a city lacking a physician,[6] for that would mean that people could not take reasonable care of their bodies, which belong to God. This appreciation of medicine has led to a virtual love affair between Jews and medicine over the last 2,000 years, and it means that Jews trust medicine—and use it extensively—when they encounter medical problems, including those involving sex or procreation.

3. Sex has two goals, the pleasurable bonding of the couple and procreation. The Torah includes a number of sexual prohibitions regarding with whom one may have sex[7] and at what times during the woman's menstrual cycle,[8] but it also includes two positive commandments. One, the very first commandment mentioned in the Torah, is "Be fruitful and multiply" (Gen 1:27). Although the command is given to both the first man and woman, and although both are clearly necessary to produce children, for exegetical and possibly for moral reasons the Rabbis of the Mishnah and Talmud asserted that only the man was obligated to fulfill this commandment.[9] Among the moral concerns were the facts that the man was going to have to support his children and so he had to be commanded to procreate against his economic self-interest, and that pregnancy endangers a woman and so it would not be fair to command her to have children. In any case, as we shall see, this rabbinic decision has important consequences for the use of contraceptives, for it makes it much easier to allow women, who have no duty to procreate, to use them than it is to justify their use by men.

A man fulfills his duty to procreate, according to Jewish law, when he produces one boy and one girl,[10] thus imitating the way that God created humans "male and female" (Gen 1:27). Because the Jewish tradition sees children as a great blessing, however, men were supposed to try to have as many children as possible, in fulfillment of two biblical verses—"God did not create it [the earth] a waste, but formed it for habitation" and "Sow your seed in the morning [that is, in your youth], and do not hold back your hand in the evening [that is, in later years]."[11]

Sex, however, is not exclusively for procreation; it is also for the mutual bonding of the couple, emotionally as well as physically. The Rabbis derive this notion from Exodus 21:10, according to which a man owes his wife "her food, her clothing, and her conjugal rights."[12] As they usually do with regard to any commandment, they then define exactly how this commandment may be fulfilled by determining how often a man must offer to engage in sexual relations with his wife. They maintain that it depends on the degree to which his job enables him to be home at night, and that consequently a man may not change his job to one that will bring him home at night less often without his wife's permission. Conversely, men also have rights to sex in marriage, but, remarkably, the Talmud already prohibits marital rape,[13] which was not prohibited in any American state until 1975 and not in all American states until 1993.[14] If his wife repeatedly refused to engage in conjugal relations, then, the Mishnah's remedy was that he could diminish what he owed her in divorce by a certain amount each week until he could divorce her without paying her anything and marry someone else,[15] for he too has a right to sexual satisfaction in marriage. This recognition of the role of sex in a couple's physical satisfaction and emotional bonding, together with their respect for medicine, has made Jews quite willing to use medical and psychological interventions to overcome sexual dysfunctions, and to use artificial reproductive techniques to overcome infertility.

4. *The status of the embryo/fetus.* Exodus 21:9–10 says that if two men who are fighting hit a pregnant woman who miscarries, then if there is no other injury to her, the assailant must pay compensation for the lost fetus "to be based on a reckoning"—presumably depending on how far along she was in the pregnancy. But if there is other injury to the woman, then the remedy is "life for life, eye for eye, etc." The Rabbis later interpreted "eye for an eye" to mean monetary compensation in lieu of physical retribution,[16] but the Torah is clearly distinguishing the status of the woman, who is a full human being, from that of the fetus, who is not. This fact leads the Rabbis to rule that if a woman is having difficulty in childbirth, those attending her must dismember the fetus within her (safe Caesarian sections were not available until the late 1940s), for she is a full-fledged human being and the fetus is not.

The fetus becomes a human being when its head—or, in a breach birth, its shoulders or, according to some, the greater part of its body—emerges from the vaginal canal. At that point, if doctors cannot save them both, the usual rules of triage apply—namely, that they should save the one whom they have the better chance of saving.

Before birth, the Rabbis divided pregnancy into two stages. During the first forty days, the embryo is "simply liquid"[17]; from then on it is "like the thigh of its mother."[18] Note that unlike modern obstetricians, who count from the woman's last period, resulting in a forty-week pregnancy, and unlike modern geneticists, who count from conception, resulting in a thirty-eight-week pregnancy, the Rabbis were probably counting from the first period that the woman missed, so that their "forty days" is approximately fifty-four days of gestation. That is so because they could have known what the fetus looks like only from the miscarriages they witnessed. During the first month of pregnancy, a miscarriage is simply a heavy menstrual flow. During the second month it looks like a clump of cells. It is only after that—roughly at fifty-four days of gestation—that the fetus gains a bone structure, so that a miscarriage at that point has bone, flesh, and even hair. At that stage, given that it comes from the groin area of the body, it does indeed look like its mother's thigh. Thus, unlike American law, which sees the fetus as part of the mother and therefore, with some limitations in some states, subject to her discretion until the moment of birth, and unlike current Roman Catholic authorities, who maintain that the fertilized ovum is already a full human being, Jewish tradition takes an intermediate, developmental position, in which the embryo over time emerges from "simply liquid" to "the thigh of its mother" to a full-fledged human being. As one might expect, this view will have significant implications for Judaism's view of abortion and embryonic stem cell research.

BIRTH CONTROL

Jewish sources from as early as the second century describe methods of contraception. A rabbinic ruling from that time prescribes the use of such methods when pregnancy would endanger either the woman or the infant she is nursing.[19] Subsequent rabbinic opinion splits between those who sanction the use of contraception only when such danger exists and those who mandate it then but allow it for other women too.

If couples are going to use contraceptives, Jewish law prefers those that prevent conception in the first place over those that abort an already fertilized egg, because, as will be discussed in the next section, in most cases Jewish law forbids abortion. The most favored form of contraception from a Jewish perspective is thus the diaphragm, for it prevents conception and has little if any impact on the woman's health. If the contraceptive pill or implant is not counterindicated by the woman's age or body chemistry, those are usually the next most favored forms of contraception. RU486 and any other means of retroactively aborting an embryo are, from this understanding, considered legitimate only when pregnancy would threaten the mother's physical or mental health, as defined in the ways discussed in the next section.[20]

The only nonpermanent, male form of contraception currently available is the condom. As was noted above, in Jewish law the male is legally responsible for propagation, and that fact argues against the man using contraception, at least until he has fulfilled that duty.[21] Condoms, moreover, sometimes split or slip off,[22] and even if they remain intact and in place, they do not always work. Nevertheless, condoms must be used if unprotected sexual intercourse poses a medical risk to either spouse, for condoms do offer some measure of protection against the spread of some diseases, and the duty to maintain health and life supersedes the positive duty of the male to propagate.[23]

It should be noted, though, that rabbis from past centuries who permitted contraception for nontherapeutic reasons never anticipated that Jews would postpone having children as long as many Jewish couples now do. Even with modern medical advances, the late teens and the twenties are biologically still the best time for the human male and female to conceive and bear children.[24] Those who wait until after those ages to try to procreate often have infertility problems.[25] This means that even if young couples choose to use contraceptives for a time, they are well advised, both medically and Jewishly, not to wait too long.

There are, of course, good reasons why so many Jews wait so long. In addition to long-term schooling, in which Jews engage at far higher percentages than the general population,[26] most women in our society find that they must earn money to support themselves and their families, just as their male partners or husbands do, and so they often try to get their careers up and running before bearing children. Moreover, many people who would love to find a mate and get married in their early twenties may not be so fortunate, and once out of college it is often difficult for them to meet someone they want to marry. The painful reality of infertility and the increased likelihood of birth defects as one ages, though, argue strongly for seeking a mate and procreating earlier than most Jews now do.

Infertility is not only a great source of pain for the couples involved, it is also a demographic problem of major proportions for the Jewish people. Christians make up a third of the world's population, Muslims about 22 percent. Jews, numbering just over 13 million, are only two-tenths of one percent.[27] Furthermore, because of the factors described above, the reproductive rate among North American Jews is only 1.8 (where 2.1 is required for replacement),[28] and among Israeli Jews it is about 2.0. Add to that the effects of intermarriage and assimilation, and there is a real possibility that Jews and therefore Judaism will not survive for many more generations. The contemporary, demographic problem of the Jewish people, then, must also be a factor that figures into the thinking of Jews using contraception.

As is true for other highly educated communities, Jews have been concerned about the world's overpopulation since the 1960s, and sometimes that is another factor that convinces couples not to propagate altogether or to have only one child. Jews, though, constitute only two-tenths of one percent of the world's population, and so even if the entire Jewish population were to be eradicated, that loss would do almost nothing to resolve the overpopulation problem. To do that, we need to raise the standard of living of poor populations, teach people how to use birth control and provide it to them cheaply, and change the policies of some groups that forbid artificial forms of birth control. Eliminating Jews and, with them, Jewish culture is not an effective or wise way of resolving the very real problem of world overpopulation.

On the contrary, given the demographic crisis of the Jewish community, rabbis are currently encouraging couples who can propagate to consider having three or four children. As Maimonides says, "If one adds a soul to the People Israel, it is as if s/he has built an entire world."[29] In the current Jewish demographic crisis, doing so is all the more imperative. Thus although a couple's first two children fulfill the commandment (*mitzvah*) to procreate, the Conservative Movement's Committee on Jewish Law and Standards has approved a rabbinic ruling urging couples to have one or more additional children who are also "*mitzvah* children," both in the original sense of that word meaning "commandment" in that Jewish law requires couples who can to have more than the minimum number of two, and also in the sense of "*mitzvah*" as "good deed," in that they are helping to make Jewish physical continuity, and therefore Jewish religious and cultural continuity, possible.[30]

As Jewish communities have increasingly come to realize, the Jewish pattern of long-term education and the Jewish demographic crisis must also be factors in communal planning. Many adult Jews are now meeting each other through commercial dating websites focused on Jews, and Jewish communities are creating programs to help young adult Jews meet each other. To encourage young Jewish couples to have children, the family and community must share in the financial burden of raising them. So, for example, the Talmud imposes a duty on grandparents to educate their grandchildren in the Jewish tradition,[31] just as it obligates parents to do so, and so grandparents with the means are increasingly being educated to contribute to the tuition for their grandchildren's Jewish education. Some Jewish day schools, camps, and youth group programs are giving discounts for each additional sibling.[32] Moreover, Jews, acting out of their own best interests and out of Jewish values are increasingly supporting profamily legislation such as laws that provide for family leaves for both mothers and fathers and for high-quality, affordable day care.

All this means, then, that young marrieds, especially those who marry in their late twenties or later, should use contraceptives for family planning purposes only for a very short time, if at all. In the end, the Jewish tradition thinks of children—and many people experience them—as a true blessing from God.

ABORTION

Because Jewish law perceives the woman as a full-fledged person and the fetus as not of that status, abortion is required when the woman's life or health is at stake, with rabbis variously interpreting how serious a threat the fetus must be to the woman's health in order to require an abortion. When the woman has a condition that puts her more at risk than a normal pregnancy would be—if, for example, she has diabetes—then she may choose to accept that risk and go ahead with the pregnancy (but consult her doctor much more often than usual), or she may choose to abort the fetus in order to avoid the risk.

What about mental health as a rationale for abortion? Rabbi David Feldman summarizes the evidence as follows:

> Precedent for equating mental health with physical health comes from a late-seventeenth-century Rabbi... On the basis of Talmudic teaching, Rabbi Israel Meir

Mizrachi argued that serious danger to mental health (*tiruf da'at*) is tantamount to risk to one's physical wellbeing, and issued a permissive ruling...At least one Responsum (dated 1913), applied it specifically to the matter of abortion.[33]

Mental health as a justification for abortion, though, has generally been construed rather narrowly, especially in the Orthodox community, so it would not justify abortion, for example, simply because the woman does not want to have another child. That would be a good reason to use contraception, but not retroactively to abort. (In the Reform movement, where individual autonomy is a major value, rabbis discourage abortion when it is contemplated for this reason, but they maintain that it is ultimately and properly the individual woman's choice.[34])

In modern times, with the advent of techniques to test embryos for genetic diseases, some rabbis in the Orthodox community, and most in the Conservative community, would permit an abortion when the fetus has a lethal genetic disease such as Tay-Sachs or Familial Dysautonomia. When the disease is debilitating but the child will have more or less normal life expectancy, some rabbis permit, and others forbid, abortion directly on the grounds of the disease. The problem with that approach, however, is that it inevitably involves sensitive and controversial judgments; when is a disease sufficiently serious to warrant an abortion, and when not? And which rabbi, if any, has the authority to make that judgment?

More commonly, then, rabbis use the maternal (and paternal) reactions to the fetus's disease to determine whether it should be aborted. So, for example, Rabbi David M. Feldman, a Conservative rabbi who wrote the first comprehensive treatment of abortion in Jewish law, has written that if such a woman tells him that suffering from Down Syndrome will be terrible for her child, he would tell her that that may or may not be so, but in any case that is not a reason to abort. If the same woman, however, tells him that she is going crazy over the thought of bearing a Down Syndrome child, he would tell her that that is indeed an acceptable justification to abort. In the first case, she was talking about her child's feelings and the future, neither of which she knows; in the second case, she was describing her own present feelings, and Rabbi Feldman would therefore invoke her mental health to justify an abortion.[35]

This writer would instead ask the couple to talk to three other couples who are raising children with Down Syndrome so that they know what it is really like and not what they imagine it to be. Then, if the couple believes that they really cannot raise such a child, I would consider that a sufficient reason to abort the fetus, based on the mother's and father's mental health. (As we shall see in the last section of this chapter, couples with family histories of these diseases increasingly engage in preimplantation genetic diagnosis precisely to avoid the need for aborting a fetus with such a disease.)

In sum, the Jewish tradition requires abortion when the mother's life or her physical or mental health is at stake. Judaism sanctions abortion when the mother's physical or mental condition makes pregnancy more risky than it normally is. Abortion, though, is generally prohibited as an act of self-injury (not murder, because the fetus is not a human person who bears the legal protections against murder until birth), and the burden of proof is always on the one who wants to abort.

Embryonic Stem Cell Research

Stem cells are those cells that produce more than one kind of cell. Adult stem cells—called that if they come from any born human being from infancy through adulthood—are produced, for example, from bone marrow, which manufactures four different kinds of blood cells, and from skin, which produces three kinds of skin cells. Embryonic stem cells come from the inner cell mass of embryos that are five or six days old. At that stage, the embryo has produced a circle with cells inside it; if the embryo is in a woman's womb, the circle will become the placenta, attaching the embryo to the woman's body to provide the nutrients necessary for the embryo to develop, and the cells inside the circle (the "inner cell mass") will ultimately become all the cells in the infant's body. As such, these cells are "pluripotent"—that is, they are able to produce many different kinds of cells, including those that will ultimately become the infant's heart and circulatory system, its nervous system (brains, spinal cord, and neurons), its respiratory system, its bone structure, and so on.

Because embryonic stem cells are more flexible than adult stem cells, they hold out more promise for producing cures for a variety of serious and even life-threatening illnesses. If we could figure out how cells "decide" to differentiate into the specific cells they become, we might be able to produce cardiac cell lines, for example, that could cure the damage brought on by a heart attack or stroke, or neurological cells to cure a spinal cord injury or Alzheimer's. Embryonic stem cells also turn off, so that we get one head and not more, and if we could determine the mechanism that turns them off, we would have the ultimate cure for cancer, which is precisely the production of too many cells of a given type. Thus while research using adult stem cells holds out some promise and certainly should be pursued, embryonic stem cell research is even more promising, as demonstrated not only by the pluripotency of the cells, but by a number of animal studies in which they actually did cure some diseases.[36]

The embryos used for such research are donated by couples who created them in an effort to overcome infertility through in vitro fertilization (IVF) but who have now had as many children as they want or have given up on having their own biological children. The choice, then, is either to discard the remaining embryos or to donate them to research. (Creating embryos for purposes of research might involve other objections, but that has not been the question at issue because of the availability of embryos created for infertility treatments.)

The problem with embryonic stem cell research is that in order to carry on such research, one must remove the inner cell mass from an embryo, which kills the embryo. The question, then, is the status of the embryo. Although Church Fathers as important as Augustine and Aquinas viewed the fetus developmentally,[37] very much as the talmudic Rabbis did, Roman Catholic doctrine over the last several centuries has classified the embryo in a woman's uterus as a full human being, as a result of the invention of the microscope, and Catholic authorities construe embryonic stem cell research as murder. In recent years they have extended that concept even to embryos in a Petri dish, where there is no chance whatsoever for the embryos to become a human being unless they are implanted into a woman's womb.

As we saw above, on the basis of Exodus 21 and their own observation of miscarriages, the Rabbis of the Mishnah and Talmud instead viewed the fetus developmentally, with embryos less than forty days old—and certainly those at five or six days of gestation—classified as "simply liquid." They were clearly well aware that in a woman's womb some of that "liquid" may become a human being, but to classify it as such so early in pregnancy is to confuse a potential state with an actual one. In fact, we now have good hormonal studies to indicate that as many as 80 percent of fertilized egg cells in a woman's womb will miscarry,[38] and so even there one has only a one in five chance that the embryo will become a human being. In a Petri dish, that chance is zero. At the same time, the Jewish tradition includes a strong mandate to seek to cure (or at least mitigate the effects of) diseases, and the embryos in question would otherwise simply be discarded. Therefore, rabbis across the denominations have ruled that until and unless embryonic stem cell research proves to be unsuccessful in producing the cures it promises, engaging in such research is not only permissible, but desirable.[39]

Infertility

A surprising number of biblical figures had fertility problems. Abraham and Sarah, Rebekah and Isaac, Rachel and Jacob, and Elkanah and Hannah (who ultimately bore the prophet Samuel) all had difficulties.[40] No other culture's sacred scripture focuses so extensively on infertility.

What can we learn from this? First, that children are precious. Indeed, the Jewish tradition sees them as a great blessing. In part this is so because of the psychological growth and joy they bring to their parents. In addition, of course, the future of Judaism and the Jewish people depends on procreation. But the very difficulty that so many couples have in conceiving and bearing children is itself a mark of how precious they are when they come.

Second, the biblical stories amply indicate that infertility causes immense tensions in a marriage. Infertile couples begin to question who they are individually as a man or woman and what their future together holds. Worse, couples seeking to become pregnant have the equivalent of a final examination each month, and if they are having difficulties conceiving, they will fail many of those examinations. Nobody likes to fail, least of all in a matter as important and personal as childbearing. Some couples break up over this issue, and those whose marriages survive must revise their hopes and dreams of their lives together.

In our own time, Jews are especially troubled by this problem, in part because of Jewish genetic diseases but primarily because Jews have adopted the American ideology that makes *work* the fundamental source of one's identity and pride. As was noted earlier, this situation leads Jews to engage in extended education and to postpone marriage until the late twenties or later, producing low birth rates and problems with infertility.

Another factor that contributes to infertility is that men commonly believe that infertility is only a woman's problem, that only women have a biological clock for procreation. Actually, about a third of infertile couples are so because of a problem in the woman; a third because of a problem in the man; and a third because of a problem in both or for reasons that are unclear.[41] Age is not the only factor in infertility, but it complicates all the rest in both men and women and makes it harder to fix.

Yet another part of the American milieu that deceives Jews is its emphasis on technology as the cure for all that ails us. Jews have greatly honored medicine for the last two thousand years, and many young Jewish adults now trust that at whatever age they want to bear children, medicine will enable them to do so. Although infertility specialists have made great strides in making it possible for many couples to bear children, they cannot do that for everyone, and the younger the couple is, the greater the chance that the new techniques will work.

To respond to the problems infertility poses for both couples and the Jewish people as a whole, Jews are becoming aware that they need to take a number of steps (described more fully in my book *Love Your Neighbor and Yourself: A Jewish Approach to Modern Personal Ethics*).[42] Among them are these: ensuring that Jewish teenagers choose colleges where there are many Jews, for social as well as educational and religious purposes; communicating that it is not too early to look for a spouse while in college, and if one finds one, it is not too early to marry and begin to have children in graduate school, for the pressures of graduate school are no greater than those of the first years of one's job; creating methods for those beyond college to meet other Jews; and providing affordable and good day care arrangements and tuition aid for Jewish day schools, supplementary schools, and camps so that young couples are not deterred by the costs of having three or four children. At the same time, because the emphasis on children in the Jewish tradition only exacerbates the problems of infertile Jewish couples, steps to encourage couples to procreate must be balanced by measures to make infertile couples feel valued, including a clear statement that like all obligations in Jewish law, the duty to procreate ceases to apply to those who cannot fulfill it through no fault of their own. Couples *may* avail themselves of the many assisted reproduction techniques

(ARTs) now available—although Orthodox authorities generally prohibit the use of donor sperm or eggs, and, in any case, there are some special issues with using them that the couple needs to confront—but from the point of view of Jewish law they *need not* do so.⁴³

Genetic Testing

Beginning with amnioscentesis, developed in the 1960s, and followed by corrianic villae sampling and sonograms, among other techniques, modern science has provided us with mechanisms to know much more about the genetic structure of the fetus than our ancestors did. Like every new ability, this development raises the question about when it is appropriate to use it, and when not, for just because we can do something does not mean that we should. Jews use these new techniques and thus encounter their moral ambiguities more than most other subsets of the population, in part because of their commitment to medicine but also because of those genetic diseases to which Jews are especially predisposed.

The Torah already indicates its displeasure when Jews marry outside the community,⁴⁴ and endogamy increasingly became the norm in the Second Temple period and beyond.⁴⁵ Because Muslim and especially Christian regimes under whose authority Jews lived during the Middle Ages and as late as the twentieth century forced Jews to dwell in small, concentrated areas, and because Jews never were a large percentage of the world's population, they suffer more than other communities from the founder effect—that is, the continuation of genetic abnormalities over generations. Ashkenazic (northern and eastern European) Jews are at greater risk than the general population especially for six or eight such diseases and to a lesser extent for as many as ten more; Sephardic Jews (from the Mediterranean Basin) are at risk for two others. Some of these diseases, such as Tay-Sachs and Familial Dysautonomia, are lethal, killing their victims often in the first years of life but sometimes not until their teens; others, such as Gaucher's Disease, do not shorten life span but are debilitating and expensive to treat.⁴⁶

To combat these diseases, Jews have developed several strategies. When the tests for Tay-Sachs were created in the early 1970s, Jews aggressively encouraged their young couples to be tested for it before procreating. If both members of a couple tested positive, until the 1990s the only thing they could do was to have the woman undergo an amniocentesis in the fifth month of pregnancy and then, if the child was going to have the disease, abort it. Because Orthodox rabbis generally approved of abortion only for maternal reasons and not for fetal conditions, a program called *Dor Yesharim* was initiated in that community, in which young people who were contemplating marriage would need to get the approval of a particular member of the community who had access to all the Tay-Sachs results of everyone who was tested so as to avoid marriages of two carriers. As a result of these measures in the Orthodox and non-Orthodox communities, Tay-Sachs has been effectively eliminated as a Jewish genetic disease within a generation—although Jews still need to be tested to see if they are carriers.

In October 1989, scientists first successfully used preimplantation genetic diagnosis (PGD) to test embryos for a genetic disease so that they might choose only unaffected embryos to implant in the woman's uterus.[47] This procedure, widely available since the early 1990s, is expensive—although not nearly as expensive as caring for a child who has the disease—and it does not work for all genetic diseases, but this new technology has enabled couples who are both carriers of a genetic abnormality to have normal children without abortion.

The problem is that once you can test for lethal and debilitating diseases, you can also test for many other traits, such as gender, that are not diseases at all, and you can also test for some disabilities, such as deafness, that some in the disabled community see as devaluing them by trying to rid society of those affected. Furthermore, once you go beyond lethal and severely debilitating diseases (such as Fragile X Syndrome), where, if anywhere, do you draw the line as to what is morally appropriate? Is this, as some have feared, the new, effective methodology to engage in eugenics in order to create "the designer child"—however that is defined? Concerns such as these have led Rabbi Mark Popovsky, for example, to write a rabbinic ruling for the Conservative Movement's Committee on Jewish Law and Standards that limits the appropriate use of PGD to lethal and severely debilitating diseases.[48]

THE BLESSINGS OF SEX AND CHILDREN

In the end, it is important to remind readers that Jewish responses to issues at the beginning of life come out of a strong conviction that God has indeed blessed us in giving us sexual pleasure and children and that, as in all other forms of medicine, we act as God's partners and agents in enabling people to overcome whatever difficulties they have in these areas. It is appropriate, then, to end this chapter with the Psalmist's description of these blessings:

> Blessed are all who revere the Lord,
> who follow in His ways.
> You shall enjoy the fruit of your labors,
> you shall be happy, you shall prosper.
> Your wife shall be like a fruitful vine within your house,
> your children like olive shoots round about your table…
> May you live to see children's children. May there be peace for the people Israel.[49]

Notes

1. For example, Deuteronomy 10:14; Psalms 24:1.
2. B. *Shabbat* 129b.
3. Leviticus 26:16; Deuteronomy 28:22, 59–61.
4. Exodus 15:26; Deuteronomy 32:39; cf. Isaiah 19:22; 57:18–19; Jeremiah 30:17; 33:6; etc.
5. B. *Bava Kamma* 85a, 81b; B. *Sanhedrin* 73a, 84b (with Rashi's commentary there). See also *Sifrei Deuteronomy* on Deuteronomy 22:2 and *Leviticus Rabbah* 34:3. Nahmanides, *Kitvei Haramban*, Bernard Chavel, ed. (Jerusalem: Mosad Harav Kook, 1963 [Hebrew]), Vol. 2, p. 43; this passage comes from Nahmanides' *Torat Ha'adam (The Instruction of Man), Sh'ar Sakkanah (Section on Danger)* on B. *Bava Kamma*, chap. 8, and is cited by Joseph Karo in his commentary to the *Tur, Bet Yosef, Yoreh De'ah* 336. Nahmanides bases this interpretation on similar reasoning in the talmudic passages cited above. See also *Sifrei Deuteronomy* on Deuteronomy 22:2 and *Leviticus Rabbah* 34:3.
6. B. *Sanhedrin* 17b with regard to "students of the Sages"; J. *Kiddushin* 66d, with regard to all Jews.
7. For example, Leviticus 18, 20.
8. See Leviticus 15:19–32, esp. 19–24.
9. B. *Yevamot* 65b; B. *Kiddushin* 35a; M.T. *Laws of Marriage* 15:2; S.A. *Even Ha-Ezer* 1:1, 13.
10. M. *Yevamot* 6:6 (61b); M.T. *Laws of Marriage* 15:4; S.A. *Even Ha-Ezer* 1:5. There was some debate about this, however; see Elliot N. Dorff, *Matters of Life and Death: A Jewish Approach to Modern Medical Ethics* (Philadelphia: Jewish Publication Society, 1998), p. 336, n. 9, repeated in Elliot N. Dorff, *Love Your Neighbor and Yourself: A Jewish Approach to Modern Personal Ethics* (Philadelphia: Jewish Publication Society, 2003), pp. 275–76, n. 61.
11. B. *Yevamot* 62b and M.T. *Laws of Marriage [Ishut]* 15:16) encourage as many children as possible on the basis of Isaiah 45:18 and Ecclesiastes 11:6.
12. Some biblical scholars think that the Torah's word here, *onata*, means conjugal rights; others think that it means housing; and still others think that it means ointments. See Nahum Sarna. *The JPS Torah Commentary: Exodus* (Philadelphia: Jewish Publication Society, 1991), p. 121. The Rabbis, however, understood it to mean conjugal rights (M. *Ketubbot* 5:6), and that is what is controlling for Judaism.
13. B. *Eruvin* 100b; *Leviticus Rabbah* 9:6; *Numbers Rabbah* 13:2; M.T. *Laws of Ethics* 5:4; M.T. *Laws of Marriage* 14:15; M.T. *Laws of Forbidden Intercourse* 21:11; S.A. *Orah Hayyim* 240:10; S.A. *Even Ha-Ezer* 25:2, gloss.
14. In Common Law, in force in North America and the British Commonwealth on many matters, the very concept of marital rape was an impossibility. Thus Sir Matthew Hale, Chief Justice in seventeenth-century England, wrote in his classic treatise, *Historia Placitorum Coronae*, that "The husband cannot be guilty of a rape committed by himself upon his lawful wife, for by their mutual matrimonial consent and contract the wife hath given up herself in this kind unto her husband, which she cannot retract." In December 1993 the United Nations High Commissioner for Human Rights published the Declaration on the Elimination of Violence Against Women (www.unchr.ch/huridocda/huridoca.nsf/(Symbol)/A.RES.48.104. En?Opendocument). This establishes marital rape as a human rights violation. As of 1997, however, UNICEF reported that just seventeen nations had criminalized marital rape. In 2003, UNIFEM reported that more than fifty nations had done so. In the United States, in 1975 South Dakota was the first state to remove the husband's

protection from prosecution; by 1993 all fifty states had done so, but in thirty of them the husband still was exempt from prosecution if he did not have to force his wife to have sex—if, for example, she was unconscious or asleep, or if she was mentally or physically impaired. See Raquel Kennedy Bergen, "Marital Rape: New Research and Directions," http://www.vawnet.org/applied-research-papers/print-document.php?doc_id=248 (accessed June 8, 2012).

15. M. *Ketubbot* 5:7.
16. M. *Bava Kamma* 8:1, and see the Talmud thereon.
17. B. *Yevamot* 69b.
18. B. *Hullin* 58a and elsewhere.
19. T. *Niddah* 2; B. *Yevamot* 12b, 100b; *Ketubbot* 39a; *Niddah* 45a; *Nedarim* 35b. On this entire topic, see David M. Feldman, *Birth Control in Jewish Law* (New York: New York University Press, 1968), chaps. 9–13, esp. pp. 185–87. (The subsequent, paperback edition, published by Schocken in 1973, is called *Marital Relations, Birth Control, and Abortion in Jewish Law*, and so is the revised 1996 edition published by Jason Aronson and now Rowman and Littlefield.)
20. For a recent, comprehensive review of available forms of contraception and Jewish law, see Miriam Berkowitz and Mark Popovsky, "Contraception," at http://www.rabbinicalassembly.org/sites/default/files/public/halakhah/teshuvot/20052010/Contraception%20Berkowitz%20and%20Popovsky.pdf (accessed June 8, 2012).
21. The language of the Mishnah (M. *Yevamot* 6:6) suggests that the man may use contraceptives after fulfilling the commandment with two children. It reads: "A man may not cease from being fruitful and multiplying *unless* he has children. The School of Shammai says: two males; the School of Hillel says: a male and a female." As is noted in note 11 above, however, this was not the position of later Jewish law (B. *Yevamot* 62b; M.T. *Laws of Marriage [Ishut]* 15:16), which encouraged as many children as possible on the basis of Isaiah 45:18 and Ecclesiastes 11:6.
22. British researchers, citing World Health Organization statistics and their own study of 300 men at a south London clinic, have suggested that the failure of condoms may be due largely to the use of the same size for all men, a size too small for one-third of the men of the world. See "One Size of Condom Doesn't Fit All," *Men's Health*, March 1994, p. 27.
23. For more on the Jewish imperative of safe sex, see Michael Gold, *Does God Belong in the Bedroom?* (Philadelphia: Jewish Publication Society, 1992), pp. 112ff.
24. The optimal age is twenty-two: *The Columbia University College of Physicians and Surgeons Complete Guide to Pregnancy*, as quoted in Beth Weinhouse, "Is There a Right Time to Have a Baby? The Yes, No, and Maybe of Pregnancy at 20, 30, 40," *Glamour*, May 1994, pp. 251, 276, 285–287, which presents a helpful description of the physical factors in pregnancy through a woman's twenties, thirties, and forties. Infertility increases with age: 13.9 percent of couples in which the wife is between thirty and thirty-four are infertile; 24.6 percent where the wife is between thirty-five and thirty-nine; and 27.2 percent where the wife is between forty and forty-four. See U.S. Congress, Office of Technology Assessment, *Infertility: Medical and Social Choices*, OTA-BA-358 (Washington, DC: U.S. Government Printing Office, May 1988), pp. 1, 3, 4, and 6.
25. Carl T. Hall, "Study Speeds Up Biological Clocks: Fertility Rates Dip After Women Hit Age 27," *San Francisco Chronicle* (April 30, 2002), citing a study of 782 European couples using only the rhythm method of contraception, published on that date in the journal *Human Reproduction*; available at http://www.sfgate.com/

cgi-bin/article.cgi?file=/chronicle/archive/2002/04/30/MN182697.DTL (accessed April 3, 2011). See also Elizabeth Heubeck, "Age Raises Infertility Risk in Men Too: Risks Associated with Men's Biological Clocks May Be Similar to Women's," citing 2003 and 2004 studies published in the *Journal of Gynecology, Human Reproduction Update*, and the *Journal of Urology*, available at http://www.webmd.com/infertility-and-reproduction/guide/age-raises-infertility-risk-in-men-too (accessed April 3, 2011).

26. "More than half of all Jewish adults (55%) have received a college degree, and a quarter (25%) have earned a graduate degree. The comparable figures for the total U.S. population are 29% and 6%." (No authors stated), *The National Jewish Population Survey 2000-2001* (New York: United Jewish Communities, 2003), p. 6, available at www.UJC.org/njps/pdf (accessed April 3, 2011).

27. The best estimate of the current number of Jews in the world is 13,089,800. See Sergio Della Pergola, "World Jewish Population," *American Jewish Yearbook 2006* (New York: American Jewish Committee, 2006), vol. 106, pp. 559–601, esp. p. 571. With the world's population at 6.477 billion in 2006, and now over 7 billion, Jews are 2.02 per 1,000 of the world's population—that is, approximately 0.2 percent of the world's population.

28. [No author listed.] *The National Jewish Population Survey 2000-2001: Strength, Challenge and Diversity in the American Jewish Population* (New York: United Jewish Communities, 2003), p. 4; available at http://www.ujc.org/page.html?ArticleID=33650 (accessed April 3, 2011).

29. M.T. *Laws of Marriage* 15:16. Maimonides' theme of a whole world being created with the birth of a child is echoed in M. *Sanhedrin* 4:5, "If anyone sustains a soul within the People Israel, it is as if he has sustained an entire world," and the converse appears in B. *Yevamot* 63b: "If someone refrains from propagation, it is as if he commits murder (literally, 'spills blood') and diminishes the image of God."

30. Kassel Abelson and Elliot N. Dorff, "Mitzvah Children," available at http://www.rabbinicalassembly.org/sites/default/files/public/halakhah/teshuvot/20052010/mitzvah_children.pdf (accessed July 14, 2011).

31. B. *Kiddushin* 30a.

32. On the duty to educate children and its costs today, see Dorff, *Love Your Neighbor* (at n. 10 above), pp. 143–54.

33. David M. Feldman, *Birth Control in Jewish Law* (New York: New York University Press, 1968), p. 286. The talmudic sources he cites are B. *Yoma* 82a, 83a, and 83b. The 1913 *responsum* is *Responsa L'vushei Mordekhai, Hoshen Mishpat*, #39. See also Daniel Schiff *Abortion in Judaism* (New York: Cambridge University Press, 2002).

34. Mark Washofsky, *Jewish Living: A Guide to Contemporary Reform Practice* (New York: UAHC Press, 2001), pp . 242–45.

35. David M. Feldman, "This Matter of Abortion," in his *Health and Medicine in the Jewish Tradition: L'Hayyim—To Life!* (New York: Crossroad, 1986), pp. 79–90, esp. pp. 87–88; reprinted in *Contemporary Jewish Ethics and Morality: A Reader*, Elliot N. Dorff and Louis E. Newman, eds. (New York: Oxford University Press, 1995), pp. 382–91, esp. pp. 388–89.

36. For more on the science of embryonic stem cell research, see "Stem Cells: A Primer," National Institutes of Health, May 2000, pp. 1–2, http://stemcells.nih.gov/info/basics/ (accessed July 15, 2011).

37. See the testimony of Margaret Farley to President Clinton's National Bioethics Advisory Commission, in *Ethical Issues in Human Stem Cell Research*, Volume III: Religious Perspectives (Rockville, MD: National Bioethics Advisory Commission,

June 2000), pp. D1–D5, http://bioethics.georgetown.edu/pcbe/reports/past_commissions/nbac_stemcell3.pdf (accessed April 3, 2011).

38. Allen J. Wilcox et al., "Incidence of Early Loss of Pregnancy," *New England Journal of Medicine* 319: 189–94 (1988).

39. The official Conservative/Masorti position: Elliot N. Dorff, "Stem Cell Research," at http://www.rabbinicalassembly.org/sites/default/files/public/halakhah/teshuvot/19912000/dorff_stemcell.pdf. The official Reform position: Mark Washofsky, "Human Stem Cell Research," in *Reform Responsa for the Twenty-First Century*, Mark Washofsky, ed. (New York: Central Conference of American Rabbis, 2010), pp. 121–42, available for a fee at www.ccarnet.org, under the heading "Rabbinic Materials" and the subheading "Responsa." The Orthodox community is too splintered to have one official position, but Rabbi Moshe Tendler, a biologist at Yeshiva University and an influential Orthodox voice in bioethics, has strongly endorsed it; see his testimony before President Clinton's National Bioethics Advisory Commission, in *Ethical Issues in Human Stem Cell Research, Volume III: Religious Perspectives* (Rockville, MD: National Bioethics Advisory Commission, 2000), pp. H-1-5, available at http://bioethics.georgetown.edu/nbac/stemcell3.pdf (accessed April 14, 2011).

40. Genesis 15:2–4; 18:1–15; 25:21; 30:1–8, 22–24; 35:16–20; 1 Samuel 1:1–20.

41. "Infertility," www.womenshealth.gov (National Women's Health Information Center of the U.S. Department of Health and Human Services, Office on Women's Health), esp. p. 5.

42. Elliot N. Dorff, *Love Your Neighbor and Yourself* (at note 10 above), pp. 95–111.

43. For more on Jewish norms relevant to the use of artificial techniques of reproduction, and the range of positions on the use of donor gametes, see Elliot N. Dorff, *Matters of Life and Death: A Jewish Approach to Modern Medical Ethics* (at note 10 above).

44. See, for example, Genesis 24 and 27:46–28:5 for the measures taken by Abraham and Sarah and by Rebekah and Isaac to make sure that their sons married within their clan, and see Genesis 26:35 for the displeasure that Rebekah and Isaac have when Esau marries Hittite women—so much so that Esau takes an additional wife from Ishmael's daughters to placate his parents (Gen 28:6–9). That said, the Bible records many men who married outside the tribe, including Moses himself (Exod 2:21) and later leaders of the Jewish people, in some cases for apparently political reasons (e.g., Judges 3:6; Ruth 1:4; 2 Samuel 3:3, 11:3; 1 Kings 3:1, 7:14, 9:1; 1 Chronicles 2:17). Still, both Moses (Exod 34:16; Deut 7:3–4) and Joshua (Josh 23:12) declare God's commandment not to marry Canaanite women.

45. Ezra and Nehemiah, in the fifth century BCE, require Jewish men who want to move from Babylonia to Israel to rebuild the Jewish community there to divorce their non-Jewish wives; see Ezra 9 and 10, and Nehemiah 13:13–30.

46. For a thorough description of Jewish genetic diseases, see Batsheva Bonne-Tamir and Avinoam Adam, eds., *Genetic Diversity Among Jews: Diseases and Markers at the DNA Level* (New York: Oxford University Press, 1992).

47. A. H. Handyside, J. G. Lesko, J. J. Tarín, R. M. Winston, and M. R. Hughes (September 1992), "Birth of a normal girl after in vitro fertilization and preimplantation diagnostic testing for cystic fibrosis." *New England Journal of Medicine* 327 (13): 905–9. doi:10.1056/NEJM199209243271301. PMID 1381054.

48. Mark Popovsky, "Choosing Our Children's Genes: The Use of Preimplantation Genetic Diagnosis," http://www.rabbinicalassembly.org/sites/default/files/public/halakhah/teshuvot/20052010/Popovsky_FINAL_preimplantation.pdf (accessed April 3, 2011).

49. Psalms 128:1–3, 6. For lack of space, this volume does not include a chapter on the ethics of parent-child relationships. For a discussion of a Jewish view of filial and parental duties, see Elliot N. Dorff, *Love Your Neighbor and Yourself* (at note 10 above), chap. 4; and Elliot N. Dorff, *The Way Into Tikkun Olam (Repairing the World)* (Woodstock, VT: Jewish Lights, 2005), chaps. 9 and 10.

Suggestions for Further Reading

Because positions on these matters depend generally on one's approach to Jewish law, I have identified the movement affiliation of each of the authors on this list, when clear and relevant, so that readers can read their works in that light.

Bleich, J. David. 1998. *Bioethical Dilemmas: A Jewish Perspective*. Hoboken, NJ: Ktav. [Orthodox]

Cardin, Nina Beth. 1999. *Tears of Sorrow, Seeds of Hope: A Jewish Spiritual Companion for Infertility and Pregnancy Loss*. Woodstock, VT: Jewish Lights. [Conservative]

Dorff, Elliot N. 1998. *Matters of Life and Death: A Jewish Approach to Modern Medical Ethics*. Philadelphia: Jewish Publication Society. [Conservative]

———. 2003. *Love Your Neighbor and Yourself: A Jewish Approach to Modern Personal Ethics*. Philadelphia: Jewish Publication Society, esp. chaps. 3 and 4.

Feldman, David M. 1968. *Birth Control in Jewish Law*. New York: New York University Press. (Subsequently republished by Schocken in 1974 and by Jason Aronson [now Rowman and Littlefield] in 1996 as *Marital Relations, Birth Control, and Abortion in Jewish Law*.) [Conservative]

Feldman, David M. 1968. 1986. *Health and Medicine in the Jewish Tradition*. New York: Crossroad. [Conservative]

Feldman, Emanuel, and Joel B. Wolowelsky, eds. 1997. *Jewish Law and the New Reproductive Technologies*. Hoboken, NJ: Ktav. [Orthodox]

Gold, Michael. 1988. *And Hannah Wept: Infertility, Adoption, and the Jewish Couple*. Philadelphia: Jewish Publication Society. [Conservative]

Jacob, Walter, and Moshe Zemer. 1995. *The Fetus and Fertility in Jewish Law: Essays and Responsa*. Pittsburgh: Freehof Institute of Progressive Halakhah. [Reform]

Mackler, Aaron L., ed. 2000. *Life and Death Responsibilities in Jewish Biomedical Ethics*. New York: The Jewish Theological Seminary of America. [Conservative]

Rosenberg, Shelley Kapnek. 1998. *Adoption and the Jewish Family: Contemporary Perspectives*. Philadelphia: Jewish Publication Society.

Rosner, Fred, and J. David Bleich, eds. 2000. *Jewish Bioethics*. Hoboken, NJ: Ktav. [Orthodox]

Schiff, Daniel. 2002. *Abortion in Judaism*. Cambridge, UK, and New York: Cambridge University Press. [Orthodox]

Steinberg, Avraham. 2003. *Encyclopedia of Jewish Medical Ethics*. Fred Rosner, trans. Jerusalem and New York: Feldheim Publishers. 3 vols. [Orthodox]

Washofsky, Mark. 2000. *Jewish Living: A Guide to Contemporary Reform Practice*. New York: UAHC Press, esp. chap. 6, "Medical Ethics." [Reform]

CHAPTER 18

JEWISH BIOETHICS
THE END OF LIFE

DANIEL B. SINCLAIR

Introduction

The Jewish legal tradition (*halakhah*) contains a rich storehouse of precedents and principles for the treatment of the dying, and contemporary writers in all the modern branches of Judaism draw their inspiration from these sources. In general, active euthanasia and suicide, including physician-assisted suicide, are prohibited in both the Orthodox and Conservative (called "Masorti" outside of North America) movements,[1] but these prohibitions are regarded as only starting points in Reform Judaism. The withdrawal of basic life support is generally prohibited, although, as will be seen below, there are specific situations in which this prohibition may not apply. Withholding treatment from a dying patient is generally permitted, although here too there are some differences of opinion in relation to the scope of the permission to withhold life support.

Some liberal writers interpret talmudic narratives recounting the role of prayer in the deaths of various rabbis in the Talmud (B. *Ketubbot* 104a; B. *Avodah Zarah* 18a) in such a way as to conclude that both active euthanasia and suicide are permitted.[2] This chapter, however, reflects the traditional *halakhic* view according to which interpretations of talmudic narratives do not override *halakhic* norms. Hence, the only legitimate conclusion that may be drawn from these narratives is that it is permitted to pray for the death of a suffering, terminally ill patient.[3] In the present writer's view, the subordination of narrative to norm in this context provides a truer fit with the traditional methodology of Jewish law, and, as Louis Newman has suggested, modern Jewish ethics is all about achieving the best fit with Jewish tradition: "When contemporary Jewish authorities armed with a body of traditional Jewish sources confront a contemporary moral problem, the decision that they reach, through interpretation and application of those sources, will be guided by a sense of what 'fits' the tradition."[4]

This chapter begins with a brief sketch of the historical development of the *halakhic* position regarding the terminally ill patient, and a statement of the contemporary Orthodox consensus on this issue. The position adopted by the the Conservative/Masorti movement is also noted. It then proceeds to make two claims. The first is that patient autonomy at the end of life is a significant *halakhic* value and extends to the withholding, and arguably also to the withdrawing of basic life-support. The second, responding to the view that the criminal law in Common law systems is too blunt an instrument for dealing with the whole range of euthanasia cases, especially those of a morally challenging nature, is that an approach based upon the more richly textured *halakhic* position regarding the killing of a fatally ill individual (*terefah*) may provide a better way for dealing with such cases. These claims are presented in the context of a tightly reasoned *halakhic* framework in the belief that as such, they will succeed in passing Orthodox muster. At the same time, their somewhat radical substance will hopefully resonate with most of the mainstream positions in the more liberal movements.

Finally, reference will be made to legal provisions relating to the treatment of the terminally ill in Israeli law. The underlying theme of these provisions is the attempt to provide a synthesis between *halakhah* and democracy, which is, after all, one of the major concerns of modern Jewish ethics. How that balance plays out in Diaspora Jewish communities will also be noted.

THE DYING PERSON AND JEWISH LAW

In the past, the dying individual—*goses*—was identified by physical features such as a death rattle and the inability to swallow. According to a sixteenth-century authority, Rabbi Joshua Falk Katz, a *goses* is a person who will not survive for more than three days.[5] In modern times the traditional symptoms have been replaced by more sophisticated medical criteria, and in terms of the time frame, the majority of contemporary *halakhic* authorities believe that a *goses* may survive for several months and even a year. Under Israel's Terminally Ill Patient Law, 2005, a terminal patient is defined as one whose life expectancy is less than six months (sec. 8a).

Precipitating the death of a *goses* is an act of murder.[6] An impediment to death may, however, be removed. For example, according to the thirteenth-century work *Sefer Hasidim*,[7] it is mandatory to remove a woodchopper from the vicinity of the *goses*, because it was believed at the time that the sound of chopping was instrumental in preventing the soul from departing from the body; hence the presence of the woodchopper constituted an impediment to death. For a similar reason, salt is not to be put on the tongue of the *goses*. Moving the *goses* from place to place, even for the purpose of ensuring a timely death, is forbidden by the *Sefer Hasidim* for fear that any such movement may precipitate death. According to Rabbi Moses Isserles, a prominent sixteenth-century authority, if salt is placed on the tongue of the *goses*, it may be gently brushed off.[8] The distinction made in the *Sefer Hasidim* between removing an impediment to death, which is permitted, and precipitating death, which is prohibited, became the cornerstone of the *halakhah* regarding the treatment of the dying in Jewish law.

In the modern period, the focus of the *halakhic* discussion has shifted from woodchoppers and salt to respirators and artificial nutrition and hydration. As a result, the distinction between precipitation of death and impediment-removal is now expressed in medical terms. The dominant Orthodox view is that medical treatment calculated to provide a temporary cure, which in effect merely prolongs dying, is regarded as an impediment to death and may be withheld or even withdrawn. Treatment directly aimed at maintaining the *goses*'s basic physical needs—that is, respiration, nutrition, and hydration—is not regarded as an impediment and consequently ought not to be withheld.[9]

A good example of a medical treatment that falls into the category of impediment removal is given by Rabbi Shlomo Zalman Auerbach, a leading Orthodox Israeli authority in the second half of the twentieth century, who wrote that it is not mandatory to amputate the gangrenous leg of a patient dying from terminal cancer if he objects to the operation. Removing the leg will not change the prognosis and, in effect, only serves to delay death. It is, however, forbidden to withhold artificial nutrition, hydration, or respiration from a dying patient until the establishment of death.[10]

It is also important to emphasize that according to the overwhelming majority of contemporary Orthodox halakhists, there is no difference between natural and artificial life support, and neither form may be discontinued until the establishment of death.

The Conservative Movement's Committee on Jewish Law and Standards validated two rulings on December 12, 1990, that agree in about 80 percent of the issues but disagree in the remainder. One ruling, by Rabbi Avram Reisner,[11] takes the same stand as that of the Orthodox rabbis described above. The other, by Rabbi Elliot Dorff,[12] maintains that artificial nutrition and hydration are to be regarded as medicine, not food, because they lack some of the most important characteristics of food—variations in texture, temperature, and taste—and they do not come into the body the way food normally does, and so artificial nutrition and hydration, as well as machines and medications, may be withheld or withdrawn if it is in the patient's best interests to do so.

Patient Autonomy at the End of Life

A unique contribution to this field of Jewish law was made by Rabbi Moses Feinstein, the leading *halakhic* authority in North American Orthodoxy in the latter half of the twentieth century. In a *responsum* dealing with the treatment of the dying patient, Rabbi Feinstein emphasizes the importance of not doing anything to traumatize such a person by imposing unwanted treatment, including actual life support—artificial respiration, nutrition, and hydration. Regarding a competent adult patient who objects to being connected to an intravenous feeding device, Rabbi Feinstein rules that "one may not apply physical force to an adult to make him accept nutrition, especially if he believes it is causing him harm."[13] This is so because the trauma of coercion in such a situation endangers the patient's physical and mental health, and as a result it is more than likely to precipitate his or her death.

Support for this position is found in the Talmud with respect to dying individuals who wish to dispose of their property even though the formal means for so doing, such as valid witnesses and formal deeds, are unavailable to them. The Talmud rules that the wishes of such individuals are to be respected, and the property is transferred in accordance with their wishes, despite the lack of the usual formalities. Any refusal to implement the express desire of the dying person is likely to cause him or her grave mental distress, and this in turn may lead to a deterioration of the patient's condition to the extent of precipitating death.[14] Rabbi Feinstein opines that the medical treatment of the dying is undoubtedly worthy of even more serious consideration—as far as trauma avoidance is concerned—than the disposition of the person's property. Hence the wishes of the patient in this case are to be respected, and he is not to be fed forcibly.

Rabbi Feinstein's decision is radical in permitting the withholding of actual life support, that is, nutrition. As is pointed out above, the general consensus among Orthodox authorities in the past was that such basic life-necessities may not be withheld unless death has been established. Rabbi Feinstein deviates from this consensus and permits the withholding of artificial nutrition from a competent *goses*.

Rabbi Feinstein's decision is also original in that it places the focus entirely upon the wishes of the patient. In relation to this focus, it is tempting to link this *responsum* with an earlier one in which he argues, in effect, that Jewish law does recognize a limited form of patient autonomy.[15] In that *responsum*, the question concerned a patient who was offered a rather risky treatment that would, if successful, significantly increase both his life expectancy and his quality of life.[16] The problem was that the risk of death was far higher than 50 percent, and the accepted position under Jewish law is that the obligation to preserve life applies equally to the short and to the long term. A treatment that does not have even a 50 percent chance of success would seem to fall short of the necessary statistical qualifications for justifying the risk, and there are precedents to the effect that in this type of situation, the best course is that of inaction.

Nevertheless, Rabbi Feinstein rules that the decision lies in the hands of the patient, and he is permitted to choose the chance of a significant improvement to his life expectancy and quality of life, notwithstanding the high risk. Rabbi Feinstein points out that the desire for improved quality of life and an extended life-expectancy is common to people everywhere, and in this respect, the case pits two legitimate values against each other.[17] The way that the *halakhah* chooses to resolve the conflict between the two values is to let the patient decide. Clearly, if the patient decides not to undergo the highly risky treatment but to remain with his short-term, low-quality life, his wishes must also be respected.

Rabbi Feinstein reinforces his argument with a gloss on the theological principle of the Divine ownership of human life.[18] In a rather dramatic statement, he claims that in this type of situation, "people become the owners of their bodies with respect to improving the quality of their lives," and, in effect, God transfers His title in that patient's life to him and makes the patient the arbiter of his fate. In other words, Rabbi Feinstein contends that in hard cases, the Divine will makes itself known in the form of the patient's wishes. In pastoral terms, an important ramification of Rabbi Feinstein's position is that rabbis consulted regarding the treatment of a terminal patient must ascertain the wishes of the patient and factor them into their *halakhic* decisions.

Finally, it is important to note that Rabbi Feinstein's limited notion of patient autonomy lies at the heart of Israel's 2005 Terminally Ill Patient Law.[19] The Law begins by presuming that every terminal patient wishes to live, but it then allows the rebuttal of this presumption by the terminal patient himself, or by means of an advance directive or a health proxy.[20] The rebuttal option derives its *halakhic* legitimacy from Rabbi Feinstein's approach, according to which artificial feeding may be withheld if this is in accordance with the wishes of the patient. This approach also underlies the legitimacy of advance directives and health proxies for Orthodox Jews in accordance with the regulations drawn up under the law.[21]

The 2005 Law is specific with regard to the situations in which life support may be withheld or withdrawn. In accordance with Rabbi Feinstein's position, the law permits the withholding of all life support from a competent patient who refuses to accept it.[22] In Section 16, the Law permits the withdrawal of all treatment of a periodic, as opposed to a continuous nature; hence life support, which is by nature continuous, may not be withdrawn until the establishment of death.[23]

The Law does, however, permit "refrain[ing] from restarting continuous life support that was terminated...in a manner that does not contravene any legal provision."[24] The phrase "in a manner that does not contravene any legal provision" refers to the option promised in the notes to the draft law proposing that a timer be developed that would bring one cycle of continuous treatment to an end, and, in a halakhically acceptable manner, prevent another cycle kicking into action.[25] In other words, there is a potential *halakhic* option for collapsing the distinction between withholding and withdrawing by converting every withdrawal of a continuous treatment into a withholding of the treatment. No such timer has yet been used, first, because it is difficult to accept that life and death decisions involving terminal patients may be resolved on the basis of a timer alone, and second, because the best of machines do not always function properly, and the consequences of a technical glitch in this context are indeed grave.

Finally, a question arises as to the scope of Rabbi Feinstein's original ruling: is it limited to withholding life support, or would it also apply to its withdrawal? It is certainly arguable that the concern for trauma prevention would apply equally to a case in which a feeding tube had already been connected as well as to the initial hookup. In general, it would appear that the distinction between withholding and withdrawing here tends to become highly artificial, since, in effect, the decision not to connect the patient to life support leads to death in exactly the same way as its withdrawal results in the patient's demise.

The Human *Terefah*

In addition to the *goses*, there is another *halakhic* category that is relevant to the dying and their treatment—the *terefah*. A *terefah* is an individual who is suffering from a fatal condition and, on the basis of the best medical evidence, whose death is expected to occur within approximately twelve months. Unlike the *goses*, the murderer of a *terefah* is treated differently from the killer of a regular person, and he is exempt from the death penalty normally administered by the court for murder. The explanation given by the Talmud for this exemption is that the death penalty is administered only for the taking of a viable life. Since the death of the *terefah* is inevitable, the killer cannot be said to have taken a viable life. In the words of the commentators on the Talmud, "the killer of a *terefah* has, in fact, killed a dead man."[26]

The *halakhah* does, however, make it very clear that it is morally wrong to kill a *terefah* in a wanton manner, and one who does so is liable to death at the hands of Heaven.[27] From the fact that the killer of a *terefah* is subject to a Divine penalty, Rabbi Moses Feinstein deduces that there is also a *halakhic* prohibition on killing a *terefah*.[28]

Nevertheless, there are circumstances in which the death of a *terefah* may be brought about in order to save viable life. A classical case in talmudic literature is that of a group of defenseless travelers who are surrounded by armed brigands and offered a grim choice: either they hand over one member of the group to the slaughter, or they will all die.[29] The unanimous decision in that case is that it is forbidden to pick an individual and hand him over merely because of a calculation based upon numbers of lives that may be saved by his sacrifice. However, a difference of opinion exists where the brigands request a specific individual. According to one view, this request makes all the difference, and the named person may be handed over in order to save the whole group. This ruling is based upon a biblical precedent (2 Samuel 20) and also upon the moral intuition that it is heinous to pick a victim and hand him over to the slaughter, but justifiable to hand over a marked man.[30]

One of the medieval commentators on the Talmud, Rabbi Menahem Meiri, raises the issue of giving up a *terefah*:

> And it seems quite clear that in the case of the travelers, if one of them was a *terefah*, then he may be given up in order to save the lives of the rest, since the killer of a *terefah* is exempt from the death penalty."[31]

According to Rabbi Meiri, the *terefah* status also produces the "marked man effect." The life of the *terefah* is clearly inferior to that of a viable individual, since there is no death penalty for his murder. In the travelers' dilemma there is a morally arguable case for giving up one person to save a whole group. The *terefah* state is the extra factor, just like the naming of a particular individual. Hence, we have an example of how the exemption of the killer of a *terefah* from capital punishment becomes an operative factor in a case of tragic choice.

Rabbi Meiri's position is further explicated by Rabbi Joseph Babad's interpretation of the talmudic dictum upon which the principle of the inviolability of individual human lives is based, that is, "How do you know that your blood is redder? Perhaps the blood of the other person is redder?"[32] Rabbi Babad argues that by virtue of his fatal defect, the blood of a *terefah* is indeed "less red" than that of a viable individual; consequently, he may be sacrificed in order to save the rest of the group.[33]

Not all authorities are in agreement with Rabbi Meiri's conclusion. Rabbi Ezekiel Landau, for example, states that "the very idea that a *terefah* might be killed for the sake of preserving a viable life is unheard of."[34] Rabbi Landau's position is, however, qualified by later *halakhic* authorities in such a way that Rabbi Meiri's position remains viable.[35]

What is the relevance, if any, of the *terefah* to voluntary euthanasia? At first sight, the answer is none at all. In the cases of tragic choice and medical dilemmas cited above, the law of the human *terefah* is applied in order to strike a balance between competing claims to life. The conclusion in each case is that the non-*terefah* takes precedence over the *terefah*. However, in none of these cases is the law governing the killing of a *terefah* applied where the sole result is the death of the *terefah*. In every case, it is for the sake of saving viable life that the law of the *terefah* swings into operation.

Notwithstanding this rather compelling argument, there are isolated voices in both the Orthodox[36] and Conservative[37] camps in support of the idea that in the case of a human *terefah* patient who is undergoing great suffering, it ought to be possible to put the exemption of his killer from capital punishment into practice, and rule leniently, at least in terms of withdrawing life support prior to the establishment of death, and in an indirect manner. The use of the *terefah* category in this regard is nevertheless highly controversial, and it has indeed come under heavy criticism.[38]

Terefah and the Terminally Ill

In 1412 a Spanish Jewish physician by the name of Joshua Lorki converted to Catholicism. He assumed the name Geronimo de Santa Fé and became an implacable enemy of Judaism. Immediately after his conversion, he published a polemical pamphlet seeking to demonstrate that the Talmud was a morally offensive work. One of the doctrines cited in this pamphlet was the exemption of the killer of a *terefah* from the death penalty, which Lorki claimed was thoroughly immoral; he also pointed out that non-Jewish law recognized no such exception to criminal liability in the law of homicide.[39]

The Jewish response appeared in the form of a work entitled *Milkhemet Miztvah* by Rabbi Solomon b. Simon Duran, a fifteenth-century Algerian authority. In addition to attacking the lax morals of the Christian clergy, R. Duran also dealt with the specific points raised by Lorki. Rabbi Duran observed that the legal exemption of the killer of a *terefah* is not a blanket permission to kill any *terefah* in sight, but rather, a means of making the law of homicide, and particularly the mandatory death sentence, more flexible in difficult cases. The very same result, observed Rabbi Duran, is achieved in non-Jewish law by means of royal clemency. Rabbi Duran went even further in suggesting that the approach of Jewish law is preferable, since it does not give the impression that the course of justice is being perverted. Pardoning a convicted killer creates the impression—particularly in the minds of the victim's family—that a legally culpable individual has escaped without any penalty. In Jewish law, by contrast, exemption from the death penalty is an integral part of the law, and consequently its application is not perceived as a departure from the idea of justice.[40]

The point of citing this observation here is not to decide which legal system is superior, but merely to observe that both Jewish and non-Jewish law recognize the tension arising in difficult cases between the need to protect the value of human life by executing every killer in society, and the need to temper the strict demands of law and justice in morally challenging situations by leaving certain acts of homicide unaffected by conventional criminal law sanctions. The sole difference between Jewish and non-Jewish law to emerge from Rabbi Duran's remark is in relation to the means to be adopted in order to overcome this tension.

A nice illustration of the use of the royal pardon in morally hard circumstances is the famous nineteenth-century case of *R. v. Dudley and Stephens* (1884)14 QBD 273. In that case, the captain and first mate of a ship that capsized at sea on the way from England to Australia killed and ate the cabin boy in order to survive. The deed was done after eighteen days in an open boat, during which the supplies of food and water had run out and all the survivors were in poor physical shape. The cabin boy was in worse physical shape than any of the other sailors. Four days after the cabin boy had been killed and eaten, the survivors of the shipwreck were rescued. The accused were indicted for murder and were found guilty and sentenced to be "hanged by the neck until dead." They were, however, promptly pardoned by Queen Victoria.

The Court was not prepared to accept a defense of necessity, and this stance has remained the mainstream position in the Common law, despite attempts by eminent jurists to use the defense in the context of voluntary euthanasia. This position was concisely summed up by U.S. Supreme Court Justice Benjamin Cardozo, the famous American judge who wrote that there is no "principle of human jettison" in the Common law.[41]

The Court in the shipwrecked mariners case was not prepared to make any concession on the necessity argument on the basis of the fact that the boy's physical condition was much worse than that of the grown men on board, and that he was the closest one to death. The non-Jewish legal tradition mentioned by Rabbi Duran and exemplified by the decision in *R. v. Dudley and Stephens* (1884) 14 QBD, 273, refuses to budge from the principle that all intentional acts of killing are murder, irrespective of the physical condition of the victim. Jewish law, on the other hand, would likely have taken into account the victim's physical condition and used it to categorize him as a *terefah*. From the perspective of Jewish law, it may be argued that as a *terefah*, the sailors ought never to have been charged with murder in a regular court of law.

The refusal of the Common law to recognize necessity as a defense to a murder charge, while relying on the royal prerogative of mercy or its modern equivalents to remove the moral sting from this refusal, has been characterized as lacking in intellectual force:

> When, however, all is said and done, probably the most persistent English attitude to the problem raised by the necessity plea—intellectually unsatisfying though it may be—is that hard cases are best dealt with by the prerogative of mercy.[42]

Contemporary Common law possesses a number of methods in addition to the prerogative of mercy to deal with the moral tension inherent in the area of voluntary euthanasia. These include policy decisions not to prosecute physicians who engage in voluntary euthanasia; unconvincing findings by juries that such physicians did not intend the deaths of the deceased; the jury's return of verdicts of manslaughter or other lesser offenses; and extremely light sentences handed out by judges to those doctors actually found guilty of murder. These methods, which open up a wide gap between the law in theory and its practical application, clearly fall into the category of the "intellectually unsatisfying." Indeed, it is the dissatisfaction with the existence of this gap that, *inter alia*, underlies much of the contemporary criticism of the application of the criminal law to cases of medical euthanasia.[43]

Returning to Jewish law, the category traditionally deemed applicable to the dying has been that of the *goses*. As was already observed, the relevant principle governing the treatment of the *goses* is that he is to be considered as "a living being in all respects." This principle undoubtedly reflects a past age in which the dying person lay on his death-bed at home, surrounded by family and friends, and in many cases issued final instructions and requests. This is clearly not the case today, when most people end up dying in hospitals under very different circumstances. It may be argued that in the context of the new era of medicalized dying, there is room for the *terefah* category, particularly in relation to the criminalization of euthanasia. It is certainly possible in contemporary medicine to determine whether a sick, hospitalized patient is likely to die within twelve months. It would also follow that in accordance with the law of the *terefah*, termination of treatment impeding the death of a terminal patient, or for that matter, taking more active steps resulting in his death, would not constitute homicide punishable by human courts. In other words, those involved in "mercy-killing" cases ought to be treated not as regular murderers, but as individuals subject to Divine jurisdiction and, of course, to the strictures of their own moral consciences. Now, we have already seen that *halakhic* authorities do their utmost to ensure that no credence is given to the idea that it is halakhically permissible to kill a *terefah*. Nevertheless, it is surely arguable that in the context of the formal institutions of criminal justice, the killer of a *terefah* in a hard case ought to be treated more leniently than that of a regular person. As was pointed out by Rabbi Solomon Duran, this leniency is in place precisely in order to provide the criminal law with a certain amount of flexibility in difficult cases.

This is not an idea that is easily applicable to a modern, pluralist society subscribing to a wide range of moral values, but even in such a society, it is not totally without merit. In institutional terms, it may very well require the hearing of mercy-killing cases by bodies other than regular criminal courts. One possibility would be to try such cases before special tribunals, and if at any stage it became evident that the case was more appropriate for a regular court, it would be possible to transfer it accordingly. In any case, since a description of the practical aspects of such a tribunal is beyond the scope of this chapter, we will conclude with the observation that if it is accepted that the standard rules of criminal law in Common law jurisdictions are too blunt an instrument for dealing with what is broadly termed "mercy killing," then the *terefah* category in Jewish law may be of some help in moving toward a better approach.

In the Conservative Movement, in one of the two rabbinic rulings on end-of-life care that the Movement's Committee on Jewish Law and Standards approved,[44] this is indeed the approach that Rabbi Elliot Dorff has taken, but in some ways he has gone further than the above analysis would suggest, and in some ways he has not gone as far. Once a person has become a *terefah*, he would allow withdrawing not only machines and medications, but also artificial nutrition and hydration. On the other hand, in another rabbinic ruling,[45] he makes it clear that he does not allow assisted suicide. Thus he stretches the permission for what is sometimes called "passive euthanasia" about as far as it can go while still maintaining the ban against "active euthanasia."

In any case, while in Israel the new law described above, although based on Jewish sources, governs all citizens of Israel—Jewish or not, religious or not—in the Diaspora the laws of each nation govern its citizens' options in matters of death and dying. In some jurisdictions (e.g., the Netherlands, Oregon) the law permits assisted suicide under specific circumstances. In the United States, as in most Western jurisdictions, the law permits withholding or removing machines and medications from patients, including nutrition and hydration,[46] when doing so is in the patient's best interests, as determined by the patient's advance directive or by the patient's surrogate decision maker. Jews living in such jurisdictions take advantage of these leniencies or choose not to do so depending on their own individual choice, which is sometimes guided by rabbis from the specific form of Judaism to which they subscribe.

NOTES

1. For the official Conservative/Masorti position, see "Statement on Assisted Suicide," in *Responsa 1991–2000 of the Committee on Jewish Law and Standards of the Conservative Movement*, Kassel Abelson and David J. Fine, eds. (New York: Rabbinical Assembly, 2002), pp. 398–99, also available at http://www.rabbinicalassembly.org/sites/default/files/public/halakhah/teshuvot/19912000/assistedsuicide.pdf (accessed June 12, 2012). The rabbinic ruling to which it refers and on which it is based is Elliot N. Dorff, "Assisted Suicide," in ibid., pp. 379–97; also available in his book on Jewish medical ethics, *Matters of Life and Death: A Jewish Approach to Modern Medical Ethics* (Philadelphia: Jewish Publication Society, 1998), pp. 176–98, and at http://www.rabbinicalassembly.org/sites/default/files/public/halakhah/teshuvot/19912000/dorff_suicide.pdf (accessed June 12, 2012).
2. Byron Sherwin, *In Partnership with God* (Syracuse, NY: Syracuse University Press, 1990), pp. 94–98; Peter Knobel, "Suicide, Assisted Suicide, Active Euthanasia," in *Death and Euthanasia in Jewish Law*, Walter Jacob and Moshe Zemer, eds. (Pittsburgh: Freehof Institute of Progressive Halakhah, Rodef Shalom Press, 1995), pp. 27ff.
3. Rabbenu Nissim, *Nedarim* 40a.
4. Louis E. Newman, "Woodchoppers and Respirators: The Problem of Interpretation in Contemporary Jewish Ethics," in Elliot N. Dorff and Louis E. Newman, eds., *Contemporary Jewish Ethics and Morality: A Reader.* (New York: Oxford University Press, 1995), p. 154.
5. *Perishah, Yoreh Deah* 339:5.
6. B. *Sanhedrin* 78a; M.T. Laws of Murder and the Preservation of Life 2:7.
7. Section 722.
8. S.A. *Yoreh Deah* 339:7, gloss.
9. Rabbi Immanuel Jakobovits, "The Law Relating to the Precipitation of the Death of a Hopeless Patient Who is Undergoing Great Suffering" (Heb.), *Hapardes* 31 (1957), pt. 1, pp. 28–31; pt. 3, pp. 16–19.
10. *Responsa Minhat Shlomoh*, no. 91.
11. Avram Israel Reisner, "A Halakhic Ethics of Care for the Terminally Ill," in *Responsa 1980–1990 of the Committee of Jewish Law and Standards of the Conservative Movement* (New York: Rabbinical Assembly, 2005), pp. 467–518.; also available at http://www.rabbinicalassembly.org/sites/default/files/public/halakhah/teshuvot/19861990/reisner_care.pdf (accessed June 12, 2012).
12. Elliot N. Dorff, "A Jewish Approach to End-Stage Medical Care," in ibid., pp. 519–80; also available at http://www.rabbinicalassembly.org/sites/default/files/public/halakhah/teshuvot/19861990/dorff_care.pdf (accessed June 12, 2012), and, in a somewhat updated form, in his book *Matters of Life and Death: A Jewish Approach to Modern Medical Ethics* (Philadelphia: Jewish Publication Society, 1998), chaps. 7–9.

13. *Responsa Iggrot Moshe, Hoshen Mishpat* 2 no. 74.
14. B. *Bava Batra* 147b, 156b; B. *Ketubbot* 70a.
15. It is necessary to distinguish between autonomy as a systemic value in the legal system as a whole and R. Feinstein's autonomy, which functions as a specific *halakhic* solution to rare and particularly difficult cases. In this respect, R. Feinstein's autonomy is of a limited nature; also see David Shatz, "Concepts of Autonomy in Jewish Medical Ethics," *Jewish Law Annual* 12 (1997), pp. 3 ff.
16. *Responsa Iggrot Moshe, Yoreh Deah* 3 no. 36.
17. According to Rabbi Feinstein, the desire to choose a risky therapy for the sake of greater quality of life is a valid one even though its source lies in universal practice rather than in any *halakhic* source. Rabbi Feinstein's proof for this claim is derived from the talmudic discussion of the prohibition for a Jew to go to a heathen practitioner for medical treatment. The reason for this prohibition is the fear that in the course of the treatment, the heathen would kill the Jew. The Talmud (B. *Avodah Zarah* 27b) restricts the prohibition to a case in which the Jew will live even if the disease remains untreated. If, however, it is certain that without the requisite medical treatment, the Jew will die, he may then seek treatment from a heathen physician. To the objection that short-term survival is a *halakhic* value and therefore ought not to be endangered by visiting the heathen physician even if death is the inevitable result, the Talmud responds with a biblical passage in which it is clear that short-term survival may, indeed, be sacrificed for the mere chance of long-term viability. This passage is the biblical account of the four lepers who chose to throw themselves on the mercy of the Arameans even though they would thereby prejudice their short-term lives (2 Kings 7:4). According to the rabbinic tradition, the four lepers were Gehazi, the rapacious steward of the prophet Elisha, and his three sons, who were also implicated in his villainy (B. *Sotah* 47a; Radak, 2 Kings 6:27). Rabbi Feinstein raises the question as to how the Talmud can rely upon the calculations of sinful people in order to derive a *halakhic* norm. His answer is that in matters of universal rationality such as the choice between preserving short-term life at all costs and risking it for the sake of possible salvation—even if the chances of the latter are very slim—Jewish law focuses on the rationally compelling nature of the choice and disregards the spiritually flawed personalities of those making that choice. In these matters, *halakhah* recognizes the validity of choices based upon a universally compelling logic, i.e., "what most people would think."
18. M.T. Laws of Murder and the Preservation of Life 1:4.
19. The Chair of the Draft Law Committee, Prof. Abraham Steinberg, is an expert in the field of biomedical *halakhah*, and the *halakhic* background to the Draft Law that was accepted by the vast majority of the mixed religious and secular committee, is analyzed in his article: "The Halakhic Basis for the Terminally Ill Patient Draft Law," *Assia* 71–72 (1993:25–39) (Hebrew). Rabbi Feinstein is cited on almost every page, and his pervasive influence on the provisions of the Draft Law is patent.
20. Sections. 4–7.
21. Sections. 30–44.
22. Section 15.
23. Section 21.
24. Ibid.
25. *Responsa Tzitz Eliezer* 13 no. 89. As Rabbi Elliot Dorff reports, this is also an option that Rabbi Immanuel Jakobovits suggested in a lecture to physicians and other interested parties at Cedars-Sinai Medical Center in Los Angeles in 1983.

26. *Yad Remah, Sanhedrin* 78a; *Shittah Mekubetzet, Bava Kamma* 26a.
27. M.T. Laws of Murder and the Preservation of Life 2:8: *Resp. Ahiezer, Yoreh Deah* no.16.
28. *Responsa Iggrot Moshe, Yoreh Deah* 3, no.36.
29. J. *Terumot* 8:4; Tosefta *Terumot* 7:20.
30. The other view maintains that the named person may be given up only if he is subject to the death penalty. Maimonides rules in accordance with the latter view (Laws of the Foundations of the Torah 5:5) and his ruling is followed by the majority of *halakhic* authorities (*Bayit Hadash, Yoreh Deah* 153; *Turei Zahav, Yoreh Deah* 157:7). It is arguable, however, that if the entire group is liable to perish, then the marked individual is "subject to the death penalty" merely by being part of the group. It is on the basis of this argument that R. Simon Efrati (*Resp. Migei Hahareigah* no.1) ruled that a man hiding in an underground bunker with a group of Jews during the Holocaust was halakhically justified in bringing about the death of a crying baby by stuffing a rag in its mouth in order to prevent the discovery of the entire group by the Germans. Since all the group members, including the baby, would have been exterminated immediately upon discovery, the baby was considered to be subject to an objective "death penalty"; hence, its sacrifice was justified in accordance with Maimonides' ruling. Obviously in this case the baby's cries produced the "marked man" effect.
31. *Bet Habehirah, Sanherin* 74a.
32. B. *Sanhedrin* 74a.
33. *Minhat Hinukh* no. 296.
34. *Responsa Noda Biyehudah* 2, *Hoshen Mishpat* no. 59.
35. See, for example, *Responsa Bet Yizhak, Yoreh Deah* 2 no. 162, and *Responsa Yabia Omer* 4, *Even Haezer* 1.
36. N. Z. Goldberg, "Terminating Artificial Respiration in the Case of a Fatally Ill Patient in Order to Save a Potentially Viable Individual," (Heb.) *Emek Halakhah Assia* 1 (1986) 83. The somewhat controversial nature of this position is reflected by the fact that Rabbi Goldberg's article is presented together with numerous critical notes by Rabbi Levi Yizhak Halperin, who is of the opinion that the law of the *terefah* has absolutely no relevance for the treatment of the terminally in Jewish law.
37. Elliot N. Dorff, "A Jewish Approach to End-Stage Medical Care," *Conservative Judaism* 43 (1991), p. 32. See especially n. 66. Available also in his book *Matters of Life and Death* (see note 1 above), chaps. 7–9 (where the note is n. 56 on pp. 376–77), and at http://www.rabbinicalassembly.org/teshuvot/docs/19861990/dorff_care.pdf.
38. For example, on December 12, 1990, the Conservative Movement's Committee on Jewish Law and Standards approved both Rabbi Dorff's *responsum*, which employs the *terefah* category (see previous note), and also a *responsum* by Rabbi Avram Israel Reisner, who opposes it: "my fundamental objection to taking this tack is that to do so is to permit the hastening of the death of patients by vacating their lives in theory in advance. This is (a) (pernicious) (b) (unseemly) (c) (wrong.) Yes, such precedent exists in the literature.... If you kill a *terefah* can you be found guilty?... No. But there is no implication that such murder is permissible.... Rabbi Elliot Dorff, basing himself on the work of Rabbi Dr. Daniel Sinclair, has argued this case elegantly. Notwithstanding the persuasiveness of his prose, the fundamental flaw remains. It devalues life in order to attain its end." Avram Israel Reisner, "A Halakhic Ethic of Care for the Terminally Ill," *Conservative Judaism* 43 (1991), n. 39; Rabbi Reisner's *responsum* is also available at http://www.rabbinicalassembly.org/teshuvot/docs/19861990/reisner_care.pdf (accessed March 7, 2011).

39. *De Judaeis Erroribus Ex Talmuth*, published in *Biblioethera Maxima Veterum Patrum* 3 (Frankfurt, 1602).
40. *Milhemet Mitzvah* 32b, s.v. *ve'od heshiv*.
41. Benjamin Cordozo, *Law and Literature and Other Essays and Addresses* (New York: Harcourt, Brace, and Company, 1931; republished, Littleton, CO: F. B. Rothman, 1986), p. 113.
42. P. Glazebrook, "The Necessity Plea in English Criminal Law," *Cambridge Law Journal* (1972a), pp. 118–19.
43. See: M. Otlowski, *Voluntary Euthanasia and the Common Law* (New York: Oxford University Press, 1997), pp. 185–86. In this context, it is noteworthy that in 2001 the English Court of Appeal (*Re A (Children) [2001] 2 WLR 480*) broke with this longstanding refusal on the part of the Common law to recognize necessity as a defense to an act of homicide when it permitted the separation of newly born, conjoined twin girls sharing one sound heart. One functioning heart cannot support two little girls, and at some later stage both would have died as a result of heart failure. The direct result of the surgical separation of the twins, however, would be the death of the weaker one, who relied upon her stronger sister's heart for her life-blood. The court decided to permit the operation using, *inter alia*, the "lesser of the two evils" argument and the *halakhic* concept of the "marked man" in the travelers' dilemma referred to above; see: D. Sinclair, *Jewish Biomedical Law: Legal and Extra-legal Dimensions* (New York: Oxford University Press, 2003) 219–24.
44. See notes 38 and 39 above.
45. See note 1 above.
46. *Cruzan, by Her Parents and Co-Guardians, v. Director, Missouri Department of Health*, 497 U.S. 261 (1990).

Suggestions for Further Reading

Bleich, J. David. 1998. *Bioethical Dilemmas*. Hoboken, NJ: Ktav, chaps. 3–4.

Dorff, Elliot N. 1998. *Matters of Life and Death: A Jewish Approach to Modern Medical Ethics*. Philadelphia: Jewish Publication Society, esp. chaps. 7–9.

Dorff, Elliot N. 1998–1999. "Assisted Suicide," *Journal of Law and Religion* 13:263–87.

Jacob, Walter, and Moshe Zemer, eds. 1995. *Death and Euthanasia in Jewish Law*. Pittsburgh: Freehof Institute of Progressive Halakhah.

Jakobovits, Immanuel. 1959, 1975. *Jewish Medical Ethics*. New York: Bloch Publishing Company.

Lesnick, H. 2010. *Religion in Legal Thought and Practice*. Cambridge: Cambridge University Press, chap. 9.

Lichtenstein, Y. S. 2008. *Suicide: Halakhic, Historical, and Theological Aspects*. Tel Aviv: Hakibbutz Hameuhad Publishing House (Hebrew).

Newman, Louis E. 1995. "Woodchoppers and Respirators: The Problem of Interpretation in Contemporary Jewish Ethics." In *Contemporary Jewish Ethics and Morality: A Reader*, Elliot N. Dorff and Louis E. Newman, eds., pp. 140–60.

Novak, David. 2007. *The Sanctity of Human Life*. Washington, DC: Georgetown University Press.

Reisner, Avram Israel. 1991. "A Halakhic Ethics of Care for the Terminally Ill," *Conservative Judaism* 43:3, pp. 52–91.

Resnicoff, S. 1998–1999. "Jewish Law Perspectives on Suicide and Physician Assisted Dying," *Journal of Law and Religion* 12:2, pp. 289–349.

Sherwin, Byron. 1990. *In Partnership with God*. Syracuse, NY: Syracuse University Press, chap. 5.

Sinclair, Daniel. 2003. *Jewish Biomedical Law: Legal and Extra-Legal Dimensions*. Oxford and New York: Oxford University Press, chaps. 4–5.

Zohar, Noam. 1997. *Alternatives in Jewish Bioethics*. Albany: State University of New York Press, chap. 2.

CHAPTER 19

JEWISH BIOETHICS
THE DISTRIBUTION OF HEALTH CARE

AARON L. MACKLER

FOUNDATIONAL Jewish values, discussed in previous chapters, shape Jewish understandings regarding the distribution of health care.[1] Among these, the Book of Genesis (1:27) teaches that God created humans in God's image, *betzelem Elohim*. The ancient Rabbis and later Jews have treasured this verse as expressing the intrinsic value and dignity of each human being. The Mishnah proclaims:

> Therefore was a single man [Adam] created, to teach you that anyone who destroys a single person from the children of man is considered by Scripture as if he destroyed an entire world, and that whoever sustains a single person from the children of man is considered by Scripture as if he sustained an entire world; and for the sake of peace among people, that no one could say to his fellow, my ancestor was greater than your ancestor;... and to proclaim the greatness of the Holy One, blessed be He, for man stamps many coins with the same die and they are all the same as one other, but the King of the kings of kings, the Holy One, blessed be He, stamps every man with the die of the first man and not one of them is the same as his fellow.[2]

The Bible and later Judaism understand this fundamental, divine value of each person and related values to require support to meet the needs of the poor. The Torah mandates practices in the context of a farming community. The corners of one's fields, gleanings, and forgotten produce are to be left for the poor to take, in addition to a tithe for support of the needy.[3] Rabbinic Judaism developed the Hebrew Bible's value of justice (*tzedek*) and institutions for support of the needy into *tzedakah*. That which is to be given to the poor never simply belonged to the giver, but was always God's, and was owed to the needy as their right.[4] Codifying traditions that go back to the Talmud and beyond, the *Shulhan Arukh*, the authoritative sixteenth-century code of Jewish law, states that "each individual is obligated to give *tzedakah*.... If one gives less than is appropriate, the courts may administer lashes until he gives according to the assessment, and the courts may go to his property in his presence and take the amount that it is appropriate for him to give."[5]

Jewish tradition does not provide a precise definition of "need" but offers paradigmatic examples, such as food, clothing, shelter, furnishings, and requirements of a family life.[6] The Talmud sets broad parameters for the extent of support in its exegesis of Deuteronomy 15:8, "You shall surely open your hand to him, and shall surely lend him sufficient for his need (or lack), according as he needs (lacks)." "'Sufficient for his lack'–you are commanded to support him, and you are not commanded to enrich him; 'according as he lacks'–even a horse to ride and a servant to run in front of him."[7]

Extraordinary needs are considered in the traditional category of *pidyon shevuyim*, the redemption of captives, such as those captured by slave traders or unjustly held prisoner. Moses Maimonides explains the special importance of aiding such individuals. "A captive falls in the category of the hungry and the thirsty and the naked, and stands in danger of his life."[8]

Traditional sources emphasize the urgency of the imperative to save lives and redeem captives, though they acknowledge limits. "One does not redeem captives for more than their monetary worth [as slaves] on account of *tikkun olam*," the "improvement of the world" and proper ordering of society. This provision dates back to the Mishnah, and the Talmud debates whether such a limit could be justified as protecting the community from onerous burdens, or as avoiding incentives for future hostage taking. The *Shulhan Arukh*, following Maimonides and other codifiers, accepts only the latter justification.[9]

The imperative to save life is powerful. The Book of Leviticus (19:16) commands, "Do not stand idly by the blood of your neighbor." The *Shulhan Arukh* specifies an application for health care: "The Torah gave permission to the physician to heal; moreover, this is a *mitzvah* [a commanded act] and is included in the category of saving life, and if the physician withholds his services, it is considered as shedding blood."[10] Physicians (and by implication other health care professionals) are urged to provide needed care to patients, without charge if necessary.[11] In the nineteenth century, Rabbi Eleazar Flekeles ruled that free care of the poor was not only a benefit to be expected from a virtuous physician, but a *halakhic* obligation enforceable by a (religious) court.

In twentieth-century Israel, Rabbi Eliezer Yehudah Waldenberg accepts this ruling but notes problems in enforcement even within a traditional Jewish community. The basis for the ruling, he observes, is that when an individual cannot afford to pay for medical care, the community (represented by the court) acquires the obligation for that person's healing. The community's responsibility reasonably falls on the physician more than on anyone else because of the physician's special knowledge and ability. Waldenberg asserts that while a virtuous physician is encouraged to provide charitable care, this can be enforced as a legal responsibility only in a community that has just one physician. In contemporary communities, with more than one physician, possible means to ensure needed care include appropriating money from the general *tzedakah* fund, conducting a special appeal, equitably apportioning cases to all physicians for treatment on a *pro bono* basis, and establishing a special fund for payment of physicians' fees.[12]

The imperative to save life plays a central role in shaping the distribution of health care. Powerful forces in the tradition would prioritize acute care necessary to save life. Contemporary rabbi and physician Avraham Steinberg acknowledges that "no country in the world can provide for all the medical needs of all its citizens in an equal manner," so rationing is unavoidable. At the same time, he insists that "vital medical services" cannot be compromised. "Society should be obligated to supply basic and vital needs to all its citizens equally."[13]

Other thinkers elaborate on the implications of unavoidable limits. Rabbi Elliot Dorff argues that other cases where the Jewish community faced scarcity—namely, supporting the poor and redeeming captives—should be used to create guidelines for determining the priorities and responsibilities for payment in our day.[14] Rabbi Noam Zohar states that the Talmud's concern for *tikkun olam* would require limitations on a community's provision of health care:

> The Jewish tradition postulates a strong obligation to provide for the basic needs of all members of society, and particularly for those whose needs involve mortal risk. This obligation devolves both upon individuals and upon the community as a political collective.
>
> At the same time, the tradition recognizes that this strong obligation cannot be deemed absolute. Sometimes, the community should refuse to lay out an enormous sum (in ransom), even though this may entail the death of a particular person. Limitations can be justified by concern over depletion of public funds, and also over future escalation in the requirements for life-saving expenditures.[15]

Zohar appeals to traditional precedents that call for managing market forces and imposing limits on profits for essential items such as basic food.

While acknowledging the imperative to save lives, Rabbi Yuval Cherlow argues that it could be appropriate to give priority to expenditures that promote the quality and not only the quantity of life. An identified patient in need should be helped, but formulating policies and planning involve not actual patients, but "statistical patients"; it is anticipated that some future patients will not receive some treatments, but in social planning no identified patients are deprived.[16] Cherlow suggests that there is not a sharp division between treatment to save life and that to improve the quality of life. As one example, a medication to reduce nausea accompanying chemotherapy directly improves the quality of life, and it may lead patients to accept chemotherapy, serving healing and extension of life as well as adding to its quality.[17] Also, suffering often will weaken a patient, and may even lead the patient to seek death. Further, some sources of the tradition indicate that extreme suffering may be even worse than death. Treatments to reduce suffering may be acceptable, even if there is some risk of shortening life.[18]

More generally, a government may legitimately pursue other important goals rather than devoting all resources exclusively to saving life. Similarly, individuals are not required to spend all of their money for another person's treatment even if doing so could save that person's life. Likewise, an individual should avoid harm to self but may legitimately choose to pursue activities and goals other than maximizing longevity. *Halakhah* accords significant priority to reducing suffering.[19] Others agree that society as a whole has legitimate interests and need not always give priority to the needs of an individual. The Talmud records a view that if two cities share a source of water, one may use water for laundry even if doing so interferes with the other's obtaining water for drinking[20]; authorities disagree about the extent to which laundry is important to preserving health and life, and whether the other town could obtain water for drinking from a less convenient source.[21]

Many authors agree that effective preventive care should be provided to the population generally, before people become ill and are patients, even if this does not fit the rescue paradigm as clearly as does acute care. A practical reason is that much preventive care is cost-effective. Moreover, prevention of illness provides important benefits and reduces suffering for individuals and loved ones.[22]

Finally, diverse authors acknowledge that contemporary national governments differ from the religious court discussed in classical sources. Cherlow notes that the government of Israel legitimately gives weight to the well-being and dignity of its citizens, as well as their diverse desires.[23] Authors in other nations, such as the United States, emphasize that the distribution of health care involves not only religious obligations, but responsibilities of justice that are incumbent on any society. They urge that Jewish understandings of justice contribute to a broader national dialogue.[24]

Notes

1. See also Aaron L. Mackler, *Introduction to Jewish and Catholic Bioethics: A Comparative Analysis* (Washington, DC: Georgetown University Press, 2003), pp. 3–15, 191–92, and Elliot N. Dorff, *Matters of Life and Death: A Jewish Approach to Modern Medical Ethics* (Philadelphia: Jewish Publication Society, 1998), pp. 14–33.
2. M. *Sanhedrin* 4:5.
3. Leviticus 19:9–10, Deuteronomy 14:28–29, 26:12.
4. See Aaron L. Mackler, "Judaism, Justice, and Access to Health Care," *Kennedy Institute of Ethics Journal* 1 (1991), p. 145. On the Jewish requirement to support the needy generally and the way that affects health care, see Elliot N. Dorff, *To Do the Right and the Good: A Jewish Approach to Modern Social Ethics* (Philadelphia: Jewish Publication Society, 2002), chap. 6; and Elliot N. Dorff, *The Way Into Tikkun Olam (Repairing the World)* (Woodstock, VT: Jewish Lights, 2005), chap. 5.
5. S.A. *Yoreh De'ah* 248:1.
6. Ibid., 251:1.
7. B. *Ketubbot* 67b.

8. M.T. *Laws of Gifts to the Poor* 8:10; see also S.A. *Yoreh De'ah* 252:1.
9. M. *Gittin* 4:6, B. *Gittin* 4:6, S.A. *Yoreh De'ah* 252:4, Mackler, "Judaism, Justice" (at note 4 above), p. 148.
10. S.A. *Yoreh De'ah* 36:1.
11. Elliot N. Dorff and Aaron L. Mackler, "Responsibilities for the Provision of Health Care," in *Responsa 1991-2000: The Committee on Jewish Law and Standards of the Conservative Movement*, Kassel Abelson and David J. Fine, eds. (New York: Rabbinical Assembly, 2002), pp. 328-30. Also available at http://www.rabbinicalassembly.org/sites/default/files/public/halakhah/teshuvot/19912000/dorffmackler_care.pdf (accessed June 12, 2012).
12. Eliezer Yehudah Waldenberg, *Ramat Rahel*, published with *Tzitz Eliezer* 5, *responsum* # 24. (1985, Hebrew); Mackler, "Judaism, Justice" (at note 4 above), pp. 149-50.
13. Avraham Steinberg, *Encyclopedia of Jewish Medical Ethics*, Fred Rosner, trans. (Jerusalem: Feldheim, 2003), vol.1, p. 42.
14. Elliot N. Dorff, *Matters of Life and Death* (at note 1 above), pp. 287-89, 300-306.
15. Noam Zohar, "A Jewish Perspective on Access to Health Care," *Cambridge Quarterly of Healthcare Ethics* 7 (1998), p. 264.
16. Yuval Cherlow, "Including Treatment to Improve Quality of Life in the Health Basket," *Tehumin* 28 (2008, Hebrew), pp. 384-85.
17. Yuval Cherlow, "How We Struggled and How We Decided" (Hebrew) http://www.themedical.co.il/Article.aspx?itemID=1377, posted November 9, 2008.
18. Cherlow, "Including Treatment," (at note 16 above), pp. 385-91.
19. Ibid., pp. 385-87.
20. B. *Nedarim* 80b.
21. Discussed in Steinberg, *Encyclopedia* (at note 13 above), vol. 1, pp. 45-46.
22. See, for example, Dorff and Mackler, "Responsibilities" (at note 11 above), p. 322; Steinberg, *Encyclopedia* (at note 13 above), vol. 1, pp. 43-46; and Cherlow, "How We Struggled" (at note 17 above).
23. Cherlow, "Including Treatment" (at note 16 above), pp. 385-89.
24. Dorff and Mackler, "Responsibilities" (at note 11 above), pp. 333-35; Mackler, *Introduction* (at note 1 above), pp. 194-95, 224-31.

Suggestions for Further Reading

Cherlow, Yuval. 2008a. "How We Struggled and How We Decided." (Hebrew) http://www.themedical.co.il/Article.aspx?itemID=1377, posted November 9, 2008.

Cherlow, Yuval. 2008b. "Including Treatment to Improve Quality of Life in the Health Basket," *Tehumin* 28: 383-91. (Hebrew)

Dorff, Elliot N. 1998. *Matters of Life and Death: A Jewish Approach to Modern Medical Ethics*. Philadelphia: Jewish Publication Society, pp. 279-310.

Dorff, Elliot N. 2006. "'These and Those Are the Words of the Living God': Talmudic Sound and Fury in Shaping National Policy." In *Handbook of Bioethics and Religion*, David E. Guinn, ed. New York: Oxford University Press, pp. 143-68.

Dorff, Elliot N., and Aaron L. Mackler. 1998. "Responsibilities for the Provision of Health Care," *Responsa 1991-2000: The Committee on Jewish Law and Standards of the Conservative Movement*, Kassel Abelson and David J. Fine, eds. New York:

Rabbinical Assembly, 2002, pp. 319–36. Also available at http://rabbinicalassembly.org/sites/default/files/public/halakhah/teshuvot/19912000/dorffmackler_care.pdf

Mackler, Aaron L. 1991. "Judaism, Justice, and Access to Health Care," *Kennedy Institute of Ethics Journal* 1: 143–61.

Mackler, Aaron L. 2003. *Introduction to Jewish and Catholic Bioethics: A Comparative Analysis*. Washington, DC: Georgetown University Press.

Novak, David. 2007. *The Sanctity of Human Life*. Washington, DC: Georgetown University Press, pp. 91–110.

Steinberg, Avraham. 1994. *Encyclopedia of Jewish Medical Ethics* (Hebrew). Jerusalem: Schlesinger Institute, s.v. "Allocation of Scarce Resources," 4: 245–72.

Steinberg, Avraham. 2003. *Encyclopedia of Jewish Medical Ethics*. Translated by Fred Rosner. Jerusalem: Feldheim, s.v. "Allocation of Scarce Resources," 1: 40–50.

Waldenberg, Eliezer Yehudah. 1985. *Ramat Rahel*, published with *Tzitz Eliezer* 5, *responsum* # 24. (Hebrew)

Zohar, Noam. 1998. "A Jewish Perspective on Access to Health Care," *Cambridge Quarterly of Healthcare Ethics* 7: 260–65.

Zoloth, Laurie. 1999. *Health Care and the Ethics of Encounter: A Jewish Discussion of Social Justice*. Chapel Hill: University of North Carolina Press.

CHAPTER 20

JEWISH BIOETHICS
CURRENT AND FUTURE ISSUES IN GENETICS

LAURIE ZOLOTH

INTRODUCTION

Jewish bioethics, in Jews' literature and discourse, has reflected deeply on the issues raised by the emerging science of human genetics and genomics. First, the particularity, individuality, and heritability of DNA stand in the popular imagination for the essential part of being itself.

Second, the discovery that molecular genetics affects illness and that distinctive genetic markers are indicators of risk plays a complex and heavily freighted role within the Jewish community. The modern story of genetic screening often begins with the classic success narrative of the Jewish community's response to the gene for Tay-Sachs carrier status. When this fatal degenerative disease, which devastates babies (who appear perfectly healthy at birth) within four years, was found to have a genetic cause, rabbis, community leadership, and physicians called for an immediate population screening. Tay-Sachs testing is still routine for all adolescent Ashkenazi Jews, a sort of a rite of passage of adulthood. This contemporary experience of genetic screening provides a successful test case for the mobilization of an entire community, the leadership of scholars, and the active rethinking of traditional norms to support new understandings of molecular genetics. With new advances in genetic testing, links of genes to diseases of adult life present far greater questions.

Third, while all bioethicists raise concerns about what is called "The Shadow of the Past," meaning the use of genetics as a part of the Nazis' justifying narrative for the genocidal destruction of European Jewry, Jewish bioethicists are bound to a particular attention to the possibility of genetic abuse.

All three factors play a significant role in the ethical issues in reflection on the genetic future by Jewish scholars. But as our most basic conceptions of health, illness, and normalcy are challenged by such new understandings, how ought Jewish scholars to respond? While Jewish texts and tradition clearly point toward support for all advances in medical technology that might save a life, Jewish history is shadowed by this darker narrative, that of the dangers of genetic markers that are linked to race and ethnic community. How can these complex ethical appeals lead to a public discourse about the goal, meaning, and obligations that we carry when we alter the human genetic structure in our struggle for health? What are the correct boundaries of the research goals? How can the Jewish population involved in testing for BRCA [breast cancer] markers honor both the claims of history and the vision of a scientific imperative? How far should we go in using genetics to assert a person's Jewish identity?

Naming and Being

Identity in America is a complex question. In large part, I know who I am, and you know who you are, because of how you are named by the ones who created you and who first loved you. This, of course, is not so different from the biblical story of naming. Just as creatures are called into identity and into meaning by the Yearning One, children are named into identity by parents who give them the sign that one hopes is descriptive, interpretive, or persuasive.

Genetics is, among many other things, a way to name and describe the processes that make us distinctive and particular. In the words of many who describe the genetic mapping projects, knowing and naming can help us "crack the code of Life," or "tell us who we are and why we behave the way we do," or "explain our traits." The genetic explanation—and here I am not thinking of the reductionist causality of one gene making one behavior—allows an understanding that genes, proteins, and the environment intricately signal one another and hence "write" the narrative of human action. The idea that inheritable characteristics determine family ties is an old notion, but the idea that membership in a class of others is similarly determined is an idea that gained ground only in the eighteenth century, when colonial expansion raised the problem of including others into categories of science.

Membership and with it moral status and social privilege become linked not to narratives of place, dress, or speech, but rather to something more tangible, the phenotype of persons. This physicality of how we knew what was valid, the link of the true with the observation of physical facticity, has transformed both the science and the polity of modernity. Identity is paradoxical for Americans, and in particular for American Jews, whose very entrance to an American future was predicated on losing aspects of identity such as place, language, and tradition. It is a country premised on the idea that who you were does not matter, who your parents were is not the determinant factor in this new land, all of which was challenging for the Jewish family. For many, this radical change in the role of one's heritage would mark the interruption of centuries of closed familial possibilities and yet enable the possibilities of shifting identity that urban and industrial concentrations required. Yet the mutable, spontaneous, and creative reimagining of the self has collided with another narrative, that of a deeply preorganized and highly structured internal code, a code which, for better or for worse, is passed between generations.

Hence, Jews in modernity hold two things in tension—that we are free of all previous and unchosen commitments, and that we are increasingly to be understood as having our fate scripted into our very cells. In thinking about what it means to reflect on identity in this way, one can reflect on how identity is shaped and altered by a genetic understanding. Yet the Jewish view of commitments themselves is also shaped by commitments to the Jewish tradition, text, and history.

The Essential Commitments of Jewish Bioethics

News about advances in medical science and the ability to craft human response to illness, disability, and disease are usually greeted with swift positive reaction in the Jewish community. This is in large part due to the normative response of the Jewish tradition to the mandate to heal the sick and nurture the vulnerable. It is also due in large part to Jewish optimism about the possibility of continuous *tikkun olam*, the acts of redemptive justice by which human persons use every single insight, skill, and creative impulse to repair the brokenness of the world. The constantly grounding, basic theological claims of Jewish thought can be summarized as follows:

First, it is the duty of each person to heal, to restore what is lost, including lost function or health, and to not "stand idly by the blood of your neighbor, (Lev 19:16)." Visiting, caring for, and healing the sick are not a subversion of God's edict but are rather the fitting response in the dialogic relationship between persons and God, the way that a Jew answers tragedy with faith, justice, and compassionate action together with a deep sense of reflection and humility. It is the liturgical response to the query of the Day of Atonement, Yom Kippur, when Jews ask—who will be "written in the book of life?" in a life in which all will experience loss and despair, and the burdens of illness will be borne without reason? The prayer that announces the inevitability of fate and the litany of dangers ("who by water, and who by beast, and who by plague?") also contains the rejoinder—*tefillah, tzedakah*, and, *teshuvah*[1] (prayer, charity, and repentance). It is the responsibility of the entire community to address the needs of the vulnerable, and it is of particular importance in Jewish law to tend to the needs of the sick. Rabbinic thought likens this responsibility to that of the farmer with a vineyard that he constantly prunes and tends[2]; medieval philosophers such as Maimonides remind us of the constant need for careful attention to preventive health,[3] and modern scholars[4] pay close attention to the duty to heal the sick, allowing and in fact mandating the full range of science and technology if it can be claimed to save a life—*pekkuah nefesh*. This mandate allows even acts normally unpermitted: working with the sick as a health care provider even on the Sabbath, using otherwise prohibited foods for the purpose of healing, or relaxing rules regarding contraception for a woman who is ill.[5]

Second, traditional Jewish law reminds us that our bodies belong, not "to" us, in the way that modernity claims for us autonomy, but "to" God. Elliot Dorff frames this idea as having a lease with conditions of use, and among these is the requirement that we seek to preserve health.[6] From the tradition of Maimonides, the eleventh-century Jewish physician,[7] we learn details of preventive care and of the physician's duty to use both natural and artificial means to affect illness and to work as an agent of God in the use of research, observation, and reason in the act of healing.

Third, the human body is good, the condition of the self is not fallen, the body and the self are not separate, and each of us, no matter what body we bear, is an image of God's presence. To save even one life is "to save a world"[8]; hence, procedures that could save a life are not only permitted, but mandated acts. Other arguments, especially arguments in theory or of later temporal concerns, would not stand against this mandate, and it is this argument that has driven acceptance of medical genetics even against other valid social fears. The need to help this good body far overrides inchoate fears about the future of the "human germ-line." In fact, many of the fears associated with genetic engineering—for example, the worry that some parents will enhance their prodigy to give them an unfair advantage—are so speculative as to be irrelevant when weighed against possible therapeutic uses. This position too is rooted in talmudic dicta that suggest that the danger that is present far overweighs even a greater danger that is only possible. [9]

Fourth, all people are obligated by basic rules of engagement and covenant. We are in general mandated to be for the poor, to stand against cruelty, and to be stewards within a condition that is essentially exilic. In this, we are understood to be on a progressive historical journey—bound East of Eden, into the plains of community, society, and the diversity of language. And Jews are bound in an additional way by their story of slavery and Exodus and the taking on of what Levinas called the commandments as "the responsibility for each other's responsibility," the ceaselessness of justice. This general dictum of stewardship and the progressive and historical nature of human knowledge shape the Jewish response to the natural world and the scientific, empirical task of understanding it and working with it. Medicine is firmly held in this larger tradition of stewardship.

Further, the tradition is framed in terms that are first, textual, second, discursive and of course, argumentative, and finally legal. Hence, when a new insight or research truth is claimed, this fact is then considered in light of the hermeneutic circle of text and debate in which response is made and justified in the terms of case-based precedent. This method of discourse is the primary basis for Jewish ethical response, and it assumes that cases will emerge from the scientific process that will change our moral understanding of the universe.

Applying These Tenets to the Specific Case of Breast Cancer Genetics

Given all of these general axioms as prelude, we can turn our attention to the complex responses evoked by the extraordinary new understandings in the field of cancer genetics as an example of how a promising, visionary effort of science that carries our best hopes for understanding, preventing, and treating cancer also raises complex ethical issues. .

As is indicated above, it was this very optimism and traditional faith in medicine that led to the classic success story of medical molecular genetics, Tay-Sachs. The Jewish community was quick to respond to the call for population-based Tay-Sachs testing. Traditional texts were mobilized to support testing and prenatal diagnosis, even selective abortion of an affected fetus. Virtually every pulpit issued the call, and every Jewish synagogue and communal center became a testing center. It is assumed that Jews of childbearing age know their Tay-Sachs status, and genetic tracking and testing have dramatically reduced the incidence of Tay-Sachs disease in the Jewish community.[10] In fact, the stored blood samples from that experience were used as the basis for some of the initial research for BRCA 1 and BRCA 2, the genes that have been shown to indicate increased risk for breast cancer.

Hence, we face a paradox: Tay-Sachs testing not only created the tissue sample banks from which to draw data; it created a precedent for calling for ethnically named populations, Ashkenazi Jews, to volunteer for testing. In fact, an ad in the *New York Times* calling for Jewish volunteers for BRCA testing, for Gaucher's and Canavan screening, and most recently for screening for cognitive disorders such as depression and schizophrenia, has become a commonplace.[11]

Facts about the Incidence of Cancer in Ashkenazi Jews

But of all of the speculative data that may yet be solidified about genetic links to behavioral diseases and disorders, the data that link increased risk of breast, ovarian, and colon cancers to specific genes seem to be the strongest. The proportion of high-risk families with BRCA 1 and 2 mutations that are linked to breast cancer does in fact vary widely among ethnic populations.[12] Two mutations of BRCA1—185delAG and 5382insC—are common in Ashkenazi Jews, with a combined frequency of 1 percent. About 20 percent of Ashkenazi Jewish families with two cases of breast cancer, one of which was diagnosed before the age of fifty, carry a mutation in BRCA1 or BRCA2. The risk of breast cancer in female BRCA1 mutation carriers is estimated to be 87 percent before age seventy.[13] The risk of ovarian cancer in this population is 39 percent.[14] In Ashkenazi Jews, the 617delT mutation is found in 24 percent of high-risk families, and in 6 percent of unselected breast cancer patients.[15] The 185delAG mutation produces a protein that is only 3 percent of the normal tumor suppressor gene BRCA1, rendering it unlikely to function normally, and these genetic shifts are found to be strongly linked not only with breast cancer, but with ovarian and colon cancers as well, in significant numbers.[16] Current research results are not in complete agreement, but they indicate that approximately 1 in 40 Ashkenazi women may carry one of the three known BRCA mutations, and that as much as 15 to 20 percent of all breast cancer in Ashkenazi Jewish women may be linked to hereditary genetics.[17] Recent research has indicated that the presence of the mutation in breast cancer patients is also an adverse prognostic factor. The probability of death in the first five years in the mutation-positive group tested was 35.7 percent, and in the mutation-free group, it was 4.3 percent.[18] Women who do not have a family history of breast or ovarian cancer but carry the mutation have a 56 percent chance of breast cancer, as opposed to a 13 percent chance in those without the mutation, and they have a 16 percent chance of ovarian cancer as opposed to a 1.6 percent chance.[19]

These numbers seem significant to researchers, and further, because they have been widely reported in the popular press, Jewish women's perception of their risk—and the perception of the men who love them—is deeply significant. Reaction to these statistics has been swift. Breast cancer is culturally framed as the new epidemic, appearing on the cover of magazines, becoming the subject of poplar culture and the arts, and, alongside AIDS, it has reshaped the way that Americans perform illness and death as both public and political acts. Opposition to breast cancer is seen as a sort of political cause; pink ribbons signal opposition to the disease and affiliation with those who are fighting it, worn in the same way as buttons to support candidates are worn.

The sense of epidemic is quite real. Breast cancer is the most commonly diagnosed form of cancer in the developed world, and the second most common cause of death for American women. There are 180,000 new cases a year.[20] In the wake of the most recent findings, the Jewish community leadership began to raise a call for immediate action on behalf of the Jewish community that was most affected by the data.

In April 1998 The National Institutes of Health leadership, including Francis Collins and Richard Klauser, director of the National Cancer Institute, addressed forty Jewish leaders, ranging from Orthodox to secular,[21] to assuage fears that discrimination, stigmatization, and marginalization could arise from these reports. Hadassah, the largest Jewish women's organization in the United States, has taken the issue as a central concern, focusing both local and national conferences on the topic. When one attends this organization's gatherings, one is handed both the traditional appeals for Israel support and brochures explaining risk factors and human genetics. But despite reassurances from the NIH that "genetic groups do not mean ethnic groups" (Klausner) or the equally firm but entirely contrary reassurance that cultural norms and not ethnicity just make it seem as if ethnic groups are genetic groups ("Jews are not afraid of volunteering for studies," "Jews trust medicine and like to be studied"), and despite the fact that availability of the Tay-Sachs samples might have "merely caused Jews to be first to be studied" (Collins),[22] the unease about the meaning of this work persists. What grounds the alarm?

MARKED AND NUMBERED IN THE GOLDEN LAND: THE CERTAINTY OF SCIENCE

The idea that the marked body of the Jew or the "different blood" of the Jew is linked to the Jew's marginal and precarious existence is nothing new. There is a historical link between molecular genetics and its applications of naming and noting social difference. Sander's work has extensively explored the European fascination with the Jew, the one who is marked with a secret defect, despite the appearance of assimilated normalcy. Under even the bourgeois clothing, the defective disorder could be found; linked to the oddity of the circumcised genitalia, or to the syphilis, or hysteria, the mark would ultimately be uncovered. Fearful of the discrimination that the large noses or large breasts might provoke, plastic surgery emerged to alter the body part that named the Jew as different, and as ill. Gilman notes too that radical surgery cured the despair caused by such discrimination.

In truth, then, physicians did in fact make the claim that the hereditary aspects that framed affective disorders could be changed by new medical advances. If you could change how the patient looked, changed traits that are clearly hereditary, then you could change her affect. In the nineteenth century, to be cut into a more "normal" visage reduced your risk for the Jewish diseases, especially for depression.

In the United States, the notion that Jewish genetic heritage was problematic, pathological, and socially dangerous to the "body politic" and surely not quite American was a standard of the popular rhetoric of the eugenics movement. Consider this quote from Dr. J.G. Wilson, writing in *Popular Science Monthly*. Wilson was the U.S. Public Health Service doctor in charge of standing at the gates of America, examining immigrants on Ellis Island in New York, the major portal for Ashkenazi Jews, hence the official voice of the new medicine in the *goldena medina* [Yiddish for "the golden land"]:

> If the science of eugenics deserves any practical application at all, it should insist upon a careful study of the...Jews, (because) the Jews are a highly inbred and psychopathically inclined race (whose defects) are almost entirely due to heredity...the general paranoid attitude of the race is shown in an almost universal tendency to fail to appreciate the point of view of one who opposes them.[23]

In other words, as Martin Pernick points out in his book about American eugenics, if Jews disagreed about the notion that they were inferior genetically, that position too could be seen as a universal pathology—anger, fear, and distrust of medicine seen as just more mental illness.[24] This view of the dark, defective Jew structured a system of quotas, elaborately reinforced by "scientific" IQ testing, that gave further evidence of hereditary feeblemindedness when Jews and other new immigrants struggled through language and culture to interpret the tests and failed.

Throughout the early twentieth century, this stance continued. Eugenics was championed not only by conservative or nativist forces, but by leaders of the Progressive movement as the correct, health-conscious, and socially responsible response to the public justice issues inherent in all diseases. This idea, that all disease had a social consequence and a social risk-benefit cost that ought to be a matter of public policy, was a formative notion of the health care systems, begun in the progressive era, that served the immigrant Jews. And the response of the American Jew was to embark on the "love affair" with all things American, to engage in the flight from traditional memes that marked the American Jewish leadership so strongly, in an attempt to leave the hereditary nature of the visible lifeworld of Judaism behind, to be in another family, the American one, with blondness, small noses, and whiteness as the markers.

The Record of Memory: State and Identity

But it was the mid-twentieth century that transformed eugenics from essentially a health fad, reported in Kellogg's newsletters, to murderous state policy. It is the link between eugenics, naming, and racism to extermination that created the shadow of the Holocaust that haunts all post-Shoah discourse. It is this shadow that one feels as the statistics of the Jewish links to genetic illness are numbered, and most of all this fear, of tagging, marking, and counting, that troubles even the use of genetics in cancer research. It is part of the cultural trope in the post-Shoah generations of Jews.

Consider the following image: as visitors walk into the first exhibits in the Holocaust Memorial Museum in Washington DC, they are directed past a large, bulky machine. It is one of the original computers, made by the German division of IBM, and its first use was to punch out and record German identity cards on which were noted, with precision, the markers of ethnic identity.

Across from the computer is a case that displays the hair swaths that were used to compare hair color and curliness so the computer could record this as well. Jew; curly, brown, and so forth. There are calipers to measure the Jewish nose and ~ze" (the distance between the eyes and how they are set) versus the Aryan nose ⁔. It is an eerie prelude to the piles and piles of Jewish hair, and the piles and 'eglasses that one will see later in the museum. The brown curly hair was collected in mountains to sell as mattress stuffing after it was shorn off the heads of the prisoners, just before they were gassed and burned, with technology developed and manipulated by the physicians that first used it in medical eugenics, and whose twinning experiments, and now whose research interest in cancer, we can still access if we choose. None of this history and none of these images are far from this generation of young adult Jews, and the resonance between the "defective" Jews of the Nazi imagination and the defective, marked genes of the Ashkenazi Jew called for by today's researchers seems clear. When one goes to the Internet, to medline, and types in "Jews," one now gets article after article with this genre of headline:

"New Defect Found In Ashkenazi Jews"
"Second Breast Cancer Gene Flaw Found in Jewish Women"
"Gene-Defect Rate Reportedly High in Jewish Women with Ovarian Cancer."

At stake in this consideration of the issue is not only how the issue is framed and what terms are used, but in the persistent question of privacy and the state. This too is raised by the image of the computer in the museum and the stack of punch cards that sit beside it. Exactly how much information is public, or is defining, or is in the records of the state in the way that other signifiers of our identity are recorded, and who will have access to all of this recording of data?

Who Is the Jew: Chosenness and Inclusion

The problem of the link between genetics and the ethnic, tribal nature of the Jew is not a new one. The long-standing uneasiness about ethnicity and chosenness versus conversion and inclusion of the stranger has existed in Jewish tradition since biblical times. It can be seen in the paradox of Ishmael, or the contradiction at the center of the Book of Ruth. We are enjoined both to avoid sexual encounter with the other, especially the Moabite women, yet a Moabite woman, Ruth, converts to Judaism and is genetically linked to David, upon whose genetic lineage tradition accords the Messiah-yet-to-come. We are enjoined never to draw attention to the convert in traditional Jewish life, and to consider the Jew-by-choice equal in all religious respects to the Jew by birth. Yet Jews struggle over the issue of matrilineal (and hence incontrovertible, at least until the advent of IVF and surrogacy) genetic descent. The recent advances in genetics that show the persistence of particular genetic patterns on the Y chromosome of the Kohanim, or hereditary priests, and that reveal that this pattern is found even in the African Lemba tribe who claim

Jewish ancestry,²⁵ are a powerful indication of the very narrative that the National Cancer Institute hopes will "break down." But the recent press of genetics in these examples has rather convincingly shown exactly the opposite, solidifying our sense of the link between ethnicity and genetic heritages.

The sense that one is fated to carry on a genetic and ethnic legacy that the statistics seem to indicate, that one is included in a specific and inescapable history, has caught many off guard, especially in an assimilated, up-to-date America that prizes the autonomous ability to completely control one's life. Here, one could buy a new future like another commodity, or be reborn from the impoverished immigrant as anything one chooses—Zen, or Sufi, or Republican. However, the one thing that one cannot be reborn into is a new genetic history. The statistics seem to suggest to modern Jews that no matter how far you run from the old neighborhood, you cannot hide from your collective fate; despite any attempts to hide who you are, your Jewish identity is permanently and inevitably revealed.

Jewish Mothers and Their Daughters

The advances in cancer genetics carry an additional concern, for the cancer is breast cancer, the new epidemic, and the battleground of the illness is the inscribed female body, the most public and fetishized, and yet the most private part of the body. Further, breast cancer erupts into American society in deep cultural unease about Jewish women at precisely the point of the visible contention—the breast. It is the Jewish mother, with her smothering, exaggerated breasts, and the frigid, withholding Jewish American Princess daughter, with her denial of sexuality, that is the modern American caricature of the Jew. As powerfully as the shifty Shylock haunted popular culture, it is the consuming Jewish mother rather than the German iconography of the hooked nose peddler that haunts it now. Portnoy's mother, Mrs. Robinson, and the mother of the Seinfield universe are the standing joke of popular culture. The link between the breast and the passing on of this fate from mother to daughter reifies the thematized relationship: the mother had a disease of mothering, she is a sick mother (breastfeeding or ovary production as the sites for the cancer), and hence the daughter's only choice is to prophalactically remove her own markers of sexuality and femininity, breasts and ovaries. She becomes the embodiment of the not-mother, all erotic surface denied, and thus her very ability to be either sexual or a mother is at risk.

All of this, then, unfolds within the context (the bosom!) of the family, with the attendant issues of guilt, intergenerational responsibility, and the complexity of survival, always an issue for Jews after the Shoah. I am not suggesting that these narrative themes of difference, genocide, or mothers are the *primary* issues, merely that they are a part of the inchoate ground of culture, internal psychodynamics and family responses that help us to understand the limits of the formal ethical discourse or the *halakhic* norms in this intricate, unfolding science. To be fully cognizant of what is meant by a Jewish response will go far beyond the usual textual search, which would stress the necessity of healing, of rescue, and of the primacy of medicine to a far more complex reflection on culture and meaning.

CLINICAL IMPLICATIONS AND EMERGING ETHICAL ISSUES

Cancer genetics has arisen rapidly as a new issue of both feminist and Jewish concern. The science has brought us to a particular place in our technologically limited medical universe, however. How will our new understandings of population-based epidemiology and its link to ethnicity alter classic ethical norms based on individual informed consent, the physician-patient relationship, and parental decision-making in genetic prenatal testing?

The first issue concerns adult women at risk for BRCA variations. Three issues emerge. The first are new calls for genetic testing for all Jewish women. Unlike the cost-effectiveness of testing all women, testing targeted populations (an unfortunate name in this context) might allow early intervention. Testing raises the inevitable issues of consent, truth-telling, and privacy. The best research is done with the most family members sampled. Short of compelling people to submit to research, what moral resources should be brought to bear on families or communities to participate? Until this year, the only prophylaxis was bilateral breast removal, and this was the option that has been taken in larger number each year.[26] New research with tamiloxafin suggests other alternatives. How will testing be done, how funded, and with what results? Once the test is positive, how will the discussion of prophylaxis be framed? How will treatment options be paid for in a country in which access to insurance can be tenuous at best and in which a preexisting condition can be cause for exclusion for coverage?

The evidence suggests that if the rabbinic and lay leadership can be convinced that a specific testing program could lead to the saving of a life, then the support of even a dramatic and sweeping population-based response should be undertaken. But unlike Tay-Sachs, even carrier status is a marker of the strong possibility of significant illness, not inevitable illness, and this probability, but uncertainty, of illness has implications not only for insurance actuaries and employers, but for family, friends, and potential partners. How will the community bear the weight of this foreknowledge? Surely new variations on the commandment to "be with," to visit, to witness the suffering and support the sick will need to be developed. Strong internal traditions of support despite fragility, which were classically a part of the communal traditions at an earlier historical period, will have to be renegotiated, without nostalgia, and with new intentionality.

Linked to this issue are articles in the literature about how prognosis can be linked to genetic predisposition. This link raised, for this author, complex issues of treatment, outcomes, and "medical futility."[27][28] If the treatment for a specific cancer can be shown to be statistically unsuccessful, should the treatment be offered in the hope that it will work for some minority? Is it just to alter treatment standards on the basis of such studies, only offering treatments with resounding success rates? Ought health care resource allocation decisions be based on such factors? Can such studies, which are also affected by socioeconomic class status, by social support structures, and by intangibles such as faith, in addition to a genetic marker, ever be unbiased? How can we protect women from not only the classic discrimination in employment and insurance, but even from treatment withholding or withdrawal rooted in such futility arguments? How ought we to triage limited resources? Whose voice should count, and to what extent, as we make these decisions?

Treatment of existing conditions is only the first step. As prenatal testing for a wide spectrum of genetic disorders becomes commonplace, social pressure will emerge, given all the factors mentioned above, for prenatal testing for BRCA carrier status. Prenatal testing issues raise other significant problems. Multigene genetic testing is now available and can be tailored to ethnic-specific mutations, hence the tests for Tay-Sachs, Gaucher's, and cystic fibrosis (CF). Here again, the Ashkenazim present what is called in the literature a "unique opportunity" to study a population at "increased risk for several recessively inherited disorders... about 1 in 8 Ashkenazi Jewish individuals is a carrier of either TSD, CF or GD."[29]

Studies in 1997 of couples who were considering prenatal testing revealed significant trends. Of the couples interviewed after testing, of note is the fact that 37 percent " strongly favored" and 11.2 percent "somewhat favored" termination of a pregnancy if the fetus was found to have Gaucher's disease, a mild, treatable endocrine disorder, and 58.9 percent strongly favored and 18.3 percent somewhat favored termination of fetus with Cystic Fibrosis, which may or may not express as illness, and which ranges in severity. Nearly all (80.5 percent strongly and 8.1 percent somewhat) favored termination of a Tay-Sachs fetus.

What would be the results if we were to add screening for BRCA mutations known to give a strong predisposition for hereditary cancers? Would we advocate the termination of female fetuses with the variant? Ought we as a society offer this choice, and whose decision will it be to make that policy? Would early detection allow for interventions in the other risk factors, diet, environment, and the like? Or, as with Tay-Sachs, if we could choose against such an embryo among a series from which we would choose some to implant, ought we avoid this condition altogether?

Moreover, issues concerning the use of testing begin earlier, if one is a member of certain circles of Jews in which marriages are arranged, factoring into the arrangement family status, health conditions, and ability to raise children in a traditional Jewish home. Elsewhere I have noted the use of genetic testing by the group known as "Dor

Yeshurin" (Generation of the Righteous), who began their work under the premises of the Tay-Sachs rubric and now test for several disorders prior to making matches. Such a practice, clearly begun to avoid the deliberate matching of couples with Tay-Sachs carrier status, now has far wider implications, raising the issue of stigma and risk.

Further issues await us. Since Ashkenazim are so available as research subjects, will the use of the insights and policies we create for cancer genetics be the template for the predisposition for the affective or cognitive disorders now being tested, including depression, schizophrenia, ADD, violent behaviors, and the full range of the psychopathologies that were assumed at Ellis Island? Will our determination to end the devastation of cancer open a door to another, darker room of possibilities? If we eliminate genetic variations, or the humans who carry them, who and what exactly are we losing? Why is it that these variants, these "Jewish defects," are so common, and to what else might this phenomenon be linked?

Where can we search for answers? At least in part, the answer will be found in the classic logic of text. Since so much of this discourse is about the Jew as pathological, or as a victim of fate, unwillingly marked, "who shall live, and who shall die," it is critical to return at this juncture to the traditional liturgical response of Yom Kippur in which this very notion is addressed. I noted in the beginning of this chapter that even once one's personal fate is sealed annually, and that fate cannot be fundamentally avoided, it can be ameliorated by community action, which mitigates the "stern decree" of illness or a bad fate.

How is this done? The liturgical text notes three methods. *Tefillah*: meaning prayer, in a faithful community and for collective search for meaning, is the first. *Tzedakah*: meaning both justice and world repair, including charity or some concrete action to make a world that cares for the poor and for the stranger. *Teshuvah*: meaning both being able to rethink one's actions with humility, and to literally "turn around" and begin again when you have gone wrong, to have the wisdom to understand if you have gone astray.

To begin to answer the difficult ethical questions will mean being equally clear about this aspect of what is carried by the Jewish tradition. We must pay attention not only to the mark of the genetic carrier, but to the textual resources that have allowed this specific community to answer the hardness of fate with resistance, endurance, and faith.

Ethicists are supposed to stand at such doorways and passages, peering around the next corner, imagining the secrets, fearing the worst, checking the monsters under the bed. When I first wrote about the ethical issues raised by genetics and Jews, my own children were small. I wrote about genetics because it was spoken of in the secular world in all the ways that theologians write of the future—the possibility of repair, of corrupted texts that are redeemed, of family, legacy and promises. As I wrote, they would cry out for me in the night, and I would go to them, wondering what they heard, in their worlds beyond mine, their quality of being-into-the future into which they will carry my, and their, and their people's broken and encircled DNA codes.

Now it is years later; they are grown with children of their own, and the puzzles of genetics are only inches closer to being solved. Ethicists write of theology and philosophy from these broken bodies, write of the elusive speech of God, the encoded word of God, and the love of the knowledge of the universe in which we struggle to read the text that is all around us. We are words from a body, in the way that Jews are a faith from within an embodied people. For Jews, the world comes with maps drawn up, another sort of codes to decipher, the biblical and talmudic records of struggles, the history and the commanded act of justice. These are the traces of light into this darkness, the room, which for Jews is only dimly illuminated, both with the memory of the fires of destruction, the bodies of the lost Jews gone in a blaze of hatred for the genetically different, and with the incandescence of our responsibility for ourselves and for the world.

Notes

1. See the Yom Kippur Liturgy, Mahzor, Soncino Press.
2. *Midrash Temurrah*, as cited in *Otzar Midrashim*, J. D. Eisenstein, ed. (New York: Hebrew Publishing Company, 1915), vol. II, pp. 580–81.
3. M.T *Laws of Ethics (De'ot)* 3:3. See also *Medicine and Jewish Law*, Fred Rosner, ed., (Northvale, NJ: Jason Aronson, 1990).
4. Avraham Steinberg, *Jewish Medical Law*, as compiled from Eliezer Waldenberg's *Tzitz Eliezer*, David Simons, trans. (Jerusalem: Gefen Publishing, 1980).
5. Immanuel Jakobovits, *Jewish Medical Ethics* (New York: Bloch, 1959).
6. Elliot N Dorff, *Matters of Life and Death:A Jewish Approach to Modern Medical Ethics* (Philadelphia:Jewish Publication Society. 1998), p. 15, and see generally Introduction and chaps. 1–2 for a description of the fundamental beliefs of Judaism that affect medicine and health care.
7. Fred Rosner, *Medicine in the Misneh Torah of Maimonides* (New York: Ktav, 1984).
8. M. *Sanhedrin* 4:5.
9. Although there are no texts that address the use of research science specifically, the Talmud is replete with stories about the general ability of the Rabbis to examine closely the abortus itself or closely to observe specific medical conditions. On the other hand, there are no *halakhic* texts that forbid basic research either. David Bleich notes that these phenomena are characteristic of several modern problems in medicine, where there are no clear textual referents. In a recent work he has used texts that refer to the necessity to build fortification around cities. The community must build walls in the face of danger, but the obligation that the community has to protect itself against "imminent danger" does not extend to danger that exists in the not-yet-existing future. Hence, by extrapolation, genetics work that promises the very real chance of saving a life is an obligation to pursue even in the face of other theoretical dangers. See J. David Bleich (Biolaw, Volume II) and J David Bleich, *Contemporary Halakhic Problems* 11:74–80.
10. In the year 2000, Michael Kaback reported that in the United States and Canada, the incidence of Tay-Sachs Disease in the Jewish population had declined by more than 90 percent since the advent of genetic screening. See Michael M. Kaback, "Population-Based Genetic Screening for Reproductive Counseling: The Tay-Sachs

Disease Model," *European Journal of Pediatrics* **159**: S192–S195 (December 2000). doi:10.1007/PL00014401. PMID 11216898. On January 18, 2005, the Israeli English language daily *Haaretz* reported that as a "Jewish disease" Tay-Sachs had almost been eradicated. Of the ten babies born with Tay-Sachs in North America in 2003, none had been born to Jewish families. In Israel, only one child was born with Tay-Sachs in 2003, and preliminary results from early 2005 indicated that none were born with the disease in 2004: see Tamara Traubman, "Tay-Sachs, The 'Jewish Disease,' Almost Eradicated," *Haaretz* (2005–01–18).

11. This leads to speculation about what the impact of such ads might be on the reader. Who are all of these depressed, unbalanced Jews the doctors are seeking?
12. Israela Lerer, et al., "The 8765delAG mutation in BRCA2 is common among Jews of Yemenite Extraction," letters, *American Journal of Human Genetics*, Volume 50 (June 1992), pp. 272–74.
13. Foulkes et al., "Germ-line BRCA1Mutation Is an Adverse Prognostic Factor in Ashkenazi Jewish Women with Breast Cancer," *Clinical Cancer Research* 3 (December 1997), pp. 465–69.
14. L. Robles-Díaz, D. J. Goldfrank, N. D. Kauff, M. Robson, and K. Offit, "Hereditary Ovarian Cancer in Ashkenazi Jews," Clinical Genetics Service, Department of Medicine, Memorial Sloan-Kettering Cancer Center, 1275 York Avenue, New York, NY 10021, USA.
15. C. I. Szabo and M-C King, "Population Genetics of BRCA1 and BRCA2," *American Journal of Human Genetics*, 60:1013–20 (1997).
16. Robles-Díaz (at note 14 above).
17. Ibid. See also Jaya M. Satagopan, et al., "The Lifetime Risks of Breast Cancer in Ashkenazi Jewish Carriers of BRCA1 and BRCA2 Mutations," *Cancer Epidemiology, Biomarkers and Prevention*, Vol. 5 (2010).
18. Foulkes, "Germ-line" (at note 13 above).
19. "Cancer Risk from Breast Cancer Gene Alterations in the Jewish Community," NCI Fact Sheet: Cancer Net from the National Cancer Institute (May 1999).
20. *National Action Plan on Breast Cancer*, National Institutes for Health, National Cancer Institute, November 23, 1997.
21. Meredith Wadman, "Jewish Leaders Meet NIH Chiefs on Genetic Stigmatization Fears," *Nature*, Vol. 392 (April 30, 1998), p. 851.
22. Ibid.
23. As cited in Martin S. Pernick, *The Black Stork* (New York: Oxford, 1996), p. 56.
24. Ibid.
25. M. G. Thomas, T. Parfitt, D. A. Weiss, K. Skorecki, J.F. Wilson, M. le Roux, N. Bradman, and D. B. Goldstein, "Y chromosomes traveling south: the cohen modal haplotype and the origins of the Lemba—the 'Black Jews of Southern Africa,'"PMID:10677325[PubMed – indexed for MEDLINE] PMCID: PMC1288118.
26. John Gever, "Survival Gain Seen with Prophylactic Breast Removal," 2010–02–25T04:26:31–04:00, Breast Cancer.Org. website.
27. Denise Grady, "Lymph Node Study Shakes Pillar of Breast Cancer Care," *New York Times*, February 8, 2011.
28. Susan Rubin, *When Doctors Say "No"* (Bloomington: Indiana University Press, 1998). Rubin deals with the emerging use of the term "medical futility" to limit treatment.
29. Christine Eng et al., "Prenatal Genetic Carrier Testing Using Triple Disease Screening," *Journal of the American Medical Association*, Vol. 278, No. 15. (October 15, 1997).

Suggestions for Further Reading

Davis, Dena S. 2001. *Genetic Dilemmas: Reproductive Technologies, Parental Choices, and Children's Futures.* New York: Routledge.

Davis, Dena S., and Laurie Zoloth. 1999. *Notes from a Narrow Ridge: Religion and Bioethics.* Hagerstown, MD: University Publishing Group.

Feldman, David M. 1968. *Birth Control in Jewish Law: Marital Relations, Contraception, and Abortion as Set Forth in the Classic Texts of Jewish Law.* New York: New York University Press. Reprinted as *Marital Relations, Birth Control, and Abortion in Jewish Law.* New York: Schocken, 1974.

Freedman, Benjamin. 1999. *Duty and Healing: Foundations of a Jewish Bioethics.* Charles Weijer, ed. and Introduction. New York: Routledge.

Green, Ronald Michael. 2007. *Babies by Design: The Ethics of Genetic Choice.* New Haven, CT: Yale University Press.

Holland, Suzanne, Karen Lebacqz, and Laurie Zoloth, eds. 2001. *The Human Embryonic Stem Cell Debate: Science, Ethics, and Public Policy.* Cambridge, MA: MIT Press.

Woodruff, Teresa, Laurie Zoloth, Lisa Campo-Engelstein, and Sarah Rodriguez, eds. 2010. *Oncofertility: Ethical, Legal, Social, and Medical Perspectives.*

Zohar, Noam. 1997. *Alternatives in Jewish Bioethics.* Albany: State University of New York Press.

Zohar, Noam. ed. 2006. *Quality of Life in Jewish Bioethics*, Lanham, MD: Lexington Books.

CHAPTER 21

JEWISH BUSINESS ETHICS

BARRY J. LEFF

Rabbi Yisrael Salanter had a student who was a *shohet*, a kosher butcher, who once came to him with a problem. He said, "Rabbi, I've been a *shohet* for many years, and as I grow older I become more concerned about my responsibilities. I'm so worried that I'm going to cause someone to eat nonkosher meat that I want to change careers: I want to give up being a *shohet*, and instead go into business." Rabbi Salanter asked him if he was an expert on the laws of *shehitah*, of kosher slaughter. The student replied, "Of course, I'm a *shohet*, I've been studying *shehitah* for years." The rabbi asked, "Are you expert in the laws of business?" To which the student replied, "No, of course not. Who bothers to learn *Hoshen Mishpat* (the Jewish laws dealing with business)?" The rabbi said, "Wait a minute, I don't get this. Here you are, you're an expert in the laws of *shehitah*, yet you are ready to give it up because of your fear of sinning. Yet you know nothing about the *halakhah* (laws) of business, and you want to go into business? All the more so you should worry about sinning!"

Many people assume that to be "religious" one must be punctilious about ritual commandments. Everyone knows that one must also be ethical to be religious, but they often assume that everyone "knows" how to be ethical in business, that it does not require a great deal of training. The truth is quite the opposite. Business is a complex process with competing values present in many situations, and so the moral course of behavior is not always intuitive.

Business ethics, a complicated topic from its very origins, is made even more so by rapidly evolving technology. Technology makes it possible to steal at the speed of light from the comfort of your own home. Technology makes it easier to defraud people, to steal intellectual property, to cause economic damage. Technology also makes theft possible on a scale unheard of in times past. In March 2010 a computer hacker was sentenced to twenty years in prison for stealing credit card information on 40 million people. The Boston Globe reports that according to the U.S. government, "retailers, banks, and insurers lost hundreds of millions of dollars in the data theft."[1] In a case involving sums that are truly staggering, rogue trader Jerome Kerviel cost his employer, SociétéGénérale, 4.9 billion Euros. His actions were not theft—he did not steal the money to put it into his account—but they were clearly unethical as they involved "breach of trust, computer abuse, and forgery."[2]

In addition to facilitating theft on a grand scale, evolving technology can make it difficult to figure out what is the moral thing to do in a complex situation. Is it theft to download a music file? To give a friend a copy of a software program? Is it ethical for an employer to snoop around on employees' Facebook pages, or to look up someone's Facebook account as part of a screening process for prospective employees? May an employer read employees' emails, or track their computer usage?

To answer such moral questions, the Jewish tradition uses the Torah (the five books of Moses) as our "grundnorm," the "Constitution," the basis for our legal system. An obvious question is "How can a 3,000-year-old book inform our thinking on the most modern and complex of ethical conundrums?"

While technology has evolved rapidly, human nature, alas, has not. The Torah tells us that after God destroyed the world in the flood, He said to Himself, "I will not again curse the ground because of man, for the inclination of man's heart is evil from his youth."[3] It has long been known that businesspeople in particular can be tempted to evil: hence the Torah contains, among other laws, warnings against using false weights and measures. That champion of capitalism, Adam Smith, also recognized the problem: "People of the same trade seldom meet together, even for merriment and diversion, but the conversation ends in a conspiracy against the public, or in some contrivance to raise prices."[4]

In an article in the *Harvard Business Review*, Albert Carr claims that a business's only responsibility is toward its shareholders. As a result, for Carr, "moral" is defined as "legal"; he writes, "The basic rules of the game have been set by the government, which attempts to detect and punish business frauds. But as long as a company does not transgress the rules of the game set by law, it has the legal right to shape its strategy without reference to anything but its profits." Carr believes businesses should do whatever they can to maximize profits, with the only moral concern to be to work within the boundaries of the law.

Carr wrote those words over forty years ago, in 1968. The business world seems much more enlightened today. In the wake of numerous major business scandals—Enron, Global Crossing, and Worldcom, to name just a few—society has come to recognize that business has responsibilities to parties other than shareholders, including customers, employees, and society as a whole. In the wake of major ethical failings on the part of large corporations, the law, at least in the United States, has also been greatly strengthened to encourage –and even mandate—moral behavior with the passage of a variety of laws, especially the Sarbanes-Oxley Act in 2002. In the wake of "aggressive accounting" practices intended to mislead the public, Section 303 of the Act states:

> It shall be unlawful, in contravention of such rules or regulations as the Commission shall prescribe as necessary and appropriate in the public interest or for the protection of investors, for any officer or director of an issuer, or any other person acting under the direction thereof, to take any action to fraudulently influence, coerce, manipulate, or mislead any independent public or certified accountant engaged in the performance of an audit of the financial statements of that issuer for the purpose of rendering such financial statements materially misleading.[5]

The business community itself also seems increasingly conscious of its obligations toward constituencies in addition to shareholders. At a commencement address given at Northeastern University on May 14, 2010, Kenneth Channault, CEO of American Express, said:

> Business exists because society allows us to exist; and in exchange for that permission to pursue profits, business must behave and act in ways that protect and enhance the world we live in. In other words, a business exists to serve its customers and the communities in which it operates. You can't just look at the bottom line.[6]

The Jewish tradition agrees that business has responsibilities beyond the bottom line. The tradition strongly disagrees with Albert Carr: simply obeying secular law is not good enough. The Talmud, a vast repository of rabbinic wisdom, theology, and law that is the foundation for modern Judaism, tells us that when a person passes away, the first question the soul is asked is, "Did you conduct your business affairs with integrity?"[7] It is not, "Did you observe the rituals?" "Did you eat only kosher food?" or "Did you observe the Sabbath?" The most important question is held to be "Did you conduct yourself ethically in your business dealings?"

How do we determine what defines "ethical" in a given situation? Obviously no one book (and even less an article!) can have all the answers. Instead, we need to understand certain basic principles and then learn how to apply them to a given situation. This chapter will address the following broad issues: (1) how Judaism deals with the issue of business ethics within a religious framework; (2) a discussion of fundamental principles of business ethics found in the Jewish tradition; and (3) some contemporary applications to illustrate how Judaism's understanding of business ethics is applied to contemporary situations.

Multiple Approaches to Jewish Law

Judaism has a body of law, called *halakhah*, which contains rules not only for ritual behavior but moral behavior as well. A full discussion of the different approaches to *halakhah* taken by the different movements within Judaism—Conservative, Modern

Orthodox, Reconstructionist, Reform, Renewal, Ultra-Orthodox, and so on—would be far beyond the scope of this chapter. To vastly oversimplify, the various forms of Orthodoxy and Conservative Judaism posit that following *halakhah* is obligatory; the other streams of Judaism tend to believe that, at least when it comes to ritual rules, *halakhah* is "advisory."

Within the Orthodox and Conservative camps, there are three approaches regarding what to do when there seems to be a conflict between *halakhah* and our sense of what is moral:

1. One approach says *halakhah* defines what is moral, so by definition there can be no conflict. If the *halakhah appears* immoral to us, it is simply a problem of perspective or understanding. If we truly understood God's will, we would not see a conflict.
2. A second approach says that if *halakhah* and morality are in conflict, morality trumps *halakhah*, and one should act morally despite the law ("civil disobedience").
3. A third school of thought would say that the *halakhah* should be adjusted to adapt to our evolving understanding of what is moral, which is guided by the Jewish tradition and *halakhic* precedent, but which also receives input from other sources.

In general—but only in general—Orthodox Jews follow the first approach, Reform Jews follow the second, and Conservative/Masorti Jews follow the third. Because the author of this chapter belongs to the third school of thought, that is the perspective from which the discussion will evolve.

Fundamental Principles

As a starting point Jewish law holds that it is a religious obligation to obey the laws of the land in which we live or do business. This is called *dina d'malkhuta dina*, "the law of the land is the law," a principle first articulated by the sage Samuel in the third century C.E.[8] Nahmanides, a thirteenth-century rabbi, succinctly describes the principle: "The law of the land is the law; all levies, property taxes, and laws that are judgments of the king that is customary (for kings) to impose on their kingdoms are the law, for all people in the kingdom accept the laws and statutes of the king willingly."[9]

Exceptions would be made if the law itself were immoral or contrary to the Torah. As was mentioned earlier, a Jewish approach to business ethics disagrees strongly with Albert Carr: obeying the secular law is a requirement, but it is only the starting point. We may impose requirements above and beyond what the secular law permits. If secular law says it permissible to steal in certain situations, we still would not permit or condone stealing.

A second fundamental principle of Jewish business ethics is that ethics is fundamentally a discussion of responsibilities, not rights. Ethics attempts to address the proper way in which to conduct ourselves. The *halakhic* system is well suited to a discussion of ethics, because it too is focused on responsibilities, not on rights. So, for example, Jewish law asserts that businesses have responsibilities to many other people. An employer has certain responsibilities toward employees, customers, society, and even competitors. Employees have responsibilities toward their employers and co-workers.

More specifically, the employer is obligated to provide a fair wage, offer decent working conditions, and pay employees on time. The employee, in turn, is obligated to provide the employer a day's work for a day's wages. *Halakhah* is so sensitive to this obligation that it eases certain religious ritual requirements so that employees do not waste their employer's time. For example, there is prescribed form of blessing to say after a meal. Employees who are working are told to recite an abbreviated form of the blessing to avoid causing the employer to lose any more time of his employees' work than necessary to fulfill this ritual requirement.[10]

The Jewish system of business ethics thus envisions a world of "fettered capitalism." The rabbis of the talmudic era recognized the benefits of capitalism and competition. Yet they were also aware that "the inclination of man's heart is evil from his youth,"[11] and they put constraints on business aimed at achieving an environment that is just toward all. Business owners have responsibilities beyond themselves and their partners, and beyond their employees. They also have obligations to their customers (e.g., to sell at a fair price). Overcharging is forbidden. Interestingly, customers also have obligations toward vendors: underpaying is also forbidden![12] Business owners also have an obligation to society and must repair any harm they cause to public spaces.

Lo Tignov—Do Not Steal

We now will explore some of the key precepts of Jewish business ethics. The list below is in no way comprehensive. These are just some examples of Jewish moral norms that have very common applications in the business world. There are many other "general ethical" rules that might be described, but these will suffice to give readers a sense of some of the norms of Jewish business ethics and how the tradition developed them to apply to multiple contexts. In each section below, after describing the norm, the chapter will suggest several ways to apply these general principles to some contemporary issues in business ethics. After discussing some central Jewish precepts in Jewish business ethics, we will provide some examples of contemporary rabbinic rulings on specific topics in business ethics to give readers a sense of how much this is a living part of the Jewish tradition in our own times.

The first norm is *lo tignov*—Do not steal. Everyone knows that this is one of the Ten Commandments. What may be less well known is that the rabbis have traditionally held that the "Do not steal" in the Ten Commandments refers to stealing people, that is, kidnapping. They derive this meaning because all the other "do not's" in the Ten Commandments are capital offenses, and kidnapping is the only form of theft that is a capital offense.[13] Ordinary theft of property is forbidden on the basis of several other verses in the Torah that explicitly forbid theft of objects such as sheep and cattle.[14]

More specifically to our interest in business ethics, the Torah is aware that commerce can provide special temptations to cheat, and so we are warned "You shall not have in your bag different weights, a large and a small. You shall not have in your house different measures, a large and a small. You shall rather have a perfect and just weight, a perfect and just measure shall you have; that your days may be lengthened in the land that the Lord your God gives you."[15]

These verses from the Torah teach us that it is not acceptable to cheat. If you are selling a pound of olives, you are obligated to deliver a full pound of olives. Obviously, this concept extends to other forms of business cheating and shortcuts. You are obligated to deliver "the full measure" of what the client buys. This is readily understood to include quality as well as quantity: a discussion in the Talmud shows that when people pay for a specific product—vinegar, medium-quality wine, or select wine—they are entitled to receive what they purchased.[16]

The concept of "do not steal" is extended beyond the theft of physical objects to include intangibles. We are forbidden to engage in *geneivat da'at*—deception, literally "stealing the mind," creating a false impression, or misleading people. The Talmud explicitly states that such deception is forbidden, and it specifies that one may not deceive "idol worshipers," which is to say not only gentiles, who are also ethical monotheists, but anyone at all.[17]

There are several examples of forbidden deception in the Talmud that we can use to extrapolate to contemporary situations. Some of these examples are:

- Letting a guest think you are opening a barrel of wine in his honor, when you plan to open the barrel anyway. This act would deceive the guest to think you thought he was worth a great expense, and it might prompt the guest to think that he must treat you with the same degree of honor the next time you are a guest in his home.
- Inviting someone to a meal when you know he will say no. (Does "let's do lunch" sound familiar?) Another contemporary equivalent would be offering to open a very expensive bottle of wine for a guest you are certain will say no.
- Giving some meat to a gentile and allowing him to think it is kosher and therefore more expensive than nonkosher meat when it is not. Even though the gentile is not required to follow the kosher dietary laws, you may not deceive him in this way, both because he may inadvertently give it to a Jew thinking it is kosher, and because you are misleading him into thinking you are more generous than you are.
- Inviting someone to anoint himself with oil when you know the jar is empty.

- Offering many gifts to someone if you know he will not accept. Note that exceptions would probably be made for cultures where it was expected both to make the offer and to reject it, since there is no deception in that context.[18]

Contemporary applications abound:

- Misleading advertising. This is a complex area that requires careful case-by-case consideration. Although it is forbidden to make false claims or to mislead intentionally, it is permitted to make your product look/sound as attractive as possible. There are those who might argue, for example, that advertisements for cars showing sexy women getting out of the cars are misleading because they imply that if a man buys that car, he will attract that kind of woman. I would disagree, because I do not think anyone believes a man's buying the right car will lead to sexy women throwing themselves at him; rather the manufacturers are trying to convey a certain image, to appeal to a particular demographic, and that is not forbidden.
- Concealing flaws. For example, if you were selling a used car, it would be forbidden to put extra heavy weight oil in the car to conceal the fact that the car had an oil leak.
- Misleading financial statements. Any actions that would cause potential investors to think the company is financially healthier than it is to encourage them to invest is forbidden. For example, if a client asks a company to invoice them before the end of the year so that it uses up the prior year's budget, even though the goods are not shipped until later in the following year, it would be forbidden to claim all of that revenue without booking a corresponding liability for the goods not yet shipped. Failure to do so would artificially inflate the receiving company's profits, because they will have recorded the revenue but not yet recorded the associated expenses.

Ona'at Mamon—Price Fraud

Ona'at mammon (price deception or price fraud) is a very important prohibition that teaches us that we have to "play fair." The concept is related to theft, although unlike *geneivat da'at* (deception), *ona'at mammon* is a specific prohibition found in the Torah. Leviticus 25:14 states, "When you sell anything to your neighbor or buy anything from your neighbor, you shall not deceive one another."

The Mishnah articulates very specific guidelines as to what constitutes price fraud: selling an object for more than 1/6 above what it is "really" worth. Interestingly—and very much at odds with our normally accepted ideas about fairness in pricing—it is equally forbidden to *underpay*. Paying more than 1/6 *below* the real price is also forbidden, and such a transaction can be legally nullified. A reasonable profit is allowed, and some variation in pricing is acceptable, but overall prices should be "fair."

One of the biggest problems in applying this principle is determining what constitutes the "same product." Two stores may be selling what appears to be the same product, but one store might provide a better warranty, or have different payments terms, or offer much better customer service, and so on, all of which could be sufficient to say that the product is not exactly the same and a price differential greater than 1/6 is justified.

Hasagat G'vul—Honoring Boundaries

Another principle related to theft is *hasagat g'vul*, or "moving boundaries." *Hasagat g'vul* provides an excellent illustration of how a concept has evolved over time: from a simple rule in the Torah not to steal land by moving a boundary marker, the tradition has evolved into a prohibition against unfair competition, and then this is further extended to protect intellectual property.

Hasagat g'vul literally means "moving a boundary," and the concept is rooted in a prohibition found in the Torah: "You shall not remove your neighbor's landmark.."[19] In other words, do not steal his land by moving the landmarks used to delineate the boundaries of his field.

The Talmud extends this concept to tradespeople and competition. In the Babylonian Talmud, *Bava Batra* 21b, we find the following teaching: "If a resident of a *cul de sac* sets up a mill to grind grain for others, and then a fellow resident of the *cul de sac* comes and sets up a mill in the same street, the law is that the first one can stop the second one, for he can say to him 'You are cutting off my livelihood!'" The same discussion in the Talmud brings another example—namely, that fishermen have to respect each other's fishing areas, even though the fish themselves are ownerless: "Fishing nets must be kept away from [the hiding place of] a fish [that has been spotted by another fisherman] the full length of the fish's swim."

The Rabbis did, however, recognize that competition can be a good thing, bringing lower prices, and that other people—competitors—are entitled to make a living as well. The Talmud provides several examples of limits to the ability to argue "you are interfering with my livelihood." This is one of them:

> Certain basket-sellers brought baskets to Babylon [to sell]. The townspeople came and stopped them [because they did not want the competition], so they [the basket sellers] appealed to Ravina. He said, "They have come from outside [the town], and they may sell to the people from outside [the town]. This restriction, however, applies only to the market day, but not to other days; and even on the market day only for selling in the market, but not for going round to the houses."[20]

We can see in this example that the Rabbis were concerned about balancing the livelihood of the local basket-sellers against the desire of the townspeople for competition and the ability of the itinerant basket-sellers also to make a living.

In the last few hundred years, the principle of *hasagat g'vul*, not to move boundaries, has even been extended as a rationale for the protection of intellectual property. The Rabbis see it as a natural extension: since the Talmud, for example, expressed a concern about protecting the livelihood of a fisherman who had invested effort in a particular fish run, it follows that we should also protect the livelihood of someone who has invested effort in creating something new, such as a book, a song, or an invention.

Respecting boundaries is a fundamental principle that applies to many of our business relationships. Some of the ways this principle finds expression in contemporary business situations are these:

- One must honor confidentiality agreements between an employer and employee, or between companies.
- One must have respect for the intellectual property rights of others.
- Anti-competitive behavior—for example, using predatory pricing to drive competitors out of the market so you can raise your prices afterward—is prohibited.

The balance the Rabbis tried to strike in extending the concept of *hasagat g'vul* to unfair competition is exactly what antitrust laws try to accomplish—to permit competition but to put limits on competition to avoid situations that are patently unfair.

Lo Titein Mikhshol—Do Not Put a Stumbling Block before the Blind

Another fundamental principle that highlights our responsibilities toward others is the concept of "Do not put a stumbling block before the blind." The Torah commands this: "You shall not curse the deaf, nor put a stumbling block before the blind, but shall fear your God; I am the Lord."[21] In addition to the literal meaning of the verse, referring to physically blind people, the Rabbis of the Talmud interpret "blind" metaphorically: they take it to mean anyone who is unaware of something, who does not see something, who has a "blind spot." With this principle, the Jewish tradition raises our responsibilities toward others to quite a high level: we are not allowed to do things that would cause someone else to sin, that would cause someone else to do something wrong. We are commanded not to give bad advice.

There are many examples given in the Talmud, including these:

- Do not offer a Nazirite (someone who has taken a vow not to drink wine) a glass of wine.[22]
- Do not offer to lend—or ask to borrow—money at interest because you would cause the other person to violate the prohibition on lending money to a fellow Jew at interest (the Rabbis eventually did find ways to allow lending at interest).[23]

- One should not entrust animals to a shepherd if there is a good chance he will allow the animals to graze on someone else's property, thus stealing the grass on which the animals graze.[24]

Contemporary ways this principle may be applied include these:

- There are many situations where being in violation of the prohibition on deception (see above) would also result in placing a stumbling block before the blind, such as creating misleading financial statements, or misleading advertising, where the actions could cause someone to be "blind" to the actual financial health of a company or the worthiness of a product and to harm himself as a result.
- A salesperson recommending an item because he gets a bigger commission on it, not because it would be best for the client, violates this norm. It is not forbidden for a manufacturer to encourage the sale of certain of their products over others. What is forbidden, where the line gets crossed, is when the best needs of the client are ignored in the process.
- Offering a bribe or kickback is also banned by this rule. An employee is supposed to be working in the best interests of his employer, not to line his own pockets. If you offer someone a bribe, you are causing him or her to stumble because he or she will no longer be acting in the best interests of his or her employer.

Contracting

One of the most basic features of the business world today is the contract. Whenever two companies enter into a business relationship, a contract defines the terms of the deal and generally specifies what happens if something goes wrong. Contracts are common with consumers as well; one of the most common forms of contract nowadays governs the purchase of software. The manufacturers generally state that by opening the package or clicking "purchase," the buyer is in essence entering into a contract with the seller and is agreeing to abide by the terms of the sale and the restrictions on making copies. The acceptability and authority of such "shrink-wrap" contracts are complex issues in both American and Jewish law.

The Jewish approach to contracting is similar to the approach highlighted above regarding all business transactions: "play fair." Two basic rules in a Jewish approach to contracts are: (1) deception is forbidden; and (2) you have to have a "meeting of the minds."

- *Mi'dvar sheker tirhak*—"Stay far from a false matter" (Exod 23:7). The Rabbis of the Talmud, in tractate *Shevu'ot* (oaths), explicitly apply this rule of the Torah to settling a variety of disputes. For example, they say this:

- How do we know that if three persons have a claim of a hundred *zuzim* against one person, one should not be the litigant, and the other two, the witnesses, in order that they may extract the hundred *zuzim* and divide it? Because it is said: "From a false matter keep far."[25]
- The Rabbis also acknowledge, however, that in normal daily life there may be some exceptions. So, for example, when Shammai opposes calling an ugly woman a "beautiful bride," in keeping with "Keep far from a false matter," his colleague, Hillel, retorts that she is surely beautiful in the eyes of the groom, so it is no sin to praise her to the groom.
- *Mekah ta'ut*—an erroneous transaction. If two parties make an agreement but it turns out that one of the basic assumptions was wrong, the deal is null and void. The Talmud gives an example of a person who thought he had some excess money, contracted with his partners to use that money to pay their tax bill, but later found out that he did not actually have any excess money. The Rabbis called this a flawed transaction and cancelled the contract.[26]

SOME EXAMPLES FROM CONTEMPORARY RABBINIC RULINGS

We can now proceed to describe some examples from contemporary rabbinic rulings about specific issues to illustrate that Jewish business ethics was not just a matter of concern in the past but rather occupies contemporary rabbis and lay Jews as well. We will develop one example in some depth of how Jews apply all of this ancient wisdom to contemporary situations that were beyond the imagination of the Rabbis of centuries ago—namely, the issue of intellectual property—and then we will note several other examples to illustrate how contemporary rabbis have applied to modern times the Jewish tradition's sources and values on business ethics.

What wisdom would the Jewish tradition bring to the question of whether it is permissible to trade digital music files with your friends? Many young people today (and some not so young) claim that there is nothing wrong with swapping music files on sites such as the now-defunct Napster. Among various rationales presented are these: (1) No one is actually harmed, because you are not physically "taking" anything from anyone; (2) the person copying the file was not going to buy it anyway; (3) the trade provides more exposure for the artist's music, so you are actually "helping" the artist.

In my rabbinic ruling, "Intellectual Property: Can you steal it if you can't touch it?" I argue that it is wrong to engage in such file-swapping. Some of the arguments can be a bit technical. For those interested, the full paper is available online at the link cited in this note.[27]

First and foremost, there is the principal of *dina d'malkhuta dina*, "the law of the land is the law." We are required to follow the laws of the places where we live, unless such laws directly contradict Torah law. Thus, just the fact that it is easy to circumvent a law does not mean it is acceptable to do so.

But beyond the obligation to be a law-abiding citizen, there are several principles we can apply from within the *halakhic* system as well.

The first question that had to be addressed was the status of intangibles under *halakhah*. There are talmudic statements that would seem to weigh against giving intangibles any consideration; these are offset by the principle that we follow *minhag ha—makom,* local custom, and it is certainly not only a local custom but virtually a global custom to treat intellectual property (IP) as something valuable that is, and should be, legally protected. The status of intangibles such as IP under *halakhah* has evolved accordingly.

Secular law has taken two different approaches to the protection of intellectual property. In America and most common-law countries, IP laws are based on a "public good" argument, that there is a benefit to the public to encourage invention and innovation by offering this protection. In Europe and elsewhere, the laws are more often based on a "moral right" argument, that an inventor/author has a moral right to "own" his intellectual creations.

Both approaches can also be seen in a Jewish approach to the issue. Similar to the European "moral right" argument, we can invoke *hasagat g'vul*, the principle discussed above of respecting boundaries, to say that the inventor/author has a moral right to a livelihood from the things in which he or she has invested time and creativity. Presumably because there are more Jewish authors than Jewish inventors, the *responsa* literature contains many more references to copyright issues than to patent issues. In one of the rare rabbinic rulings addressing patent issues, Rabbi Ovadiah Yosef, the most important living rabbi for those of the Sefardi (Mediterranean) Jewish tradition, stated this: "When a person invents new technology and patents a particular subject, no one is permitted to distribute it without permission of the inventor because of *hasagat g'vul*."[28]

Additionally, there are those who have argued that the author has a right to what is called *shi'ur b'kinyan,* a "limited sale" –that is, that when he sells something, he can place limits and restrictions on the sale, that the seller can determine just what it is he is selling. Therefore he can sell the right to listen to something, but not the right to copy it as part of the sales contract. This situation is similar to the idea in secular law that the sale of something like a video or music CD may include some rights ("fair use") but not other rights (making unlimited copies).

Ever since at least the seventeenth century, rabbis have recognized that there is a public good served by encouraging the publication of books. For centuries it has been common for rabbis to write letters of recommendation that would be printed in a book of Torah learning. Around the seventeenth century it started to become common for rabbis to include in their letters of recommendation a statement prohibiting anyone else from publishing the book, usually for a specified number of years, in order to allow the publisher to recoup its costs. In this case, the rabbis were not concerned with the "moral rights" of the author: they were concerned with the public good of having more works of Torah published. Along these lines, a nineteenth-century rabbi, the Hatam Sofer, wrote this:

> If we were not to close the door in the face of other publishers [i.e., prohibit competition], which fool would [undertake the publication of Judaica and] risk a heavy financial loss [lit., "a loss of several thousands"]? The publication [of Jewish works] will cease, God forbid, and Torah [study] will be weakened. Therefore, for the benefit of the Jewish people and for the sake of the exaltation of the Torah, our early sages have enacted [this ban]..."[29]

In some cases the rabbis added colorful warnings invoking curses and "serpent's bites." This example illustrates how *halakhah* has evolved over time, bringing to bear over 3,000 years of thinking on ethical issues to the most contemporary of problems.

Other contemporary examples, taken from the *responsa* of Judaism's Conservative and Orthodox movements, of how a Jewish approach to business ethics balances the needs of the individual and the needs of society or others include these:

- May an employer monitor an employee's email? The conclusion is "yes," provided that the employer notifies the employees ahead of time that such monitoring may occur.[30]
- Does an employee have a responsibility to report wrongdoing on the part of his/her employer? The conclusion is "yes," although he does not have to destroy his/her livelihood to save others from a minor financial loss.[31]
- Is there an obligation to pay workers a "living wage"? The conclusion is yes, that Jewish tradition mandates not only a minimal "living wage," but that even the lowest-level workers must be treated with dignity and respect.[32]
- Should a businessperson who is a manager, not an owner of a business, behave ethically even if doing so will cost his employers money? The conclusion is yes, it is inconceivable that society would hold to ethical principles and then create an entity (the corporation) that is exempt from those principles.[33]

In all fairness, it should also be noted that just as is the case in the secular court system, where different judges may come to different conclusions about the same set of facts, opinions may vary regarding specific situations. But the basic principles of balancing competing interests and seeking an outcome that is "fair" are universal in Judaism's approach to business ethics.

Conclusion

We can see that the Jewish approach to business ethics does not impose one-sided support for any particular group (employers vs. employees, individuals vs. society), but rather is an attempt to find a nuanced balance between competing interests so that the final conclusion represents a solution readily recognized as just. This attempt to balance competing needs is illustrated by Hillel's famous maxim from *Pirkei Avot (Ethics of the Fathers)*: "If I am not for myself, who will be for me? And if I only care for myself, what am I?"[34] More than a slogan, "Justice, justice you shall pursue"[35] is the overall guiding principle for Jewish ethics.

On an individual level we are charged to go beyond simply being just; we must also be compassionate, going *lifnim meshurat hadin*, beyond the strict "letter of the law." An example is given in the Talmud of workers who broke a barrel of wine. Even though by strict *halakhah* the workers could have had their wages docked, they complained, "We are poor, and if you withhold our wages, we cannot eat." When the business owner consulted his rabbi, he was told, "Go and pay them [their full wages]." The owner asked "Is that the law?" "It is indeed," the rabbi continued, "[for we are enjoined to] Keep the path of the righteous."[36] The Jewish tradition thus envisions a world where in business as in all other areas of life, we act *lifnim meshurat hadin*, beyond the strict letter of the law, to create a world of peace, harmony, and compassion.

Notes

1. "TJX Hacker's 'Lieutenant' Gets 7-Year Sentence," *The Boston Globe*, March 30, 2010. Online at http://www.boston.com/business/articles/2010/03/30/tjx_hackers_lieutenant_gets_7_year_sentence_for_role_in_credit_card_data_theft/.
2. "French Rogue Trader Jérôme Kerviel Sentenced to Jail and €4.9bn Fine," *The Guardian*, October 5, 2010. Online at http://www.guardian.co.uk/business/2010/oct/05/jerome-kerviel-jail-sentence.
3. Genesis 8:21.
4. A. Smith, *An Inquiry Into the Nature and Causes of the Wealth of Nations* (Chicago: University of Chicago Press, 1776/ 1952), p. 55.
5. Section 303, H.R. 3763, a.k.a. "The Sarbanes-Oxley Act of 2002."
6. http://www.youtube.com/watch?v=Misqgyf5rPQ, time 9:10.
7. B.*Shabbat* 31a.
8. B. *Gittin* 10b, B. *Nedarim* 28a. See also S.A. *Hoshen Mishpat* 369:6.
9. *Responsa* of Ramban (Nahmanides), *siman* 46 (Hebrew).
10. B. *Berakhot* 16b.
11. Genesis 8:21.
12. B. *Bava Metzia* 49b.
13. B. *Sanhedri* 86a.
14. For example, Exodus 21:37; Leviticus 19:11.
15. Deuteronomy 25:13–15.
16. B. *Bava Metzia* 73b.
17. B. *Hullin* 94a.
18. All of the above examples also come from B. *Hullin* 94a.
19. Deuteronomy 19:14.
20. B. *Bava Batra* 22a.
21. Leviticus 19:14.

22. B. *Pesahim* 22b.
23. B. *Bava Metzia* 75b.
24. B. *Bava Metzia* 5b.
25. B. *Shevu'ot* 31a.
26. B. *Gittin* 14a.
27. Barry Leff, "Intellectual Property: Can you steal it if you can't touch it?," (approved by the Conservative Movement's Committee on Jewish Law and Standards, December 12, 2007), http://www.rabbinicalassembly.org/sites/default/files/public/halakhah/teshuvot/20052010/leff_IP.pdf.
28. Ibid., p. 15.
29. *Hatam Sofer* 6:57.
30. Elliot Dorff and Elie Spitz, "Computer Privacy" (approved by the Conservative Movement's Committee on Jewish Law and Standards, March 13, 2001,http://www.rabbinicalassembly.org/sites/default/files/public/halakhah/teshuvot/19912000/dorffspitz_privacy.pdf (accessed June 25, 2012).
31. Barry Leff, "The Requirement to Report Employer Wrongdoing," (approved by the Conservative Movement's Committee on Jewish Law and Standards, December 12, 2007), http://www.rabbinicalassembly.org/sites/default/files/public/halakhah/teshuvot/20052010/leff_whistleblowing.pdf (accessed June 25, 2012).
32. Jill Jacobs, "Work, Workers and the Jewish Owner" (approved by the Conservative Movement's Committee on Jewish Law and Standards, May 28, 2008), http://www.rabbinicalassembly.org/sites/default/files/public/halakhah/teshuvot/20052010/jacobs-living-wage.pdf.
33. "Asher Meir, Value Conflicts in Jewish Business Ethics: Social Versus Fiduciary Responsibility," published onine at http://www.jlaw.com/Articles/fiduciary.html.
34. M. *Avot* 1:14.
35. Deuteronomy 16:20.
36. B. *Bava Batra* 83a. The biblical verse cited is Proverbs 2:20.

Suggestions for Further Reading

Bodner, Yisroel Pinchos. 2003. *Halachos of Other People's Money*. Jerusalem: Feldheim.

Dorff, Elliot N. 2001. "Judaism, Business, and Privacy." In Herman and Schaefer, eds., *Spiritual Goods*. An expanded form of this article appeared in his book, *For the Love of God and People: A Jewish Approach to Modern Personal Ethics*. Philadelphia: Jewish Publication Society, 2003, chap. 2.

Dorff, Elliot N. 2005. "Nonprofits and Morals: Jewish Perspectives and Methods for Resolving Some Commonly Occurring Moral Issues." In *Good Intentions: Moral Obstacles and Opportunities*, David H. Smith, ed. Bloomington: Indiana University Press.

Dorff, Elliot N. 2009. "Donations of Ill-Gotten Gain." http://www.rabbinicalassembly.org/sites/default/files/public/halakhah/teshuvot/20052010/Dorff_Donations%20of%20Ill-Gotten%20Gain.FINAL.062909.pdf (accessed June 25, 2012).

Dorff, Elliot N., and Elie Kaplan Spitz. "Computer Privacy and the Modern Workplace" http://www.rabbinicalassembly.org/sites/default/files/public/halakhah/teshuvot/19912000/dorffspitz_privacy.pdf (accessed June 25, 2012).

Green, Ronald M. 2001. "Guiding Principles of Jewish Ethics." In Herman and Schaefer, eds., *Spiritual Goods*.

Herman, Stewart W., with Arthur Gross Schaefer, eds. 2001. *Spiritual Goods: Faith Traditions and the Practice of Business*. Charlottesville, VA: Philosophy Documentation Center.

Jacobs, Jill. 2008. "Work, Workers, and the Jewish Owner." http://www.rabbinicalassembly.org/sites/default/files/public/halakhah/teshuvot/20052010/jacobs-living-wage.pdf. and see the responses of Elliot Dorff and Marc Gary on the same website.

Jacobs, Jill. 2009. *There Shall Be No Needy: Pursuing Social Justice Through Jewish Law and Tradition*. Woodstock, VT: Jewish Lights.

Leff, Barry. 2007. "Intellectual Property: Can You Steal It If You Cannot Touch It?" http://www.rabbinicalassembly.org/sites/default/files/public/halakhah/teshuvot/20052010/leff_IP.pdf (accessed June 25, 2012).

Leff, Barry. "Whistleblowing: The Requirement to Report Employer Wrongdoing." http://www.rabbinicalassembly.org/sites/default/files/public/halakhah/teshuvot/20052010/leff_whistleblowing.pdf (accessed June 25, 2012).

Levine, Aaron. 1980. *Free Enterprise and Jewish Law: Aspects of Jewish Business Ethics*. New York: Ktav and Yeshiva University Press.

Levine, Aaron. 1987. *Economics and Jewish Law: Halakhic Perspectives*. New York: Ktav and Yeshiva University Press.

Levine, Aaron. 2000. *Case Studies in Jewish Business Ethics*. New York: Ktav and Yeshiva University Press.

Levine, Aaron. 2005. *Moral Issues of the Marketplace in Jewish Law*. Brooklyn, NY: Yashar Press.

Spitz, Tzvi. 2001. *Cases in Monetary Halachah*. New York: Mesorah Publications.

Tamari, Meir. 1986. *With All Your Possessions: Jewish Ethics and Economic Life*. New York: Free Press.

Tamari, Meir.1991. *In the Marketplace: Jewish Business Ethics*. New York: Feldheim.

Tamari, Meir. 1995. *The Challenge of Wealth: A Jewish Perspective on Earning and Spending Money*. Northvale, NJ: Jason Aronson Press.

Teutsch, David A. 2007. *Organizational Ethics and Economic Justice*. Wyncote, PA: Reconstructionist Rabbinical College.

Zoloth, Laurie. 2001. "Her Work Sings Her Praise: A Framework for a Feminist Jewish Ethic of Economic Life." In Herman and Schaefer, eds., *Spiritual Goods*.

In addition, readers may want to consult the following websites for rabbinic rulings and/or articles from particular points of view:

Conservative: http://www.rabbinicalassembly.org/jewish-law/committee-jewish-law-and-standards

Orthodox: www.jlaw.com. Reform: www.ccarnet.com/responsa.

CHAPTER 22

JEWISH SEXUAL ETHICS

DANYA RUTTENBERG

THERE is a famous story in the Talmud[1] about a curious student who takes his studies past the point of what might generally be considered in good taste. Kahane, the yeshivah boy in question, hides under the bed of his teacher, deliberately listening in on the master's lovemaking with his wife. He is shocked by the way they chat and joke together during the coital act but tries his best to remain unnoticed. To no avail, however; in one dramatic moment, his presence—and *hutzpah*—are revealed.

> "Kahane, are you there?" his teacher thunders. "Leave now, because it is rude!"
> "It is not, and I will not," Kahane calmly replies, "for this is Torah, and I must learn."

In Judaism, every aspect of human life is a holy piece of Torah, worthy of thought, study, and consideration—and sex is certainly no exception. The Talmud compares the penis sizes of its most venerated sages[2] and discusses in euphemistic, but excruciating, detail the positions in which a married couple is permitted to make love.[3] Jewish law devotes pages and pages to the prohibition against sex with a menstruant, down to instructions on how to comport oneself if, mid-coitus, it appears that the female partner has just gotten her period.[4] One law code tells us that a widow should not own a dog, because, it seems, there is some suspicion about what a woman who has already tasted the pleasures of the flesh might do with her pet.[5]

In some ways, the tradition's approach to carnal matters appears to be steeped in the wisdom of the ages, and sometimes it seems out of step with our contemporary ethos. Needless to say, there are (as with most things) many shades of gray between these two extremes. Jewish sexuality is nothing if not complex. The Jewish tradition has always been one of continual unfoldings, of each generation commenting and building on those who had come before. And so too is it with us today, as feminism and postmodernism, queer theory, and new reconsiderations of gender have helped us to push our understandings of Jewish sexual ethics further than ever before.

This chapter will outline a few major concepts in Jewish sexual ethics—those that are critical for any real understanding of the classical sources, those that reflect the major issues related to sexuality today, and, of course, those that are of eternal relevance, that speak most closely to the issues with which human beings with bodies and sexual desires will always grapple. This is not a comprehensive examination by any means, either in breadth or in depth; it is rather meant to be a starting point for further discussion and study. The ideas discussed here are, as will soon become evident, rooted in the classical sources and concepts that form the foundation of Jewish thought and practice.

Extramarital Sex and Marriage

Jewish sources, it may be fair to suggest, presume marital union to be the ideal state in general, and certainly for intimate relations. The Talmud quotes Rabbi Tanhum in the name of Rav Hanilai, "Any man who has no wife lives without joy, without blessing, and without goodness."[6] Similarly, "Rabbi Elazar said, If a single man comes to a single woman [for sexual relations] without the intention of marriage, he makes her into a licentious woman."[7]

And yet, the tradition also acknowledges the reality of sex outside of marriage, regarding it with some ambivalence. Rav Amram responds to Rabbi Elazar's statement above somewhat unequivocably: "The law is not according to Rabi Elazar."[8] Elsewhere in the Talmud, sages debate whether a person might ever intentionally have sex without the intention to effect betrothal: "The House of Shammai say that a man [is willing to] make his acts of sexual intercourse the intercourse of licentiousness, while the House of Hillel say that a man does not [want to] make his acts of intercourse the intercourse of licentiousness."[9] More strikingly, the Talmud also includes this story: Rav, whenever he happened to visit [the town of] Dardeshir, used to announce, "Who would be mine for the day?" So also Rabbi Nahman, whenever he happened to visit Shekunzib, used to announce, "Who would be mine for the day?"[10] Biblical, rabbinic, and medieval sources all mention the category of the *pilagesh*, the concubine/mistress, a woman with whom a man might have an ongoing nonmarital sexual relationship, whether or not he was married to another woman.

And yet the sources also raise the possibility that a woman who has premarital sex might be ineligible to marry a member of the priestly class.[11] They also state clearly that either a man or woman who has sex with multiple partners creates serious social havoc, as lack of clarity about paternity (in the case of a woman) and lack of awareness of possible children fathered (in the case of a man) open the possibility of incestuous relations between two people who are unaware that they have a shared parent.[12]

As is the case in many traditional cultures, Jewish male sexual activity is not read the same way as a woman's sexual activity is; it does not impact his future marital prospects, either in regard to the priestly class or because of virginity status, though a female virgin's dower was twice that of a nonvirgin's. There is also no male equivalent of the *pilagesh* (a concubine) for either married or unmarried women.

In the past, marriages commonly occurred just a few years after puberty, but today couples usually marry in their twenties or later. Moreover, given the improved status of women in relationships and in the culture in general, the prevalence of love relationships rather than arranged matches, and many other factors, nonmarital relationships—which have always been a reality—have claimed a new place in the broader culture, and in Jewish life more specifically. Elliot Dorff, in *This Is My Beloved, This Is My Friend: A Rabbinic Letter on Human Intimacy*,[13] articulates several values that might inform extramarital relations, including regarding oneself and one's partner as created in God's image, respect, honesty, concern for health and safety, and interest in the Jewish nature of the relationship. Or, as Sara Meirowitz puts it:

> We can begin to think of non-marital sexuality as containing within it the potential for holiness. We create holiness in every interaction with another human being, when we connect with the spark of divinity in emotional, spiritual, or sexual ways. In our times, when life is long but childbearing years are few, we should empower ourselves to connect deeply with others and feel the range of experiences that come from different intimate connections.[14]

The Jewish wedding—particularly the first stage, the betrothal (*kiddushin*), now included as the first half of a wedding ceremony—invites discussion. The Mishnah reports, regarding betrothal, that "a woman is acquired in three ways …. She is acquired through money, through a contract, or through sexual intercourse."[15] What is this acquisition? Some argue that the groom purchases the bride outright, looking to the way in which the Mishnah and Talmud draw parallels between this acquisition and the acquisition of a slave, animal, or land.[16] Others—Judith Romney Wegner most famously—argue that he acquires not her being, but rather her sexuality, the right to monogamy.[17] For example, the Talmud states that the betrothal ritual renders the woman forbidden to other men just as an object dedicated to the Ancient Jerusalem Temple is forbidden for all other purposes.[18]

In betrothal (*kiddushin*), the bride's consent is required, though her speech is not: "Silence is akin to consent."[19] Additionally, only the husband can give a writ of divorce to the wife, a feature of Jewish law that has left some women trapped in unfortunate or even tragic situations when a husband is unable or unwilling to do so, or will do so only on specific, possibly untenable, conditions. If *kiddushin* is performed, then Jewish law mandates that the marriage be ended by means of the traditional divorce proceedings (or the death of the husband).

In recent years in our contemporary culture, there has been a rise in scholarly interest and creativity around the many questions that *kiddushin* raises around women's active participation and equal status. Rachel Adler crafted a *Brit Ahuvim*, a Lovers' Covenant, to be used in place of *kiddushin*[20]; Dov Linzer suggests a model in which the woman has more of an active role in *kiddushin* than is traditional[21]; Meir Simhah Feldblum proposes a ceremony called *Derekh Kiddushin* ("In the Manner of *Kiddushin*"), which uses a talmudic framework to sidestep the technical performance of *kiddushin*.[22] Others suggest a variety of other solutions, including a mutually performed *kiddushin*, the uttering of vows instead of *kiddushin*, and a mutual exchange of rings.[23] In addition, to avoid cases where a woman is "anchored" (*agunah*) to her former husband because he cannot or will not divorce her in Jewish law, despite a divorce decree in civil law, since 1969 the Conservative rabbinate has used a *t'nai b'kiddushin*, a condition of betrothal, that both members of the couple sign before their marriage to remove that possibility, and when that has not been done in a particular instance, the Conservative rabbinate will annul the marriage, employing the power granted by the Talmud to contemporary rabbis to do that in such cases. Modern Orthodox rabbis in recent years have also adopted such a condition to *kiddushin*, and Reform rabbis consider the divorce in civil law to be sufficient as a divorce in Jewish law as well.

Consent and Pleasure

Within, or even outside of, a marital relationship, it could certainly be contended that the cornerstone of Jewish sexual ethics is the high value placed on consensual pleasure. As such, it should perhaps first be noted that, since the time of the Torah, Judaism has considered consent to be a necessary and immutable precondition of sexual relations.[24]

The Mishnah and Talmud acknowledge that sexual assault causes not only physical pain, but emotional suffering and humiliation that need to be compensated appropriately,[25] and that consent given partway through an act of intercourse does not mitigate the fact that consent was not given initially.[26] Moreover, the long-standing *halakhic* prohibition against marital rape dates back to the Talmud[27]; for comparison, it might be useful to note that a mere seventeen countries of the United Nations had official criminalization of marital rape as recently as 1997 and that it was not criminalized in all fifty states of the United States until 1993.[28]

In other words, consent has long been a precondition of Jewish sexual behavior, and, more than that, full presence of mind during the sexual act is considered an important principle. One talmudic source, repeated in the later codes,[29] suggests that "one should not drink out of one goblet and think of another" and that one should not have sex in a situation that involves anger, fear, intimidation, disdain, mistaken identity, unresolved disagreements, or intoxication, or after a decision to end the relationship has been made. All of these conditions might prevent a couple from engaging in a loving, fully present connection.

If both partners are emotionally on the same page, however, sex is, in various places in the sources, described as a wonderful, praiseworthy act. More than that, sexual service is considered a nonnegotiable part of the marital relationship. The Torah articulates three basic obligations of the husband to the wife: *she'er* (food), *kesut* (clothing), and *onah* (sexual intimacy), which were then codified in the standard Jewish wedding contract (*ketubbah*). *Onah* literally translates as "time period," referring to the duration of time between sexual encounters, and is understood to refer to conjugal rights as a whole. The Mishnah fleshes out the notion of sexual duty in Tractate *Ketubbot*: "Students may leave to study Torah without the permission [of their wives] for thirty days; laborers, for one week. The times for conjugal duty prescribed in the Torah: for those with independent means, every day; for laborers, twice a week; for donkey drivers, once a week; for camel drivers, once in thirty days; for sailors, once in six months. These are the rulings of Rabbi Eliezer."[30] The relationship between sexual duty and occupation is so fundamental that the Talmud even clarifies that a husband must acquire the consent of his wife if he wants to change to a more lucrative occupation that demands less time at home, since some women prefer less money "with frivolity" to more money "with abstinence."[31]

Onah, this notion that a couple should come together as often as is possible—and that, verily, the husband is the one who owes the wife a regular degree of sexual service—is often cited as proof that Judaism has a fairly "sex-positive" take on relationships. Feminist theologian Judith Plaskow, for example, writes that "the laws of *onah* represent a remarkable concern with and accommodation to female sexuality as well as appreciation of sexuality generally."[32]

However, some scholars note that reading *onah* can be somewhat complex. The Mishnah [33] states that the courts will reduce the *ketubbah* of a woman who refuses to have sex with her husband by a certain amount each week (and, as a parallel, the husband who refuses sex with his wife must add to her *ketubbah*)—and later Jewish law[34] clarifies that if she states that he is repugnant to her, she may possibly be granted a divorce, but she will certainly be sent out without the *ketubbah* monies necessary for her survival without male protection and income. Melanie (Malka) Landau writes, "Male access to ongoing heterosexual sex from their partners is secured through the guise of a commandment incumbent on the male to pleasure his wife."[35]

Rachel Biale, on the other hand, understands *onah* as less of a challenge to the principle of consent than as a concession to the curse of Eve ("Your desire shall be for your husband, and yet he shall rule over you," Genesis 3:16). Biale writes that, according to the Rabbis' understanding, "the woman's punishment is that she is unable to fulfill her desire; she does not have the boldness to initiate sex or ask for it."[36] She argues that the Rabbis believed that women were by nature simultaneously full of sexual passion and deeply inhibited. As such, she suggests, the concept of *onah* was created to enable functional marital sexual relationships.

Sexual pleasure can be seen as another value whose threads run through many of the sources. For example, once married, a couple, if together at an appropriate time (see below), is permitted to make love in any position they desire. The Talmud writes:

> Our Sages said ... a man may do whatever he pleases with his wife [in intercourse]: A parable; Meat that comes from the butcher may be eaten salted, roasted, cooked or seethed; so with fish from the fishmonger.... A woman once came before Rabbi and said, "Rabbi! I set a table before my husband, but he overturned it." Rabbi replied: "My daughter! The Torah has permitted you to him. What then can I do for you?" [37]

Here the classic metaphor of food for sex is used to tell us that once a couple is permitted to engage sexually, they have quite a bit of leeway in what they do. In fact, it is even permitted to "turn the tables," generally interpreted as either vaginal sex with the woman in the "top" position or engaging in anal sex.[38] This latter reading is of particular interest given that "spilling the seed" (generally interpreted as depositing semen anywhere other than the vagina, even if contraceptives are used) is generally frowned upon in the sources (see below). However, for example, the medieval commentary of Tosafot on the Talmud writes that, "It is not considered like the [forbidden] act of Er and Onan unless it is his intention to destroy the seed and it is his habit always to do so. However, if it is occasional that the desire of his heart is to come upon his wife in an unnatural way, it is permitted."[39]

This permissive passage is also of interest given that, as will be discussed below, homosexual anal sex is considered problematic by many sources. It should also be noted that of the ways one could cook the various kinds of meat—obtained, presumably, from a kosher butcher—one does not find "with milk or cheese" on the list. Even here, not everything goes: within certain "kosher" parameters, one may engage sexually as one pleases, but there are in fact parameters. (Consent, of course, is one major one, as is the question of whether the two people in question are permitted to engage in intercourse on the basis of their marital or relational status, for Jewish law prohibits adultery and incest.)

Some have rightly criticized the ways in which this text seems to treat the wife as an object; she is, after all, compared to meat or fish, and her desires are hardly the subject of inquiry here. Daniel Boyarin acknowledges this point but writes:

> This is a reflection of the overweening androcentrism of the discourse as a whole, not *necessarily* a statement that husbands do not need to take account of their wives' needs ... [Th]is ... does not translate into a statement that a woman is a pure sexual object, but only that the Torah does not get involved in the bedroom. The eating metaphor here must be read within the rich field of metaphors in which sex and eating are mutually mapped on to each other.[40]

Another oft-cited text on pleasure is the thirteenth-century Kabbalistic work, *Iggeret HaKodesh* (*The Holy Letter*); its authorship is uncertain, but some attribute it to Nahmanides. The *Iggeret* suggests—in sharp contrast to Maimonides, who claimed that "sanctification consists in absence of sensuality"[41]—that intimate relations between husband and wife are indeed sacred. For the author of the *Iggeret*, the spiritual consciousness of both parties has an impact on the nature of the future child. In this evocative passage, for example, we see that the *Iggeret* recommends foreplay and female orgasm:

> You ought to engage her first in matters that please her heart and mind and cheer her in order to bring together your thought with her thought and your intention with hers. And you should say such things, some of which will urge her to passion and intercourse, to affection, desire and lovemaking, and some of which will urge fear of heaven, piety and modesty. You should attract her with charming words and seductions and other proper and righteous things as I have explained. And do not possess her while she is asleep because the two intentions are not one and her wish does not agree with yours.... Finally ... do not hasten to arouse your passion until the woman's mind is ready, and engage her in words of love so that she will begin to give forth seed first and thus her seed would be like matter and your seed like form, as it is said, "when a woman gives forth seed and bears a male child."[42]

The *Iggeret*'s interest here is certainly in the Kabbalistic union of the male and female aspects of the Divine and the way that fulfilling the commandment of *onah*, according to David Biale, "makes it possible to transform the physical pleasure into a desire for heaven."[43] We also see here the medieval notion that a woman's orgasm will lead to conception. Although this text neither unequivocally embraces bodily desire nor puts the emphasis on women's pleasure for its own sake (but rather, for conception), the influence of this text—and its emphasis on foreplay, orgasm, and the sacred encounter between lovers—on later generations of Jews of many backgrounds is formidable. In many ways, the *Iggeret* won the pleasure war over Maimonides, to the (literal) gratification of many generations.

MENSTRUAL SEPARATION

One would be remiss, in a discussion of Jewish sexual ethics, not at least to mention the principle of ritual menstrual separation and the complex issues that it raises.

The Torah, in a number of places, describes the notions of *tum'ah* (ritual impurity or unfitness) and *toharah* (ritual purity or fitness) The state of *tum'ah* is contracted in a variety of ways: eating nonkosher animals, coming into contact with a corpse, becoming ill with a disease often translated as leprosy (that was most certainly not like the leprosy we know today), or having particular bodily emissions. One could also contract *tum'ah* by coming into certain forms of contact with someone else who was *tameh* (the male adjectival form of the noun *tum'ah*) or *te'mei'ah* (the female adjectival form). Generally speaking, this state was of little consequence, except for the critical fact that, during the biblical era, one who was in a state of *tum'ah* was unable to offer sacrifices at the ancient Jerusalem Temple.

Menstruation was one of a number of genital emissions that could cause a person to contract *tum'ah*; male ejaculation and either male or female irregular "flux" emissions (from illness, miscarriage, and so forth) also did so. *Tum'ah* could be contracted from another person, and though in Leviticus 15 the consequences of this contraction are described in the simple language of cause and effect, the Torah (Lev 18:19; 20:18) twice explicitly prohibits sex with a menstruant.

During the Rabbinic era, normal menstruation and the irregular "flux" states became conflated, as the Rabbis decreed that a woman must—as the Torah commands for a woman with an irregular "flux"[44]—wait an extra week after the cessation of her regular menstrual period.[45] By the time of the Mishnah, it is also simply presumed that a menstruant must immerse in water before she would once again be permitted to engage in sexual relations, as the Torah obligates one who experienced an irregular "flux" emission from illness, miscarriage, or some other nontypical occurrence to immerse in water before resuming sexual relations.[46] As such, according to post-Rabbinic traditional practice, a couple does not engage in sexual relations while a woman is menstruating (which, according to Ashkenazi practice, lasts a minimum of five days) and for seven days thereafter. At the end of this period, she immerses in the ritual bath and is once again permitted to engage in marital relations with her husband.

This practice of sexual separation during menses has been controversial among many feminists. There are those who repudiate the practice entirely, such as Rachel Adler, who writes:

> The Israelite purity symbolism that associates masculinity with fertility and control, and feminism with death and disorder, constructs a culture in which men dominate women. This polarization of the symbolic meaning of gender is intensified by developments in Rabbinic and post-Rabbinic Judaism: Purity laws affecting men became atrophied, while those affecting women are elaborated and made more stringent.... I do not believe the laws of purity will ever be reinstated, nor should they be. The worlds reflected in such rules are not worlds we inhabit. Neither should we seek to replicate such worlds. They are unjust.[47]

Other feminists, such as Haviva Ner-David, find beauty and "spiritual power" in the notion of ritually marking the body's cycles and the sexual ebb and flow in her marriage. She writes:

> An approach to sexuality within marriage that limits permissible sex to only certain times during the month can be a positive or a negative influence on not only the couple's sex life, but on their relationship in general—depending on the couple's spiritual and emotional attitude towards this sexual regimen.... There is something that works for me in the together/apart cycle inherent in the *nidah* ritual.... But in order for this ritual to survive in an authentic and sincere way, it is our responsibility as women to reclaim this ritual and reinterpret it, express what it means for us in the 21st century.[48]

Ner-David suggests, as do some others working on this issue today, that one way to reclaim this practice is to abandon the Rabbinic addition of the extra week of abstention—that one week of separation, as described in the Torah, is spiritually, emotionally, and sexually sufficient,[49] they claim—and the original conflation of regular menses and irregular flux should be rejected on the grounds that it casts healthy menstruation as an infirmity and it creates a problem known as "*halakhic* infertility."

Halakhic infertility, Ner-David explains, happens when a "woman who keeps the extra seven days ovulates before the time in which she is eligible to go to the *mikveh*, therefore missing her chance to conceive. As most women age, their periods tend to be shorter and their ovulation time earlier. Therefore, *halakhic* infertility is even more common now than ever, for women are having children later in life now than they ever have before."[50] Rather than encouraging women to preserve the extra week of abstention and treat the ovulation timing issue with hormones, as many Orthodox and ultra-Orthodox rabbis suggest they do today, these feminists encourage women who choose to keep the laws of menstrual separation to keep only the original biblical week of separation, especially if adding the additional Rabbinic week will prevent a woman from getting pregnant if she so desires.[51]

Ner-David also suggests that both partners immerse in the *mikveh* at the appropriate time, creating an increased sense that this is a *mitzvah* connected to the sexual relationship as a whole, rather than one incumbent upon the woman alone.[52]

MASTURBATION

In Genesis 38 we find the story of Onan, who was obligated through the principle of levirate marriage to produce an heir with his brother's widow, Tamar. Onan, who did not want to conceive a child who would be considered his brother's rather than his own line, "spilled his semen on the ground" (Gen 38:9). This act was "bad in God's eyes" (Gen 38:10), and Onan was killed.

Although this story is about interrupted coitus and not masturbation, its negative view of "spilling semen" is considered the basis for the prohibition against male masturbation (hence the term "onanism"). The Mishnah and Gemara elaborate on this prohibition,[53] as does later Jewish law.[54] Female masturbation is almost never mentioned, though the Talmud does describe one woman's practice of having intercourse with a phallus-like object in negative terms.[55]

Today more people describe masturbation as a positive, healthy part of human sexuality. Elliot Dorff suggests that masturbation should be permitted on the grounds that its physiological ill effects, as described by doctor and important legal authority Maimonides, have since proven to be untrue.[56] Rebecca Alpert points out that the connection between the story of Onan and masturbation is not necessarily one to be taken for granted. She writes, "What was Onan's crime? The most obvious conclusion is that it was his refusal to comply with the task his father set for him, which was to impregnate Tamar. So although the term 'onanism' should refer to a refusal to follow orders or to take a stance against the custom of levirate marriage, it refers instead to the method Onan used to accomplish this act, namely, 'letting his seed go to waste.'"[57] She suggests that masturbation should be reframed in Jewish life based on Jewish values, including those of self-care, self-knowledge, preparation for connection with others, and privacy.[58]

Procreation

The obligation to procreate is derived from God's mandate, in Genesis 1:28, to "Be fruitful and multiply." The Rabbis interpreted this as being incumbent upon men alone, exempting women from the obligation.[59] Several possible explanations are offered for this interpretation of the command. One talmudic explanation takes an essentialist approach, noting that the complete verse states, "Be fruitful and multiply; fill the Earth and conquer it" (Gen 1:28) and that "it is the nature of a man to conquer, but it is not the nature of a woman to conquer," and therefore the commandment of procreation does not apply to women.[60]

Rabbi Meir Simcha of Dvinsk (nineteenth to twentieth century), on the other hand, suggests that this exemption was, rather, meant for the protection of women, for "The Torah did not burden a Jew with an obligation that he (*sic*) is physically unable to handle.... Therefore, regarding women, who are endangered during pregnancy and childbirth, the Torah did not obligate them to procreate."[61] Still others cite the ways in which lineage is established through the male line (see, for example, Gen 25:19) and the fact that parental obligations are incumbent upon the father[62] to wonder if women's exemption from procreation reflects a *halakhic* sense that the children are more strongly identified with their father.[63] Still others suggest an economic interpretation: because Jewish law obliges the father to support his children, Jewish law had to impose a duty to procreate on the man to overcome his economic self-interest. Finally, some suggest a physical reason to impose the duty of procreation on the man—namely, that he had to choose to participate in conjugal relations with his wife in order for procreation to take place.[64]

Jewish law describes the fulfillment of this *mitzvah* as fathering one son and one daughter,[65] and many commentators describe it as an important commandment indeed. The sixteenth-century legal code, the *Shulhan Arukh*, for example, opens its section on marital relationships with the laws of procreation, and states:

> Every man is obligated to marry a woman in order to be fruitful and multiply, and whoever does not occupy himself with being fruitful and multiply—it is as if he has spilled blood, lessens the Divine Image, and causes the *Shekhinah* (Divine Presence) to go away from Israel.[66]

And yet the Bible contains many stories of infertility, as described in the stories of Sarah, Rebecca, Rachel, Hannah, Samson's mother, and Mihal, among others, and much has been written in contemporary times about the use of artificial reproductive techniques (ARTs) now available to infertile couples.[67]

Even in the talmudic era, methods of birth control were known and used with permission.[68] One important source states, "Three [categories of] women use a contraceptive absorbent in their marital intercourse: a minor, a pregnant woman, and a nursing woman."[69] Debates in later Jewish legal sources questioned whether these three categories of women—all of whom were believed either to be endangered or possibly to endanger an existing fetus or child with a subsequent pregnancy—were *permitted* to use contraception (in which case other women might not be permitted) or were *required* to do so (in which case other women might be permitted to do so). Ultimately, Jewish law makes room for the use of several types of birth control,⁷⁰ and many argue that even condoms—once discouraged as a form of "spilling seed"—should be permitted on the grounds that, in a world in which AIDS is a reality, their use is consistent with Judaism's principle that saving life trumps most other commandments.⁷¹

SAME-SEX RELATIONSHIPS

Another issue that has been of significant interest over the last generation is the status of same-sex relationships. The Torah in Leviticus states, "Do not lie with a man as one lies with a woman; it is an abomination" (Lev 18:22). In another verse (Lev 20:13), the Torah repeats the injunction, but specifies that "the two of them have done an abominable thing; they shall be put to death—their bloodguilt is upon them."

Rabbinic and later *halakhic* sources generally interpret these verses to prohibit male same-sex relationships. Lesbian sexual activity is not mentioned in the Torah and is forbidden almost as an afterthought in later sources. Specifically, the Talmud describes female same-sex activity as "mere obscenity" that does not disqualify a woman from marrying a member of the priestly class,⁷² and Maimonides says that though female same-sex sexual activity is technically forbidden, "there is no specific biblical prohibition, and it is not called 'intercourse' at all."⁷³ In other words, though lesbians today must also contend with a discouraging textual tradition, the strength of the prohibitions against them are much lighter and easier to address from a legal standpoint than those regarding gay men.

Many have struggled with a way to deal with these prohibitions—both those against lesbian activity and particularly those against gay male sexual engagement. Some have looked to a historical perspective as a way to understand the Leviticus verses in context, arguing, for example, that the activity prohibited is actually that of idolatry—that the verses impugn the Canaanite practice of cultic prostitution. This reading is supported by the talmudic statement, "What is meant by *to'evah* (abomination)? '*To'eh attah bah* (you shall go astray because of it.).'"⁷⁴ This statement suggests that the problem of homosexuality is that it might lead to idolatry. Others posit that the prohibition is against rape and humiliation,⁷⁵ since the idea of two men coming together for a loving, long-term partnership may have been unheard of in the Ancient Near East, and evidence exists—the Sodom story in Genesis (19:1–14), for example—of homosexual intercourse used as a form of dominance. Some suggest that the verse can more precisely be defined as prohibiting anal sex, suggesting that Jewish communities should embrace and sanctify same-sex relationships and that Jewish gay male couples should refrain from engaging in that one specific act, and this has become one officially accepted position of the Conservative Movement.⁷⁶

Still others, including theologian Judith Plaskow, critique the attempt to find permission for same-sex relationships in ancient sources. At the end of the day, she suggests, homosexual relationships should be validated regardless of whether or not the tradition originally allowed for them (and, she suggests, it probably did not). She writes, "Perhaps if we focused less on the justification of gay and lesbian existence in relation to certain texts and more on the fruits of sexual relationships for self and community, we would better be able to ... encourage the intimacy and mutuality that distinguish holy sexuality."[77]

Whatever the philosophical approach one takes to the sources, it should be noted that homosexual Jewish life has flourished in unprecedented ways over the last twenty or thirty years. Synagogues, prayer books, study groups, spirituality retreats, literature, rituals, theology, activism, curriculum, and more have emerged in great volume, not only expanding the range of religious possibilities for gay-identified Jews, but impacting the broader Jewish culture in a significant way as well.

Gender Identity and Sexuality

While issues around gender identity are, by and large, entirely separate from issues around sexuality—how one inhabits one's own body and gender does not, after all, necessarily impact whom one desires as a sexual partner—they are often conflated in contemporary discourse. Rather than risk the topic's exclusion entirely from this volume, I will briefly address the subject.

The Mishnah and Talmud discuss two, and possibly as many as four, types of intersex persons—people born with (presumably genital, hormonal, and/or chromosomal) sex characteristics that complicate their easy categorization into "male" or "female." Though their status challenges the gender roles so prevalent in Rabbinic literature, the sources affirm their humanity and integrate them into the existing system. For example, the Mishnah states, "An *androgynos* [a person of one of these intersex categories] is in some respects legally equivalent to men, and in some respects legally equivalent to women, in some respects legally equivalent to [both] men and women, and in some respects legally equivalent to neither men nor women.... The androgynos ... dresses like men, marries but is not taken in marriage like men."[78]

As Elliot Rose Kukla observes of this text, "Not only is a person who is neither male nor female allowed to be a fully sexual being worthy of companionship in Jewish sacred texts, the androgynos is *presumed* to be one."[79] Kukla then asks:

> [H]ow does the androgynos' presence in marriage impact the way we have understood the gender hierarchy between husband and wife in traditional Judaism? Once the androgynos marries a woman, does that mean that the couple is permitted to engage in all forms of sexual intimacy, with all possible combinations of genitalia? If so, how does this impact Jewish law prohibiting homosexuality? More generally, how does the presence of a gender nonconforming sexual being disrupt

the heterosexual and misogynist assumptions underlying a traditional Jewish view of sex and love?[80]

Certainly, it can be said that the tradition both carved out an informed sexual and romantic space for those who do not fit easily into the gender binary, and that these people implicitly challenge some of Judaism's existing assumptions and understandings around sex and relationships.

There are a variety of opinions regarding the status of a transgendered person—one whose gender identity does not conform easily to the sex assigned at birth. Rabbinic rulings in the late twentieth century by several major religious authorities, including Eliezer Waldenberg among the Orthodox and Mayer Rabinowitz in a ruling endorsed by the Conservative Movement's Committee on Jewish Law and Standards, suggest that a transgender person's status should reflect the chosen gender rather than the presumed sex.[81]

Most critically, however, as Noach Dzmura writes, "No part of a person's gender identity need remain hidden in Jewish space … it is untenable for a Jew who wants *in* to be locked away from the beauty of Judaism, to be barred from the joy and solace of family, communal ritual, or social activity. There should be no gender-based … barrier to the Divine or to the synagogue."[82] As with gay Jewish life, a whole range of ritual innovations has begun to emerge from transgender and intersex Jews and Jewish communities, and it will undoubtedly have a marked impact on Jewish life in years to come.

Conclusion

As we have seen, Jewish sexuality is expressed in a number of different ways in traditional sources. Some principles may seem more immediately accessible to our twenty-first-century sensibility, and others have been the beneficiaries of the bounty of interpretation, creativity, and even textual activism available over the centuries and in contemporary life.

When Kahane, the student in the story mentioned at the beginning of this chapter, attempts to listen in on his teacher, he learns that the great sage—who had presumably been married for many years—partakes of his sexual relationship with great gusto and zeal, "as though he had never before tasted food." In Judaism, sex is meant to be not only enjoyed, but savored, fully present, with a "beginner's mind" even many years into the relationship. And yet the student was able to teach the master as well, with his rejoinder that "This too is Torah." From this not only do we learn that sexuality is embraced as sacred, but that, in Judaism, every generation has the ability to teach the generation before.

The Jewish project of engaging sexuality in a way that creates holiness, intimacy, connection, and integrity is an ongoing one. And each generation, in its way, finds a way to receive this Torah anew.

Notes

1. B. *Berakhot* 62a.
2. B. *Bava Metzia* 84a.
3. B. *Nedarim* 20b.
4. S.A. *Yoreh De'ah* 185:4.
5. S.A. *Even Ha-Ezer* 22:18.
6. B. *Yevamot* 62b.
7. B. *Yevamot* 51b.
8. Ibid.
9. B. *Gittin* 81b.
10. B. *Yevamot* 37b.
11. B. *Yevamot* 51b.
12. B. *Yevamot* 37b.
13. Elliot N. Dorff, *This Is My Beloved, This Is My Friend: A Rabbinic Letter on Intimate Relations* (New York: Rabbinical Assembly, 1996). The letter may also be found as chapter 3 of Dorff's book, *Love Your Neighbor and Yourself: A Jewish Approach to Modern Personal Ethics* (Philadelphia: Jewish Publication Society, 2003).
14. Sara N. S. Meirowitz, "Not Like a Virgin: Talking About Nonmarital Sex," in Danya Ruttenberg, *The Passionate Torah: Sex and Judaism* (New York: New York University Press, 2009). p. 180.
15. M. *Kiddushin* 1:1.
16. M. *Kiddushin* 1:2–6; B. *Kiddushin* 2a–b.
17. Judith Romney Wegner, *Chattel or Person? The Status of Women in the Mishnah* (New York: Oxford University Press, 1992), pp. 43–45.
18. B.*Kiddushin* 2a–b.
19. B. *Yevamot* 87b.
20. Rachel Adler, *"Brit Ahuvim*: A Marriage Between Subjects," in her *Engendering Judaism: An Inclusive Theology and Ethics* (Philadelphia: Jewish Publication Society, 1998).
21. Dov Linzer, "Towards a More Balanced Wedding Ceremony," *JOFA Journal* [of the Jewish Orthodox Feminist Alliance], 4:2 (Summer 2003), pp. 4–7.
22. Meir Simhah Feldblum, "Ba'ayot Agunot uMamzerim," *Dine Yisra'el* XIX (5757–5758).
23. For more on some of these approaches, see (http://alternativestokiddushin.wordpress.com/ (Accessed 6/12).
24. See, for example, Deut 22:25–27, B. *Eruvin* 100b, B. *Ketubbot* 51b.
25. B. *Ketubbot* 39a–b.
26. B. *Ketubbot* 51b.
27. B. *Eruvin* 100b.
28. "Spousal Rape Laws: 20 Years Later," *Victim Policy Pipeline*, (Winter 1999/2000), National Center for Victims of Crime, http://www.ncvc.org/ncvc/main.aspx?dbName=Document Viewer&DocumentID=32701 (accessed March 1, 2011).
29. B. *Nedarim* 20b, codified in M.T, *Issurei Biah (Forbidden Forms of Sexual Intercourse)* 21:12.
30. M. *Ketubbot* 5:6.
31. B. *Ketubbot* 62b.
32. Judith Plaskow, *Standing Again at Sinai: Judaism from a Feminist Perspective* (San Francisco: HarperSanFrancisco, 1990), p. 180.
33. M. *Ketubbot* 5:7.

34. B. *Ketubbot* 63b and M.T. Laws of Personal Status (*Hilkhot Ishut*) 14:8–9.
35. Melanie (Malka) Landau, "Good Sex: A Jewish Feminist Perspective," in Ruttenberg, *The Passionate Torah* (at note 14 above), pp. 97–98.
36. Rachel Biale, *Women and Jewish Law: The Essential Texts, Their History, and Their Relevance for Today* (New York: Schocken, 1995). p 122.
37. B. *Nedarim* 20b.
38. See, for example, Rashi on B. *Nedarim* 20a and Daniel Boyarin, *Carnal Israel: Reading Sex in Talmudic Culture* (Berkeley: University of California Press, 1993), pp. 10, note 1, 112–13.
39. Tosafot, B. *Yevamot* 34b.
40. Boyarin, *Carnal Israel* (see note 38 above), pp. 116–17.
41. Maimonides, *The Guide for the Perplexed*, Part. III, chap. 33.
42. *Iggeret HaKodesh, The Holy Letter: A Study in Medieval Jewish Sexual Morality, Attributed to Nahmanides*, Seymour J. Cohen, trans. (New York: Ktav, 1976), chap. 6. At the end of this passage, the author is quoting Leviticus 12:2.
43. David Biale, *Eros and the Jews: From Biblical Israel to Contemporary America* (Berkeley: University of California Press, 1997), p. 107.
44. Leviticus 15:28; see Tirzah (leBeit Yoreh) Meacham, "An Abbreviated History of the Development of the Jewish Menstrual Laws," in Rachel Wasserfall, ed., *Women and Water: Menstruation in Jewish Life and Law* (Waltham, MA: Brandeis University Press. 1999), p. 24. See also Haviva Ner-David, "Reclaiming Nidah and Mikveh Through Ideological and Practical Reinterpretation," in Ruttenberg, ed., *The Passionate Torah* (at note 14 above), p. 123.
45. B. *Niddah* 66a.
46. Leviticus 15.
47. Rachel Adler, " 'In Your Blood, Live': Re-Visions of a Theology of Purity," in Debra Orenstein and Jane Rachel Litman, eds., *Lifecycles: Jewish Women on Biblical Themes in Contemporary Life*. (Woodstock, VT: Jewish Lights, 1997), Vol. 2, pp. 203, 205.
48. Haviva Ner-David, "Reclaiming Nidah and Mikveh Through Ideological and Practical Reinterpretation," in Ruttenberg, ed., *The Passionate Torah* (at note 14 above), p. 116.
49. See, for example, the three rabbinic rulings accepted by the Conservative Movement's Committee on Jewish Law and Standards on September 13, 2006, as acceptable ways of observing these laws: Miriam Berkowitz, "Reshaping the Laws of Family Purity for the Modern World," available at http://www.rabbinicalassembly.org/sites/default/files/public/halakhah/teshuvot/20052010/berkowitz_niddah.pdf (accessed May 9, 2011); Susan Grossman, "Mikveh and the Sanctity of Being Created Human," available at http://www.rabbinicalassembly.org/sites/default/files/public/halakhah/teshuvot/20052010/grossman_niddah.pdf (accessed May 9, 2011): and Avram Israel Reisner, "Observing Niddah in Our Day: An Inquiry on the Status of Purity and the Prohibition of Sexual Activity with a Menstruant," available at http://www.rabbinicalassembly.org/sites/default/files/public/halakhah/teshuvot/20052010/reisner_niddah.pdf (accessed May 9, 2011). See also Blu Greenberg, *On Women and Judaism: A View from Tradition* (Philadelphia: Jewish Publication Society, 1981), p. 121. Greenberg's suggestion of returning to the biblical practice of a *niddah*'s waiting for only one week is more tentative ("At certain stages of life, and for certain people …"), but she does open it as a possibility, which is particularly notable given how early into the Jewish feminist conversation she suggests it, and given her esteemed position within Orthodoxy. See Blu Greenberg, *On Women and Judaism: A View from Tradition* (Philadelphia: Jewish Publication Society, 1981), p. 121.

50. Ner-David, "Reclaiming" (at note 48 above), p. 125.
51. This is the focus of Rabbi Susan Grossman's rabbinic ruling; see note 49 above.
52. Ner-David, "Reclaiming (at note 48 above), pp.132–33.
53. M. *Niddah* 2:1; B. *Niddah* 13a–b.
54. For example, S.A. *Even Ha-Ezer* 23:2.
55. B. *Avodah Zarah* 44a.
56. Elliot Dorff, "A Jewish Perspective on Birth Control and Procreation," in Ruttenberg, ed., *The Passionate Torah* (at note 14 above), pp.158–59. See also Elliot N. Dorff, *Matters of Life and Death: A Jewish Approach to Modern Medical Ethics* (Philadelphia: Jewish Publication Society, 1998), pp. 116–20.
57. Rebecca Alpert, "Reconsidering Solitary Sex from a Jewish Perspective," in Ruttenberg, ed., *The Passionate Torah* (at note 14 above), p. 182.
58. Alpert, Rebecca. "Reconsidering Solitary Sex from a Jewish Perspective," in Ruttenberg, *The Passionate Torah* (at note 14 above), pp. 187–89.
59. M. *Yevamot* 6:6.
60. B *Yevamot* 65b.
61. His Torah commentary, Meshekh Hohmah, on Gen. 9:7.
62. B *Ketubbot* 65b; B. *Kiddushin* 29a.
63. Dov Linzer, "Women and the Mitzvah of *Pru u'Rvu*," *Kol Chovevei Torah*, Vol. I, Issue 4.
64. Both the economic and physical explanations are suggested by Elliot N. Dorff, *Matters of Life and Death* (at note 56 above), p. 335, note 8.
65. M. *Yevamot* 6:6.
66. S.A. *Even Ha-Ezer* 1:1.
67. For more on Jewish norms relevant to the use of artificial techniques of reproduction and the range of positions on the use of donor gametes, see Elliot N. Dorff, *Matters of Life and Death* (at note 56 above), chaps. 3 and 4.
68. M. *Shabbat* 14:3, B. *Yevamot* 12b, 65b, B. *Shabbat* 110b–11a.
69. B *Yevamot* 12b. General scholarly consensus is that a *mokh* was a tuft of wool or cotton inserted vaginally to absorb semen.
70. See, for example, Moshe Feinstein, *Iggerot Moshe, Even Ha-Ezer*, Part 4, response 34.
71. For the principle that saving a life supersedes most other commandments, see B. *Yoma* 85a-b, B. *Sanhedrin* 74a–b. For modern sources that apply that principle to the use of condoms in the age of AIDS and other sexually transmitted diseases, see (in alphabetical order) Miriam Berkowitz and Mark Popovsky, "Contraception," accepted by the Committee on Jewish Law and Standards of the Conservative Movement on December 14, 2010, available at http://www.rabbinicalassembly.org/sites/default/files/public/halakhah/teshuvot/20052010/Contraception%20Berkowitz%20and%20Popovsky.pdf (accessed on June 7, 2012); Yitzchok Breitowitz, "AIDS: A Jewish Perspective," in *Jewish Law*, accessed at http://www.jlaw.com/Articles/aids.html on December 29, 2010; Elliot N. Dorff, "A Jewish Perspective on Birth Control and Procreation," in Ruttenberg, ed., *The Passionate Torah* (at note 14 above), p. 162; and Z. S.Soshard, "Machalat AIDS B'Mishpachah," appearing in medethics.org.il, accessed at http://www.medethics.org.il/articles/ASSIA/ASSIA61–62/ASSIA61–62.11.asp on December 29, 2010.
72. B *Yevamot* 76a.
73. M.T. Laws of Forbidden Intercourse (*Issurei Biah*) 21:8.
74. B *Nedarim* 51a.
75. For example, Steven Greenberg, *Wrestling with God and Men: Homosexuality in the Jewish Tradition* (Madison: The University of Wisconsin Press, 2004), pp. 204–7.

76. This is one reading of B. *Sanhedrin* 54a. Joel Roth rejects this interpretation; see his "Homosexuality Revisited," accepted by the the Committee of Jewish Law and Standards of the Conservative Movement on December 6, 2006, available at http://www.rabbinicalassembly.org/docs/Roth_Final.pdf (accessed March 1, 2011). Elliot N. Dorff, Daniel Nevins, and Avram Israel Reisner, however, argue for it; see their "Homosexuality, Human Dignity and Halakah: A Combined Responsum for the Committee on Jewish Law and Standards," accepted by the the Committee of Jewish Law and Standards of the Conservative Movement on December 6, 2006, available at http://www.rabbinicalassembly.org/docs/Dorff_Nevins_Reisner_Final.pdf (accessed March 1, 2011).
77. Judith Plaskow, *The Coming of Lilith: Essays on Feminism, Judaism and Sexual Ethics* (Boston: Beacon Press, 2005), p. 192.
78. M *Bikkurim* 4:1–2.
79. Elliot Rose Kukla, "'Created by the Hand of Heaven': Sex, Love and the Androgynos." in Ruttenberg, ed., *The Passionate Torah* (at note 14 above), p. 93.
80. In Ruttenberg, *The Passionate Torah* (at note 14 above), p. 194.
81. Eliezer Waldenberg, 10 *Tzitz Eliezer* 25:26, 6. Mayer Rabinowitz, "The Status of Transsexuals," http://www.rabbinicalassembly.org/sites/default/files/public/halakhah/teshuvot/20012004/rabinowitz_transsexuals.pdf (accessed June 17, 2012).
82. Noach Dzmura, *Balancing on the Mechitza: Transgender in Jewish Community* (New York: North Atlantic Books, 2010), p. xv.

For Further Reading

Adler, Rachel. 1997. "'In Your Blood, Live': Re-Visions of a Theology of Purity." In *Lifecycles: Jewish Women on Biblical Themes in Contemporary Life*, Debra Orenstein and Jane Rachel Litman, eds. Woodstock, VT: Jewish Lights, 1997, Vol. 2. Pp. 197–204.

Adler, Rachel. 1998. *Engendering Judaism: An Inclusive Theology and Ethics*. Philadelphia: Jewish Publication Society.

Berkowitz, Miriam, and Mark Popovsky. 2010. "Contraception." Accessed at http://www.rabbinicalassembly.org/sites/default/files/public/halakhah/teshuvot/20052010/Contraception%20Berkowitz%20and%20Popovsky.pdf on June 7, 2012.

Biale, David. 1997. *Eros and the Jews: From Biblical Israel to Contemporary America* Berkeley: University of California Press.

Biale, Rachel. 1995. *Women and Jewish Law: The Essential Texts, Their History, and Their Relevance for Today*. New York: Schocken.

Borowitz, Eugene. 1969. *Choosing a Sex Ethic: A Jewish Inquiry*. New York: Schocken.

Boyarin, Daniel. 1993. *Carnal Israel: Reading Sex in Talmudic Culture*. Berkeley: University of California Press.

Breitowitz, Yitzchok. [no date listed]. "AIDS: A Jewish Perspective." In *Jewish Law*, accessed at http://www.jlaw.com/Articles/aids.html on 12/29/10.

Cohen, Seymour, trans. 1976. *Iggeret HaKodesh: The Holy Letter: A Study in Medieval Jewish Sexual Morality, Attributed to Nahmanides*. New York: Ktav. [Hebrew and English].

Dorff, Elliot N. 1996. *This Is My Beloved, This Is My Friend: A Rabbinic Letter on Intimate Relations*. New York: Rabbinical Assembly. The letter may also be found as chapter 3 of Dorff's book *Love Your Neighbor and Yourself: A Jewish Approach to Modern Personal Ethics* (Philadelphia: Jewish Publication Society, 2003).

Dorff, Elliot N. 1998. *Matters of Life and Death: A Jewish Approach to Modern Medical Ethics.* Philadelphia: Jewish Publication Society.

Dorff, Elliot N., Daniel Nevins, and Avram Israel Reisner. 2006. "Homosexuality, Human Dignity and Halakah: A Combined Responsum for the Committee on Jewish Law and Standards." Accessed at http://www.rabbinicalassembly.org/sites/default/files/public/halakhah/teshuvot/20052010/dorff_nevins_reisner_dignity.pdf on June 7, 2012.

Dzumra, Noach. 2010. *Transgender in Jewish Community: Balancing on the Mechitza.* Berkeley, CA: North Atlantic Books.

Feldblum, Meir Simhah. "Ba'ayot Agunot uMamzerim." *Dine Yisra'el* XIX (5757–5758) [Hebrew].

Greenberg, Blu. 1981. *On Women and Judaism: A View from Tradition.* Philadelphia: Jewish Publication Society.

Greenberg, Steven. 2004. *Wrestling with God and Men: Homosexuality in the Jewish Tradition.* Madison: The University of Wisconsin Press.

Grossman, Susan. "Mikveh and the Sanctity of Being Created Human," available at http://www.rabbinicalassembly.org/sites/default/files/public/halakhah/teshuvot/20052010/grossman_niddah.pdf (accessed May 9, 2011).

Linzer, Dov. "Women and the Mitzvah of *Pru u'Rvu*," *Kol Chovevei Torah*, Vol. I, Issue 4. Tishrei 5767/October 2006.

Linzer, Dov. 2003. "Towards a More Balanced Wedding Ceremony." *JOFA Journal* [of the Jewish Orthodox Feminist Alliance] 4:2 (Summer).

Plaskow, Judith. 1990. *Standing Again at Sinai: Judaism from a Feminist Perspective.* San Francisco: HarperSanFrancisco.

Plaskow, Judith. 2005. *The Coming of Lilith: Essays on Feminism, Judaism and Sexual Ethics.* Boston: Beacon Press.

Reisner, Avram Israel. "Observing Niddah in Our Day: An Inquiry on the Status of Purity and the Prohibition of Sexual Activity with a Menstruant," 2006. available at http://www.rabbinicalassembly.org/sites/default/files/public/halakhah/teshuvot/20052010/reisner_niddah.pdf (accessed June 7, 2012).

Roth, Joel. "Homosexuality Revisited," 2006. available at http://www.rabbinicalassembly.org/sites/default/files/public/halakhah/teshuvot/20052010/roth_revisited.pdf (accessed June 7, 2012).

Ruttenberg, Danya. 2001. *The Next Wave of Jewish Feminism: Yentl's Revenge.* Seattle: Seal Press.

Ruttenberg, Danya. 2009. *The Passionate Torah: Sex and Judaism.* New York: New York University Press.

Schneer, Caryn, and David Schneer, eds. 2002. *Queer Jews.* New York: Routledge.

Wasserfall, Rachel, ed. 1999. *Women and Water: Menstruation in Jewish Life and Law* Waltham, MA: Brandeis University Press.

Wegner, Judith Romney. 1992. *Chattel or Person? The Status of Women in the Mishnah.* New York: Oxford University Press.

CHAPTER 23

JEWISH ENVIRONMENTAL ETHICS

INTERTWINING *ADAM* WITH *ADAMAH*

ARTHUR WASKOW

JEWISH ethical outlooks on the relationship between humanity and the earth can be seen to develop in four epochs or aspects of Jewish history:

1. The biblical period, when the people of Israel was an indigenous farming and herding people with strong awareness of its connection to the ecosystems of the land of Israel as grounding for its economic and spiritual well-being—indeed, the central aspect of its relationship with God.
2. Rabbinic Judaism, when Jews were dispersed in many lands, rarely responsible for shaping land policy in any of them, and much more oriented to words of prayer and Torah study and the shaping of ethical patterns within the Jewish community as paths for connection to God.
3. Modernity, including both the Zionist movement, in which Jews reconnected with the land of Israel and originally showed deep concern for the actual land, earth, water, and air of the land of Israel but gradually committed themselves to industrialism as a basic economic framework; and Diaspora communities similarly committed themselves to

4. What might be called Eco-Judaism, arising mostly in the American Diaspora as hypermodernity seemed to approach the point of self-destruction, endangering the web of life on Earth and calling forth a sense of crisis in the human–earth relationship.

As is clear in other chapters in this book, Jewish ethics is often articulated in Jewish law, and there are indeed Jewish laws relevant to ecology, from the Torah down to our own day. Jewish ethics, though, is also rooted in the Jewish tradition's theology, history, proverbs, prayers, patterns of study, and stories.¹ In this review of Jewish "earth–human" ethics, we will focus on what three central biblical stories—the Garden of Eden, the Flood, and the Plagues of Exodus—tell us about Jewish ecological ethics as the Torah itself tells those stories and as the later rabbis interpreted and expanded them, with special concern for the emerging ethics of Eco-Judaism. In so doing, I will be illustrating how the Jewish tradition uses *midrash*, interpretation of texts and their literary nuances, in discovering meanings in sacred texts that make them ever relevant to us in changing times and circumstances. Then I will very briefly develop one of the Torah's laws on ecology and an emerging interest on the part of some Jews to understand God differently, in order to reflect our current ecological understanding of life as one integrated whole. I hope thus to demonstrate how Jewish stories, law, and theology are all relevant to ecology.

Eden/Plagues/Shabbat/New Eden

Eden

The story of Eden begins by pointing us toward the close relationship between humans and the earth:

> And YHWH [the Name of God that can only be pronounced by breathing with no vowels, thus "Yahhh, Breath of Life"] formed the *adam* [human earthling] from the *adamah* [humus-earth] and blew into his nostrils the breath of life; and the human-earthling became a living being." (Gen 2: 7)
>
> [These odd translations of *adam* and *adamah* are intended to heighten in English the interrelationship that the Torah—indeed, the Hebrew language itself—teaches so simply. Indeed we do have in English the word "earthling" to mean "human being" and the word "humus" to mean a kind of earth, but each of them is a highly specialized word.]

What "*adam*" and "*adamah*" teach is deeply different from what the word "environment" teaches. The "environment" is in the "environs"—out there, separate from us. The very words *adam* and *adamah* are intertwined, and they should teach us not only about language but about the reality that language tries to describe in words.

Then we proceed to the story of Eden. God—the Truth and Reality of life—says to the human couple who together make up the human race: "Here there is overflowing abundance. Eat of it, of every tree of the Garden, in joy!—But you must also learn self-restraint. Do not gobble up all this abundance. The fruit of one tree you must not eat." But they abandon self-restraint. They eat of the one tree they have been told to leave uneaten.

And their greed ruins the abundance. So—says God/Reality—they must work with the sweat pouring down their faces just to wring from the earth enough to eat, for it will give forth thorns and thistles, both an economic and an ecological disaster.

Yet there are ways to go beyond this disaster—by growing up still further, into a fuller maturity.

Shabbat: Take One

Growing further began, says the Torah, in the early days of the Wilderness trek, just after the Breath of Life freed ancient Israelites from the power-greedy Pharaoh who enslaves human beings and brings plagues upon the Earth. The first discovery of these runaway slaves is the Shabbat [Sabbath] that comes with manna—a taste of rest from endless toil, and a gift from the abundant earth. For manna is the food that the earth gives freely, so that eating it barely requires any work at all (Exod 16:14–30). With the manna comes the information that on the morning of each sixth day, the manna will come in a double portion so that no one will have to do even the light work of gathering it on the seventh day, Shabbat.

It is as if the first realization of a people newly freed—even before they have their Great Encounter with God at Sinai—is that there must be time to rest and reflect, for otherwise they are still in slavery. If the deep misstep of Eden was refusing to restrain human inclinations to gobble up the Earth, then Shabbat comes as a time for choosing self-restraint—not a grim ascetic self-restraint, but one of joyful abundance in community. And since the mistake of Eden was overeating, then this partial reversal must come with a different kind of eating.

Says Isaiah (51:3): "*Vayasem midbarah k'eden v'arvatah k'gan YHWH*." "You turn the barren place to Eden, and the desert to a garden breathing Life."

Pharaoh and the Plagues

By its placement of the manna/Shabbat story immediately after Pharaoh's power dissolves in the Reed {Red} Sea, the Torah is suggesting that we can grow beyond the disaster of Eden only if we act to free *adam* and *adamah* from domination by the Pharaohs of each generation. So let us look at the teachings that flow from the story of Pharaoh's effect upon the earth.

Moses called upon Pharaoh to obey God's will and let the Hebrews go free from their forced labor, but Pharaoh refused. As Moses began to invoke God's pressure to make Pharaoh change his mind, the Torah says that Pharaoh—time after time—hardened his own heart against compassion for the Hebrews and against obedience to God's warnings.

How do we understand this pressure from God, the ten smitings of the land of Egypt, *Mitzrayyim*, literally, the Tight and Narrow Space—what we conventionally call the Ten Plagues? Were the Plagues magic, "miracles" handed down by a Supernal King, a Super-Pharaoh in the sky? Or were they the emerging consequences of tyranny, the evidence that the Interbreathing of all life brings about torment and rebellion of the Earth when human beings are oppressed? In a generation that watches a profit-mad oil company ignore all warnings, safety standards, and precautions so as to maximize its profits from an oil well a mile deep under-sea, and this attitude brings death upon its own workers, disaster to the ecosystem, and economic paralysis to the region—it is easier to see how YHWH, interconnecting all life, responds to unaccountable power with uncountable plagues.

For arrogance is not only a moral and spiritual malady. It breeds stupidity. Those who are utterly convinced of their own absolute rightness cannot hear the warnings of others, cannot pay attention to the signals from the world around them, cannot learn from their own mistakes. How did this attitude work in the tale of ancient Egypt?

First came the "plagues"—ecological disasters. The rivers became poisonous, undrinkable. Frogs swarmed everywhere and then died in stinking heaps. Vermin swarmed. Venomous bloodsucking flies followed. Mad cow disease descended. Airborne infections raised boils on everyone. Unprecedented hailstorms signaled radical climate change, shattering grass, grain harvests, trees, animals.

To the bafflement of Pharaoh and his advisers, Moses and Aaron had evidently become experts in the ecological balance. Again and again, their warnings had been borne out. Now they warned that the ecosystem was so ruined that a monstrous plague of locusts was about to strike.

And in this critical moment, Pharaoh's own advisers shrieked at him—"Do you not know that Egypt is destroyed?" (Exod 10:7). But Pharaoh hardened his heart once more, and the locusts came. And after that, so darkened were the eyes of all the people that the land itself was darkened as a thick dust swallowed up all vision. And then came an illness that left no house untouched by death.

How were Moses and Aaron able to foretell disaster? Why did Pharaoh fail? What glimmer of reality spoke through the king's advisers?

For Pharaoh, the "plagues" were a startling series of singular accidents. "Stuff happens." That was all. Each one was scary, but it did not portend another—or a broken system.

Moses and Aaron saw a deeper truth. They saw and felt the interconnections that weave the world together. They understood that "YHWH" was the Interbreathing of all life. They may not have understood the details of how smashing a butterfly far up the Nile could bring down hailstorms on the country's farmland—but they knew that it could happen. They understood that oppressing and enslaving workers, forcing them to work the land beyond its limits, would leave the land defenseless against a horde of locusts. That was their advantage over Pharaoh and over his advisers, who could through sleight of hand make a serpent appear where a staff had been—but could not cure tormented cattle from mad cow disease.

Finally, the advisers admitted their incapacities, spoke aloud Reality—and were ignored. The morning after they told Pharaoh he was destroying Egypt, his hardness-addicted heart drove him to march forward on the road to ruin.

This kind of response has not been limited to one millennium, one country, or one form of government. The dangers of top-down, unaccountable, irresponsible power transcend the borders and the centuries. In the epoch when the excesses of modernity are bringing danger to the planet, what are we to learn as a Jewish ethic? Hearken to the warnings of those who focus on the Breath of Life that intertwines us all.

Can we learn from this old story to look beyond specific issues—this war or that highway, this tax cut or that coal plant—to the issue of unaccountable power? Of power as pyramidal in its top-down shape as ancient pyramids?

How do we resolve the apparent conflict between two quite different biblical teachings: one, that the Flood and its global ecological disaster came about from the widespread *hamas* [destructive] behavior of the human species as a whole, and the other, that the Plagues came about as a result of a ruler's arrogance and stubbornness? On one hand, all are responsible; on the other hand, the powerful are especially guilty.

The metaphor of "addiction" may help us. In regard to mass public addiction, some point to the overburning of fossil fuels as the deep problem. Others point to the oppressive power of Big Oil, Big Coal, and their governmental allies as the source of danger. If we agree that large publics are indeed addicted, we can also say that some great power centers act like "drug lords" and "drug pushers," just as Big Tobacco engendered and facilitated the nicotine addiction of millions.

The spiritual-ethical responsibility of Jews and other religious communities to free people from personal addiction—one kind of idolatry—can be complemented by their spiritual-ethical responsibility to free people from oppressive power centers—another kind of idol.

Shabbat, Take Two: Sabbath, Sabbatical Year, and Jubilee

The Torah sets forth a time-tempered rhythmic process of economic, ecological, and political action that is intended to preserve abundance and that warns of utter disaster if the balance is undone.

When we look for what we might call the "eco-Judaism" of biblical Israel, one of the most notable teachings about the relationship between the human community and the earth is the teaching of *Shabbat* (the Sabbath), the *shmitah* or Sabbatical year, and the Jubilee year.

Every seventh day, every seventh year, and the year after every seventh cycle of seven years (the fiftieth year), the human community is to pause from work, not merely to rest from physical labor, but also to renew itself, to achieve "release" or "self-reflection" or "detachment" or "holiness." And as the community rests, so does the earth—animals and vegetation are also released.

Indeed, it is almost impossible to disentangle the implications of this whirling spiral of Shabbats for *adamah*, the earth, from its implications for *adam*, the human community. The Bible connects this rhythm both to revitalization of the earth and to human freedom and equality.

As we have already seen, the Shabbat of the seventh day comes first into human ken, along with manna, just after the liberation of the Israelites from slavery.

When the Torah describes the second revelation of Shabbat—the one at Sinai—it gives two different ways of understanding it. One (Exod 20:8–11) focuses on Shabbat as a reminder of God's Creation of the entire "natural" world, in which the cosmos itself needs and celebrates rest and renewal as an organic reality. In the second version (Deut 5:12–15), the main reason for the existence of Shabbat is said to be as a reminder of liberation from slavery in the Narrow Place, *Mitzrayyim*, Egypt. It is a way of making sure that even in a society where some become indentured servants, "your male and female servants may rest as one-like-yourself."

In the larger spiral of the seventh year, the Hebrew Bible insists that the sabbatical year be one not only of release from work, but release from debt (Deut 15:1–11). And for the fiftieth year, the year of Jubilee, the Bible makes its most radical demand for political, social, and economic change:

> You shall count off seven sabbaths of years, seven times seven years.... Then you shall make proclamation with the blast of the *shofar* [ram's horn].... On the Day of Atonement you shall make proclamation with the horn throughout all your land. And you shall make holy the fiftieth year, and proclaim release throughout the land to all the inhabitants thereof. It shall be to you a jubilee [or "a home-bringing," according to Everett Fox's translation in *The Five Books of Moses*, drawing on the Hebrew roots beneath the word *yovel*], so you—every one of you—shall return to your own ancestral holding, every one of you, to your family.... You shall not sow, nor reap what grows, nor gather the grapes of the unpruned vines.... And the land shall not be permanently sold—*For the land is Mine. You are strangers and visitors with Me*.[2]

A radical social transformation! Not only are debts periodically annulled, but once a generation, the rich give up whatever extra land they have acquired, and the poor who have lost their family plot return to it.

Shabbat is not only a blessing for *adam*. Says Leviticus, "But in the seventh year there shall be a Sabbath of Sabbath-ceasing *for the land*, a Sabbath of YHWH."[3] Not for the sake of humanity alone comes restfulness, but for the earth as well, in direct relationship with YHWH.

What is the content of this restful-time?

> Your field you are not to sow, your vineyard you are not to prune, the aftergrowth of your harvest you are not to harvest.... It shall be a Sabbath of Sabbath-ceasing for the land. You may eat whatever the land during its Sabbath will freely produce—you, your male and female servants, your hired hand, resident-settlers

who sojourn with you, and your domestic cattle and the wild-beasts in your land may eat all its yield.⁴

And if they failed to do this, what would happen? The very next chapter, Leviticus 26, describes the consequences:

> But if you do not obey Me and do not observe all these commandments, if you reject My laws and spurn My rules, so that you do not observe all My commandments and you break My covenant.... Then I, I Myself, will make the land desolate, so that your enemies who settle in it will be appalled at the desolation in it. And you I will scatter among the nations; I will unsheathe the sword against you, so that your land becomes a desolation and your cities become a wasteland.
>
> Then shall the land make up for its sabbath years throughout the time that it is desolate and you are in the land of your enemies; then shall the land rest and make up for its sabbath years. Throughout the time that it is desolate, it shall observe the rest that it did not observe in your sabbath years while you were dwelling upon it .... For the land shall be forsaken of them, making up for its sabbath years by being desolate of them, while they atone for their iniquity; because—yes, because!—they rejected My rules and spurned My laws.⁵

According to the ecological theory and experience of ancient Israel, the need for Sabbath-restfulness, for a rhythm of Doing and Being, is not merely a superficial wistfulness. It is a law of gravity: the Earth does rest. If you rest with it, celebrating joyfully, then all is harmonious and happy. But if you try to prevent it from resting, it will rest anyway—upon your head, through famine, drought, exile, desolation—it *will* rest.

And the very last chapter of the Hebrew Scriptures, Chronicles 36: 20, claims to report:

> Those who survived the sword he [Nebuchadnezzar] exiled to Babylon, and they became his and his sons' servants till the rise of the Persian kingdom, in fulfillment of the word of YHWH spoken by Jeremiah, until the land paid back its sabbaths; as long as it lay desolate it kept its sabbath, till seventy years were completed.

The cycles of Shabbat, sabbatical year, and Jubilee are not static. The Bible does not imagine that the earth can be renewed, the land can be shared, and justice can be achieved once and for all. And it does not imagine that a little change, year after year, can make for real renewal. The Jubilee says that for six years of every seven it is all right for some to accumulate wealth and some to lose it, and for the earth to be forced to work under human command—but that once every seventh year there must be a major healing, and once every generation there must be a great transformation. And that each generation must know it will have to be done again, in the next generation.

How does the cycle feel when the Jubilee itself comes around at last? There stands the land untilled as it stood the year before, the seventh seventh year. Two years in a row untilled. Imagine how strange (and how anciently familiar) the land would look: more than a touch of wilderness. More than a touch of the land that nomads remember.

Everyone would learn that the biggest "action" of all is not to act.

Not acting!—How fearful the farmers who tried to live by this teaching! The farmer might fear that waiting two years in a row would bring ruin. But the Bible asserts, and modern science confirms, that letting the land lie fallow is a crucial part of its restoration. What looks like a famine in the short run is necessary to prosperity in the long run. Trusting in God and practicing science are not contradictory.

The Jubilee stands beyond the politics of guilt and rage. It does not ask for the rich to give their land away in fear or guilt; it does not ask the wretched of the earth and the prisoners of starvation to rise in rage to take back the land from the swollen rich.

Instead, the Jubilee proclaims a "release," a Shabbat, for everyone, a release for the rich as well as the poor. The rich are released from working, bossing, increasing production—and from others' envy of them. The poor are released from working, from hunger, from humiliation and despair—and from others' pity of them. Both the rich and the poor are seen as fully human, as counterparts to be encountered—not as enemies or victims to be feared or hated.

Perhaps that is why the Jubilee Year begins not at the New Moon of the seventh month, not on Rosh Hashanah when the fiftieth year itself begins, but ten days later—on Yom Kippur, the Day of Atonement (Lev 25:9–10), when the community has already purged itself of guilt and rage. Thus Jubilee is both the final healing gift of the people to God to complete the old cycle, and God's first blessing to the people and the earth, in the new cycle.

But the sabbatical year, with its annulment of debt, and the Jubilee, with its redistribution of land, were not based only on the "science" of letting land lie fallow to recover its fertility, or on the "religion" of recognizing God's image in every human being and in the breathing earth. They may also have appealed to "politics"—the class interests of a large group of independent small farmers who wanted to prevent the emergence of a permanent, ever-fattening class of large landholders who could lord it over them, on the one hand, and a class of permanent slaves or debtors who would undercut their income, on the other.

What is the Torah's economic/ecological vision? We might call it a "pulsating" rather than an expanding or exploding system. It bears a family resemblance to what some economists and ecologists today call "sustainable" economies, which can meet their people's needs year after year, generation after generation, by restoring the earth to the same degree that they deplete it. This is definitely not the same as the goal of economic growth.

And the great sabbatical spiral renews human community as well. Here we see the Torah's vision of social justice through its focus on "resting," not only from the physical work of tilling the land, but from the political and social work of building institutions and concentrating capital. Stop work for even just one day, and for that day hierarchy dissolves: No boss, no employee. Stop work for an entire year, and the institutions of society—normally so useful—periodically dissolve. People are freed up, the imagination is freed up, the Breathing-Spirit of the world blows where it likes.

For the "eco-Judaism" of the Bible, spiritual enrichment is profoundly connected with limiting the society's exploitation of the earth, and both of these are intimately intertwined with limiting the mastery of the rich and powerful over the poor. And the energy flows in all directions through this organic whole. In one direction, only the spiritually well fed can ease their hunger for land, for wealth, and for power. In another direction, only those who rest from working the earth and from amassing wealth can get in deepest touch with God. In still another direction, the greed and envy that push people toward overworking the land cannot end unless everyone knows there is no point to envy: debts will be annulled and the land will be redistributed.

At another level, the sabbatical process shapes time into a spiral. For the Jews, the cycles of the earth, the moon, and the sun became not endlessly repetitive circles, unchanging, year after year after year. Nor did Jewish time ignore these cycles and turn time into a straight line always going forward, defined simply by historical and social change.

What the Shabbats of the seventh day and the seventh year accomplished was making a turn possible from one level to another of the repetition of the days and years. Taking time for reflection, for digestion of the last six days or years, made it possible to "repeat" them in a new key, at a new level, to learn from them so as not to have to repeat them, and to integrate the forward reach of historical, personal, and social change into the rhythms of forever. As in a spiral, Jewish time went backward in order to go forward.

Shabbat Throughout the Generations

If this theory of the origins and intentions of biblical "eco-Judaism" is correct, it teaches us a still deeper truth, one of method as well as content. We know that when, two thousand years ago, the Jewish people faced a great economic, political, and scientific transformation in the form of Greco-Roman Hellenistic civilization and its shattering of biblical society, their response was the creation of talmudic/rabbinic Judaism (and their contribution to the creation of Christianity and Islam). They responded by adopting some of the approaches of this new Hellenistic ability to control the earth and human beings, but also by infusing it with the more ancient wisdom of the Torah—wisdom of Being as well as Doing, Loving as well as Controlling.

In the rabbinic period of Jewish history, the sabbatical (*shmitah*) year and the *yovel* (home bringing) year were relegated to anachronisms by being limited to the land of Israel, even as Jews spread widely around the world. Since they had little or no power to enact or enforce such broad edicts, there was no point in trying.

The seventh-day Shabbat became even more elaborately defined than in the Bible, as it became crucial in marking the distinction between Jewish and other communities. Its meaning became focused on communal ethics and practice rather than on an ethical relationship to the earth.

As post-rabbinic modernity became a dominant mode of Jewish thought and behavior, Shabbat was often abandoned. In an industrial world, it seemed to be a waste of time—time to work, to add income, to accumulate wealth and power or stave off starvation.

In the early days of nineteenth- and twentieth-century Eco-Judaism, however, an effort began to redefine Shabbat as in part a path of respect and celebration for the Earth. Samson Raphael Hirsch in *The Jewish Sabbath*, Abraham Joshua Heschel's *The Sabbath*, and Erich Fromm's *You Shall Be as Gods* all took this tack. They found audiences from publics that were beginning to sense both the spiritual exhaustion and the ecological devastation wrought by societies that never made Shabbat.

Perhaps the most thorough biblical exploration of Eden Renewed is the Song of Songs, in which the relationship between *adam* and *adamah* is peaceful, even playful, and the hint of the Shabbat that comes with manna is fulfilled in an atmosphere that is almost wholly Shabbat. It is not surprising that the rabbis appointed the Song to be chanted during Passover, that the mystics of Safed decided 500 years ago it should also be chanted every Friday evening as Shabbat began, and that in the era of Eco-Judaism it has become a touchstone for the fusion of body and spirit, earth and human.

Sacred Offerings and Sacred Seasons

Throughout the biblical period, the relationship between the clan of Abraham (who become the Children of Israel) and their God is carried out through interactions with aspects of the earth—rocks and mountains; water, which is so scarce because the rain is so sparse throughout the Middle East; and the soil, from which springs food (flocks, grain, fruit).

One way of making this relationship holy, as we have seen, is through the rhythms of rest that reaffirm that the earth belongs to YHWH. Another way is the series of sacrificial offerings. All of them are food: grain, meat, fruit, bread, pancakes, and, once a year, water and wine. The Hebrew for them, *korbanot*, is from the root that evokes "nearness": they are all ways of coming near to God, and the word also echoes the Hebrew for "guts, intestines," where food is turned into body. We come near to God by connecting our holy food-processing innards to the Holy One Who breathes all life into food, all food into life.

The *korbanot* suffuse all aspects of life—dawn, morning, afternoon, nightfall; moments of guilt, sorrow, well-being—but they are especially elaborated for holy festivals that follow the dance of Earth, Sun, and Moon.

Given the sacred importance of this earth–human relationship, it is not surprising that the Bible's most dreadful tale of ecological disaster is one in which water ceases to be scarce and instead overwhelms all land, all life: the Flood.

What ethical practices can we learn from that story? The Torah's teaching about how to prevent the Flood is far less explicit than how to deal with it once it is on the way.

What ethical failure led to the Flood? Vaguely, the Torah specifies only *hamas*—ruination, perhaps connected with "heat." Humanity at large, not a central institution or person, was to blame.

The Rabbis usually asserted that the universe is built on "measure for measure": God's rewards and punishments fit our actions. So the Rabbis asked, "Since the purging of the earth came through water, what was being wrongly done through water?" And they answered that before the Flood, all the species were mixing the water of their semen with each other. This water washed away all biological boundaries, confounding the clarity of God's creation; so God sent a Flood of water to wash away all boundaries.[6]

Today we know that few species can mix together and propagate in this way. But we have also invented "genetic recombination," by which indeed the genes of one species can be introduced inside the DNA of another. Should we take the fantasy of the Rabbis as a warning to explore this new technology with the greatest care, if at all, lest we bring upon ourselves a global disaster?

The very fact of the biblical Rainbow Covenant and the inclusion within it of not only all humans but "every breathing life-form with you" (Gen 9:8–17) hints that covenanting itself is an ethical path, a way of preventing eco-disaster. The Rabbis maintained that God made a covenant with all Children of Noah, consisting of seven commandments.[7] In creating that list of commandments, the Rabbis seem to assume that the provisions of basic justice—forbidding murder and theft, requiring that all societies establish courts of justice—may establish an ethical system that will prevent a future Flood. Their only direct rule connecting human with other life is that the biblical permission to eat animals is limited by prohibiting eating part of a living animal.

When it comes to mitigating disaster rather than preventing it, we learn more. Noah is not an expert on rain, or ships, or animals. He is simply a righteous person, and some of the rabbinic commentators conclude that he is not even extraordinarily righteous, but only middling righteous, compared with those around him.[8] Thus the Noah story teaches that when all life is in danger, any of us who regard ourselves as simply reasonably decent people—"middling righteous"—are obligated to act.

What must Noah and his family do? They must preserve all life. The first "species preservation act" turns out to be the command of God to Noah that a pair of every species be rescued aboard the Ark. Today this command might suggest an ongoing commitment to prevent the mass extinction of species that human expansiveness and lack of self-restraint are causing.

The story of the Flood begins and ends with affirmations of the importance of the seasons and the flow of time. Alone among all the tales of Genesis, it specifies crucial dates: when the rain began to fall, when the waters stopped their rising, when dry ground first appeared, when the Ark landed. From start to finish, the story takes one lunar year plus eleven days—exactly one solar year.

What are we to learn from this? In the age of modernity, the sacred cycles of time have been thwarted. We have let our desire for "productivity" destroy our sense of holy time and holy cycles. We have become so drunk on our new ability to produce goods that we have forgotten to rest, reflect, contemplate, meditate, celebrate.

This hyperproductive mode, in which time is only a raw material of production, has taken us to the brink of hyperdestruction. In a world that discards meditation and celebration as—literally—a waste of time, the H-bomb, destruction of the ozone layer, acid rain, deforestation, and the climate crisis are all inevitable. The Flood and the Rainbow remind us that we must renew the cycles and our celebration of them in order to live.

Noah's own name means "the restful one." Only willingness to rest can save all life. And the covenant itself is not between God and humankind alone: "all breathing life" is enfolded in it.

Noah celebrated the renewal of all life after the Flood by building a sacred slaughter-site and lifting up to YHWH, the Breath of Life, those animals and fowl that were "pure" for eating, to reconnect the Earth with God.[9] If we come back from this mythic tale of Earth shattered and renewed to the Bible's commonplaces of everyday life in the midst of the relationship between *adam* and *adamah*, what do we find?

Over and over again, wellsprings are seen as a place of sacred connection with the Divine. Hagar's seeing *Be'er Lahai Roi*, the Well of the Living One Who Sees Me[10]; Abraham's oath at *Be'er Sheva*[11]; the marriage moments of Isaac[12] and Jacob[13] and Moses[14]; the crucial moments in the Wilderness when God tells Moses how to bring forth water from a rock[15]—all testify that water must be seen as sacred. The Second Temple practice of pouring offerings of water into a spout next to the sacred Altar—as Rabbi Akiba explained, pouring water to remind God to pour out the water of rain[16]—carries this knowledge to its highest expression.

Jacob's recognition of *Beth El*, the House of God, by anointing a rock with olive oil,[17] and the revelation of the Ten Utterances upon the Mountain of God (and the inclusion of salt in the Temple offerings) recognize that what moderns might see as "dead" minerals are filled with Divine life.

The offerings at the Mishkan in the Wilderness[18] and at the shrines in Shiloh[19] and Jerusalem[20] are mostly grain, fruit, and meat, the foods that spring from the soil of the land of Israel. Even pancakes—"fine flour mixed with oil and spice, then turned to smoke upon the Altar"[21]—are a path to God.

This practice taught that the relationship between *adam* and *adamah* was the expression of relationship with God. So it is not surprising that biblically, and then in rabbinic tradition, elaboration of proper and improper foods, what was and was not kosher to eat, took on immense importance in defining a sacred life. Animals described by their relationship to earth, sea, and air embodied into intimate human relationship those three primal aspects of God's process of creation.

Separating mammalian foods of life (milk) and death (meat) became a marker of sacred imitation of the God Who gave life or decreed death.

Although rabbinic Judaism focused on the sacred uses of the mouth to chant words of prayer and passages of Torah and midrash much more than eating as a way of connecting with God, choosing what to eat never lost its sacred power in rabbinic practice. Not until modernity became a central theme of much of Jewish life did "secular" Jews and "Reform" Jews put aside eating as a sacred connection with the Earth and God. And even where Jews kept kosher practice alive, its function as part of intimate community weakened through the establishment of corporate institutions instead of local rabbis to authorize and administer *kashrut*.

In the era of Eco-Judaism, as it became clear that human consumption—"eating"—of coal and oil, uranium and plastics, was gobbling up the earth beyond the mouthing of food, the question arose whether consuming these other products should be done in an "eco-kosher" way. Was energy derived from nuclear power plants "eco-kosher"? Was wine for *Kiddush* drunk from nonrecyclable styrofoam cups "eco-kosher"? Was meat "eco-kosher" if it came from animals slaughtered in accordance with *halakhah* but only after being fed all their lives with antibiotics and being restrained from running freely in pastures, so as to increase the weight of their saleable flesh?

The Festivals: Seasons of the Moon, the Sun, the Earth

In the Torah, the festivals are described as being closely related to the agricultural cycle and the cycles of the moon. The full moon of spring begins Pesah, and approximately coincides with the shepherds' moment of lambing (whence the "*pesah*" offering) and the farmers' moment of the sprouting of barley (whence the "*matzah*" practice). Forty-nine days of the barley harvest climax with the spring wheat and the Shavuot festival of "first fruits." On the full moon of fall comes the festival of harvest fullness—Sukkot—as this double fullness takes its place not only in the solar-agricultural cycle but also in the special lunar cycle of the seventh "moonth," alongside its new moon (Rosh Hashanah), its waxing moon (Yom Kippur), and its disappearing moon (Shmini Atzeret).[22]

These Torah festivals are followed by other special days in the Jewish calendar: Tisha B'Av, at the fiercely hottest moment of the year, connecting a Babylonian solar-scorching sacred day with the burning of the Temple in Jerusalem; Purim, a festival of spring fever and hilarious rebellions against wintry authority justified by the story of Esther; Hanukkah, lighting a growing bank of lights during what is (in the northern hemisphere) the darkest time of sun and moon; Tu B'Shvat, which began as the fiscal-year date for tithing fruit.

In rabbinic tradition, many of these festivals and fasts were explained with little connection to the cycles of the earth, sun, and moon. (Shavuot, for example, became the festival for the revelation of Torah.) Many were defined as responses to a political or historical event, or given spiritual meaning divorced from the earth.

As parts of the Jewish people began to move out of the Rabbinic mind-set and culture into modernity, industrialization became a central concern of both Zionism and large Diaspora communities. Though early Zionism included outlooks like that of A.D. Gordon that showed deep concern for the actual land, earth, water, and air of the Land of Israel, three factors changed this: the desire to shift aspects of the Land (for example, a unique version of forestation) to mark Zionist and then Israeli turf as distinguished from previous or continuing Palestinian turf; the push toward industrialization as a necessity of competition in the "developed" world; and the concern for military effectiveness during seemingly permanent war status. All of these thrust Israeli society toward an industrial model in which ecological considerations became a low priority.

Variants of Jewish Modernism in the Diaspora similarly focused on emulating the surrounding cultural and economic goal of industrialization. This involved the abandonment of both the biblically and rabbinically rooted concern for nonhuman life forms and the Earth as an ecosystem.

In parts of the Zionist movement, some of the agricultural meanings of some of the festivals were renewed—for example, Shavuot as "first fruits" by agrarian *kibbutzim*. Tu B'Shvat was focused on the reforestation of land held by the Jewish settlements in Palestine, and later in the State of Israel—though, as is clear in hindsight, the forests were often grown without attention to ecological good sense.

With the emergence of Eco-Judaism, many of these holy times were redefined as earth-connected. Hanukkah's deep roots in darkness were reemphasized, along with Tu B'Shvat as a sacred celebration of precious trees, Sukkot as a time to save the earth from industrially generated carcinogens as well as from locusts and drought, Tisha B'Av as grief for the destruction of the Holy Temple of Earth herself, Pesah as a time to free the Earth and Humanity as a whole from Pharaonic powers in Big Corporations and Big Government that through oppressive arrogance were bringing modern plagues upon the planet (undrinkable water, extreme "hailstorm" weather, unprecedented insect invasions, mad cow disease, and so on).

Just as the approach of Eco-Judaism sought to unify the ecological with the spiritual, it sought to unify "ritual" with "ethical action." So observance of the festivals became occasions for public action to change corporate or governmental public policy.

TREES: DO NOT DESTROY

What seems in the Torah a specialized and therefore rather minor edict about behavior toward the earth becomes a much broader one in rabbinic Judaism. The Torah says, "When you besiege a city, making war against it, you shall not destroy its trees.... for is the tree of the field human that you should besiege it? Only trees that you know do not bear fruit may you destroy."[23]

The rabbis of the Talmud concluded that if we must not destroy enemy fruit trees even in wartime, then all the more must we take care not to waste them, or any life-forms, or even human-made objects, in time of peace: *Bal tashhit*! ("Do not destroy!"). At the same time, having broadened the command so much, they also made clear that it was wasteful use, not all use, that they were prohibiting, that indeed God sees it as a sin not to take advantage of the joys God provided in the world God created.[24]

So a calculus of when the destruction of trees, or furniture, or clothing, might be worthwhile when their destruction protected or healed human beings or gave them joy became a constant dance of rabbinic *halakhah*. Confronted in the twentieth century with the charge that biblical Judaism and Christianity had, through the teaching "Fill the earth and subdue it,"[25] encouraged destruction of nature by human beings, some rabbis responded by citing *Bal tashhit*. But on careful examination, it was realized there was much more apologia than accuracy to this way of exculpating Judaism. Appeals to the biblical traditions cited above were much more accurate.

Nevertheless, the principle raised some interesting questions. Its origins in the protection of trees struck a sensitive nerve in the midst of wars when the U.S. government and the government of Israel were destroying, respectively, Vietnamese and Palestinian trees, and when other nations paid no heed to the trees that they were destroying not only in war, but in clearing rain forests and other stands of trees to exploit the land for commercial purposes. As modern science discovered the planetary importance of trees in absorbing carbon dioxide and breathing out oxygen, applying "Do not destroy" to forests and to broader swathes of the planetary ecosystem attracted more attention and encouraged the emergence of Tu B'Shvat not only as a day for planting trees in the land of Israel, but also as a day for honoring and protecting trees around the world.

As climatologists focused on the worldwide danger of "global warming" and a "climate crisis" arising from deforestation and the overburning of fossil fuels, both the obscure holy day of Tu B'Shvat and the dictum of *Bal tashhit* grew more important in Jewish ethics.

In one tiny corner of the world of "postmodern" Eco-Judaism, the role of trees in *bal tashhit* led to a seed of potential interest, both in content and process. In a synagogue school class of twelve-year-olds studying Judaism and the "environment," the question arose how to think about the scientific fact that all trees are "fruitful" of the crucial oxygen that all animals need to breathe and that balances (or tries to balance) carbon dioxide in the atmosphere. Knowing what we know now, must we forebear from cutting down all trees, not only those producing the kind of fruit the Torah had in mind (olives, figs, etc)? After arguing the question, the class concluded that human beings could not, need not, eschew the cutting of all trees—but that we should commit ourselves to plant at least one new tree for every one cut down. This solution is an interesting example of applying the *halakhic* method to new circumstances.

Theology and the Name of God

Early in Torah, God appears often to the Patriarchs and Matriarchs as *El Shaddai*, usually translated as "God Almighty" but, because *shadayim* is the Hebrew word for breasts, it may mean "the God of Breasts," bearing nourishment from the Earth as prosperity and fertility for Israelites. Then in the crisis moment heralded by the Burning Bush, God drops "El Shaddai" and tells Moses two "new" Divine Names: *Ehyeh Asher Ehyeh*, "I Will Be Who I Will Be," and "*YHWH*." Rabbinic Judaism turned the latter into "*Adonai*, Lord," and in the classical form of rabbinic blessing, "*Melekh*, King."

In the modern, industrialized period of Jewish thought and practice, these ways of understanding God were either dropped entirely in favor of atheism (being replaced by the "Historical Dialectic" of Marx or the "Invisible Hand" of Adam Smith) or turned into a mumbled rote with little meaning in prayers recited not "by heart" but "by memory." Even in the modernized Judaism of Mordecai Kaplan's Reconstructionism, which redefined God as "the sum of all natural processes that allow human beings to become self-fulfilled," during prayer the metaphors of God as "Lord" and "King" were preserved (perhaps as fossils held in amber).

But the postmodern emergence of feminist forms of Judaism and Eco-Judaism sought other metaphors for use in prayer. Two that have begun to win broad attention and use are deeply rooted in the natural world: *Eyn ha'hayyim*, "Wellspring of life," and *Ru'ah ha-Olam*, "Breath/Wind/ Spirit of the universe." Along with these have come a flood of theologies that draw on the Hassidic *Alz iz Gott*, "All is God," in new ways, emphasizing the immanent or panentheist way of experiencing God, rather than transcendence. All these approaches encourage an ecological ethic that does not restrict the *tzelem elohim*, the "Image of God," to human beings alone, as biblical and rabbinic Judaism seem to have assumed.

If these theologies keep growing in acceptance, they are likely to continue changing the Jewish ethics of relationship between *adam* and *adamah* in directions ever more attuned to their interwovenness.

Notes

1. For a discussion of how each of these sources serves as a source of Jewish moral norms and ethical vision, see Elliot N. Dorff, *Love Your Neighbor and Yourself: A Jewish Approach to Modern Personal Ethics* (Philadelphia: Jewish Publication Society, 2003), Appendix. For a comparison of the moral implications of the central stories of Judaism, Christianity, and the United States, see Elliot N. Dorff, *To Do the Right and the Good: A Jewish Approach to Modern Social Ethics* (Philadelphia: Jewish Publication Society, 2002), chap. 1.
2. Leviticus 25:8–11, 23.
3. Leviticus 25:4.
4. Leviticus 25:4–7.

5. Leviticus 26:14–16, 32–35, 43.
6. B. *Rosh Hashanah* 12a: Rav Hisda said: "With hot liquid they sinned, and with hot liquid they were punished. With hot liquid they sinned—namely, with sexual transgressions."
7. B. *Sanhedrin* 56a–b.
8. B. *Sanhedrin* 108a; *Genesis Rabbah* 30:9.
9. Genesis 8: 20–22.
10. Genesis 16:14.
11. Genesis 21:31.
12. Genesis 24, esp. 24:11–27 and 24:42–48.
13. Genesis 29:1–12.
14. Exodus 2:15–21.
15. Numbers 20:7–13; cf. Deuteronomy 3:23–29.
16. B. *Rosh Hashanah* 16a.
17. Genesis 28:18.
18. Leviticus, chaps. 1–9.
19. 1 Samuel 1:24–25.
20. 1 Chronicles 23: 28–29; 2 Chronicles 7: 4–7; Ezra 6:17, 7:17; Nehemiah 10: 33–37; M. *Tamid passim*; B. *Zevahim*, chap. 5, *passim*.
21. Leviticus 2:1–3.
22. See Leviticus 23; Numbers 28–29; and Deuteronomy 16 for a description of these holy times mandated by the Torah.
23. Deuteronomy 20:19–20.
24. B. *Bava Kamma* 91b. For the prohibition itself, see also B. *Shabbat* 67b, 129a, 140b; B. *Kiddushin* 32a; and B. *Hullin* 7b.
25. Genesis 1:28.

Suggestions for Further Reading

Benstein, Jeremy. 2006. *The Way into Judaism and the Environment.* Woodstock, VT: Jewish Lights Publishing.

Bernstein, Ellen. 1987. *The Trees' Birthday: A Celebration of Nature: A Tu B'Shvat Haggadah.* Mt. Airy, PA: Turtle River Press.

Bernstein, Ellen. 2005. *The Splendor of Creation: A Biblical Ecology.* Cleveland: Pilgrim Press.

Biers-Ariel, Matt, Deborah Newbrun, and Michal Fox Smart. 2000. *Spirit in Nature: Teaching Judaism and Ecology on the Trail.* Springfield, NJ: Behrman House.

Eisenberg, Evan. 1998. *The Ecology of Eden.* New York: Alfred A. Knopf.

Elon, Ari, Naomi M. Hyman, and Arthur Ocean Waskow, eds. 2000. *Trees, Earth, and Torah: A Tu b'Shvat Anthology.* Philadelphia: Jewish Publication Society.

Gendler, Everett. 1971. "On the Judaism of Nature." In *The New Jews*, James A. Sleeper and Alan L. Mintz, eds. New York: Random House, pp. 233–43.

Sasso, Sandy Eisenberg. 1996. *A Prayer for the Earth: The Story of Naamah, Noah's Wife.* Woodstock, VT: Jewish Lights Publishing.

Schwartz. Richard H. 1987. *Judaism and Global Survival.* New York: Atara Publishing.

Tirosh-Samuelson, Hava, ed. 2002. *Judaism and Ecology: Created World and Revealed Word.* Cambridge, MA: Harvard University Press.

Troster, Lawrence. 1991. "Created in the Image of God: Humanity and Divinity in an Age of Environmentalism." *Conservative Judaism* 44:1 (Fall), pp. 14–24.

Waskow, Arthur. 1982. *Seasons of Our Joy*. New York: Bantam. 2nd ed., 1990. Boston: Beacon Press; 3rd ed., 2012. Philadelphia: Jewish Publication Society.

Waskow, Arthur. 1995. *Down-to-Earth Judaism: Food, Money, Sex, and the Rest of Life*. New York: William Morrow.

Waskow, Arthur., ed. 2000. *Torah of the Earth: Exploring 4,000 Years of Ecology in Jewish Thought*. Woodstock, VT: Jewish Lights Publishing, 2 vols.

http://www.theshalomcenter.org/treasury/5

http://www.jewcology.com/

CHAPTER 24

JEWISH ANIMAL ETHICS

AARON S. GROSS

THE DIVERSITY OF JEWISH ANIMAL ETHICS

Ethically charged engagements with animals permeate Jewish traditions, beginning with the Bible. Compassion (*rahamim*) for animals is deeply interwoven with the Pentateuchal narrative where God creates humans and animals on the same day and gives them the same blessing (Gen 1:24–28); grants humans dominion over animals but also commands them to be vegetarian (Gen 1:26–30)[1]; holds both humans and animals (*kol basar*) culpable for the earth's corruption (Gen 6:12); is angered by human craving for meat (*basar*) (Num 11:33); (reluctantly?) allows humans to eat all living things within a sacrificial system that includes an absolute prohibition on consuming blood as a permanent symbol of the sanctity of life (Gen 9:3–5)[2]; covenants with all creation (Gen 9:8–17); and ordains specific legal protections for animals in both the Exodus and Deuteronomic legal codes—including commanding Sabbath rest for all Israelites, their human slaves, and their large domestic animals (Exod 20:10, 23:12; Deut 5–14). The Prophetic texts of the Bible continue many of these themes, for example by offering visions of the coming messianic age that imply a return to Edenic vegetarianism (Isa 11:6–7, Joel 4:18, Amos 9:14, and Hosea 2:24). In the *Ketuvim* (Writings), the Psalms are especially dense with images of animal praise of God and God's care for animal life (e.g., Psalms 65:14; 148:10–13); Proverbs argues that the righteous are attentive to animal welfare (Prov 12:10); Job extols the ability of animals to teach humans (12:7–8) and is told by God that the fantastic animal, behemoth, is "the first of God's work" (40:19); and Ecclesiastes even questions the degree to which animals (*behemah*) are inferior to humans

(Eccles 3:19). Indeed, the dominant image of God in the Bible is as a shepherd of God's human flock generally and of Israel in particular (Gen 48:15; Isa 40:11; Ps 23:1)—an image that uses the relationship between humans and farmed animals to describe the ideal human–divine relationship.

Classical rabbinic texts, biblical commentators, and liturgists expand this robust combination of both *halakhic* (Jewish legal) and *aggadic* (nonlegal) attention to animals found in the Bible.[3] All comprehensive rabbinic legal compendiums incorporate animal ethics.

The Jewish concern for animal welfare continues in medieval and modern Jewish sources, both religious and secular. For example, tales of compassion for animals are a regular feature of contemporary Orthodox hagiographies.[4] The value of animal life is a recurring theme in the work of modern literary adepts such as Franz Kafka, Nobel Laureate Shmuel Yosef Agnon, and a handful of major figures in Yiddish literature including Nobel Laureate Isaac Bashevis Singer. Animal ethics has increasingly been enshrined in Israeli law and remains a prominent theme among secular and other "problematically" Jewish thinkers such as Walter Benjamin, Max Horkheimer, Jacques Derrida, and Peter Singer. Moreover, this ethical regard for animals takes on distinctive forms in specific historical movements, most notably in the various forms of Jewish mysticism, in ethical movements like Mussar, and in responses to catastrophic destruction. Because of length limitations, the distinct ways in which each of these Jewish voices expresses concern for animal welfare will of necessity be conflated here.

While keeping this diversity in mind, the chief aim of this chapter is to utilize a largely synchronic and text-based analysis to describe the constraints of the mainstream of Jewish animal ethics and provide a phenomenological taxonomy that allows us to comprehend the fundamental basis for compassion to animals. In order to allow space to touch on pragmatic questions of responsibility, the chapter will give special attention to farmed animals. We will proceed through the detour of a story.

Imagining Jewish Animal Ethics

In the talmudic tractate *Bava' Metzi'a'* (32a–32b) we encounter the most extended discussion of the most important question regarding the *halakhic* status of Judaism's broad principle of animal protection: is the general Jewish law not to cause suffering to living creatures without cause (known as *tza'ar ba'alei hayyim*) a "Torah law" or a "rabbinic law"? If it is a Torah law, then the commandment has great authority—greater than the vast body of Jewish law proclaimed by rabbinic traditions. Though "it is the virtually unanimous opinion of rabbinic decisors"[5] in later periods that this principle of minimizing pain to animals is a Torah law, the debate in the Talmud itself is left unresolved. Roughly fifty folios later, as if in response to this unresolved debate, we are told of a curious interaction between a nameless calf and the editor of the Mishnah, Rabbi Judah haNasi (second century).[6]

The story contains two parts. In the first, Rabbi Judah is punished for his lack of compassion to a calf being led to slaughter:

> A calf being lead to *shehitah* [Jewish religious slaughter] broke away, hid its head in the folds of Rabbi's garment, and wept. He said to it: "Go. For this you were created." [The heavenly court] said [in response]: "Since he had no compassion, let him face sufferings." (B. *Bava Metzi'a'* 85a)

The second part of the story explains why Rabbi Judah's sufferings ultimately ended:

> One day Rabbi's female servant was sweeping the house. Some infant rodents were scattered [from their nest], and she swept them up. He said to her: "Let them go. As it is written: 'His compassion is over all His works'" (Ps. 145:9). They said: "Because he was compassionate, let us be compassionate to him" (B. *Bava Metzi'a'* 85a).

This story creates a dialectical juxtaposition of two different sentiments, both put in the mouth of Rabbi Judah: "Go. For this you were created," and "His compassion is over all His works" (Ps. 145:9). Though the force of this story is to highlight the importance of compassion for animals, the idea that animals are created for the sake of humans, a prevalent view in the Talmud, is never denied.

So, to paraphrase the philosopher of animal ethics, Mary Midgley, why do animals matter?[7] The major fault line in answering this question is the issue of whether animals were created by God only for humans, or whether they have inherent worth. Further, what responsibilities does Jewish animal ethics impose on us?

The Horizons of Jewish Animal Ethics

In light of the biblical and rabbinic sources mentioned above, there is no question about *whether* animals matter, but only why and how. Abraham Ibn Ezra (1089–1164) goes so far as to include animals in the command to "Love your neighbor as yourself" (Lev.19:18).[8] Moses Hayyim Luzzatto (1707–1746) makes compassion for animals a basic virtue.[9] Noah Cohen concludes that the classical rabbis see compassion for animals as "categorical and undeniable.... not a proposition to be proved."[10] This notion constitutes the opening horizon of Jewish animal ethics: our treatment of animals matters. Human–animal relations are an important religious issue.

While it is clear that animals matter, it is equally clear that there is widespread agreement in rabbinic sources that whatever human and Jewish responsibilities there are to protect the *lives* of animals, such protections should not preclude the use of animals for legitimate human *interests*, such as—paradigmatically—satisfying the desire to eat *basar*, flesh. This principle, rarely explicit but constantly operative, constitutes the closing horizon of Jewish animal ethics. One can argue that Judaism is a tradition friendly to and even encouraging of ethical vegetarianism (though this is a position many would dispute), but one cannot persuasively argue that traditional and modern forms of Judaism demand a complete ban on meat consumption such as, for example, we find in several South Asian traditions. Significantly, some powerful minority streams within Judaism would insist that consuming meat is in principle unethical—a moral compromise—and would argue that vegetarianism is an ideal even though not a mandatory practice. These minority streams, perhaps as old as the book of Genesis, are found in traces throughout the Talmud and classical commentaries on the Bible[11] and are vibrant in Jewish materials throughout modernity.[12] In light of the way in which Judaism has evolved over time, there is no reason these now marginal views could not one day become dominant.[13]

This simultaneous insistence on both the value of animal lives and the greater value of human well-being is articulated in a dialectical fashion throughout Jewish texts by juxtaposing countervailing principles of, on the one hand, *kindness* to animals (often coupled with an emphasis on human creatureliness), and, on the other hand, human *ascendancy*, (often coupled with an emphasis on human distinctiveness).[14] We have in fact already seen this dialectical strategy in the story of Rabbi Judah and in Genesis's juxtaposition of God's violent command to dominate ("master" and "rule") animals with a command to be vegetarian. As the modern Orthodox rabbi Irving (Yitz) Greenberg explains, "The Jewish strategy was to combine human activism and restraint, yoking mastery over nature with reverence for the natural order."[15]

Why Animals Matter: To Benefit Humans

When the tradition emphasizes the ascendency side of the dialectic, compassion for animals is understood to be for the sake of the human being, but when the kindness side of the dialect is highlighted, animals are granted a value independent of human beings. Both strains serve as foundations for Jewish animal ethics.

Three distinct but overlapping Judaic ideas point to the value of compassion for animals for the sake of humanity: the ideas that (1) compassion to animals is rewarded (as in the story of Rabbi Judah), (2) morally outstanding individuals spontaneously show compassion to animals, and (3) sensitivity to animals promotes sensitivity to other humans.

The first idea can be found in the Deuteronomic Code itself where the command to drive away a mother bird before taking her eggs (birds become distressed when their eggs are taken)—a paradigmatic example of compassion for animals in later Jewish traditions—is followed by the phrase "in order that it may go well for you" (Deut 22:7). Thus we read in the Talmud that "anyone who is compassionate to creatures receives compassion from the heavens, and anyone who is not compassionate to creatures does not receive compassion from the heavens" (B. *Shabbat* 151b).[16] Similarly, in *Midrash Tehillim*, the rabbinic commentary on the Book of Psalms, Abraham concludes that Noah and his sons came forth alive from the ark "only [!] because they gave alms [to animals]" (Ps 37).[17] In the legal code of Rambam (Moses ben Maimon, or "Maimonides," 1135–1204), the *Mishneh Torah*, we read, "He who shows mercy to animals will in turn be shown mercy by God."[18] *Sefer Hasidim*, a thirteenth-century text of German Jewish pietists, asserts that "A person who hurts an animal needlessly will receive the same punishment" (§482).[19]

The second theme noted above, that compassion for animals is a quality inherent in the righteous person, is articulated most famously in the book of Proverbs: "The righteous person knows the needs [*nefesh*, literally "soul"] of his animal" (Prov 12:10). The same conception seems to be operative in Genesis (24:44), where Abraham's servant Eliezer determines that Rebecca—a paradigm of the good wife—is a suitable spouse for Isaac when she provides water not only for him, but also, without prompting, for his camels. We also find it in rabbinic texts, such as *Midrash Tanhuma* (Noah 5), where both Noah and Joseph are deemed righteous men "because they nourished creatures." Perhaps most strikingly, *Exodus Rabbah* (2:2) relates that both Moses and David—the paradigmatic male leadership of Israel—were tested by God through how they functioned as shepherds.

The third theme, that compassion for animals actively promotes kindness to other humans, is articulated by Ramban (Moses ben Nahman, "Nahmanides," 1194–1270) in his commentary on both the Deuteronomic law that one must drive away a mother bird before taking her eggs (22:7) and the prohibition on killing a mother and its young on the same day (Lev 22:28). Ramban goes out of his way to argue that the reason for the law of the mother bird is not—despite the suggestion of some Jewish sources (including Rambam[20])—the undeniable suffering of the mother bird. *Sefer ha-Hinnukh* (thirteenth century), which provides a numbered, systematic commentary on each of the 613 commandments of the Torah, cites Ramban's view with approval: God's "compassion does not extend over [individual] creatures with animal souls [but only over entire species]...for if so, *shehitah* [Jewish ritual slaughter of animals] would have been forbidden. Indeed, the reason for the restriction [i.e., of driving away the mother bird] is to teach us the quality of compassion" (Mitzvah 545).[21] And referring to the commandment in Deuteronomy 25:4 not to muzzle a domestic animal during its work (thus causing the animal suffering by tempting it with food it cannot eat), another law paradigmatically associated with compassion for animals, *Sefer ha-Hinnukh*, makes the case that "from its root the commandment serves to teach us to make our souls beautiful ones...by accustoming us to this even with animals, which were created only to serve us" (Mitzvah 596).

Why Animals Matter: The Inherent Value of Animal Creation

Other streams, by contrast, champion the inherent, divinely established worth of animals by emphasizing (1) God's care for animals, (2) animals' praise of God,[22] and (3) ways that animals are imbued with and reflect the divine.[23] Many of these images are found in the Psalms, such as the aforementioned "His compassion is over all His works" and, at the end of the same Psalm, "And all flesh [*basar*] will bless His holy name forever and ever" (145:21). Significantly, Psalm 145, which incorporates all three themes and is recited three times in the daily liturgy, is regularly used as a proof text demonstrating God's concern for animals. For example, in the rabbinic text *Tanhuma*, Psalm 145:9 is cited to prove that unlike human beings, who, when aboard a ship caught in a storm, will toss their possessions and animals overboard, God, by contrast, "shows compassion to animals in the same way He shows compassion to people " (*Noah* 6).

Another widely cited example of the first theme, divine concern for animals, is Psalm 147:9, which praises God as the one "Who gives to the animals their food, to young ravens what they cry for." An interesting intensification of this theme is the idea that God cares so much for animals that unethical humans are saved for their sake. Thus in *Genesis Rabbah* we read that God grants the wicked kingdom of Alexander rain only for the sake of animals: the verse "Human and animal You save, Adonai" (Ps 37:7) is reinterpreted by the text to mean, "Human *for the sake of* animal You save, Adonai" (33:1). The Maharal (Judah ben Bezalel Löw, ca. 1520–1609) provides the most explicit articulation of animals having an inherent value rooted in divine concern, "Everything, like grasses and fruits, were created for the sake of animals, which are flesh, for He gave them everything to eat, as the verse states, 'I give you...' [Gen 1:29]. From this you see that everything else was created for the animals, while the animals were created in the world for their own sake" (*Be'er Ha-Golah*).[24]

Examples of the second theme, the tradition of animals (and other parts of the natural world) praising God, are frequent in Psalms, such as the exhortations of Psalm 148—"Praise Adonai ... wildlife and all animals, creeping things, and birds of wing.... Let them praise the name of Adonai" (148: 7–13), and Psalm 150, the concluding line of the entire book, "Let all that breathes praise Adonai" (150:6). The theme also "occurs quite frequently in talmudic and midrashic literature,"[25] such as the talmudic interpretation of 1 Samuel 6:12, in which two cows pulling the Ark of the Covenant "turned their faces toward the Ark and sang a song [praising God]" (B. *Avodah Zarah* 14b). The Rabbis go on to debate precisely what song the cows sang! The most dramatic example of this theme is found in *Perek Shirah*—a text of uncertain origin that consists of six chapters containing verses beginning with the formula "The such-and-such says..." and then putting a quotation from the Bible, most frequently Psalms, in the mouth of an animal, plant, or other part of the natural world. For example, "The hen is saying, 'He gives food to all flesh [*basar*], for his covenant-love [*Hesed*] is eternal' [Ps 136:25]." *Perek Shirah*'s influence is considerable in part because of the long-standing practice in some Jewish communities of incorporating it into daily prayer, one chapter for each weekday.

Overlapping these traditions are texts that address the third theme, that animals are imbued with and reflect the divine. Psalm 104:24 declares that God fashioned all creatures with wisdom. The Talmud, going further, maintains that each creature consented to the form God gave it, implying that God conferred with the animals (B. *Hullin* 60a). This ability to reflect a part of the divine wisdom hovers in the background of the numerous classical rabbinic stories of animal sagacity. For example, *Pesikta Rabbati*, a sixth- or seventh-century redaction of earlier rabbinic materials, tells a story of a cow who, when sold to a gentile, still refused to work on the Sabbath and ultimately so impressed its new owner with its piety that the new owner converted to Judaism and became a great rabbi (14).[26] In some of these stories animals behave ethically and show an awareness of God when humans do not. Thus "Balaam's ass" sees a divine messenger on the road when Balaam is unable to do so (Num 22:21–28), and in the Talmud we read that while the humans of today are like donkeys when compared with the previous, morally superior generation, they are "not like the donkeys of R. Hanina and R. Pinhas ben Ya'ir," who refused to eat untithed barley and therefore are, the text seems to imply, our moral superiors (B. *Shabbat* 12b). Moses Cordovero (1522–1570), returning to the story of Rabbi Judah and the calf, argues that "the Supernal Wisdom is extended to all created things—minerals, plants, animals, and humans.... In this way man's pity should be extended to all the works of the Blessed One just as the Supernal Wisdom despises no created thing.... This is the reason our holy teacher was punished for his failure to have pity on the young calf that tried to hide near him."[27]

Human Responsibility for Animals

The two roots of compassion for animals delineated in the previous two sections produce two fundamental Jewish responsibilities that humans have toward animals: (1) to protect a precious and imperiled human "sentiment of compassion" that flows simultaneously toward both humans and animals,[28] and (2) to protect animals from humans where economic incentives make abuse likely. Significantly, these responsibilities are among the very few that some rabbinic traditions extend to all humanity. Thus Saadiah Gaon (ca. 882–942), for example, argues that gentiles will be rewarded for observing the commandment to chase away the mother bird.[29] A stronger statement of the universality of this obligation is the mishnaic prohibition against eating a limb from a living animal, one of the seven "Noahide laws," understood as obligatory for all humanity.[30] While this prohibition is justified in a variety of ways, compassion for animals is a common rabbinic explanation. This inclusion of animal protection in the Noahide laws, at least for those who see a humane impulse behind it, implies that treatment of animals is one marker of whether a person or nation is "civilized" and thus fully human. As Jordan Rosenblum argues, the Tannaim understood this law as a basic taboo "that distinguishes a civilized person from an animal."[31] Compassion toward animals is thus configured as basic to the humanity of humans.

Meat as an Ethical Problem

Rather than survey core areas of human responsibility to animals, I will limit this discussion to animals that are eaten as food, commenting on both classical texts and the contemporary state of affairs. Jewish traditions tend to view the act of killing animals as acceptable but morally fraught. Thus the Talmud dictates that one should not eat meat unless one craves it and kills the animal on one's own (B. *Hullin* 84a), has wealth (B. *Hullin* 84a[32]), and is educated (B. *Pesahim* 49b). Some intellectual streams go further and view meat-eating as a divine compromise, understanding *kashrut* (Jewish dietary law) as a vehicle intended to limit meat eating or even encourage us toward vegetarianism. The most influential modern exponent of this idea was almost certainly Rabbi Abraham Isaac Kook (1865–1935), the first Ashkenazic Chief Rabbi of pre-state Israel.[33] Meat is an ethical problem both because it ends an animal's life, and God "did not create His creatures to die" (*Midrash Aggadah* to Genesis 1:29),[34] and because killing poses a threat to human moral development. This is perhaps the logic behind the Mishnah's assertion that "the best of the butchers is a partner of Amalek [the arch-enemy of Israel]" (M. *Kiddushin* 4:14).[35] In this way, the first ethical obligation in relation to eating animals is *restraint*.

At the same time, another strain in the Jewish tradition mandates eating meat (often "meat and wine") on the Sabbath, and, in some versions, on other celebratory holidays as well, as part of the way the holiday is made special. Thus Rabbi J. David Bleich, a contemporary Orthodox authority, maintains that vegetarianism is, at most, permissible—and there are rabbinic authorities whom he quotes who deny that—and certainly not mandatory.[36]

THE IDEAL OF AN ANIMAL'S GOOD DEATH

If one does eat meat, we can subdivide the ethical responsibilities into those that pertain to the animal's life and those relevant to the animal's slaughter. Taking the latter first, one important responsibility concerns the damage potentially done to the slaughterer's ability to cultivate compassion. For this reason diverse Jewish traditions argue that only men of high ethical caliber should be slaughterers (*shoh'tim*)—men who can resist the callousness that killing animals may engender. In one widely circulated modern image, the Baal Shem Tov (Israel ben Eliezer, 1698–1760) is said to have been so sensitive a butcher that he whetted the blade used for slaughter with his own tears. This said, I am aware of no evidence that steps are taken by modern industrial kosher slaughterhouses to ensure that their *shoh'tim* are sensitive to animal suffering. Lack of confidence in humane slaughter, among other factors, has prompted an increasing number of contemporary Jews to exert considerable effort to arrange for an individual *shohet* to slaughter an animal for them or pay a premium to a handful of small distributors that give special attention to finding *shoh'tim* sensitive to animal suffering.[37]

Another responsibility is to provide the animal a good, relatively quick death. This idea is often expressed in manuals used to train *shoh'tim*, which have historically cited Rambam's position[38] that *shehitah* functions to prohibit cruelty. Unlike the practice of selecting particularly sensitive individuals to serve as *shoh'tim*, the technical rules of *shehitah* are enforced in contemporary kosher slaughter. However, if we rely on peer-reviewed essays by recognized experts in humane slaughter, in particular the work of Dr. Temple Grandin, we have strong evidence suggesting that kosher slaughter is not any more humane than is usual in the United States or Europe.[39] Moreover, a high-profile 2004 video of the kosher slaughter methods employed at what was then the largest glatt kosher cattle slaughter facility in the United States revealed that the plant was systematically removing the trachea and esophagi of cattle after *shehitah* but before loss of consciousness. I mention this egregious case of animal abuse, which is not representative of kosher slaughter, in order to contextualize the response of kosher certification companies who, when challenged, argued publicly that animals killed in this manner were considered kosher and that, indeed, no amount of animal suffering, no matter how extreme, would have any bearing on whether these companies certify a product as kosher. While this procedure is technically consistent with *halakhah*, where the law requiring compassion for animals and *shehitah* are legally distinct domains, it is profoundly at odds with popular Jewish understandings, and many in the Jewish community responded with shock. The same 2004 scandal of animal abuse also seems to have played a key role in inspiring Jews to reassert the traditional ties between kosher practice and animal ethics. For example, novelist and National Jewish Book Award-winner Jonathan Safran Foer produced a widely distributed video entitled "If This Is Kosher..." protesting the incident and making a case for Jewish vegetarianism. And at an institutional level we could point to the Conservative Movement's historic development of an ethical certification (*Magen Tzedek*, "shield of justice") that would be provided to select food products beyond the usual kosher certification and would address ethical issues including animal welfare. We can conclude that the ideal of providing animals a good death is very much a living one, however imperfectly it is put in practice.

The Ideal of a Life Free of Unnecessary Suffering

The same is not true of Jewish traditions that provide an animal a good life. The vast majority of unnecessary animal suffering on today's ubiquitous "factory farms" occurs not at the slaughterhouse, but on the farm itself while the animal is being raised. One egregious example is the suffering caused by the common practice of confining animals in spaces so small that they cannot extend their limbs for long periods of time, or, as in the case with egg-laying hens, during most of their lives. Since in a previous era abuses such as confining animals to a point of near immobility would have led animals to be unproductive or die, there was no need for legal measures to prevent such abuse; having a productive animal generally was consistant with providing the animal good welfare. Today, by contrast, sick and suffering animals may actually be more profitable than healthy ones.

This important observation has been advanced by the prominent animal welfare advocate, philosopher, and "father of veterinary medical ethics,"[40] Dr. Bernard Rollin, a secular Jew who spent twelve years in *yeshivah* (Orthodox religious school).[41] Rollin has argued throughout his career of more than thirty years that the major problems of farmed animal welfare today are the result of a failure to update our ethics to take into account our contemporary situation. In today's factory farms unnecessary animal suffering is at least as likely to occur on the farm as it is during slaughter, and responding to this new situation is arguably the most important aim of contemporary animal ethics, including Jewish animal ethics. Ninnety-eight percent of the interactions that U.S.citizens have with animals are with those raised for food,[42] and 99 percent of these animals are raised on factory farms.[43] Nonetheless, no movement of Judaism in the United States or Israel has attempted to develop policy on the systematic suffering inflicted upon animals on factory farms *during their lives*. This situation is likely to change in the near future, and already a committee of the Rabbinical Assembly, the organization of Conservative rabbis, is at work on just such a document as part of its *Magen Tzedek* program to certify foods as meeting ethical as well as ritual standards.

An important resource in formulating a response is the broad legal principle expressed by the rabbis of the Talmud as a command not to cause *tza'ar*—literally "suffering" and understood to mean suffering that does not advance some legitimate human good—to *ba'alei hayyim*—to "living beings." The *Rishonim* (leading rabbinic authorities of the eleventh to sixteenthth century) associate a variety of laws with this principle. Frequently cited examples include the prohibition against plowing with two animals of unequal strength (paradigmatically an ox and donkey), which causes the weaker animal to suffer (Deut 22:10), and the already mentioned prohibition on muzzling an ox as it labors (Deut 25:4)—rabbinically expanded to include all animals. Arguably the most prominent such law, found in both versions of the Decalogue, dictates that animals too are to be included in Sabbath rest (Exod 20:10, Deut 5:14).

All of these laws are expanded by rabbinic traditions, creating a massive body of legal material regarding Jewish and human responsibilities to animals. Thus, for example, the participation of animals in the rest of the Sabbath has led both ancient and contemporary rabbis to be lenient in permitting activities that are otherwise prohibited on Shabbat if they function to relieve animal pain (*tza'ar ba'alei hayyim*). And Rashi, commenting on Exodus 23:12, interprets the command to include not simply freedom from labor, but a positive state of contentment, and he thus rules that animals normally must have access to pasture on the Sabbath.

Such laws demonstrate a concern for animal lives that takes into account diverse forms of harm such as that caused by the behavior of other animals, by emotional factors, or by constant exertion without respite. While forged largely in relation to laboring animals, the basic thrust of these laws—concern for the physical, social, and emotional lives of animals—would today be most applicable to the systematic forms of abuse inflicted upon farmed animals being raised for meat, milk, and eggs.

Conclusion

In closing, I will venture beyond the descriptive task that has driven this discussion by asking what insights might the ethico-legal traditions documented here provide if we took seriously Rollin's caution that the fundamental nature of animal abuse has changed with the rise of new technologies—and, to extend his argument, the rise of new forms of forgetting the suffering of animals and hiding it from view.[44] Although it is beyond the scope of this chapter to document, it is of great significance that it is being published at a time when factory farming has created a historically unprecedented degree of suffering for billions of animals. We would do well to think deeply about this misery and our societal, if not individual, complacency and complicity with it. Why? "Morality resides there, as the most radical means of thinking about the finitude we share with animals, the mortality that belongs to the very finitude of life, to the experience of compassion."[45] The talmudic story of Rabbi Judah and the calf with which this chapter began is sometimes read as a caution: even individuals of great moral stature may too readily draw on parts of the Jewish tradition that serve humans ("Go. For this you were created") while forgetting those that serve our humanity ("His compassion is over all His works").

In Jewish tradition the human is "responsible for the universe, the hostage of the creature ... asked to account for things ... he did not will."[46] We are responsible both because animals matter and because human compassion itself is at stake. In our response to the new challenges posed by modernity to Jewish animal ethics, we risk both animal lives and that most exalted state of ethical achievement that we call, perhaps too audaciously, being human.

Notes

1. Genesis 1:29–30 is interpreted with near unanimity by classic Jewish and Christian biblical commentators as indicating that God originally commanded humans to be vegetarian.
2. See Jacob Milgrom, *Leviticus 1–16*, Anchor Bible Series (New York: Doubleday Dell Publishing Group, 1991), pp. 718, 733, 735, 736, 741; Mary Douglas, *Leviticus as Literature* (Oxford: Oxford University Press, 1999), p. 137.
3. For a systematic analysis of one such interpretive expansion see Jeremy Cohen, *Be Fertile and Increase, Fill the Earth and Master It: The Ancient and Medieval Career of a Biblical Text* (Ithaca, NY: Cornell University Press, 1989).

4. Arguably the best-known such hagiographical story is about the founder of the Mussar movement, Israel Salanter, who is said to have spent the evening of Yom Kippur rescuing a lost calf while his congregation waited for him.
5. David J. Bleich, "Judaism and Animal Experimentation," in *Judaism and Environmental Ethics*, Martin D. Yaffe, ed. (Lanham, Boulder, New York, Oxford: Lexington Books, 2001), pp. 356–57.
6. Also see *Genesis Rabbah* 33:3.
7. Mary Midgley, *Animals and Why They Matter* (Athens: University of Georgia Press, 1984).
8. Elijah Judah Schochet, *Animal Life in Jewish Tradition* (New York: KTAV, 1984), p. 263.
9. Moshe Hayyim Luzzatto, *The Path of the Upright = Mesillat Yesharim*, Mordecai Menahem Kaplan, trans. (Northvale, NJ: Jason Aronson, 1995), p. 155.
10. Noah J. Cohen, "*Tsa'ar Ba'ale Hayim*—the Prevention of Cruelty to Animals" (Ph.D. dissertation, Catholic University of America, 1959).
11. Yael Shemesh, "Vegetarian Ideology in Talmudic Literature and Traditional Biblical Exegesis," *Review of Rabbinic Judaism* 9 (2006).
12. Arguably the most articulate contemporary voice of this historically persistent minority position is the Yiddish writer and Nobel laureate Isaac Bashevis Singer: "I feel that since I'm a vegetarian that not only man, but even animals belong to my community. They suffer just as we do. They are made of blood and flesh." Janet Hadda, *Isaac Bashevis Singer: A Life* (Madison: University of Wisconsin Press, 2003), p. 144.
13. In entertaining this possibility I follow Jacques Derrida, who speaks of "a war (*whose inequality could one day be reversed*) being waged between, on the one hand, those who violate not only animal life but even and also this sentiment of compassion, and, on the other hand, those who appeal for an irrefutable testimony to this pity." Jacques Derrida, *The Animal That Therefore I Am*, David Wills, ed. and Marie-Louise Mallet, trans., Perspectives in Continental Philosophy (New York: Fordham University Press, 2008), pp. 28–29.
14. Aaron Gross, "The Question of the Animal: Dietary Practice, Ethics, and Subjectivity" (Ph.D. dissertation., University of California, 2010), chap. 6.
15. Irving Greenberg, *The Jewish Way* (Northvale, NJ: Jason Aronson, 1998), p. 105.
16. Unless otherwise indicated, Hebrew translations are my own.
17. *The Midrash on Psalms*, trans. William Gordon Braude, 2 vols., vol. 1, Yale Judaica Series (New Haven, CT: Yale University Press, 1959), p. 422.
18. *Kinyan, Hilkhot Avadim* 9:8. As translated in Schochet, *Animal Life in Jewish Tradition*, p. 202.
19. Yehudah HaChassid, *Sefer Chasidim: The Book of the Pious*, trans. Avraham Yaakov Finkel (Northvale, NJ: Jason Aronson, 1997), p. 270.
20. See *Moreh Nebukim* (*The Guide for the Perplexed*) 3:48.
21. My own translation has benefited from the annotated English translation of Charles Wengrov: *Sefer Ha-Hinukh*, trans. Charles Wengrov (Jerusalem & New York: Feldhaim, 1988).
22. For examples see Louis Ginzberg, *The Legends of the Jews*, Henrietta Szold and Paul Radin, trans. (Skokie, IL: Varda Books, 2003), pp. 43–46; Dov Neumon, "Motif-Index of Talmudic-Midrashic Literature" (Ph.D. dissertation, University of Michigan, 1954), pp. 224–28.
23. This threefold typology is indebted to the work of Kimberley Patton. See Kimberley Patton, "He Who Sits in the Heavens Laughs: Recovering Animal

Theology in the Abrahamic Traditions.," *Harvard Theological Review* 93, no. 4 (2000), p. 409.
24. As translated in Shemesh, "Vegetarian Ideology" (at note 11 above), p. 146.
25. Ginzberg, *The Legends of the Jews* (at note 22 above), p. 45.
26. For an extensive list see Neumon, "Motif-Index of Talmudic-Midrashic Literature"(at note 22 above), pp. 215–18.
27. Moses Cordovero, *The Palm Tree of Deborah*, Louis Jacobs, trans. (New York: Sepher-Hermon, 1981), pp. 83–84 (chap. 3, in Hebrew).
28. The idea of a "sentiment of compassion" that, like animals, needs protection is helpfully theorized by Jacques Derrida, from whom I take this phrase. See Derrida, *The Animal That Therefore I Am* (at note 13 above), pp. 28–29.
29. See Schochet, *Animal Life in Jewish Tradition* (at note 8 above), p. 263.
30. T. *Avodah Zarah* 8:4; B. *Sanhedrin* 56b.
31. Jordan Rosenblum, *Food and Identity in Early Rabbinic Judaism* (Cambridge, New York: Cambridge University Press, 2010), p. 71.
32. Also see Rashi on Deutoronomy 12:20.
33. More recent examples include the modern Orthodox Rabbi Shlomo Riskin, who writes that "the dietary laws are intended to teach us compassion and lead us gently to vegetarianism" (Shlomo Riskin. "A Sabbath Week–Shabbat Ekev," *The Jewish Week*, August 14, 1987), and the influential liberal Rabbi Arthur Green, who has described vegetarianism as a "*kashrut* for our age." Arthur Green, *Seek My Face, Speak My Name* (Northvale, NJ, London: Jason Aronson, 1992), pp. 87–89.
34. As cited in Shemesh, "Vegetarian Ideology" (at note 11 above), p. 146.
35. *The Mishnah*, Jacob Neusner, trans. (New Haven, CT: Yale University Press, 1988), p. 498. This saying is cited with this meaning in *Sefer haḤinnukh* (Mitzvah 545).
36. David J. Bleich, "Vegetarianism and Judaism," in *Judaism and Environmental Ethics*, Martin D. Yaffe, ed. (Lanham, Boulder, New York, Oxford: Lexington Books, 2001).
37. For an anecdotal description of this phenomenon see Samantha M Shapiro, "Kosher Wars," *The New York Times Magazine*, October 12, 2008.
38. *Moreh Nevukhim* (*The Guide for the Perplexed*) 3:26, 48.
39. Temple Grandin and Joe Regenstein, "Religious Slaughter and Animal Welfare," in *Meat Focus International* (Wallingford UK: CAB International, 1994).
40. Bernard E. Rollin, *Putting the Horse before Descartes: My Life's Work on Behalf of Animals* (Philadelphia: Temple University Press, 2011), p. 29.
41. Yeshivah was largely a negative experience for Rollin, but he notes that he did learn "logic and humor to fight those in power." *Ibid.*, p. 243.
42. David Wolfson and M. Sullivan, "Foxes in the Henhouse," in *Animal Rights: Current Debates and New Directions*, Cass R. Sunstein and Martha Nussbaum, eds. (Oxford: Oxford University Press, 2005), p. 206.
43. Farm Forward, "Homepage," http://www.farmforward.com/.
44. For contemporary applications of the idea that we "forget" animal suffering, see Jonathan Safran Foer, *Eating Animals* (New York: Little, Brown and Company, 2009), pp. 197–98; and Derrida, *The Animal That Therefore I Am* (at note 13 above), p, 26.
45. Derrida, ibid., p. 28.
46. Emmanuel Levinas, *Nine Talmudic Readings*, A. Aronowicz, trans. (Bloomington: Indiana University Press, 1990), p. 170.

Suggestions for Further Reading

Bleich, David J. 2001. "Judaism and Animal Experimentation" and "Vegetarianism and Judaism." In *Judaism and Environmental Ethics*, Martin D. Yaffe, ed. Lanham, Boulder, New York, Oxford: Lexington Books.

Cohen, Noah J. 1959. *"Tsa'ar Ba'ale Hayim*—the Prevention of Cruelty to Animals." Ph.D. dissertation., Catholic University of America.

Derrida, Jacques. 2008. *The Animal That Therefore I Am*, David Wills, trans and Marie-Louise Mallet, ed. New York: Fordham University Press.

Gross, Aaron. 2010. "The Question of the Animal: Dietary Practice, Ethics, and Subjectivity." Ph.D. dissertation, University of California.

Levinas, Emmanuel. 1990. "The Name of a Dog, or Natural Rights." In *Difficult Freedom: Essays on Judaism*. Baltimore: Johns Hopkins Press.

Schochet, Elijah Judah. 1984. *Animal Life in Jewish Tradition*. New York: KTAV.

Schwartz, Richard. 2001. *Judaism and Vegetarianism*. New York: Latern.

Sears, David. 2003. *The Vision of Eden: Animal Welfare in Jewish Law and Mysticism*. New York: Orot.

Slifkin, Natan. 2006. *Man and Beast: Our Relationships with Animals in Jewish Thought*. New York: Yasha Books/Lamda Publishers.

Telushkin, Joseph. 2006. *A Code of Jewish Ethics: Vol. 2, Love Your Neighbor as Yourself*. New York: Bell Tower.

Waldau, Paul, and Kimberley Patton, eds. 2006. *A Communion of Subjects: Animals in Religion, Science, and Ethics*. New York: Columbia University Press.

CHAPTER 25

JEWISH ETHICS OF SPEECH

ALYSSA M. GRAY

SPEECH differentiates human beings from other living beings and, in the Jewish view, makes us similar to God. In the Torah, God is said to have carried out the work of creation through speech, and the Rabbis later describe the Divine creation as having taken place through "Ten Sayings" (M. *Avot* 5:1). The second creation narrative's account that "man became a living being" after God blew into his nostrils (Gen 2:7) is rendered by the Aramaic Targum Onkelos as "and it [=God's breath] was in [the first] man as a speaking spirit." Human speech can be creative, like God's; witness the Jewish legal recognition that through speech human beings can change—*re-create*—the statuses of people (e.g., through vows of Naziriteship), animals (e.g., through designation as sacrifices), or things (e.g., through designation as *tzedakah*, charity). Human speech can also be the equivalent of murder (B. *Bava Metzia* 58b). Of human beings, then, it can justifiably be said that "Death and life are in the power of the tongue" (Prov 18:21) and that "When [the tongue] is good, there is nothing better; when bad, there is nothing worse" (*Leviticus Rabbah* 33:1).

This chapter will survey a Jewish ethics of speech under the following headings: (1) Jewish legal and ethical norms pertaining to bad language and speech about other people; (2) holy speech; and (3) speech that is beneficial to society or other people. Throughout, it will consider the different voices within Jewish sacred literature, including voices that express ethical considerations bound to very particular—and sometimes difficult—historical contexts.

Legal and Ethical Norms Pertaining to Bad Language and Speech about Others

1. Bad language. The Talmud (B. *Shabbat* 33a) teaches that "bad language" (*nivlut peh*) causes a number of horrors in the world (citing Isa 9:16). Rav Hanan b. Rava points out in a seemingly disjointed observation that everyone knows why the bride enters the bridal chamber and that one who was Divinely decreed to enjoy seventy good years would suffer a complete reversal of fortune as a result of bad (in this case, sexual) language in speaking to or about the bride and groom. Rashi explains Rav Hanan b. Rava to mean that everyone knows why the bride enters the bridal chamber, and so there is no need for that to be spelled out. A person whom Heaven had decreed would enjoy seventy good years will forfeit them should he unnecessarily and indelicately explain the open secret of what goes on in the bridal chamber.

On B. *Ketubbot* 8b and in the manuscripts of B. *Shabbat* 33a, the first part of Rav Hanan b. Rava's statement is curiously doubled: "whoever speaks obscenely and brings an obscenity out of his mouth." Rabbi David Halevy (1586–1667) later explained that sometimes people utter bad language with no ill intent. Therefore, according to Halevy, Rav Hanan b. Rava doubled his statement to indicate that the dire punishments for bad language fall only on those who intentionally cause obscenities to come out of their mouths (*TaZ* to S.A. *Yoreh Deah* 124:1, n. 1). Halevy's comment is a thoughtful gloss on an apparent redundancy, but it goes against the grain of the talmudic passage, which makes no distinction between intentional and unintentional uses of bad language.

2. Lying and related issues (misleading people, permitting the drawing of false inferences, bending the truth for praiseworthy reasons). The Torah clearly prohibits lying in several places: "You must not carry false rumors" (Exod 23:1); "Keep far from a false charge" (Exod 23:7); and "You shall not deal deceitfully or falsely with one another" (Lev 19:11). While eschewing lies is necessary for the maintenance of trust among people, thus making human society possible, the Rabbis recognized that not every untruth is an evil to be avoided, nor every truth necessary to reveal.

According to a story on B. *Sanhedrin* 97a, Rava at first despaired of finding truth in the world. He then learned of another rabbi who never told lies and who had settled in a town called "Kushta" ("truth"). No one in Kushta ever told lies or died prematurely. The Kushtan rabbi married and had two sons. One day a neighbor called for his wife, who was washing her hair. The rabbi thought it inappropriate to mention that fact, and so (falsely) stated that his wife was not present. His two sons died, and when the townspeople investigated this unheard-of tragedy and learned how it had come about, they asked him to leave Kushta. The story's point is that absolute truth cannot abide an untruth told even for a virtuous purpose, and human life itself cannot be sustained within the realm of absolute truth.

This latter rabbinic insight appears in a number of places in the Talmud and post-talmudic literature where the point is not necessarily that physical human life is endangered by absolute truth, but that absolute truth may endanger human relations, emotions, and psyches. For example, *Genesis Rabbah* 48:18 points out that while the matriarch Sarah had included her husband's advanced age along with her own as the reason she could not conceive (Gen 18:12), God reported her statement to Abraham as mentioning only her own age (Gen 18:13). The *midrash* points out that the Torah altered her statement in order to keep peace between them. B. *Yevamot* 65b also refers to Joseph's brothers' reference to their deceased father's nonexistent request that Joseph forgive them (Gen 50:15–17), as well as to Samuel's misleading Saul as to the real purpose of his coming to see him (1 Sam 16:2)—which was to inform him of God's rejection. In the first and third of these biblical examples, it is God Himself Who utters or suggests the untruth. Referring to Genesis 50:15–17, Rabbi Il'a states that it is permitted to alter a statement for the sake of peace, while Rabbi Nathan relies on 1 Samuel 16:2 in asserting that it is a *mitzvah* to do so. The passage on B. *Yevamot* 65b closes with reference to God's shading of the truth in Genesis 18:13, thus tipping the scale in Rabbi Nathan's favor.

In a well-known talmudic exchange (B. *Ketubbot* 16b–17a), Bet Shammai and Bet Hillel disputed concerning "how one dances before the bride"; that is, with what language does one praise a bride? Bet Shammai held that the bride should be praised as she is, while Bet Hillel proposed that every bride be praised as "beautiful and pious." Bet Shammai objected that if the bride were in fact lame or blind, such a song would be false and the singer(s) would violate Exodus 23:7. Nevertheless, Jewish law mandates that one "dances before the bride" after the manner of Bet Hillel.

Interaction with the critically ill, the dying, and their families is another arena in which the weighing of absolute truth versus shading the truth is required. If the close relative of a sick person dies, she is not to be told, lest her psyche be shattered by the news (B. *Mo'ed Katan* 26b). Discussion of a dying person's need to recite the personal confession, the *viddui*, is not to be held in the presence of people whose emotional reaction may cause pain to the dying person (S.A. *Yoreh De'ah* 338:1).[1]

Thus far we have considered situations of shading the truth for a praiseworthy or protective purpose. Difficult historical circumstances, notably episodes of anti-Jewish persecution, also yielded legal rulings on shading the truth. Rabbi Joseph Karo (1488–1575) rules in S.A. *Yoreh De'ah* 157:2 that while a Jew is forbidden to say he is a non-Jew in order to escape death, he may disguise himself as a non-Jew during a time of persecution. The difference is that by disguising himself he is not verbally declaring himself to be a non-Jew; rather, he is permitting those who see him to draw that (false) inference themselves. Rabbi Moses Isserles (ca. 1525–1572) goes one step further in his gloss on that paragraph, allowing a Jew in a time of danger to utter an ambiguous statement about his religious identity to which he attaches one meaning while the persecutor attaches another.

Moving on from shading the truth to overt deception, B. *Pesahim* 113b states that the person who says one thing while thinking another is one of three types of people whom God hates. Apropos that statement, B. *Hullin* 94a declares that one may infer from the sage Samuel's example that he holds that it is forbidden "to 'steal the mind of creating beings,' even idolaters." "Stealing the mind" (*geneivat da'at*) means deception. Further down that page, the Talmud quotes T. *Bava Batra* 6:14, in which R. Meir says, *inter alia*, that a person should not urge his peer to dine with him when he knows that the strenuously proffered invitation will not be accepted. The deception in this case is that the invitee has been made to believe that his presence at the meal was urgently desired, whereas this is not the case. Maimonides (1138–1204) collects examples of prohibited deception in a passage which he closes as follows: "And even one word of [deceptive] enticing and of deceit is forbidden. Rather [one should have only] lips of truth, and a firm spirit, and a heart pure of all deceit and chicanery" (M.T. *Laws of Ethics* 2:6; see also *Laws of Sale* 18:1).

Historical circumstances also influenced talmudic and post-talmudic reflection on deception. M. *Nedarim* 3:2 states that one may avow to tax collectors, *inter alia*, that items are not taxable—when in fact they are. The Jerusalem Talmud (J. *Nedarim* 3:4, 38a) quotes scholars who assert that such a vow is permissible at a "time of danger" (=persecution) but that taxes collected pursuant to a fixed law of the government must be paid. The Babylonian Talmud (B. *Nedarim* 28a) reconciles this *mishnah* with Samuel's well-known declaration (e.g., B. *Bava Kamma* 113b) that "the law of the land is the law," making it clear that the only tax-collector who may be deceived is either one who simply seizes whatever he wishes, or one who has set himself up in business and is not appointed by the government. These principles made their way into the classic codes (Arba'ah Turim ["Tur"], *Hoshen Mishpat* 369; S.A. *Hoshen Mishpat* 369:6).

3. *Gossip (rekhilut).* Leviticus 19:16 commands, "Do not go around as a talebearer (*rakhil*) among your people." Tale-bearing, or gossip, refers to telling stories about others that are true (at least in the speaker's mind) and not necessarily negative or degrading to the subject (M.T. *Laws of Ethics* 7:2). The Jerusalem Talmud interprets the verse's *rakhil* with reference to *rokhel*, a peddler: one should not be like a *rokhel* who bears the burden of one person's words and carries them to another (J. *Peah* 1:1, 16a). Maimonides (M.T. *Laws of Ethics* 7:1–2) employs strong language in writing of gossip, pointing out that it is a "great sin" which can cause the "killing of souls" and can "destroy the world." He specifically calls attention to the case of Doeg the Edomite (1 Sam 22:9–19). Doeg informed King Saul that Ahimelech, a priest in Nob, had assisted the then-fugitive David. This information was true (per 1 Sam 21:2–10) and was not *prima facie* negative about either Ahimelech or David; yet this information enraged Saul, who ordered Doeg to kill all the priests in Nob. Thus, according to Maimonides, the prohibition of gossip is appropriately placed alongside the command "Do not stand idly by your brother's blood" (Lev 19:16).

Another issue with the gossipmonger is that she may reveal what should be kept private. M. *Sanhedrin* 3:7 quotes Leviticus 19:16 and Proverbs 11:13 ("A base fellow [*rakhil*] gives away secrets, but a trustworthy soul keeps a confidence") in order to make the point that a judge should not reveal after the rendering of a verdict that he had voted that a party should not be held liable while the others had voted for liability. In a related vein, Rabbi Shabtai HaKohen (1621–1662; *Shakh* to S.A. *Hoshen Mishpat* 19:1, n. 2) later points out that these verses prohibit a judge from commenting to a person who had come before the court that another judge did not adjudicate him fairly. Tur *Hoshen Mishpat* 19 also derives the rule that if a party asks the court for a written judicial opinion following the rendering of the verdict, the written opinion must be issued without the names of which judges took which position.

Classical rabbinic literature also ponders the relevance of gossip to personal status issues. M. *Gittin* 9:9 rules that if word spreads around town that a certain single woman has been betrothed, or that a married woman has been divorced, that information is sufficient to establish the women's marital status, provided that the story is not accompanied by other details that undermine or complicate the fixing of status. Both Talmuds (J. *Gittin* 9:8, 50d and B. *Gittin* 89a) are uncomfortable with the *mishnah*. The latter presents a dispute over whether or not we "invalidate the story" (literally, "voice"), followed by accounts of many instances in which the local tale is not given legal credence. Both Talmuds' efforts to limit the legal significance of these "stories around town" show the rabbis' awareness of the pervasiveness and power of such speech.

4. *Slander (hotza'at shem ra) and negative yet true statements about another (lashon ha-ra).* Spreading false information about another *(hotza'at shem ra)* is forbidden (M.T. *Laws of Ethics* 7:2). *Lashon ha-ra* (literally, "evil tongue") differs from slander and gossip in that not only are the statements about the other true, but they are negative (e.g., M.T. *Laws of Ethics* 7:2). Maimonides states that it is forbidden to live in the neighborhood of those who speak *Lashon ha-ra* and even more so to sit with them and hear their words (M.T. Laws of Ethics 7:6). Negative yet true speech spoken directly to the subject of the speech is not *Lashon ha-ra* (B. *Arakhin* 15b), nor is such speech *Lashon ha-ra* when spoken by the subject himself in the presence of three people, since by speaking to three, the speaker himself denigrates himself *(d'mitamra b'apei telata)*.

T. *Avodah Zarah* 1:10 and 14 also mention a subcategory of *lashon ha-ra* called *avak lashon ha-ra*, literally "the dust" of *lashon ha-ra*—speech that is not quite *lashon ha-ra*, but is similar to it. *Avak lashon ha-ra* is one of three sins that no one can avoid every day (B. *Bava Batra* 164b–65a). Defining *avak lashon ha-ra* out of the Tosefta and Talmuds is difficult, and Maimonides collects a number of examples in order to standardize the definition. The Tosefta illustrates *avak lashon ha-ra* as speaking praise of one's fellow, which Maimonides sensibly interprets to mean that one should not praise a person in the presence of those who hate him, which will undoubtedly cause them to veer off into speaking ill of him (M.T. *Laws of Ethics* 7:4).[2] Rabbi Samuel b. Meir (b. 1085, to B. *Bava Batra* 165a, s.v. *avak lashon ha-ra*) defines it by reference to an exchange between Rava and Abaye on B. *Arakhin* 15b. There, Rava defined *lashon ha-ra* as a statement such as "There is fire in So-and-so's house." Abaye objected that this was simply reportage, but the response is that the statement implies that So-and-so is wealthy enough that he can always keep a fire burning to cook the food he always has. Although neither the printed edition nor the manuscripts of B. *Arakhin* 15b refer to Rava's case as an example of *avak lashon ha-ra*, Rabbi Samuel b. Meir interprets it that way. Other examples of *avak lashon ha-ra* presented by Maimonides are someone saying that he does not wish to speak about what happened with So-and-so (inviting conversation about what did happen); someone asking rhetorically, "Who can say how So-and-so is in the condition he is in?" (inviting conversation); or someone speaking *lashon ha-ra* in a light manner or with feigned unawareness that the speech is indeed *lashon ha-ra*.

As is its way with behaviors it wishes either to encourage or to discourage, the Babylonian Talmud includes traditions that make extreme claims about the evil of *lashon ha-ra*. Rabbi Yohanan quotes Rabbi Yose b. Zimra as teaching that one who speaks *lashon ha-ra* is like one who denies the fundamental principle (of the existence of God), citing Psalms 12:5: "They say, 'By our tongues we shall prevail; with lips such as ours, who can be our master?'" (B. *Arakhin* 15b). The verse connects the use of the tongue to rebellion against God, but the link to *lashon ha-ra* is a purely rabbinic invention. Similarly, Resh Lakish states that speakers of *lashon ha-ra* amass sins going all the way up to heaven (*ibid.*), and Rav Hisda in the name of Mar Ukba quotes God as declaring that He and the speaker of *lashon ha-ra* cannot both abide in the world (*ibid.*). In light of these traditions, it is hardly surprising that a Tanna of the school of Rabbi Ishmael teaches that the speaker of *lashon ha-ra* amasses sins corresponding (in severity) to the three cardinal sins—murder, idolatry, and sexual immorality—which a Jew should rather die than commit (e.g., B. *Sanhedrin* 74a–75a).

The Babylonian Talmud and medieval legal sources also refer to the related notion *kala d'lo paseik* ("a voice that does not cease"), local discussion about individuals that may in fact be true and that may have negative legal repercussions for the subjects of the talk. Two examples must suffice. Rabbi Jacob b. Asher (ca. 1269–1343) summarizes a *responsum* of his father, Rabbi Asher b. Yehiel (ca. 1250–1327), about a man, "Reuben," concerning whom there was a *kala d'lo paseik* that he was having relations with a servant girl. Rabbi Asher ruled that the rumor alone was sufficient for the court to compel him to expel her from his house (Tur, *Even Ha-ezer* 26). Rabbi Jacob also ruled that at a time when a Jewish court can adjudicate capital cases (*dinei nefashot*), the court in its discretion may inflict corporal punishment even without fully vetted eyewitness testimony if there is a *kol she'eno posek* as to an individual, and reason to suspect that he has violated Jewish norms and deserves punishment (Tur, *Hoshen Mishpat* 2).

5. *Oppressive speech (ona'at devarim).* A *baraita* on B. *Bava Metzia* 58b roots the prohibition of oppressive speech in Leviticus 25: 17: "Do not wrong one another, but fear your God; for I the Lord am your God." M. *Bava Metzia* 4:10 begins with an example of "oppressive speech" in a commercial context: a person should not inquire about an item's price if he has no intention of buying it. The *mishnah* also prohibits reminding the penitent of his prior bad deeds and reminding the convert of his ancestors' non-Jewish past. The aforementioned *baraita* on B. *Bava Metzia* 58b goes further than the *mishnah*. The *baraita* directs that if a convert comes forward to study Torah, one should not say to him, "The mouth that ate [forbidden foods] comes to study [the] Torah that was given from the mouth of the Power [God]!" Also, if illnesses come upon a person or he has buried his children, speaking to him in the manner of Job's companions (Job 4:6–7) is considered oppressive speech: "Is not your piety your confidence.... Think now, what innocent man ever perished?"

Three talmudic sages go so far as to say that oppressive speech is even worse than commercial overreaching. One reason given for this comment is that Leviticus 25:17 (oppressive speech) says "but fear your God," an admonition missing from Leviticus 25:14 (commercial overreaching). A second reason is that while commercial overreaching is only a matter of money (*b'mamono*), oppressive speech is something one does with oneself (*b'gufo*). Ultimately, the *baraita* says that the matter of oppressive speech is given over to the heart. R. Vidal di Toulousa (fourteenth century), commenting on M.T. *Laws of Sale* 14:18, explains that a person may claim that the words he had spoken were intended for good, or that he had meant something other than what the hearer thought. Whatever the speaker claims about his own speech, ultimately God will look to the inner intentions behind what was said.

The Talmud on B. *Bava Metzia* 58b–59a juxtaposes a discussion of embarrassing someone in public ("whitening their face") to the treatment of oppressive speech. Embarrassing someone in public is also linked to a prohibition against calling someone by an evil name. The Talmud asks why the latter is singled out, being a subset of the former, but the response is given that even if a person has become accustomed to being called by that name, one who uses it is still guilty of publicly embarrassing him. This latter point is psychologically insightful: at the stage at which someone is no longer visibly embarrassed by the name, he is probably so humiliated that he no longer reacts to it.

Speech Considered to be Holy

In chapter 231 of Tur *Orah Hayyim*, Rabbi Jacob b. Asher writes that a person should pursue all activities—even quotidian activities, including speaking—with the intention of serving God. As to speech, Rabbi Jacob points out that it goes without saying that slurs (*lashon ha-ra*) and bad language (*nivlut peh*) are to be avoided. What does require emphasis is that (even) in speaking of the words of sages, one's intention should be that this speech is in or will lead to service of God. Disciplining oneself to engage in holy or beneficial speech is a form of *bildung*, part of the individual's training in holy behavior and character. Similarly, on B. *Arakhin* 15b a Torah scholar's preemptive remedy for *lashon ha-ra* is said to be engagement in Torah study—the use of speech for a holy purpose. Torah study is thus a suitable starting-point for a discussion of holy speech.

In the introduction to his book *Ketzot Hahoshen*, R. Aryeh Leib Heller (1745–1813) quotes a teaching from the *Zohar* that one who utters an innovative insight in Torah thereby creates a new world, for that insight (literally "word") ascends to God, Who takes and kisses it and protects it from jealous angels until the time comes to make from it a new heaven and earth. Heller observes that in light of the cosmic significance of such speech, a person should tremble at the thought of what may happen should he speak "things that are not so" about the

Torah—an inevitable occurrence, given that we think with our fallible human intellects, which cannot grasp the truth of the Torah in full. Heller's response is that Torah is meant by God to be understood by human beings according to the determinations of the fallible human intellect—even if the results so obtained do not correspond with what we might call "absolute Truth."

Heller's kabbalistic reflections are part of an older legal tradition of tolerance of different views—notably exemplified by the Babylonian Talmud's multivocality—although Jewish legal tradition does not see "freedom of speech" in the Western (or at least American) sense as an absolute value. For example, following the Torah, the Talmud explores the prohibitions of blasphemy (e.g., B. *Sanhedrin* 55b–56a), although it also permits the "rebellious elder" (Deut 17:8–13) to teach his rejected view as a theoretical matter, albeit not as practical law (B. *Horayot* 2a). Moreover, the Talmud has a heavenly voice proclaim, "These and these are the words of the living God" (B. *Eruvin* 13b) about the disputing Houses of Hillel and Shammai—although the law follows the former. The thirteenth-century "Maimonidean Controversy" over Maimonides' philosophical project is testimony to the limits on free expression in Jewish history, yet this and other limits on expression exist in unresolved tension with the recognition by some that human minds will produce various truths that should be allowed expression.

Apropos of holy speech, rabbinic Judaism also requires that *berakhot* (blessings) be recited prior to the performance of certain commandments and prior to various personal experiences (such as, *inter alia*, eating, drinking, hearing good news, smelling good smells, or seeing a great sage). Blessings recited over the performance of *mitzvoth* are short theological exercises, reminding the Jew as she prepares to perform a *mitzvah* that the people Israel are sanctified by commandments and commanded to do the particular act.

Blessings recited over personal experiences may be vehicles for the expression of different emotions, lenses through which parts of the natural environment may be viewed religiously, or expressions of gratitude to God for providing the conditions that allow for human life. As an example of blessings over personal experiences, we may note the Mishnah's direction (M. *Berakhot* 9:5) to bless God on the bad just as one blesses God over the good; although the blessings are different, one should accept the blessings' precipitating occurrences with equal equanimity (B. *Berakhot* 60b).

As to the natural environment, Rabbi Yehudah teaches that one who sees the Great Sea (=the Mediterranean) at intervals (defined on B. *Berakhot* 59b as every thirty days) should bless God "Who made the Great Sea" (M. *Berakhot* 9:2). The Babylonian Talmud prescribes a short prayer to be recited on entering the privy (B. *Berakhot* 60b), as well as another to be recited upon leaving it (*ibid.*) Similarly, the Talmud also prescribes a list of blessings to be recited upon rising, dressing, and preparing for one's day (*ibid.*).

In a related vein, the obligation to engage in prayer (e.g., M.T. *Laws of Prayer* 1:1) is also an obligation to use speech for a holy purpose. Taking as an example the central Jewish prayer, the weekday *Amidah*, it consists of nineteen blessings that fall into three categories: praise of God (three blessings), petitions (thirteen blessings), and expressions of gratitude to God (three blessings). This structure encodes both religious and ethical insights, which ultimately are one: God is not to be addressed only with petitions, but also with praise and gratitude. Praise and gratitude are types of speech that are to be directed at other human beings, not just God (e.g., B. *Berakhot* 58a).

Holy speech is not to be uttered in just any place. A person must not study (or even think of) Torah, recite the *Shema*, or pray in a lavatory or any filthy place (e.g., B. *Berakhot* 22–26). Moreover, not all speech should be uttered at just any time. The Sabbath is to be sanctified with one's speech, as well as in other ways. On the basis of Isaiah 58:13 (*v'daber davar*—"nor strike bargains," literally, "and speaking of a thing"), B. *Shabbat* 113a–b concludes that one's Sabbath speech should not be like one's weekday speech. Drawing from the context of the entire verse, Maimonides rules that a person must not discuss his business affairs on the Sabbath (M.T. *Laws of the Sabbath* 24:1), nor even engage in too much idle chatter on that day (*ibid*. 24:4). Rabbi Moses Isserles wrote in his glosses on S.A. *Orah Hayyim* 307:1 that people who enjoy doing so are permitted to gather on the Sabbath to discuss the news of the day, but those who do not enjoy such discussions should not engage in them. Similarly, *Mishneh Berurah* (Orah Hayyim 307:1, n. 3) rules that one should not discuss upsetting topics on the Sabbath.

An interesting exception to the notion that business affairs must not be discussed on the Sabbath is the principle that one may verbally stipulate *tzedakah* (charity) for the poor on the Sabbath (e.g., B. *Shabbat* 150a). The legal justification for this allowance is not entirely clear (see *Bet Yosef* to Tur *Orah Hayyim* 306:6). From an ethical perspective, we see that this legal allowance places the needy ahead of a pietistic limitation on Sabbath-day speech.

Speech Beneficial to Other Human Beings and to Society

Rabbi Yitzhak teaches how one should speak to the poor: one should commiserate with them and will be blessed with eleven blessings for doing so—five more than one who merely gives a coin (B. *Bava Batra* 9b). Maimonides takes this notion further in M.T. *Laws of Gifts to the Poor* 10:4, ruling that one must give to the poor joyfully and with a pleasant countenance, while decrying the poor person's plight with him. *Leviticus Rabbah* 34:4 provides a negative example of an imagined diatribe directed at a poor person by a person of means: "Why don't you go to work and get food? Look at those hips! Those legs! That fat body! Those lumps of flesh!"[3] According to the *midrash*, God will eventually punish the person who speaks this way.

Private reproof of a peer and social protest are complex and even potentially dangerous—although valuable—types of speech. The Talmud takes the Torah's command to "Reprove your kinsman" (Lev 19:17) as the source for the notion that one must reprove a peer who is observed doing something unseemly (B. *Arakhin* 16b). Maimonides interprets this precept to mean that one who sees his peer sinning, or following "a path that is not good," must bring him back to the good and inform him that he is sinning (M.T. *Laws of Ethics* 6:7). Leviticus 19:17 closes with the admonition "but incur no guilt because of him," which the Talmud interprets to mean that one must not reprove a person in a manner that causes "his face to change," that is, humiliates him, as evidenced through his changed facial complexion (B. *Arakhin* 16b). Maimonides takes this command a step further in *ibid.* 6:8, where he rules that it is forbidden to "humiliate a [fellow] Jew, and all the more so in public." Such humiliation is a "great sin" although it cannot be punished by a human court. A person must reprove another in private with gentle words, letting him know that the reproof is only for his own good (*ibid.* 6:7).

The complexity of human motivations and interactions makes the task of "reproof" exceedingly difficult. Rabbi Eleazar b. Azaryah is reputed to have wondered aloud if anyone in his generation really knew properly how to reprove, while Rabbi Tarfon wondered if anyone really knew properly how to accept reproof (B. *Arakhin* 16b).

Maimonides closes his discussion of reproof in *ibid.* 6:7 by noting that "whoever is able to protest and does not is punished with them, since he could have protested them." His source is a lengthy talmudic section beginning on B. *Shabbat* 54b, where scholars teach that whoever is able to protest the actions of his household, town, or the entire world and does not do so will be punished along with them. While Leviticus 19:17 and the ensuing talmudic and Maimonidean discussions of "reproof" contemplate a private context of two people, B. *Shabbat* 54b–55a, with its reference to protesting the actions of "the people of [the protester's] town" or "the entire world," apparently contemplates social criticism on a broader scale. In the continuing discussion on 55a, the point is made that such protest is necessary even if it is ultimately unheeded, since no person knows in advance that his protest will in fact go unheeded. Awareness of societal wrongdoing thus compels speech.

Medieval sources extend this discussion. According to one fifteenth-century ethical handbook, silence can be taken as acquiescence and even tacit encouragement by those whose conduct should be protested (*Orhot Tzaddikim, Sha'ar Hahanifut*). On the other hand, both *Orhot Tzaddikim* and the thirteenth-century *Sefer Mitzvot Gadol* (in positive commandment #11) declare that if one is certain that his protest will not be heeded, then one should keep silent even in the face of deliberate transgressions, because a person is obligated not to say something that will not be heeded (B. *Yevamot* 65b). *Sefer Mitzvot Gadol*'s comments come in the context of a discussion of Jewish ritual behavior, so it is possible that the author's view is that while silence about ritual transgression in the face of nearly certain rejection of the protest is justified, protest about other societal wrongs must be made regardless. This distinction does not necessarily work for *Orhot Tzaddikim*, but taking the views of the two compilations together, it may be inferred that discretion and judgment about means and ends are a crucial part of the ethics of protest.

B. *Shabbat* 54b–55a includes an interesting story that became important in a sixteenth-century scholar's assessment of his obligation to speak out on behalf of the vulnerable. Rav Yehudah was sitting before his teacher Samuel when a woman came and screamed before him—presumably to get justice from him. Samuel ignored the woman—to Rav Yehudah's astonishment—commenting that "your superior (=Samuel) will be punished with cold [water], while your superior's superior (=Mar Ukba) will be punished with hot [water]." Samuel went on to explain that he ignored the woman because she should have turned to Mar Ukba, his superior in the Babylonian judicial hierarchy. Reflecting on this story centuries later in his *responsum* 24, Rabbi Solomon Luria (ca. 1510–1573) wondered why Samuel implied he would be punished (even slightly), for he could not administer justice in place of Mar Ukba. Luria concluded that the woman wanted Samuel to advocate for her to Mar Ukba, but he held back out of concern that Mar Ukba would be offended by his intervention. Applying this analysis to himself, Luria concluded that he could not act like Samuel; rather than refuse to be involved, Luria would respectfully yet forcefully advocate for (in his case) a widow, although her case was already pending before a sitting judge. In closing his *responsum*, he points out that it is the obligation of "everyone whom the Creator has graced with the wisdom of the Torah" to "to turn [things] upside down for the merit of widows and orphans" in a manner that does not undermine the authority of a sitting judge on a case.

Conclusion

The literatures from which this survey of a Jewish ethics of speech have been drawn demonstrate, through the literary forms in which they present the material, that a Jewish ethics of speech emerges out of reflection on the nuances and sheer messiness of concrete human interactions. Maimonides' (and others') systematization of these principles was not a deduction from first principles, but an induction from the stories and scriptural interpretations found in late antiquity's rabbinic literature.

Reflecting on the many voices encountered in this chapter, we see that a Jewish ethics of speech is as concerned with what should or must be said as with what should not be said. Moreover, a Jewish ethics of speech includes not only speech between individuals, but even what might in other contexts be called political speech or public opinion. Throughout, a Jewish ethics of speech is animated by a religious sense that speech is a point of similarity between the Divine and humanity; that is the fundamental principle, to which all the rest may be seen as commentary.

Notes

1. The passage refers specifically to women, children, and the ignorant as people whose emotional reaction may be hurtful to the dying individual.
2. The definition of *avak lashon ha-ra* is somewhat different on J. *Pe'ah* 1:1, 16a. Maimonides appears to have set aside the Jerusalem Talmud's understanding in favor of the Tosefta's and possibly the Babylonian Talmud's (cf. B. *Arakhin* 15b).
3. Translation adapted from Judah J. Slotki, trans., *Midrash Rabbah: Leviticus* (London and New York: Soncino, 1983), p. 430.

Suggestions for Further Reading

Brown, Benjamin. "From Principles to Rules and from Musar to Halakhah: The Hafetz Hayim's Rulings on Libel and Gossip," *Diné Israel* 25 (2008), pp. 171–256.

Crane, Jonathan. "Defining the Unspeakable: Incitement in *Halakhah* and Anglo-American Jurisprudence," *Journal of Law and Religion*. XXV:2 (2009–2010), pp. 329–56.

Dorff, Elliot N. *The Way Into Tikkun Olam (Repairing the World)*. Woodstock, VT: Jewish Lights, 2005, chap. 4.

Kimelman, Reuven. "The Rabbinic Ethics of Protest," *Judaism* 19:1 (Winter 1970), pp. 38–58.

Telushkin, Joseph. *Words That Hurt, Words That Heal: How to Choose Words Wisely and Well*. New York: Harper, 1998.

Teutsch, David. *Ethics of Speech*. Philadelphia: Reconstructionist Rabbinical College Press, 2008.

CHAPTER 26

JEWISH POLITICAL ETHICS IN AMERICA

JILL JACOBS

The United States presents a fundamental challenge to Jewish identity. For most of history, Jews have viewed the Diaspora as a place of exile. Petitions for a return to Jerusalem appear within the daily liturgy. The yearly holiday cycle includes four fast days that commemorate the destruction of the Temple. Traditional Jewish writings tend to portray the secular government as a force to be pacified, paid off, and avoided. At worst, secular governments have overtaxed, oppressed, murdered, and exiled their Jews. At best, these governments have ignored the Jews or allowed them some degree of autonomy. While the classical principle *dina d'malkhuta dina* (the law of the state is the law), demands adherence to secular law, this principle has traditionally been applied only to economic matters, and primarily to ones that affect relationships with non-Jews. On internal Jewish matters, Jews have usually tried, to the extent possible, to govern themselves in accordance with Jewish law.[1]

In the United States, Jews have fully integrated into all areas of national life. The largest Jewish community in the world, American Jews occupy some of the highest positions in politics, business, and education, and they have experienced virtually no state-sponsored anti-Semitism since the middle of the twentieth century. The central question for American Jewish political thought, then, is whether to approach the United States as just one more foreign government, or whether this state—and therefore Jewish involvement therein—should be considered fundamentally different from other places where Jews have lived.

Some American Jewish thinkers see America as a different kind of Diaspora—one that has become the center, rather than the periphery. Others view the comfort of America skeptically and warn that the situation could deteriorate at any moment.

These two disparate attitudes lead to four basic approaches to engaging the American political state: (1) Jews should participate in American politics in service of Jewish self-interest; (2) political participation replaces religion; (3) the United States is a step in the march toward messianic redemption; and (4) Jews should involve themselves in American politics, as Jews, for the betterment of all. After examining some representative voices of these four approaches, I will look at variations on the Jewish Prayer for the Government recited by American communities as a manifestation of the Jewish debate about how to approach the U.S. political system.

Shtadlanut: The Classical Diaspora Approach

The classic diaspora approach to secular states has been *shtadlanut*, appeals to the government to protect the Jews. This model begins with two assumptions: first, that the Jewish sojourn in any given country will be only temporary, and, second, that foreign governments cannot be trusted to look out for the best interests of the Jews. Beginning in medieval Europe, each community would appoint *shtadlanim*, politically savvy individuals charged with advocating on behalf of the Jews to the political authorities. In nineteenth-century Poland and Germany, political parties such as Agudath Israel took over this traditional role from local appointees, but these groups still acted with a focus on serving the self-interests of the Jewish community.[2]

In twentieth and twenty-first century America, the role of the *shtadlanim* has largely been played by the Big Three Defense organizations—the Anti-Defamation League, the American Jewish Committee, and the American Jewish Congress (which laid off most of its staff and suspended operations in 2010 but in May 2011 announced plans to relaunch in the unspecified future). These organizations look to the U.S. government to protect Jews from hate crimes, to guarantee religious freedom, and to guard the separation of Church and State lest Christian practices be forced on Jews. The oldest of these organizations, American Jewish Committee, was founded in 1906 in the wake of pogroms in Europe, for the purpose of protecting Jews at home and abroad. The German Jewish immigrant community had typically shied away from involvement in public life, fearing a backlash from native-born citizens who might see such involvement as evidence that Jews could never be full Americans.[3] Accordingly, AJCommittee, which they founded, pursued quiet dealings with governmental authorities rather than public shows of Jewish political power. A few years later, the lynching of the Jewish businessman Leo Frank and the AJCommittee's hesitance to take public action in response, prompted the establishment of the Anti-Defamation League, founded to fight anti-Semitism and bigotry. In 1918, Eastern European Jewish leaders, classically shut out of the German-led AJCommittee, founded the American Jewish Congress.

In a view consistent with the *shtadlanut* approach to government, Louis Marshall (1856–1929), one of the founders of the American Jewish Committee, argued against political action that might suggest that Jews have "interests different from those of other American citizens." Jews, however, should "unite for the purpose of aiding all Jews who are persecuted, or who are suffering from discrimination in any part of the world, on account of their religious beliefs; and we can at the same time unite for the purpose of ameliorating the condition of our brethren in faith, who are suffering from the effects of such discrimination directly or indirectly."⁴ In this formulation, Jewish engagement with the American political system should be limited to quiet attempts to persuade the government to alleviate the suffering of Jews at home or abroad. Such political work should complement internal fundraising efforts on behalf of Jews who are suffering.

A variation on the *shtadlanut* method to Jewish political engagement replaces direct petition on behalf of the Jewish community with the establishment of political alliances with other communities. This approach acknowledges the difference between the more homogenous culture of European countries and the multiethnic reality of America. Those who engage in this approach partner with the communities deemed to share critical interests with the Jews for the primary purpose of advancing the internal interests of the Jewish community.

Replacing Judaism with Universal Political Ideals

Some American Jews have argued that neither Judaism nor other religions have a place in an enlightened secular state. This position finds its roots in Baruch Spinoza, who described Judaism as the remnant of a theocratic tradition that makes no sense outside the context of a Jewish political state. For Spinoza, the biblical God functioned as the leader of a Jewish state, whose law was *halakhah* (Jewish law). Absent a Jewish state, God has no power, and *halakhah* loses its authority.

In the late nineteenth and early to mid-twentieth century, many American Jews embraced radical social movements, including socialism, communism, and anarchism. The specific outlooks of these movements differed, as did the Jewish backgrounds, observances, and ethnic identifications of their adherents. But in the Jewish context, all of these movements began with the demand for Jews to ally themselves with other members of the working classes and to assume that Judaism as a religion has little to contribute to the current political debate.

In 1895 Abraham Cahan (1860–1951), who would later become the editor of the *Forverts*, the preeminent Yiddish Socialist newspaper, wrote the following words in commemoration of the fifth anniversary of *Di Arbeter Tsaytung* (*The Workers' Newspaper*):

> The little Jewish soul, which five years ago was shrunken and pressed down in the narrow confines of the old, moldy little Jewish world, is today as broad as the

entire world. It used to be engraved in old faint letters: "The little Jews are my people, the Land of Israel is my small sliver of the world, and the Five Books of Moses is my religion." But now honest, large, golden letters sparkle: "Humanity is my people, the wide world is my fatherland, and helping everyone to advance toward happiness is my religion!"⁵

Before the encounter with socialism, Cahan declared, Jews were small-minded, inward-facing people, held captive by adherence to an ancient law. Socialism freed Jews to pursue a greater good and to see themselves as part of a worldwide human community. Jews, according to Cahan, must be involved in the project of creating a just society, but they should do so primarily as human beings rather than as Jews.

For some radical political thinkers, organizing Jews into their own political societies and writing and giving speeches in Yiddish served only the practical purpose of engaging an immigrant community not yet fluent in English and American culture. Others, though, argued that Jews could make a particular contribution to radical causes. Rose Pastor Stokes (1879–1933), first a socialist and then a communist leader, commented, "I believe ... that the Jewish people, because of the ancient and historic struggle for social and economic justice, should be fitted to recognize a special mission in the cause of the modern Socialist movement."⁶ Like Cahan, Stokes showed little interest in Jewish religious practices or teachings. She maintained, however, that the historical experience of Jews should inspire Jews to involve themselves in socialism and should give Jews a unique perspective on the experiences of suffering and oppression.

While Cahan and Stokes dismissed religious practice and teachings as largely irrelevant to modern political struggles, the anarchist Emma Goldman (1869–1940) characterized both religion and the state as equally responsible for subjugating the individual. She wrote, "Just as religion has fettered the human mind, and as property, or the monopoly of things, has subdued and stifled man's needs, so has the State enslaved his spirit, dictating every phase of conduct."⁷ Subscribing to the anarchist agenda necessitated a rejection of all structures that threatened to suppress the expression of individual freedom. While Goldman and other anarchists spoke openly of their Jewish heritage and organized through Jewish circles, they held up anarchist beliefs as the new religion by which Jews should engage with the world.⁸

America as Part of Destiny

Proponents of the two categories discussed above essentially treat the United States as they would any other Diaspora community. These thinkers may advocate more or less religious practice, national solidarity, and involvement in political affairs, but they make little theoretical distinction between the situation of Jews in the United States and elsewhere. For the *shtadlanim*, America differs only insofar as the government is more open than European governments to satisfying Jewish self-interest. The socialists, communists, and anarchists kept their eye on a worldwide human movement rather than a specifically Jewish or American one.

In contrast, a number of nineteenth- and early-twentieth-century writers proposed that the United States plays a unique, and perhaps even divinely ordained, role in the history of the Jewish people. For some, this means that America represents the realization of the political ideals of the Torah. Others, especially in the Orthodox world, speculate that God placed the Jewish people in America in order to save them from murderous trends in Europe.

For Oscar Straus (1850–1926), the U.S. Secretary of Commerce and Labor under President Theodore Roosevelt, and the first Jewish Cabinet member, biblical Israel provided the democratic model for modern American government. He wrote:

> The republicanism of the United States is the nearest approach to the ideals of the prophets of Israel that ever has been incorporated in the form of a State.... Ours is peculiarly a promised land wherein the spirit of the teachings of the ancient prophets inspired the work of the fathers of our country.... The Protestant, the Catholic, and the Jew, each and all need the support and the sustaining power of their religion to develop their moral natures and to keep alive the spirit of self-sacrifice which American patriotism demands of every man, whatever may be his creed or race, who is worthy to enjoy the blessings of American citizenship.⁹

Straus here simultaneously described the United States as the fulfillment of the divine vision for the world and explained why Judaism and other religions remain relevant. The ancient prophets, he said, devised the philosophical system that eventually found concrete application in the establishment of the United States. Lest one conclude that the realization of the prophetic dream should mean the end of Judaism, he added that religion plays an essential role in instilling the personal characteristics necessary for one to be a productive citizen of America. To engage as a Jew in American politics, one need only practice Judaism and follow the democratic ideals of the state.¹⁰

In *They Who Knock at Our Gates*, a defense of immigration written toward the end of the mass migration of Eastern European Jews to New York, Mary Antin (1881–1949) similarly described the United States in Jewish religious terms. Rather than portray the United States as the fulfillment of the prophetic promise, she saw it as part of a divine plan for the world. Thus, she wrote "I have chosen to read the story of '76 as a chapter in sacred history; to see Thomas Jefferson in a class with Moses, and Washington with Joshua; to regard the American nation as the custodian of a sacred trust, and American citizenship as a holy order."¹¹ And: "Once the thunders of God were heard on Mount Sinai, and a certain people heard, and the blackness of idolatry was lifted from the world. Again the voice of God, the Father, shook the air above Bunker Hill, and the grip of despotism was loosened from the throat of panting humanity. Let the children of the later saviors of the world be as faithful as the children of the earlier saviors and perhaps God will speak again in times to come."¹² In this reading, the story of America becomes the sequel to the biblical narrative of striving for the promised land, and the American people as a whole become the inheritors of the Jewish covenant. Indeed, Antin called her 1912 memoir of immigration to America *The Promised Land*.

Perhaps the most famous proponent of the idea that Judaism provided the model for American democracy was Justice Louis Brandeis (1856–1941), the first Jew appointed to the Supreme Court. Though Brandeis did not grow up with a strong religious background, he discovered his Judaism as an adult and eventually became a staunch supporter of the Zionist movement. In a 1915 speech to the Conference of Eastern Council of Reform Rabbis, Brandeis articulated his understanding of the parallels between Jewish and American traditions, and of the role of Jews in the American state:

> America's insistent demand in the twentieth century is for social justice. That also has been the Jews' striving for ages. Their affliction as well as their religion has prepared the Jews for effective democracy. Persecution broadened their sympathies. It trained them in patient endurance, in self-control, and in sacrifice. It made them think as well as suffer. It deepened the passion for righteousness.
>
> Indeed, loyalty to America demands rather that each American Jew become a Zionist. For only through the ennobling effect of its strivings can we develop the best that is in us and give to this country the full benefit of our great inheritance.[13]

Here Brandeis attempted to reconcile two seemingly contradictory elements of his outlook on Judaism and America. On the one hand, he viewed participation in American democracy as the fulfillment of a Jewish ideal. The Jewish historical experience, he suggested, has made Jews uniquely suited for political life in America. At the same time, he advocated for the creation of a Jewish state in Palestine, not so that American Jews will move there, but as a means of guaranteeing a safe haven for Jews from other parts of the world. In response to any concern that Zionism might lead to dual loyalties, Brandeis argued—a bit counterintuitively—that through the project of seeking a Jewish state for others, American Jews will develop the wherewithal to be more valuable contributors to the American state.

Another approach to the uniqueness of America appears in the writings of post-Holocaust Orthodox leaders who characterize America as a *malkhut shel hesed*—literally, a kingdom of kindness—where God placed the Jews to save them from destruction at the hand of the Nazis. This portrayal reflects the experience of *Haredi* (ultra-Orthodox) communities, most of whom arrived after World War II and proceeded to re-create their European communities and *yeshivot* (Torah study centers) in America. In one *teshuvah* (legal opinion), Rabbi Moshe Feinstein (1895–1986), who is generally credited with coining this term, prohibited *yeshivot* and other religious institutions from defrauding the government on the basis that the United States has acted beneficently toward the Jewish people. Here, he spoke of the "loving kindness of our government, the United States of America, where God, who is to be praised, in God's great mercy, brought the remainder of the refugees of the Jews of Europe and the remainder of the great Torah scholars and their students to reestablish the old centers of Torah from Europe, as well as new centers." Describing the United States as a "kingdom of loving kindness (*malkhut shel hesed*), whose entire purpose is to benefit all of the residents of the country," he instructed religious leaders to "pray for the peace of the country and for all who occupy positions of leadership, that they should be blessed with all blessings."[14]

Jews Need to Change America

As Jews have become increasingly secure in America, many on both the left and the right have advocated applying Jewish law and philosophy to contemporary political questions in such a way as to transform American society to benefit Jews and non-Jews. This approach, like the *shtadlanut* described earlier, views Jewish self-interest as a major goal of political involvement, but unlike that strictly self-serving approach, this one emphasizes the betterment of all humanity as a Jewish goal in itself.

Proponents of this approach fall into two major camps: those who base their position on religious/ideological grounds, and those who emphasize historical/political factors. The former advocate bringing Jewish laws and moral principles into the American public square. The latter stress the Jewish historical experience of oppression and argue that this experience should compel Jews to unite with other minority groups to fight oppression.

One of the strongest voices of the religious/ideological camp was the Lubavitcher Rebbe, Menachem Mendel Schneerson (1902–1994), who believed that Jews have a responsibility to ensure that non-Jews follow the seven Noahide laws. These laws, which the rabbis of the Talmud understood God to have given Noah upon his descent from the Ark, forbid murder, theft, idolatry, blasphemy, incest, and eating a limb from a living animal; and they mandate the establishment of courts of law. For Schneerson, adherence to these laws was a necessary precondition of an ethical society.[15] He wrote, "Without [the Noahide] laws as a bedrock of government, a society will either have despotism, where individuals' lives are compromised and possibly abused, or anarchy, where every person pursues his or her own needs without regard for the law."[16] With these laws as the foundation, he continued, "The United States must continue to use its influence to inspire other nations in the areas of education and human rights.... The leaders of the world must encourage their constituents to live by G-d's divine laws, which will enable them to use their personal freedom to usher in a true unity between man and man, community and community, nation and nation.... The government of every nation must now prepare to do everything possible to finally bring peace to the entire world."[17] Jewish participation in national politics, then, not only serves Jewish self-interest, but also contributes to the larger goal of bringing peace to the world.

Rabbi Mordecai Kaplan (1881–1983), the founder of the Reconstructionist Movement, also proposed introducing Judaism into the American public sphere, but he focused on distilling general moral principles from Judaism rather than imposing particular laws. In Kaplan's view, the Founders established the doctrine of separation of Church and State in order to encourage the creation of a new American civil religion that would replace the supernatural religions of the past. Instead, though, the Establishment clause has created a "religious vacuum,"[18] as nationalism has grown, unchecked by religious ethics. Therefore, he wrote:

> [T]he primary task of American Jewry is to have the belief in God motivate the following objectives: 1) the utilization of our material progress for purposes of

peace and for the enhancement of human life; 2) the pursuit of the human sciences and arts with a view to the elimination of poverty, ignorance, and disease, and to the creation of opportunities for everybody's material, intellectual, emotional and spiritual self-fulfillment; 3) the limitation of the sovereignty of the nations, and the translation of their economic interdependence into a workable program for the free exchange of goods and services on a world scale; 4) the inculcation in the individual of a sense of responsibility for doing his personal share toward making the world the better and happier for his having lived in it.

The second task of American Jewry is to advocate an indigenous civic religion for the American people that shall act as a unifying influence, uniting all Americans regardless of race, creed or status without being authoritative or coercive. That task involves the incorporation into American institutions and practices of those principles in Jewish religion which have a universal import and are therefore transferable to other civilizations.[19]

Religious commitments, Kaplan suggested, should compel Jews to work to create a better world. Unlike the radicals of the nineteenth and early twentieth centuries, Kaplan believed that Judaism could contribute a particular and valuable perspective to American public life. Study of Jewish law and traditions, he posited, would yield a set of general moral principles that could be applied to the creation of an American civil religion. Through this argument, Kaplan found a middle ground between the radical rejection of religion as an obstacle to human progress, and the religious view voiced by Schneerson that America should follow specific biblical laws.

Occupying a space between Schneerson and Kaplan, the philosopher David Novak (b. 1941) defines the paradox of Jewish involvement in the public sphere as "the problem of submitting Jewish public policy to criteria that are not Jewish and which are taken to transcend Judaism. Is not any such acknowledgment a recipe for the self-destruction of Jewish independence? But, on the other hand, without the acknowledgment of some kind of general morality, how can Jews possibly participate in a society with non-Jews, indeed, in a society where the vast majority of the citizens are non-Jews?"[20] By way of solution, he distinguishes among three driving forces in Jewish political involvement: Torah, self-interest, and general morality. He explains, "The solution to the above paradox is to see Jewish agreement to certain general standards of morality to be partial rather than all-inclusive. Jews can agree to general moral standards when these standards are not presented as being universal in the sense of being total, and when these standards are not presented as being ultimate in the sense of even being most important."[21] He extracts these universal moral principles from the Noahide laws, commenting, "Even though a Noahide-like morality can be learned by ordinary human reason, the historical fact is that it is usually learned through religious tradition ... the sense of absolute obligation ... is best inculcated when morality is learned as that which is the direct will of God to human beings, and which is transmitted by religious traditions based on revelation."[22] In any given political decision, Novak says, Jews should balance communal self interest, Torah law, and general moral principles. In this way, Jews can participate fully in the American public square without putting aside specifically Jewish interests or religious law, but also without trying to impose religious law on all Americans.

Whereas Kaplan and Novak focus on what Judaism can teach America regarding general moral principles, Rabbi Elliot Dorff (b. 1943) envisions a two-way learning process, through which Jews bring Jewish teachings into the public square, while also learning from the religious teachings of other groups:

> No religion should determine national policy as a matter of right, but each religion must enter the fray of public debate if that discussion is to reflect the nation as a whole and if it is to attain the richness that only multiple parties with differing views can give it ... We Jews may believe that Judaism represents the best articulation of God's wishes for us, and we may live by that belief and even be prepared to die for it; but we must simultaneously recognize that no human being is omniscient, that human knowledge on every subject, including God's will, is limited, and that others may have insights from which we can learn.[23]

In Dorff's conception, Judaism offers not only general moral principles, but specific laws and wisdom that can and should influence the public debate. The solution to Novak's paradox, then, is not to distinguish between Jewish law and moral teachings, but to recognize that each religious tradition contributes uniquely to the conversation. In the context of any given decision, Jews may stick to Jewish law, may learn from other traditions, or may find a synthesis between the two.

In contrast to these efforts to bring Jewish religious principles into the public square, more historical-minded Jewish thinkers argue that Jews should involve themselves in the public sphere as a means simultaneously of preserving Jewish self-interest and of promoting larger societal interests. Morris Raphael Cohen (1880–1947), the professor at the center of the famous Jewish intellectual circle at City College, wrote:

> When we protest or fight against vicious discrimination or rowdy efforts to deprive us of our equal rights as citizens, we are not only defending our legitimate interests as Jews, but are also helping our fellow citizens to preserve the integrity of the traditional American way of life. We are preserving it against those who would pervert and overthrow it in the interests of racial strife and group hatreds which have at all times been destructive of humane civilization ... Our natural allies, not only in this country but throughout the world, are those who still believe in individual freedom and the toleration of conscientious differences of opinion. We dare not abandon the cause of liberalism. For if that fails in this country, we as a minority group, and ultimately all respect for human rights, are doomed.[24]

Unlike the *shtadlanim* who focus primarily on Jewish self-interest or the radicals who speak almost exclusively of general human concerns, Cohen saw the alliance between Jews and liberals (defined as the defenders of individual freedom) as serving two equally valuable purposes: the protection of Jews as a minority group, and the preservation of human rights in general. These two goals, he proposed, are wholly dependent on one another.

Similar to Cohen's approach, Melanie Kaye/Kantrowitz (b. 1945) has argued more recently that Jews, along with other minority groups and the economic underclass, suffer oppression in America. Ending this oppression, she explains, will require Jews to view their own liberation struggle as part of a larger movement:

Nor do I believe that we can fight anti-Semitism or racism without attacking the systematic economic injustice that is American capitalism. Racism, because in the U.S., racism is so often expressed in economic terms with economic consequences; Anti-Semitism because in Christian culture, Jews are identified with evil and treachery in general and with money in particular. Anti-Semitism links Jews with wealth and power in order to protect all those with wealth and power. Only by labeling anti-Semitism clearly and unequivocally as pernicious slime will capitalism be properly revealed as a maker of injustice and as a source of increasing human misery.[25]

For Kaye/Kantrowitz, the defeat of anti-Semitism can be accomplished only through the transformation of a capitalist system that produces economic injustice and that allows portrayals of Jews as moneygrubbers to thrive. Like Cohen, she does not view Jewish self-interest and the interests of humanity as competing agendas, but rather as inseparable goals. In involving themselves in the public sphere, then, Jews should simultaneously identify themselves as Jews driven by Jewish history and interest, and pursue changes that benefit all of humanity.

In the contemporary world, Jewish politicians often speak of the social justice commitments they learned from Judaism as the motivating force in their public involvement. While not necessarily agreeing with Cohen and Kaye/Kantrowitz's politics, these elected officials maintain that a commitment to Judaism and a commitment to America complement, rather than contradict, one another. Referring to her Jewish heritage and to her early Zionist involvement, Representative Bella Abzug (1920–1998) remarked, "It made me a political activist, it kept me a rebel."[26] In her political work, she continued, she refused to accept that support for Israel might preclude support for human rights. Thus, she defended Israel against condemnation by the United Nations, while refusing to give in to those who pressured her to temper her opposition to the Vietnam War lest President Nixon penalize Israel and the Jewish community as a result.[27] In a more religious vein, Senator Joseph Lieberman (b. 1942) commented, "I don't call my rabbi every time I have to cast a vote, but the values I've learned are part of me—beginning with the basic fact that I believe in God and that all are equal because all are creations of God."[28] And Representative Gabrielle Giffords (b. 1970), shot in January 2011 by a gunman who may have been at least partially motivated by anti-Semitism, credited her public involvement to "the values, instilled in me by my Jewish relatives, of tolerance, of understanding, and of a deep desire to assist and to educate others."[29] For these elected officials and others, involvement in the public sphere stems from and even strengthens their identification as Jews without replacing a commitment to Jews and to Judaism.

Coda: American Jews and the Prayer for the State

Since medieval times, the Jewish Sabbath service has included a prayer for the secular government. The traditional form of this prayer, known as "*Hanoten teshuah*," literally, "The One who brings deliverance," codified in the sixteenth century, requests divine protection for the secular leader and pleads that he and his ministers have mercy on the Jewish people. This prayer represents *shtadlanut* translated into liturgy: the assumption is that the Jews can expect no better than a government that leaves the Jews alone.

In the United States, many Jewish communities have composed new versions of this prayer for the government. These newer liturgies reflect a growing comfort in the United States, as well as an accompanying sense that Jews bear responsibility for the well-being of the state, that they are not simply supplicants for the good graces of the government. For example, one version of the prayer, composed by Rabbi Max Lilienthal for a nineteenth century Orthodox *siddur* (prayer book) pleads,

> Look down from Your holy dwelling and bless this land, the United States of America, whereon we dwell. Let no violence be heard in their land, wasting and destruction within their boundaries ... May their seed be known among nations and their offspring among peoples, and all that see them shall acknowledge them, for You will have blessed them. Amen.[30]

Here, the blessing for the success of the United States and its people does not appear to be grounded only in Jewish self-interest. Certainly, Jews will fare better in a country not racked by violence, but pure self-interest does not appear to be the prime motivation of the author of the prayer or the worshiper he imagines using this prayer.

Other prayers take a step further and challenge the United States to live up to an ideal of pluralism, justice, and equality. For instance, the 1916 prayer book of the Reform synagogue in Charleston, South Carolina, thanked God who "hast removed the intolerance of bigotry far from out this happy republic, and hast relieved the people from the yoke of political and religious bondage" and prayed that "sentiments of charity and friendship unite them as citizens of one common country."[31] An Orthodox prayer book printed the same year is even more explicit in asking that "this blessed country continue to be an asylum for the fugitives of religious and political persecution, who seek shelter under its lucid banner."[32] And a somewhat earlier Reform *siddur* went beyond simply asking God to help the country to live up to its ideals, instead demanding that the Jewish community take responsibility for guiding the United States toward a better future, saying "Thou hast appointed us, the people of Thy prophetic hope, the first born nation of liberty, to lead the van of all who would pilgrim on toward this glorious goal ... Help maintain our country the bulwark of freedom, the home of virtue, and an altar of true piety."[33]

In the late twentieth and early twenty-first century, the versions of the prayer for the state printed in American liberal prayer books have focused more on a vision for the United States and on the Jewish community's role in realizing this vision, and less on concern for the safety and security of the Jewish community itself. For example, the standard text used in Conservative synagogues requests divine blessing "for our country—for its government, for its leaders and advisors, and for all who exercise just and rightful authority. Teach them insights from Your Torah, that they may administer all affairs of state fairly, that peace and security, happiness and prosperity, justice and freedom may forever abide in our midst."[34]

Similarly, the Reconstructionist prayer book asks, "Let your blessing pour out on this land and on all officials of this country who are occupied, in good faith, with the public needs ... Please, WISE ONE, God of the lifebreath of all flesh, waken your spirit within all inhabitants of our land, and plant among the peoples of different nationalities and faiths who dwell here, love and brotherhood, peace and friendship."[35]

Mishkan Shalom, the new Reform siddur, places responsibility for creating a better country both on the leaders of the country and on individuals, asking "Teach us to give thanks for what we have by sharing it with those who are in need. Keep our eyes open to the wonders of creation, and alert to the care of the earth. May we never be lazy in the work of peace.... Grant our leaders wisdom and forbearance. May they govern with justice and compassion."[36]

These prayers for the state reveal a uniquely American perspective on the role of Jews in public life. Rather than limit themselves to begging the secular government to spare the Jewish community from destruction, expulsion, or a punishing tax burden, the communities that recite these prayers portray themselves as active participants in American democracy. In American public life, as reflected in these prayers, Jews simultaneously pursue internal communal interests while also bringing Jewish teachings, history, and commitments to bear in the pursuit of a better life for all.

Notes

1. See, for example, Gil Graf, *Separation of Church and State: Dina De-malkhuta Dina in Jewish Law 1750–1848* (Tuscaloosa: University of Alabama Press, 2003), and Shmuel Shilo, *Dina De-malkhuta Dina* (Jerusalem: Academic Press, 1974) (Hebrew).
2. Alan Mittleman, *The Politics of Torah: The Jewish Political Tradition and the Founding of Agudat Israel* (Albany, NY: SUNY Press, 1996).
3. Naomi W. Cohen, *Encounter with Empancipation: The German Jews in the United States 1830–1914* (Philadelphia: Jewish Publication Society, 1984), pp. 129–39.
4. Charles Reznikoff, ed., *Louis Marshall: Champion of Liberty* (Philadelphia: Jewish Publication Society, 1957), vol. 1, p. 22. See also, Leo Pfeffer, *Religion, State, and the Burger Court* (Amherst, NY: Prometheus Books, 1985). Pfeffer (1910–1993), the longtime general counsel of AJCongress and the director of the organization's Commission on Law and Social Action, maintained that any state involvement in religion—even on a nonpreferential basis—violates the Establishment Clause.
5. Quoted in Tony Michels, *A Fire in Their Heart: Yiddish Socialists in New York* (Cambridge, MA: Harvard University Press, 2005), p. 1.
6. Joyce Antler, *The Journey Home: Jewish Women and the American Century* (New York: Simon and Schuster, 1997), p. 82.
7. "Anarchism: What It Really Stands For," in *Red Emma Speaks: An Emma Goldman Reader*, AlixKates Shulman, ed. (Amherst, NY: Humanity Books, 1998), p. 68.
8. Paul Avrich, *Anarchist Portraits* (Princeton, NJ: Princeton University Press, 1988), chap.13, "Jewish Anarchism in the United States," pp. 176–99.
9. Oscar Straus, "American Judaism," in *The American Spirit* (New York: The Century Co, 1913), pp. 291–92.
10. Ironically, at approximately the same time as Straus wrote about the similarity between Jewish and American values, Hermann Cohen was asserting the same

parallelism between Jewish and German culture and arguing, in words that resemble Straus's comments about America, that Jews have finally found their national and moral homeland in Germany—words that admittedly startle Jews who lived during or after the Holocaust, and that pose questions about Straus's analysis of America. See Hermann Cohen, *Reason and Hope: Selections from the Jewish Writings of Hermann Cohen*, Eva Jospe, trans. (New York: Norton [B'nai Brith Heritage Series], 1971), "German and Jewish Ethos I and II," pp. 175–88. I would like to thank Elliot Dorff for pointing out this comparison to me.

11. Mary Antin, *They Who Knock at Our Gates* (Boston: Houghton Mifflin, 1914). p. 27.
12. Ibid., pp. 142–43.
13. Louis D. Brandeis, "The Jewish Problem: How to Solve It." Speech to the Conference of Eastern Council of Reform Rabbis, April 25, 1915. Available at: http://www.law.louisville.edu/library/collections/brandeis/node/234 See also Stephen W. Baskerville, *Of Laws and Limitations: An Intellectual Portrait of Louis Dembitz Brandeis* (Cranbury, NJ: Associated University Presses, 1994).
14. *Igg'rot Moshe Hoshen Mishpat* 2:29.
15. Jan Feldman, *Lubavitchers as Citizens: A Paradox of Liberal Democracy* (Ithaca, NY: Cornell University Press, 2003), p. 47.
16. Simon Jacobson, *Toward a Meaningful Life: The Wisdom of the Rebbe Menachem Mendel Schneerson* (New York: William Morrow, 1995), pp.163–64.
17. Ibid. pp. 168–69.
18. Mordecai Kaplan, *The Greater Judaism in the Making: A Study of the Modern Evolution of Judaism* (New York: The Reconstructionist Press, 1960), p. 476.
19. Ibid. pp. 476–77.
20. David Novak, "Toward a Jewish Public Philosophy in America," in Alan Mittleman, Robert Licht, and Joathan D. Sarna, eds., *Jews and the American Public Square: Debating Religion and Republic* (Lanham, MD: Rowman & Littlefield, 2002), p. 344.
21. Ibid., p. 345.
22. David Novak, "A Jewish Policy on Church–State Relations," in Alan Mittleman, ed., *Religion as a Public Good* (Lanham, MD: Rowman & Littlefield, 2003), pp. 152–53.
23. Elliot N. Dorff, "Jewish Tradition and National Policy," in Daniel H. Frank, ed., *Commandment and Community: New Essays in Jewish Legal and Political Philosophy* (Albany, NY: SUNY Press, 1995) pp. 104–5. See also the later, expanded version of his approach in Elliot N. Dorff, *To Do the Right and the Good: A Jewish Approach to Modern Social Ethics* (Philadelphia: Jewish Publication Society, 2002), chap. 4: "'The King's Torah' Judaism and National Policy," pp. 96–113. See also Jill Jacobs, *There Shall Be No Needy: Pursuing Social Justice Through Jewish Law and Tradition* (Woodstock, VT: Jewish Lights, 2009), pp. 214–21, for a related take on Jewish participation in public discourse.
24. Morris Cohen, *Reflections of a Wondering Jew* (Boston: Beacon Press, 1950), pp. 3–4.
25. Melanie Kaye/Kantrowitz, *The Issue Is Power: Essays on Women, Jews, Violence, and Resistance* (San Francisco: Aunt Lute, 1992), p. 133.
26. "Bella on Bella," *Moment Magazine*, February 1976, p. 28.
27. Ibid., pp. 28–29.
28. Sheri Silverman, "Joseph Lieberman Brings Jewish Values to U.S. Senate," *Washington Jewish Week*, July 31, 1998. Available at: http://www.vanguardnewsnetwork.com/wolzek/2000_LiebermanGoyReference.htm (accessed July 3, 2011)
29. Danielle Cantor, "Interview with Gabrielle Giffords," *Jewish Women Magazine* (Spring 2007). Available at: http://www.jwi.org/Page.aspx?pid=1954 (accessed July 3, 2011). Bella on Bella," *Moment Magazine*, February 1976, p. 28.Ibid., pp. 28–29.Sheri

Silverman, "Joseph Lieberman Brings Jewish Values to U.S. Senate," *Washington Jewish Week*, July 31, 1998. Available at: http://www.vanguardnewsnetwork.com/wolzek/2000_LiebermanGoyReference.htm (accessed July 3, 2011).Danielle Cantor, "Interview with Gabrielle Giffords," *Jewish Women Magazine* (Spring 2007). Available at: http://www.jwi.org/Page.aspx?pid=1954 (accessed July 3, 2011).
30. Rabbi Max Lilienthal, "*Ribbon Kol Ha-olamim,*" in Henry Frank, *Tefilot Yisra'el: Prayers of Israel with an English Translation* (New York: Henry Frank, 1848/49), pp. 198–99, as translated and quoted by Jonathan Sarna in his essay, "A Forgotten 19th-Century Prayer for the United States Government," in *Hesed ve-Emet: Studies in Honor of Ernest S. Frerichs*, ed. J. Magness and S. Gitin (Athens, GA: Scholars Press, 1998), 431–40.
31. Sabbath service of the Reformed Society of Israelites in Charleston (New York: Bloch Publishing, 1916).
32. Julius Silberfeld, *The Sabbath Service: Arranged and Revised, with Special English Prayers and Responsive Readings* (New York: Bloch Publishing, 1923), p. 187.
33. Emil Hirsch, *Olat Tamid* (1896) in Barry Schwartz, "Expressions of Civil Religion in Jewish Prayer for the Government," *Journal of Reform Judaism* 37 (Spring 1990), pp. 5–11.
34. Jules Harlow, ed., *Siddur Sim Shalom* (New York: Rabbinical Assembly, 1985), p. 415.
35. David Teutsch, ed., *Kol HaNeshama: Shabbat and Festivals* (Elkins Park, PA: Reconstructionist Press, 2004), p. 418.
36. Elyse Frishman, ed., *Mishkan Tefillah* (New York: CCAR Press, 2007), p. 376.

Suggestions for Further Reading

Dorff, Elliot N. 2002. *To Do the Right and the Good: A Jewish Approach to Modern Social Ethics*. Philadelphia: Jewish Publication Society, esp. chap. 4.

Goldberg, J .J. 1997. *Jewish Power: Inside the American Jewish Establishment*. New York: Basic Books.

Graf, Gil. 2003. *Separation of Church and State: Dina De-malkhuta Dina in Jewish Law 1750–1848*. Tuscaloosa: University of Alabama Press.

Jacobs, Jill. 2009. *There Shall Be No Needy: Pursuing Social Justice Through Jewish Law and Tradition*. Woodstock, VT. Jewish Lights.

Jacobs, Jill. 2011. *Where Justice Dwells: A Hands-On Guide to Doing Social Justice in Your Jewish Community*. Woodstock, VT. Jewish Lights.

Michels, Tony. 2005. *A Fire in Their Heart: Yiddish Socialists in New York*. Cambridge, MA: Harvard University Press.

Mittleman, Alan. 2003. *Religion as a Public Good: Jews and Other Americans on Religion in the Public Square*. Lanham, MD: Rowman & Littlefield.

Mittleman, Alan, Jonathan D. Sarna, and Robert Licht. 2002. *Jewish Polity and American Civil Society: Communal Agencies and Religious Movements in the American Public Sphere*. Lanham, MD: Rowman & Littlefield.

Mittleman, Alan, Jonathan D. Sarna, and Robert Licht. 2002. *Jews and the American Public Square: Debating Religion and Republic*. Lanham, MD: Rowman & Littlefield.

Novak, David. 2005. *The Jewish Social Contract: An Essay in Political Theology*. Princeton, NJ: Princeton University Press.

Walzer, Michael. 2006., *Law, Politics, and Morality in Judaism*. Princeton, NJ: Princeton University Press.

CHAPTER 27

JEWISH POLITICAL ETHICS IN ISRAEL

REUVEN HAMMER

The creation of the State of Israel as "a Jewish state in the Land of Israel," in the words of Israel's Declaration of Independence, created a situation unprecedented in Jewish history. While Jews in Israel face the same ethical problems as Jews everywhere else in such matters as medical dilemmas and business ethics, the creation of a Jewish polity added a new dimension that is not to be found where Jews are simply part of a general population. It is those areas that will be addressed in this chapter.

For the first time a sovereign political entity was established by the Jewish People that was to be governed by a democratically elected parliamentary system totally secular in nature in which all the citizens of the State, Jews and others, were to be granted equal civil rights. The State, in the words of the Declaration, would "uphold the full social and political equality of all its citizens, without distinction of race, creed or sex," and it would guarantee all Arab inhabitants "full and equal citizenship and due representation in all its bodies and institutions."

The "Jewish" ethical aspect of the State was enunciated by the statement that the country would "be based on the precepts of liberty, justice and peace as envisioned by the prophets of Israel." By referring to "the prophets of Israel" rather than "the Jewish tradition" or "the precepts of Judaism," the founders were deliberately distancing themselves from the Jewish religion as expressed through the codes of law and the works of ethics and philosophy that had developed over the two thousand years of exile—that is, rabbinic Judaism—and were basing themselves solely on the ethics of the prophets.

This perspective reflected the prevailing secular ethos of political Zionism that tended to view the new settlement as a direct continuation of the last period of Jewish independence, the time of the Second Temple, and to disparage the exile and anything created there. Secularism, furthermore, under the influence of Western

Enlightenment, tended to view the prophets as the greatest teachers of ethics and to look upon the Torah and rabbinic writings and teachers as representatives of outmoded religious ritual.

Religion and State

Once the Jewish settlement, known in Hebrew as the *yishuv*, became a state in 1948, ethical problems arose. In what way was the state connected to the Jewish People? What were the rights of non-Jewish residents? Could they be full citizens, could they vote, could they own land and serve in official state capacities? The Israel Declaration of Independence settled these questions in theory by its statement, quoted above, that Israel would "uphold the full social and political equality of all its citizens, without distinction of race, creed or sex." In practice, however, there remained difficulties for many years because until 1966 Arab sectors remained under military rule in accord with Defense Emergency Regulations. Although these were administered with great care and with a light hand, they nevertheless placed these communities in a different status than Jewish areas and controlled freedom of movement.[1] Arabs were also exempted from military service, thus drawing a major distinction between Jewish and Arab citizens, albeit one that Arabs desired. Discrimination in land purchase was illegal, but land owned by the Jewish National Fund had been designated for Jewish settlement and was not available to Arabs. In practice, Arabs frequently felt discriminated against, much as minorities in other countries are, in ways that are controlled not governmentally but socially, influenced by religious beliefs that sometimes differentiate between Jews and non-Jews. Attempts were made to alleviate this situation, as will be discussed below.

Who Is a Jew?

The Jewish nature of the State was also expressed through the "Law of Return," passed by the Knesset on July 5, 1950. It stated unequivocally that "Every Jew has the right to come to this country as an *oleh* [immigrant]." The question immediately arose as to who is a Jew? The position of the government was that anyone who declared him/herself to be a Jew and did not practice any other religion was to be accepted as a Jew for this purpose. This decision did not put an end to the discussion, especially in Orthodox circles.

Jewish Law does not consider children of a Jewish father to be Jewish if their mother is not. Thus a specific question that arose was what to do with children of a non-Jewish mother who were raised as Jews? Could they be registered as Jews in the national registry? In 1958 then Prime Minister David Ben Gurion put that question to Jewish scholars in Israel and abroad. Their answers were published in a book entitled *Jewish Identity: Modern Responsa and Opinions*.[2] The responses are what would have been expected. Both Orthodox and Conservative authorities, whether rabbis or not, would not accept the registration of children of gentile mothers unless they were converted. The attitude toward conversion and the strictness of the requirements for conversion, however, varied.[3] Among the nonobservant there were various opinions. Some called for registering them as Jews under nationality but not under religion, or even to eliminate the category of religion altogether.[4] Yehzkiel Kaufman, a secular Jewish Bible scholar instead strongly favored requiring conversion, although castigating the Chief Rabbinate for being overly strict in its requirements.[5] Mordecai Kaplan, the founder of the Reconstructionist Movement, suggested registering these children not as Jews but as "Jewish residents."[6] Justice Haim Cohen, however, found precedents in Jewish law that he asserted would permit registering the children as Jews.[7] In 1970, after prolonged and bitter debates, the law was amended specifically to give the right of emigration to descendants of a Jew to the third generation[8] and also to define "who is a Jew" as "a person who was born of a Jewish mother or has become converted to Judaism and who is not a member of another religion."

Despite this legislation, the bitter debate over "who is a Jew" has continued. Several attempts were made to modify the law by defining conversion as being "according to Jewish Law," a code phrase for being recognized by Orthodox authority. The opposition to such a change, so far successful, has come from secular forces and especially from the Conservative and Reform Movements in Israel and throughout the world, whose conversions then would not have been recognized.

The question of who is a Jew was posed by the scholar and philosopher Eliezer Schweid in an essay entitled, "What Does It Mean to Be a Jew?"[9] He describes three approaches to this problem: the religious, the secular-nationalist, and the cultural. Schweid's suggestion is that all must learn to appreciate and accept the other and find whatever common ground is possible. His contention is that a rebirth of Jewish culture and creativity is needed and that this is a long and difficult process that can be done only in Israel, where there is "a Jewish community leading a full and independent life."[10]

A major conflict erupted in 1997 over the Jewishness of adopted children converted in Israel by a religious court of the Masorti/Conservative Movement. The Ministry of the Interior had refused to register them as Jews in their Identity Cards and in the Population registry, contending that the Law of Return applied only to those who were converted overseas. The case was taken to the Supreme Court. In response, religious political parties introduced legislation that would have barred the recognition of any conversions other than those of the Chief Rabbinate. They threatened to topple the government if this legislation was not passed. World Jewry was up in arms, and in order to avoid a conflict, Prime Minister Benjamin Netanyahu appointed a commission under Yaakov Neeman, including representatives of the Conservative and Reform Movements, to study the question of the recognition of non-Orthodox conversions in Israel.[11] The commission discussed the possibility of a trial period in which there would be a joint effort among the various streams of Judaism to educate toward conversion, with an Orthodox Rabbinical Court of a more open and liberal nature performing the actual conversion. The rejection of this suggestion by the Chief Rabbinate, accompanied by a verbal attack on both non-Orthodox movements, resulted in the commission's never completing its work and never issuing a formal report. Instead the court cases were reinstated and were successful in attaining State recognition of these conversions. The controversy over conversion and which conversions should be recognized by the State for purposes of citizenship, however, remains, and new attempts to change the situation continue to be made by Orthodox religious parties.

A Jewish and Democratic State

"Israel is a Jewish and democratic state" has become a well-accepted mantra, proclaimed in two Basic Laws promulgated by the Knesset in 1992 and proposed in 2011 as the central part of an oath to be taken by non-Jews becoming Israeli citizens. Although the phrase appears nowhere in the Declaration of Independence, it can be said to stem from that document, which both "declares the establishment of a Jewish State," speaks of the government as being "an elected body," and guarantees liberty, justice, and full social and political equality for all its citizens.

The combination of Jewish and democratic has been seen as containing an inner contradiction and has required frequent elucidation. If truly democratic, is it not a state of all its citizens, Jewish and non-Jewish? If so, how is it Jewish? If Jewish, can it be democratic given that Judaism is a religious-legal system that is based not upon the equal rule of all its citizens to determine the law but upon the authority of rabbinic sages who are bound by Torah-based Jewish law? Or does "Jewish and democratic" mean that it is a compromise between these two sets of values? This tension, which has never been resolved, informs much of the political debate in Israel.

The Israel Democracy Institute published a volume of essays by prominent leaders of all sectors devoted to this question of defining "the identity and character of the State of Israel through scrutiny of the expression 'a Jewish and democratic state.'"[12] The variety of opinions expressed therein includes those who deny the idea of a Jewish state, preferring "the state of the Jews"[13]; those who see problems with the very term "Jewish and democratic"[14]; those who state clearly that "we put our emphasis on 'a Jewish state,' and if 'a democratic state' runs counter to this" they will do everything possible to "underscore the Jewish nature of the state"[15]; and, the direct opposite of this last stance, those who see democracy as the prime value since "democracy today is legitimate in its own right…and does not require the legitimacy of the Torah handed down by Moses."[16]

Many Orthodox contributors attempted to demonstrate that the very basis for democracy is found in Jewish doctrines such as the concept that humans are created in the image of God,[17] or that Judaism is opposed to totalitarianism and "the democratic concept of government is the closest among all the forms of government to being a suitable solution from a religious Jewish perspective."[18]

One of the most articulate contributors to the symposium was Professor Aviezer Ravitsky. He views the tension as being not between Jewish identity and democracy, but between Judaism and democracy.[19] Ravitsky emphasizes the fact that the new Jewish state is "an extraordinary historical phenomenon, never before envisioned in Jewish literature," which "took the sources by surprise."[20] For him, this is both a problem and an opportunity for creativity. Judaism teaches that "Divine authority has ceded political authority to human beings,"[21] and what is required now is to seek "to fuse two ethical worlds that have left their stamp" upon us as Jews and as modern people.[22]

Is there a solution to this ethical-political dilemma? Some see it in the writing of a constitution, which, according to the Declaration of Independence, was mandated to be completed no later than October 1, 1948. Israel's founders presumed that this constitution would delineate once and for all the nature of a Jewish and democratic state. The constitution has yet to be created, however, because it entails painful compromises. The religious would have to agree that the government and the laws are built on secular, democratic foundations, while the secular and non-Jewish population would have to agree that Isarel's Jewish identity is found in the calendar, its national symbols, and in its embracing, but not imposing, Jewish tradition and religion.[23]

The democratic nature of the state is also difficult to define. Democracy generally means a government elected by the citizens, with each citizen of age having an equal vote. By this criterion Israel is undoubtedly democratic. There are, however, certain problems in this regard. Because the British ruled Israel from 1918 to 1948, Israel inherited the British system of parliamentary democracy, but chose to have the representatives elected through party lists by proportional representation, and thus no specific representative is actually elected by constituents. Some parties are more democratic in their selection process than others. Ultra-Orthodox party lists are basically selected by the rabbinic authority or authorities, and no women are permitted to be selected. Because a government must command at least one more than half of the delegates to the Knesset (Parliament), and because no party has gained that number of votes on its own, governments are inevitably the result of coalitions, so that minority parties, generally but not exclusively religious parties, have greater influence on policies and legislation than their numbers would indicate. Furthermore although theoretically Arab parties could be part of a coalition, in fact they have never been so, although individual Arabs, members of major Zionist parties, have participated as government ministers.

JEWISH LAW IN THE STATE OF ISRAEL

The new State of Israel was intended by its founders to be a Jewish state, but its citizenry was not exclusively Jewish, and its laws were to be democratically determined by officials elected by all citizens, Jews and Arabs alike. What, then, was to be the status of Jewish Law—*halakhah*—in Israel? Jewish Law as such was not declared to be the law of the state, not only because of non-Jewish citizens, but also because the majority of Jewish citizens were opposed to being governed by religious law interpreted by religious authorities. Indeed the role of Jewish Law within the State of Israel has constituted one of the basic sources of conflict within Israel since its founding.

The founders of the State, led by David Ben Gurion, attempted to maintain unity and avoid a culture clash by agreeing to the maintenance of the "status quo" in religious matters. Whatever was the accepted practice at the time of the founding of the State in 1948 would remain. Thus secular Israeli Jews would not nullify any existing religious practices, and the religious would not demand any new laws to enforce religious practices. For example, since there was public transportation in Haifa on the Sabbath at that time, it would continue, but since there was none in Tel Aviv or Jerusalem, none would be permitted. Although there was a general effort to adhere to this agreement, it did not prevent attempts by either party to gain ground, and indeed the "status quo" has been more honored in the breach than in the observance, with each side castigating the other for attempting to make changes.[24]

One of the major sources of contention is the Sabbath, which is the national day of rest. Questions concerning the opening of stores and businesses on the Sabbath, the employment of Jews, and the opening of cultural and entertainment places remain very much in flux. Attempts by the Israel Democracy Institute and others, so far unsuccessful, to formulate and legislate a constitution for Israel have all had to wrestle with the role of religion in marriage and divorce and the observance of the Sabbath. A document prepared by Professor Ruth Gavison and Rabbi Yaakov Medan proposed a compromise, but it has not found wide support from either side.

Following the creation of the State, subsequent legislation granted certain powers to ecclesiastical authorities, establishing a Chief Rabbinate that has exclusive jurisdiction over such matters as marriage and divorce. The same powers were granted to religious authorities of other religions as well. This setup followed the pattern that had existed since the days of Turkish rule before 1918, thus continuing the status quo. Thus Israel has no civil marriage. It is the secular State, however, that grants this authority and that theoretically could nullify it as well. In effect, then, the Chief Rabbinate and those who serve under it are exercising civil authority in their rulings regarding the personal status of Israeli Jews, even though they are basing them upon Jewish religious law.

In a similar vein, Ben Gurion granted an exemption from army service to ultra-Orthodox yeshivah students. Mistakenly he assumed that this was for a very small number of people, but it has become a major source of friction as the number of such students has multiplied many times over so that today a sizable number of young men do not serve, much to the chagrin of those who do. In 1999, by which time there were over 30,000 yeshivah students exempted from army service, a law proposed by Justice Tzvi Tal was passed aimed at finding a way to encourage more to serve voluntarily, but so far few have done so. The Tal law was also intended to find a way to bring more of the ultra-Orthodox men into the work force, for the ethos that all males should spend their entire lives in Torah study and not engage in work produced a burden on the taxpayer who had to subsidize this study and the families of these students, thus creating a burden on the entire economy. The Tal law became inoperative in the summer of 2012 and the entire question was opened for discussion once again.

The question of the role of traditional civil Jewish Law—known in Hebrew as *ha-mishpat ha-'ivri*—in the Jewish State has been equally problematic. It was clear from the beginning that Israel would not be governed by Jewish religious law. Religious Zionists, who would have wanted it otherwise, were faced with a practical dilemma; they were in a minority and could not insist that Jewish traditional laws become the laws of the State. The more ultra-Orthodox compromised, seeing Israel as a reality forced upon them that they could use for their own purposes while never really acknowledging its legitimacy as a Jewish state. The more modern and progressive looked upon this secular state as a stage in the ultimate redemption, with the goal of legislating as much of Jewish practice as possible. The dilemma of observant Jews was further aggravated by the fact that Jewish tradition was in no way prepared to deal with the realities of a modern state.

For the entire period beginning with the destruction of the Temple and of Jerusalem in 70 C.E. Judaism had been the religion of a people living in exile, a minority ruled by others. Its spiritual leaders were rabbis, and its self-governing regulations were based on such rabbinic works as the Mishnah and the Talmud. Therefore the Jewish polity never developed a philosophy or set of regulations that dealt realistically with the problems of sovereignty, including controlling a territory under modern conditions, ruling as a majority while dealing with the rights of a minority, and creating rules for the State other than Jewish law because the majority of Jews did not observe it. Even the sections of Jewish law that dealt with such issues as kingship or warfare did so on a theoretical basis, not having to take reality into account.

Very few Israeli thinkers, religious or secular, have dealt seriously with these complex issues. Among them was Professor Daniel Elazar, who attempted to mine the traditions of Judaism for political implications and who founded The Jerusalem Center for Public Affairs, which was dedicated to this purpose. To this end he produced a number of studies of Jewish polity in biblical times and beyond, as well as a series of books devoted to this topic.[25] Elazar's contention was that the idea of covenant was central to Jewish polity which was "clearly republican...whose leaders are drawn from and are penultimately responsible to the people. Ultimately, all are responsible to God."[26] There has always been a delicate balance of power between those who derive authority from God and those who derive authority from the people. Interestingly enough, Elazar thought that this balance was "reflected in modern Israel in the deference shown those recognized as representatives of normative Judaism, which goes beyond the demands of coalition politics."[27] The covenant idea and the republican tendency in normative Judaism could serve as the basis of Jewish self-governance in a modern state as well.[28]

One of the modern rabbinical authorities studied by Elazar, in his attempt to make Judaism appropriate for a modern state and to find a way in which both Jewish nationalism and the Jewish religion could work together rather than conflict, was Rabbi Haim Herschensohn (1856–1930). Born in Safed, he eventually left what was then Palestine for the United States because of the opposition of the ultra-Orthodox to his ideas. Under the sponsorship of Elazar's Center, Professor Eliezer Schweid published an extensive study of this largely forgotten rabbi's writings and philosophy.[29]

Herschensohn, while devoutly Orthodox in practice and opposed to reformists movements, was radical in his approach. He attempted to "lay a *halakhic* [Jewish Law] foundation for a democratic, theological, and political regime" in the new Jewish State that he believed would be formed.[30] He recognized that the new state would require many changes in order to deal with the needs of sovereignty in a new age with its economic, social, political, scientific and philosophical problems. He viewed the modern world not as a threat, but as a challenge. The new secular accomplishments had to be incorporated into Judaism's Torah so that they would all come together in the new state.[31] He was concerned that proper *halakhic* responses would have to be formulated to deal with such questions as the use of electricity on the Sabbath, the role of women, and the equality of Jews and non-Jews. He was confident that decrees that were no longer relevant could be cancelled and that once the spirit and attitude of Jewish Law were properly discerned, ways would be found to make it relevant, to lighten its burdens, and to create a democracy based on Torah.[32] Unfortunately his attitude did not prevail among religious authorities, and his work remained largely unknown among the secular as well.

Yeshaiyahu Leibowitz, a well-known and highly controversial Orthodox scientist and philosopher, also discussed these problems over the years in articles, books, and public appearances. For example, in discussing the problem of the Sabbath in the modern State of Israel, he stated that the central problem was not the observance or lack thereof, but the fact that the religious leaders had never seriously tackled the problem of what the Sabbath rules must be in order to accommodate the running of a state, as well as the needs of the community and of the economy as they now had to be conducted. Instead they have made do with the use of the "Sabbath gentile," often simply the secular Jew, who will do what must be done while permitting the observant Jew the luxury of obeying all the Sabbath regulations.[33] The religious sector, he contended, must present a constructive plan for conducting a modern state in accordance with the Torah in which religious people could take part along with all others in whatever had to be done on the Sabbath and other holy days. Instead, the religious establishment simply worries about its own needs, making certain that observant Jews will not have to work on the Sabbath, castigating those who do not observe it, and permitting others to do the needed work without which the state and the economy would collapse.[34]

In the Zomet Institute for Halakhah, headed by Rabbi Israel Rosen, an attempt was made to find technical ways to create or modify appliances and machinery that might be needed on the Sabbath within the framework of strict *halakhah*. The

Institute did not make any attempt, however, to revise any Sabbath regulations to meet the needs of a state. Most Orthodox authorities simply ignored the problems and concentrated on the ways in which an observant Jew could avoid transgressing the laws while living in a secular society.

For many religious Jews, the desideratum would be for Israel to be ruled by Jewish Law, and indeed some sectors of Israeli society turn to Rabbinic Courts to adjudicate their problems whenever possible, even though these courts have no official status to rule on these matters. Only in matters of personal status is Jewish Law the official law of the land applied through rabbinical courts.

A policy was nevertheless enunciated giving Jewish Law the status of "the main but not the only or binding source"[35] for adjudicating cases when Knessest legislation does not speak to the case. Professor Menahem Elon, later a justice of the Supreme Court, advocated giving Hebrew Law the same status as British Common Law in such cases. Undoubtedly there are sections of this law regarding civil matters and business law, for example, that could serve well.[36] On the other hand, there are parts of this law that could be seen as discriminatory against non-Jews and other parts that do not speak to modern conditions. Moreover, once these precedents are used by civil rather than religious courts and interpreted in ways other than those indigenous to Jewish law, they cease to be "Hebrew Law."

It is interesting to note that Hebrew Law is nowhere specifically invoked in one of the most important ethical documents produced in Israel, *The Ethical Code of the Israel Defense Forces (IDF)*. This code, entitled *The Spirit of the IDF*, certainly holds the Israeli soldier to the highest possible ethical standards of conduct as a serviceman or woman in peace or in war. The document begins by stating that it draws its basic principles from three sources:

1. The tradition of the Jewish People throughout its history.
2. The tradition of the State of Israel, its democratic principles, laws, and institutions.
3. The tradition of the IDF and its military heritage as the Israel Defense Forces.

Yet, for whatever reason, the code never cites any specific sources of its basic principles. Although it is said to draw on the "tradition of the Jewish People," it never quotes from any such source, neither biblical nor rabbinic, even though the question of conduct in warfare is discussed at length in these sources. One reason may be that this was supposed to be basically a secular document. Another might be that within the vast corpus of Jewish sources, there are concepts that would no longer be considered ethically acceptable. For example, in 2010 a Hebrew volume was published entitled *Torat Ha-melekh [The Laws of the King]*, written by two well-known rabbis of the extremist right wing, which stated that Jewish Law's prohibition against murder applied only to Jews, spoke derogatorily about non-Jews, and permitted the killing of non-Jewish babies since "it is clear that they will grow to harm us." The authors and others who endorsed the book were investigated by the Israeli government, and prominent rabbis contended that this was a distortion of Jewish Law. Many others denounced the book. Major controversy arose, however, since there were many rabbinical authorities who contended that the government should not investigate the authors and certainly not arrest them, since they were simply quoting Jewish Law. Indeed, for many Israel citizens from the Ultra-Orthodox sectors, the tension between secularism and religion is such that their recognition of the State and its authority is partial at best, seeing it as a reality that cannot be ignored but not the desideratum, which would be a theocratic state governed and bound by Jewish law.[37]

This tension came to a boiling point during the evacuation of Jewish settlers in the Gaza Strip. Army troops, many of whom were Orthodox, were called upon to enforce this evacuation. When rabbinical authorities, often teachers of these same soldiers, ruled that the evacuation was a violation of Jewish law, the soldiers were faced with the dilemma of obeying the state or obeying their rabbis—in essence obeying the Torah. Some asked to be excused from this task, and the army seemed to go out of its way to avoid a conflict. The settlers themselves and their civilian supporters, however, opposed the army, sometimes violently, when being evacuated.

Israel and the Arab World: Ethical Dilemmas

The very existence of Zionism and then of the State of Israel has presented Israel with ethical dilemmas that have caused critics to question the existence of the State. Hertzel Fishman, a well-known Jewish thinker and educator, pointed to "three basic moral considerations" of the Arab-Israel conflict: Israel's moral right to exist in the Holy Land, supplanting the hundreds of thousands of Arabs who fled the country; the Palestinian demand for national self-determination in territories occupied by Israel since 1967; and the nature of Israel's military response to Arab violence.[38]

Fishman's general position is that although states must be concerned first and foremost with their own best interests, ethical considerations cannot be ignored. In the case of Israel and the Arabs, there are frequently conflicting rights that each side must take into account when relating to the other. Fishman recognizes that the Jewish claim to a homeland in the land of Israel conflicts with Arab national rights in Palestine, but he believes that in this case the Jewish claim has greater validity because it is essential to the physical and cultural survival of Jews and Judaism, while Palestinians are still part of a large Arab nation.[39] Nevertheless, it is morally correct for Israel to recognize the legitimacy of the Palestinian claim and to come to a compromise. "In the realistic, power-oriented world of international politics, the value of compromise—acknowledging the partial rights of a political opponent—is as close as one can get to an expression of morality."[40]

Concerning Palestinian self-determination, Fishman recognizes the security problems involved and the difficulties presented by Arab attitudes toward Israel, but he concludes that although self-determination is not "necessarily morally superior to maintaining Israel's relative security... Israel must be aware of the growing nuclear capabilities of Arab and Muslim states; the quicker a political settlement can be achieved with the Palestinians and Syria, the greater the likelihood of avoiding a nuclear confrontation."[41]

Finally Fishman admits that "as in every army, there are individual officers and soldiers who deviate from IDF policy... such abuses reflect human frailty, not army policy."[42] He further points out the many times when the IDF has taken disciplinary steps so that flaws and misdeeds are acknowledged and corrected.

Yeshaiyahu Leibowitz, on the other hand, took an extreme and very pragmatic view of this matter. Immediately after the Six Day War in 1967 he advocated leaving all the territories (with the exception of Jerusalem) without making any peace agreements. He did not believe that there was any possibility of such an agreement in the foreseeable future and that remaining there would be the end of the Jewish State because of the incorporation of such a huge Arab population. Either that or Israel would become an apartheid state, and the army would become just another conquering army of occupation. Such a situation would be ruinous to Jewish ethical morality.[43]

Tensions continue to exist between Jews and Palestinian Arabs who are not citizens of Israel in the areas that came under Israeli control after 1967, both because of the presence of the army and the need to prevent terrorist actions and because of the conflicts between Israelis who have created new settlements there and the existing population. There are, however, many groups of Jews in Israel who attempt to see to it that the high standards of morality and ethics associated with Judaism and with the Israel Defense Forces are maintained and who protest whenever actions are taken that seem to violate ethical rules. As long as the conflict continues to be unresolved, these issues will arise, with the built-in safeguards of Israeli law and the Israel justice system to prevent gross violations of human rights.

Notes

1. Howard M. Sachar, *A History of Israel* (New York: Alfred A. Knoff, 1976), pp. 384ff.
2. Sidney B.Honig, ed., *Jewish Identity: Modern Responsa and Opinions* (New York: Feldheim, 1965).
3. See, for example, the article by Prof. Ernst Simon, identified with the Conservative Movement, in ibid., pp. 152–61.
4. Ibid., pp. 132 and 206.
5. Ibid., pp. 142ff.
6. Ibid., p. 235. Harry Wolfson of Harvard preferred the term *gerim gerurim*, meaning self-made converts, or, even better, "Hebrew," ibid., p. 243.
7. Ibid., pp. 247–61.

8. This was influenced by the fact that the infamous Nuremburg Laws of the Nazi regime had included these non-Jewish descendants of Jews in the list of those to suffer discrimination and, eventually, extermination. The Law of Return would guarantee that never again would there be a situation when those persecuted as Jews did not have a refuge to which they could flee.
9. *Israel at the Crossroads* (Philadelphia: Jewish Publication Society, 1973), pp. 9–42.
10. Ibid., p. 42.
11. It should be noted that the writer was the head of that rabbinical court and served on the Neeman Commission.
12. Joseph E. David, ed., *The State of Israel: Between Judaism and Democracy* (Jerusalem: The Israel Democracy Institute, 2003), p. 9.
13. Anita Shapira, in ibid., p. 19; Menachem Brinker, in ibid., p. 88, Asa Kasher, in ibid., p. 124, Haim Cohn, in ibid., p. 187.
14. Ruth Gavison, in ibid., p. 343.
15. Rabbi Israel Meir Lau, in ibid., p. 38.
16. Yaakov Katz, in ibid., p. 80.
17. Rabbi Aharon Lichtenstein, in ibid., p. 106.
18. Yoel Ben-Nun, in ibid., p. 148.
19. Ibid., p. 264. See also his listing on various articles on the subject on p. 280, n. 20.
20. Ibid., p. 271.
21. Ibid., p. 272.
22. Ibid., p. 279.
23. See, for example, Dahlia Scheindlin, "The Problem Is Constitutional," *Haaretz*, August 6, 2010.
24. Ibid., pp. 376ff.
25. Daniel J.Elazar,, *Covenant and Polity in Biblical Israel: Biblical Foundationa and Jewish Expressions* (New Brunswick, NJ, and London: Transition Publishers, 1995).
26. Ibid., p. 437.
27. Ibid.
28. See esp. ibid., pp. 440, 456, and 457.
29. Eliezer Schweid, *Democracy and Halakhah* (Lanham, MD, New York, and London: University Press of America, on behalf of The Jerusalem Center for Public Affairs, 1994).
30. Ibid., p. xv.
31. Ibid., p.23.
32. See, for example, ibid., pp. 42, 64, 68, and 86.
33. Yeshayahu Leibowitz, *Judaism, The Jewish People and the State of Israel* (Jerusalem: Schocken Publishers, 1975), pp. 108ff (Hebrew).
34. Ibid., pp. 110ff.
35. *Encyclopedia Judaica* (Jerusalem: Keter, 1972), 12:148.
36. Ibid., pp. 149–51.
37. See Charles S. Liebman, ed., *Conflict and Accommodation between Jews in Israel* (Jerusalem:, Keter, 1990).
38. Hertzel Fishman, *The Challenge To Jewish Survival* (West Orange, NJ: Berhman House, 1993), pp. 285ff.
39. Ibid., p. 287.
40. Ibid., p. 288. See also Schweid (at note 29 above), p. 136, for a similar position.
41. Ibid., p. 295.
42. Ibid., p. 299.
43. Leibowitz, *Judaism* (at note 33 above), pp. 418–31.

Suggestions for Further Reading

David, Joseph E. 2003. *The State of Israel: Between Judaism and Democracy*. Jerusalem: The Israel Democracy Institute.

Elazar, Daniel J. 1995. *Covenant and Polity in Biblical Israel: Biblical Foundationa and Jewish Expressions*. New Brunswick, NJ and London: Transition Publishers.

Elon, Menchem. 1994. *Jewish Law*. Philadelphia: Jewish Publication Society.

Fishman, Hertzel. 1993. *The Challenge to Jewish Survival*. West Orange, NJ: Berhman House.

Gafni, Isaiah, and Gabriel Motzkin, eds. 1987. *Priesthood and Monarchy: Studies in the Historical Relationships of Religion and State*. Jerusalem: Shazar Center for Jewish History.

Honig, Sidney B., ed. 1965. *Jewish Identity: Modern Responsa and Opinions*. New York: Feldheim.

Leibowitz, Yeshaiyahu. 1975. *Judaism, The Jewish People and the State of Israel*. Jerusalem: Schocken Publishers (Hebrew).

Liebman, Charles, ed. 1990. *Conflict and Accommodation between Jews in Israel*. Jerusalem: Keter.

Ravitsky, Aviezer, ed. 2005. *Religion and State in Twentieth Century Jewish Thought*. Jerusalem: Israel Democracy Institute.

Sachar, Howard M. 1976. *A History of Israel*. New York; Alfred A. Knoff.

Schweid, Eliezer. 1973. *Israel at the Crossroads*. Philadelphia: Jewish Publication Society.

Schweid, Eliezer. 1994. *Democracy and Halakhah*. Lanham, MD, New York, and London: University Press of America, for the The Jerusalem Center for Public Affairs.

CHAPTER 28

JUDAISM AND CRIMINAL JUSTICE

LAURIE L. LEVENSON

INTRODUCTION

It is nearly impossible to describe in one chapter how great a contribution Judaism has made to criminal justice systems throughout the world. The central contribution has been the ethical precepts that individuals have free choice and are therefore individually accountable for their actions. As fundamental as this sounds, free choice and individual accountability are the ethical pillars of nearly all modern criminal justice systems. In fact, they are so fundamental that many assume there can be no criminal justice system without these principles.

However, history has proven the contrary. There have been criminal justice systems that operate much more like civil justice systems—their only goal is to balance the losses in nature. Thus, for example, if a person of one tribe injures or kills a person of another tribe, the victim's tribe may exact revenge against any member of the other tribe. There is no effort to hold the individual offender accountable.

From the first chapter of the Torah, Judaism sets forth the paradigm for a criminal justice system that develops into nuanced laws throughout the Bible, the Talmud, and later Jewish legal literature. Adam and Eve are expelled from the Garden of Eden when they choose to eat the forbidden fruit;[1] Cain is punished when, acting upon very human emotions of anger and jealousy, he chooses to kill his brother, Abel.[2] All individuals are accountable for their own acts. Moreover, they are accountable not just to the victim or to the victim's family. They are also accountable to the community and, ultimately, to God.

Judaism also recognizes that a criminal justice system is more than just a list of prohibitions and punishments. There are two other key elements that must be considered: compassion and the moral value of fair process. The role of compassion in tempering the law is not just to limit the punishment of the offender. Rather, it is to put into practice the fundamental principle that one of the goals of criminal justice is to rehabilitate the offender—to find good in someone who has done bad and, if possible, rehabilitate that individual by appealing to that goodness.

The role of a fair process is to bring legitimacy to the criminal justice system. Before society can condemn an individual's actions, there must be a process that rises above mere revenge and seeks to evaluate not only what happened, but why it happened.

Judaism's approach to criminal justice is anything but simplistic. The details are important because they recognize that no two crimes are the same, even when they offend the same law. Individual accountability is inextricably linked to individual circumstances. The goal is to provide a justice system in which the most basic moral judgments are embodied in the law but the application of those standards can be tailored to individual circumstances.

Before we delve deeper into Judaism's approach to criminal justice, it is worth noting that many of the approaches that we call "Jewish" have always been recognized, by Jews at least, as universalistic morals. Thus, according to the rabbinic tradition, long before God prohibited murder in the Ten Commandments, God did so in the Noahide code governing all human beings.[3] In that same code, God demands the establishment of laws and courts. This chapter therefore does not suggest that Judaism owns a monopoly on criminal justice. Nor does it suggest that the biblical model for criminal justice should apply directly to cases today. Furthermore, it does not discuss or advocate for how criminal justice should be implemented in the Jewish State of Israel. Rather, it describes the ethical basis in the Torah and Talmud of Judaism's criminal justice system and suggests how some of Judaism's principles and procedures can help us form a viable and ethically based criminal justice system today.

Is Punishment Ethical?

The initial question that must be asked of any criminal justice system is: "What gives us the right to punish?" After all, in the early biblical stories, it is God who metes out punishment. God expels Adam and Eve; God curses Cain.[4] One could argue that God acts as a model for the authority in any society; what God can do, so can the controlling powers of a community. But Judaism does not rely on the power model for justice. Rather, justice derives from covenant—the social contract individuals have with God and with each other.

Thus, the key laws governing the criminal justice system are set forth in Exodus and Deuteronomy after Jews have become a people. They are no longer governed by the laws of a foreign ruler. They must have laws by which they can govern themselves. There were many models of criminal justice they could have chosen. Some were as simple as allowing victims' families to avenge the blood of their loved ones. But that is not a criminal justice system; that is human behavior and emotions unchecked by society or a legal system, barely distinguishable from the way animals react when one of their own is injured.

Judaism seeks to elevate a criminal justice system. It is not reactive; it is proactive. The goal is to control aberrant behavior and provide a society where accountability is based upon reason and moral imperatives, not just emotional reaction. The right to punish derives from the natural right of members of a community to protect their community. Retribution (deriving from "retribuo"—Latin for "I pay back") authorizes punishment as a way to repair the harm an individual has caused, not just to another individual, but to society by undermining its laws. Because an individual has accountability for his actions, he is obliged to acknowledge his transgressions and, to the extent possible, repair the damage he has caused not only to the direct victims of his actions but also to the moral fabric of society.

It is, of course, a separate matter to define what kind of punishment will serve these goals. The famous *lex talionis*, "eye for eye, tooth for tooth,"[5] encapsulates Judaism's approach to punishment. Punishment should be in direct response and proportional to the harm caused. While the Rabbis later converted this biblical demand into a system of monetary compensation,[6] the principle remains the same. Punishment may not actually repair the damage done (an eye for an eye does not replace an eye, and neither does money), but it does reinforce the laws of society and eliminate the need for the victim or victim's family to seek revenge. Retribution differs from revenge because it is restrained and meted out by neutral parties. In this way, criminal justice is fundamentally different from other areas of the law, where the parties themselves may resolve their differences. Criminal justice requires that society, as represented by its courts and judges, reaffirm the standards of society and determine what conduct deserves moral condemnation.

Although retribution is the principle justification for punishment, there are other reasons as well. Criminal laws must serve to deter future violations by the offender and other individuals. Deterrence, too, operates on the assumption that the individual has the free will to decide to break the law. Knowing the consequences, a rational person will not violate those laws and suffer the consequences. Although it is unethical to punish an innocent individual merely to show the power of the state, a corollary benefit of punishing a guilty offender is that others will use their free will and reason to make different, lawful decisions.

Finally, Judaism recognizes that punishment may serve to repair the individual, not just society. In this way punishment is closely tied to the concept of *teshuvah*—repentance (literally, "return").[7] To be accepted back into society, an individual must acknowledge his transgressions and make amends. Punishment offers a way for the individual to start that process. Judaism's model for criminal justice, therefore, rests on two principles—*din* (judgment) and *rahamim* (compassion). By their nature, human beings will transgress and must be punished. However, a criminal justice system is different from a system of vengeance because it examines each case individually, with an eye toward compassion and a goal of rehabilitation.

Fundamentally, Judaism assumes the human responsibility of enforcing laws but asserts that they were established initially by God and are still ultimately enforced by God.[8] The concept of Divine Justice accomplishes two goals. First, it adds legitimacy and a moral imperative to punishment. Second, it tempers the vengeful urge for victims, or those representing them, to transform the criminal justice system into a mere vehicle for revenge. Without punishment, there is no commitment to the morality that binds us as a society.

These are firm theoretical justifications for punishment. The problem today is that there is often little evidence that the manner by which we choose to punish (primarily by incarceration, a punishment relatively unknown in biblical times) actually accomplishes these goals. Judaism sets up ideals that can be fruitfully used as criteria by which to measure the punishments meted out by present-day criminal justice systems.

Capital Punishment

The death penalty is first stated in Genesis 9:6: "Whoever sheds the blood of a man, By man shall his blood be shed; For in His image of God, did God make man." Yet, the Torah does not stop there. It is chock-full of offenses punishable by death. Capital punishment is designated for crimes ranging from intentional murder[9] to sexual offenses[10] to even cursing one's parents.[11] It is also prescribed for theological offenses such as idolatry,[12] sorcery and witchcraft,[13] and violating the laws of the Sabbath.[14] There are at least thirty-six offenses for which the Torah authorizes the death penalty.[15] In modern times it is difficult to countenance such a system.

To understand the morality of biblical death penalty law, one must put it in context. In biblical times, there were no prisons. The options for punishment were fairly limited—flogging, execution, or fines. The offenses designated for capital punishment were those that threatened the lives of individuals or the very ethical and religious life of Jewish society.

Capital punishment for murder represents the basic ethical principle that each life is valuable. Absent extraordinary circumstances, there is no right to take another person's life. Executing the offender will not bring back the lost life, but it will reestablish the basic principle that intentional killing is wrong. It will also serve the fundamental practical purpose of preventing blood feuds.

Capital punishment for idolatry and certain prohibited sexual offenses serves to save the spiritual life of a community. While one can certainly debate which, if any, of these transgressions should still lead to the death penalty today, Judaism recognizes that life serves no purpose unless it is imbued with a fundamental morality. If one wants to be Jewish, one cannot be an idolater. If one wants to be Jewish, one cannot engage in sexual acts that threaten the propogation and moral norms of the Jewish people.[16]

Judaism's discomfort with its own capital punishment laws is well-known. In the modern State of Israel, the death penalty may be invoked for only two crimes: genocide and treason during times of actual war. Moreover, the Torah itself, and the Rabbis to a greater extent, adopted procedural rules designed to make the death penalty a rarity. Two witnesses to the crime are required.[17] They may not be related to each other or to the defendant.[18] No circumstantial evidence is permitted.[19] A person may not be executed unless he has been warned by two witnesses before committing the offense.[20] A person may not be executed as a result of the testimony of an informant[21] or a confession.[22] A person may not be executed unless deliberations are conducted in a manner designed to find the redeeming value in the human being, including a requirement that the accused be set free if the vote to convict is unanimous, because the accused is entitled to at least one advocate among the panel of judges.[23] As the Mishnah records, a court that executes a person once in seven years is said to be "a bloody court"; Rabbi Elazar ben Azariah would make that once in seventy years; and Rabbis Tarfon and Akiba say they would never impose the death penalty.[24]

Viewed in this context, Judaism's designation of certain crimes as capital offenses represents not law in practice but rather an ethical ranking of violations. Some offenses pose a greater danger to individuals and societies than do others. The Jewish people reserve the right to protect themselves, but that protection must be both just and compassionate. The debate in Jewish sources and in modern times about capital punishment indicates that its use may be too high a price to pay for protecting us, even from serious harm, because it asks us as a society to engage in behavior that we otherwise condemn. Society wants to hold individuals responsible for their actions, but it too must be held responsible for its judgments. Discriminatory enforcement and errors in imposing the death penalty are too costly to measure or tolerate.

When Is a Person Criminally Responsible?

Judaism's focus on personal responsibility also leads to interesting rules regarding causation, joint offenders, criminal intent, and defenses. Judaism is extraordinarily careful not to hold a person liable for the criminal actions of another. Even a person who hires another to commit an offense is not responsible for the offense unless that person directly participates in the criminal behavior. Conversely, an offender is responsible for his acts, even if another person solicited him to commit them.[25]

Judaism does not ignore that there may be group criminality. Thus, when an offense is committed by joint offenders, all of them are liable if the offense could not have been committed without their participation.[26] However, in an effort to distinguish itself from a system that just feeds blind vengeance, the Talmud provides that when a man is beaten to death by several people, none of them is criminally liable unless the identity of the person who inflicted the last stroke can be determined or if the death would not have occurred but for the participation of all of the attackers.[27]

Judaism's imperative of individual culpability adds an important ethical dimension to its criminal laws. Especially in times when groups, domestic or foreign, are perceived as threatening a community's safety, there is a natural inclination to judge a person on the basis of his ethnicity or affiliations, and there are times when the Torah condemns entire nations.[28] Yet, Judaism's focus on individual culpability tempers this natural inclination to blame someone on the basis of who they are rather than what they did.

Moreover, Judaism places high value on an individual's intent in deciding whether that person is criminally culpable. Generally, bad thoughts alone are insufficient for criminal culpability. As the Talmud emphasizes, no person is criminally responsible for any act unless he did that act willfully.[29]

As a corollary, Judaism affords defenses to those who do not make a free decision to violate the laws. A person ignorant of the law cannot be punished, unless the circumstances indicate that he must have been aware—either from prior experiences or from the current circumstances—of what the law required. Unlike many other criminal justice systems, in Jewish law ignorance of the law is an excuse[30] because a person has not made a conscious decision to violate the law.

Duress, mistake, unconsciousness, involuntary intoxication, infancy, and diminished capacity are all defenses created to avoid condemning an individual who did not freely and consciously decide to violate the laws.[31] Yet these defenses were carefully tailored so they would not excuse those who willfully choose to violate the laws, even if they do so in unusual situations. For example, the Talmud provides that there are three grave offenses a defendant may not commit, even when coerced by the threat of death: idolatry, adultery/incest, and homicide.[32] Forcing people to make hard choices is not the same as taking away people's free will. If anything, these are situations where individuals most need the directive of the law to make an ethical decision, at least as ethics is understood by the community that has set those standards.

The Jewish law of self-defense also reinforces the basic ethical principles set forth in the Torah. Life is sacred. No one has the right to take a life unless a just distinction can be made between the life taken and the life saved. What is that fundamental distinction? In order to save one's own life, an individual may kill an attacker. Thus the Talmud says, "If someone comes to kill you, rise up and kill him first."[33] But self-defense can be used only as a last resort. It is not an excuse for vigilantism.[34]

In practical terms, this rule can raise significant issues for today's world. May one shoot a known terrorist or murderer because he is likely to attack in the future? The killing would not be justified if the goal were to avenge lives already lost; that is the role of a criminal justice system. However, if the threat to others is imminent (a term admittedly difficult to define), then killing the pursuer in self-defense or in defense of another may be justified. Each case will depend on its facts. Judaism starts with the ethical principle that life is sacred, and it then constructs laws that preserve that principle.

A "Victimless" Crime?

In today's society, where people are often disconnected from their community, a discussion of "victimless crimes" may have traction. Judaism's approach to criminal justice is based on its more communitarian understanding of who we are. The designation of certain acts as violating society's ethics makes the community, not just an individual, one of the victims of every crime. By their very nature, actions designated as crimes harm the moral fabric of society.

Moreover, in Judaism people do not have the right to consent to harm. Given that each person is made in the image of God[35] and belongs to God,[36] we have a fiduciary duty to maintain our own life and health as well as that of others. Therefore the Mishnah prohibits self-injury,[37] and modern rabbinic rulings include in that category repeated drunkenness, illegal drug use, mutilation, and even unsafe sexual activity.[38]

In Judaism, a person does not stand alone. Each individual is derived from the divine, and each individual is part of the whole community. The individual does not have the right to harm the whole, or diminish the divine, by acts that society has deemed harmful.[39]

Judaism's Lessons for the *Content* of Criminal Justice Systems

It is actually remarkable how much Judaism's ancient laws and stories regarding crimes can help guide justice systems today.[40] Not all are a perfect fit, but many offer fundamental lessons.

Consider, for example, Judaism's harsh view of kidnapping. In biblical times, it was considered a capital offense to kidnap a human being for gain. As recalled in the story of Joseph,[41] kidnapping and selling a person into slavery not only harms that individual and his family, but may actually alter the course of history. Abduction is stealing a human being. Because the Torah elsewhere prohibits stealing goods,[42] the Rabbis, who assume that there is nothing superfluous in God's teachings in the Torah, interpreted the prohibition against stealing in the Ten Commandments[43] as a ban against kidnapping.[44] Couched between the two commandments against murder and adultery, both capital offenses, kidnapping too was held to be a capital offense.[45]

Jewish law on assault demonstrates the transition from the strict law of *talion* (a limb for a limb) to a more sophisticated system focusing on the needs of the victim. Rather than ordering that the defendant suffer the same wounds as those inflicted on the victim, the court imposes monetary damages.[46] The amount of these damages depends on both the nature of the injury and the defendant's intent when committing the assault.[47] While today we generally focus on incarceration as the punishment for assault, the recent movement toward victim restitution can be traced to Jewish law's efforts to shift the focus of punishment from physical punishment to compensation for victims.

The Talmud discusses in detail the complexities of making the victim whole through the law of *shinnui* (the transmutation of property while it has been in the defendant's possession).[48] In the criminal law context, Jewish law is based upon the admonition in the Bible that a thief "shall pay double unto his neighbor."[49] Theft and robbery, in the context of fraudulent and oppressive dealings with others, are considered noncapital larceny.[50] Judaism offers a model for a criminal justice that focuses more on compensation to the victim than harsh physical punishment for the defendant.

Yet it would be wrong to assume that Judaism's ancient criminal laws are always a perfect fit for today's society. Jewish laws on sexual offenses reflect the morality of the times in which they developed. Some sexual offenses in the Bible are punishable by death.[51] By contrast, the trend today, even in those countries that retain the death penalty, is to not impose capital punishment for sexual offenses.[52] Moreover, Jewish law prohibits many sexual activities, including consensual acts with nonmarried partners, that today's secular laws may allow.[53] The biblical laws on rape and sexual assault seem antiquated when they call upon women to resist their attackers, cry out for help, and be amenable to "punishment" of the defendant by requiring him to marry the victim or pay a fine.[54] These ancient laws do not fit today's culture because they come from a time when women were often considered a type of property.

So what do these laws teach about Judaism and the content of criminal justice? They teach us, first, that while Judaism offers some valuable lessons about the operation of a criminal justice system, it does not offer magical formulas for a peaceful and just society. The greatest value that Judaism offers for establishing a criminal justice system is not in the details of its individual prohibitions or exceptions. Rather, it is an ethics-based system that holds its laws out as representative of its ethical values. Within that system, the focus is as much on the needs of the victim as it is on society's need to punish the defendant.

Second, Judaism's approach to criminal law is a system that demonstrates the value of *a structure* that has absolute prohibitions (e.g., the Ten Commandments), affirmative obligations (e.g., the duty of a witness to testify),[55] and interpretive commentary (including, Midrash Halakhah, Mishnah, Talmud, and later rabbinic teachings in codes and legal rulings). In itself, this structure has been replicated in many criminal justice systems with the adoption of criminal codes, interpretations by the judges, and regulations guiding application of the codes. These transform criminal sentences from the arbitrary decisions of judges to the rule of law.

Third, Judaism sets an important example of a criminal justice system that seeks to *individualize justice*. The Torah announces that "Parents shall not be put to death for [the crimes of] their children, nor shall children be put to death [for the crimes of] their parents; a person shall die only for his own crime."[56] In contrast, crimes of attaint under English law, in which family members could be executed for the treachery of other family members, had to be specifically abrogated by the United States Constitution.[57]

Judaism's effort to individualize justice applies not only to punishment, but to defining crimes in the first place. The clearest example may be the laws of homicide. The shedding of blood is the subject of the first admonition of a criminal nature in the Bible: "Whoever sheds the blood of man by man shall his blood be shed; for in His image did God make men."[58] Murder is prohibited by the Ten Commandments (Exod 20:13; Deut 5:17), and it is marked as a capital offense in Exodus 21:12.

However, long before secular systems sought to differentiate among offenders, Jewish law had already done so. Not all homicides are treated the same. Distinctions are made according to the crucial element of the defendant's intent. In Judaism, the death penalty is prescribed for murder only if it is willful.[59] The Torah articlulates a distinction between premeditated murders and accidental killings. Today we might speak of the difference between deliberate killings (murder) and accidental killings (manslaughter or negligent homicide). Both are deserving of punishment, but they are not deserving of the same punishment. The Torah provides for Cities of Refuge, to which an offender could flee if he accidentally killed another human being.[60] In those cities, the accidental killer would be safe from avengers, at least pending an assessment of whether he had killed intentionally. The unintentional killer would then have to reside there until the current High Priest died, at which point he could leave the city and be legally protected from avengers for the rest of his life.

Judaism's nuanced approach to the accidental killer teaches several important lessons regarding criminals and homicide. First, although there is no formal presumption of innocence in the Torah, an offender is not presumed guilty. Cities of refuge allow the hand of vengeance to be stayed until the facts can be ascertained. Second, accidental killings are fundamentally different from intentional murders. What makes them different? The same thing that underlies the overall justification for punishment—a directive to punish people on the basis of their choice to do evil, not just the harmful consequences of their actions.

Finally, it suggests that even those who have committed irreversible harm can be reintegrated into society. Rather than being a purely backward-looking view of retribution, Judaism allows the hope of redemption. Cities of Refuge are the closest that Jewish tradition comes to incarceration, and they work to provide a period of atonement.

Few criminal justice systems today speak of the redemptive power of the law. Soaring recidivism rates suggest just the opposite. Judaism offers a different model. Offenders are held accountable, but so are those who would seek justice. Engaging in criminal justice is a holy pursuit whose success is measured by whether the defendant is treated fairly, regardless of the nature of his offense.

Judaism's Lessons for the *Process* of Criminal Justice

Judaism views criminal justice as more than just a ledger of laws. Criminal justice is a process; its fairness depends on how the laws are administered, not just on what they state. Thus, judges play a critical role in the Jewish justice system. Moses judged cases even before the revelation of the Ten Commandments at Mount Sinai.[61] Later, God directed Moses to appoint judges.[62] People, not God, determine the fate of other human beings. Indeed, perhaps the most crucial aspect of Judaism's approach to the criminal justice system is not the content of its laws, but its insistence that those who participate in the criminal justice system have the integrity and ethics to apply them honestly.

To ensure the justice of judicial procedures, Judaism sets forth intricate procedural rules for criminal cases. From the nature of the oath, to what qualifies as evidence, Judaism has constructed criminal procedures that are designed to lead to honest and just verdicts. Consider just a few examples.

1. *The role of judges in deciding what is just.* Judaism embraces the use of judges, not jurors, to decide criminal cases, and so the quality of justice depends on the quality of the judges. The Torah already requires that they have high moral character and wisdom.[63] Maimonides summarizes the later rabbinic tradition in asserting that judges must have seven fundamental qualities: wisdom, humility, fear of God, disdain of money, love of truth, love of people, and a good reputation. They must also, as he explains, have practical life and family experiences. They must be aware of the "absurdities" of idolatry and magic so as not to fall victim to them. They must be people of stature so that their judgments are accepted. And they must judge in a manner likely to lead to a just verdict. A judge must show patience, indulgence, humility, and respect for persons when sitting in court. A judge must always hear both parties to the case, and he must not discriminate for or against any of the parties. A judge must deliberate with care but not delay in pronouncing his verdict. He must assume the responsibility to render an individual opinion and not rely on the opinion of even more prominent judges.[64]

Just as criminals must accept individual responsibility for their acts, so must those who judge them. The model for judges is set forth in the Torah. God is the ultimate judge, but God was never intended to be the sole judge for people's actions. Human beings are authorized and expected to perform that function.[65] The goal of a criminal justice system in Judaism has always been to have human judges act with the humility of humans and with the wisdom, patience, and compassion of God.

2. Burdens of proof, evidence, and witnesses. In addition to recognizing that the quality of justice depends on the qualities of those dispensing it, Judaism also offers the insight that justice does not exist in the abstract but is directly dependent upon the quality of evidence presented and the procedures used to present it. The Torah established that at least two witnesses were required for any conviction.[66] Because their word would prescribe the minimum burden of proof, the Rabbis established intricate laws to ensure the greatest possible reliability of those witnesses. Witnesses could not use hearsay; they had to be competent; they could not be informants; they were subject to vigorous cross-examination; their testimony could not be contradicted if it was to be the basis of judgment; affirmative efforts had to be made to solicit witnesses for the defense; and confessions in criminal cases were inadmissible.[67]

Each of these rules reflects an important judgment about the type of procedure most likely to lead to a just verdict. The Torah itself sets forth layers of protection to guard against the corruption of witnesses and the courts;[68] the Rabbis added even more.[69]

Even in modern times, there are constant debates as to what kind of tribunals should be used for criminal cases. The recent debate over how international tribunals should operate, or whether military tribunals should be used to try alleged terrorists, raises these same fundamental questions. Judaism not only offers examples of procedures still used today, but more fundamentally it teaches that a verdict is only as legitimate as the procedures that are used.

"Justice, Justice Shall You Pursue"

Perhaps the greatest contribution of Judaism to the study of criminal justice is the recognition that the pursuit of justice is difficult and ongoing. There are many explanations of the famous verse in the Torah, "Justice, justice shall you pursue."[70] Why, the Rabbis ask, was the word "justice" repeated in that verse? One might say that the biblical admonition is an attempt to obtain justice both for the individual victim and for society. Others argue that the repetition emphasizes the difficulty in obtaining justice at all. Still others contend that many types of justice might apply in an individual case.[71]

In reality, it might not be possible to articulate one clear standard of justice applicable to every case. What is important is its pursuit. Judaism's extensive laws reflect a dedication to a criminal justice system that serves the needs of the community while being fair to an offender. "Free choice" forms the fundamental basis for any criminal justice system—the free choice of the defendant to violate the laws and the free choice of society to seek vindication through fair treatment of the defendant. Both must be judged for their exercise of free choice by wisely chosen courts using fair procedures.

NOTES

1. Genesis 3:23.
2. Genesis 4:11–13.
3. B. *Sanhedrin* 56a–b.
4. Genesis 4:10–11.
5. Exodus 21:24.
6. M. *Bava Kamma* 8:1.
7. For a discussion of the various steps required of individuals by the Jewish doctrine of return, see Elliot N. Dorff, *Love Your Neighbor and Yourself: A Jewish Approach to Modern Personal Ethics* (Philadelphia: Jewish Publication Society, 2003), chap. 6. For a discussion of how that doctrine applies to communities, see Elliot N. Dorff, *To Do the Right and the Good: A Jewish Approach to Modern Social Ethics* (Philadelphia: Jewish Publication Society, 2002), chap. 8.
8. Haim M. Cohn, "Divine Punishment," in *The Principles of Jewish Law*, Menachem Elon, ed. (Jerusalem: Encyclopedia Judaica, 1975), p. 522.
9. Exodus 21:12.
10. Leviticus 20:10–21.
11. Exodus 21:27; Deuteronomy 21:18–21.
12. Deuteronomy 5:8.
13. Leviticus 20:13.
14. Exodus 31:14.
15. Hyman E. Goldin, *Hebrew Criminal Law & Procedure* (New York: Twayne Publishers, Inc., 1952), p. 26.
16. Leviticus 20:2.
17. Numbers 35:30–34; Deuteronomy 17:5; 19:15.
18. M. *Sanhedrin* 3:4.
19. M. *Sanhedrin* 4:5.
20. Deuteronomy 19:15.
21. Haim H. Cohn, "Informer" in *The Principles of Jewish Law* (at note 8 above), pp. 507–8.
22. *Ein adam masim atzmo rasha* ("A person may not make himself a criminal"), says the Talmud at B. *Yevamot* 25b, B. *Ketubbot* 18b, and B. *Sanhedrin* 9b and 25a. Confessions in civil matters, however, were legally determinative: *hoda'ah k'me'ah edim dami* ("Confession is like a hundred witnesses"); see B. *Gittin* 40b and 64a, B. *Kiddushin* 65b, and B. *Bava Metzia* 3b.
23. B. *Sanhedrin* 17a.
24. M. *Makkot* 1:10.
25. B. *Kiddushin* 42b–43a; B. *Bava Kamma* 51a, 79a; B. *Bava Metzia* 10b; *et al.* (*ein shali'ah l'devar aveirah*).
26. M.T. *Shabbat*. 1:15–16.
27. B. *Sanhedrin* 78a; M.T. *Laws of Murder* 4:6–7.

28. For example, entire nations were at times condemned in the Bible. These include Amalek (Exod 17:8–16; Deut 25:17–19) and the seven Canaanite nations (Num 33:50–56; Deut 7:1–6; 12:29–13:1; 20:10–18), and Midian (Num 31).
29. B. *Avodah Zarah* 54a; B. *Bava Kamma* 28b; M.T. *Laws of the Fundamental Principles of the Torah* 5:4; *Laws of Courts* 20:2.
30. See, for example, M. *Shabbat* 7:1.
31. Haim M. Cohn, "Criminal Responsibility," in *The Principles of Jewish Law* (at note 8 above), pp. 471–74.
32. B. *Sanhedrin* 74a.
33. B. *Sanhedrin* 72a.
34. M. *Sanhedrin* 8:7; B. *Sanhedrin* 73a–74a. If one kills the pursuer unnecessarily, one is liable for the death penalty; see ibid. 74a.
35. Genesis 1:27; 5:1.
36. Deuteronomy 10:14; Psalms 24:1.
37. M. *Bava Kamma* 8:6.
38. See, for example, David Novak, "Alcohol and Drug Use in the Perspective of Jewish Tradition," in *Addictions in the Jewish Community*, Stephen Jay Levy, ed. (New York: Federation of Jewish Philanthropies of New York, 1986), pp. 245–64; Basil F. Herring, *Jewish Ethics and Halakhah for Our Time: Sources and Commentary* (New York: Ktav and Yeshuva, 1984), pp. 221–43; and Elliot N. Dorff, *Matters of Life and Death: A Jewish Approach to Modern Medical Ethics* (Philadelphia: Jewish Publication Society, 1998), pp. 17–18, 249–52.
39. One is allowed, though, to take the risks that most people take, such as driving a car. The principle is announced in B. *Shabbat* 129b.
40. For a discussion of the various sources of Jewish ethics, including law, narratives, and others, and how they interact with each other, see Dorff, *Love Your Neighbor and Yourself* (at note 7 above), Appendix.
41. Genesis 37.
42. Leviticus 19:13.
43. Exodus 20:13; Deuteronomy 5:17.
44. *Mekhilta*. Mishpatim, 5.
45. Exodus 21:16.
46. M. *Bava Kamma* 8:1; B. *Bava Kamma* 83b–86b.
47. M. *Bava Kamma* 2:6.
48. *Shitah Mekubbezet*, Bava Kamma 66a, 96a–b.
49. Exodus 22:8.
50. B. *Sanhedrin* 86a.
51. Leviticus 20.
52. Kennedy v. Louisiana, 554 U.S. 407 (2008).
53. Mark Dratch, "Sexual Abuse and Marital Rape," (2006), http://www.jsafe.org/pdfs/pdf_032206_2.pdf (accessed July 21, 2011), p. 2.
54. Deuteronomy 22:28–29 ("and she shall be his wife, because he humbled her; and he may not put her away all his days"); Haim H.Cohn, "Sexual Offenses" (1952), in Elon, ed., *The Principles of Jewish Law* (at note 8 above), p. 485. He notes there that apart from specified acts, "rape as such is not a criminal offense in Jewish law" but requires compensation to the victim.
55. E.g., Leviticus 5:6–13; Numbers 5:5–8.
56. Deuteronomy 24:16.
57. See U.S. Const. Article I, § 9.

58. Genesis 9:6. The term is first used in Genesis 4:8.
59. Exodus 21:12, 14; Leviticus 24:17, 21.
60. Exodus 21:13; Numbers 35:30–34; Deuteronomy 19:1–13.
61. Exodus 18:13–27.
62. Deuteronomy 16:18.
63. Exodus 18:21; Deuteronomy 1:13–14.
64. M.T. *Sanhedrin [Laws of Courts]* 2:1–7.
65. In Exodus 18 and Deuteronomy 1:12–17, Moses establishes judges on his own authority; in Deuteronomy 16:18–20 he asserts the duty to establish courts in each jurisdiction for the generations to come; and in Deuteronomy 17:8–13 the judges are given ultimate authority to determine matters of law, not just matters of fact.
66. Numbers 35:30–34; Deuteronomy 17:5; 19:15.
67. For a summary of these rules, see M.T. *Laws of Evidence* generally, but especially chaps. 1–5, 17, and 22.
68. For example, Deuteronomy 16:18–20; 19:16–20.
69. For a summary of such added layers of protection against corrupt courts, see M.T. *Sanhedrin [Laws of Courts]*, chaps. 20, 21, and 24.
70. Deuteronomy 16:20; see also 25:1–3.
71. David Rosen, "The Mission of Jewish Responsibility—'Justice, Justice Shall You Pursue,'" August 2004. Keynote Address at the Cape Jewish Board of Deputies Centenary.

Suggestions for Further Reading

Bleich, J. David. 1983. *Contemporary Halakhic Problems*, Vol. II. New York: Ktav Publishing House, esp. pp. 341ff.

Block, Richard A. 1999. "Capital Punishment." In *Crime and Punishment in Jewish Law: Essays and Responsa*. Walter Jacob and Moshe Zemer, eds. New York: Berghahn Books, esp. pp. 70–71.

Cytron, Barry D., and Earl Schwartz. 1986. *When Life Is in the Balance: Life and Death Decisions in Light of the Jewish Tradition*. New York: United Synagogue of Conservative Judaism Department of Youth Activities, esp. pp. 191ff.

Dorff, Elliot N. 2002. *To Do the Right and the Good: A Jewish Approach to Modern Social Ethics*. Philadelphia: Jewish Publication Society, chap. 5, "Procedural Justice: Making a Fair Decision."

Dorff, Elliot N. 2003. *Love Your Neighbor and Yourself: A Jewish Approach to Modern Personal Ethcis*. Philadelphia: Jewish Publication Society, chap. 6, "The Elements of Forgiveness."

Dorff, Elliot N., and Danya Ruttenberg. 2010. *Jewish Choices, Jewish Voices: Social Justice*. Philadelphia: The Jewish Publication Society of America.

Elon, Menachem, ed. 1975. *The Principles of Jewish Law*. Jerusalem: Encyclopaedia Judaica.

Gordis, David M., ed. 1991. *Crime, Punishment and Deterrence: An American-Jewish Exploration*. Los Angeles: Wilstein Institute.

Pritikin, Martin. 2006. *Punishment, Prisons, and the Bible: Does "Old Testament Justice" Justify Our Retributive Culture?* 28 Cardozo L. Rev. 715.

Rosenberg, Irene Merker, Yale L. Rosenberg, and Bentzion S. Turin. 2000. *Murder by Gruma: Causation in Homicide Cases Under Jewish Law*, 80 Boston Univ. Law Review 1017.

Schwartz, Helene E. 1976. *Justice by the Book: Aspects of Jewish and American Criminal Law*. New York: Women's League for Conservative Judaism.

Vorspan, Albert, and Eugene J. Lipman. 1957. *Justice and Judaism: The Work of Social Action*. New York: Union of American Hebrew Congregations, esp. pp. 70–88.

CHAPTER 29

JEWISH ETHICS AND WAR

ASA KASHER

Introduction

It would be helpful to delineate the family of topics that should be discussed under the seemingly simple title of this chapter. I will first do it by briefly elucidating the notions of "ethics" and "morality," and "Jewish ethics and morality."

We use "ethics" in reference to some conception of proper behavior of persons in a certain capacity, be it one's profession, one's affiliation, or one's role in some sphere. Accordingly, "medical ethics" is a conception with respect to proper behavior of persons in their professional capacity as physicians or nurses, and "command ethics" is a conception of proper behavior of persons in their professional capacity as military commanders. Similarly, "police ethics" is a conception of proper behavior of persons *qua* police officers, and "company ethics" of a certain company is a conception of proper behavior of persons affiliated with the company as directors or employees. Playing a role in a certain sphere of activity is here on a par with acting in a professional capacity or *qua* affiliated to an agency or company. Thus, "parliamentary ethics" is a conception of proper behavior of persons who play the formal role of a member of parliament, and "parenthood ethics" is a conception of proper behavior of men and women who play the informal role of parents.

Notice that each of the ethics conceptions mentioned is different from the other ones, though there is usually some overlap. One expects to find the value of *integrity* and related norms in the conception of every field of ethics, but whereas command ethics and parliamentary ethics usually include *leadership*, medical ethics and company ethics usually do not.

Unlike ethics, which is here confined to activity in a certain capacity, "morality" here relates to human activity in general. The commandment "You shall not murder" applies under all human circumstances, irrespective of profession, affiliation, or role. In this chapter, "morality" is a conception that guides persons in maintaining commitment to protection of human dignity. It is assumed that such a conception can be used in shaping proper human activity and interaction. Since activity under a certain capacity is usually an activity of human beings in an interaction, what is required on grounds of morality constitutes a part of what is required by the ethics of activity under that capacity. A military commander ought to respect and protect the human dignity of his troops, both on grounds of morality and command ethics (of military forces in democratic states), but his general commitment to the value and norms of *leadership* rests on command ethics and not on morality.

When should a conception of ethics or morality be described as "Jewish"? My use here of the attribute of "being Jewish" will rest on the following considerations: First, there is a distinct Jewish people; there is a distinct Jewish religion; and there is the State of Israel, which identifies itself and is recognized by almost all of the nations as a Jewish state. Second, the Jewish people includes numerous ethnic groups, but they form a family of groups that bear significant resemblance to each other. Similarly, there are a variety of Jewish religious denominations, but they also form a family, whose members are much closer to each other than they are to any distinctly non-Jewish religious denomination. The State of Israel has an intricate institutional structure and a rich society of citizens, but it has an identity at least parts of which can be shown to be unique. Thus, finally, a conception of ethics or morality will here be regarded as "Jewish" if it is characteristic of the Jewish people during a certain significant period of its existence, or of the Jewish religion, as expressed in Hebrew Scriptures (the *Tanakh*), other major religious texts, or in practice, or of the State of Israel.

The following discussions will be confined to explicit reference to warfare and to peace, within the framework of each of these three components—people, religion, and state.

A Biblical Conception: During War

The most conspicuous presentation of a Jewish biblical conception of a religious duty to restrain warfare is a cluster of commandments in Deuteronomy 20, the fifth book of the Pentateuch, the Torah, which Jews regard as the fundamental and most sacred part of the Bible. The activities to be governed by these commandments are: waging a war, exempting some combatants from participating in it, offering the enemy peaceful surrender, treating captives and booty, and conducting a siege. Additional Deuteronomy 21 verses govern the case of a combatant desiring to have a captive beautiful woman as a wife. The ethics of warfare embodied in these norms rests on a fundamental religious strategy that permeates the whole body of Jewish commandments: Jews may be involved in every human sphere of activity, whether individual or collective, except for idol worship, but their activity within each sphere is significantly restrained. Thus, for example, setting a siege around a town is permitted, being an ordinary, nonidolatrous act of warfare, but a siege ought not to involve cutting down fruit trees.

Any moral evaluation of this ethics of warfare should consist of two parts: a moral evaluation of the imposed constraint, and a moral evaluation of what is permitted. The first evaluation involves the following consideration: If (a) the cause of war is good, and (b) a constraint imposed on warfare activities does not eliminate the ability to gain victory, then (c) the imposed constraint presumably helps alleviate the calamities of war and therefore (d) is morally worthy. It seems that the Deuteronomy 20 "you shall not" constraints are all morally commendable.

The second evaluation focuses on the constrained dimension of the sphere of activity in order to determine whether it permits activities that are morally unjustifiable. The results of this evaluation of the norms of Deuteronomy 20 are mixed. On the one hand, the exemption of certain men, such as one "who has betrothed a wife and has not taken her," delineates the corps of combatants in a just and effective way. On the other hand, the association of proclaiming peace with the requirement "that all the people that are found therein shall serve you at forced labor " (v. 11) is indeed morally unjustifiable. Other commandments are even worse, for example, the norm that when a town will make no peace, "you shall put all its males to the sword" (v. 13).

Because Deuteronomy 20–21 is an element of the Jewish Holy Writ, a question arises as to what lessons should be drawn, within the Jewish religious tradition, from the ethical norms of these chapters. A plausible answer would involve a clarification of the above-mentioned fundamental Jewish religious strategy: Except for idolatry, Jews may be involved in every human sphere of activity, as it is practiced under the circumstances, but the activity within each sphere is significantly restrained. This is why the Bible includes, for instance, norms of slavery and norms of marriage and divorce that prescribe unequal treatment of persons according to their gender. The same applies to warfare practices. The moral evaluation of the constrained activities permitted by Jewish biblical ethics is actually a moral evaluation of warfare practices of the time. Accordingly, current Jewish warfare ethics should rest on a modern conception of warfare, one that embodies some variant of the Just War doctrine, and imposes constraints on its application. Unlike Deuteronomy 20–21, it will involve, for example, a principle of distinction between combatants and others and be as morally justifiable as Just War norms.

This is one example of a much larger phenomenon—namely, that what constitutes the Jewish tradition, and Jewish ethics in particular, is not the Bible alone, but rather is based on how rabbis and lay Jews have interpreted and applied the Bible and subsequent traditions over the centuries. This includes not only how Jews have developed their tradition internally, but also what they have learned from others and made part of the Jewish tradition—in this case, Just War theory.

LATER CONCEPTIONS: WAGING WAR

During the twentieth century it became customary to draw a distinction between norms related to a decision to wage a war (*jus ad bellum*) and norms pertaining to activities conducted by troops during a war (*jus in bello*). This distinction induced further distinctions regarding agents complying with these norms and the types of violations. Although many of these distinctions are morally dubious, at least to a certain extent, they have become part and parcel of international law of warfare.

Deuteronomy 20–21 include norms of both kinds. During later periods these norms were clarified and expanded. The most important discussions by ancient and medieval Jewish authorities focused on the religious status of wars of different types. Most prevalent is the distinction between "commanded wars" (*milhemet mitzvah*) and "permitted wars" (*milhemet reshut*), but the nature of each type of war is not crystal clear. The notion of "obligatory wars" (*milhemet hovah*) also appeared in early discussions, but it was usually interpreted as delineating the same class of wars as the notion of "commanded wars."

Maimonides provides a relatively clear characterization of the different types of war in his code of Jewish law, the *Mishneh Torah*, in the section "Kings and their Wars": "And what is a commanded war? This is a war against the seven [Cannanite] nations and a war against the Amalekites and a war to deliver Israel from an enemy attacking them" (5.1). As he later points out, the war against the seven nations took place in biblical times and has no current significance, in particular because the major cause of war against these nations was their idolatrous nature and because those nations have disappeared. Nor does the war against the Amalekites bear any present significance, for they too have disappeared—although some later interpreters understand "Amalek" to apply to all enemies of the Jews. A war to deliver Israel from an enemy attacking them is indeed a war of self-defense, which is obligatory from a religious point of view as well as from moral and prudential points of view.

It is noteworthy that Maimonides does not mention among the commanded wars one that is meant to conquer the land of Israel. Although some authorities, such as Nahmanides, expressed the opposite view, it is commonly held that proposed attempts in our time to extend the borders of the State of Israel into other parts of the land of Israel are not a case of a "commanded war."

Maimonides' characterization of "permitted war" is seemingly of a political rather than religious nature: "a war that [the king] conducts against the other nations, to extend the borders of Israel and enhance his greatness and prestige"(ibid.). The king may implement such a war plan only if the 71-member religious court (Sanhedrin) allows it and it is approved by God speaking through the High Priest's breastplate (the *urim v'tumim*). Examples of permitted wars are those waged by King David, to the extent that they were not wars of self-defense. It must be recalled, however, that David told Solomon he had been divinely forbidden from building the Temple, because "you have shed blood abundantly, and have made great wars" (1 Chron 22:8 and also 28:3). According to an ancient Aramaic translation of Psalm 60, in one war David's corps suffered 12,000 casualties. Maimonides' deeper view of such "permitted wars" can be read in the last sentences of the previous section: "Everything [the king] does should be for Heaven's sake, and his tendency and thought should be to enhance the religion of truth" (4.10). Wars for enhancing the king's prestige are not for Heaven's sake and are therefore not permitted but rather forbidden, and all "permitted wars" are banned also because both the Sanhedrin and the High Priest's breastplate no longer exist.

Although a notion of "forbidden wars" has not been introduced into discussions of the types of war, it is plausible to maintain that from the point of view of Jewish religious tradition all wars are forbidden unless they are wars of self-defense. Commanded and permitted wars of other kinds are now obsolete and banned.

Is there a Jewish ethical attitude toward preemptive and preventive wars?

If the notion of "preemptive war" refers to an action of self-defense, when war is the last resort of defense against an imminent attack or one that is bound to happen unless aborted by an active defense, then the permission and indeed command to engage in wars of self-defense provide a simple affirmative answer. If the notion of "preventive war" refers to a war of self-defense when the war is not the last resort against a future attack, then again a simple answer follows, this time a negative one. If a war is not the last resort under the circumstances, then blood is going to be unnecessarily shed, which is never justifiable.

During recent decades military forces were deployed in some cases of humanitarian intervention that involved combat. Usually such wars cannot be portrayed as wars of self-defense. Are they justifiable? Although there is no official Jewish view of such interventions, a starting point can be offered. It is the biblical precept "you shall not ... stand against the blood of your neighbor" (Lev 19:16). That verse is usually interpreted as pertaining to proper interactions between individuals—that, for example, one must seek to rescue a person who is drowning or accosted by highway robbers (B. *Sanhedrin* 73a)—but it can and should serve as grounds for a conception of proper humanitarian intervention in telling us that we as a society may, and maybe even should, engage in such wars if there is no alternative to protecting innocent lives.

Jews in Wars

Before the State of Israel was founded, Jews had served in military forces of states in which they resided as citizens. Under such circumstances Jews participated in wars waged by the heads of the states that tolerated Jewish residence or even citizenship in the lands under their control. Naturally, common participation in national military forces made it possible for a perspective to emerge of Jewish participation in such activities.

The Camp of Israel (in Hebrew: *Mahaneh Yisrael*), written by a rabbi of high authority, Israel Meir HaCohen (Kagan) of Radin and published first in 1881, was meant to provide Jewish troops with guidelines on participation in military affairs. The author's assumptions about military activity, mentioned in passing in his book, were general: (1) a national military force is under the control of the head of state; (2) military activities put the life of participants in jeopardy; (3) it is the duty of a combatant to overcome the enemy or at least not be captured by it; (4) there is a variety of military occupations; and (5) military activity usually involves daily maintenance of armament.

On the background of such a thin conception of military activity, the book guides Jewish troops along a path that involves two major norms. The first one, taken for granted and only briefly mentioned, is the talmudic principle of "the law of the land is the law" (B. *Nedarim* 28a; B. *Gittin* 10b; B. *Bava Kamma* 113a; B. *Bava Batra* 54b–55a), that is, the law of the land is binding from the Jewish religious point of view as well. The principle applies to every sphere of activity that is essentially governmental, including principles of warfare. It does not apply to Jewish rituals, such as the contents of the prayer books. Accordingly, for example, if the law of the land requires compliance with some variant of Just War Doctrine, which is Catholic in origin, then Jewish troops should strictly observe it.

The major point made in *The Camp of Israel*, though, is that a Jewish soldier ought to behave as much as possible as the rest of the Jews do in noncombat situations. He should do his best to observe the Jewish precepts related to the Sabbath and Jewish holidays and to eating only kosher food. The book is actually a manual of relevant Jewish precepts, trying to teach Jewish troops in much detail how to maximize observance of these precepts.

A significant part of the book is devoted to slippery slope arguments: Conditions of military activity are prone to enhance improper behavior, unless virtues of self-restraint are nurtured, mostly by means of observing the precepts, which usually involve self-restraint. The discussion of virtues emphasizes *comradeship*, but not any of the other military virtues, such as *courage*.

The emerging conception is that of participation without responsibility. The portrayed conception of *The Camp of Israel* had nothing to say about the principles of waging war or conducting it. It is the responsibility of the head of state to set the principles, and it is the duty of the Jewish troops to be obedient. Responsibility is confined to individuals making genuine efforts to observe the Jewish precepts to the maximal extent possible. Although the whole book is addressed to troops, it could have served Jews whose missions were not in warfare but, say, in forestry.

Israel: Prospective Religious Conceptions

The conception expressed in *The Camp of Israel* presupposed the general principle of "the law of the land is the law." It exempted the Jews from shouldering responsibility to develop and elaborate "the law of the land" with respect to warfare. Someone else had done that, and they must comply. Jewish political independence rendered obsolete that exemption from responsibility for evaluating the justifications for going to war in the first place and one's conduct during war. In a Jewish state "the law of the land" is the law that Jews have established and enforce. The prospective transformation was radical: from participation without responsibility to participation on grounds of responsibility.

Several rabbinical scholars met the challenge of forthcoming Jewish political independence and military responsibility and suggested principles of Jewish warfare for the State of Israel, just before or shortly after its independence had been proclaimed. Some of them shared with *The Camp of Israel* its naïve conception of military activity and the major interest in conditions that would enable a Jewish soldier of the Jewish state to observe the religious precepts to a highly significant extent. However, some additional principles of proper warfare were also suggested.

An interesting example is the book *The Law of the Military in Israel*, by Rabbi Alter David Regensberg, a student of the former Chief Rabbi, Rabbi Avraham Yitzhak HaCohen Kook. The book, published in Jerusalem in 1949, is an annotated code that consists of twenty sections, each containing several general principles or particular norms. The annotation justifies every item on grounds of authoritative religious sources.

The suggested code requires that certain values, all common in ordinary codes of military ethics, be embodied in the conduct of commanders and troops. *Courage*, *discipline*, and *professionalism* are explicitly mentioned. *Protection of combatant life* is a most interesting value that is implicitly expressed in two norms: First, "The Commander in Chief should not send people to war [jeopardizing their lives] without any strategic calculation [compelling reasoning that they would succeed]" (15:4), drawn from the 2 Samuel 11 story of King David's war in which Uriah was killed. Second, "The military should be trained in all warfare tactics; but training should not involve a danger of injury, let alone jeopardy to life" (2:1–2), drawn from the 2 Samuel 1:18 phrase "to teach the children of Judea [how to operate a] bow" and from talmudic critical discussions of a noncombat practice used by Ben Kuziva ("Bar Kokhvah," during the 130s C.E.) that involved cutting off the fingers of combatants.

The code includes a major *ad bellum* principle, drawn from Deuteronomy: "When you come to a city to fight against it, then proclaim peace to it" (20:10). It is important to notice that the principle is suggested in the code for all types of war. The same attitude is manifest in the Just War principle of "Last Resort": war should not be waged if the conflict can be resolved without it.

Some *in bello* principles as well appear in the code, varying in their moral validity. Obviously acceptable is the principle that forbids killing POWs and that requires that they be well taken care of (16:1–2), drawn from talmudic and later discussions of some biblical stories. Thus, biblical stories that involve killing POWs are implicitly evaluated either as wrong or as not setting a binding or even commendable precedent.

A principle suggested and used in the code is, frankly, morally unacceptable: "It is allowed to use in fighting the enemy all means at our disposal," and consequently, "It is allowed to kill them by hunger or thirst or any other kind of causing death." Present ethical principles and international laws of armed conflict forbid the use of certain types of weaponry and certain kinds of warfare methods, even if intended to alleviate the calamities of war. The annotation of the code does not endorse imposing such restrictions on warfare. The simple explanation is that the author had not been able to justify such an attitude on grounds of authoritative sources, but perhaps the date of the code, a few years after the Holocaust and World War II, also influenced the attitude of the author. His detailed conceptions of war and military force and his deep sense of responsibility for the decision to wage war are accompanied by an inclination to allow Jews to use any means to defend themselves. As much as such an inclination seems natural, it should be restrained very carefully in practice.

Pre-Israel "Purity of Arms"

The period of the British Mandate over Palestine, created by the League of Nations after World War I (1920) and lasting until the State of Israel was proclaimed (1948), was marked by numerous cases of violence involving two or three of the parties present at the time—namely, the British Mandate government, Arab organizations, and Jewish[1] ones. Among the major events were the 1929 Arab riots, during which sixty-seven Jews were massacred in the town of Hebron/al Halil, and the 1936–1939 Arab Revolt that involved many terrorist attacks against Jews.

Jewish political movements and organizations resorted to a variety of defensive and offensive practices. The dominant Jewish policy at the time included an ethical conception of proper usage of force, a tenet that has exerted much influence over the paramilitary and then military activities of the major Jewish forces. The policy was dubbed "Restraint" (in Hebrew, *havlagah*). It confined activities to defensive ones and emphasized the moral duty to avoid attacking noncombatants. In the words of Berl Katznelson, an intellectual leader of the Zionist Labor Movement at the time, "Restraint is a political and moral method, emerging from our history and circumstances, our character and present conditions of warfare." In particular, "Restraint means that our arms ought to be pure. We train to use arms, we bear arms, we face those who attack us, but we do not want our arms to be stained by innocent blood" (Proceedings of the twenty-first Zionist Congress, August 20, 1939).

The conception of the *purity of arms* was not self-evident. It was opposed to the conception of revenge of "an eye for an eye," which prevailed in the Middle East (and still does among several communities), even though it creates a vicious cycle of bloodshed. More important, it opposed a suggested strategy of deterrence, which seemed to some parties to be reasonable, even though it shares an immoral ingredient with terrorism. The dominant conception of *purity of arms* established firm ethical principles of self-restraint, including a principle of the immunity of noncombatants from deliberate attacks and a principle of ethical integrity that forbids adoption of immoral elements used by an enemy but allows accommodation to the nature of threats caused by the enemy. Such principles have remained a major part of military ethics in Israel.

Israel: Military Rabbinate

Since the very beginning of the IDF (Israel Defense Force), there has been a Military Rabbinate unit, headed by a Major General or Brigadier General. During most of its history, that unit acted on a par with ordinary military chaplaincy in Western democratic states, rendering religious services to persons in military uniform to the extent required. In the context of Israel, this has meant not only maintaining synagogues and conducting services, but also regulating the *kashrut* of military kitchens, given the IDF decision to have a single, kosher system of kitchens for all troops and commanders. A unit within the Military Rabbinate has been in charge of military funerals and involved to a certain extent in identifying casualties.

During recent decades there have been attempts on the part of the Military Rabbinate to become involved in educational activities related to the troops' morale, though usually such activities are carried out by commanders with the help of a separate Education Force. Such activities brought the military rabbis closer to spheres of ethical considerations outside the confines of observing Jewish ritual precepts. Interestingly, the rabbis made no significant novel contribution to the development of IDF ethics, though, unlike the author of *The Camp of Israel*, persons of religious conviction who serve in the IDF undoubtedly share with their fellows a strong sense of responsibility with respect to all aspects of IDF mission and activity.

However, some minor developments have taken place as expected. An example can be found in a book entitled *Military Law [drawn] from Its Source*, which is a 2010 manual for religious troops, compatible with the Military Rabbinate regulations. It was written by Rabbi Y. T. Rimon, who had served as a combatant in an IDF Armor brigade. Male religious troops, who were educated in all-male high schools and colleges, find themselves serving and even carrying out missions together with women. Although many rabbis have opposed female military service, the book outlines (pp. 265–69) ethically reasonable manners of conduct that enable women and religious men to serve together, giving priority to mission considerations while making efforts not to violate any religious precept.

Israel: The IDF Code of Ethics

Between 1991 and 1994 the IDF developed its own code of ethics, eventually entitled "The Spirit of the IDF: Values and Basic Principles." This period of time followed the years of the Palestinian popular uprising of the late 1980s, but the latter events played no role in the decision to develop such a code or in its values and basic principles. The suggestion to have a code of ethics was first made by an IDF Major General, Ilan Biran, as one of many lessons he had drawn from a year-long visit to the U.S. Marines. Although at that time most of the state organs, governmental bodies, and public institutions did not have a code of ethics, the suggestion to have an IDF one was soon adopted by the Chief of Staff at the time, Lieutenant General Ehud Barak, and the Generals. As Chief of Personnel, Major General Yoram Yair was in charge of the process, and Professor Asa Kasher headed the committee that wrote and revised drafts.

The adoption of the proposed code is best explained in terms of the maturation of the State of Israel. The judiciary and the Mossad, a secret service agency (on a par with the CIA), introduced their codes of ethics at about the same period, and numerous others followed the IDF and these other agencies in developing their own ethical codes and eventually also their programs of implementation.

The IDF code of ethics contains eleven annotated values and thirty-four basic principles. Values in any military code of ethics reflect the mission of the military force and the conditions required for discharging it. Hence, the IDF code of ethics contains the mission values of *loyalty* and *responsibility* and the condition values of *courage* (under the IDF traditional title of *perseverance*), *discipline*, and *comradeship*, as well as *professionalism*, *reliability*, and *setting a personal example* (of proper conduct).

Another value requires a person in military uniform to see him/herself as a representative of the IDF and the State of Israel under all circumstances of military activity. This value does not commonly appear in other codes of ethics, but it is a natural expression of the democratic nature of the State of Israel.

Two additional values have drawn particular attention and have been argued to implicitly reflect the Jewish background of military activities of the IDF: *human life* and *purity of arms*. Neither value is listed among the values of other military forces of democratic states. The annotation of the *human life* value uses the expression "sanctity of human life" in an attempt to emphasize that though warfare involves much jeopardy to human life, military activity should be planned and carried out in a manner that aims to accomplish the missions assigned while minimizing casualties among the troops and collateral damage among enemies.

Among the basic principles is one that imposes a significant restriction on jeopardizing troops: Risking one's own life and that of one's subordinates is justifiable only when one is facing an enemy force, usually in combat, or rescuing human life. (Recall the above-mentioned norm of *The Law of the Military in Israel*, according to which it is forbidden to jeopardize the life of troops during drills.)

As we saw in the previous section, the *purity of arms* value is drawn from the Jewish policy of Restraint during the 1930s. Among the basic duties that follow from this value is compliance with international law of international armed conflicts, as interpreted by Israeli authorities.

Both values reflect deep Jewish roots, viz., those of justifiable self-restraint and of saving human life. These values are evident in both the religious tradition of Judaism and the humanistic tradition prevalent in the movements of secular Zionism.

During 2000 the code was somewhat revised. Among the current list of values is protecting "*human dignity*," an expression that has become part of Israel's constitutional, fundamental law "Human Dignity and Liberty." Another value that has been added is *love of homeland*. Arguments against the implausible inclusion of any "love"-value in a code of ethics were overruled by political considerations.

ISRAEL: THE ETHICS OF FIGHTING TERRORISM

Since August 2000, Israelis have become targets of Palestinian terroristic activities that regularly and deliberately disregarded the immunity of noncombatants from attacks. The Palestinians have used two methods in particular. First, suicide/homicide bombers infiltrated into Israel or Israeli settlements in the occupied territories in order to explode their bombs in crowded areas and cause as many casualties as possible. Second, missiles or rockets, usually launched from Palestinian residential areas in the Gaza Strip, hit Israel in an attempt to cause death, injury, damage, and terror among Israelis. The second method has been also used by the Lebanese terrorist and guerilla branch of Hizballah.

International law as well as the IDF Code of Ethics were devised and phrased with international armed conflict in mind. For example, the principle of distinction between combatants and noncombatants, implemented by practical steps such as distinguishing between persons who wear uniforms and bear arms and those who do not, cannot be implemented under the new circumstances without causing either significant collateral damage or the failure to accomplish necessary military missions to protect Israel's citizenry, leading to the death of Israel's own citizens. The existing ethical guidelines needed to be extended according to the new circumstances of fighting terrorism.

Every military force of a democratic state has grappled with the difficulties caused by the new circumstances. Within the IDF, a new doctrine, consisting of a systematic family of principles of fighting terrorism, was devised, presented, and implemented. The doctrine was developed by an IDF College of National Defense team, led by its commander at the time, Major General Amos Yadlin, later the IDF Chief of Intelligence, and Professor Asa Kasher. The doctrine was developed as a set of consequences of "The Spirit of the IDF" and is definitely compatible with it.

One of the novelties of the doctrine is the priority of protecting Israel's forces over minimalizing collateral damage during anti-terrorist action, in an area not under Israel's effective control, whose inhabitants have been effectively warned, by a variety of methods, to evacuate a building or a neighborhood that it is about to be the site of military activity. The norm rests on the Jewish and Israeli sense of graded responsibility to human life, which rejects any trace of a conception of terrorists as state instruments.. This principle caused some controversy, but the authors of the doctrine have not been convinced by the criticism. There are reasons to assume that similar principles are used by anti-terrorist forces of other democratic states, under similar circumstances.

Peace

A general view of war implies a general view of peace. Jewish ethics of war is directly related to what may be called the "Jewish ethics of peace."

The first component of the Jewish ethics of peace is expressed in famous biblical verses: "To every thing there is a season, and a time to every purpose under the heaven... a time of war and a time of peace" (Eccles 3:1 and 8). If this is interptreted as a description of what happens in life, it is just a pessimistic observation about human affairs, but under a deeper, normative interpretation this is a religious rejection of both pacifism and militarism. Under some circumstances, war is appropriate; under others, peace should prevail.

In the biblical verse a symmetry between war and peace is presented in a religious pursuit of the middle course. More elaborate presentations give priority to peace (without becoming committed to pacifism). The best example is the *Chapter of Peace*, a collection of sayings of "sages" of the second and third centuries c.e., all beginning with the words "great is peace," compiled during later centuries. It praises peace on each and every dimension of existence. Thus, for example, "Rabbi Joshua [of the first century c.e.] said: Great is peace, for Israel is [also] called peace, as it is written 'For as the seed of peace [the vine shall give her fruit]' (Zekh 8:12). To whom befits peace, [if not] the children of peace?" (14). Even though there is "time of war," the essence of the existence of Israel is peace.

Suggestions for Further Reading

Baron, Salo W., George S. Wise, and Lenn Goodman, eds. 1977. *Violence and Defense in the Jewish Experience*. Philadelphia: The Jewish Publication Society of America.
Cohen, Stuart A. 2007a. "The Quest for a Corpus of Jewish Military Ethics in Modern Israel." *The Journal of Israeli History* 26:1, 35–66.
Cohen, Stuart A. 2007b. "The Re-Discovery of Orthodox Jewish Laws Relating to the Military and War in Contemporary Israel: Trends and Implications." *Israel Studies* 12:2, 1–29.
Dorff, Elliot N. 2002. "A Time for War and a Time for Peace: The Ethics of War and International Intervention." In Elliot N. Dorff, *To Do the Right and the Good: A Jewish Approach to Modern Social Ethics*. Philadelphia: The Jewish Publication Society pp. 161–82.
Dorff, Elliot N., and Danya Ruttenberg, eds. 2010. *Jewish Choices, Jewish Voices: War and National Security*. Philadelphia: Jewish Publication Society.
Edrei, Arye. 2005. "Divine Spirit and Physical Power: Rabbi Shlomo Goren and the Military Ethics of the Israel Defense Forces [sic]." *Theoretical Inquiries in Law* 7:1, 257–300.
Goren, Shlomo. 1983–1992. *Response to War: Responsa on Matters of the Military, War and Security* [Hebrew]. Tel Aviv: Yediot Aharonoth, vols. I–IV.
Hager-Lau, Yehoshua. 1993. *Courage and Humility, Security, Military, and War in Maimonides' View* [Hebrew]. Beit Yatir, Israel: Hamekhinah HaKedam Tzvait Yeshivatit.
Kagan, Israel Meir HaCohen of Radin. 1881. *The Camp of Israel* [Hebrew]. Warsaw. http://www.hebrewbooks.org/33289.
Kasher, Asa. 1996. *Military Ethics* [Hebrew]. Tel Aviv: Ministry of Defense.
Kasher, Asa, and Amos Yadlin. 2005. "Military Ethics of Fighting Terrorism: An Israeli Perspective." *Journal of Military Ethics* 4:1, 3–32, 60–70.
Nardin, Terry, ed. 1996. *The Ethics of War and Peace, Religious and Secular Perspectives*. Princeton, NJ: Princeton University Press.
Niditch, Susan. 1993. *War in the Hebrew Bible, A Study in the Ethics of Violence*. New York and Oxford: Oxford University Press.
Ravitzky, Aviezer. 1996. "Prohibited Wars in the Jewish Tradition." In Terry Nardin, ed., *Ethics of War and Peace*, pp. 115–27.
Regensberg, Alter David. 1949. *The Law of the Military in Israel* [Hebrew]. Jerusalem: Mossad Harav Kook.
Rimon, Yosef Tzvi. 2010. *Military, Law [drawn] from Its Source* [Hebrew]. Tel Aviv: Yediot Aharonot, Merkaz Halakhah ve-Hora'ah, and Yeshivat Har Etzion,, vols. I–II.
Sperber, Daniel, ed. 1979. *Great Is Peace. Perek Ha-Shalom from the Talmudic Tractate Derekh Eretz Zuta*. Jerusalem: Massada Press and Golden Pages.
Walzer, Michael. 1996. "War and Peace in the Jewish Tradition." In Terry Nardin, ed., *Ethics of War and Peace*, pp. 95–114.
Walzer, Michael. 2010. "War in the Jewish Tradition." In *Jewish Choices, Jewish Voices: War and National Security*, Elliot N. Dorff and Danya Ruttenberg, eds. Philadelphia: Jewish Publication Society, pp. 59–63.

BIBLICAL SOURCES: RABBINIC AND SELECTED MEDIEVAL CITATIONS

TANAKH

Genesis

1:24–28	419
1:26–30	419
1:26–27	44
1:27	314, 345, 478
1:28	392, 415
1:31	44
2:7	44, 402, 433
3:23	371
4:7	44
4:11–13	371
5:1	477
6:5	44
6:12	419
8:21	44, 368
9:1–7	44, 45, 97
9:3–5	419
9:6	44, 475, 480
18:13	435
18:17–20	45
18:23–25	244
18:25	45
20:11	36
25:32	232
30:2	88
37	478
38:9	391
42:18	36
50:15–17	435

Exodus

1:21	36
2:11–12	90
2:11–17	92
2:13	91
2:15–17	90
4:14	88
7:3–5	44
10:1–2	44
10:7	404
12:38	46
12:44	47
14:13	91
19:5–6	38
19:6	40, 45
20	38
20:2–3	39
20:5	39
20:10	47
20:12	39
20:13	477, 478
21:2	47
21:9–10	315
21:10	315
21:12	374, 477, 480
21:13	479
21:16	478
21:19–20	314
21:20–21	47
21:24	372
21:26–27	47
21:27	374
22:8	478
22:20	39, 46, 47
22:21	297
22:22	296
22:23	39
22:25–26	46
22:26	88
22:30	40
23:1	434
23:7	376, 434, 435
23:9	39, 47
23:12	45, 47
23:16	47
24:3	38

24:7	38, 290
30:33	46
31:14	474
34:6	94

Leviticus

2:1–3	412
11:7	86
18:4	86
18:19	390
18:22	228, 234
18:26	47
19	36–8
19:10	47
19:11	434
19:13	38, 478
19:14	38, 375
19:16	38, 230, 346, 353, 436, 491
19:17	441
19:18	35, 140, 143, 314, 421
19:33–34	46, 47
20	479
20:2	476
20:10–21	374
20:13	393, 475
20:18	390
20:24, 26	66n24
22:28	423
23:22	47
24:17	480
24:19–20	59–60
24:21	480
24:22	47
25:4	406
25:8–11	406
25:10	90
25:14	374, 439
25:17	438, 439
25:23	406
25:39–42	47
25:42	39, 47
25:45	47
25:55	39
26	38, 406

Numbers

1:51	46
11:4	46
11:33	419
35:15	47
35:30–34	475, 480

Deuteronomy

4:5–8	40
4:8	244
4:15	287
4:37	40
5:7	478
5:8	474
5:9	39
5:15	39
5:16	39
5:17	477
6:4	88, 306
6:5	40, 41, 143
6:10–11	39
6:17–18	42
7:1–4	46
7:6	40
7:10	39
7:13	40
8:11–18	39
10:14	478
10:15	40
10:17–18	40
10:18–19	40–1, 46, 47
11:10–13	40
12:12	47
12:18	47
12:20	87
13:5	173
13:6	39
14:2	40
14:21	40
14:29	39, 47
15:3	46
15:7	88
15:8	88, 346
15:10	39
15:12	47
15:13–15	39
16:11	47
16:14	47
16:20	380
17:5	476
17:7	39

17:8–13	440
17:15	46
19:9	39
19:14	374
19:15	476
20:10	493
20:11	489
20:13	489
20:16–18	46
20:19–20	414
21:18–21	60, 374
21:21	39
22:2	314
22:7	39, 422
22:11	86
22:28–29	479
23:6	40
23:20–21	46
24:17	47
24:10–13	38
24:17	38
25:5	86
25:13–15	372
25:15	39
25:18	36
26:16	86
27:17	38
28	38
28:9	94, 173, 174
29:13, 28	29n16
30:19	44
31:9–13	24n20
32:15	39

Joshua

9:1	46

Judges

21:25	44

1 Samuel

1:18	493
2:25	45
16:2	435
21:2–10	436
22:9–19	436

1 KINGS

5:10	42
9:20–21	46

2 Kings

24:20	45

Isaiah

1:2–3	39
1:10–17	41
2:2–5	46
5:1–7	41
5:3	403
6:8	289
6:9–10	45
33:15	88
43:4	40
49:6	45
58:2–10	41
58:13	441

Jeremiah

2:5–8	39
7:25	44
9:22–23	94
9:23	41
11:13	41
17:21–27	41
24:7,	45
25:4–7	44
26:5	44
31:3	40
31:31–34	45
32:39	45

Ezekiel

16	39
18:5–9	41

Hosea

2:22–23	41
6:6	41
10:1	41
11:1	40
13:4–6	39

Amos

1:1–2:8	41
2:10–12	39
8:5	41

Jonah

3:8	45

Micah

4:1–3	46
6:8	90, 92
6:8–9	41

Zechariah

8:21–22	46
14:9	46

Psalms

8:5	291
12:5	438
19:2	173
19:8–10	24n36
24:1	477
29:4	257n43
31:3	88
88:3	88
104:24	424
118:1	245
128:1–3, 5	323
136:1	245
136:25	424
145:16	88
145:21	424
147:9	424
148:7–13	424
150	424

Proverbs

1:1–3	42
1:7	36, 42
2:6–9	42
6:17	88
6:32	42
8	36
10:20	43
11:13	436
12:10	423
13:11	88
13:19	42
15:14	43
18:21	433
19:20	36
21:4	88
21:13	88
98:9	45
40:19	419
145:9	421
146:9	47

Job

1:1	44
4:6–7	438
9:22	43
26:4	87
32:8	87
33:20	87
42:7–8	43

Ecclesiastes

2:24–25	43
3:1	498
3:8	498
3:12–13	43
3:19–22	43
5:7	43
7:9	87
7:15	43
7:16–18	43
9:2–3	43

Nehemiah

5	46

1 Chronicles

22:8	491
28:3	491
36:20	407

MISHNAH

Berakhot

9:2	440
9:5	440

Pe'ah

1:1	24n22, 66n25

Bikkurim

4:1–2	394

Shabbat

1:15–16	477

Yevamot

6:6	59, 326n21

Nedarim

3:4	436

Gittin

9:9	437

Kiddushin

1:7	55
4:14	426

Bava Kamma

2:6	479
4:3	62
8:1	60, 474, 479
8:6	478
8:7	24n32

Bava Metzi'a

4:10	24n33, 438

Bava Batra

6:14	435

Sanhedrin

3:4	476
3:7	436
4:5	61, 327n29, 348n2, 476
8:7	477

Makkot

1:10	476
3:16	66n25

Avodah Zarah

2:1	62

Avot

1:2	53
1:6	53
1:7	53
1:14	377
1:16	294
1:18	53
2:1	24n30, 53
2:9	53
2:13	53
2:16	64n13
4:2	24n31
4:6	53
4:12	53

Horayot

3:7–8	249

BABYLONIAN TALMUD

Berakhot

16b	371
59b	440
60b	440

Shabbat

12b	425
31a	37
33a	434
33b–34a	66n27
54b–55a	442
88a	290
88b–89a	291
127a	24n23
113a–b	441
151b	422

Eruvin

13b	235, 440
54a–b	233

Pesahim

22b	375

49b	426
50b	24n29
113b	435

Yoma

9b	58
38b	24n31
67b	244
86b	24n31

Rosh Hashanah

12a	417n6

Moed Katan

26b	435

Hagigah

14a-15a	66n26

Yevamot

12b	392
25b	476
37b	384
51b	384
62b	315
65b	435
69b	317

Ketubbot

8b	434
8b-9b	59
16b-17a	435
18b	476
67b	348n7

Nedarim

23a	492
28a	370, 436
51a	393

Nazir

23b	66n25

Sotah

14a	24n15, 173

Gittin

10b	370, 491
14a	377
34a	229–30
36a	248
61a	63
81b	384

Kiddushin

31a	55
42b-43a	476

Bava Kamma

26a	335
28b	476
38a	65n22
51a	476
79a	476
83b-86b	378
113a	492
113b	436

Bava Metzia

5b	376
10b	476
30b	58
32a-32b	420
49b	371
58b	433, 438
58b-59a	439
73b	372
75b	375
85a	24n26, 421
89a	437

Bava Batra

9b	441
21b	374
22a	374
54b-55a	492
83A	380
164b-165a	437

Sanhedrin

9b	476
17a	476

BIBLICAL SOURCES

19a	24n26
25a	476
56a	97
56b	472
72a	477
73a	491
73a-74a	477
74a	336, 477
74a-75a	438
78a	335, 477
86a	372, 479
97a	434

Avodah Zarah

14b	424
18a	330
54a	477

Horayot

2a	440

Makkot

7a	248

Shevuot

31a	377

Hullin

60a	424
84a	426
94a	372, 435

Arakhin

15b	437, 438, 439, 441–2

Niddah

20b	246

TOSEFTA

Yevamot

8:5	59
8:7	66n27

Gittin

3:18	63

Sanhedrin

11:6	60
13:2	63

Avodah Zarah

1:10	437

ADDITIONAL RABBINIC MATERIAL

Genesis Rabbah

44:1	66n32
33:1	424
48:18	435

Exodus Rabbah

47:3	66n32
2:2	423

Leviticus Rabbah

13:3	66n32
33:1	433

Song of Songs Rabbah

1:15	66n32

Sifra to Leviticus

112c	66n32

Avot de-Rabbi Natan

A41	66n27

MAIMONIDES

Mishneh Torah

SEFER HAMADDA

Foundations of the Torah

5:4	477

Ethics

1:5–6	173
2:6	436
6:7	441
7:2	436, 437

7:4	437
7:6	437

Torah Study

4:1	24n27

Repentance

8:1–2	101n52
9:2	94

SEFER ZMANIM
Sabbath

24:1	441
24:4	441

SEFER NASHIM
Women

15:16	315

SEFER ZERAIM
Gifts to the Poor

6:7	441–2
6:8	441
8:10	348n8
10:4	441

SEFER NEZAKIM
Murder

4:6–7	477

SEFER KINYAN
Sale

14:18	439

Slaves

9:8	423

SEFER SHOFTIM
Courts

2:1	94
20:2	477

Kings and Their Wars

4:11	491
5:1	490
8:11	97

Sefer Ha-mitzvot

Positive Commandment 8   173

COMMENTARY ON THE MISHNAH
Pe'ah

1:1	93

Guide for the Perplexed

1:2	100n39
1:54	174
2:33	100n39
3:32	251
3:54	100n40

Shulhan Arukh
Orah Hayyim

307:1	442

Yoreh De'ah

36:1	349n10
124:1	434
157:2	435
248:1	348n5
338:1	435

Even ha-Ezer

1:1	392

Hoshen Mishpat

369:6	436

Subject Index

R. Abaye, 437
Abraham Cahan, on socialism, 447–8
Abortion, 318–20, 323, 362; Feinstein on, 172; Waldenburg on, 172.
Abzug, Bella, on political ethics, 453
adam (human being), 410, 412
Adler, Rachel, 218, 273, 276–7, 280
Aggadah, 58, 230, 232
Agunah (the "chained" wife), 253–4n7
Akedah (the "binding" of Isaac), 254n15
Albo, Joseph, 97
Albright, Madelyn, 187
Alpert, Rebecca, 280–1
Altmann, Alexadner, 86, 87
Amalek, 251, 252
American Jewish Committee, 446–7
American Jewish Political Ethics, 445–56 *passim*; anarchism in, 448; biblical narratives in, 449; diaspora in, 446; prayer for the government in, 450, 454–6; *shtadlanut* in, 446–7, 455;
Anarchism, *See* American Jewish political ethics.
Animal Ethics, compassion in, 419, 421–5, 427; meat in, 421–2, 425–6; *Shehitah* (ritual slaughter), 423, 427; vegetarianism in, 419, 421–2
Antin, Mary, 449
Antisemitism, 196–7; in American Jewish political ethics, 445–6, 454
Arabs, in Israel, 458, 459, 467, 468;
Aristotle, 94, 102–3, 105, 111
Avot (Mishnaic tractate), 52–4, 73
Avot d'Rabbi Natan, 293–5

Babad, Joseph, 336
Baeck, Leo, 211
Bahya ibn Pakuda, 81n9, 81n10, 88–9. *See also* Hovot ha-Levavot.
Bauer, Yehuda, 187, 194
Ben Azzai, 66n27
Benamozegh, Elijah, on ethics, 124; on *mussar*, 123–4; universality in, 124
Bedersi, Abraham, 95–6
Berman, Donna, 281–2
Biale, David, 125
Biale, Rachel, 387
Biblical Criticism, in Conservative Judaism, 233–4

Bioethics, 313–24, 330–9, 345–8, 351–64 *passim*; body in, 313, 357; embryo in, 315, 316; embryonic stem cell research in, 320–1; in Israel, 331, 334, 335, 339; personal identity in, 352 3; sex in, 314–5, 325n12
Birth control, 316–8
Blasphemy, 441
Bleich, J. David, 364n9; on vegetarianism, 426
Body, *See* Bioethics.
Borowitz, Eugene, 5, 56, 215–6; on covenant, 216
Brandeis, Louis, 449
Breast Cancer, 355–7, 360–2
Bribery, 376
Buber, on Cohen, 143; dialogic principle of, 142–3; existentialism of, 141, 143; on I-It, 142; on I Thou, 142–3; on Jewish law, 144–5; and Rosenzweig, 139; on revelation, 142–3
Business Ethics, 367–80 *passim*; competition, 374; contracts in, 376; deception in, 372; employers and employees in, 230, 371; fairness in, 376; "stumbling block before the blind" and, 375–6; in the Talmud, 369

Carr, Albert, on business ethics, 368–9
Capital punishment, 475–6
Catholic Church, 195–6
Cherlow, Yuval, on health care, 347
Chiasm, in the Hebrew Bible, 37
Chofetz Chaim (Israel Meir HaCohen Kagan), on war, 492
Cicero, 86, 94
Cohen, Hermann, Buber on, 143; ethical monotheism of, 137; on ethics, 134–7; on equality, 136; and the God-idea, 135–7, 153; on Jewish law, 144–5; on Maimonides, 210; on the "Other," 135–7; on reason, 135; on the stranger, 136; universalism of, 136
Cohen, Morris Raphael, on political ethics, 453
Cohen, Richard A., 290
Commandments, 12, 36–41, 55–6, 74, 94–6, 128, 134, 440; Heschel on, 160–1; Kaplan on, 152, 261–2; Lazarus on, 134; Levinas on, 354; to procreate, 318, 326n21; "rational" and "auditory", 85–6, 89–90, 92; reasons for, 55–6, 75
Committee on Jewish Law and Standards, 234–5, 332, 342n38

Conservative Judaism, 201, 263; biblical criticism in, 233–4; commandments in, 227, 231; ethics in, 255–36 passim; and *magen tzedek*, 230, 427–8; universalism in, 226; value pluralism in, 235–6; See also Committee on Jewish Law and Standards; Dorff, Elliot; Roth, Joel; Tucker, Gordon.
Conversion, in Israel, 460–2
Covenant, 12, 38, 39–40, 63; Borowitz on, 216; Elazar on, 464; and the Holocaust, 192; Levinas on, 290
Creation, Rosenzweig on, 139; Soloveitchik on, 175
Crescas, Hasdai, 96
Criminal Justice, "cities of refuge" in, 480; compassion in, 475; fairness in, 473, 483; role of God in, 473, 481–2; judges in, 481–2; personal responsibility in, 472, 476, 477, 480; punishment in, 474, 479; self-defense in, 477–8; *teshuvah* (repentance) in, 474; vengeance in, 474–5, 477

David, 490–1
Death, precipitating, 331; impediment to, 332
Deception, See Speech ethics.
Democracy, in Israel, 462–4, 466; Spinoza on, 106, 110
Derrida, Jacques, 430n13
Desire, 388
Dewey, John, 260–1
Dialogic Principle, of Buber, 141–2
Dina d'malkhuta dina ("the law of the land is the law"), in business ethics, 370, 378; in political ethics, 445; in war, 492
DNA, 351
Dorff, Elliot, on bioethics, 332, 339, 354; on ethical theories, 231, 233, 237n27–8; on halakhah, 231, 238n46; on health care, 347; on homosexuality, 228–9, 233, 236n12, 238n43; on political ethics, 452
Duran, Simon, 337, 339

Earth, See Environmental Ethics.
Ecclesiastes, ethics in, 43
Elazar, Daniel, on covenant, 465
Elisha b. Abuyah, 66n26
Enlightenment, 20, 460. See also Haskalah (Jewish Enlightenment).
Environmental Ethics, 401–15 passim; *adam* (human being) in, 410, 412; earth in, 402, 403, 406–7, 410, 414; Eco-Judaism and, 402, 409, 410, 413, 415; Jewish calendar and, 413–4; Shabbat and, 403, 405–9
Equality, Cohen on, 136; in Jewish feminism, 273; Spinoza on, 106–07
Esau, 232
Ethics, Cohen on, 134–7; in Conservative Judaism, 225–38 passim; in the Hebrew Bible, 35–50 passim; in Jewish feminism, 272–83 passim; Kook on, 167–9; law and, 15–9; ontology and, 169–70, 174; postmodernism and, 287–97 passim; prayer and, 13; in Reconstructionist Judaism, 259–69 passim; and sacrifice, 176–9; as a science, 157; Solovetichik on, 168–9, 173, 174, 176–9; study and, 13–15; theology and, 12–13. See also American Jewish Political Ethics; Animal Ethics; Bioethics; Business Ethics; Criminal Justice; Environmental Ethics; Jewish Political Ethics in Israel; Mussar; Sexual Ethics; Speech ethics; War.
Eugenics, 358–9
Euthanasia, 336, 339
Evil, Heschel on, 161–2; Kaplan on, 161; Soloveitchik on, 178
Existentialism, of Buber, 141, 143
Ezrat Nashim, 283

Fackenheim, Emil, on the Holocaust, 190–1; on liberalism, 215
Falk, Marcia, 278
Fatally Ill Patient (*goses*), 335–6, 38
Feinstein, Moshe, on abortion, 172; on bioethics, 333–5, 341n17; on the United States as *malkhut shel hesed*, 450
Feldman, David, 319
Feminism, See Jewish feminism.
Fetus, 315, 320
Fishman, Hertzel, on Jewish political ethics in Israel, 467
Flood, 405, 411–2
Foer, Jonathan Safran, on animal welfare, 427
Foucault, Michael, 293, 294, 300n34
Free Will, 44

Garden of Eden, 44, 402, 403
Genetic testing, 323
Genetics, 352, 354
Genocide, 198–9
Gentiles, 55, 61, 461, 467
Ger, 39, 46–7, 49n19
Gersonides, 95–6
Gilman, Sander, 357
God, 416; Cohen on, 135–7, 153; fear of, 35, 36, 43, 45; as healer, 314; Heschel on, 158–60; image of, 158, 162; justice of, 35–9, 43, 45, 158; Kaplan on, 153–6; love of, 141; in Reconstructionist Judaism, 260; and speech ethics, 439–40; Spinoza on, 103, 153
Goldman, Emma, 448
Goses (fatally-ill patient), 335–8
Gossip, 436–8
Greenberg, Blu, 276
Greenberg, Irving, on the Holocaust, 191–2

Hadot, Pierre, 293, 300n34
Halakhah, 54–9, 62–3, 72, 73–5, 79; in bioethics, 330–9 passim; in Conservative Judaism,

225-38 *passim*, 370; in Jewish feminism, 273, 276, 278, 282; Kook on, 179, 183n75; in Orthodox Judaism, 210, 215, 370; in Reconstructionist Judaism, 262, 265; Soloveitchik on, 175, 178-9
Halberstam, Chaya, 295-6
Halevi, Judah, 89-90, 92
Halevy, David, 434
Halkin, Simon, 71
Hanan b. Rava, 434
Hartman, Tova, 279
Hasidism, and *mussar*, 128-30
Haskalah (Jewish Enlightenment), and *mussar*, 118, 128-9
Hatam Sofer, on printing and publication rights, 378
Health care, 345, 347-8
Hereditary traits, 357
Heschel, Abraham Joshua, 233-4; on the commandments, 160-1; ethics of, 162; on evil, 161-2; on God, 158-60; on the prophets, 158-9; relationship with Mordecai Kaplan, 151-2; on the state, 159-60; theocentricity of, 160-2
Hesed, 94
R. Hillel, 435
Hirsch, Emil, 212
Hirsch, Samson Raphael, on *mussar*, 125-6
Hirschensohn, Hayim, on Jewish political ethics in Israel, 466
Hoffman, Lawrence, 217, 218
Holdheim, Samuel, 210
Holocaust, 160; bystanders in, 194; and the Catholic Church, 195-6; and ethics, 186-20 *passim*; and the State of Israel, 187-9; and "superfluous populations," 197-8; survival in the, 187-9; Wiesel on, 192-3
Homosexuality, in Conservative Judaism, 228, 231-4, 236n12; in Reconstructionist Judaism, 266; in sexual ethics, 393-4
Hosea, ethics in, 41
Hovot ha-Levavot (Bahya Ibn Pakuda), 71, 74, 75, 78, 81n9, 82n10, 89
Human Rights, in rabbinic literature, 61-2
Humanism, of Mordecai Kaplan, 162
Hume, David, 307
Humiliation, in speech, 441-2
Hutner, Isaac, on *imitatio dei*, 181n42

I-It, in Buber, 142
I-Thou, in Buber, 142-3
Ibn Daud, 91-2, 94
Ibn Ezra, on liberty, 90-1
Ibn Gabirol, 82n11; ethics of, 87-8
Ibn Shemtov, 97-8
Idealism, 135
Identity, Jewish. *See* Jewish Political Ethics in Israel.

Imitatio dei, 244; as commandment, 181n33; Hutner on, 181n42; Maimonides on, 173; Soloveitchik on, 173, 175-7. *See also* God.
Infertility, 317, 321-2; halakhic, 390-1
Intellectual property, 374, 377-8
Isaiah, ethics in, 41
R. Ishmael, 296-7
Israel (Biblical land), 40
Israel (people), 39-41, 62
Israel (State), halakha in, 463-8; Jewish feminism in, 275; War in, 493-9. *See also* Jewish Political Ethics in Israel.
Isserles, Moses, 435

Jacob (Patriarch), 232
Jacob b. Asher, 438-9
James, William, 260
Jewish feminism, activism in, 282, 283; and agunah, 283; equality, 273; and ethics, 272-83; and halakhahh, 273, 276, 282; and lesbianism, 274-5, 280-1; in Orthodoxy, 276, 279; in Reform, 218. *See also* Women.
Jewish law. *See* Halakhahh.
Jewish Political Ethics in Israel, 459-69 *passim*; Chief Rabbinate in, 462, 463; Israel Defense Forces in, 467, 469; Jewish identity in, 458-61, 463
Job, 43-4
John XXIII, 196
John Paul II (Pope), 196
R. Judah Ha-Nasi, 11, 420-1
Judah b. Shmuel b. Kalonymus, 76
Jubilee, 406-8
Justice, 102, 354, 408; in bioethics, 345-6, 354; divine, 35-9; and the environment, 408; social, 230-1, 448, 454

Kabbalah, 75-7, 79-80; commandments in, 76-7; ethics in, 71-81 *passim*; Kook on, 167; Krochmal on, 125; in *mussar*, 122, 124, 127; and sex, 389. *See also* Sifrut ha-Musar.
Kant, Immanuel, 85, 307; ethics of, 135; Soloveitchik on, 171-2
Kaplan, Mordecai, on American Judaism, 450-1; on the commandments, 152, 261-2; on ethics, 157; on evil, 161; on God, 153-6; on Jewish civilization, 152, 260; relationship with Abraham Joshua Heschel, 151-2; on revelation, 152; on the state, 152-3
Katz, Steven, 161
Kavanah (intention), 74
Kaye/Kantorowitz, Melanie, on political ethics, 452-3
Kidnapping, 478
Klepfisz, Irena, 282
Kohler, Kaufmann, on ethics, 208; on halakhahh, 211; on Zionism, 211

Kook, Abraham Isaac, 257n47; on ethics, 167–9, 179; on halakhah, 179, 183n75; and kabbalah, 167; on natural morality, 171, 180; on slavery, 170, 183n74; on vegetarianism, 426; on women's education, 183n76
Krochmal, Nathan, on kabbalah, 125; on *mussar*, 124–5
Kugel, James, 36
Kukla, Elliot Rose, 394–5

Landau, Yehezkel, 231–2, 336
Lashon hara, 437–8, 439
Law, *See* Commandment (divine law) and Halakhah (rabbinic law).
Law of Return, 460, 470n8
Lazarus, Moritz, on commandments, 134; on ethics, 207–08
Leibowitz, Yeshayahu, on Jewish political ethics in Israel, 466, 469
Lesbianism, in Jewish feminism, 275–6; 280–1. *See also* homosexuality.
Levinas, Emmanuel, 106; on commandment, 354; and ethics, 287–91
Leviticus 19, 36–7
Lex talionis ("eye for an eye"), 59–60, 474, 479
Life Support, 332–5
Lifnim meshurat ha-din ("beyond the letter of the law"), 57–8, 67n39, 72–3, 243, 261; in business ethics, 380
Love, commandment of, 143–4; in the Hebrew Bible, 35, 36, 37, 40–1, 46–7; Spinoza on, 112
Luria, Isaac, 77, 83n28
Luzzato, Samuel David, and *mussar*, 121–3, 130
Lying, 434–5, 436
Lyotard, Jean-François, 287

MacIntyre, Alasdair, 264
Maharal, 424
Maharsha (Samuel Edels), 102–3
Mamzerut, 229
Maimonides, 75, 92–5, 98, 101n52, 102, 105, 109, 342n30; on attributes of action, 173–4; Cohen on, 210; on health, 354; on homosexuality, 393; on sex, 388–9; on *shehitah*, 427; Soloveitchik on, 173–4; on speech ethics, 436, 442; on war, 490–91
Mar Ukba, 443
Marriage, 386–7
Marton, Kati, 187
Mamzerut (bastardy), 253–4n7; in Conservative Judaism, 229
Masturbation, 391
Masturbation, 391
Medicine, 313–4
R. Meir, 436
Meiri, Menachem, 69n55, 336
Mendelssohn, Moses, 98, 119, 126
Meyer, Michael, 220
Middat hasidut ("the way of the pious"), 243

Milgrom, Jacob, 37
Misleading speech, *See* Speech ethics.
Mitnagdim, 130
Morality, *See* Ethics.
Moses, 91, 92, 404
Mussar, Benamozgh on, 123–4; Hasidism and, 128–30; and the *Haskalah*, 118, 128–9; Hirsch on, 125–6; kabbalah and, 122, 124, 127; Krochmal on, 124–5; Luzzato on, 121–3, 130; Salanter on, 127–30
Mysticism, Kaplan on, 156; Kook on, 168

Na'aseh ve-nishma ("we will do and we will hear" Ex. 24,7), 290, 291
Nachmanides, 314, 370, 423
Natural law, 85–6; Spinoza on, 104–5
Nazism, 197
Necessity Defense, 337–8
Neeman Commission, 461
Neighbor, love of, 140–1
Neo-Orthodoxy, 125
Ner-David, Haviva, 390–1
Newman, Louis, on bioethics, 330–1
Niebuhr, Reinhold, 160
Nietzsche, Friedrich, 91
Noahide, 62–3, 97, 425, 451, 452
Non-Jews. *See* Gentiles.
Novak, David, on political ethics, 452

Ontology, *See* Ethics, Ontology.
Organ Donation, 230
Orthodox Judaism, 20–1, 263; accommodationism in, 251–2; commandments in, 245–6; ethics in, 241–53 *passim*; feminism in, 276, 279; halakhah in, 241–53 *passim*, 370; Haredi, 241–2; indeterminacy in, 247–8; modern 241–2; revelation in, 241; values in, 248–50, 256n35
"Other", Buber on, 144; Cohen on, 135–7, 144; Rosenzweig on, 139–40, 144; Soloveitchik on, 176
Ozick, Cynthia, 273

Palestinians, 468–9
Particularism, in rabbinic literature, 60–3
Patient Autonomy, 333–4
Pharaoah, 44
Philosophy, Spinoza on, 108–09
Pikkuah nefesh, 354
Pittsburgh Platform, 210, 212, 215
Plagues, 403–5
Plaskow, Judith, 278, 393
Plato, 87, 90, 91; *Euthyphro*, 134
Pleasure, 387–8
Postmodernism, "care of the self" in, 294; covenant in, 290; and Jewish ethics, 287–97 *passim*; "totality" in, 286–9, 294; truth in, 291, 295–6. *See also* Levinas, Emmanuel; Foucault, Michael.

Power, Samantha, 199
Price fraud in, 373
Printing and publication rights in, 378–9
Procreation, 392–3
Protest, *See* Speech ethics.
Proverbs, ethics in, 42
Providence, 159

Radday, Yehuda, 37
Rape, 386, 479
Rashi, 428
Rationalism, 123
Rava, 437
Ravitsky, Aviezer, on Jewish Political Ethics in Israel, 463
Rawls, John, 264
Reason, 85, 89, 121; Cohen on, 135; and revelation, 172
Rebellious son, 60
Reconstructionist Judaism, commandments in, 261; ethics in, 259–69 *passim*; functionalism in, 260; God in, 260; halakhah in, 262, 265; homosexuality in, 266; values-based decision-\ making in, 266–9
Redemption, Rosenzweig on, 139
Reform Judaism, 21–2, 41; authenticity in, 217–8; autonomy in, 215; and civil rights, 213–4; and ethics, 206–20 *passim*; and halakhah, 210, 215, 370; Kantian ethics in, 207, 209, 217; social justice in, 212–3; *tikkun olam* in, 207; universalism in, 208; Zionism in 211, 219.
Regensberg, Alter David, on war, 493–4
Reisner, Avram, on bioethics, 332
Reproof, *See* Speech ethics.
Revelation, Buber on, 142–3; Kaplan on, 152; in Orthodox Judaism, 241; and reason, 172; Rosenzweig on, 139; Soloveitchik on, 173; Spinoza on, 109
Riskin, Shlomo, on vegetarianism, 431n33
Rollin, Bernard, on animal welfare, 428–8
Rosenzweig, on command, 139–41; on creation, 139; on Jewish law, 144–5; on love, 140–1; on the "Other," 139–40; on philosophy, 138–9; on redemption, 139; on revelation, 139
Ross, Tamar, 277
Roth, Joel, on halakhah, 231; on homosexuality, 228; on women and the rabbinate, 227–9, 237n16, 238n44
Rubenstein, Richard, on the Holocaust, 197–8
Ruth, 359

Saadiah Gaon, 75, 82n11, 172, 425; ethics of, 84–7
Sacrifice, Soloveitchik on, 176–9
Salanter, Israel, on business ethics, 367; on mussar, 127–30; on the soul, 129
R. Samuel, 435–6, 442–3
Samuel b. Meir, 437
Sarbanes-Oxley, and business ethics, 368–9
Schofer, Jonathan, 293–5

Scholem, Gershom, 71–2, 81n1
Schneerson, Menachem Mendel, 451
Schweid, Eliezer, on Jewish political ethics in Israel, 461
Sefirot, 77, 80
Sexual Ethics, 383–95 *passim*; gender in, 385, 394; Maimonides on, 388, 389; menstrual separation in, 389–90, 397n49; same-sex relationships in, 393–4
Shabbati Zevi, 82–3n17
Shammai, 435
Shehitah (ritual slaughter), *See* Animal Ethics.
Sifrut ha-musar (ethical literature), 71, 72, 73–4, 75, 78–81
Silverman, William, 219
R. Simeon, 297
Sin, Kaplan on, 161
Singer, Isaac Bashevis, on vegetarianism, 430n12
Slander, 437
Slavery, in the Hebrew Bible, 39, 46–7, 49n20; Kook on, 179, 183n74
Smoking, prohibition of, 230
Social Gospel, 211
Socialism, in American Jewish political ethics, 447–8
Socrates, 85
Soloveitchik, Joseph, on the commandments, 174; on creation, 175; on ethics, 168–9, 173, 174, 177; on ethics and sacrifice, 176–9; on evil, 178; on free will, 172; on halakhah, 172, 175, 178–9; on *imitatio dei*, 173, 175, 176–7; on Kant, 171–2; on Maimonides, 173–4; on natural morality, 170; on women's education, 183n74
Stokes, Rose Pastor, 448
Straus, Oscar, 449
Speech ethics, 433–443 *passim*; beneficial speech in, 441; deception in, 435–6; holy speech in, 439–41; language in, 433, 439; Maimonides on, 435, 436, 437, 441, 442; misleading speech in, 435; oppressive speech in, 438–9; protest, 441, 442; reproof, 441, 442
Speech-thinking, in Rosenzweig's thought, 138–9
Spinoza, Benedict, 101n13, 446; on civil law, 104; on *conatus* (power), 103, 105, 107, 110; on democracy, 106, 110; on divine law, 107; on equality, 106–07; on ethics, 111–12; on God, 103, 107–08, 153; on natural law, 104–5; on Nature, 103–4, 108; on obedience, 105–7; on polity, 104–09; on the social contract, 109
Spirituality, 74, 75, 76, 79–80
Steinberg, R. Avraham, on health care, 347
Stranger, *See* Ger and "Other".

Tal Law, 465
Tay-Sachs, 351, 355, 361, 362, 364n10
Theft, 371–2
Terefah (Terminally-Ill Patient), 331–3, 337–9
Terrorism, 497–8

Ticktin, Esther, 273
Torah, 14, 255n23; in Conservative Judaism, 233, 234; as *grundnorm*, 369; in Reconstructionist Judaism, 260
Trees, 414–5
Tribalism, *See* Particularism.
Tucker, Gordon, on halakhah, 231, 235, 238n49
Tzimtzum (God's "self-contraction"), 175, 176

Universality, in Benamozegh, 124; in Cohen, 137; in the Hebrew Bible, 45–6; in rabbinic literature, 60–3; in Reform Judaism, 208

Vegetarianism, *See* Animal Ethics.
Virtue, 102

Waldenburg, Eliezer, on abortion, 172; on health care, 346–7
War, in the Bible, 487–8; commanded, 490; ethics of, 487–99 *passim*; human dignity in, 497; human life in, 493, 496; and the IDF, 495–9; Just, 489–90; Maimonides on, 490–1; morality of, 488, 489; norms of, 489; and peace, 493, 498; permitted, 490; preemptive, 491; preventive, 491; "purity of arms" in, 495, 496–7; restraint in, 494–5, 497; and the State of Israel, 488, 493–9

Wiesel, Elie, on the Holocaust, 192–3
Wilson, J.G., on Jewish genetics, 357
Wisdom, 42
Wise, Isaac Mayer, 209
Wise, Stephen, 211–2
Wissenschaft des Judentums (Science of Judaism), 123
Women, and commandments, 55, 227, 228; and Conservative Judaism, 226–7, 229, 237n16, 238n44; marginalization of, 273, 276; subordination of, 272, 273, 274, 276, 277, 278, 283

Yetzer (inclination), 53, 64–5n13, 294, 295
Yirat shamayim (fear of heaven), 251
R. Yohanan b. Zakkai, 58, 226
R. Yose Ha-Gelili, 295
Yosef, Ovadiah, on intellectual property, 378

Zionism, 459; in American Jewish political ethics, 450; and environmental ethics, 414; and the Holocaust, 187; Kohler on, 211; in Reform Judaism, 211, 219; in Reconstructionist Judaism, 261
Zohar, 76, 77, 80
Zohar, Noam, on health care, 347
Zoloth, Laurie, 280